Autism
A Sensorimotor Approach
to Management

Editor

Ruth A. Huebner, PhD
Professor
Department of Occupational Therapy
Eastern Kentucky University
Richmond, Kentucky

AN ASPEN PUBLICATION®
Aspen Publishers, Inc.
Gaithersburg, Maryland
2001

B S

Library of Congress Cataloging-in-Publication Data

Autism : a sensorimotor approach to management / editor, Ruth A. Huebner.
p. cm.
Includes bibliographical references and index.
ISBN 0-8342-1645-0
1. Autism. 2. Sensorimotor integration. 3. Sensorimotor cortex—Diseases. I. Huebner, Ruth A.
RC533.A88 A98 2000
616.89′82—dc21   00-058298

Orders: (800) 638-8437
Customer Service: (800) 234-1660

About Aspen Publishers • For more than 40 years, Aspen has been a leading professional publisher in a variety of disciplines. Aspen's vast information resources are available in both print and electronic formats. We are committed to providing the highest quality information available in the most appropriate format for our customers. Visit Aspen's Internet site for more information resources, directories, articles, and a searchable version of Aspen's full catalog, including the most recent publications: **www.aspenpublishers.com**
Aspen Publishers, Inc. • The hallmark of quality in publishing
Member of the worldwide Wolters Kluwer group.

Editorial Services: Timothy Sniffin
Library of Congress Catalog Card Number: 00-058298
ISBN: 0-8342-1645-0

Printed in the United States of America

1 2 3 4 5

4/19/02

Contents

Contributors

Grace T. Baranek, PhD, OTR/L
Assistant Professor of Occupational Science
Section Head of Occupational Therapy
Center for Development and Learning
University of North Carolina at Chapel Hill
Chapel Hill, North Carolina

Rita D. Brockmeyer, BA, EMT-P
Mother of child with autism
Eastern Kentucky University Autism Group
Richmond, Kentucky

Myra Beth Bundy, PhD
Assistant Professor of Psychology
Eastern Kentucky University
Richmond, Kentucky

Connie Donaldson, MA
Special Education Teacher
Jessamine County School System
Lexington, Kentucky

Leah S. Dunn, OTR/L, BCP
Occupational Therapist
Winchester, Kentucky

Winnie Dunn, PhD, OTR, FAOTA
Professor and Chair
Department of Occupational Therapy
    Education
University of Kansas Medical Center
Kansas City, Kansas

Rose M. Geis, MS, CCC/SLP
Senior Speech-Language Pathologist
Child Evaluation Center
University of Louisville
Louisville, Kentucky

Charlotte A. Hubbard, PhD
Assistant Professor
Speech-Language Pathologist
Communication Disorders Program
Eastern Kentucky University
Richmond, Kentucky

Ruth A. Huebner, PhD, OTR
Professor
Department of Occupational Therapy
Eastern Kentucky University
Richmond, Kentucky

Jean Kalscheur, MS, OTR/L
Associate Professor of Occupational
    Therapy
Eastern Kentucky University
Richmond, Kentucky

Gary W. Kraemer, PhD, OTR
Professor and Chair
Kinesiology and Occupational Therapy
    Program
University of Wisconsin-Madison
Madison, Wisconsin

Shelly J. Lane, PhD, OTR/L, FAOTA
Professor and Chair
Department of Occupational Therapy
Virginia Commonwealth University
Richmond, Virginia

Elaine Fehringer Leone, MA, OTR/L
Assistant Professor of Occupational
    Therapy
Eastern Kentucky University
Richmond, Kentucky

Penelope McMullen, MA
Co-Director of Loretto Tutor Team
Santa Fe, New Mexico

Debra B. Reinhartsen, MEd, CCC/SLP
Speech/Language Pathologist
Center for Development and Learning
University of North Carolina at Chapel Hill
Chapel Hill, North Carolina

Sandra L. Rogers, PhD, OTR/L
Assistant Professor of Occupational
    Therapy
The Ohio State University
Columbus, Ohio

Lisa A. Ruble, PhD
Assistant Professor of Pediatrics
Treatment and Research Institute for
    Autism Spectrum Disorders
Child Development Center
Vanderbilt University Medical Center
Nashville, Tennessee

Kay Rydeen, MOT, OTR/L
Occupational Therapist
United States Army Health Clinic—
    Educational and Developmental
    Intervention Services
Mannheim, Germany

**Colleen M. Schneck, ScD, OTR/L,
    FAOTA**
Professor of Occupational Therapy
Eastern Kentucky University
Richmond, Kentucky

Lonnie L. Sears, PhD
Associate Professor and Pediatric
    Psychologist
Child Evaluation Center
University of Louisville
Louisville, Kentucky

Kim Sturmfels-Hall, OTR/L, ATP
Occupational Therapist
Formerly of Bluegrass Technology Center
Lexington, Kentucky

Scott D. Tomchek, MS, OTR/L
Chief Occupational Therapist
Child Evaluation Center
University of Louisville
Louisville, Kentucky

Suzanne W. Wannamaker, MS, OTR/L
Occupational Therapist
Exceptional Children Services
Guilford County Public School Systems
Greensboro, North Carolina

Preface

In 1968, about the time I began a part-time college job working in a Madison, Wisconsin, residential research and treatment center with children who had autism, there was very little research on autism and Dr. A. Jean Ayres (the founder of sensory integration) was just coming into her productive stride. Excitement about behaviorism, advances in brain research, new medications, and innovations in neurorehabilitation techniques abounded. Institutionalization was "beginning the end" of its era, and health care was on the cusp of sweeping changes. There was a contagious optimism that therapy could shape behavior, normalize brain structure, and cure, or at least substantially reduce, the impairments of neurological disorders. Amidst this historic time, occupational therapists, psychologists, and researchers from many fields labored largely independently of each other to actualize these dreams about autism, each convinced that their specialty was prominent. In the 1980s and 1990s, demands arose for proof of outcomes in health care and education service delivery, the realities of the human aspects of neurological disorders were manifested in our schools and communities rather than hidden in our institutions, and sweeping changes occurred in the neuro-sciences with the advent of brain imaging techniques. Isolated professional efforts, although yielding valuable results, were inadequate to meet these challenges or interpret the burgeoning research.

As an occupational therapist and a psychologist, my view of autism today is interdisciplinary in focus and tempered by my experiences with families and people with autism. In designing *Autism: A Sensorimotor Approach to Management,* I strove to bring together the expertise of many professionals, parents, and people with autism to shed light on the sensory and motor aspects of autism. As children, we "play" with visual loss in the dark, with blindfolds, or walking with our eyes closed. But it is very difficult to imagine sensory abnormalities such as defensiveness to touch, fear of movement, a desire to smell objects, or hypersensitive hearing. It is easier to observe and imagine difficulties in language expression than to imagine an existence where sensory processing results in a fragmented or troublesome perception of the world. Sensory perception is taken for granted; it is just there. There are authors who believe that there are few sensory processing or motor deficits associated with autism; they may be right. Others feel that sensory abnormalities are a marker of autism but do not distinguish autism from other disorders; they also may be right. There are authors who espouse that sensory abnormalities are a core deficit of autism in the same class as communication and social interaction deficits; again, they may be right. The presence and management of the sensorimotor deficits of autism has engendered controversy, debate, and sometimes censorship of sensory integrative treatment.

A primary goal of this book was to compile in a single source literature to address the questions surrounding the sensorimotor deficits of autism and to generate new questions and paradigms. Each author aspired to create a comprehensive, well-referenced, and well-written book that integrates multiple ideas and areas of research. Compiling and synthesizing this work has been a labor of love and joy. This book is a beginning, the first of its kind to examine the research from many fields and apply it to understanding the sensorimotor dysfunction of autism. It may generate more questions than answers and more challenges than acclaims. But any dialogue or debate that results from this book may spur more refined theories, terminology, and management approaches. People with autism and their families may be the ones who ultimately benefit. So, let the debate begin!

A second goal of this book was to explore a theoretical framework and suggest specific techniques to plan and structure the sensory environment for children, adolescents, and adults with autism. A change in paradigm is inherent in adopting the sensorimotor approach to management of autism. In this approach, the behavior of children, adolescents, and adults is considered communication that may shed light on their sensory experiences. Using the sensorimotor approach requires being open to this com-

munication and believing that people with autism and their families have expertise. Planning and structuring a sensory environment for people with autism is done in order to enhance learning, elicit adaptive responses, and promote engagement in occupation—the tasks of life. Ultimately the goal of this approach is to help children and adults learn how to self-regulate their sensory responses to achieve independently an optimal level of functioning. In this book, we advocate using the sensorimotor approach to elicit an adaptive response, enhance learning or social interaction, or to facilitate engagement in occupation. For example, modifying the environment to provide sensory supports is done to enhance learning, not to reward inappropriate behavior or to engage in solely for pleasure. We do not believe that a sensorimotor approach to autism can cure autism. We do believe that multiple approaches are needed, in conjunction with a carefully applied sensory analysis and attunement to motor needs, to promote function optimally. Because the concern of occupational therapy is the functional performance of the tasks of life (occupation), we have included ideas for enhancing occupation in many domains of life.

In developing a book that integrates the literature from many fields and the expertise of researchers, professionals, parents, and people with autism, extensive variability in the text is unavoidable. There are approximately four levels of writing complexity inherent in this book. The first level, such as in Chapter 3, Neuropsychological, Findings, Etiology, and Implications for Autism includes a synthesis of extensive research and, in this case, neurological findings. The literature and synthesis of this literature are complex. A second level of complexity, for instance in Chapter 2, Diagnostic Assessment of Autistic Disorder, consists of an integration of the literature but conveys specific techniques for assessment or management that are more concrete. At a more pragmatic level, Chapter 9, Integration of Sensorimotor and Speech-Language Therapy, and Chapter 13, Play: Engaging Young Children with Autism, as examples, are written by clinicians and include applications to case examples. Finally, chapters such as Chapter 18, My Greatest Wish: "I Must Play! I Must Play! I Must Play!", are written by people about their direct experiences with autism. These final chapters contain very little referencing to previous literature. With just this caveat to consider about the text, the book could seem to lack a focus, to be a hodgepodge of information. But upon reading it, the views of all of these experts flow together to create a rather profound exploration of the sensorimotor aspects of autism and the application of management strategies to improve function. The varying levels of complexity are necessary to comprehensively cover the scientific, clinical, and human aspects of this topic.

There are a few chapters that deserve a special highlight because of their preeminent and original contributions to autism. These are listed here:

- Dr. Colleen M. Schneck, in Chapter 5, The Efficacy of a Sensorimotor Treatment Approach by Occupational Therapists, explores the efficacy of a sensorimotor approach while summarizing a large number of studies, producing a long awaited synthesis of this literature.
- Dr. Sandra L. Rogers, in Chapter 6, Sensory Integration in Child-Centered Therapy, presents a vivid and pragmatic guide to direct therapeutic intervention using child-centered sensory integration therapy.

- Dr. Ruth A. Huebner and Dr. Gary W. Kraemer, in Chapter 7, Sensorimotor Aspects of Attachment and Social Relatedness in Autism, integrate the literature on attachment and sensorimotor deficits to develop a theoretical framework and pragmatic techniques for enhancing social interaction.
- Dr. Myra Beth Bundy, in Chapter 11, Integration of Sensorimotor and Psychoeducational/Behavioral Interventions, creates a comprehensive synthesis of ideas from behavioral and sensory approaches from the view of psychology.
- Dr. Grace T. Baranek and her colleagues, in Chapter 13, Play: Engaging Young Children with Autism, contribute one of the most complete expositions of play in autism available; their work should serve as a foundation to clinical practice and research for years to come.
- Professor Jean Kalscheur, in Chapter 15, Assistive Technology for Persons with Autism, applies her solid background in assistive technology with innovative ideas for improving function in autism.
- Rita D. Brockmeyer, in Chapter 17, Parenting, Advocacy, and Living a Full Life, and the aforementioned Chapter 18, shares her expertise as a parent and a playful person in a delightful, yet sobering, insight into parenting and play in autism.
- Chapter 19, The Effects of the Autism Experience on Life View and Philosophy: A Glimpse from One Side of the Looking Glass, is a unique and powerful compilation of the narratives from parents, family members, and adults who have been touched by the experience of autism.
- Penelope McMullen, in Chapter 20, Living with Sensory Dysfunction in Autism, tells her story and inspires re-

spect for the resilience of people with autism.

- And finally, Barbara Moran's cover art conveys the social experiences of people with autism through her artistic and compelling drawings of cathedrals, refrigerators, and stop lights.

I hope you enjoy this book, use it to improve the lives of people with autism, and begin to think about autism in a slightly different manner. Thank you.

Ruth A. Huebner

Acknowledgments

The culmination of a project of this magnitude engenders reflection on the many people who have helped me come to this point in my life. There are far more people than I could ever thank in a single page.

First, there are all the people with autism and their families who have taught me so much over my years of practice. From Wendy and Ryan who both must be middle aged now, to Mark and David and others who are now in adulthood, and to my recent encounters. I especially want to thank Rita D. Brockmeyer, a parent of a child with autism. She has inspired the best work from many professionals; she asks hard questions that stimulate thought and then she supports you as you struggle to find the answer.

Secondly, there are many authors who have contributed to this book. I want to especially thank Scott D. Tomchek for his early brainstorming. The faculty of the Eastern Kentucky University Autism and Related Disorders Group has been a steadfast support. The excellence of this book developed because of the commitment of each author to producing a scholarly book, despite many rewrites and revisions, that we can all be proud of. My gratitude to these authors is profound.

The editors at Aspen Publishers have been persistent mentors in my first experience as a book editor. Amy Martin approached me to do this book and then stayed with me through more than two years of hard work and writing. Amy's support has been the single most powerful influence in completing this book in a timely and thorough manner.

Then there are the social supports. My husband, Herb, has been an enthusiastic cheerleader, never asking for anything and seeming to enjoy the journey as much as I have. We have had a great life together.

PART 1

Understanding Autism and the Sensorimotor Findings in Autism

CHAPTER 1

Introduction and Basic Concepts

Ruth A. Huebner and Winnie Dunn

CHAPTER OBJECTIVES

At the completion of this chapter, the reader will:

- Understand and appreciate the historical trends in autism and the historical foundation of sensory integration theory.
- Discuss the current symptoms, incidence, and prognosis for autism.
- Identify the differential diagnostic criteria for autism and related disorders.
- Understand the concepts of child-centered and occupation-based intervention.
- Discuss the symptoms of regulatory disorders and the related sensory and motor difficulties of autism.
- Know the process of neural development and the assumptions of neural plasticity.
- Understand the features and importance of sensory processing in daily life.
- Appreciate the factors that can lead to a loss of objectivity regarding treatment interventions.

INTRODUCTION

The *Diagnostic and Statistical Manual of Mental Disorders* (*DSM-IV*; American Psychiatric Association, 1994) includes the autistic spectrum disorders under the broad category of Pervasive Developmental Disorders (PDD). Each of the disorders is characterized by delays and qualitative deviations in social interaction, communication, and restricted behavior or interests with an onset in the first years of life. The PDD category includes these disorders: Autistic Disorder, Rett's Disorder, Childhood Disintegrative Disorder, Asperger's Disorder, and PDD Not Otherwise Specified (NOS). The term *autistic spectrum disorders* refers to all of these pervasive developmental disorders, which are expressed in a wide range of severity and functional deficits. In this book, we use the term *autism* primarily to refer to autistic disorder but also to this entire range of PDD; the term *autism* is least applicable to Rett's Disorder.

The purpose of this chapter is to develop a framework for understanding the sensorimotor approach to serving people with autism and their families. To accomplish this task, we divided the chapter into sections. The first section explores the historic and current understanding of autism, including a discussion of the complexity of differential diagnosis, the expression of autism as a spectrum disorder, the epidemiology of autism, and the prognosis. Following the exploration of the historical and current understanding of autism, we present an overview of the philosophy of occupational therapy, the premises of sensory integration theory, the neurological foundations for sensorimotor interventions, and the findings from studies of sensory processing. Finally, a framework for analyzing both the potential benefits and risks of any intervention, with cautions for parents and professionals, is presented.

Each of the topics we present in this chapter has been subject to scholarly and clinical debate. These debates originate from the conscientious and scholarly disagreements that are inherent to any large body of research with findings that can be logically attributed to multiple causes, yielding differing conclusions. This type of debate may ultimately produce an improved understanding of autism (Brown & Bambara, 1999) and improved rigor in research. Disagreements also arise from flaws in research methodology, omitting variables such as family variables in research, inconsistent description of treatment methods or participant characteristics, commonalities in intervention approaches despite purported differences, and limited attention to the effects of extraneous variables (Prizant & Rubin, 1999). To advance our knowledge, we reviewed literature most pertinent to understanding the sensorimotor approach to management and recognized and shared these sources of debate throughout this chapter.

HISTORICAL AND CURRENT CONCEPTS IN UNDERSTANDING AUTISM

Historical Perspective

Kanner (1943) and Asperger (1944) both used the word *autistic* to describe the marked problems with social interaction seen in the children they described. These original descriptions of social and language behaviors and paradoxical responses to sensory stimuli among children with autism remain today as remarkably accurate. However, this historical work also inspired myths and misconceptions about autism. Speculation that all children with autism have average intellectual potential, that autism is not associated with medical conditions, and that children with autism are found in families with highly successful fathers have been disproved. Using the thinking of the time, which minimized the importance of biological factors in psychiatric disorders, Bettelheim (1967) advanced the erroneous theory that autism could be attributed to deficits in child care and parent-child interaction. As an appreciation of the child's influence on the parent-child interaction grew, it was apparent that cold and autistic parent-child interactions did not produce autism. As the evidence of neurological dysfunctions in children with autism mounted, it was also apparent that autism was a neurological disorder.

Kanner continued to follow the children from his original study and other children for years; the results of this longitudinal work (Kanner, 1973; Kanner & Eisenberg, 1956) still profoundly influence the field. In 1973, Kanner lamented the limited progress made in understanding autism and the hodgepodge of theories of etiology and treatment that marked the first 30 years of the study of autism. At that time, no neuroimaging studies on autism existed, nor was autism included in the *Diagnostic and Statistical Manual*. In 1980, the *DSM-III* (APA) included, for the first time, infantile autism as a diagnosis in a new class of disorders, the pervasive developmental disorders. This marked a major change in the direction of research. Scientists began to agree on diagnostic criteria and use these to describe the persons they studied. Diagnostic criteria enabled physicians and psychologists to identify children with a spectrum of autistic disorders and clarified the difference between childhood schizophrenia and autism. Although not without limitations, ongoing refinements have been applied to DSM criteria for PDD through two revisions since 1980 (see Volkmar & Lord, 1998, for a recent review of these revisions).

Since 1980, the amount of research has exploded, with 2,509 articles on autism indexed in the PsychLit database in this 20-year period. This research, although unwieldy and sometimes marked by false trails of reasoning and misleading findings, greatly expanded our understanding of the etiology of autism and the interdisciplinary treatment of autism explored in this book. Still, Rapin (1994) acknowledged that a diagnosis of autism is "the schizophrenia or cancer of the developmental disorders" (p. 2) because of its history of criminalizing parents and its association with behaviors that are socially unacceptable and difficult to manage. Nonetheless, Rapin implored professionals, the public school system, and insurance companies to recognize that there is no longer any rational reason to shun this diagnosis.

Our experience in working with parents, some of whom contributed to this book, is that they no longer tolerate the shunning of their children nor hide in shame from this

diagnosis. These parents are optimistic. They do not believe that a magic bullet will cure their child. Rather, they are optimistic that their own efforts, their coordination with multiple service providers, environmental supports, ongoing research, contributions to the literature, and careful trials of intervention strategies will lead to better management and improved quality of life for their children. There are many reasons to be optimistic. For example, the National Institutes of Health has designated 27 million dollars over the next five years for research on autism. Parent-sponsored groups such as the National Alliance for Autism Research (NAAR) and Cure Autism Now (CAN) are spurring many into action. Efforts abound to integrate the literature and establish research hypotheses that combine the wisdom of multiple disciplines and research findings that have withstood the test of time. Rapin and Katzman (1998) said it best: "The time seems ripe for an all-out attack on autism" (p. 7). Thus, in one sense, the historical work of Kanner and Asperger continues to guide our understanding, but, in another, we seem on the verge of major advancements in autism research. Much of this potential for advance is founded in an integrative approach to the literature (e.g., Bailey, Phillips, & Rutter, 1996) and guided by consistent diagnostic criteria for systematic description of persons with autism.

Differential Diagnosis

The category of PDD within the *DSM-IV* includes the five disorders listed earlier. Although these disorders overlap with each other and with similar disorders, each has unique diagnostic criteria that differentiate it from the others; these are described in the following section. There is a danger in presenting only the differential criteria for diagnostic categories. Such a presentation may seem to belittle the need for a thorough diagnostic process using the full range of diagnostic criteria, and it ignores that these disorders are complex and require careful attention and skill to differentiate in clinical practice. Nonetheless, we present differential criteria here to highlight the spectrum of autism and autismlike disorders; they are necessarily abbreviated and simplified for clarity. Ruble and Sears (2000) review differential diagnosis in more depth in Chapter 2. Differential diagnostic criteria are displayed in Table 1–1.

Autistic Disorder

Autistic Disorder is sometimes referred to as *pure*, *Kanner-type*, or *primary* autism.

The expression of the symptoms of Autistic Disorder along a wide spectrum depends on factors such as a person's chronological age, developmental level, and the presence of other disorders. The expression of autistic symptoms changes with age. For example, restricted and repetitive behaviors are uncommon in toddlers, but repetitive stereotypic behaviors gradually emerge and tend to peak at five to seven years of age. As the child grows older, restricted interests often change from simple interests (such as lining up blocks) to more sophisticated or complex interests, such as restricted preoccupations with art, music, math, television characters, or other specific topics (Lord, 1995). The expression of autistic symptoms tends to decrease and social functioning tends to im-

Table 1–1 Differential Diagnostic Criteria of PDD and Related Non-PDD Disorders

PDD* Disorder	Differential Diagnostic Criteria
Autistic Disorder	Social and communicative skills are lower than cognitive level.
Childhood Disintegrative Disorder	Autistic regression after two years of entirely normal development including speech in sentences.
Asperger Syndrome	Absence of retardation and significant language disorder with severe impairment of social interaction and restricted interests.
Rett's Syndrome	Girls with a neurological disorder and decelerated head growth.
Pervasive Developmental Disorder NOS	Subthreshold autism; diagnostic criteria for autistic disorder are not met.
Non-PDD Disorder	Differential Diagnostic Criteria
Reactive Attachment Disorder	Autisticlike condition associated with inadequate or abusive parenting.
Stereotypic Movement Disorders	Driven quality of self-stimulatory and/or self-injurious behavior associated with severe retardation or sensory losses (e.g., blindness).
Childhood Schizophrenia	Associated with delusions, disorganized thinking, or hallucinations developing later in childhood than autism.

*PDD = Pervasive Developmental Disorder.

Based on the *Diagnostic and Statistical Manual IV* (American Psychological Association, 1994) and related literature.

prove as children acquire language and learn to influence their environments (Rapin, 1997). At adolescence, the expression of autism may worsen with a deterioration in behavior, increased depression or anxiety, and for about 25% of persons the onset of seizures. However, some adolescents develop insight into their social differences and actively try to develop skills to fit in social environments (Kanner, 1973). In adulthood, the expression of autism is markedly variable depending on myriad factors; the process of maturation tends to be nonlinear, with occasional setbacks even for the most successful adults (MacDonald, 1998). Because of these developmental changes, the period between four and five years, when autistic symptoms are strongest, is used as a standard age in determining severity of autism by some authors (e.g., Volkmar & Lord, 1998).

Developmental level and comorbidity with mental retardation also influences the expression of autism. In previous research, mental retardation was found to be a comorbid condition in about 75% of cases (*DSM-IV*). Presently, the actual incidence of mental retardation among persons with autism is not known and is the subject of debate. The term *mental retardation* itself is misleading because individuals with autism and mental retardation are very different from individuals with mental retardation only. The pattern of adaptive and intellectual functioning for people with autism is an uneven rather than a flat profile, as seen in mental retardation, with some skills being stronger and others skills being weaker (Carter, Gillham, Sparrow, & Volkmar, 1996). Most commonly, visual skills are stronger than language skills, and daily-living adaptive behaviors are stronger than social adaptive behaviors. The frequency of symptoms such as stereotyped behaviors and self-injurious behavior increases with more severe mental retardation (Willemsen-Swinkels, Buitelaar, Dekker, & van Engeland, 1998). Because of this complex interaction with cognitive abilities, the diagnosis of Autistic Disorder is made relative to the person's overall intellectual functioning; the social and communicative deficits must be more severely impaired than intellectual capability (Volkmar & Lord, 1998). Autistic Disorder may be also present with other disorders, such as Attention Deficit Hyperactivity Disorder (ADHD), Learning Disabilities, Fragile-X Syndrome, and other neurological conditions that influence the clinical profile and expression of autism.

Other Pervasive Developmental Disorders

The following disorders fall within the PDD category of *DSM-IV* but are not Autistic Disorder; Volkmar and Lord (1998) described these as nonautistic PDD. Childhood Disintegrative Disorder (also called Heller's syndrome) is marked by insidious or sudden massive autistic regression (language, behavior, motor skills, and cognition) after entirely normal early development until at least two years of age, including the ability to speak communicatively in sentences (Rapin, 1997). According to Rapin, this disorder may be associated with seizures and have an overall poorer outcome than autistic disorder; however, it is indistinguishable, after the onset, from Autistic Disorder. Although about 30% of parents report a period of regression occasionally associated with a stressful event for their child (referred to as *autistic regression*; Rapin, 1997), the regression in Autistic Disorder occurs before two years of age (Rapin & Katzman, 1998).

Asperger Syndrome merits particular attention because it is sometimes confused with high-functioning autism or mild autistic disorder (Volkmar & Lord, 1998). However, the diagnosis of Asperger Syndrome must include an absence of both retardation and significant language disorder. The defining characteristics are severe impairment of social interaction and a restricted pattern of behaviors, interests, or activities. The clinical picture of this syndrome may include lower nonverbal intelligence than verbal skills (a reverse pattern of that often seen in Autistic Disorder) and significant motor incoordination.

Rett's syndrome occurs only in girls and is diagnosed by decelerated head growth, loss of purposeful hand movements, and severe retardation. Although Rett's syndrome is a neurological disorder quite different from autism in pathology and course of the disorder, it may appear to be Autistic Disorder at the onset before careful physical examination. The diagnostic category PDD-NOS was included in *DSM-IV* to encompass subthreshold cases of autism when some criteria for Autistic Disorder are not met (Volkmar & Lord, 1998). Mayes, Volkmar, Hooks, and Cicchetti (1993) found that children diagnosed with PDD-NOS showed less severe disturbance in relatedness then children diagnosed with autism, but more need for routine and order than children with language disorder.

Related Non-PDD Conditions

Other conditions that share characteristics with the category of PDD but are not PDD include Reactive Attachment Disorder, which is autisticlike behaviors associated with inadequate or abusive parenting. Stereotypic Movement Disorder is associated with repetitive, seemingly driven, motor behavior such as hand shaking, body rocking, head banging, or self-biting and occurs most often with mental retardation or severe sensory impairments such as blindness, especially in environments that are low in stimulation. In this disorder, stereotypic movements may increase with painful conditions such as an ear infection. Childhood Schizophrenia is defined by delusions, disorganized thinking, or hallucinations, which are not present in autism; schizophrenia develops later in childhood than autism.

The Incidence of Autism

Originally, autism was thought to be a very rare disorder. Since this early work, diagnostic procedures, diagnostic criteria, and descriptive research on autism have clarified our understanding of autism and changed the methods and improved the reliability of professionals who diagnose it. In 1988, Gillberg estimated that autism occurred in 4.0–6.7 children per 10,000. In 1998, Rapin and Katzman estimated that autism affected at least 1 or 2 persons in 1,000, a 100–200% increase in the reported incidence of autism since 1988. The U.S. Department of Education reported a 173% increase in autism between the 1992–1993 school year and the 1997–1998 school year. There has been much speculation on the cause of this increase, but no definitive answers. Rapin (1997) attributed the increase to the identification of less severely affected children due to the more specific criteria of *DSM-IV*. It may be that physicians and psychologists are less reluctant to assign this diagnosis because they understand the more subtle expression of autism and have more rating scales and diagnostic measures available to them (Gillberg, Steffenburg, & Schaumann, 1991; Volkmar & Lord, 1998). Or, more children may be visible as they are served in community settings rather than institutions. Howlin and Goode (1998), for instance, found that, prior to 1980, nearly 55% of children with autism were institutionalized; currently, that rate is estimated at 8%. Or, there may be an actual increase in the incidence of autism associated with some environmental risk factor. The popular press has carried stories of clusters of autism—for example, in Trenton, New Jersey, that are being investigated as possibly related to environmental toxins. Another theory, advanced by Bernard Rimland, contends that autism results from the overuse of childhood vaccinations (Manning, 1999).

Nonetheless, across countries and in the United States, Rapin (1997) found that the incidence of autism was consistently 1 to 2 per 1,000. In sharp contrast, Fombonne (1998) summarized the results of many epidemiology studies from a sample of more than 4 million children and estimated the incidence of autism between 4.6 and 5.5 per 10,000. Despite this conclusion, the tables presented in Fombonne's summary (which includes the same studies reviewed by Rapin) show that the rate of autism is 1 to 2 individuals per 1,000 children across most studies. Obviously, there is no universal agreement on the incidence of autism, but it does seem clear that autism is not a rare disorder. Autism occurs at a higher rate than Down syndrome, childhood cancer, and diabetes, and is thought to be one of the most prevalent developmental disorders among children (Rogers, 1998). Because of the diagnostic confusion that has persisted over years, there are no reliable estimates of the prevalence of autism in adult populations.

Although Fombonne's (1998) conclusions are inconsistent with the work of other authors, his work includes a careful and notable review of the epidemiological research. Fombonne found that about 75% of cases on the autistic spectrum meet diagnostic criteria for Autistic Disorder, with an overall 3.7:1 male:female ratio. A bimodal peak in the onset of seizures was identified for those with Autistic Disorder; the first peak was in the first year of life and the second at adolescence, with at least 25–33% having seizures in their lifetime.

Another method of considering the incidence of autism is to examine subcategories within the broad group of PDD. Eaves, Ho, and Eaves (1994) used data generated from multidisciplinary evaluations of 166 children with autism and clustered the data using cluster analysis. Four clinically meaningful clusters were found with similar demographic characteristics in each cluster. About 55% of the sample was described as typically autistic, with a 5:1 boy:girl ratio. The second group (19%), a low-functioning group with a 1:2.5 boy:girl ratio, had marked delay reaching motor milestones and moderate to severe retardation. The third group (<10%) was the least autistic, with a 6:1 boy:girl ratio; these children demonstrated restricted interests, sensory preoccupations, a short attention span, and tantrums. The last group (17%), a high-functioning group with a 3:1 boy:girl ratio, included less than half who were aloof and only one who was nonverbal. However, nearly all children in this last group displayed language perseveration, pragmatic language disorders, narrowed interests, and more externalizing behavior such as aggression.

Greenspan and Weider (1999) described a functional developmental approach to classifying children with autism. In this approach, the diagnosis was considered secondary to the primary functional expression of problems. For example, children with functional problems in motor planning disorders (a primary concern) may be diagnosed as having autism, cerebral palsy, or learning disabilities. This functional approach is consistent with the sensorimotor approach to management; both encourage solutions to functional problems rather than solutions based on diagnosis. Using this approach, Greenspan and Weider analyzed the developmental patterns of 200 children diagnosed with severe disabilities in relating to others and communicating. Four subtypes of children were identified. Children classified as Type I made rapid progress and exhibited stronger auditory skills than visual-spatial skills; they showed mixed responses to sensory stimuli. In the Type II subtype, children made slow, consistent progress; they showed stronger visual processing than auditory processing and underreactive responses to sensory input. Children classified as Type III were characterized by moderate to severe auditory and visual-spatial processing difficulties; they required sustained, consistent input to make slow progress. However, they sometimes read words and recognized logos. In the Type IV subcategory, children showed severe motor planning and oral motor difficulties, with a strength in visual processing. They tended to rely on visual cues and limited signing, or on single words, to support their lower-functioning abilities.

Prognosis

Functional outcomes for adults with autism are as highly varied as the autistic spectrum. In Kanner's (1973) meticulous records of the adult outcomes for the 96 children he studied, 12 did very well; 11 held jobs, often at a lower level than their qualifications, 7 had their own homes, and 1 was married, with a child. Adults in this successful group had few close relationships, although some belonged to social clubs. The remaining children were variously dependent as adults, living either with their parents, in sheltered communities, or in institutions. Overall, about 50% of the 96 people with autism were functioning relatively well in their home or in the community with supports. Asperger (see Frith, 1991, for a translation) found a variable outcome as well, but children with Asperger Syndrome more often succeeded in vocational areas related to their restricted interests.

Howlin and Goode (1998) reviewed outcome studies from more than 40 years of research from many countries; they compared findings in the past 15–20 years with earlier findings. Overall, their findings suggested that outcomes for autism are improving in more recent studies. According to Howlin and Goode, about a third of children with autism were able to care for themselves and achieve some independence in adulthood; they were likely to have some friends, live independently or semi-independently, and succeed at some kind of work. Marriages were very rare and almost two thirds had no friends. The rates of those with a poor outcome, who were likely to be dependent on families or living in residential settings, ranged from 16% to 74% of the samples in the studies reviewed. Similar variability of rates was found for the development of any speech or useful conversational speech. Some individuals had a very poor outcome, with seizures, major behavioral problems, and continued dependency. In their summary of these widely differing findings, Howlin and Goode estimated that about 55% achieved a good to fair outcome and 45% achieved a poor outcome. Nearly 70% had some good to fair functional language; the rest had poor to absent speech. Nearly 18% worked in some capacity; 11% were in their own home. In adulthood, there was an increased risk for affective disorders, especially depression and anxiety, with some studies reporting an increased suicidal tendency. No objective evidence that people with autism are more prone to criminal behavior than any other group was found (Howlin & Goode).

Factors associated with more positive outcomes for children with autism include the development of at least simple communicative language by the age of five to six years, the ability to score within the mildly retarded or above range on nonverbal tests of ability, the development of some social skills (Howlin & Goode, 1998), the early ability to sequence actions (motor planning), and an ability to imitate others (Greenspan & Weider, 1999). Having both autism and a significant learning disability was associated with poorer outcomes (Frith, 1991). In most studies, girls have a more unfavorable outcome, but these studies may have included girls with Rett's syndrome, complicating comparisons (Howlin & Goode). Kanner (1973) believed the presence of some specialized interest was associated with a more favorable outcome.

Examining variables that influence outcomes in this manner is helpful, but it is also constricting because these variables are outside of our control and provide little information about how to influence outcome through intervention. Greenspan and Weider (1999), for instance, found that early involvement in structured programs that engaged people with autism with others in a joyful manner was associated with a more positive outcome. An alternative model, proposed by Ruble and Dalrymple (1996), considers outcomes as a composite of competencies as judged by others (e.g., ability to work) and quality of life as judged by the person with autism. Ruble and Dalrymple proposed that positive quality of life outcomes include having opportunities for participating in activities with family members or friends, participating in holidays and other celebrations, being active in the community, working at a job they like, learning about the world through experiences, having choices and respected opinions, having responsibilities at home, having possessions and space to be alone, and receiving adequate information to make choices. When

applying these quality-of-life criteria to a group of 46 people with autism (mean age 17.1 years) who had neither a normal social life nor independence, they found that the highest quality of life was associated with having at least one advocate who enjoyed being with them, social acceptance, a variety of experiences, social experiences with others, and some form of work. The prognosis for children who are diagnosed with autism today is likely to be different from the prognosis of previous generations because of improved early intervention, early diagnosis, expanded resources available to families and professionals, and the consideration of quality of life outcomes from a person-centered perspective.

Personal reports of people with autism also enlighten us about the lifespan experiences of autism and possible outcomes. Grandin (1992), for example, described her own development from a withdrawn nonverbal child with autism to an adult with an earned doctorate and a successful career in designing livestock equipment. Mentors, teachers, and family members encouraged her to explore her strong interests, which were intrinsically motivating for her. The expansion of these restricted interests allowed her to excel. Nonetheless, during adolescence she experienced intense periods of anxiety and benefited from medications to reduce this. Her early sensory experiences were marked by tactile defensiveness, intense auditory sensitivity, and a craving for deep pressure touch. She described her way of learning and understanding as "visual thinking"; she thinks and sees in pictures without words or language. Although Grandin describes a positive outcome, persons who develop well and achieve a good outcome, nonetheless, experience a lifelong struggle of managing and overcoming the sensory, social, and communication problems of autism (MacDonald, 1998).

THE PRINCIPLES OF OCCUPATIONAL THERAPY

Sensorimotor Definition and Historical Roots

With this basic understanding of autism as a background, we now explore the principles of occupational therapy and occupational therapy using a sensorimotor approach for children and adults with autism. The term *sensorimotor* refers to a broad class of both sensory and motor difficulties and related treatment methods spanning a full range of interventions that originally arose from sensory integration theory and neurodevelopmental theories. Subtle variations of sensorimotor intervention are described by different authors; the distinctions between these variations and strategies are explored in other literature (e.g., Murray & Anzalone, 1991) and in Chapter 5 of this text. For example, sensory integration theory originally emphasized active experienced-based learning but, more recently, passively administered sensory stimulation has been included. The primary focus of this book is on understanding the sensory and motor characteristics of persons with autism, the effect of these characteristics on function, and the application of sensorimotor treatment strategies. As the body of literature regarding interventions for sensory and motor difficulties expands, so has related terminology. Table 1–2 includes a listing of common sensory and motor difficulties that can be found in autism and related disorders. These terms are defined and intervention strategies are broadly described.

Much of the credit for highlighting sensory needs and sensory responses as important in child function/dysfunction belongs to Jean Ayres (1972a, 1979), who was an occupational therapist and leader in child development. Although Ayres pioneered the emphasis on sensory input and sensory responses, her work also addressed the influence of primitive motor reflexes, motor output, and motor planning on function for children and adolescents. Her writings and research uniquely highlighted the role of body-centered sensations from the tactile, vestibular, and proprioceptive systems that complemented the emphasis on visual and auditory processing within other disciplines. The work of Ayres paralleled the work of authors of the time, such as Erikson (1963) and Maslow (1970), who emphasized stage models and hierarchical models of development, with a premise that prerequisite skills are necessary to achieve optimal higher-order functioning. Ayres's work was also in alignment with that of Piaget (1971), who valued and highlighted the role of sensory experiences in promoting development. The neuroscience investigators of her time, and the work of neurodevelopmental clinicians such as the Bobaths, profoundly influenced Ayres's theory development (Ayres, 1974). Although the theoretical work of all of these classic authors has been debated and modified, these original works continue to influence education, psychology, and occupational therapy practice.

Occupational Therapy and the Sensorimotor Approach

The work of Ayres and current authors (e.g., Fisher, Murray, & Bundy, 1991; Parham & Mailloux, 1996) forms the foundation for sensory integration theory; however, this is but one theory that guides the practice of occupational therapy and sensorimotor management for persons with autism. Occupational therapy treatment is fundamentally child-centered or person-centered treatment—that is, the occupational therapist believes that the child or person has the necessary resources for adaptation, growth, and change; these resources need to be elicited and developed through

Table 1–2 Sensory and Motor Difficulties and Related Intervention Guidelines

Functional Difficulty	Definition and Description	Systems Involved	Intervention Strategies
Arousal Modulation (also termed state regulation) Problem— Regulatory disorder	Ability to regulate the state of readiness and excitation of the nervous system. Varies on at least two continua of attention and affective responses.	Multiple structures and processes in the brain modulate brain activity to control excitation level.	Provision of external controls of the environment to compensate for regulatory disorders. Maintenance of optimal state of arousal to promote neural development and learning. Learn self-regulation strategies.
Sensory Modulation Problems— Decreased sensory registration or sensory defensiveness	Capacity to internally regulate the amount and intensity of sensory input. Difficulties seen in hyporeactivity (decreased registration) or hyperreactivity (defensiveness) to sensory input.	Touch, smell, taste, sound, vision, movement of the body, or movement against gravity.	External control of environment with carefully graded sensory input to improve self-regulation ability (usually involves providing more sensory input) or to compensate for inadequate sensory modulation.
Sensory Processing Problems—All of the above plus decreased discrimination	Ability to register, decode, comprehend, and differentiate sensory input, sensory sequences, and sensory patterns.	All of the above plus visual-spatial and language processing.	Simplify or amplify sensory input; graded teaching of processing. (e.g., visual motor skills). Environmental modification to support function.
Sensory Integration	Ability to organize the input from multiple senses for use in adaptive responses.	All sensory input including input from muscles, joints, and vestibular (gravity) receptors.	Facilitate active output by the child and enhance adaptive responses through graded sensory input.

continues

Table 1–2 continued

Functional Difficulty	Definition and Description	Systems Involved	Intervention Strategies
Sensory—Affective Processing (Greenspan & Weider, 1999)	Ability to process and react to affect and link affective intent to responding.	Integration of multiple cues from voice, body language, touch, etc., to gain affective meaning. Highly integrative response.	Multiple interventions all involving carefully graded intense affective contact.
Soft Neurological Signs	Findings that indicate less than optimal functioning of the brain. Sensory, motor, and dysmorphic (frontal upsweep) characteristics that are subtly apparent in most individuals but may be more prevalent and severe in autism and other developmental disorders.	Muscle tone, incoordination, visual tracking, primitive reflex integration, tremors, crossing the body midline, proximal muscle instability, etc.	Improve proximal motor stability, integration of more primitive patterns through active inhibitory techniques and skill development. Using compensatory strategies to bypass problems.
Imitation (Smith & Bryson, 1994)	Capacity to sense and then produce a response similar to that modeled by another person or thing (e.g., facial expression, action, or sound). May diminish social and play development if impaired.	Outcome of sensory integration, social representations of others, and multiple sensory and motor aspects.	Requires more intensive and structured teaching of skills, simplification of responses, and use of strongest sensory modality (e.g., vision). Increase salience of stimuli (e.g., exaggerate actions or responses).

continues

Table 1–2 continued

Functional Difficulty	Definition and Description	Systems Involved	Intervention Strategies
Motor Planning and Sequencing	Capacity to sequence actions, behaviors, words, images, and thoughts to produce a coherent and understandable outcome.	May affect all aspects of responding (output), from motor, language, and affective to constructional output.	As above. Careful teaching of one step; chaining responses. Simplifying motor output. Use of strongest sensory modality. Compensatory strategies.

Summarized from the works of Greenspan & Weider, 1999; Koomar & Bundy, 1991; Parham & Mailloux, 1996; Smith & Bryson, 1994.

the therapist-person interaction and guided treatment. These concepts emerged from the work of numerous theorists, beginning with Rogers (1969). This fundamental person-centered belief is expressed by the occupational therapist through his or her sensitivity to the nonverbal communication of the child, careful observations of the child's responses to environmental stimuli, and recognition that therapy is both guided by the therapist and child-directed (Koomar & Bundy, 1991). Person-centered practices coupled with sensory supports form the scaffolding that empowers the person with autism to take risks and learn (Tickle-Degnen & Coster, 1995).

Occupational therapy practice is also occupation based—that is, focused on the ability of any person to engage in the tasks of life. In an occupation-based approach, the diagnosis is far less important than the functional or social problems that inhibit or constrain a person's full participation in life. In the sensorimotor approach, the adaptive skills and behaviors of people are fostered through engaging in the tasks of life (occu-

pation). For the young child, play, self-care, language development, social attachment, exploration, and motoric responses are the meaningful occupations of life. As the child enters school, learning, skill development, and friendships are the occupations of life. From adolescence through young adulthood, the occupations of life include preparation for work and independence, social interaction, and later intimate attachment with peers. All of these tasks of life, or occupations, are the concerns of occupational therapy and are discussed in this book with respect to autism. The sensorimotor approach to management is one method to reduce the barriers to occupation.

To accomplish the development of skills for occupation, occupational therapists use remediation techniques to reduce impairments, compensatory techniques to bypass activity or participation impairments, and prevention techniques. In the case of children with autism, the occupational therapist focusing on remediation of a sensory modulation dysfunction may, for instance, carefully grade sensory input to diminish sensory defensiveness while enhancing attachment, play, or language production. In focusing on the motor aspects of autism, the occupational therapist may seek to improve proximal muscle stability to enhance coordination, visual tracking, or oral motor control. In addition and, often, simultaneously, the occupational therapist may seek to bypass the sensorimotor difficulty to improve participation and occupation. For example, the environment can be modified (e.g., dim lighting) to diminish sensory overload or a safe space provided in which the child can calm himself or herself when needed. Clothing might be altered to bypass sensory defensiveness from irritating fabrics, or simplified to teach dressing and self-care. Occupational therapists are also committed to prevention of secondary problems, often through collaboration with others. In the case of autism, collaborators might include the parents, multiple professionals, school personnel, and community-based supports joined to encourage adjustment, normalization of the environment, successful inclusion, and, ultimately, full participation in life.

Within the context of autism, the sensorimotor approach to management refers to the full range of methods to diminish sensory and motor problems and to enhance occupation and engagement in the tasks of life. Although the exact nature of sensory and motor dysfunction is currently being described, as many as 90–100% of children with autism experience sensory processing deficits (Eaves et al., 1994; Kientz & Dunn, 1997) and motor impairments (Jones & Prior, 1985). The sensorimotor approach was designed to address these sensory and motor manifestations, just as the behavioral approach was designed to address the behavioral manifestations of autism. This approach to the management of autism and related disorders is neither a cure for autism

nor a complete picture of the needs of people with autism. Nonetheless, a fundamental regard for the sensory and motor needs of people with autism can be incorporated into the home, preschool, classroom, and community settings, just as a fundamental regard for language development, behavioral control, and learning ideally permeate these environments. As demonstrated in this book, the sensorimotor approach can be used to complement structured behavioral interventions, educational approaches, speech and language therapy, and a host of other interventions. In this approach, a fundamental philosophy prevails that respects communication, often conveyed through behavior rather than words, about people's sensory and motor experiences. For example, children who engage in rocking and twirling behavior may be communicating a need for vestibular stimulation. We can meet the sensory need in a more acceptable manner and in a way that engages the child with others. For example, we could encourage the child to sit in a rocking chair or a swing while learning language or self-care.

Occupational Therapy Practice for Persons with Autism

Several recent studies highlight the practice of occupational therapy with people who have autism. Watling, Deitz, Kanny, and McLaughlin (1999) surveyed 72 occupational therapists experienced in autism treatment and found that sensory integration was the dominant theoretical framework used. However, this approach was combined with a developmental and a behavioral approach by more than 70% of respondents, suggesting an integrated and holistic framework for therapy. Additionally, occupational therapy practices included both a 1:1 focus of intervention (82%) and frequent collaboration with speech pathologists (98%), schoolteachers (84%), and psychologists (64%) during evaluation and, similarly, during intervention. Case-Smith and Miller (1999) surveyed 292 occupational therapists in school system practice and found that they applied sensory integration and environmental modification in their direct and consultative roles with children with autism. Huebner and Healander (in preparation) studied the clinical reasoning of 170 occupational therapists with an average of 11.6 years of experience in occupational therapy and 6.2 years of experience with autism. When asked about the unique contributions of occupational therapy to the treatment of autism, more than 90% responded that occupational therapists contribute an understanding of how sensory processing and sensory modulation disorders affect behavior, communication, and functional skills. These consistent findings demonstrate that occupational therapists use a broad sensorimotor framework in their work with people who have autism, collaborate with others, explore problems, and provide education of others from a consistent person-centered focus and philosophy.

BASIC CONCEPTS OF THE SENSORIMOTOR APPROACH

Historical Underpinnings

Historically, several clinicians and scholars developed neurorehabilitation treatment techniques based in neuroscience at the same time that Ayres was working. Much of this work was clinic-based work with adults and children who had neurological disorders, such as cerebral palsy or cerebrovascular accidents (see Farber, 1982). Margaret Rood and her colleagues pioneered the use of techniques in both occupational and physical therapy to inhibit abnormal sensory and motor responses and facilitate more normal responses. The use of specific sensory input devices such as vibrators, brushes, and dynamic stretches in sensorimotor therapy stems from the assumptions inherent in the work of Rood that providing carefully graded sensory and especially tactile (touch) input may enhance neurological function and motor abilities. Ayres expanded on the work of Rood to include vestibular stimulation through balance and whole-body motions and proprioceptive stimulation of muscles and joints through movement and resistance to enhance neurological maturation and motor abilities.

The work of the Bobaths, from the United Kingdom, profoundly influenced the treatment of children (see Bly, 1991, for a review) in both occupational and physical therapy. The Bobaths underscored the importance of proximal stability with the idea that mobility (ambulation and fine motor movements in the hand and mouth) is superimposed on stability (most often, proximal control in the trunk, shoulder girdle, pelvis, neck, and some facial muscles)—that is, mobility skills such as writing, cutting with scissors, and articulating sounds are dependent on stability in the trunk, shoulder girdle, neck, and facial musculature. The Bobaths and other rehabilitation theorists emphasized the hierarchical development of balance and coordination, with primitive reflexes (as seen in the newborn) forming a foundation for equilibrium reactions (such as riding a bike). For children with more severe neurological disorders, the Bobaths' neurodevelopmental theory stressed that primitive reflexes that persist beyond normal development or reappear with brain injury interfere with skills development and needed to be inhibited and/or integrated. Integration of primitive movement patterns was enhanced by actively assuming motor patterns opposite the reflex pattern and then facilitating equilibrium responses. Patterns opposite reflex patterns, or reflex-inhibiting postures, usually involve motions using proximal (toward the center of the body) muscle control. For example, actively assuming and holding prone extension (see Figure 1–1) in a swinging net while tossing objects toward a target, or pulling into supine flexion (see Figure 1–2) on a therapy ball simultaneously integrates primitive reflex patterns and strengthens proximal muscles while encouraging equilibrium responses and visual tracking (a fine coordinated motion) (see Koomar & Bundy, 1991, for other examples). This proximal muscle control and strength then provide the

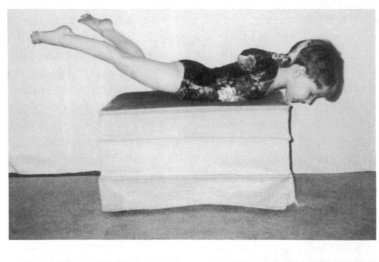

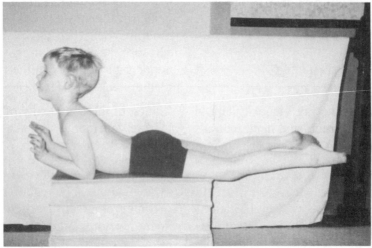

Figure 1–1 Prone extension posture held by a 4-year-old without autism and an 8-year-old with autism. The boy with autism is unable to assume the posture with his upper and lower body. Prone extension posture against gravity uses strength in all proximal muscles of extension.

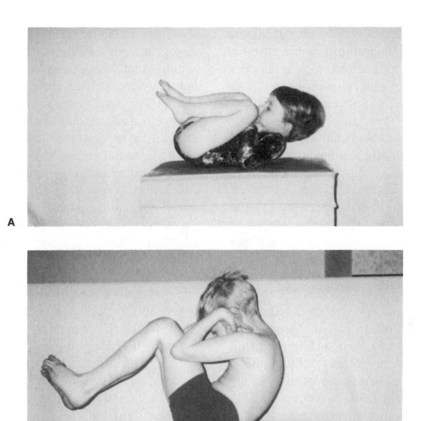

Figure 1–2 Supine flexion posture held by a 4-year-old without autism and an 8-year-old with autism. Supine flexion posture against gravity uses strength in all proximal muscles of flexion.

stability for coordinating visual tracking, oral motor skills, speech, and hand motions (all mobility patterns). A second principle of treatment is that responses are learned by experiencing and doing motions (Dutton, 1998)—that is, to learn normal movement, one must experience increasingly normal movement patterns.

Much of the earlier work of the theorists in neurorehabilitation interventions was based on premises of a linear or hierarchical system of brain processing, with less appre-

ciation of the complexity of brain function. As the development of sensory and motor patterns is understood from the perspective of learning theory and dynamic systems theory (e.g., Thelan, 1995), our understanding of the multicausal, multidimensional, and self-organizing nature of brain development has also emerged and been incorporated into sensorimotor theories. Dynamic systems theory and sensory integration theory share the belief that all people have some innate capacity to organize their behavior in response to changes in the environment; this self-organization capability is harnessed by the occupational therapist working in a person-centered and occupation-centered approach to therapy (Spitzer, 1999). The person-centered approach enhances the therapist-child relationship and the parent-child relationship so that the emotional support provides scaffolding that supports the person in taking risks, trying challenging tasks, and experiencing mastery (Tickle-Degnen & Coster, 1995). Specific motor learning theories are based on the principles of teaching motor skills in such a way that learned skills persist and generalize to different contexts. These theories add the concepts to the sensorimotor approach of providing different types of feedback to learners to enhance their performance abilities. Feedback such as knowledge of the results of one's actions, knowledge of how to perform, and altering practice schedules may achieve optimal learning and harness self-organizing capabilities (Guiffrida, 1998).

Sensory Integration Processes

Sensory integration, in the broad sense, refers to the processes that are common to all forms of learning and the primary functions of the brain (Kolb & Whishaw, 1996). It is the taking in of sensory input, the processing of input in the brain, and the organization of a response, which is expressed as behavior and learning. Each sensory system is similarly organized. Sensory receptors, which may be specialized for detecting unique aspects of each sensory input (e.g., bitter taste receptors, color detectors), respond to a particular intensity or characteristic of a stimulus. The number and distribution of sensory receptors determine the amount of sensory discrimination possible at any site. For example, numerous touch receptors and proprioceptors in the fingers facilitate exact discrimination of small coins and finely coordinated motion for activities like touch typing. Sensory receptors convert, or transduce, a sensation to a usable stimulus for processing in the brain.

Once a sensation is converted to an electrical impulse (action impulse) for brain processing, it is relayed through multiple neurological sites. At each site, action potentials converge with other sensory input, inhibitory impulses, motor neurons, and multiple other inputs that modulate (dampen or exaggerate) the action potential. Action potentials are received by the nervous system and acted on in ways that are not totally understood—but, once perceived, a response to a sensory input is organized, resulting in an identifiable response (e.g., a thought, reflex withdrawal from pain, a word, or an action) and/or a change in the threshold sensitivity of the sensory receptor, neuron, or neural system. Thus, sensation is received, converted, processed, modulated, and acted on; this process is referred to as *sensory integration* or *sensory processing*. Figure 1–3 shows an example of a typical neuron (brain cell) and illustrates the dendrites, which receive input from multiple sources and the axon, which conducts the action potential. The myelin on the axon speeds the electrical action potential. In any small section of the brain, hundreds of neurons connect with all parts of the brain through dendritic sprouting and axonal connections. Neurotransmitters carry the action potential from one cell to another. The web of dendritic sprouting is continuously changing in response to environmental (experiences) and internal (thoughts) stimulation.

When sensory input is appropriately discriminated and modulated, the person has

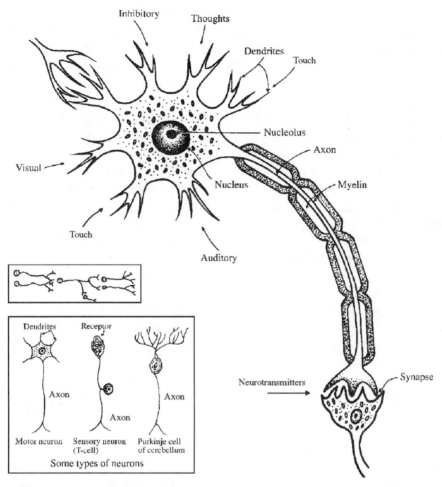

Figure 1–3 Typical neuron. *Source:* Reprinted from S.D. Gertz, *Neuroanatomy Made Easy and Understandable,* 6th, ed., p. 3, Aspen Publishers, Inc.

the opportunity to construct a reasonable response to that sensory input. However, if a person processes sensory input either poorly (e.g., has low vision) or differently (e.g., has sensory hypersensitivity), then the response that the person can create to the sensation is likely to be seen as unusual by others. If a person perceives sensation very differently, as in autism, then the person is likely to respond differently and has a diminished or altered ability to discover and master the environment. Because of the power of sensory

input, extremes of sensory processing, such as finding movement or touch noxious, are likely to be associated with a very different perception of life and barriers to engaging in the tasks of life (occupation).

THE FOUNDATIONS OF SENSORY INTEGRATION

Sensory integration theory (Fisher & Murray, 1991) is based on an understanding of brain-behavior relationships and rooted in neuroscience. This theory attempts to explain normal sensory functioning, dysfunctional sensory integration processes, and techniques to guide intervention. In the past 10 years, the wealth of information coming from neuroscience is so vast that the theoretical base of sensorimotor interventions is rapidly evolving and changing. The principles of sensory integration and other sensorimotor interventions are based in neuroscience, and so, as neuroscience knowledge expands, we can identify more refined ways to interpret people's behaviors from a sensorimotor perspective and create a more substantial rationale for sensorimotor interventions. In this section, we introduce key information from the literature on neural plasticity, sensory processing, and arousal regulation that informs us about the nervous system's methods for taking in, understanding, and using information for functioning in daily life.

Neural Plasticity

The term *neural plasticity* refers to the brain's ability to change or be modified both in response to normal developmental processes and to a range of sensory input including visual images, social interaction, and educational techniques. Learning, the development of new skills, is the behavioral output of neural plasticity and is sometimes used synonymously (Churchland, 1986). Sensory integration theory and practices are based on the assumption that experiences modify brain structure and function in either an adaptive or maladaptive manner (Fisher & Murray, 1991). Although the assumption of neural plasticity is stated more formally in theories such as sensory integration, this assumption is also fundamental to education and all learning.

Developmental Processes Related to Plasticity

In the young child, neural plasticity results, in part, from typical developmental processes in the brain. At the time and site of each developmental process, brain maturation is both most vulnerable to insult and most amenable to optimal influences. Kolb and Whishaw (1996) described five processes of brain development that contribute to neural plasticity. Cell production occurs in the first half of gestation within specialized brain tissue; these cells then migrate from the sites where they were produced to their final location. Cell migration continues until eight months of postnatal age, with the final cortical layer of cells migrating last. Errors or truncation (restriction) of cell production or migration can occur in response to any disease, genetic disorder, or infection affecting the brain during these developmental processes (Coleman, 1994).

As cells migrate to their target sites, axons sprout from the neurons. The processes of axonal growth, dendritic growth, and synaptic formation underlie the differentiation and specialization of brain sites. Axonal development proceeds in a manner yet unknown, but axons migrate through obstacles or to new locations in the presence of brain injury. Dendritic growth, or the branching out of the axon, includes both processes of developing dendritic density and pruning or shedding dendritic spines. This process continues throughout life and can be enhanced by stimulation and diminished with sensory deprivation or brain injury (Kolb & Whishaw, 1996). Synaptic formation is a process of establishing contact between the dendrites, axon, or cell body of neurons; the synapse is the site of neurotransmitter releases that influence the action potential of receptor neurons. These processes of dynamic brain restructuring through synaptic formation and pruning, which are the foundation of neural plasticity in older children and adults, continue in the presence of appropriate stimulation and health well into the 60s and, probably, indefinitely (Kolb & Whishaw, 1996).

Myelination, a maturation process of the brain, involves surrounding axons with an insulation that speeds the transmission of impulses. The extent of myelination is one indicator of relative maturity in the brain. Developmental processes of myelination, which begin in the second half of gestation, continue well into the third and fourth decades of life, with the reticular formation and intracortical association areas being fully myelinated last (Westman, 1990).

Although there is the possibility for continued brain differentiation throughout life, peak periods of brain growth or growth spurts in children occur at 3 months to 1.5 years, 2–4 years, 6–8 years, 10–12 years, and 14–16 years (Kolb & Whishaw, 1996). The first four brain spurts correspond to the four main stages of intellectual development described by Piaget (1971) and correlate with the emergence of skills such as state regulation, attachment, language, and abstract reasoning (Kolb & Whishaw).

The Impact of Experience on Neural Plasticity

A growing body of research suggests that autism in children reflects neurological immaturity, a failure of brain development in early gestation (e.g., Bauman & Kemper, 1994; Coleman, 1994; Courchesne, Townsend, & Saitoh 1994; Poustka, 1998; Rapin & Katzman, 1998). Thus, children with autism are likely to be endowed, biologically and naturally, with differences in brain structure and function. Given an underlying difference in brain development (nature), theories and findings related to neural plasticity (sometimes termed the *biodynamic systems model*) highlight the effects of experiences and context (nurture) on the development of learning. Within the biodynamic system model, there is no inherent deterministic developmental process of brain function. Rather, both small changes early in development and small differences in neural structures are thought to be associated with large effects over time, because small changes alter the developmental trajectory (e.g., Cicchetti & Tucker, 1994; Perry, Pollard, Blakley, Baker, & Vigilante, 1995; Thelan, 1995). In this dynamic view of brain function and development, the individual's experiences and active strivings for mastery alter brain development throughout the life course.

Much of the support for the premise that "the mechanisms of plasticity cause the brain's anatomical differentiation to be dependent on stimulation from the environment" (Cicchetti & Tucker, 1994, p. 537) comes from studies of the neurobiology of trauma, deprivation, or psychopathology, or from studies in learning and memory. We are beginning to understand the effects of experiences on the long-term potentiation (active readiness) or long-term depression (inhibition) of learning and memory (Post & Weiss, 1997; Post, Weiss, & Leverich, 1994), suggesting that experiences remodel both individual neurons and influence entire neural networks and neural integration. Studies in affective disorders suggest that a sensitization of neurons and networks from repeated stress, recurrent depressions, or small electrical differences (electrophysiological kindling) ultimately changes the brain microstructure, resulting in an increased sensitivity to stress, trauma, or seizures, with a cascade of subsequent neurobiological events through the lifespan. This kindling effect is proposed by Waterhouse, Fein, and Modahl (1996) as a possible mechanism for the sudden early regression seen in some children with autism and the onset of seizures. In response to a single major traumatic experience, recurrent milder trauma, or continuous experiences of anxiety and hyperarousal, changes in the brain result in persistent states of anxiety or dissociation (Perry et al., 1995). Thus, early negative experiences alter the microstructure and networks of the brain, so that the brain is more vulnerable to succeeding negative experiences.

As our understanding of the neural plasticity of the brain evolves, it becomes increasing clear that experiences are critically important in shaping the nervous system responsiveness. For the person with autism, the sensorimotor approach to management emphasizes sensory and motor experiences, and seeks to promote a positive experience for the child. There is abundant and growing understanding of how experiences influence neural development (Cicchetti & Tucker, 1994; Kandel, Schwartz, & Jessell, 2000), but we need to continue to collect evidence about the relationships between nervous system activity and both general human experiences and sensorimotor interventions. Currently, drawing conclusions about the effects of sensorimotor interventions on specific neural structures is unwarranted (Fisher & Murray, 1991) and highly speculative, because neuroscience does not have any unified theory about brain processes and function (Churchland, 1986). Nonetheless, the sensorimotor approach to management is based on the ideas that sensory and motor experiences have the potential to positively or negatively influence neural structures and subsequent behavior and function. We also believe that individuals' adaptive responses—that is, functional and appropriate behavior—reflect the evidence of improved sensory integration and mobilize their self-strivings for development. For example, if a child who is withdrawn and isolated due to sensory overload actively interacts with others (if only briefly) when environmental demands are simplified, he or she emits an adaptive response reflecting more typical sensory processing, and the positive experience may elicit additional efforts toward learning. Over time, adaptive or maladaptive neuronal models of behavior, interaction, response to sensory input, and sensory processing patterns are established and reinforced.

Sensory Processing

Researchers have been fascinated with the role of sensory processing in human behavior for more than a century. In the late 1800s, researchers were emphasizing sensation as "the key to the mind" and reported that all sensory systems shared three features: They required a physical stimulus to activate, the nervous system had to transform the stimulus into a neural impulse, and the nervous system had to create a response to the stimulus in the form of a perceptual event of a conscious experience of sensation (Gardner & Martin, 2000). We know now that these sensory data are critical for the nervous system; they form the basis for our plans about movement, emotional responses, and cognitive problem solving (Kandel, Schwartz, & Jessell, 2000).

Children and adults have characteristic ways of processing sensory information. For some people, particular sensory experiences are pleasurable, while the same sensory events are innocuous or noxious for others. Each way of responding to or experiencing sensation may have a corresponding pattern of behavior. Zuckerman (1979) studied the phenomenon of "sensation seeking" and its impact on behavioral responses and optimal arousal for performance; other authors have examined features of high sensitivity to sensation. For example, in a preliminary study, Reich (personal communication) found that people with a high need for structure and who dislike disruptions also score high on "sensory sensitivity" and "sensory avoidance"' on the Adult Sensory Profile, a measure of people's responses to sensory events in daily life. He found that the items "Having an Orderly Life" and "Wanting Structure" were positively correlated with "sensory avoidance" and negatively correlated with "sensory seeking" behaviors. Brown, Tollefson, Dunn, Cromwell, and Filion (in press) found a significant relationship between skin conductance responses and the preferred pattern of sensory processing as measured on the Adult Sensory Profile. Persons with a high physiological responsiveness to sensory stimuli also reported a high sensitivity or high need to avoid sensory experiences. Those who habituated quickly to sensory stimuli tended to either discount sensory experiences or not notice what was going on around them (i.e., low registration). McIntosh, Miller, Shyu, and Hagerman (1998) also found similar relationships in children between skin conductance responses and patterns of sensory processing.

The issue of sensory processing is a salient feature of disabilities as well. Ayres (1972a) discussed the characteristics of particular children with learning and behavior disabilities in relation to their responses to touch and movement sensations. Fisher, Murray, and Bundy (1991) and Royeen and Lane (1991) discussed the sensory processing characteristics of children who also have incoordination, emotional lability, and learning challenges. Others have hypothesized about the relationships between the behaviors and symptoms of schizophrenia and individuals' methods of processing information (e.g., Cromwell & Snyder, 1993; Brekke, Raine, Ansel, Lencz, & Bird, 1997; Brown et al., in press). Studies have reported unique patterns of sensory processing in children who have autism (Kientz & Dunn, 1997), ADHD (Bennett, 1996; Ermer & Dunn, 1998), and Fragile-X Syndrome (McIntosh et al., 1998).

Researchers have also sought to create and validate measures of sensory processing (e.g., Ayres, 1972b, 1989; Ayres & Tickle, 1980; DeGangi & Greenspan, 1989; Larson, 1982; Royeen & Fortune, 1990; Dunn, 1999). Ayres conducted a line of research studies to validate the methods of assessing children's sensory processing as part of the Southern California Sensory Integration Tests battery and the more recent Sensory Integration and Praxis Tests. These studies demonstrated the sensory processing features of children's performance by validating a link between particular sensations and particular ways of constructing movements. For example, she demonstrated that there is a relationship between somatosensory perception and one's ability to plan new motor acts (i.e., praxis). Royeen and Fortune designed a measure of touch processing for schoolchildren in which the children tell whether they are bothered by certain touch events (e.g., nails cut, hair combed, being hugged). By using this strategy, these authors tried to characterize a child's sensitivity or defensiveness to touch as a basis for testing the relationships between sensitivity to touch and certain maladaptive behaviors. DeGangi and Greenspan formulated the Test of Sensory Functions in Infants to help professionals identify children at risk for having difficulties regulating their own state of

arousal, because this can interfere with social interactions that facilitate development.
Larson designed a way to record a child's responses to sensory aspects of life, called the
Sensory History. Dunn, more recently, refined this measurement technique by conducting research on the Sensory Profile (for
children for ages 3–10), the Adult Sensory
Profile, and the Infant-Toddler Sensory Profile. These measures ask people to record
how frequently they, or their child, engage in
behaviors that indicate their high or low responsiveness to sensory events in daily life.
All of these authors have designed ways to
capture responses to sensation to enable
testing of both the relationships between
sensory responses and behavior and the impact of sensory-based interventions created
to improve functional outcomes.

Much work can be done to further establish the relationships between sensory processing and one's experiences in daily life.
The work thus far is promising in that it
confirms that the early neuroscientists' intu-
itions were correct: There *is* a primal link
between the way the nervous system receives, interprets, and uses sensory information and the way the person experiences
life events. The sensory systems provide the
only mechanism for communicating with
the brain; when this mechanism operates
differently for a person (e.g., by processing
more slowly, too quickly, distortedly, less
powerfully, too intensely), then the output
systems are likely to produce unusual results (i.e., maladaptive or ineffective behavioral responses). The more we understand
sensory processing mechanisms, the better
we can interpret the meaning of people's
behavior and design effective sensorimotor
interventions. Concepts associated with the
literature on arousal, modulation, and self-
regulation also contribute to the under-

standing of sensorimotor interventions, especially for children with autism.

Arousal, Modulation, and Self-Regulation

Arousal

Arousal is defined as a physiological state
of readiness elicited by the organism's perception of its environment (Johnson & Anderson, 1990) or as the general state of nervous system excitation that affects behavior
(Belser & Sudhalter, 1995). As summarized
in Chapter 3, numerous studies on the neuropsychology of autism implicate the neurological substrates that regulate and modulate
arousal as faulty. The neural structures that
control the state of arousal within the nervous system include brainstem structures
for alerting the neurological system, the
cerebellum for modulation sensory input
and coordinating the timing and sequence of
motor output, midbrain structures for as-
signing emotional significant and memory
to arousal, and connections to cortical areas
for planning, executing, and abstract processing. Although there is limited description of the specific arousal differences of
children with autism, difficulties with self-
modulation of arousal have been a fundamental premise supporting the use of sensorimotor interventions for people with autism
and other sensory processing disorders
(Huebner, 1992).

Arousal implies a normal state regulation
continuum, which influences both an attention continuum and an affective continuum.
Consequently, the modulation of arousal is
critical to optimal attention, learning
(Royeen & Lane, 1991), and emotional security. On the attention continuum, low
arousal is associated with drowsiness and
mental lethargy; high arousal is associated

with distractibility and flight of ideas with hyperactivity and, at the extreme, manic behavior. On the affective continuum, low arousal is associated with boredom or a sense of calm; higher arousal to hyperarousal is associated with increasing levels of excitement, anxiety to fear, and, at the extreme, terror and fight or flight. In the middle range of arousal, attention and affect are at optimal levels for function and enhanced performance and learning. Typically, people have a wide range of optimal arousal and can function adequately despite sleep deprivation or anxiety-provoking situations. In contrast, children with autism seem to have a very narrow range of optimal arousal. Royeen and Lane theorized that arousal might be considered circular for children with sensory processing disorders, who vacillate between defensive/anxious states and dormancy states. Another recently emerging theory is that hyperarousal, associated with high anxiety and distress, is more likely to be responded to with immobility (freezing) or compliant behavior (surrender) by a child because flight-or-fight is less likely to be effective for him or her. Both immobility and surrender may result in dissociation from present experiences over time (Perry et al., 1995). This link between hyperarousal and dissociation may explain the paradoxical or circular pattern observed by Royeen and Lane—that is, hyperarousal may be associated with dissociation (a response to anxiety), which may appear to be dormancy, low arousal, or even lethargy. These ideas are speculative, of course, and need further research. Nonetheless, clinical observations and reports of people with autism suggest that many people with autism experience sensations differently than others, including exaggerated and threatening perceptions of sensory input and arousal disorders. These

different experiences are likely to be stressful and cumulative over time, perhaps resulting in changes in neural sensitivity and dissociation.

State Regulation and Modulation

Understanding of the impact of disorders of arousal modulation or state regulatory disorders on infants and young children is growing. The diagnostic criteria for such regulatory disorders are defined by the National Center for Clinical Infant Programs (1994). Regulatory disorders are characterized by difficulties in regulating behavior and responses to sensory, motor, and affective input in order to organize a calm, alert, or positive affective state. The criteria for diagnosis and description of problems inherent in regulatory disorders are displayed in Exhibit 1–1.

Research evidence suggests that children with autism have regulatory disorders with diminished ability to modulate arousal. Bagnato and Neisworth (1999) found that among children between the ages of 11 and 71 months (approximately 1 and 6 years), those with autism ($n = 36$) showed the most severe regulatory disorders when compared to typical children ($n = 612$), children with developmental delay ($n = 37$), and children with Fragile-X Syndrome ($n = 12$). Children with autism experienced significant symptoms of regulatory disorders in all categories. Belser and Sudhalter (1995) found that males ($n = 10$, mean age 16 years 1 month) with Fragile-X Syndrome (often associated with autism) were more anxious during conversations and experienced more physiological arousal during eye contact with a partner than other males with developmental disabilities and similar cognitive abilities. People with autism also exhibit motor stereotypies such as hand flapping

Exhibit 1–1 Characteristics of Regulatory Disorders

Both a poorly regulated behavioral pattern and poorly modulated sensorimotor or organizational processing must be present for a diagnisis of a regulatory disorder.

Poorly regulated behavioral patterns are shown in:

- Poor state modulation (e.g., irregular breathing, easily startled, gagging)
- Gross motor disorganization, jerky or constant movements
- Poorly differentiated or limp fine-motor activity
- Problems in attending; either hyperactivity or perseveration on small details
- Affective organization; a predominant affective tone (sober, distressed), restricted range of affect, rapidly changing affect, or problems in organizing affect in relationships (clinging, avoidant, negative)
- Aggressive or impulsive behavior
- Sleep, eating, or elimination problems
- Language or cognitive difficulties

Poorly modulated sensory, sensorimotor, or processing difficulties include the following:

- Over- or underreactivity to auditory, visual, pain, touch, odor, or temperature stimuli
- Tactile defensiveness and/or oral hypersensitivity, or articulation difficulties
- Oral-motor incoordination

- Gravitational insecurity
- Poor muscle tone, motor planning, fine-motor skills, or modulation of activity
- Deficits in attention and focus not related to anxiety or interactive difficulties
- Deficits in visual-spatial processing capacities

Four subtypes of regulatory disorders are described:

1. Hypersensitivity Type: overreactive to stimuli:
   - Either a fearful and cautious behavior or a negative and defiant behavior
2. Underreactive Type
   - Either a pattern of withdrawn and difficult to engage or self-absorbed behavior
3. Motorically Disorganized, Impulsive Type
   - Either aggressive and fearless behavior or impulsive and disorganized behavior
   - Craving for sensory input
4. Other category for children who do not meet the behavioral criteria for any of the other subtypes but exhibit motor or sensory-processing difficulties

Summarized from the National Center for Clinical Infant Programs (1994).

and rocking, and may exhibit self-injurious behaviors such as hand biting. One theoretical interpretation of these stereotypies is that they are used to modulate arousal and maintain homeostasis (Berkson, 1996; Guess & Carr, 1991). Willemsen-Swinkels et al. (1998) found ($n = 10$) physiological evidence that initiation of stereotypic behavior was associated with high-arousal distressed states just prior to the stereotypic behavior in 85% of instances. Stereotypic behavior had a calming effect. However, stereotypic behaviors, in other instances, were associated with elation (possibly as an outlet for excitement) and calm states (possibly to get attention), suggesting multiple functions. The study of the states of arousal and the expression of these states for persons with autism is in its infancy, but may yield pertinent discoveries. As Donnellan (1999) so aptly summarized, in autism there are no rules; there is only complexity, because we are studying the most complex object in the universe, the human brain.

A Model for Considering Modulation and Sensory Processing

Dunn (1997) proposed a model for sensory processing that is consistent with the regulatory disorders categories just described. In this model, two primary continua are considered. The first is a neurological threshold continuum, which characterizes the amount of stimulation the nervous system requires to produce a response; the second is a behavioral response continuum, which characterizes the nature of a person's responses to environmental demands. Neurological thresholds can be high, indicating that a large amount of stimulation is necessary before the nervous system responds (e.g., habituation to stimuli) or low, indicating that the nervous system responds quickly to stimuli (e.g., sensitization). Persons can respond in a passive or an active manner to environmental demands, which are represented by the anchor points for the behavioral response continuum. Figure 1–4 illustrates Dunn's original model of sensory processing.

Once these continua are graphed as a quadrant, patterns of responsivity emerge.

The patterns illustrated on the figure represent the anchor points at the end of each continuum. Persons with high neurological thresholds to sensory input and who are passive in relation to these thresholds have *low registration*. People with very low registration demonstrate a dull affect, may be withdrawn, and seem apathetic or self-absorbed; they don't notice what is going on around them. Persons who have a high neurological threshold but who are active in relation to those thresholds are *sensation seekers*. People who seek sensation are very active, can be fidgety and excitable, and seem to be continuously engaged; they notice and enjoy every sensory stimulus that is available. People who have low neurological thresholds to sensory input and who are passive in relation to these thresholds can be called *high responders*. They are distractible, may seem hyperactive, and might complain a lot about things being bothersome; they notice sensory stimuli and "have enough" very quickly. People who have low neurological thresholds but who are active in relation to those thresholds can be called *sensation avoiders*. People who avoid sensation tend to be very rule-bound and ritualistic, pre-

Neurological threshold continuum	Behavioral response continuum	
	Passive	Active
High	LOW REGISTRATION	SENSORY SEEKING
Low	SENSITIVITY	SENSORY AVOIDING

Figure 1–4 Dunn's model of sensory processing (see Dunn, 1997). *Source:* Reprinted from W. Dunn, The Impact of Sensory Processing Abilities on the Daily Lives of Young Children and Their Families: A Conceptual Model, *Infants and Young Children,* Vol. 9, No. 4, p. 24 © 1997, Aspen Publishers, Inc.

sumably to reduce the amount of unpredictable or new stimuli around them; they know that new stimuli are unpleasant and therefore work actively to prevent them.

In research with children with and without disabilities, Dunn and colleagues found that children exhibit patterns of sensory processing behavior in daily life that are consistent with this model and, therefore, consistant with the regulatory disorder categories (see Table 1–3). Dunn and Brown (1997) conducted a factor analysis using data from the Sensory Profile, a parent reporting measure of children's responses to sensory events in daily life (Dunn, 1999), and identified nine factors that accounted for 47.4% of the variance in a national sample of children without disabilities ($n = 1,037$ children). Rather than grouping by sensory system, the items that are grouped into factors based on thresholds and responsivity to stimuli in the environment—thus supporting the concepts that one's way of responding—might be more fundamental to understanding sensory processing than the type of sensory input per se.

Kientz and Dunn (1997) compared the sensory processing patterns of children with autism ($n = 32$ children, ages 3 to 13 years) to 64 similarly aged children without autism using data from the Sensory Profile. The factor structure identified by Dunn and Brown and discriminating factors identified by Ermer and Dunn (1998) are displayed in Table 1–3 with items from the Sensory Profile that were identified in at least 50% of children with autism (Kientz & Dunn) and in subsequent data analysis. The data displayed in Table 1–3 illustrate the unique sensory processing profile of children with autism. When comparing these studies, it was noticed that the sensory processing patterns related to touch were rarely reported by parents of typical children but frequently reported by parents of children with autism. Only 31% of items related to touch had fac-

tor loadings above .50, in contrast to an average of 75% of all the items from the Sensory Profile, which loaded in the factor structure. This observation suggests that typical children experience little variability or difficulty in processing touch sensation, but children with autism frequently experience difficulty with processing touch or tactile input. Processing differences for touch sensation may be one group of sensory items that differentiates children with autism, perhaps at an early age. This speculative hypothesis requires testing, of course. Perhaps the factor structure for data from the Sensory Profile for children with autism is different than the structure found among more typically developing children. Future studies using factor analysis may yield further insights into the unique processing patterns of persons with autism.

Ermer and Dunn (1998) used a discriminant analysis to compare performance on these factors among children without disabilities, children with autism, and children with ADHD. They correctly discriminated the groups with 89.08% accuracy using the nine-factor structure. Factor 1 (Sensory Seeking), Factor 4 (Oral Sensory Sensitivity), Factor 5 (Inattention/Distractibility), and Factor 9 (Fine Motor/Perceptual) contributed most to the differentiation of groups. Children with ADHD were most distinct from children with autism on Factors 1, 4, and 9. Children with ADHD were most distinct from children without disabilities on Factor 5, while children with autism were most distinct from children without disabilities on all four of these factors. The findings support the idea that autism and ADHD present distinct sensory processing and regulation features that are characteristic of each of these disorders.

This model of sensory processing emerged from research Dunn and her colleagues conducted using various forms of the Sensory Profile. With further work

Table 1–3 Domains of Sensory Processing and Findings in Autism

Factor #	Factor Name[1]	No.	Behaviors Reported by > 50% in Autism[2]
1[3]	Sensory Seeking	25	Continually seeks out all kinds of movement.
		7	Enjoys strange noises/seeks to make noise for noise's sake.*
2	Emotional Reactivity	92	Needs more protection from life than other children.
		109	Poor frustration tolerance.
		105	Displays excessive emotional outbursts when unsuccessful at a task.
		107	Is stubborn and uncooperative.
		121	Has difficulty tolerating changes in plans and expectations.
		122	Has difficulty tolerating changes in routine.
		101	Has trouble "growing up" (e.g., reacts immaturely).
3	Low Endurance/ Tone		No behaviors noted in this category. *Most prevalent items were: seems to have weak muscles (37.5%); has a weak grasp (35%).*
4[3]	Oral Sensory Sensitivity		Shows preference for certain tastes.*
		64	Seeks out certain tastes or smells.
		58	Picky eater, especially regarding textures.
5[3]	Inattention/ Distractibility	48	Has difficulty paying attention.
		4	Is distracted or has trouble functioning if there is a lot of noise around.
		3	Has trouble completing tasks if the radio is on.
		49	Looks away from tasks to notice all actions in the room.
		6	Appears not to hear what you say (46.9%).
6	Poor Registration		No behaviors noted in this category. *Notably, children with autism were reported to have a sense of humor and an ability to perceive body language or facial gestures.*
7	Sensory Sensitivity		No behaviors noted in this category. *Although these items did not load in the factor analysis with typical children, they were present in children with autism and seem to represent sensory sensitivity. Items were: expresses discomfort during grooming; has difficulty standing in line or close to other people; avoids eye contact.*
8	Sedentary	87	Seeks sedentary play options.
9[3]	Fine Motor/ Perceptual	119	Has trouble staying between lines when coloring or when writing.
		118	Writing is illegible.

Note: No. = the item number from the Sensory Profile.

[1]Factors identified by Dunn and Brown (1997). [2]Behaviors identified by >50% parents as present in their child with autism (Kientz & Dunn, 1997) and subsequent analysis. [3]Factors that differentiated children with autism from children without disabilities (Ermer & Dunn, 1998).

Items are arranged so that the behavior most often reported is listed first in the column.

*Indicates items that were also reported by more than 20% of typical children.

Although 62.5% of parents of children with autism reported that their children were "Always 'on the go,'" 50% parents of typical children also reported this behavior (item number 90).

among her colleagues, Dunn has refined the model to continue to capture the most recent thoughts about how these complex mechanisms operate for people with and without disabilities. Figure 1–5 illustrates current hypotheses about this model. As you can see, the relationships among the parts of the model are conceived as more complex, just as the human experiences are more complex. For example, although Brown et al. (in press) identified specific patterns of skin conductance (i.e., physiological responses to sensation) that could be associated with the four quadrants on the original model (i.e., seek, avoid, low registration, and sensitivity), there was some interplay among the items in the groups. Relationships between the Sensitivity and Avoiding patterns were identified, for instance. Thus, the model displayed in Figure 1–5 includes a more fluid relationship between these parameters. Anecdotally, it may be true that sensory seekers have high and low thresholds, with the common thread that they enjoy sensory experiences—hence the more expansive pattern for sensory seeking in the model.

Researchers and experienced professionals have also speculated about the personal implications of Sensory Profile data. Some suggest that adults who have early experiences of avoiding sensations, for example, may create a lifestyle with fewer demands for responding to sensory stimulation so that daily life is easier (children have less freedom to structure their life, but adults structure much of their lives); this idea needs further investigation. The pilot study of the Infant-Toddler Sensory Profile indicated that a "body-environment" continuum should be considered—that is, that there may be a difference in how persons respond to sensations about body awareness (i.e., touch, proprioception) and sensations about mapping the environment (i.e., auditory, visual) (Dunn & Daniels, in preparation). This insight is consistent with earlier research that hypothesized that sensory processing at different levels of the nervous system may require different types of processing and intervention. For example, sensory processing related to higher brain centers (i.e., visual and auditory) may require more cognitively oriented intervention approaches, while sensory processing related to body awareness (i.e., touch, movement, body position) may profit from a sensori-

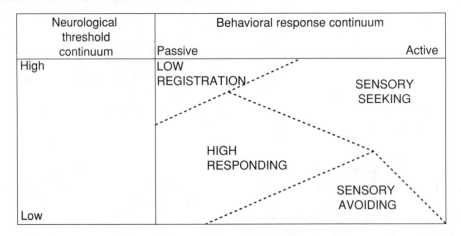

Figure 1–5 Hypothesized revision of Dunn's model of sensory processing.

motor approach (e.g., Ayres 1972a; Ayres & Tickle, 1980).

It is important to remember that each individual has a unique pattern of responses to the sensory experiences of daily life. People can have different responses based on the particular sensation (e.g., low thresholds for movement but high thresholds for sound), time of the day and biorhythms (e.g., higher thresholds after "warming up" or lower thresholds with fatigue after the day has worn on), biobehavioral state (e.g., rested or tired, hungry or satisfied, happy or anxious), cognitive appraisals (e.g., positive or negative attributions of the stimuli), or context (e.g., home, school, new social situations). It is always unwise to minimize the rich experience of humanity with a single category. This model helps us organize our thinking about sensory processing and understand the complexities of living, but models may limit the progress of knowledge development if they limit our thinking.

For example, when considering Dunn's models of sensory processing (see Figures 1–4 and 1–5), we must also consider that everyone processes sensory information in some way as part of living. It is incorrect to think of the categories of sensory processing (i.e., seeking, avoiding, high responding, low responding) as *problems* with sensory processing. It is correct to think about these categories as ways that people process information; we can observe the lives of satisfied people and see that some of them would fall into each category. Researchers must investigate the ways that people construct successful living, working, and social environments for themselves within each way of processing sensory information.

Each sensory information processing type has unique adaptive qualities. People with a low registration pattern have a high ability to focus on a particular task because they do not readily notice what is going on around them. People who are high responders do notice what is going on around them; this vigilance is critical to some tasks and contributes to precision in outcomes. People who seek sensation are able to generate ideas, and people who avoid sensation enjoy routines and may be counted on to implement structure for tasks and projects. Ultimately, each person's ability (and the family's ability) to have insight about himself or herself is most beneficial.

While considering knowledge about state regulation and sensory processing, interventions do not target changing the essential nature of the person's way of processing information. Rather, interventions incorporate our insights about the person's essential ways of regulating sensory input into the plans for improving performance in daily life. For example, for a child who is highly sensitive to sound and who has a low registration for movement, we might be sure to design a quiet place (adapting for the high sensitivity during a necessary activity of getting ready) and relocate clothing and personal hygiene items to increase the movement requirements for getting ready (designing increased-intensity vestibular input to generate more arousal for getting ready). These strategies acknowledge the child's essential sensory processing nature and find ways to use that knowledge to enable successful outcomes.

CAUTIONS FOR PROFESSIONALS AND PARENTS

Given this background, we feel ethically bound to put the sensorimotor approach to management in a context of caution that applies to all intervention strategies. A plethora of interventions has been suggested over the years to "cure" autism; unfortunately, no magic bullet has been found. The search for a cure is unique to autism when compared to other developmental disabilities and may have arisen because early descriptions theorized that autism represented a "locked-in syndrome" of a normal child. The uneven intellectual profile, with some skills being near or even above average, typical of people with autism probably reinforced this misguided notion. The search for a cure may have arisen because the social skills deficits of autism seem to violate the fundamental nature of human interaction, or because the behaviors of autism are often upsetting and troublesome, or because of the unique and sometimes isolated service provision systems for people with severe disabilities (Huebner & Emery, 1998; Jacobson, Mulick, & Schwartz, 1995). Because this search has sometimes seemed desperate, both professionals and parents have been vulnerable to testimonials and claims about cures. As we proceed into a discussion of management for autism, it is timely and wise to step back and remind ourselves of our vulnerability and the limitations of our knowledge despite years of study. Part of our vulnerability to the unproven claims of treatment effectiveness is rooted in our psychological makeup and social structure.

Because of the huge and sometimes contradictory body of literature on autism and the multiple experts who share this literature, it is probable that much of what people believe comes from a small sample of data that supports their viewpoints and is professed by an expert they believe. As Gilovich (1991) concluded from his review of the research, experts may distort the truth (intentionally or innocently) to make it more compelling, exaggerate differences to make a point, and present hypotheses as fact. The process of childhood socialization teaches us to believe what we are told, especially by experts, and to believe that they couldn't say it if it weren't so (Gilovich). This belief in experts is one source of vulnerability for professionals, service providers, parents, and persons with autism. The immense and, often, overwhelming body of literature both advances the study of autism and confuses consumers of this literature. The truth is that for all we know about autism, we have more questions than we have answers; we are sure only that no single intervention is effective for everyone with autism, at least not today.

The relationship between professionals and parents, and between professionals and people with autism is unequal (Jones et al., 1984), especially when the stigma attached to autism is severe and the needs of people are great. Thus, parents and people with autism are both vulnerable and stigmatized. Working with clients who are vulnerable and stigmatized may generate contradictory emotional responses in professionals (Gunther, 1987). Feelings of being needed and appreciated may be acknowledged; however, the helping relationship may also elicit feelings of disappointment, helplessness, resentment, or inner confusion when clients fail to make progress or to be grateful. With similar contradiction, professionals may be seen as saints by some who view work with developmental disabilities as holy and requiring great patience, or as perverts by others who view the work as distasteful (Gold & Gannon, 1994). These conflicting emotions and expectations may also promote a sense of desperation in service providers and create a vulnerability to believe unfounded claims or embrace an idea that "can't hurt."

Numerous other factors make us vulnerable to a loss of objectivity and a desire to embrace new ideas, especially with autism. These vulnerabilities may also be our strengths. For example, to work well with people who have severe disabilities one needs a sense of optimism, a desire to help, growth as a professional, persistence in the face of setbacks, and an expectation of a just world in which one is rewarded for work. These gifts and aptitudes, nonetheless, can temper our objectivity (see Huebner, 1997; Huebner & Emery, 1998, for a full review) and leave us vulnerable to self-delusion and the invention of knowledge (Donnellan, 1999). Intervention strategies are sometimes embraced because they seem plausible; treatment of a disorder is logically inferred from the symptoms (Gilovich, 1991). While logic may serve to support face validity of a management strategy, it is wise to pause and evaluate the appropriateness of a treatment and to investigate the empirical support for any intervention (Freeman, 1997; Rogers, 1998).

Worrall (1990) proposed a guide for educators and parents to use when rating therapies. The rating of an intervention is based on its congruence with common sense, its consistency with related bodies of knowledge, and the extent of objective evidence. Worrall further proposed that any intervention be viewed as suspicious when claims regarding it include (a) application to a wide range of problems, (b) the offer of a cure, (c) statements that the treatment is being suppressed by the establishment, (d) reliance on testimonial evidence, (e) promises of immediate results, and (f) descriptions using words such as *amazing* and *miracle*. Interventions with these characteristics may require more rigorous review than others. Parents and people with autism have the right to ask questions about interventions and receive complete information; professionals have the obligation to share the pros, cons, and current empirical support for every intervention strategy. In this book, we review

applications of sensorimotor interventions for children with autism. We do so knowing the empirical support for some aspects of this management approach is limited; each idea should be evaluated using the criteria just described.

Finally, we must remember to accept people as they are now. Sometimes, in the frenzy to intervene, professionals unwittingly communicate to families and people with autism that they or their child are not OK. This message can generate a great deal of anxiety and a continuous process of "doing" with, to, and for the child, when sometimes children and their families just need to *be*. Perhaps the best intervention is understanding the nature of this interesting human being and finding ways to facilitate function that honor the child's nature rather than trying to change it. Isn't that what everyone wants?

CONCLUSION

The content of this chapter is broad. We reviewed the historical underpinnings of our understanding of autism and the sensorimotor approach to management. We conclude that the current and future explosion of literature in this field will result in an even more dynamic and evolving theoretical and historical base. We reviewed differential diagnosis of the autistic spectrum disorders and related disorders. We conclude that the spectrum is wide and that differential diagnosis will continue to be refined as subtypes of autism are identified. We reviewed the prognosis and rate of occurrence for autism and find that both are increasing at a phenomenal rate for reasons unknown. We reviewed the fundamental rationale for both occupational therapy and sensorimotor interventions, including the neurobiological basis of neural plasticity. In the scientific literature and sensorimotor literature, concepts such as engagement in occupation, self-striving, adaptation, and person-centered approaches emerge as common threads purported to influence neural development and function. We reviewed the research and theoretical base describing sensory processing and find that unique patterns of sensory processing emerge that differenti-ate children with autism from children with other or no disabilities. Finally, we reminded ourselves that, for all we know, we still don't have the answers we want. Because of this, we must be cautious and vigilant in maintaining our objectivity while providing extra protection for vulnerable populations, such as persons with autism and their families.

CHAPTER REVIEW QUESTIONS

1. Identify the changes in our understanding of autism from the time of Kanner to the present time.
2. Compare and contrast differential diagnostic criteria for PDD and non-PDD conditions.
3. Describe the factors associated with improved outcomes for people with autism.
4. Define sensory processing, sensory modulation, sensory integration, and motor planning.
5. Describe the behavioral and sensory difficulties found in regulatory disorders.
6. Describe the processes of neural development and neural plasticity.
7. Discuss the relationship between sensitivity and habituation to sensory experiences and activities of daily living.
8. Discuss how the term child-centered relates to the sensorimotor approach to understanding and managing autism.
9. Define at least two intervention strategies for sensory or motor difficulties.
10. Identify personal characteristics that may make you more vulnerable to a loss of objectivity in evaluating the worth of treatment interventions.

REFERENCES

American Psychiatric Association (1980). *Diagnostic and statistical manual of mental disorders* (2nd ed.). Washington, DC: Author.

American Psychiatric Association (1994). *Diagnostic and statistical manual of mental disorders* (4th ed.). Washington, DC: Author.

Asperger, H. (1944/1991). Autistic psychopathy in childhood. Translated and annotated by U. Frith. In *Autism and Asperger Syndrome*. Cambridge: Cambridge University Press.

Ayres, A. J. (1972a). *Sensory integration and learning disorders*. Los Angeles: Western Psychological Services.

Ayres, A. J. (1972b). *Southern California Sensory Integration Tests*. Los Angeles: Western Psychological Services.

Ayres, A. J. (1974). Preface. In A. Henderson, L. Llorens, E. Gilfoyle, C. Myers, & S. Prevel (Eds.), *The development of sensory integrative theory and practice: A collection of the works of A. Jean Ayres* (pp. xi–xii). Dubuque, IA: Kendall/Hunt.

Ayres, A. J. (1979). *Sensory integration and the child*. Los Angeles: Western Psychological Services.

Ayres, A. J. (1989). *Sensory Integration and Praxis Tests*. Los Angeles: Western Psychological Services.

Ayres, A. J., & Tickle, L. (1980). Hyper-responsivity to touch and vestibular stimulation as a predictor of responsivity to sensory integrative procedures by autistic children. *American Journal of Occupational Therapy, 34*, 375–381.

Bagnato, S. J., & Neisworth, J. T. (1999). Normative detection of early regulatory disorders and autism: Empirical confirmation of DC: 0–3. *Infants and Young Children, 12*, 98–106.

Bailey, A., Phillips, W., & Rutter, M. (1996). Autism: Toward an integration of clinical, genetic, neuropsychological, and neurobiological perspectives. *Journal of Child Psychology and Psychiatry, 37*, 89–126.

Bauman, M. L., & Kemper, T. L. (1994). Neuroanatomic observations of the brain in autism. In M. L. Bauman & T. L. Kemper (Eds.), *The neurobiology of autism* (pp. 119–145). Baltimore: Johns Hopkins Press.

Belser, R. C., & Sudhalter, V. (1995). Arousal difficulties in males with Fragile-X Syndrome: A preliminary report. *Developmental Brain Dysfunction, 8*, 270–279.

Bennett, D. (1996). *Comparison of sensory characteristics: Children with and without Attention Deficit Disorder*. Unpublished master's thesis, University of Kansas, Kansas City.

Berkson, G. (1996). Feedback and control in the development of abnormal stereotyped behaviors. In R. Sprague & K. Newell (Eds.), *Stereotyped movements: Brain and behavior relationships* (pp. 3–15). Washington, DC: American Psychological Association.

Bettelheim, B. (1967). *The empty fortress*. New York: Free Press.

Bly, L. (1991). A historical and current view of the basis of NDT. *Pediatric Physical Therapy, 3*, 131–135.

Brekke, J., Raine, A., Ansel, M., Lencz, T., & Bird, L. (1997). Neuropsychological and psychophysiological correlates of psychosocial functioning in schizophrenia. *Schizophrenia Bulletin, 23*, 19–28.

Brown, C., Tollefson, N., Dunn, W., Cromwell, R., & Filion, D. (in press). The Adult Sensory Profile: Measuring patterns of sensory processing. *American Journal of Occupational Therapy*.

Brown, F., & Bambara, L. M. (1999). Introduction to the special series on interventions for young children with autism: An evolving integrated knowledge base. *Journal of the Association for Persons with Severe Handicaps, 24*, 131–132.

Carter, A. S., Gillham, J. E., Sparrow, S. S., & Volkmar, F. R. (1996). Adaptive behavior in autism. *Child and Adolescent Psychiatric Clinics of North America, 5*, 945–961.

Case-Smith, J., & Miller, H. (1999). Occupational therapy with children with pervasive developmental disorders. *American Journal of Occupational Therapy, 53*, 506–513.

Churchland, P. S. (1986). *Neurophilosophy: Toward a unified science of the mind/brain*. Cambridge, MA: MIT Press.

Cicchetti, D., & Tucker, D. (1994). Development and self-regulatory structures of the mind. *Development and Psychopathology, 6*, 533–549.

Coleman, M. (1994). Second trimester of gestation: A time of risk for classical autism. *Developmental Brain Dysfunction, 7*, 104–109.

Courchesne, E., Townsend, J., & Saitoh, O. (1994). The brain in infantile autism. *Neurology, 44*, 214–223.

Cromwell, R. L., & Snyder, C. R. (1993). *Schizophrenia: Origins, processes, treatments, and outcomes*. New York: Oxford University Press.

DeGangi, G., & Greenspan, S. (1989). *Test of Sensory Functions in Infants*. Los Angeles: Western Psychological Services.

Donnellan, A. M. (1999). Invented knowledge and autism: Highlighting our strengths and expanding the conversation. *Journal of the Association for Persons with Severe Handicaps, 24*, 230–236.

Dunn, W. (1997). The impact of sensory processing abilities on the daily lives of young children and their families: A conceptual model. *Infants and Young Children, 9*(4), 23–35.

Dunn, W. (1999). *The Sensory Profile*. San Antonio, TX: Psychological Corporation.

Dunn, W., & Brown, C. (1997). Factor analysis on the Sensory Profile from a national sample of children without disabilities. *American Journal of Occupational Therapy, 51*, 490–495.

Dunn, W., & Daniels, D. (in preparation). Development of the Infant-Toddler Sensory Profile.

Dutton, R. (1998). Neurodevelopmental theory. In M. E. Neistadt & E. B. Crepeau (Eds.), *Willard and Spackman's Occupational Therapy* (9th ed.) (pp. 545–546). Philadelphia: Lippincott.

Eaves, L. C., Ho, H. H., & Eaves, D. M. (1994). Subtypes of autism by cluster analysis. *Journal of Autism and Developmental Disorders, 24*, 3–22.

Erikson, E. H. (1963). *Childhood and society* (2nd ed.). New York: Norton.

Ermer, J., & Dunn, W. (1998). The Sensory Profile: A discriminant analysis of children with and without disabilities. *American Journal of Occupational Therapy, 52*, 283–290.

Farber, S. D. (1982). *Neurorehabilitation: A multisensory approach*. Philadelphia: W. B. Saunders.

Fisher, A. G., & Murray, E. A. (1991). Introduction to sensory integration theory. In A. G. Fisher, E. A. Murray, & A. C. Bundy (Eds.), *Sensory integration theory and practice* (pp. 3–26). Philadelphia: F. A. Davis.

Fisher, A. G., Murray, E. A., & Bundy, A. C. (1991). *Sensory integration theory and practice*. Philadelphia: F. A. Davis.

Fombonne, W. (1998). Epidemiology of surveys of autism. In F. R. Volkmar (Ed.), *Autism and pervasive developmental disorders* (pp. 32–63). New York: Cambridge University Press.

Freeman, B. J. (1997). Guidelines for evaluating intervention programs for children with autism. *Journal of Autism and Developmental Disorders, 27*, 641–651.

Frith, U. (1991). *Autism and Asperger Syndrome*. Cambridge: Cambridge University Press.

Gardner, E., & Martin, J. (2000). Coding of sensory information. In E. Kandell, J. Schwartz, & T. Jessell (Eds.), *Principles of neural science* (pp. 411–430). New York: McGraw-Hill.

Gillberg, C. (1988). Annotation: The neurobiology of infantile autism. *Journal of Child Psychology and Psychiatry, 29*, 257–266.

Gillberg, C., Steffenburg, S., & Schaumann, H. (1991). Is autism more common now than ten years ago? *British Journal of Psychiatry, 158*, 403–409.

Gilovich, T. (1991). *How we know what isn't so: The fallibility of human reasoning in everyday life*. New York: Free Press.

Gold, J. R., & Gannon, S. (1994). Countertransference in rehabilitation: Saint or pervert? *Advances in Medical Psychotherapy, 7*, 65–78.

Grandin, T. (1992). An inside view of autism. In E. Schopler & G. B. Mesibov (Eds.), *High-functioning individuals with autism* (pp. 105–126). Cambridge, MA: Perseus Publishing.

Greenspan, S. I., & Weider, S. (1999). A functional approach to autistic spectrum disorders. *Journal of the Association for Persons with Severe Handicaps, 24*, 147–161.

Guess, D., & Carr, E. (1991). Emergence and maintenance of stereotypy and self-injury. *American Journal on Mental Retardation, 96*, 299–319.

Guiffrida, C. G. (1998). Motor learning: An emerging frame of reference for occupational performance. In M. E. Neistadt & E. B. Crepeau (Eds.), *Willard and Spackman's Occupational Therapy* (9th ed.) (pp. 560–564). Philadelphia: Lippincott.

Gunther, M. S. (1987). Catastrophic illness and the caregivers: Real burdens and solutions with respect to the role of the behavioral sciences. In B. Caplan (Ed.), *Rehabilitation psychology desk reference* (pp. 219–243). Rockville, MD: Aspen Publishers.

Howlin, P., & Goode, S. (1998). Outcome in adult life for people with autism and Asperger's syndrome. In F. R. Volkmar (Ed.), *Autism and pervasive developmental disorders* (pp. 209–241). New York: Cambridge University Press.

Huebner, R. A. (1992). Autistic disorder: A neuropsychological enigma. *American Journal of Occupational Therapy, 46*, 487–501.

Huebner, R. A. (1997). Potential for help and harm: Therapeutic interactions in occupational therapy. *Developmental Disabilities Special Interest Section Quarterly, 20*(3), 1–4.

Huebner, R. A., & Emery, L. (1998). A social psychological analysis of facilitated communication: Implications for education. *Mental Retardation, 36*, 259–268.

Huebner, R. A., & Healander, J. (in preparation). Occupational therapy practice with people who have autism.

Jacobson, J. W., Mulick, J. A., & Schwartz, A. A. (1995). A history of facilitated communication: Science, pseudoscience, and antiscience. *American Psychologist, 50*, 750–765.

Johnson, A. K., & Anderson, E. A. (1990). Stress and arousal. In J. T. Cacioppo and L. G. Tassinary (Eds.), *Principles of psychophysiology* (pp. 216–252). New York: Cambridge University Press.

Jones, E. E., Farina, A., Hastorf, A. H., Markus, H., Miller, D. T., & Scott, R. A. (1984). *Social stigma: The psychology of marked relationships*. New York: Freeman.

Jones, V., & Prior, M. (1985). Motor imitation abilities and neurological signs in autistic children. *Journal of Autism and Developmental Disorders, 15*, 37–46.

Kandel, E., Schwartz, J. & Jessell, T. (2000). *Principles of neural sciences* (4th ed.). New York: McGraw-Hill.

Kanner, L. (1943). Autistic disturbances of affective contact. *Nervous Child, 2*, 217–250.

Kanner, L. (1973). *Childhood psychosis: Initial studies and new insights.* New York: Winston/Wiley.

Kanner, L., & Eisenberg, L. (1956). Early infantile autism, 1943–1955. *American Journal of Orthopsychiatry and Psychiatry, 26*, 55–65.

Kientz, M. A., & Dunn, W. (1997). A comparison of the performance of children with and without autism on the Sensory Profile. *American Journal of Occupational Therapy, 51*, 530–537.

Kolb, B., & Whishaw, I. Q. (1996). *Fundamentals of human neuropsychology* (4th ed.). New York: Freeman.

Koomar, J. A., & Bundy, A. C. (1991). The art and science of creating direct intervention from theory. In A. G. Fisher, E. A. Murray, & A. C. Bundy (Eds.), *Sensory integration theory and practice* (pp. 251–317). Philadelphia: F. A. Davis.

Larson, K. A. (1982). The sensory history of developmentally delayed children with and without tactile defensiveness. *American Journal of Occupational Therapy, 36*, 590–596.

Lord, C. (1995). Follow-up of two-year-olds referred for possible autism. *Journal of Child Psychology and Psychiatry, 36*, 1365–1382.

MacDonald, V. B. (1998). How the diagnosis of Asperger's has influenced my life. (1998). In E. Schopler & G. B. Mesibov (Eds.), *Asperger syndrome or high-functioning autism?* (pp. 367–376). New York: Plenum Press.

Manning, A. (1999, August 16). Vaccine-autism link feared. *USA Today*, D, pp. 1–2.

Maslow, A. H. (1970). *Motivation and personality.* New York: Harper & Row.

Mayes, L., Volkmar, F., Hooks, M., & Cicchetti, D. (1993). Differentiating pervasive developmental disorder not otherwise specified from autism and language disorders. *Journal of Autism and Developmental Disorders, 23*, 79–90.

McIntosh, D., Miller, L., Shyu, V., & Hagerman, R. (1998). Sensory modulation disruption, electrodermal responses and functional behavior. Manuscript submitted for publication.

Murray, E. A., & Anzalone, M. E. (1991). Integrating sensory integration theory and practice with other approaches. In A. G. Fisher, E. A. Murray, A. C. Bundy (Eds.), *Sensory integration theory and practice* (pp. 354–383). Philadelphia: F. A. Davis.

National Center for Clinical Infant Programs (1994). Axis I primary diagnosis: Regulatory disorders. In *Diagnostic classification of mental health and developmental disorders infancy and early childhood* (pp. 31–37). Arlington, VA: Author.

Parham, L. D., & Mailloux, Z. (1996). Sensory integration. In J. Case-Smith, A. S. Allen, & P. N. Pratt (Eds.), *Occupational therapy for children* (3rd ed.) (pp. 307–355). St. Louis: Mosby.

Perry, B. D., Pollard, R. A., Blakley, T. L., Baker, W. L., & Vigilante, D. (1995). Childhood trauma, the neurobiology of adaptation, and "use-dependent" development of the brain: How "states" become "traits." *Infant Mental Health Journal, 16*, 271–289.

Piaget, J. (1971). *Psychology and epistemology: Toward a theory of knowledge.* New York: Viking Press.

Post, R. M., & Weiss, S. R. B. (1997). Emergent properties of neural systems: How focal molecular neurobiological alterations can affect behavior. *Development and Psychopathology, 9*, 907–929.

Post, R. M., Weiss, S. R. B., & Leverich, G. S. (1994). Recurrent affective disorder: Roots in developmental neurobiology and illness progression based on changes in gene expression. *Development and Psychopathology, 6*, 781–813.

Poustka, F. (1998). Neurobiology of autism. In F. R. Volkmar (Ed.), *Autism and pervasive developmental disorders* (pp. 130–168). New York: Cambridge University Press.

Prizant, B. M., & Rubin, E. (1999). Contemporary issues in interventions for autism spectrum disorders: A commentary. *Journal of the Association for Persons with Severe Handicaps, 24*, 199–208.

Rapin, I. (1994). Introduction and overview. In M. L. Bauman & T. L. Kemper (Eds.), *The neurobiology of autism* (pp. 1–17). Baltimore: Johns Hopkins University Press.

Rapin, I. (1997). Autism. *New England Journal of Medicine, 337*, 97–104.

Rapin, I., & Katzman, R. (1998). Neurobiology of autism. *Annals of Neurology, 43*, 7–14.

Reich, J. (1999, November). The relationship between routinization, the need for structure, and sensory processing. Personal communication.

Rogers, C. R. (1969). *Freedom to learn.* Columbus, OH: Merrill.

Rogers, S. J. (1998). Empirically supported comprehensive treatment for young children with autism. *Journal of Clinical Child Psychology, 27*, 168–179.

Royeen, C. B., & Fortune, J. (1990). Touch inventory for elementary school aged children. *American Journal of Occupational Therapy, 44*, 155–159.

Royeen, C. B., & Lane, S. J. (1991). Tactile processing and sensory defensiveness. In A. G. Fisher, E. A. Murray, & A. C. Bundy (Eds.), *Sensory integration theory and practice* (pp. 108–136). Philadelphia: F. A. Davis.

Ruble, L. A., & Dalrymple, N. J. (1996). An alternative view of outcome in autism. *Focus on Autism and Other Developmental Disabilities, 11*, 3–14.

Ruble, L. A., & Sears, L. L. (2000). Diagnostic assessment of autistic disorder. In R. A. Huebner (Ed.), *Autism: A sensorimotor approach to management* (pp. 41–59). Gaithersburg, MD: Aspen Publishers.

Smith, I. M., & Bryson, S. E. (1994). Imitation and action in autism: A critical review. *Psychological Bulletin, 116*, 259–273.

Spitzer, S. L. (1999). Dynamic systems theory: Relevance to the theory of sensory integration and the study of occupation. *Sensory Integration Special Interest Section Quarterly, 22*(2), 1–4.

Thelan, E. (1995). Motor development: A new synthesis. *American Psychologist, 50*, 79–95.

Tickle-Degnen, L., & Coster, W. (1995). Therapeutic interaction and the management of challenge during the beginning minutes of sensory integration treatment. *Occupational Therapy Journal of Research, 15*, 122–141.

Volkmar, F. R., & Lord, C. (1998). Diagnosis and definition of autism and other pervasive developmental disorders. In F. R. Volkmar (Ed.), *Autism and pervasive developmental disorders* (pp. 1–25). New York: Cambridge University Press.

Waterhouse, L., Fein, D., & Modahl, C. (1996). Neurofunctional mechanisms in autism. *Psychological Review, 103*, 457–489.

Watling, R., Deitz, J., Kanny, E. M., & McLaughlin, J. F. (1999). Current practice of occupational therapy for children with autism. *American Journal of Occupational Therapy, 53*, 498–505.

Westman, J. C. (1990). *Handbook of learning disabilities: A multisystem approach.* Boston: Allyn and Bacon.

Willemsen-Swinkels, S. H. N., Buitelaar, J. K., Dekker, M., & van Engeland, H. (1998). Subtyping stereotypic behavior in children: The association between stereotypic behavior, mood, and heart rate. *Journal of Autism and Developmental Disorders, 28*, 547–557.

Worrall, R. S. (1990). Detecting health fraud in the field of learning disabilities. *Journal of Learning Disabilities, 23*, 207–212.

Zuckerman, M. (1979). *Sensation seeking: Beyond the optimal level of arousal.* Hillsdale, NJ: Erlbaum.

CHAPTER 2

Diagnostic Assessment of Autistic Disorder

Lisa A. Ruble and Lonnie L. Sears

CHAPTER OBJECTIVES

At the completion of this chapter, the reader will:

- Describe classification systems for diagnosing autism.
- Describe various diagnostic assessment instruments.
- Explain how to differentiate autism from other disabilities.
- Explain the symptoms of autism observed in a very young child.
- Understand the difference between assessment for establishing a diagnosis and assessment for program planning using a competency-based model.

INTRODUCTION

More than 50 years ago, Leo Kanner (1943) presented case studies of children who displayed unusual development of communication skills and a "disturbance of affective contact." These children were also noted to have odd behaviors and unusual sensory interests and an "insistence on sameness." Kanner used the term *autistic* to describe these children, borrowing from Bleuler in 1911 (1950), who used the label to describe the social withdrawal observed in schizophrenia. Particularly striking in these children was the contrast between the ability to develop affective relationships and the child's "intelligent relations to objects." Kanner recognized, as did other clinicians before him (e.g., Itard in 1828; see Carrey,

1995), that deficits in social interaction and communication can occur in individuals who may otherwise be considered intelligent based on their ability to function in nonsocial tasks. The differentiation of social competency skills and intelligence is key in making the diagnosis of autism. Determining that social and communication deficits are not due to general cognitive impairment but rather to a more specific social learning impairment is critical. This differentiation also promotes the development of an appropriate intervention program based on the individual's strengths and weaknesses.

Since Kanner's first description of autism, early identification and diagnosis improved dramatically as a result of ongoing research. Unlike 20 years ago, there are now consistent, research-based diagnostic criteria. Although presumed to be a neurodevelopmental disorder (Fisher et al., 1999), autism, it is agreed, is a clinical syndrome defined by behaviors rather than by medical tests (Freeman, 1993). Autism is expressed along a spectrum of symptoms ranging from severe to mild and varies with age and developmental level. Autism is a retrospective diagnosis; in order to make a differential diagnosis, careful assessment of developmental history is essential. Finally, the complexity of diagnostic assessment of autism is increased because the disorder frequently occurs in association with other syndromes and developmental disabilities. Recent studies suggest that the prevalence of autism may be about 1 in 1,000 (Bryson & Smith, 1998). Thus, autism is not an uncommon disorder, particularly in the caseloads of professionals providing services to children with behavioral and learning difficulties. As a result, providers working in a variety of settings require enhanced skill in identifying autism, particularly in the very young child.

The development of appropriate and specialized intervention programs is based on a diagnostic assessment, identifying the features common to autism (Schopler & Mesibov, 1988). While establishing a diagnosis does not replace the need for in-depth assessment of skills for individualized treatment planning, diagnostic assessment is a critical first step. It answers the question, "Does the child exhibit the pattern and number of symptoms to qualify for autism?" Assessment for intervention planning, on the other hand, is used to identify the unique characteristics of each child (Schopler & Mesibov). It answers the question, "What are the child's learning style, strengths, and weaknesses?" In this chapter, we review diagnostic assessment and (a) present current classification systems for establishing an

autism diagnosis; (b) provide an overview of available diagnostic instruments; (c) discuss differential diagnosis; (d) consider how to recognize autism in the very young child; and (e) present a competency-based approach intended to facilitate the translation of diagnostic information into intervention planning. In this chapter, the term *autism* is used only to refer to Autistic Disorder and not the entire autism spectrum.

CLASSIFICATION SYSTEMS

Diagnostic classification systems serve many purposes. Ideally, a classification system provides a label that facilitates communication among professionals and families, allows access to intervention services, provides a basis for research and prevention, leads to appropriate treatment planning and intervention, and provides a framework for gathering information on outcome, etiology, and associated problems. Most importantly, a label allows parents to become informed (Marcus & Stone, 1993). It gives them the basis to gather information, read, join support groups, advocate, and become organized in their efforts to develop and pass legislation. We believe that the benefits of a diagnosis far outweigh the liabilities.

Several classification systems available to clinicians are relevant to diagnostic assessment of developmental disabilities. The choice of a system usually depends on its use. School personnel, for example, classify children in order to determine eligibility for special education services. Medical personnel, on the other hand, require a classification system that permits reimbursement by insurance companies. In both cases, medical and school personnel classify children in order to identify problems and implement correct interventions that lead to optimal functioning.

Diagnostic Criteria of Autism Using
DSM-IV* and *ICD-10

The two major diagnostic classification systems in use today are the *Diagnostic and* *Statistical Manual of Mental Disorders* (*DSM-IV,* American Psychiatric Association, 1994) and the *International Classification of Diseases* (*ICD-10,* World Health Organization, 1993). These systems have

---

Exhibit 2–1 *DSM-IV* Diagnostic Criteria for Autistic Disorder

A. A total of six (or more) items from (1), (2), and (3), with at least two from (1) and one each from (2) and (3).

1. Qualitative impairment in social interaction, as manifested by at least two of the following:
   a. Marked impairment in the use of multiple nonverbal behaviors such as eye-to-eye gaze, facial expression, body postures, and gestures to regulate social interaction
   b. Failure to develop peer relationships appropriate to developmental level
   c. A lack of spontaneous seeking to share enjoyment, interests, or achievements with other people (e.g., by a lack of showing, bringing, or pointing out objects of interest)
   d. Lack of social or emotional reciprocity

2. Qualitative impairments in communication as manifested by at least one of the following:
   a. Delay in, or total lack of, the development of spoken language (not accompanied by an attempt to compensate through alternative modes of communication such as gesture or mime)
   b. In individuals with adequate speech, marked impairment in the ability to initiate or sustain a conversation with others

   c. Stereotyped and repetitive use of language or idiosyncratic language
   d. Lack of varied, spontaneous make-believe play or social imitative play appropriate to developmental level

3. Restricted repetitive and stereotyped patterns of behavior, interests, and activities, as manifested by at least one of the following:
   a. Encompassing preoccupation with one or more stereotyped and restricted patterns of interest that is abnormal either in intensity or focus
   b. Apparently inflexible adherence to specific, nonfunctional routines or rituals
   c. Stereotyped and repetitive motor mannerisms (e.g., hand or finger flapping or twisting, or complex whole-body movements)
   d. Persistent preoccupation with parts of objects

B. Delays or abnormal functioning in at least one of the following areas, with onset prior to age three years:
   1. Social interaction
   2. Language as used in social communication
   3. Symbolic or imaginative play

C. The disturbance is not better accounted for by Rett's Disorder or childhood disintegrative disorder.

Source: Reprinted with permission from the Diagnostic and Statistical Manual of Mental Disorders, Fourth Edition. Copyright 1994 American Psychiatric Association.

adopted nearly identical criteria for autism based on qualitative impairment in social interaction and communication and the presence of abnormal behavior patterns (see Exhibit 2–1). The *DSM-IV* and *ICD-10* use dichotomous criteria based on the presence or absence of a behavior. This approach has been criticized because the presence or absence of a certain behavior cannot be reliably determined. This weakness has led some researchers to develop dimensional classification approaches based on social communication skills, for example (Robertson, Tanguay, L'Ecuyer, Sims, & Waltrip, 1999). Despite this problem, however, the *DSM-IV* system has been shown to be reliable and valid when standard diagnostic procedures are followed (Volkmar, Klin, & Cohen, 1997).

Heterogeneity in Autism

In order to meet the diagnostic criteria for autism described in the *DSM-IV* and *ICD-10*, an individual must exhibit at least six behavioral symptoms with at least two impairments in social interaction and one each in the communication and repetitive behavior domain. Because a variety of combinations of impairments noted in Exhibit 2–1 can lead to a diagnosis of autism, *DSM-IV* has been referred to as a "Chinese menu" approach (Lord & Risi, 1998). Persons with autism are likely to display abnormalities across several of the behavioral domains because the criteria are not independent. A child who has difficulty sharing pleasure with others (1c), for example, also likely has impaired social-emotional reciprocity (1d). Despite the likelihood of overlap due to similar processes underlying the behavioral criteria, the *DSM-IV* and *ICD-10* allow for the inclusion of a range of behavior patterns in the autism category. This heterogeneity is observed when two individuals with autism

meet criteria under different combinations of impairments and behavioral abnormalities. One individual could be also identified with autism despite meeting different criteria at different ages (Lord & Risi, 1998; Tsai, 1992a). Thus, the diagnosis informs us of an individual's general areas of weakness but does not describe how autism is specifically manifested in that person. To move beyond the generalities inherent in the diagnostic assessment process, individualized assessments that take into account the individual's strengths and weaknesses must be conducted for program planning.

In addition to the heterogeneity that is part of the diagnosis of Autistic Disorder, the many questions about the boundaries of autism (Schopler, Mesibov, & Kunce, 1998) led to the use of the broader category Pervasive Developmental Disorder (PDD) (Rutter & Schopler, 1988). PDD is used to convey the commonalities across autism and autism spectrum disorders. Determining the boundary for Autistic Disorder versus autism spectrum disorders is complicated by issues such as the variability in symptom presentation related to the presence of associated impairments. In the cognitive domain, for example, approximately 75–80% of individuals with autism have mental retardation, based on performance on standard intelligence tests (Coleman & Gillberg, 1985). When the entire autism spectrum is considered, however (i.e., including Asperger's syndrome), less than 50% of persons with a PDD have mental retardation (Bryson & Smith, 1998).

Variability in individuals with autism has also been described according to differences in socialization patterns. While all persons with autism have social impairments, patterns of "aloof," "passive," or "active but odd" social interest may be apparent (Wing, 1988). Another source of variability is in language skills. About 50% of individuals are nonverbal or minimally verbal (Prizant, 1983). Motor abilities range considerably. Some individuals may have significant fine or gross motor impairments; others may exhibit well-developed skills (Wing, 1988). Response to sensory stimuli can differ from person to person. Some individuals may be indifferent to stimuli and others respond with distress (Coleman & Gillberg, 1985). Thus, no single behavioral impairment is observed across all individuals or across all points in time in development. As a result, diagnostic clinicians must be skilled and experienced in discriminating the variation in behavior based on a keen understanding of individual differences and developmental changes in behavior.

Diagnosis of Other Pervasive Developmental Disorders Using *DSM-IV* and *ICD-10*

The *DSM-IV* places Autistic Disorder within the category of Pervasive Developmental Disorders (PDD). Other disorders included in the PDD category are: Pervasive Developmental Disorder Not Otherwise Specified (PDD-NOS), Asperger's Disorder, Rett's Syndrome, and Childhood Disintegrative Disorder (APA, 1994). Autism is the prototypical disorder within the PDD category, while the other PDDs share features of autism, most typically the significant impairment in social interaction. Estimates of the prevalence of autism spectrum disorders are 4 to 5 in 1,000 (Bryson & Smith, 1998).

Pervasive Developmental Disorder Not Otherwise Specified

The diagnosis of PDD-NOS is typically given to a child who exhibits features of autism but does not meet full criteria for autism (APA, 1994). Not surprisingly, the diagnosis of PDD-NOS is less reliable than the diagnosis of autism based on *DSM-IV*

field trials (Towbin, 1997). Generally, persons with PDD-NOS have the core social impairments seen in autism and meet criteria for impairments in social interaction (category 1) but may not meet the remaining criteria for autism (Towbin). Thus, the diagnosis is used to identify an individual with autistic features (especially in the social realm) whose symptoms are not accounted for by another disorder (e.g., mental retardation or attention deficit hyperactivity disorder [ADHD]). Although somewhat vague, the diagnosis of PDD-NOS may be useful for intervention planning by identifying autismlike problems needing to be addressed through an individualized program (Towbin).

Asperger's Syndrome

There has been a great deal of discussion regarding the differentiation of autism and Asperger's syndrome. Hans Asperger and Leo Kanner both published accounts of children notable for features of autistic psychopathology, leading to the use of the terms *Asperger's syndrome* and *Kanner's syndrome* (or *Kanner's autism*). The history of these diagnostic terms is informative and has been well described by others (Frith, 1991). At present, it is recognized that Asperger's syndrome and high-functioning autism overlap and that their boundaries are not clear (Klin & Volkmar, 1997; Schopler, 1998). *DSM-IV* indicates that the disorders share social impairments and circumscribed interests as common features, but Asperger's syndrome is not diagnosed if the individual meets criteria for autism (APA, 1994). Although the terms are often used interchangeably, there is some indication that the two can be separated based on language skills and neuropsychological test performance. Persons with Asperger's syndrome generally have normal or near-normal scores on intelligence tests and may not have a history of developmental delays in expressive language (Volkmar, Klin, & Cohen, 1997). Asperger's syndrome may also be distinguished from autism based on relative weaknesses in visual-perceptual skills in contrast to the strengths in visual-perceptual skills often seen in autism (Klin & Volkmar, 1997). Research is needed to clarify the boundaries of these disorders. In the meantime, the terms *high-functioning autism* and *Asperger's syndrome* likely will continue to be used interchangeably by clinicians and researchers.

Rett's Disorder

Another diagnosis included in the PDD domain is Rett's Disorder (APA, 1994), which is a progressive developmental disorder of unknown origin. Rett's Disorder occurs in females and is included in the PDD category based on similarities to autism in social and language impairments (Van Acker, 1997). Also, the regression in skills acquired prior to 18 months of age that occurs in Rett's Disorder is also seen in some females with autism (Tsai, 1992b). Because of these similarities, it is especially important to include a medical evaluation as part of a comprehensive developmental evaluation when attempting to diagnose autism in young females. Differential diagnosis of Rett's Disorder is made based on the course of developmental regression, including acquired microcephaly, growth retardation, and the presence of stereotypic hand movements (Trevathan and Naidu, 1988).

Childhood Disintegrative Disorder

DSM-IV field trials suggested that children with autismlike behavioral features can be differentiated as having Childhood Disintegrative Disorder (CDD) by their unique pattern of development. In contrast to the development of children with autism, these children demonstrate normal development up to at least two years of age, followed by a severe regression in social and communication skills (Volkmar, 1994). Children with this disorder also display repetitive behavior patterns, as seen in autism, and marked deterioration in self-help skills, usually without an identified medical cause (Volkmar, 1994). CDD is rare. Differentiating CDD from autism requires a thorough developmental history to determine the age of onset of the developmental regression (Volkmar, Klin, Marans, & Cohen, 1997).

OTHER DIAGNOSTIC/ CLASSIFICATION APPROACHES

Other classification approaches have been developed in order to fill perceived gaps left by the *ICD-10* and *DSM-IV*. The field trials for the *DSM-IV*, for example, did not include children younger than four years, thus limiting its use for very young children (McBurnett, Lahey, & Pfiffner, 1993). These alternate classification approaches include: (a) the classification of the *Diagnostic and Statistical Manual for Primary Care (DSM-PC), Child and Adolescent Version*, (b) *Zero to Three Diagnostic Classification of Mental Health and Developmental Disorders of Infancy and Early Childhood*, and (c) educational classification criteria. Each approach can be differentiated based on both the training and professional orientation of the diagnostic clinician and on the purpose of the classification system.

The *DSM-PC, Child and Adolescent Version*, was developed in 1996 and produced by the American Academy of Pediatrics (Wolraich, Felice, & Drotar, 1996). The *DSM-PC* is a multiaxial classification system of child and adolescent mental diagnoses developed for use by primary care clinicians. The diagnostic criteria for Pervasive Developmental Disorders are the same as those described in the *DSM-IV* and organized under the cluster of atypical behaviors. The strength of this system is its link to *DSM-IV*, which is the classification system based on the most research. Unfortunately, this link also poses a weakness in diagnosing children with autism under age four. Researchers have expressed concerns regarding the *DSM-IV* criteria because children with autism cannot meet certain criteria and go undiagnosed due to their age, developmental delays, and/or speech delays (Stone, et al., 1999); they suggest that a different algorithm for diagnosis might be warranted for children under four years.

The Zero–Three Diagnostic Classification of Mental Health and Developmental Disorders of Infancy and Early Childhood (1995) is a multiaxial and provisional system. It takes into account changes in young children due to developmental issues and purports to be open to modifications based on research. Unlike the *DSM-PC*, which uses the same criteria described in the *DSM-IV*, the 0–3 Diagnostic Classification system uses the category Multisystem Developmental Disorder (MSDD) to capture the features of autism. The clinical and research utility of MSDD has not been investigated. Another weakness with this category is its limited recognition among researchers, clinicians, and service providers; it therefore lacks many of the features of a good classification, as described earlier.

Another independent classification system has been established by state departments of education. School personnel use these criteria to determine student eligibility for special education services. It was only in 1992 that the federal Department of Education recognized autism as a separate handicapping condition (see Exhibit 2–2). The other Pervasive Developmental Disorders, PDD-NOS and Asperger's Disorder, are not recognized as special education categories. Although autism has been defined in the Individuals with Disabilities Education Act (IDEA) (*Federal Register,* 1992, 300.7), classification or identification criteria often vary considerably by state, as states are at their own discretion to develop special education eligibility criteria using IDEA criteria as the minimal standard. Some states use *DSM-IV* criteria; others use their own criteria. Tennessee, for example, is planning to describe PDD-NOS in the autism code in order to serve these students.

Although the effects of using nonstandard criteria to identify children with autism in public schools are not known, major problems are likely to be the result. The federal Department of Education has no way of receiving accurate reports from states on the number of students with autism receiving services and the subsequent description, quality, and costs of these services. Depending on local expertise and the experience of

---

Exhibit 2–2 Federal Department of Education Criteria for Autism

Autism means a developmental disability significantly affecting verbal and nonverbal communication and social interaction, generally evident before age three, that adversely affects a child's educational performance. Other characteristics often associated with autism are engagement in repetitive activities and stereotyped movements, resistance to environmental change or change in daily routines, and unusual responses to sensory experiences.

the school psychologist and Individual Education Plan (IEP) team members, the identification of students with autism may vary widely, excluding students who exhibit the more subtle features of autism. Students with PDD-NOS or Asperger's Disorder, for example, may be deemed ineligible for school services. School personnel may not know that the intervention approaches for children with these diagnoses are essentially identical as those for autism (Attwood, 1998; Harris, Glasbert, & Ricca, 1996). If a student is performing well academically, problems with social interaction with peers and pragmatic language use may be left untreated. These skills are critical for success on the job after high school. In order to ensure that children with Asperger's syndrome receive appropriate special education services, some researchers have suggested that these students be classified under autism for educational purposes (Schopler, 1998).

DIAGNOSTIC PROCEDURES

Unfortunately, classification systems offer no guidelines for the assessment of autism (Harris, Glasbert, & Ricca, 1996). As a result, diagnosticians must receive specialized training.

Multidisciplinary Team

The assessment of children with autism requires multiple evaluators using multiple methods of gathering information. A formal diagnosis is best made by a multidisciplinary team specializing in autism (Klin & Shepard, 1994; Stone & Ousley, 1996). Such teams often include a developmental pediatrician, a psychologist, a speech and language pathologist, an occupational therapist, and an educational specialist. Assessment methods must be broad enough to gather in-

formation regarding social, communication, motor, sensory, and cognitive development. It is strongly recommended that a comprehensive approach include both a detailed standardized parental interview and a standardized observational system (Rutter & Schopler, 1988). Analysis of behavior in the natural environment is often desirable in order to assess key diagnostic features that may elude observation in the clinical setting. Components of an evaluation for autism are provided in Exhibit 2–3.

Diagnostic Instruments

Several diagnostic instruments for the assessment of autism are available and can be grouped as observational instruments, parent/teacher questionnaires, parent interviews, and interactive assessments. A summary of these instruments is provided in Table 2–1. Recent advances in two instruments, the Autism Diagnostic Interview—Revised (ADI-R) (Lord, Rutter, & LeCouteur, 1994) and the Autism Diagnostic Observation Schedule—Generic (ADOS-G) (Lord, Rutter, & DiLavore, 1998), allow for the assessment of individuals of adult or very young ages and of higher or lower cognitive functioning. Both the ADI-R, a semistructured parent interview, and the ADOS-G, a semistructured interactive observation scale, include items that correspond to *DSM-IV* criteria.

The strengths and weaknesses and the psychometric properties of these observational instruments and parent/teacher questionnaires are reviewed in detail elsewhere (Morgan, 1988; Parks,1988). Checklists such as the Childhood Autism Rating Scale (CARS) (Schopler, Reichler, & Renner, 1986), Autism Behavior Checklist (ABC) (Krug, Arick, & Almond, 1980), and Diagnostic Checklist for Behavior-Disturbed

Exhibit 2–3 Components of a Diagnostic Evaluation for Autism

Medical
- Developmental history
- Family history
- Maternal medical history
- Child medical history
- Medical and neurological evaluation

Psychological
- Nonverbal problem-solving abilities
- Verbal problem-solving abilities
- Adaptive behavior skills

- Social, communication, and other behaviors in natural and clinical settings

Speech and Language
- Receptive language abilities
- Expressive language abilities
- Pragmatic language abilities

Occupational Therapy
- Fine-motor skills
- Gross-motor skills
- Sensory-processing abilities

Children (Form E-2) (Rimland, 1971) do not take into account the wide range of differences across individuals with autism based on age and functioning level. The CARS emerges as the scale with the best-demonstrated psychometric properties (DiLalla & Rogers, 1994; Morgan, 1988) and is useful as a screening device (DiLalla & Rogers, 1994; Parks, 1988).

Assessment of Specific Criteria

Assessment of the characteristic features of autism—social and communication impairments and restricted patterns of behaviors and interests—require varied assessment approaches. Social assessment consists of two main strategies: structured and unstructured observation, and parent interview (Watson & Marcus, 1988). Reliable assessment of social development and behavior is often more difficult to achieve than judgments of impairments in communication or unusual behaviors (Lord & Risi, 1998). The impairments in social behavior are often missed by clinicians who lack experience in autism. Behaviors easier to observe, such as unusual language (echolalia) and unusual interests, are easier to assess than social behaviors. In addition, the nature of the social dif-

ficulties varies with developmental level and age. In the very young child, the social impairments may be expressed by reduced play in baby games such as peekaboo; reduced attempts to draw attention to themselves for the purpose of showing off to adults; reduced ability to imitate vocal sounds, body movements, and actions with objects; and reduced ability to point to objects, show objects, and follow an adult's point to objects for purely social reasons. Observation of the child's play skills with toys and with peers should target whether the child merely manipulates toys and plays in a solitary fashion, or whether functional toy play exists with parallel or cooperative play with peers. Social and play skills should be considered in the context of the child's developmental age.

Communication assessment should consist of informal and formal testing, observational assessment, and parent interview (Watson & Marcus, 1988). Assessment should also include information on the child's functional communication abilities (Wetherby, 1986)—that is, on the forms (*how* the child communicates), the functions or purposes (*what* the child communicates), and the contexts (*where* and *with whom* the child communicates) of communication. Young children with autism

Table 2–1 Summary of Assessment Instruments for Autism

Autism Diagnostic Instruments	Description
Observation Instruments	
Behavior Observation Scale for Autism Freeman, Ritvo, Guthrie, Schroth, & Ball, 1978	24 behaviors grouped as solitary, relationship to objects, relationship to people, and language
Behavior Rating Instrument for Autistic and Atypical Children (BRIAAC) Ruttenberg, Kalish, Wenar, & Wolf, 1977	8 scales of behaviors grouped as relationship to an adult, communication, drive for mastery, vocalization and expressive speech, sound and speech reception, social responsiveness, body movement, and psychobiological development
Childhood Autism Rating Scale (CARS) Schopler, Reichler, & Renner, 1988	15 subscales of behaviors grouped as relating to people, imitation, emotional response, body use, object use, adaptation to change, visual response, listening response, task smell, touch response and use, fear or nervousness, verbal communication, nonverbal communication, activity level, level and consistency of intellectual response, and general impressions
Ritvo-Freeman Real Life Rating Scale (RLRS) Freeman, Ritvo, Yokota, & Ritvo, 1986	5 scales of behaviors grouped as sensorimotor, social (relationship to people), affectual response, sensory response, and language
Checklist for Autism in Toddlers (CHAT) Baron-Cohen, Allen, & Gillberg, 1992	5 behaviors characterized as social interest, social play, pretend play, joint attention, and pointing to express interest
Parent/Teacher Questionnaires	
Diagnostic Checklist for Behavior-Disturbed Children (Form E-2) Rimland, 1971	80 questions concerning social interactions, speech, reaction to stimuli, intelligence, family information, and psychological development
Autism Behavior Checklist (ABC) Krug, Arick, & Almond, 1980	57 behaviors grouped as sensory, relating, body and object use, language, and social and self-help
Parent Interview Intruments	
Autism Diagnostic Interview–Revised (ADI-R) Lord, Rutter, & LeCouteur, 1994	5 sections of questions grouped as opening questions, questions on communication, social development and play, repetitive and restricted behaviors, and general behavior problems
Parent Interview for Autism (PIA) Stone & Hogan, 1993	118 questions of behaviors grouped as social relating, affective responses, motor imitation, peer interactions, object play, imaginative play, language understanding, nonverbal communication, motoric behaviors, sensory responses, and need for sameness

continues

Table 2–1 continued

Autism Diagnostic Instruments	Description
Interactive Assessment Instruments	
Autism Diagnostic Observation Schedule (ADOS-G) Lord, Rutter, & DiLavore, 1998	A 30–45-minute semistructured assessment tool for children and adults designed to evaluate communication, social interaction, play, and imaginative use of materials
Screening Tool for Autism in Two-Year-Olds (STAT) Stone & Ousley, 1997	A 20-minute semistructured screening tool for two-year-olds designed to assess motor imitation, functional play, and directing attention to objects or events of interest

demonstrate difficulty understanding and using nonverbal means, such as gestures, to communicate. Children with autism who have verbal speech may exhibit both the difficulty understanding the meaning of words and phrases (semantics) and using communication in a functional manner with others (pragmatics).

Repetitive behaviors and restricted range of activities and interests are best assessed via parent interview and observations. Resistance to change in environment and new routines and an insistence on following familiar routines demonstrate these behaviors. Parents can provide information on the child's narrow interests and unusual attachment to objects. Often, sensory input that incorporates a visual, auditory, tactile, olfactory, or motor component is either excessively sought or strongly avoided. An example of a visual interest is a child who enjoys spinning objects, twirling, and watching fans or objects that rotate. Stereotypic behaviors include jumping up and down and hand flapping when excited, flipping fingers in front of the eyes, and rocking the body.

DIFFERENTIAL DIAGNOSIS

The behavioral symptoms of young children with autism are often subtle and may be difficult to differentiate from behaviors of children with other developmental problems. It is the absence of typically developing behavior that distinguishes autism (Stone & Ousley, 1996). Differential diagnosis is based on the ability to distinguish autism from overlapping impairments such as mental retardation, developmental language disorder, attention deficit disorder, and schizophrenia. Children with autism exhibit a heterogeneous array of impairments and clinical features. Because development in cognitive abilities, receptive and expressive language skills, adaptive behavior skills, social reciprocity, sensory processing skills, and fine and gross motor abilities differ from child to child, it is important to understand the wide range of variability among children.

Mental Retardation

Mental retardation is the disability most commonly associated with autism. About 75–80% of individuals with autism demonstrate some degree of mental retardation (Coleman & Gillberg, 1985). Mental retardation is diagnosed in addition to autism when the child's mental age is significantly lower than the child's chronological age. Individuals with mental retardation but without autism, however, usually demonstrate social and communication skills on par with their mental age (Klin & Shepard, 1994). When a child's mental age is below the age when pretend play develops (less than 20 months), accurate diagnosis may be difficult (Wing, 1997). A differential diagnosis of mental retardation can be made by observing social responsiveness, a lack of dominance in repetitive activity patterns, and a level of play consistent with mental age.

A mistaken belief exists that children with autism are "untestable" and, thus, their intellectual or cognitive abilities cannot be adequately assessed (Klin & Shepard, 1994). Research, however, has shown that the intellectual or cognitive abilities of children with autism can be assessed and that the source of children's difficulties on various tasks is the child's intellectual limitations rather than volitional noncompliance (Volkmar, Hoder, & Cohen, 1985). Cognitive level can be assessed when adequate instruments are used and when the clinician is able to examine lower-level developmental skills with the use of adapted assessment techniques.

Developmental Language Disorder

To distinguish developmental language disorder from autism, the diagnostician must assess social behaviors, imaginative activities, and communication skills—in particular, nonverbal communication abilities (Campbell & Shay, 1995; Wing, 1997). The clinician should assess nonverbal use of gestures, facial expressions, and other means of communication. Children with autism exhibit a delayed and deviant pattern of language development absent compensatory nonverbal means of communication. Children with language disorder show less need for sameness and adherence to routines

and more social relatedness (Mayes, Volkmar, Hooks, & Cicchetti, 1993).

ADD/Learning Disabilities

Attention and impulse control problems and uneven learning patterns are observed in autism as well as attention deficit disorder (ADD) and learning disabilities (LD). While *DSM-III-R* indicated that ADD was excluded if a child had autism (APA, 1987), *DSM-IV* allows both diagnoses to be made. Whether or not to diagnose ADD or LD in children with autism is controversial (Volkmar, Klin, & Cohen, 1997). Persons with autism are assumed to have attention and learning problems as part of their profile (Burack, Enns, Stauder, Mottron, & Randolph, 1997; Sigman, Dissanayake, Arbelle, & Ruskin, 1997); hence, the additional diagnosis of ADD and LD may be redundant and confusing to both parents and professionals. On the other hand, multiple diagnoses may be useful for children with mixed features, such as PDD-NOS and learning and attention problems, when behavior and developmental patterns may not fit criteria for autism. Multiple diagnoses may be helpful for treatment planning for these types of children (Barkley, 1990).

Multiple diagnoses may also be helpful when the identification of a learning disability enhances treatment planning. A nonverbal learning disability (NLD) pattern is frequently observed in Asperger's syndrome and understanding the learning strengths and weaknesses conveyed by the NLD diagnosis may be useful for intervention planning (Klin & Volkmar, 1997). Another example is dyslexia. While high-functioning children with autism often have strengths in reading decoding (Minshew, Goldstein, Taylor, & Siegel, 1994), this pattern is not universal. Identifying reading decoding weaknesses with the LD diagnosis may be beneficial for the child with autism if it leads to interventions based on reading strengths and weaknesses (e.g., deficit in phonological processing).

Schizophrenia

Autism and childhood-onset schizophrenia are separate disorders based on phenomenology, genetics, and biological correlates (Kolvin, Ounsted, Humphrey, & McNay, 1971; Kolvin, Ounsted, & Roth, 1971; McKenna, Gordon, & Rapoport, 1994). Symptoms of schizophrenia include delusions, auditory or visual hallucinations, incoherence, loosening of association, catatonic behavior, unusual sensory experiences, and markedly peculiar behaviors (Volkmar & Cohen, 1991). In contrast to autism, a period of normal development is observed for at least the first five years of life in schizophrenia (Campbell & Shay, 1995). Adaptive behavior deteriorates in children with schizophrenia. Volkmar and Cohen (1991) examined the comorbidity of autism and schizophrenia and found that schizophrenia did not occur more often in autism than in the general population. Behaviors related to autism, such as social impairment, resistance to change, unusual language patterns, and unusual interests, need to be carefully assessed to avoid confusion with symptoms of schizophrenia. For example, restricted or circumscribed interests may be mistaken as delusions.

HOW EARLY CAN THE DIAGNOSIS BE MADE?

Several studies have confirmed that autism can be reliably diagnosed at a very young age (less than three years) and that the diagnosis is stable over time (Baron-

Cohen et al., 1996; Lord, 1995; 1999). However, most children ceive a definitive diagnosis until four to four and a half years (Siegel, Pliner, Eschler, & Elliot, 1988; Stone & Rosenbaum, 1988), limiting their opportunity to participate in specialized early intervention programs. Not only is an early diagnosis essential for participation in such programs, but a diagnosis also provides families a basis from which to become informed advocates for their child.

Early Diagnostic Features

To recognize autism in young children, it is necessary to have a keen understanding of the early features. Stone and Ousley (1996) summarized behaviors that differentiated those with autism less than 36 months of age from developmentally matched children. In the social domain, children with autism are more likely to show poor imitation of actions and gestures; failure to use eye contact in a social or communicative manner; a lack of response to the social bids of others; little interest in social games such as pat-a-cake or peekaboo; a preference for playing alone instead of with others; and a bland or flat facial expression. In the communication domain, delayed acquisition of speech, little use of gestures such as pointing or waving, and the child's failure to attract attention to his or her own activities, such as holding up or showing objects, are more likely to be observed. In the restricted and repetitive activities domain, repetitive motor behaviors such as spinning or finger posturing, repetitive play activities such as arranging objects into lines or patterns, attachment to unusual objects, failure to respond to sounds or his or her name being called, and unusual visual interests such as staring at lights or spinning objects are more likely to be observed. Three behaviors—impairment in peer relationships, impairment in language, and need for sameness—were not found to differentiate young children with autism from developmentally matched children (Stone & Hogan, 1993; Stone & Ousley, 1996).

Early Screening Instruments

Two screening instruments for very young children with possible autism have been developed. An instrument designed for children 18 months old, the Checklist for Autism in Toddlers (CHAT), was developed mainly for primary care clinicians (Baron-Cohen, Allan, & Gillberg, 1992). The CHAT consists of nine parent questions and five observational activities. Behaviors grouped as social interest, social play, pretend play, joint attention, and pointing to express interest in an object or event are assessed. Research conducted using the CHAT as a screen found that children identified with autism at 18 months who lacked two or more of the five types of behaviors were diagnosed with autism at 30 months (Baron-Cohen et al.). Three behaviors are thought to be predictive of a later diagnosis of autism: decreased pointing to share interest, joint attention, and pretend play. These behaviors were assessed in an extensive study of 16,000 children (Baron-Cohen et al., 1996). The CHAT correctly identified 10 of 12 children with autism who failed these three key items. Two children who were identified early were not diagnosed at followup.

Another instrument, the Screening Tool for Autism in Two-Year-Olds (STAT), is an interactive screening tool that takes less than 20 minutes to administer (Stone, 1999; Stone & Ousley, 1997). The STAT was developed for children ranging from 24 to 35 months of age and is designed for use by community child-find personnel. The STAT assesses three areas of development that differentiate young children with autism from children of similar developmental levels: motor imitation, functional play, and directing attention to objects or events of interest. In a pilot study using a clinic-based sample of children, failure on any two of the three domains of behavior correctly identified 14 out of 15 children with autism. The STAT has not been studied using population-based samples.

Both of these instruments show promise as sensitive screening instruments for young children with autism. Neither should be used, however, to replace a thorough multidisciplinary assessment. One should keep in mind that the CHAT may incorrectly identify children with autism who instead have language disorders, or miss children who later are diagnosed with autism. The STAT has not been replicated with larger samples in different settings, although work continues in this area (Stone, 1999).

COMPETENCY ENHANCEMENT

We reviewed assessment of autism for the purpose of establishing a diagnosis. Ideally, the diagnosis of autism leads to the development of an appropriate intervention program. For a comprehensive picture of the individual's strengths and weaknesses, it is necessary to conduct further assessment for program planning. We designed a framework to assist with the development of individualized programs. The Collaborative Model for Promoting Competence and Success (COMPASS) is a competence enhancement approach used (a) to conceptualize information from the diagnostic assessment into program planning, and (b) to collaboratively develop intervention strategies with parents and school personnel (Dalrymple & Ruble, 1995; Ruble & Dalrymple, 1996; Sears, Dalrymple, & Porco, 1993).

The child's team identifies the challenges to learning and the supports necessary for success (see Figure 2–1). The supports, on the left side of the scale, are the accumulation of both personal and environmental resources. Personal supports are the child's likes, preferences, and strengths. Environmental supports are the educational modifications and adaptations needed for success. Challenges, on the opposite side of the scale, are the sum of personal and environmental challenges. The personal challenges for a student with autism are the core impairments previously described. The environmental challenges are those factors that impede success, such as lack of visual or organizational supports, lack of social or communication supports, and lack of knowledge and skill to work with children with autism. Identifying the challenges with precision and accuracy is the first step in the design and implementation of supports. It becomes clear that the task of learning creates major

stresses and anxieties for a student with autism when the personal challenges are combined with the environmental challenges. The child with autism is competent when the supports counterbalance the challenges. The role of professionals working with children with autism is to understand how to identify, develop, implement, and maintain supports.

CONCLUSION

Autism is considered the most complex developmental disability. General agreement on many features of the diagnosis now exists. It is agreed that autism is a clinically defined syndrome based on behaviors, falls along a spectrum of symptom expression from severe to mild, is a retrospective diagnosis based on developmental history, and frequently occurs in association with other syndromes and developmental disabilities. The diagnosis is the critical first step in achieving appropriate intervention. While it does not replace assessment for intervention planning, di-

Supports

Personal
Supports

Environmental
Supports

Challenges

Personal
Challenges

Environmental
Challenges

Figure 2–1 Collaborative Model for Promoting Competence and Success (COMPASS). A competence enhancement approach for providing a seamless transition from diagnosis to intervention.

agnostic assessment must occur before more in-depth assessment of strengths and weaknesses. Potential benefits for the child and family are provided by a thorough diagnostic assessment where the clinician assists the family in translating the diagnosis into an effective response to the child's needs. A competency enhancement approach is one example of a positive program based on information from the diagnostic assessment. Through this model, a seamless transition from diagnosis to intervention may be possible as a result of close collaboration of family and professionals for the benefit of the person with autism.

CHAPTER REVIEW QUESTIONS

1. Which classification system is used to diagnose autism is based on the most research?
2. What criteria are used in this system to diagnose autism?
3. What are the similarities and differences of children with Autistic Disorder, Pervasive Developmental Disorder Not Otherwise Specified, and Asperger's syndrome?
4. How does Pervasive Developmental Disorder relate to Autistic Disorder?
5. What are the similarities and differences among children with autism?
6. What are the two screening instruments for autism described in this chapter?

REFERENCES

American Psychiatric Association. (1987). *Diagnostic and statistical manual of mental disorders* (3rd ed., rev.). Washington, D.C.: Author.

American Psychiatric Association. (1994). *Diagnostic and statistical manual of mental disorders* (4th ed.). Washington, DC: Author.

Attwood, T. (1998). *Asperger's syndrome: A guide for parents and professionals.* London & Philadelphia: Jessica Kingsley Publishers.

Barkley, R. A. (1990). *Attention deficit hyperactivity disorder: A handbook for diagnosis and treatment.* New York: Guilford Press.

Baron-Cohen, S., Allen, J., & Gillberg, C. (1992). Can autism be detected at 18 months? The needle, the haystack, and the CHAT. *British Journal of Psychiatry, 138*, 839–843.

Baron-Cohen, S., Cox, A., Baird, G., Sweethenham, J., Nightingale, N., Morgan, K., Drew, A., & Charman, T. (1996). Psychological markers in the detection of autism in infancy in a large population. *British Journal of Psychiatry, 168*, 1–6.

Bleuler, E. (1950). *Dementia praecox of the group of schizophrenias.* New York: International Universities Press.

Bryson, S. E., & Smith, I. M. (1998). Epidemiology of autism: Prevalence, associated characteristics, and implications for research and service delivery. *Mental Retardation and Developmental Disabilities Research Reviews, 4*, 97–103.

Burack, J. A., Enns, J. T., Stauder, J. E. A., Mottron, L., & Randolph, B. (1997). Attention and autism: Behavioral and electrophysiological evidence. In D. J. Cohen & F. R. Volkmar (Eds.), *Handbook of autism and pervasive developmental disorders* (2nd ed.) (pp. 226–247). New York: John Wiley & Sons.

Campbell, M., & Shay, J. (1995). Pervasive developmental disorders. In H. I. Kaplan & B. J. Sadock (Eds.), *Comprehensive textbook of psychiatry* (4th ed.) (pp. 2277–2293). Baltimore: Williams & Wilkins.

Carrey, N. J. (1995). Itard's 1828 memoir on "Mutism caused by a lesion of the intellectual functions": A historical analysis. *Journal of the American Academy of Child and Adolescent Psychiatry, 34*, 1655–1661.

Coleman, M., & Gillberg, C. (1985). *The biology of the autistic syndrome.* New York: Praeger.

Dalrymple, N., & Ruble, L. (1995). *Technical assistance manual on autism for Kentucky schools.* Frankfort, KY: Kentucky Department of Education.

DiLalla, D. L., & Rogers, S. (1994). Domains of the childhood autism rating scales: Relevance for diagnosis and treatment. *Journal of Autism and Developmental Disorders, 24*, 115–128.

Federal Register. (1992, September 29). Vol. 57, No. 189, pp. 44,794–44,852. Washington, DC: U.S. Government Printing Office.

Fisher, E., VanDyke, D. C., Sears, L. L., Matzen, J., Lin-Dyken, D., & McBrien, D. M. (1999). Recent research on the etiologies of autism. *Infants and Young Children, 11*, 1–8.

Freeman, B. J. (1993). The syndrome of autism: Update and guidelines for diagnosis. *Infants and Young Children, 6*, 1–11.

Freeman, B. J., Ritvo, E. R., Guthrie, D., Schroth, P., & Ball, J. (1978). The behavior observation scale for autism: Initial methodology, data analysis, and preliminary findings on 89 children. *Journal of the American Academy of Child Psychiatry, 17*, 576–588.

Freeman, B. J., Ritvo, E. R., Yokota, A., & Ritvo, A. (1986). A scale for rating symptoms of patients with the syndrome of autism in real life settings. *Journal of the American Academy of Child Psychiatry, 25*, 130–136.

Frith, U. (1991). *Autism and Asperger syndrome*. Cambridge: Cambridge University Press.

Harris, S. L., Glasbert, B., & Ricca, D. (1996). Pervasive developmental disorders: Distinguishing among subtypes. *School Psychology Review, 25*, 308–315.

Kanner, L. (1943). Autistic disturbances of affective contact. *Nervous Child, 2*, 217–250.

Klin, A., & Shepard, B. (1994). Psychological assessment of autistic children. *Child and Adolescent Psychiatric Clinics of North America, 3*, 53–70.

Klin, A., & Volkmar, F. R. (1997). Asperger's syndrome. In D. J. Cohen & F. R. Volkmar (Eds.), *Handbook of autism and pervasive developmental disorders* (2nd ed.) (pp. 94–122). New York: John Wiley & Sons.

Kolvin, I., Ounsted, C., Humphrey, M., & McNay, A. (1971). The phenomenology of childhood psychosis. *British Journal of Psychiatry, 118*, 385–395.

Kolvin, I, Ounsted C., & Roth, M. (1971). Cerebral dysfunction and childhood psychoses. *British Journal of Psychiatry, 118*, 407–414.

Krug, D. A., Arick, J. R., & Almond, P. J. (1980). Behavior checklist for identifying severely handicapped individuals with high levels of autistic behavior. *Journal of Child Psychology and Psychiatry, 21*, 221–229.

Lord, C. (1995). Follow-up of two-year-olds referred for possible autism. *Journal of Child Psychology and Psychiatry, 36*, 1365–1382.

Lord, C., & Risi, S. (1998). Frameworks and methods in diagnosing autism spectrum disorders. *Mental Retardation and Developmental Disabilities, 4*, 90–96.

Lord, C., Rutter, M., & DiLavore, P. (1998). *Autism diagnostic observation schedule—generic*. San Antonio, TX: Psychological Corp.

Lord, C., Rutter, M., & LeCouteur, A. (1994). Autism diagnostic interview—revised: A revised version of a diagnostic interview for caregivers of individuals with possible pervasive developmental disorders. *Journal of Autism and Developmental Disorders, 24*, 659–685.

Marcus, L. M., & Stone, W. L. (1993). Assessment of the young autistic child. In E. Schopler, M. E. Van Bourgondien, & M. M. Bristol (Eds.), *Preschool issues in autism* (pp.149–174). New York: Plenum.

Mayes, L., Volkmar, F., Hooks, M., & Cicchetti, D. (1993). Differentiating pervasive developmental disorder not otherwise specified from autism and language disorders. *Journal of Autism and Developmental Disorders, 23*, 79–90.

McBurnett, K., Lahey, B., & Pfiffner, L. (1993). Diagnosis of attention deficit disorders in *DSM-IV*: Scientific basis and implications for education. *Exceptional Children, 60*, 108–117.

McKenna, L., Gordon, C. T., & Rapoport, J. (1994). Childhood onset schizophrenia: Timely neurobiological research. *Journal of the American Academy of Child and Adolescent Psychiatry, 33*, 771–781.

Minshew, N., Goldstein, G., Taylor, H., & Siegel, D. (1994). Academic achievement in high-functioning autistic individuals. *Journal of Clinical and Experimental Neuropsychology, 16*, 261–270.

Morgan, S. (1988). Diagnostic assessment of autism: A review of objective scales. *Journal of Psychoeducational Assessment, 6*, 139–151.

Parks, S. (1988). Psychometric instruments available for the assessment of autistic children. In E. Schopler & G. Mesibov (Eds.), *Diagnosis and assessment in autism* (pp. 123–135). New York: Plenum.

Prizant, G. (1983). Language acquisition and communicative behavior in autism: Toward an understanding of the "whole" of it. *Journal of Speech and Hearing Disorders, 48*, 296–307.

Rimland, B. (1971). The differentiation of childhood psychoses: An analysis of checklists for 2,218 psychotic children. *Journal of Autism and Childhood Schizophrenia, 1*, 161–174.

Robertson, J. M., Tanguay, P. E., L'Ecuyer, S., Sims, A., & Waltrip, C. (1999). Domains of social communication handicap in autism spectrum disorder. *Journal of the American Academy of Child and Adolescent Psychiatry, 38*, 738–745.

Prizant, G. (1983). Language acquisition and communicative behavior in autism: Toward an understanding of the "whole" of it. *Journal of Speech and Hearing Disorders, 48,* 296–307.

Rimland, B. (1971). The differentiation of childhood psychoses: An analysis of checklists for 2,218 psychotic children. *Journal of Autism and Childhood Schizophrenia, 1,* 161–174.

Robertson, J. M., Tanguay, P. E. L'Ecuyer, S., Sims, A., & Waltrip, C. (1999). Domains of social communication handicap in autism spectrum disorder. *Journal of the American Academy of Child and Adolescent Psychiatry, 38,* 738–745.

Ruble, L., & Dalrymple, N. (1996). An alternative view of outcome in autism. *Focus on Autism and Other Developmental Disabilities, 11,* 3–14.

Ruttenberg, B. A., Kalish, B. I., Wenar, C., & Wolf, E. (1977). *The behavior rating instrument for autistic and other atypical children.* Chicago: Soelting.

Rutter, M., & Schopler, E. (1988). Autism and pervasive developmental disorders: Concepts and diagnostic issues. In E. Schopler & G. Mesibov (Eds.), *Diagnosis and assessment in autism* (pp. 15–35). New York: Plenum.

Schopler, E. (1998). Premature popularization of Asperger syndrome. In E. Schopler, G. Mesibov, & L. Kunce (Eds.), *Asperger syndrome or high-functioning autism?* (pp. 385–400). New York: Plenum.

Schopler, E., & Mesibov, G. (1988). Introduction to diagnosis and assessment of autism. In E. Schopler & G. Mesibov (Eds.), *Diagnosis and assessment in autism* (pp. 3–14). New York: Plenum.

Schopler, E., Mesibov, G., & Kunce, L. (Eds.). (1998). *Asperger syndrome or high-functioning autism?* New York: Plenum.

Schopler, E., Reichler, U. J., & Renner, B. R. (1988). *The childhood autism rating scale (CARS).* Los Angeles: Western Psychological Services.

Sears, L., Dalrymple, N., & Porco, B. (1993). Model for competence enhancement in persons with autism. *Indiana Resource Center for Autism: Newsletter.* (Available from ISDD-IRCA, 1853 E. 10th St., Bloomington, IN 47405.)

Siegel, B., Pliner, C., Eschler, J., & Elliott, G. R. (1988). How children with autism are diagnosed: Difficulties in identification of children with multiple developmental delays. *Developmental Behavioral Pediatrics, 9,* 199–204.

Sigman, M., Dissanayake, C., Arbelle, S., & Ruskin, E. (1997). Cognition and emotion in children and adolescents with autism. In D. J. Cohen & F. R. Volkmar (Eds.), *Handbook of autism and pervasive developmental disorders* (2nd ed.) (pp. 248–265). New York: John Wiley & Sons.

Stone, W.L. (1999, April). *An interactive screening tool for autism in two-year-olds.* Paper presented at the Meeting of the Society for Research in Child Development, Albuquerque, New Mexico.

Stone, W. L., & Hogan, K. L. (1993). A structured parent interview for identifying young children with autism. *Journal of Autism and Developmental Disorders, 13,* 639–652.

Stone, W. L., Lee, E., Ashford, L., Brissie, J., Hepburn, S. L., Coonrod, E., & Weiss, B. H. (1999). Can autism be diagnosed accurately in children under three years? *Journal of Child Psychology and Psychiatry, 40,* 219–226.

Stone, W. L. & Ousley, O. Y. (1996). Pervasive developmental disorders: Autism. In M. L. Wolraich (Ed.), *Disorders of development and learning* (pp. 379–405). Boston: Mosby.

Stone, W. L. & Ousley, O. Y. (1997). *STAT Manual: Screening tool for autism in two-year-olds.* Unpublished manuscript, Vanderbilt University.

Stone, W. L., & Rosenbaum, J. L. (1988). A comparison of teacher and parent views of autism. *Journal of Autism and Developmental Disorders, 18,* 403–414.

Towbin, K. E. (1997). Pervasive developmental disorder not otherwise specified. In D. J. Cohen & F. R. Volkmar (Eds.), *Handbook of autism and pervasive developmental disorders* (2nd ed.) (pp. 123–147). New York: John Wiley & Sons.

Trevathan, E., & Naidu, S. (1988). The clinical recognition and differential diagnosis of Rett syndrome. *Journal of Child Neurology, 3*(Suppl.), S6–S16.

Tsai, L. (1992a). Diagnostic issues in high-functioning autism. In E. Schopler & G. Mesibov (Eds.), *High-functioning individuals with autism* (pp. 11–40). New York: Plenum.

Tsai, L. (1992b). Is Rett syndrome a subtype of pervasive developmental disorder? *Journal of Autism and Developmental Disorders, 22,* 551–561.

Van Acker, R. (1997). Rett's syndrome: A pervasive developmental disorder. In D. J. Cohen & F. R. Volkmar (Eds.), *Handbook of autism and pervasive developmental disorders* (2nd ed.) (pp. 60–93). New York: John Wiley & Sons.

Volkmar, F. R. (1994). Childhood disintegrative disorder. *Child and Adolescent Psychiatry Clinics of North America, 4,* 119–130.

Volkmar, F. R., & Cohen, D. J. (1991). Comorbid association of autism and schizophrenia. *American Journal of Psychiatry, 48,* 1705–1707.

Volkmar, F. R., Hoder, E., & Cohen, D. J. (1985). Compliance, "negativism," and the effects of treatment and structure in autism: A naturalistic behavior study. *Journal of Child Psychology and Psychiatry, 26,* 865877.

Volkmar, F. R., Klin, A., & Cohen, D. J. (1997). Diagnosis and classification of autism and related conditions: Consensus and issues. In D. J. Cohen & F. R. Volkmar (Eds.), *Handbook of autism and pervasive developmental disorders* (2nd ed.) (pp. 5–40). New York: John Wiley & Sons.

Volkmar, F. R., Klin, A., Marans, W., & Cohen, D. J. (1997). Childhood disintegrative disorder. In D. J. Cohen & F. R. Volkmar (Eds.), *Handbook of autism and pervasive developmental disorders* (2nd ed.) (pp. 47–59). New York: John Wiley & Sons.

Watson, L. R., Lord, C., Schaffer, B., & Schopler, E. (1989). *Teaching spontaneous communication to autistic and developmentally handicapped children.* New York: Irvington.

Watson, L. R., & Marcus, L. M. (1988). Diagnosis and assessment of preschool children. In E. Schopler & G. Mesibov (Eds.), *Diagnosis and assessment in autism* (pp. 271–302). New York: Plenum.

Wetherby, A. M. (1986). Ontogeny of communicative functions in autism. *Journal of Autism and Developmental Disorders, 16,* 295–316.

Wing, L. (1988). The continuum of autistic characteristics. In E. Schopler & G. Mesibov (Eds.), *Diagnosis and assessment in autism* (pp. 91–110). New York: Plenum.

Wing, L. (1997). Syndromes of autism and atypical development. In D. J. Cohen & F. R. Volkmar (Eds.), *Handbook of autism and pervasive developmental disorders* (2nd ed.) (pp. 148–172). New York: John Wiley & Sons.

Wolraich, M. L., Felice, M. E., & Drotar, D. D. (1996). *The classification of child and adolescent mental diagnoses in primary care: Diagnostic and statistical manual for primary care (DSM-PC), child and adolescent version.* Elk Grove Village, IL: American Academy of Pediatrics.

World Health Organization (1993). *The ICD-10 classification of mental and behavioural disorders.* Geneva: Author.

Zero to Three/National Center for Clinical Infant Programs (1995). *Diagnostic classification: 0–3 diagnostic classification of mental health and developmental disorders of infancy and early childhood.* Arlington, VA: Author.

CHAPTER 3

Neuropsychological Findings, Etiology, and Implications for Autism

Ruth A. Huebner and Shelly J. Lane

CHAPTER OBJECTIVES

At the completion of this chapter, the reader will:

- Understand and appreciate the strengths and limitations of current methods for studying the neuropsychology of autism.
- Discuss the findings from neuropsychological research on the primary sites of dysfunction in autism and appreciate the integrative nature of brain dysfunction.
- Understand the strengths and limitations of several theories of etiology of autism.
- Appreciate the sensory and motor experiences of persons with autism.
- Comprehend the implications of this literature on the understanding of sensorimotor processing in children with autism.

INTRODUCTION

The term *neuropsychology* is a broad, unifying term that relates to the study and science of brain function as it influences human emotion, behavior, and cognition. Neuropsychology has developed from research on human and nonhuman populations and integrates information from anatomy, biology, physiology, physiological psychology, neurology, and psychology (Kolb & Whishaw, 1996). A neuropsychological understanding of the autistic spectrum is founded on investigations of brain structure, brain function, and behavioral output as they relate to the unique aspects of emotion, behavior, and cognition that underlie this syndrome.

Brain Function and Autism

Autism is a syndrome of complex and as yet undefined brain dysfunction that is expressed in an array of functional deficits. The search to uncover the specific anatomical site, the specific neurotransmitter deficit, or the etiology of brain dysfunctions associated with autism that would provide a clue to its prevention or treatment has been extensive. Unfortunately, findings in the literature continue to be inconsistent and inconclusive (Rapin, 1997). Because no findings from this extensive research are irrefutable, the question could be raised: Why study the neuropsychology of autism? Indeed, any individual could apply the ideas found elsewhere in this book on the management of autism without understanding this chapter.

There are many reasons that this quest to understand the autistic spectrum disorders is critical. The sensorimotor approach to assessment and management is based on an understanding of neurological development. In this approach, we consider the child's behavior, especially the young child's behavior, as a form of communication that provides insight to the sensorimotor needs of the child arising, in part, from physiological stimuli. Comprehension of the potential neurological basis of autism provides a more specific conceptual framework for appreciating behavior and making choices in how to approach or manage behavior. A thorough understanding of autism is necessary in order to choose wisely from the plethora of interventions proposed by multiple authors. The more that is known, the more able we are to judge the worth of any intervention for a particular individual. This chapter is an attempt to integrate the findings of available research. Bailey, Phillips, and Rutter (1996) promote such integrative attempts to identify research questions and generate innovative discourse about a complex disorder. Furthermore, the need is critical for research to describe and differentiate the sensory and motor profile of people with autism and to test treatment strategies based on these profiles. The information provided here may serve as a foundation for those efforts.

Limitations in Research

That said, when considering the neuropsychological research, it is important to consider the significant limitations of any single finding in the literature that may be overinterpreted in isolation. Weak research design is, unfortunately, common in the field of autism. The pronounced interest in autistic disorder is coupled with a limited number of persons with autism and diagnostic procedures that are relatively subjective; these factors make homogeneity among research subjects in any study unlikely (Lord, 1991). The study of some functions requires that participants possess adequate verbal and cognitive skills, excluding a portion of the population with autism; some studies do not include a comparison group matched for mental age, especially verbal mental age. Because participants with autism in any research project are likely to be different from participants in another research project, comparisons across studies also become muddled. Moreover, the research findings across time may not be comparable because the criteria for diagnosis of the disorder have changed through the multiple versions of the *Diagnostic Statistical Manual* (*DSM*) of the American Psychiatric Association (APA). These diagnostic changes, and the current trend toward providing an educational label of autism to children using similar but not identical criteria, further complicate generalization of research findings.

Fortunately, myriad methods are available to investigators of neurological functions; unfortunately, findings from this multiplicity of methods are not easily integrated and may lead to differing conclusions. For example, the finding of atypical neurotransmitter metabolite levels may lead one investigator to suggest that this reflects a primary alteration in the neurochemical system. Another investigator might instead look for anatomical abnormalities such as differences in cell size or cell density in sites that either produce or re-uptake the neurotransmitter. A third may take a systems approach and explain the findings based on atypical interactions between various brain systems and structures. Thus, there are often several plausible explanations for any single finding.

Perhaps an even more critical consideration is the dynamic and evolving understanding of how the brain functions and how its effects on behavior are conceptualized. The range of relationships possible between any neurophysiological response and the psychological manifestation of that response is wide. While a few neurological responses are invariant or the same under all conditions, most responses are context bound and affected by multiple variables such as stress level, expectations, medications, and cognitive activities. Because of this complexity, what may at first look like an invariant response may later be better understood to be affected by multiple variables (Cacioppo & Tassinary, 1990).

This growing awareness of the complexity of neurological functioning has stimulated and been reinforced by network models of neurological function (Churchland, 1986). In the network models, neurons are conceptualized as connected in a three-dimensional array with other neurons and other sites. For example, a single sensory input, such as a visual input, activates brain function at several sites. Functions such as modulation of sensory stimuli and motor control occur at older and newer brain structures. Thus, the brain has redundancy of function and a hierarchy of complexity (Churchland). The study of neuropsychology is further complicated by the effects of behavior on brain development; behavior and sensory experiences over time change neurological structures. As a person ages, separating primary effects of brain anatomy or physiology from secondary effects of behavior and learning becomes increasingly difficult. Although the methods of neurological investigation are quite sophisticated, they require exact and complicated protocols to administer and often prove difficult to implement when testing persons with autism. Finally, the enormous body of literature on autism supports many viewpoints. Sometimes results that have not been replicated or were later refuted are reported in current literature in support of a viewpoint that may not have withstood the test of time.

Although these multiple limitations may seem to argue against drawing conclusions from neurological research, they merely reinforce the necessity to carefully consider the results of multiple research studies. In this chapter, we review the recent findings from multiple research studies and draw tentative conclusions that have implications for sensory and motor development and management of autism. This review was based on an extensive literature search; the articles reviewed here are most current, have been cited in works across disciplines and across viewpoints, and represent a general consensus of findings. Nonetheless, the reader is cautioned that this research is dynamic, with continually emerging findings and refinement of knowledge.

The purpose of this chapter is to provide a foundation for understanding the extensive literature on the neuropsychology of autism. To do this, we have organized the chapter into these sections: the methods of studying neuropsychological function, the findings from this research during the last decade and the function of the brain related to this research, the theories of etiology that contribute to understanding autism, and the implications of this research.

METHODS OF STUDYING NEUROLOGICAL FUNCTION

The methods discussed here are roughly organized from least to most intrusive and from simplest to most dynamic. Basic descriptions of common methods of study are provided to assist the reader in understanding the literature and the research findings reported here.

Clinical Examination

Clinical examinations of psychological or physiological responses are simple noninvasive tests familiar to most of us. These examinations include neurological signs, dysmorphia (abnormality in facial or physical features), visual scanning and acuity, motor reflexes, sensitivity to touch or movement, and standardized tests of perception or cognition. Self-report instruments, checklists, and rating scales completed by parents or teachers contribute to this clinical examination. The methods discussed in Chapters 2 and 4 summarize the clinical examination methods used by psychologists and occupational therapists for children suspected of having autistic spectrum disorders. The results of clinical examination complement the findings from other forms of research and contribute to hypothesis formulation for research and management.

Physiological Measures

Closely akin to methods of clinical examination are physiological measures. The measurement of skin conductance, or electrodermal activity, is based on the principle that the skin momentarily becomes a better conductor of electricity when certain external stimuli are presented. Small electrodes are placed on the hand with a very small current running between them. In response to stimuli, small amounts of sweat are released; sweat reduces skin resistance to the electrical current and the resulting change in current is recorded and visualized. Skin conductance responses are the basis for lie detector tests and are routinely used to test

levels of arousal and anxiety. Similarly, results of an electrocardiogram (ECG) may be reported to demonstrate changes in heart rate with sensory stimulation. ECG responses are measures of the electrical activity generated by the heart muscle contraction; electrodes placed on particular points on the chest record the heart rate response. Both of these methods are relatively noninvasive, routine, and inexpensive, but could be upsetting for anyone, including a person with autism. Other physiological tests are numerous but not particularly relevant to the study of autism at this time.

Electrical Activity of the Brain

Brain electrical activity is measured primarily using electroencephalography (EEG); this technique was one of the first methods of studying the neurobiology of autism (Dunn, M., 1994). With EEG, brain activity in areas of interest is measured as the electrical potential differences between two electrodes. Recording electrodes are placed on the scalp over the cortical lobes in a standardized and conventional pattern, with each electrode labeled; brain cell activity in each area can be recorded. Results of research using EEG may report electrical abnormalities relative to specific electrode sites. For example, focal spikes (from electrical discharge in the brain) recorded from one electrode may be associated with seizures localized in a brain area. Asymmetrical responses from two electrodes on either side of the skull may be associated with activation of one portion of the brain by sensory input such as a visual or an auditory stimulus. The earliest versions of EEG produced relatively undifferentiated and global findings. Recently, however, researchers have increased the number of electrodes and added sophisticated computer analysis of data to improve spatial mapping of EEG responses, thus matching responses more exactly to brain sites (Pivik et al., 1993). Magnetoencephalogram (MEG) is similar to the EEG but detects the magnetic field generated by the brain in response to input. These magnetic fields can be pinpointed in a three-dimensional format for spatial mapping of responses in specific structures. MEG therefore offers a noninvasive and functional imaging technique. However, the magnetic fields generated by neurological activity are weak, requiring specialized rooms that exclude external electric and magnetic signals (Toga & Mazziotta, 1996).

Evoked potentials (EPs) or event-related potentials (ERPs) are slow electrical brain waves in response to a specific input; these waves are embedded in whole-brain electrical activity. Brain waves evoked in response to a stimulus are nearly identical and always in the same direction on each trial. To distinguish the slow, consistent brain wave from the surrounding brain electrical activity, several trials of the stimulus must be administered and the brain wave patterns must be averaged over these trials. Averaging of brain wave patterns from several trials nullifies random brain wave variances in positive and negative directions while elucidating the brain waves that occurred in response to a stimulus. ERPs can be used to determine the integrity of the pathways and aspects of cognitive processing (Gevins, 1996) and are labeled as visual, auditory, or tactile, depending on the sensory input. For each sensory input, predictable ERPs are defined in the literature and used for comparison. Evoked potentials may be expressed as positive (P) or negative (N), depending on their polarity, and be followed with a number (e.g., P300) that refers to the latency of the response measured as the number of milliseconds after the stimulus that the ERP occurred.

Variations from the typical strength of a response, differences in the latency of response, and reversal of the polarity of a response yield data on variations in processing (Coles, Gratton, & Fabiani, 1990). Numerous studies include tests of ERP responses in examining processing of stimuli by people with autism (Dunn, M., 1994).

Neuroimaging

Brain imaging, or neuroimaging, refers to several methods of viewing the brain structure and, sometimes, function in a two-dimensional or three-dimensional manner. The X-ray is one common method of neuroimaging that may be enhanced by injection of substances, such as dye, to visualize the vascular system. The computerized transaxial tomograph (CT scan), or computer-assisted tomograph (CAT), consists, essentially, of multiple X-rays of the brain taken at various points; the sums of the data are computer processed to examine multiple cross sections of the brain. CAT scans offer greater detail than the traditional X-ray, allowing viewers to distinguish specific structures. Because a CAT scan is, in essence, a snapshot, it reflects structure but not function of the brain (Kandel, Schwartz, & Jessell, 2000).

Magnetic resonance imaging (MRI), or nuclear magnetic resonance (NMR), relies on detecting the resonance or vibration of nerve cell nuclei in response to radio waves. MRI and NMR produce three-dimensional images of the brain. A magnetic field is applied that aligns cell nuclei in the same direction; the alignment is disrupted by the pulsation of a radio wave. The electrical signal (resonance) emitted by the cells as the nuclei return to their original position is converted into an image of the region under study (Kolb & Whishaw, 1996). Each type of atom, which corresponds to a neurochemical or tissue type, has a unique pattern of resonance, allowing researchers to match the resonance to tissue type. MRI provides a powerful imaging technique because it is noninvasive and does not expose the person to either X-rays or radioactive substances (Churchland, 1986). Similar to the comparison of ERPs to normative data, MRI responses can be compared to typical responses. *Functional MRI* refers to a group of techniques that pair studies of blood flow or diffusion of substances to measure brain activity dynamically with spatial accuracy (Kolb & Whishaw). Although promising, this technique needs to be standardized and has drawbacks related to resolution.

The positron emission tomography (PET) measures brain glucose metabolism, reflecting which parts of the brain are more active for certain tasks (Horwitz & Rumsey, 1994). Thus, this technique offers a dynamic and functional view of the brain. A glucose solution, with radioactive fluorine to produce the image, is administered. Glucose is taken up into active cells during a task and the fluorine makes this cell activity visible. Those areas of the brain with the most metabolic activity and, consequently, the most glucose uptake, emit more fluorine-induced gamma rays. These rays are computer-mapped in a process similar to that used in CT scan (Churchland, 1986). A PET scan may detect differences in function or activity of the brain that are present even if the brain appears normal on CT scan.

The single-photon emission computed tomography (SPECT) scan uses methodology similar to the PET scan; resolution is lower, but so is its cost to administer. Another emerging technique is magnetic resonance spectroscopy (MRS). MRS can be adjusted to measure different brain chemicals, oxygenation of tissues, and tissue metabolites that may implicate neurochemical actions. This may prove fruitful in understanding the dynamic processes of the brain and specific neurotransmitter use (Minshew, 1994). Neurochemical responses to sensory stimuli, for example, could be detected using MRS.

Although potentially useful, all of the brain imaging techniques require prolonged recording of responses. For example, an MRS requires 5 to 10 minutes of recording, making it difficult to obtain consistent data. These brain imaging techniques may require sedation of the individual, potentially influencing brain responses and confounding research findings.

Neurochemistry

Investigating brain neurochemistry may lead to an understanding of the functional relationships and systemic reactions within the central nervous system (CNS). Studies of neurotransmitters, their synthesis, receptor interactions, degradation, sites of release, and targets have vastly improved the understanding of wellness and disease in the CNS. However, the direct study of brain neurochemistry is necessarily invasive and not well suited to human investigation. Instead, CNS neurochemistry in humans can be studied by analysis of neurotransmitter metabolites in cerebrospinal fluid taken from the spinal column, blood, and urine to detect specific neurotransmitter markers. Findings from more detailed and invasive animal studies have provided neurochemical insights into human function, but generalizations from animal studies to humans must be made cautiously. Moreover, animal studies preclude the study of uniquely human processes such as language, abstract reasoning, and social relatedness. Neurochemical studies in both humans and animals have been used in investigations of CNS functions theoretically applicable to autism. Animal models of autism, with monkeys for example, have also been developed with analysis of resultant brain chemistry.

In addition to neurotransmitters, hormones can be studied to offer insight into CNS function. Of particular interest in the study of autism is cortisol. The release of this hormone is initiated by the amygdala and by hippocampus stimulation of the pituitary gland, which releases hormones to stimulate the adrenal cortex of the adrenal glands to release cortisol (Westman, 1990). Cortisol is released in response to stress and can be detected in the saliva using simple techniques. Although the results of cortisol studies may vary in response to chronic versus long-term stressors, or physical exercise (Kennedy, Glaser, & Kiecolt-Glaser, 1990), some studies on autism have yielded meaningful data on sensory stimulation and stress using cortisol measurement.

Autopsy and Invasive Techniques

Finally, autopsy examination has been used to compare the shape, size, cell density, and types of cells in various structures of the brain and to draw conclusions from these data. In an autopsy, the brain can be examined for large differences from other brains (e.g., size or weight), and tissue can be sectioned and examined in fine sheets for comparisons (e.g., cell density, size, numbers), recording structures (e.g., size, organization), and testing of tissue characteristics. Invasive procedures in nonhuman research may involve implanting probes into living brains or making isolated lesions of the brain to gather site-specific data. All of these methods have contributed to discerning the neuropsychology of autism. An overview of

methods for studying neuropsychology is presented in Table 3–1.

RESEARCH FINDINGS SPECIFIC TO AUTISM

We now turn our attention to the work that has been done in the investigation of autism. In addition to the criteria mentioned earlier, the literature for this review was chosen because it supports theories that persist across time and is relevant to the sensory and motor abilities of people with autism. This discussion is organized by the sites on which major neurological explanations of the etiology of autism are founded. These four explanations of autism include findings of disorders in the brain stem, cerebellum, medial/temporal lobe areas, or sites of cognitive and executive functions. This division by brain sites is necessarily imperfect and somewhat arbitrary because of the holistic functioning of the brain and the overlap of function among sites. For each neurological explanation, the neuroanatomy and function is discussed and the findings from the research literature are presented and summarized. This chapter includes research published primarily in the 1990s. For a review of earlier literature pertinent to sensorimotor management, see Huebner (1992) and Clark (1983). Structures of the brain are displayed in Figure 3–1; areas theoretically linked to autism are labeled.

Brain Stem Functions and Findings

Anatomy

The brain stem begins at the top (most caudal end) of the spinal cord and includes the medulla oblongata, the pons, and the midbrain. Within the brain stem, numerous nuclei are related to sensory and motor processing, including the cranial nerve nuclei

Table 3–1 Description of Methods for Studying Neurological Function

Method	Description	Strengths/Limitations
Clinical examination	Simple tests. Self-report instruments, checklists, rating scales, physical examination.	Typical responses; clinician can elicit cooperation. Drawing conclusions about sites of brain dysfunction is based on research, but relatively speculative.
Physiological measures	Skin conductance and electrocardiogram.	Noninvasive. Limitations as above.
Electroencephalograph (EEG)	Records electrical activity of the brain from scalp electrodes.	Simple and available test, now with improved spatial mapping and two-dimensional displays.
Magnetoencephalogram (MEG)	Records magnetic activity of the brain with three-dimensional spatial mapping.	Noninvasive. Magnetic fields are weak and recording requires specialized rooms.
Evoked potentials (EP) Event-related potentials (ERPs)	Records the speed and direction of slow brain waves in response to specific stimuli.	Test of brain dynamics, often with comparison to normative data. Confounding variables affect test results.
Computerized transaxial tomograph (CT scan); computer-assisted tomograph (CAT scan)	X-rays of the brain taken of multiple cross sections and then computer-processed to reveal three-dimensional portrait.	Three-dimensional measure. Longer testing time with confounding variables. Shows structure but not function of the brain. Radioactive materials may be injected.
Magnetic resonance imaging (MRI); nuclear magnetic resonance (NMR)	Records changes in cell alignment (resonance) when radio wave is passed through brain tissue.	Noninvasive; records responses to specific sensory input. Confounding variables may alter responses.
Functional MRI	Pairs MRI study with the study of blood flow or diffusions of substances.	Records dynamic functions of the brain. More complicated and invasive than MRI, with problems in resolution.
Positron emission tomography (PET scan)	Measures brain glucose metabolism.	Records dynamic action of the brain. Injection of dye.
Single-photon emission computed tomography (SPECT)	Simpler version of PET scan.	Less costly than PET scan, but also lower resolution.

continues

Table 3–1 continued

Method	Description	Strengths/Limitations
Magnetic resonance spectroscope (MRS)	Combines techniques to provide dynamic measurement, including neurochemical responses.	Newer technique. Requires prolonged recording, making results subject to confounding variables.
Neurochemistry	Measurement of neurotransmitters.	Direct study is invasive and mostly unsuitable for human research. Indirect study is confounded by multiple variables.
Autopsy	Examination of the brain after death. Size, structures, cell count, and characteristics can be compared to other brains.	Direct study. Invasive and confounded by cause of death. No ability to study dynamics of brain function.

Note: Spatial mapping refers to localizing the responses to specific structures within the three-dimensional structure of the brain. *Resolution* refers to the clarity of the visual display of responses. *Confounding variables* include factors such as anxiety, fatigue, distractibility, sedation, and medical disorders that alter brain responses and may be elicited by the test situation.

of 10 (of 12) cranial nerves. There are sites for producing the neurotransmitters serotonin, dopamine, norepinephrine, and epinephrine (Gilman & Newman, 1992). The reticular activating system of the brain stem is particularly relevant to the discussion of sensory responses in autism because it functions as a sensory gating center and controls sleep/alert cycles. The reticular activating system is one part of the larger state regulating system that is diagrammed in Figure 3–2; the reticular system interacts reciprocally with all other structures of the state regulating system. *State regulation* refers to the complex system that filters and modulates the constant flow of internal processes (metabolic processes and neurological stimuli) and external stimuli coming into the brain. The state regulating system filters and modulates stimuli, maintains a level of cortical tone essential for organized mental activity, and maintains homeostasis of the body (Westman, 1990). One major function of the state regulating system is to modulate arousal.

Functions of Arousal, Attention, and Sensory Modulation

Arousal is defined as a physiological state of readiness elicited by the organism's perception of its environment (Johnson & Anderson, 1990). The level of arousal is influenced by diverse factors such as genetics and temperament style, ongoing physiological state, psychological and environmental history, and the perception of control over the environment. The concepts of arousal and attention are critical to the use of sensorimotor management techniques because these interventions are based, in part, on the goal of improving sensory modulation to normalize arousal and thereby facilitate op-

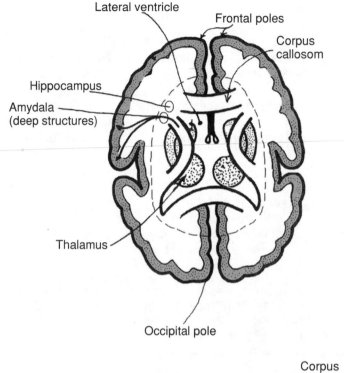

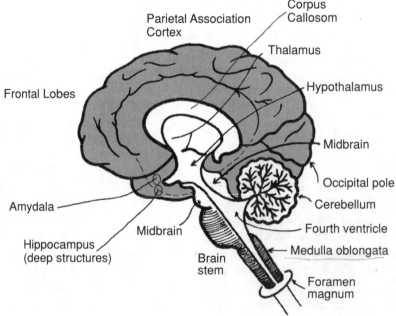

— — Dashed Area: Medial Temporal Lobe

Figure 3–1 Areas of the brain involved in autism. *Source:* Adapted from S. D. Gertz, *Neuroanatomy Made Easy and Understandable,* 6th, ed., p. 7, Aspen Publishers, Inc.

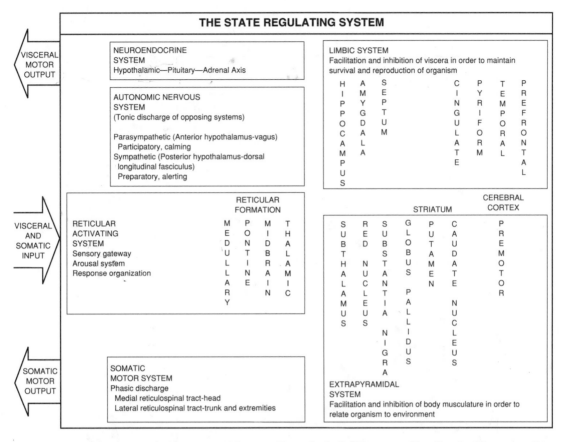

Figure 3–2 The state regulating system. *Source:* From Jack C. Westman, *Handbook of Learning Disabilities: A Multisystem Approach.* Copyright © by Allyn & Bacon. Reprinted with permission.

timal attention and learning (Royeen & Lane, 1991). Arousal varies along a continuum from the extreme of being asleep or drowsy to the opposite pole of being excited, anxious, or agitated; between these extremes is selective focused attention (Westman, 1990). Figure 3–3 depicts this continuum.

The term *arousal* implies a continuum of alertness. Inherent in this normal continuum are dimensions of attention from drowsy to vigilant and dimensions of affective responses from calm or bored to anxious or excited. Excessive arousal is associated with affective responses of distress and anxiety (Groden, Cautela, Prince, & Berryman, 1994) and sensorimotor responses of agita-

tion and distractibility. Figure 3–4 depicts four quadrants of stimulus modulation and arousal that could be used to understand difficulties with modulating arousal or maintaining state regulation. *Stimulus modulation* refers to the ability to filter and modify sensory stimuli. Miller and Lane (2000) recently described sensory modulation as an adjustment in the ongoing physiologic processes to ensure internal adaptation to new or changing sensory information. Persons with autism may fall into the category of low stimulus modulation—that is, they have difficulty modifying incoming stimuli and are easily overwhelmed—and high arousal. This processing pattern may result

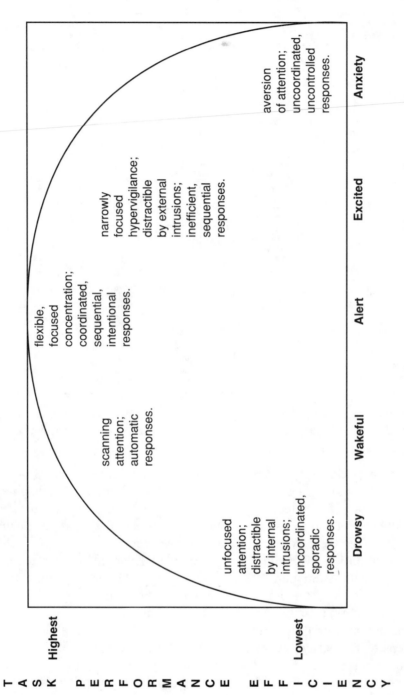

Figure 3–3 Performance continuum related to level of arousal. *Source:* From Jack C. Westman, *Handbook of Learning Disabilities: A Multisystem Approach.* Copyright ©1990 by Allyn & Bacon. Reprinted with permission. (Adpated from T. Cox, *Stress,* University Park Press, Baltimore, MD, 1978.)

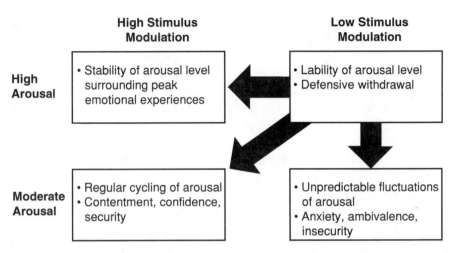

Figure 3–4 The relationship between stimulus modulation and arousal levels. Infants are presumed to move from a state of high arousal and low stimulus modulation to one of the other states during the course of development. *Source:* From Jack C. Westman, *Handbook of Learning Disabilities: A Multi-system Approach.* Copyright ©1990 by Allyn & Bacon. Reprinted by permission. (Adapted from A. Fogel, Affect Dynamics in Early Infancy: Affective Tolerance, in T. Field and A. Fogel, eds., *Emotion and Early Interaction,* Lawrence Erlbaum. Hillsdale, NJ, 1982.)

in lability of arousal for children with sensory processing disorders who, according to Royeen and Lane, seem to vacillate between defensive/anxious states and dormancy states. Westman proposed that this pattern of low stimulus modulation and high arousal is present in infants, complementing the notion that autism is a disorder of brain maturation (see later discussion). Also see Chapter 1 for a more detailed explanation of sensory processing and arousal.

This system for arousal modulation was described by Westman (1990; see Chapter 12) as a *state regulating system* and by Gray and McNaughton (1996) as a *behavior inhibition system.* Both Westman and Gray and McNaughton described the functions of this system as regulating sleep/arousal patterns, screening sensory stimuli to allow selective attention to important stimuli, regulating the amount of gross motor behavior, linking to

the emotional interpretation of sensory input, providing a background of alertness for the whole brain, and participating in planning actions.

From a neurophysiological prospective, the state regulating system receives input from and itself influences multiple structures in the brain. The neuroanatomical structures that constitute this system are described by several authors (Gray & McNaughton, 1996; Johnson & Anderson, 1990; Westman, 1990) as including the reticular activating system, a weblike structure running through the brain stem into the thalamus and other structures of the brain stem; the limbic system; portions of the neurotransmitter circuitry; the hypothalamus; and functional connections to the neocortex. Although interconnected, physiological responses to stress and anxiety vary widely depending on myriad state, behavioral, and psychological conditions. The behavioral and psychological responses to stress also vary, so correlations between physiological measures of anxiety, behavioral measures of anxiety, and psychological measures of anxiety are low, suggesting disassociation between the structures of the state regulating system (Johnson & Anderson).

Within this system, attentional and arousal responses can be either mostly involuntary or mostly voluntary and include an affective and cognitive component (Westman, 1990). Involuntary responses include reflexive orienting to stimuli, startle responses, and defensive withdrawal, and are mediated more directly by brain stem structures. More voluntary processes of attention include scanning attention, focused attention, shifting attention, and concentration; these are mediated by numerous structures in the brain. The limbic system supplies the emotional energy to attend and follow through on tasks, and assigns the emotional significance to sensory input. At the cortical level, the frontal and parietal lobes integrate sensory and motor inputs and organize strategies to initiate and execute behavior; this goal directedness sustains attention through long-term tasks. Genetic differences in temperament, early experiences with control of sensory experiences, early bereavement, and attachment experiences (see Chorpita & Barlow, 1998; Westman, 1990, for a review) are thought to be the primary influences on the neurodevelopment of the state regulating system. Depending on numerous factors, when this system is dysfunctional, people may be prone to excessive anxiety, hyperarousal or passivity, negative emotion, aggression, poor attention, distractibility, decreased initiative, and diminished goal directedness (Chorpita & Barlow).

All structures of this state regulating or behavioral inhibition system that influence arousal and attention are implicated as sites of dysfunction for autistic disorder. However, differentiating the effects of brain stem, cerebellar, midbrain/limbic/parietal, and neocortex dysfunction is difficult because of the integration of these systems. Because of this complexity, only the research on clinical observation of attention responses and findings specific to brain stem structures is reviewed in this section.

Neuropsychological Findings

People with autism may display paradoxical symptoms of attention and arousal deficits. They may be less sensitive to pain yet hypersensitive to other sensory stimuli; attention may be unusually long for self-initiated activity but very short for social interaction or specific skill development; they often experience sleep disorders; and they may avert their gaze, reacting painfully to light yet gazing for long periods at a visual display (Rapin, 1997; Rapin & Katzman, 1998). In reviewing videos of children in early life who were later found to have autism, Lelord et al. (1994) detected significant differences from normal development with decreased attention during the first and, more prominently, the second years of life, suggesting early deficits in automatic attention.

People with autism also exhibit motor stereotypies such as hand flapping and rocking, and may exhibit self-injurious behaviors such as hand biting. One theoretical interpretation of these stereotypes and some self-injurious behaviors is that they are used to compensate for modulating arousal and maintaining homeostasis in under- or overstimulating environments (Berkson, 1996; Guess & Carr, 1991). Early research focused on the brain stem as a site of dysfunction in orienting to and modulating sensory input (e.g., Ornitz, 1989). In a model developed by Ornitz, autism was attributed to disorders of sensory processing mediated by the brain stem, especially the vestibular nuclei, with a subsequent cascade of dysfunction in the higher neural structures that process and refine sensory stimuli.

Using visual and/or auditory event-related potentials, many studies (e.g., Ciesielski, Courchesne, & Elmasian, 1990; Lelord et al., 1994; Lincoln, Courchesne, Harms, & Allen, 1993; Steffenburg, 1991; Wong & Wong, 1991) have found abnormalities in processing auditory stimuli, including prolonged transmission time, smaller ERP (P300) responses, and reversed polarity of the ERPs to novel visual stimuli (reversed Nc responses). Ciesielski et al. noted that the overt performance of both groups (control and autistic) in their study was the same, but the brain wave responses were significantly different, suggesting brain stem or cerebellar abnormalities in processing. More recently, Ornitz, Lane, Sugiyama, and de Traversay (1993) studied startle modulation using EMG and found only prolongation of the unmodulated startle onset latency, which they partially and tentatively ascribed to brain stem responses.

Because the body of research on autism and neurology is large, findings of no differences between children with autism and those without and findings contradictory to those reported here can also be found in the literature (see Dunn, M., 1994, for a review). In addition, limitations of available research must be considered. For instance, ERP studies often use few electrode sites and mixed ages of participants, thus influencing the latency of the ERP (Dunn, M.). Other limitations of research examining evoked responses include undetected hearing loss in some persons with autism, dampening auditory input (Klin, 1993), and differences in expectations or difficulty of the

material, suggesting that longer latencies may indicate slower processing at other neurological sites (Coles, Gratton, & Fabiani, 1990). Despite these limitations, the study of modulation of sensory input and attention is of critical concern for individuals with autism. However, the research suggests that structures such as cerebellum, or midbrain, may be primarily involved in autistic disorder, perhaps in addition to the brain stem (Dunn, M.; Minshew & Dombrowski, 1994). Although skeptical of the brain stem hypothesis of dysfunction, Waterhouse, Fein, and Modahl (1996) include brain stem abnormal function as an associated but not a causal dysfunction for some people with autism.

Cerebellum Functions and Findings

Anatomy

The cerebellum is discussed separately here because of the importance of this structure in the literature on autism. Anatomically (see Gilman & Newman, 1992), the cerebellum is a large area on the dorsal surface of the brain with two hemispheres connected by a narrow middle portion called the vermis. The cerebellum includes a cortex of gray matter, inner white matter, and several nuclei. The Purkinje cells of the cerebellar cortex are large association neurons that receive information from visual, tactile, proprioceptive, kinesthesia, vestibular, and auditory sensation from the body, as relayed by the thalamus, reticular activating system, and vestibular nuclei (Graham, 1990). The Purkinje cells provide the last common output from the cerebellum to other parts of the brain and are one site for production of gamma-aminobutyric acid (GABA), which influences primary, inhibitory interneurons of the brain (Gilman & Newman). Figures 3–5 and 3–6 illustrate the gross anatomy and cellular structure of the cerebellum.

Functions

Historically, the role of the cerebellum in coordinating the timing of movement was emphasized. The cerebellum coordinates movement best when the conscious mind is attending to something else; conscious attempts to control coordination often override cerebellar control and impair coordination (as when one watches a full cup of coffee when carrying it) (Westman, 1990). In addition, the cerebellum is primarily a sensory afferent organ with a key role in modulating sensory input to the brain and integrating sensory responsiveness throughout the brain. One fifth of the fibers in the internal capsule are nonmotor fibers projecting from the frontal and temporal association areas to the cerebellum (Westman). Because of direct input to the cerebellum from the cochlea, it has a role in long-term habituation to the startle reflex, especially the acoustic startle response (Leaton & Supple, 1986)—which is sometimes atypical in people with autism. Deficits in cerebellar function may result in sensorimotor dysfunction including low muscle tone, poor timing and coordination of movement, slow monotone or dysarthric speech, decreased endurance (Gilman & Newman, 1992), and impaired sensory modulation (Westman).

More recent findings and formulations emphasize the higher cognitive and emotional functions of the cerebellum. Because of the findings of cerebellar dysfunction found in persons with autism and described in later sections of this chapter, Schmahmann (1994) described in detail the anatomical substrates of the cerebellum that might support nonmotor activity and higher-order behavior and learning. He concluded from an extensive review of the research literature that structures of the cerebellum are metabolically active during language tasks and during anxiety and panic states. He described afferent and efferent pathways linking cerebellar sites to structures in the pons, parietal lobes (for sensory processing), the temporal lobe, the prefrontal areas for sequencing and executive functions, the motor cortex, structures of the limbic system, and the thalamus. As Schmahmann postulated, in addition to sensory and motor control, the cerebellum may associate motions with mood states for nonverbal communication through facial and body movements. It may

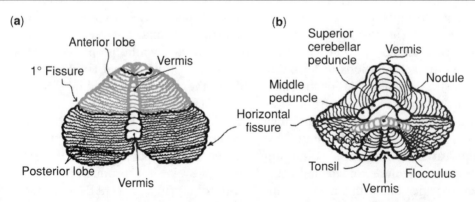

Figure 3–5 Superior surface of cerebellum (**a**) and inferior surface of cerebellum (**b**). *Source:* Reprinted from S. D. Gertz, *Neuroanatomy Made Easy and Understandable,* 6th, ed., p. 7, Aspen Publishers, Inc.

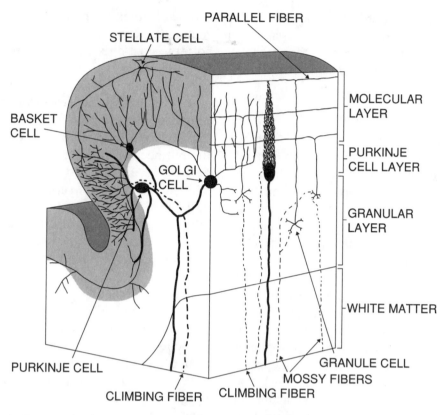

Figure 3–6 The cerebellar cortex in perspective.

be a prime regulator of the speed and consistency of cognitive processes, the timing of social interactions, such as adding prosody and intonation to express affect, and primitive defense mechanisms; it may also have a role in mediating thought, planning, strategy formation, and may serve to support nonmotor aspects of language.

Additional research demonstrates that the cerebellum has a role in learning movement patterns and pairing this learning with specific contexts. For example, children born without a cerebral cortex have learned specific motor and emotional responses to sensory stimuli and demonstrate expectations of sensory stimuli; these skills were attributed to functions of the intact cerebellum (Berntson, Tuber, Ronca, & Bachman,

1983). Studies of two persons who sustained discrete cerebellar injury found consistent deficits in ability to detect errors in performance, shift attention between sensory stimuli, use inferential reasoning, perform executive tasks (planning and sequencing), and organize visual-spatial information, especially in response to novel stimuli (Chafetz, Friedman, Kevorkian, & Levy, 1996). Holroyd, Reiss, and Bryan (1991) examined two children with Joubert Syndrome, which is marked by partial or compete agenesis of the cerebellar vermis. Behaviorally, these children displayed abnormal eye movements, hypotonia, ataxia, marked perseveration, significantly delayed expressive language and motor skills, limited social interaction, distress at certain sensory responses, and lining-up behavior despite full-scale IQs of 64 and 85. Thus, the research is beginning to demonstrate that the cerebellum has a much larger role than traditionally considered.

Neuropsychological Findings

Although Schmahmann (1994) stated that persons with autism "have no clinical deficits suggestive of cerebellar disease" (p. 195), research demonstrates significant motor deficits in autism, including the presence of choreiform movements, balance disturbances, incoordination, misarticulation and speech dysprosody, and motor dyspraxia ($n = 10$; Jones & Prior, 1985); poor visual tracking, dyspraxia, proximal muscular weakness, and incoordination ($n = 6$; Huebner, Gamradt, & Klund, ND); and increased abnormal saccadic eye movements ($n = 10$; Kemner, Verbaten, Cuperus, Camfferman, & van Engeland, 1998), that may be related to cerebellar dysfunction. In a comparison with children with mental retardation ($n = 18$) and typically developing children ($n = 166$), Kohen-Raz, Volkmar, and Cohen (1992) found postural abnormalities in the children with autism ($n = 91$) that were marked by increased lateral sway, instability in balance, and unusual postures and weight distribution over the heels and toes, suggesting postural immaturity consistent with abnormalities of the cerebellum.

Children later diagnosed with autism were observed on videotape to demonstrate differences in muscle tone and movement during the first two years of life; these motor problems, however, were less deviant than the emotional and communication differences observed (Lelord et al., 1994). Losche (1990) analyzed videotapes of children from birth through three and a half years. He compared the development of sensorimotor action complexity in several stages from contingent actions (pound the table to make noise) to goal-directed actions (solve problems) between typical children and eight children later diagnosed with autism. Losche found that the sensorimotor action complexity of children with autism was similar to typical peers during the first year of life but became strikingly different during the second. In the second year, the group with autism showed a surprising reduction in the total amount of actions that they exhibited, especially goal-directed actions, with an increase in continuous actions, which Losche attributed to the onset of stereotypies. These findings were not explained by adjusting for overall developmental delay in children with autism (Losche), but suggested an alteration in motor action development dissociated, in part, from cognitive development.

Personal reports of people with autism suggest that they experience differences in sensory processing with hyper- and hyposensitivity, sensory distortion, and overload (Cesaroni & Garber, 1991; O'Neill & Jones, 1997), and difficulty with speech production, rhythm, auditory and tactile hypersensitivity, and other sensory and motor challenges (Grandin, 1992). Although these clinical and personal accounts of sensory and motor dysfunctions may implicate the cerebellum, they are not specific to the cerebellum because neurological functions are redundant. Nonetheless, several authors (Hill & Leary, 1993; O'Neill & Jones; Smith & Bryson, 1994) suggest that the sensory and motor disturbances of persons with autism warrant more systematic investigation to determine the range and extent of abnormalities, the relationship of these to other impairments, and the influence of development and psychological factors on sensory and motor responses.

Early autopsy studies (Bauman & Kemper, 1985, $n = 1$; Ritvo et al., 1984, $n = 4$) reported a decreased number of Purkinje cells in both the cerebellar hemispheres and vermis. Findings from neuroanatomical research for persons with autism were summarized by Hass and colleagues (1996), who found 16 quantitative MRI and autopsy studies from 9 independent research groups involving more than 240 individuals, all of which demonstrated cerebellar abnormalities of varying degrees. The abnormalities found in these studies included a significant decrease in the number of Purkinje cells, atrophy of the cerebellar cortex, and differences in the size and number of neurons in the deep cerebellar nuclei, depending on the age of the individual. The findings reported by Hass et al. are consistent with the findings of Bauman and Kemper (1994; $n = 6$ at autopsy). The rate of Purkinje cell loss has been reported to be as high as 50–60% in the posterior vermis, with decreased size of the remaining cells, but less cell loss in the anterior vermis (Courchesne, Townsend, & Saitoh, 1994). These early autopsy findings were surprising to researchers and prompted a closer examination of cerebellar structure and function (Schmahmann, 1994).

Using both clinical examination and MRI, Hass et al. (1996) compared 28 children with autistic disorder to 24 normal children. They found that 95% of the children with autism exhibited at least one abnormality of cerebellar function on clinical examination, and 44% had at least one abnormality suggesting a parietal lobe dysfunction; in contrast, controls showed a very low incidence of any dysfunction. The most prevalent clinical signs were in disorders of diadokokinesis (rapid alternating movements), gait, sequential thumb-finger touching, graphesthesia, muscle tone (hypotonia), and stereognosis. Those children with autism and without retardation showed fewer signs of cerebellar dysfunction compared to children with autism and retardation. These findings are similar to many studies that found a consistent association between increasing neurological dysfunctions with decreasing intellectual abilities (e.g., review by Bailey et al., 1996). MRI findings in this study (Hass et al.) were similar to other studies by the same group of researchers (e.g., Courchesne et al., 1994) and included approximately 88–90% of subjects with cerebellar hypoplasia consistent with loss of neurons, and 10–12% with hyperplasia of cerebellar lobules VI and VII. These cerebellar abnormalities alone could account for a portion, but not all, of the symptoms evident in autism (Schmahmann, 1994).

These findings, although relatively consistent in a variety of studies, have been challenged by other authors. Minshew and Dombrowski (1994), for example, identified methodological problems inherent in the work by Courchesne and colleagues and cited several studies that failed to confirm the findings (e.g., Gaffney, Tsai, Kuperman, & Minchin, 1987; Piven et al., 1992; Ritvo & Garber, 1988). Minshew and Dombrowski conclude that the cerebellum may be abnormal in some persons with autism but that the involvement is at the cellular level (decreased number of Purkinje cells and small neuronal size); these cellular changes are evident in several structures of the brain and not isolated in the cerebellum. Waterhouse et al. (1996), although critical of the research suggesting that the cerebellum is the primary site of autistic dysfunctions, concede that many people with autism are likely to have cerebellar dysfunction. These authors include cerebellar dysfunction in their model (discussed in the following section) as a noncausal factor associated with autism, but a deficit that they believe is secondary to primary medial-temporal lobe deficits.

Medial-Temporal Lobe Functions and Findings

Anatomy

The medial-temporal lobe as a primary site of dysfunction in autism is favored by several authors (Bachevalier & Merjanian, 1994; Bauman & Kemper, 1994; Waterhouse et al., 1996). The limbic system, which is part of this structure, was implicated in early research on autism because of the social deficits and qualitative impairment in social relatedness that are fundamental to the disorder. As defined by Waterhouse et al. (1996), this system refers to structures of the temporal lobe and parietal association cortex, including the amygdala system, the hippocampal system, and the neurochemistry circuits for serotonin, oxytocin, vasopressin, and beta endorphin. This medial-temporal lobe area includes a portion of the state regulating system or behavioral inhibition system, described earlier under brain stem findings.

Findings and Implications for Functions

Theoretical and anatomical evidence for dysfunction in the medial-temporal lobe systems arises, in part, from memory research (see Bachevalier & Merjanian, 1994; Bauman & Kemper, 1994; Killiany & Moss, 1994, for reviews). These authors discuss the differences in anatomical substrates for two distinct kinds of recent memory and learning: representational or declarative memory, and habit or procedural memory. Habit or procedural memory appears relatively intact in persons with autism, who often demonstrate stronger rote and visual-perceptual memory. Representational or declarative memory, on the other hand, involves all sensory modalities and the ability to generalize information, form coherence, and attach meaning to stimuli. In their autopsy studies, Bauman and Kemper found a consistently reduced neuronal cell size and increased cell-packing density in the hippocampus, amygdala, entorhinal cortex, mammillary bodies, anterior cingulate cortex, and septum; they assign representational memory to these structures. In contrast, there were no abnormalities in the neocortex, thalamus, hypothalamus, and basal ganglia, the theoretical source of procedural or habit memory. Bauman and Kemper theorized that the dysfunction in the structures underlying procedural or representational memory may account for the preoccupation with sameness and the repetitive behavior seen in autism. With impaired representational memory but an intact habit memory, minor changes in the environment may "render that setting unrecognizable" and novel (Bauman & Kemper, p. 135). Because representational memory and learning are a later-developing system, dysfunction in it is not likely to be evident until at least 15 months of age, the age when autism often becomes evident.

To test these hypotheses about learning and memory, Bachevalier and Merjanian (1994) selectively removed the hippocampus and/or the amygdala of nonhuman primates (specifically, monkeys) at birth to simulate an animal model of autism and examine developmental changes associated with medial-temporal lobe disorders. Primates with both amygdala and hippocampus removed showed intact ability to visually match objects and form habits based on visual cues, but also had severely impaired global memory and ability to attach meaning to materials presented in all sensory channels. Socially, the primates with both structures removed were initially indistinguishable from typical primates until two to six months, when primates with lesions displayed a sharp decline in social contact, inability to initiate social contact, active avoidance of social contact, and the onset of motor stereotypes with hyperactivity. When only the amygdala was removed, the primates showed mild deficits in memory function and moderate disturbances in social interaction; the removal of only the hippocampus resulted in sparing of memory and the presence of mild social-emotional disturbances. The authors concluded that early damage to the hippocampus, amygdala, and surrounding areas produced the most severe autistic symptoms and representational memory disorders; damage to the amygdala alone was more debilitating than damage to the hippocampus alone.

Based on these findings, the authors theorized that the amount of dysfunction in these two systems may account for the variation in memory and social-emotional symptoms seen in the autistic spectrum.

Integrated Model and Neuropsychological Findings

Waterhouse et al. (1996), in an extensive and integrative review of the literature, summarized four primary dysfunctions of autism and traced these to specific sites and findings of medial-temporal lobe and parietal lobe disorder. Figure 3–7 displays the model proposed by these authors. The first dysfunction, attributed to increased hippocampal system cell packing and density, was defined as *canalesthesia*, or abnormally

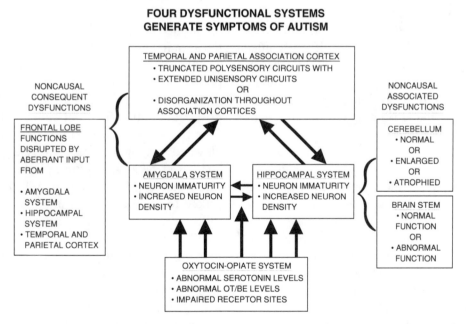

FOUR DYSFUNCTIONAL SYSTEMS GENERATE SYMPTOMS OF AUTISM

Figure 3–7 Schematic diagram of the model of four proposed core neural dysfunctions in autism: the oxytocin-opiate-(serotonin) system, the hippocampal system, the amygdaloid system, and the temporal and parietal association cortices, with associated dysfunctions in brain stem, cerebellum, and frontal lobe. OT = oxytocin; BE = beta endorphin. *Source:* L. Waterhouse, D. Fein, and C. Modahl, Neurofunctional Mechanisms in Autism, *Psychological Review 103,* pp. 457–489. Copyright © 1996 by the American Psychological Association. Reprinted with permission.

fragmented cross-modal information processing. Because increased cell-packed density prevents adequate collateral synapses between cell bodies in the hippocampus (the site of sensory integration), sensory experiences are inconsistently experienced and integrated, resulting in splintered sensory awareness and diminished ability to recognize the salience of a sensory input. Canalesthesia results in difficulty orienting to and shifting attention between stimuli and decreased working memory needed for conversation and symbolic play. Because of this splintered sensory experience, changes in the environment cannot be adequately interpreted. Any change in an environment or routine requires adjustment to constantly novel, unpredictable, and, perhaps, threatening situations. Canalesthesia, coupled with a strength in remembering visual patterns and establishing habits, may be one reason why persons with autism insist on sameness. Because of this hippocampus abnormality, persons with autism experience difficulty integrating information from several sensory channels, forming coherence about their sensory environment, judging the salience of stimuli, and attributing consistent meaning to sensory information.

A second dysfunction is defined (Waterhouse et al., 1996) as *impaired assignment of significance* to incoming sensory or social stimuli stemming from immature and cell-packed density of the amygdala. The amygdala attaches the affective significance to novel or social stimuli such as facial expression, voice quality, sensory input, rewards and punishment, and nonverbal input. Dysfunctions of the amygdala result in abnormal affect, impaired face recognition, impaired memory for the emotional content of stories, and decreased affiliative and social communication behavior. Without understanding of salience or affective significance, complex human interaction may be indeed confusing and frightening to persons with autism, and perhaps trigger avoidance.

Asociality is the third dysfunction described by Waterhouse et al. (1996). It is thought to arise from disrupted or absent levels of the neuropeptides oxytocin and vasopressin. Receptors for these neuropeptides have been found throughout the medial-temporal lobe structures and in the thalamus. These two neuropeptides regulate human social affiliation behaviors such as parental care, infant attachment, and affiliation behavior in animal models (see Chapter 7). Modahl et al. (1998) found decreased plasma levels of oxytocin among 30 children with autism compared to 30 normal age-matched controls, supporting this hypothesis. Important for understanding autism is the finding that social behavior itself enhances the additional production and release of oxytocin and vasopressin. Thus, the limited social and affiliative behavior often seen in persons with autism can lead to a further suppression of oxytocin and vasopressin (see Insel, 1997, for a recent review). Additionally, Waterhouse et al. proposed that other neurochemical changes found in some studies with autism, such as elevated serotonin levels (Anderson, 1994) and lower beta endorphin (Sandman, Barron, Chiez-DeMet, & DeMet, 1991) may be linked to oxytocin levels in some children with autism. However, the neurochemical findings relative to autism, on which this model is contingent, have been described by other authors as disappointing and inconclusive (Anderson, 1994), weak, and speculative (Rapin & Katzman, 1998).

Finally, Waterhouse et al. (1996) proposed that the fourth primary deficit of autism is *extended selective attention* resulting from maldevelopment of the parietal and temporal polysensory association areas identified in other research findings. For example, Hass et al. (1996) reported the results of several studies using MRI in which there was reduced volume in the parietal lobes and reduced size of the corpus callosum where parietal fibers are concentrated. Extended selective attention results in a narrowing of selective attention to single aspects of sensory stimuli, which are exaggerated in importance, with neglect of others aspects of the stimuli. Arising from this narrowed and exaggerated attentional focus are preoccupations with sensory stimuli, behavior, or topics of conversation; hypersensitivity to sensory stimuli; and decreased ability to recognize features of novel or significant stimuli. These authors further propose that extended selective attention can be an asset for people with autism because it may promote the development of exceptional or savant skills related to visual or auditory patterns without the distraction of gestalt processing.

Overall, Waterhouse et al. (1996) compellingly proposed that this model of medial-temporal lobe dysfunction explains most of the symptoms of autism. They added cerebellar dysfunction as existing in a subgroup with autism, explaining the motor disorders present in some persons with autism. They theorize that deficits in frontal lobe functioning stem from dysfunctional sensory information provided by the medial-temporal and parietal lobes. In this model, slowed brain stem processing may also contribute to dysfunctional processing for some persons with autism.

Cognitive and Executive Function Theories

The final group of theories about the nature of autism is supported more by clinical than by neurobiological examination. These theories add a richness to findings on the neuropsychology of autism and bridge the gap between the brain and behavior. Happe and Frith (1996) argued that complicated information processing, such as executive functioning, is unique to humans and cannot be adequately studied in either nonhuman models or by neurobiological research.

Anatomy and Function

Executive functions involve tasks often attributed to frontal lobe function, including fine motor skills, voluntary eye gaze, spontaneity, strategy formation and planning, cognitive flexibility, metacognition (thinking about thinking), and response inhibition and judgment in social and sexual behavior (Kolb & Whishaw, 1996). On cognitive testing, persons with autism often exhibit intact performance on visual-spatial tasks as well as disordered communication and language (Prior & Ozonoff, 1998). Because of this uneven profile, early investigations of autism were based on the theory that left or nondominant hemispheres were dysfunctional. However, neuroimaging studies have failed to consistently demonstrate hemispheric asymmetry or frontal lobe abnormalities in autism (Dunn, M., 1994; Piven & O'Leary, 1997). Several authors (e.g., Rumsey & Hamburger, 1988), using clinical examination, contributed to understanding the neuropsychology of autism, especially executive and language functions; their work warrants careful consideration despite a current failure to find a definitive biological dysfunction in frontal or language substrates.

Information Processing

Two recent studies examined information processing deficits related to social interaction. Ciesielski and Harris (1997) theorized that persons with autism experience the most processing difficulties on tasks that require a high degree of simultaneous processing of information and a high degree of cognitive flexibility in disengaging from one mental focus and shifting focus to a new stimulus. For example, tasks that are intellectually challenging (like block design patterns) but have well-defined rules, do not require shifting of attention, and are easier for persons with autism. The authors tested this hypothesis on 35 persons (19 with autism and 16 controls) using a large battery of neuropsychological tests. The results were independent of intellectual level but consistent with the research hypothesis. The participants with autism performed best on tests with inherent rules and less simultaneous processing and showed increased perseveration and less ability to disengage and shift attention as the degree of rule constraint declined. Similarly, Pierce, Glad, and Schreibman (1997) found that children with autism who watched videotaped vignettes of child-child interaction did well on answering questions requiring general attention. However, when they were required to use two or more cues to interpret the story, they performed significantly worse than both children with mental disability and typical children. These two groups of authors argued that the social deficits of children with autism stem from a poor ability to disengage and shift attention and attend to a multitude of dynamic events during social interaction. Although the authors conclude that these differences are consistent with involvement of the frontal subsystems, they also propose that the difficulties in attention shifting may be secondary to dysfunction in structures such as the cerebellum, brain stem, or amygdala.

Pragmatic Communication Disorders

In two related studies, Shields, Varley, Broks, and Simpson (1996a; 1996b) theo-

rized that a right hemispheric dysfunction results in deficits in pragmatic communication skills with impaired understanding of metaphors and humor. To study the communication disorders of children with autism, Shields et al. (1996a) compared four groups of 10 children each—a group with semantic-pragmatic communication disorder, a group with disorders of language phonology and syntax, a group with high-functioning autism, and a typically developing control group—on measures of functions for either the right or the left hemisphere. The results showed that children with autism and children with semantic-pragmatic communication disorders had nearly identical performances on all tests, consistent with a hypothesis of right-hemispheric dysfunction in both groups. To investigate the social communication significance of these findings, Shields et al. (1996b) hypothesized that both the children with semantic-pragmatic communication disorders and those with autism would perform most poorly in social cognition, including tests of social comprehension questions, theory-of-mind procedures, and detection of eye direction in conversation. Their findings supported the research hypothesis that both groups of children had similar difficulty with these tasks. The authors concluded that their findings were "consistent with the notion of right hemispheric dysfunction . . . but it is possible that this reflects abnormalities within a more complex functional-anatomical system" (p. 493).

Cognitive Theories

Happe and Frith (1996) reviewed three prominent and related cognitive theories about the nature of autism: cognitive theories of social impairment, decreased executive functions, and weak central coherence. The cognitive theories of social impairment posit that persons with autism lack prerequisite interpersonal relatedness skills in early development and, consequently, fail to develop adequate social interactions and insight. For instance, persons with autism have difficulty recognizing emotional expression, matching facial expressions to voice quality, sharing joint attention for social interaction, and imitating emotional responses. One component of social impairment theories is the theory of mind, which is based on the hypothesis that cognitive deficits make it difficult for people with autism to represent and think about the mental states of themselves and others (termed *mentalizing*) and to use this thinking to guide interpersonal interaction. Happe and Frith proposed that a common cognitive element accounting for the social impairments of autism is a deficit in mentalizing. The ability to mentalize about others is required for social reciprocity but does not affect the desire to have social and physical contact with others. A mentalizing defect might account for observations that children with autism enjoy tumble play with parents and comforting by others, but lack the social reciprocity necessary for interaction or pretend play.

Decreased executive functions have traditionally been considered as stemming from frontal lobe dysfunctions. Executive functions include the ability to disengage, inhibition of inappropriate responses, planning and actions, staying on task, shifting attention, and monitoring performance. *Weak central coherence* (Happe & Frith, 1996) refers to the idea that people with autism pay attention to parts rather than wholes, often missing the gist of a story and making relatively less use of context, but remember details of the story well. Both executive function deficits and weak central coherence are evident in the clinical examination of persons with autism. Although the literature from several disciplines supports the findings of disrupted executive functions and weak central coherence in autism, Happe and Frith concluded that these findings are consistent with many sites of dysfunction. As the appreciation of the complexity of neurological functions emerges, it is clear that executive functions evolve from many structures, especially in developmental disorders. These findings could also be associated with medial-temporal lobe disorder, other unidentified circuits, or the influence of neurochemical transmission (Happe & Frith).

The work of Minshew, Goldstein, and Siegel (1997) demonstrated the complementarity of biological and cognitive theories. Their study was designed to assess clinical functioning based on a wide range of theories about the primary deficits of autism using multiple measures in each of nine skill areas. Thirty-three persons who were rigorously diagnosed as having autism, without other complications and with IQ scores greater than 80, were matched with 33 normal controls. The participants with autism showed a pattern of impairments in skilled motor actions, complex memory, complex language, and abstract reasoning. However, performance in simple attention, simple memory, simple language, and visual-spatial domains was intact. These authors concluded that these findings are consistent with models suggesting abnormalities at a level of brain organization affecting multiple primary sites for tasks of complex information analysis, which develops later, while sparing simple information processing, which develops early in life.

Summary

There are four prominent and integrative theories about the neuropsychology of autism with disorders identified in: the brain stem, the cerebellum, the medial-temporal lobe and surrounding areas, and cognitive executive functions. The model proposed by Waterhouse et al. (1996) is one attempt to integrate these apparently divergent findings. Slowing of brain stem responses and neuroanatomical differences in the cerebellum with clinical evidence of dysfunction in orienting to stimuli and motor skills have been found in numerous studies. The emerging research on the role of the cerebellum is spurring a reformulation of thinking about cerebellar functions, with a greater appreciation of its complexity. The involvement of midbrain and temporal lobes in conjunction with parietal lobes seems clearly linked to autistic symptoms, but the understanding of selective attention, attentional shifts, sensory processing, neurochemistry, and the developmental processes of these structures must be refined. However, the complex system described as the state regulating system seems to be involved at all levels and may contribute to the disorders in arousal and sensory modulation that are the focus of the sensorimotor approach to management. The results of cognitive research enrich our understanding of the expression of autism, but whether these findings represent primary symptoms or secondary symptoms from dysfunction in lower neurological structures is debatable.

Many questions remain unanswered about the influence of earlier-developing structures on frontal and cortical functioning and the neurochemistry of the brain. Because early and simple cognitive processing seems spared by many accounts but sensory processing may be atypical from birth, the role of sensory processing, affective experiences, arousal, attention shifting, and imitation and motor abilities in developing these higher cognitive functions needs to be formulated. Throughout this review, consistent findings of sensory processing differences, poor sensory modulation, and motor disorders are noted that may play a critical role in development, social interaction, language and communication, cognitive functions, and the other key ways in which autism is exhibited. The presence of this consistent thread begs for a sounder research base about the sensory and motor symptoms of autism, and the implications of these for social, affective, and communication abilities.

It is clear that autism is not a disorder of one portion of the brain; rather, multiple, perhaps related, systems are involved. A key that has potential for linking these theories may lie in an understanding of brain maturation, which is discussed in the following sections along with other theories of etiology.

THEORIES OF ETIOLOGY

A question always seems to arise after a discussion of the research on the neuropsychology of autism. That question—What causes autism?—is unanswered. The earlier thought that autism was a failure of attachment due to parental inadequacy has been disproved, and the understanding of autism as a developmental disorder stemming from brain involvement has been demonstrated (Rapin, 1997). We now know that autism does not result from a postnatal injury to the brain, although some children may regress after a period of seemingly normal development (Rapin & Katzman, 1998). Other than hearing loss in some individuals (Klin, 1993), there is no evidence that sensory receptors are atypical. Much of the research conducted during the 1980s was directed to finding a marker, neurological site, neurochemical abnormality, or other single cause of autism. However, the theories about the neuropsychology of autism just reviewed are compelling and all suggest that there is diffuse system involvement, implying either an etiology affecting several neurological sites simultaneously, or a heterogeneous etiology. Both of these hypotheses are explored in the following sections. The literature is divided into three sections based on three prominent etiological theories: neurological immaturity, heterogeneous etiology, and other etiology.

Neurological Immaturity

If autism is the result of a diffuse dysfunction amid distributed neurological networks, the prevailing hypothesis expressed by a number of authors (e.g., Bauman & Kemper, 1994; Courchesne et al., 1994; Rapin & Katzman, 1998) is that autism reflects neurological immaturity, a failure of brain development. This conclusion stems from the cytopathological findings at several sites in the brain, including the cerebellum, amygdala, limbic system, and hippocampus. These structures are found to have reduced numbers of neurons, increased cell density, and truncated dendritic growth that could be associated with truncation of brain development. Evidence from several studies reveals that the brain is often larger, also suggesting a disorder of genesis (Poustka, 1998; Rapin & Katzman, 1998) and placing the timing of the truncated development in or before the second trimester of fetal development.

Truncation of development during a critical developmental period may result in the pattern of diffuse brain dysfunctions identified in this literature review. During specific critical periods of brain development, cells in the nervous system go through three stages: proliferation, migration to their mature sites, and differentiation or pruning (more cells are produced than used). At these critical periods, the neurons and sites

undergoing neurogenesis are both most plastic and most vulnerable to insult; cell proliferation and migration are completed by the end of the second trimester of gestation (Coleman, 1994; Westman, 1990). A genetic marker might trigger a truncation of migration (a preferred theory), proliferation, or differentiation. Alternatively, a genetic predisposition might be triggered by an environmental or infectious event during a critical period and have an impact on entire systems of brain function. With truncation of brain development, dysfunction in one system is also likely to secondarily affect other systems dependent on that system for input. In this model, the cortex and later-developing neurological structures are theoretically involved secondarily as a cascade of symptoms unfolds with child maturation and increased environmental demands. Although, truncation of brain development is thought to occur early, Coleman (1994) prefers the second-trimester etiology theory because most children with autism are without the facial dysmorphia associated with a first-trimester insult (as in Down syndrome). Facial dysmorphia usually occurs in the first trimester of development.

Heterogeneous Etiologies

An alternative explanation of any heterogeneous or spectrum disorder is that it results from subcategories of autism with differing etiologies and individual expression of symptoms, such as are seen in cerebral palsy (Goodman, 1989). Eaves, Ho, and Eaves (1994) used data generated from multidisciplinary evaluations from 166 children with autism and clustered the data using cluster analysis. Four clinically meaningful subdivisions of autism were found that did not differ in demographic characteristics of the children. About 55% of the sample was described as typically autistic, with a 5:1 boy:girl ratio; these children were aloof, passive, with an abnormal quality of speech, although almost all were verbal. Fewer than half were distressed over change, but 89% showed motor stereotypies or sensory preoccupations. The children in this group were low in aggressive and hyperactive tendencies, but they were socially isolated. The second group (19%) was a low-functioning group with a 1:2.5 boy:girl ratio, with marked short attention spans, delayed motor milestones, tantrums, and moderate to severe retardation. Ninety percent were nonverbal and 97% were aloof and unaware. The incidence of self-abuse and self-stimulating behaviors were highest in this group. The mothers of these children reported more breathing difficulty or distress at birth.

The third group (<10%), the least autistic, had a 6:1 boy:girl ratio; only one child in this group was nonverbal. The children in this group demonstrated restricted interests, sensory preoccupations, a short attention span, hyperactivity, impulsiveness, and tantrums. Although they had limited social play and no friends, they were more sociable and aware of social interaction than children in the first two groups. The family histories of this third group were more positive for learning difficulties and genetic defects. The last group (17%), with a 3:1 boy:girl ratio, consisted of the higher-functioning group; fewer than half were aloof and only one was nonverbal. Almost all had both motor dysfunction and sensory stereotypies and restricted interests. This fourth group was clearly different from the other groups; they were social, verbal, and brighter (active, but odd), but nearly all had abnormal language with echoing, perseveration, and pragmatic communication disorders; difficulty with conversation; narrow interests; more externalizing behavior, such as aggression; and more often had a higher verbal IQ than

performance IQ. Although not highlighted by these authors, the data also demonstrated that more than 90% of individuals in every group displayed sensory preoccupations. Sensory dysfunction was consistently present at the same or higher level than disorders of social interaction and peer friendships, suggesting that sensory preoccupations exist as a fundamental problem across subtypes of autism.

Other Explanations

Genetic disorders, medical conditions, environmental factors, and subclinical epilepsy are somewhat related explanations of the etiology of autism. Genetic predispositions are a favored theory of etiology expressed almost universally by the authors reviewed in this research. Autism is associated with many genetic disorders, such as Fragile-X disorder and tuberous sclerosis, syndromes such as Angelman's syndrome, autoimmune disorders, and other disorders (see Huebner, 1992; Piven & Folstein, 1994; Poustka, 1998; and Rapin, 1997, for reviews). These disorders may be present in 10–30% of cases of autism, but they are not unique and invariant causes of autism (Rapin, 1997). Genetic theories of predisposition, without significant genetic disorders, are based on findings of an increased incidence of autism in siblings and twins. The family aggregation of an increased incidence of speech and language disorders, deficits in executive function, incidents of autisticlike social deficits in first-degree relatives, and higher rates of affective disorders, especially among families of children with more classic autism, suggest a common genetic substrate (Piven & Folstein; Rapin & Katzman, 1998). Environmental factors may also play a role, with reports of more second-trimester bleeding in mothers, and an excess of births in March, perhaps reflecting viral infections (Coleman, 1994) or a genetic predisposition that is susceptible and expressed only in response to an environmental stressor.

One other condition that has received limited study is the presence of subclinical epilepsy, especially in children who show regression after normal development; this possibility should be considered in diagnostic procedures (Rapin, 1997). Waterhouse et al. (1996) proposed that the amygdala and hippocampus are most susceptible to subclinical seizures that they describe as resulting from kindling sensitivity. Kindling sensitivity is a process in which subtle bursts of electrical stimulation, repeated over time, result in a decreased threshold for seizures or other abnormalities (Post, Weiss, & Leverich, 1994). Theoretically, subclinical seizures in the amygdala and hippocampus would gradually diminish their function and result in the onset of clinical seizures later in life.

DISCUSSION

Summary and Implications

This literature review reflects substantial progress in our understanding of autistic disorder over the past 8–10 years since it was last formally reviewed (see Huebner, 1992) and a paradigm shift in understanding the functions of the human nervous system. In research conducted during the 1980s or earlier, the diagnostic criteria for autism were changing and the studies were often poorly designed, with little attention given to differentiating between autism and associated disorders such as mental retardation and Fragile-X disorder. Earlier research was also marked by simplistic thinking both about autism and neurological functioning (Minshew et al., 1997) and was based on the assumption that a direct relationship could be drawn between symptoms and a single site of neurological dysfunctions. Following this line of logic, studies often focused on testing a single hypothesis in isolation. These research trends reflected a linear model of neurological function rather than an understanding of the interconnectiveness and redundancy of function in the brain (Churchland, 1986). Although there was great excitement about the potential power of emerging technological sophistication applied to the study of autism in early research, little attention was paid to the methodological pitfalls and limitations of this technology. Furthermore, earlier research was often based on adult models of brain injury, with limited understanding of the developmental functions of the brain.

The research reviewed for this chapter, most of which was published in the 1990s, reflects a far greater sophistication in the understanding of neurological function and demonstrates substantial progress in addressing these limitations in the field. Many papers presented integrated models. As Bailey et al. (1996) submitted, willingness to accept the ideas that complex systems are marked by coherence through interaction, that a hierarchy exists in a network, and that dynamic processes change over a lifetime is increasing. This basic shift in philosophy seems to underlie the ambitious attempts to integrate the literature reported here and reflects the awareness that "autism has been the subject of more systematic research, across a wider range of domains, than any other child psychiatric disorder" (Bailey et al., p. 117). Although these integrative papers do not fully address all of the questions about autism, they provide hypotheses for future research and for intervention.

This change in research paradigm and the search for etiology has been accompanied by a change in understanding of treatment. An original hypothesis about the etiology of autism posited that persons with autism were essentially normal but developed autism due to inadequate parental skills. If this hypothesis were true, than changing these parental patterns or reliving early experiences in a therapeutic way might unleash the normal potential of individuals locked in an autistic shell. Alternatively, if a single abnormal site of autism or single theory of etiology were discovered, then a single diagnostic test or single treatment could be directed toward remediation or compensation. Stemming from these earlier formulations of the etiology of autism is the myth that a single magic bullet might unlock the hidden potential of people with autism. This myth has driven the development of a plethora of ineffective treatments for autism (Huebner & Emery, 1998). If the formulations of autism that are now emerging were linear, then the search for the magic bullet could continue. However, the current integrative thinking about the etiology of autism also necessitate an integrative approach to treatment. Treatment, then, falls within the realm of education, therapeutic intervention, and rehabilitation systems; it must be based on a philosophy of family- and child-centered teams engaged in consistent hard work across a lifetime.

Directions for Interventions

Linking brain deficits to symptoms in autism has proved difficult (Waterhouse et al., 1996), and linking brain deficits to treatment is even more challenging. Nonetheless, the research reviewed here clearly suggests a pattern of disturbances in sensory processing, arousal, disengaging and shifting attention, motor dysfunction, cognition, language, and social interaction and affiliative processing founded on faulty organization and, possibly, truncated development of the nervous system. It is clear from this list that current concepts of sensorimotor management need to be integrated into other systems of intervention from multiple disciplines. In an integrative spirit, the findings from much of the research reviewed are presented in Table 3–2, with implications for sensorimotor management based on these findings proposed. These proposals have not been fully tested in clinical outcomes research.

Here are some implications of these findings. If early experiences with control over sensory experiences and attachment influence subsequent development of the behavioral inhibition or state regulating system (Chorpita & Barlow, 1998), then it is particularly important to be sensitive to a child's sensory needs and to help develop an ability to satisfy these needs by the primary caregivers. If social interaction facilitates the neurochemistry and sensory processes that enhance further social affiliation (Waterhouse et al., 1996), then carefully grading sensory processing to enhance social interaction is critical to development. If deficits in weak central coherence are present in people with autism (Happe & Frith, 1996), then it may be necessary to simplify environments, exaggerate nonpreferred sensory stimuli to diminish this problem, or reduce nonpreferred stimuli to encourage adaptation and function. If more than 90% of children in the autistic spectrum experience sensory preoccupations (Eaves et al., 1994), then the need for research in this area has been neglected for too long.

Studies of sensory processing by occupational therapists contribute to our understanding of the sensory processing challenges faced by persons with autism. Kientz and Dunn (1997) compared scores on the Sensory Profile (Dunn, W., 1994) from 32 children (ages 3–13) with autism or pervasive developmental disorder to scores from

Table 3–2 Literature Findings with Implications for Sensorimotor Management

Author/s	Design	Findings	Implications for Sensorimotor Management
Bachevalier & Merjanian, 1994	Nonhuman primate research. Removal of hippocampus and/or amygdala at birth.	Removal of both structures resulted in severe social dysfunction but intact ability to match objects and form habits based on visual cues.	Stronger visual processing and matching abilities may be present and useful in skill development.
Bailey et al., 1996	Integrative literature review.	Several theories of etiology exist that may result in hypothesis-driven research.	Bring together different areas of expertise in research and literature synthesis in autism. Supports need for careful study of the sensory and motor dysfunctions of autism.
Bauman & Kemper, 1994	Autopsy of brain; *n* = 6 with autism.	Cerebellum: decreased number of Purkinje cells, reduced cell size. Limbic system: increased cell-packed density in hippocampus and amygdala, small cells, decreased dendiritic growth.	Decreased functioning of cerebellum may result in motor dysfunction. Reduction of dendritic branching and cell size may reduce ability to integrate sensory information. Supports need for sensorimotor interventions.
Chorpita & Barlow, 1998	Integrative literature review.	Experiences with control of sensory experiences and attachment promote development of the state regulating system.	Anxiety may be reduced and self-regulation enhanced by opportunities for early control and success in attachment relationships.
Ciesielski & Harris, 1997	Clinical examination; *n* = 19 with autism, *n* = 16 normal controls.	Persons with autism performed best on tasks with rules and limited need to shift attention. Difficulty in selective inhibition and disengagement to shift focus.	Structure and rules may improve performance. Additional support is needed to shift attention and discover rules in abstract material. Complex tasks could be simplified for mastery.

continues

Table 3–2 continued

Author/s	Design	Findings	Implications for Sensorimotor Management
Eaves et al., 1994	Cluster analysis of data from $n = 166$ children with autism.	Four subtypes of autism identified. All groups had over a 90% incidence of sensory preoccupations. This consistency of sensory preoccupations was higher and more consistent than language or social symptoms.	Sensory preoccupations are a distinct and consistent symptom of autism. Different treatments may prove useful for different types of autism.
Gray & McNaughton, 1996	Integrative literature review.	Described the functions of the behavior inhibition system.	This system provides a framework for understanding arousal and modulation of arousal to promote function and learning.
Happe & Frith, 1996	Integrative literature review.	Three cognitive theories are emerging: mentalizing impairment, executive dysfunction, and weak central coherence.	Supports need for persons with autism to be specifically taught about social interaction and how others think and feel. They may benefit from being specifically helped to develop cognitive flexibility. Context cues may need to be exaggerated and highlighted.
Hass et al., 1996	$n = 28$ persons with autism, $n = 24$ normal controls. MRI comparisons. Additional clinical assessment of cerebellar functions.	Pattern of either hypoplasia (88–90%) or hyperplasia (10–12%) found in cerebellum. 96% of persons with autism showed at least one sign of cerebellar dysfunction.	Motor disorders found in this study associated with cerebellar function included hypotonia, dysprosody, incoordination, easy fatiguability, gait disturbances, and disorders of stereognosis. Supports need for sensorimotor interventions.

Kientz & Dunn, 1997	Comparison of Sensory Profiles: n = 32 children with autism, n = 64 typical children.	Children with autism were significantly different from typical children in all aspects of sensory processing.	Problems with sensory awareness, sensory modulation, sensory integration, motor skills, and social affective interaction are hallmarks of autism. Supports need for sensorimotor interventions.
Minshew et al., 1997	Clinical neuropsychology test battery, n = 33 with autism, n = 33 matched controls.	Widespread deficit in complex reasoning, complex memory, complex language function, and skilled motor tasks. Decreased capacity for complex information processing. Intact simple information processing.	Supports need for simplification of teaching, including chaining techniques, simplification of environment, gradual development and introduction of reasoning and language skills. Supports need for compensations for motor impairments and sensorimotor interventions.
Schmahmann, 1994	Integrative literature review.	Cerebellar functions include aspects of cognition, language, and timing and sequencing of a variety of responses.	Supports need to investigate timing and sequencing difficulties and interventions for improving these skills.
Waterhouse et al., 1996	Integrative literature review.	Canalesthesia—that is, failure to integrate sensory experiences. Impaired assignment of significance to sensory stimuli. Asociality or reduced reciprocal engagement. Extended selective attention with exaggerated and narrow sensory experiences.	Need for careful study of sensory integration and careful grading of input based on child's responses. Careful attention to the affective responses of the child to sensory stimuli. More consistent social stimuli. Affiliation should be a goal in all management strategies. Gradual introduction of variations on preferred sensory input to expand flexibility.

64 typically developing children (ages 3–10). They found that children with autism were significantly different from typical children in all sensory categories, including activity level; perception of auditory, visual, touch, and taste/smell; perception of movement and body position; and emotional social processing. When compared to typical children, at least 50% of the children with autism displayed poorer functioning with a lot of noise around; discomfort during grooming (e.g., face washing), standing in line, and being close to other people; difficulty paying attention, tolerating changes, and making friends; and avoidance of eye contact. The parents reported that their children with autism needed more protection from life than other children, were slow to grow up, were stubborn and uncooperative, had poor frustration tolerance, and had trouble staying between the lines when coloring or writing. These findings suggest consistent problems with sensory awareness, sensory modulation, sensory integration, motor skills, and affective interaction.

From a sensorimotor viewpoint, the neuropsychological findings presented here highlight the need to carefully consider the sensory experiences of the child and use and study sensory modulation techniques like deep touch-pressure, a positive emotional tone, environmental simplification, and reduction of sensory defensiveness (Royeen & Lane, 1991). Royeen and Lane stressed the importance of the limbic system in sensory processing; this system assigns the affective meaning to incoming stimuli. When one considers that fragmented and inconsistent sensory experiences in people with autism are likely to be perceived as overwhelming, continuously novel, or exaggerated (because of narrow attention), then the affective label assigned to that stimulus is likely to be negative and engender a threat, elicit anxiety,

overarousal, and avoidance. Furthermore, if the cycle early in life begins with subtly different social interaction with parents and differences in sensorimotor experiences, then the likelihood of adequate social interaction will diminish, further compromising the formation of dendritic connections and levels of neurotransmitters (Waterhouse et al., 1996) and, subsequently, producing a cascade of increasing symptoms. Interventions using sensory integration theory are based on the premise that modulating arousal and attention through carefully graded sensory input to optimize focused attention may assist learning and stimulate function within this social integrative and social affective system.

Research from many fields is likely to affect our understanding of sensorimotor management strategies. For example, Ozonoff (1995) found that persons with autism perform better on the Wisconsin Card Sorting test when it is administered in a computer format. Although she was investigating the reliability of research findings, her own findings highlight the need to "remove unintentional task demands, decompos[e] complex tasks into component operations, and purify cognitive constructs" (p. 498). These recommendations also relate to sensorimotor management. Social or sensory input may impose unintentional demands; complex movements and sensory stimuli might need to be simplified to improve learning and function. Field et al. (1997) demonstrated that structured touch therapy improved attention, reduced touch aversion, and reduced withdrawal behavior, perhaps by reducing anxiety and stress, supporting the role of carefully graded input to improve function.

It is also likely that some children and adults with autism have cerebellar dysfunction. These problems with hypotonia, dysprosody and timing deficits, proximal instability, poor visual tracking, and poor sensory modulation are seen clinically and further compromise social interaction, attachment, and function (Huebner & Thomas, 1995). From a management viewpoint, the findings of cerebellar dysfunction are logically followed by treatment strategies. These might include developing tonic postural extension and flexion, equilibrium reactions, ocular movements, motor planning, and fine (hand, mouth, and eye coordination) motor prerequisites and motor skills (Koomar & Bundy, 1991). In addition, the inclusion of techniques based on neurodevelopmental treatment, described in this book, may be used to manage and remediate problems associated with cerebellar disorders.

Smith and Bryson (1994) underscored the need for research in the area of sensory and motor development by stating that "no study has systematically examined the relative motoric and praxis (imitative gesture and object use) abilities of individuals with autism and Asperger's syndrome and related them to the pattern of other skills" (p. 268). An expanded understanding of the effects of sensory and motor impairments on cognitive, language, and social functions might shed light on the factors underlying the impairments of autism and its management.

CHAPTER REVIEW QUESTIONS

1. Compare and contrast the information that is obtained from EEG, CAT scan, MRI, and PET scan methods of studying the brain and its function.
2. Describe the functions of the state regulating system.
3. Describe the traditional functions and the emerging understanding of the cerebellum and relate that the sensory and motor difficulties seen in persons with autism.
4. Identify and define the four functional problems theorized to stem from medial-temporal lobe dysfunction as defined by Waterhouse et al., and relate these problems to possible sensory experiences of persons with autism.
5. Differentiate between procedural and representative memory and relate these types of memory to the behaviors of persons with autism.
6. Describe the tenets of the theory of mind and use this to explain the social impairments of persons with autism.
7. Differentiate the major premises of three theories on the etiology of autism.
8. List several implications of the research reviewed here for an understanding of the sensorimotor approach to management of autism.

REFERENCES

Anderson, G. M. (1994). Studies on the neurochemistry of autism. In M. L. Bauman & T. L. Kemper (Eds.), *The neurobiology of autism* (pp. 227–242). Baltimore: Johns Hopkins University Press.

Bachevalier, J., & Merjanian, P. M. (1994). The contributions of medial-temporal lobe structures in infantile autism: A neurobehavioral study in primates. In M. L. Bauman & T. L. Kemper (Eds.), *The neurobiology of autism* (pp. 146–169). Baltimore: Johns Hopkins University Press.

Bailey, A., Phillips, W., & Rutter, M. (1996). Autism: Toward an integration of clinical, genetic, neuropsychological, and neurobiological perspectives. *Journal of Child Psychology and Psychiatry, 37,* 89–126.

Bauman, M. L., & Kemper, T. L. (1985). Histoanatomic observations of the brain in early infantile autism. *Neurology, 35*, 866–874.

Bauman, M. L., & Kemper, T. L. (1994). Neuroanatomic observations of the brain in autism. In M. L. Bauman & T. L. Kemper (Eds.), *The neurobiology of autism* (pp. 119–145). Baltimore: Johns Hopkins University Press.

Berkson, G. (1996). Feedback and control in the development of abnormal stereotyped behaviors. In R. Sprague & K. Newell (Eds.), *Stereotyped movements: Brain and behavior relationships* (pp. 3–15). Washington, DC: American Psychological Association.

Berntson, G. G., Tuber, D. S., Ronca, A. E., & Bachman, D. S. (1983). The decerebrate human: Associative learning. *Experimental Neurology, 81*, 77–88.

Cacioppo, J. T., & Tassinary, L. G. (1990). Psychophysiology and psychophysiological inference. In J. T. Cacioppo & L. G. Tassinary (Eds.), *Principles of psychophysiology* (pp. 3–33). New York: Cambridge University Press.

Cesaroni, L., & Garber, M. (1991). Exploring the experience of autism through firsthand accounts. *Journal of Autism and Developmental Disorders, 21*, 303–313.

Chafetz, M. D., Friedman, A. L., Kevorkian, C. G., & Levy, J. K. (1996). The cerebellum and cognitive function: Implications for rehabilitation. *Archives of Physical Medicine and Rehabilitation, 77*, 1303–1308.

Chorpita, B. F., & Barlow, D. H. (1998). The development of anxiety: The role of control in the early environment. *Psychological Bulletin, 124*, 3–21.

Churchland, P. S. (1986). *Neurophilosophy: Toward a unified science of the mind/brain*. Cambridge, MA: MIT Press.

Ciesielski, K. T., Courchesne, E., & Elmasian, R. (1990). Effects of focused selective attention tasks on event-related potentials in autistic and normal individuals. *Electroencephalography and Clinical Neurophysiology, 75*, 207–220.

Ciesielski, K. T., & Harris, R. J. (1997). Factors related to performance failure on executive tasks in autism. *Child Neuropsychology, 3*, 1–12.

Clark, F. (1983). Research on the neuropathophysiology of autism and its implications for occupational therapy. *Occupational Therapy Journal of Research, 3*, 3–22.

Coleman, M. (1994). Second trimester of gestation: A time of risk for classical autism. *Developmental Brain Dysfunction, 7*, 104–109.

Coles, M. G. H., Gratton, G., & Fabiani, M. (1990). Event-related brain potentials. In J. T. Cacioppo & L. G. Tassinary (Eds.), *Principles of psychophysiology* (pp. 413–455). New York: Cambridge University Press.

Courchesne, E., Townsend, J., & Saitoh, O. (1994). The brain in infantile autism. *Neurology, 44*, 214–223.

Dunn, M. (1994). Neurophysiologic observations in autism and implications for neurological dysfunction. In M. L. Bauman & T. L. Kemper (Eds.), *The neurobiology of autism* (pp. 45–65). Baltimore: Johns Hopkins University Press.

Dunn, W. (1994). Performance of typical children on the sensory profile: An item analysis. *American Journal of Occupational Therapy, 48*, 967–974.

Eaves, L. C., Ho, H. H., & Eaves, D. M. (1994). Subtypes of autism by cluster analysis. *Journal of Autism and Developmental Disorders, 24*, 3–22.

Field, T., Lasko, D., Mundy, P., Henteleff, T., Kabat, S., Talpins, S., & Dowling, M. (1997). Brief report: Autistic children's attentiveness and responsivity improve after touch therapy. *Journal of Autism and Developmental Disorders, 27*, 333–338.

Gaffney, G. R., Tsai, L. Y., Kuperman, S., & Minchin, S. (1987). Cerebellar structure in autism. *American Journal of Diseases in Children, 141*, 1330–1332.

Gevins, A. (1996). Electrophysiological imaging of brain function. In A. W. Toga & J. C. Mazziotta (Eds.), *Brain mapping the methods* (pp. 259–276). San Diego: Academic Press.

Gilman, S., & Newman, S. W. (1992). *Essentials of clinical neuroanatomy and neurophysiology* (8th ed.). Philadelphia: F. A. Davis.

Goodman, R. (1989). Infantile autism: A syndrome of multiple primary deficits. *Journal of Autism and Developmental Disorders, 19*, 409–424.

Graham, R. B. (1990). *Physiological psychology*. Belmont, CA: Wadsworth.

Grandin, T. (1992). An inside view of autism. In E. Schopler & G. B. Mesibov (Eds.), *High-functioning individuals with autism* (pp. 105–126). New York: Plenum.

Gray, J. A., & McNaughton, H. (1996). The neuropsychology of anxiety: A reprise. In D. A. Hope (Ed.), *Nebraska Symposium on motivation: Perspectives* on anxiety, panic, and fear (vol. 43, pp. 61–134). Lincoln: University of Nebraska Press.

Groden, J., Cautela, J., Prince, S., & Berryman, J. (1994). The impact of stress and anxiety on individuals with autism and developmental disorders. In E. Schopler & G. B. Mesibov (Eds.), *Behavioral issues in autism* (pp. 177–194). New York: Plenum.

Guess, D., & Carr, E. (1991). Emergence and maintenance of stereotypy and self-injury. *American Journal on Mental Retardation, 96*, 299–319.

Happe, F., & Frith, U. (1996). The neuropsychology of autism. *Brain, 119*, 1377–1400.

Hass, R. H., Townsend, J., Courchesne, E., Lincoln, A. J., Schreibman, L., & Yeung-Courchesne, R. (1996). Neurological abnormalities in infantile autism. *Journal of Child Neurology, 11*, 84–92.

Hill, D. A., & Leary, M. R. (1993). *Movement disturbances: A clue to hidden competencies in persons diagnosed with autism and other developmental disorders*. Madison, WI: DRI Press.

Holroyd, S., Reiss, A. L., & Bryan, R. N. (1991). Autistic features in Joubert Syndrome: A genetic disorder with agenesis of the cerebellar vermis. *Biological Psychiatry, 29*, 287–294.

Horwitz, B., & Rumsey, J. M. (1994). Positron emission tomography: Implications for cerebral dysfunction in autism. In M. L. Bauman & T. L. Kemper (Eds.), *The neurobiology of autism* (pp. 102–118). Baltimore: Johns Hopkins University Press.

Huebner, R. A. (1992). Autistic disorder: A neuropsychological enigma. *American Journal of Occupational Therapy, 46*, 487–501.

Huebner, R. A., & Emery, L. (1998). A social psychological analysis of facilitated communication: Implications for education. *Mental Retardation, 36*, 259–268.

Huebner, R. A., Gamradt, J., & Klund, M. (ND). *Wisconsin Sensorimotor Pointing Assessment: Application to adults with autism*. Manuscript in preparation.

Huebner, R. A., & Thomas, K. R. (1995). The relationship between attachment, psychopathology, and childhood disability. *Rehabilitation Psychology, 40*, 111–124.

Insel, T. R. (1997). A neurobiological basis of social attachment. *American Journal of Psychiatry, 154*, 726–735.

Johnson, A. K., & Anderson, E. A. (1990). Stress and arousal. In J. T. Cacioppo & L. G. Tassinary (Eds.), *Principles of psychophysiology* (pp. 216–252). New York: Cambridge University Press.

Jones, V., & Prior, M. (1985). Motor imitation abilities and neurological signs in autistic children. *Journal of Autism and Developmental Disorders, 15*, 37–46.

Kandel, E. R., Schwartz, J. H., & Jessell, T. M. (2000). *Principles of neural science* (4th ed.). New York: McGraw-Hill.

Kemner, C., Verbaten, M. N., Cuperus, J. M., Camfferman, G., & van Engeland, H. (1998). Abnormal saccadic eye movements in autistic children. *Journal of Autism and Developmental Disorders, 28*, 61–67.

Kennedy, S., Glaser, R., & Kiecolt-Glaser, J. (1990). Psychoneuroimmunology. In J. T. Cacioppo & L. G. Tassinary (Eds.), *Principles of psychophysiology* (pp. 177–190). New York: Cambridge University Press.

Kientz, M. A., & Dunn, W. (1997). A comparison of the performance of children with and without autism on the Sensory Profile. *American Journal of Occupational Therapy, 51*, 530–537.

Killiany, R. J., & Moss, M. B. (1994). Memory function and autism. In M. L. Bauman & T. L. Kemper (Eds.), *The neurobiology of autism* (pp. 170–194). Baltimore: Johns Hopkins University Press.

Klin, A. (1993). Auditory brain stem responses in autism: Brain stem dysfunction or peripheral hearing loss? *Journal of Autism and Developmental Disorders, 23*, 15–35.

Kohen-Raz, R., Volkmar, F. R., & Cohen, D. J. (1992). Postural control in children with autism. *Journal of Autism and Developmental Disorders, 22*, 419–432.

Kolb, B., & Whishaw, I. Q. (1996). *Fundamentals of human neuropsychology* (4th ed.). New York: W. H. Freeman.

Koomar, J. A., & Bundy, A. C. (1991). The art and science of creating direct intervention from theory. In A. G. Fisher, E. A. Murray, & A. C. Bundy (Eds.), *Sensory integration theory and practice* (pp. 251–314). Philadelphia: F. A. Davis.

Leaton, R. N., & Supple, W. F. (1986). Cerebellar vermis: Essential for long-term habituation of the acoustic startle response. *Science, 232*, 513–515.

Lelord, G., Herault, J., Perrot, A., Garreau, B., Barthelemy, C., Martineau, J., Bruneau, N., Sauvage, D., & Muh, J. P. (1994). What kind of markers in childhood autism? *Developmental Brain Dysfunction, 7*, 53–62.

Lincoln, A. J., Courchesne, E., Harms, L., & Allen, M. (1993). Contextual probability evaluation in autistic, receptive developmental language disorder, and control children: Event-related brain potential evidence. *Journal of Autism and Developmental Disorders, 23,* 37–58.

Lord, C. (1991). Methods and measures of behavior in the diagnosis of autism and related disorders. *Psychiatric Clinics of North America, 14,* 69–80.

Losche, G. (1990). Sensorimotor and action development in autistic children from infancy to early childhood. *Journal of Child Psychology and Psychiatry, 31,* 749–761.

Miller, L. J., & Lane, S. J. (2000). Toward a consensus in terminology in sensory integrative theory and practice: Part I: Taxonomy of neurophysiological processes. *Sensory Integration Special Interest Section Quarterly 23,* 1–4.

Minshew, N. J. (1994). In vivo brain chemistry of autism: Magnetic resonance spectroscopy studies. In M. L. Bauman & T. L. Kemper (Eds.), *The neurobiology of autism* (pp. 86–101). Baltimore: Johns Hopkins University Press.

Minshew, N. J., & Dombrowski, S. M. (1994). In vivo neuroanatomy of autism: Neuroimaging studies. In M. L. Bauman & T. L. Kemper (Eds.), *The neurobiology of autism* (pp. 66–85). Baltimore: Johns Hopkins University Press.

Minshew, N. J., Goldstein, G., & Siegel, D. J. (1997). Neuropsychologic functioning in autism: Profile of a complex information processing disorder. *Journal of the International Neuropsychological Society, 3,* 303–316.

Modahl, C., Green, L., Fein, D., Morris, M., Waterhouse, L., Feinstein, C., & Levin, H. (1998). Plasma oxytocin levels in autistic children. *Biological Psychiatry, 43,* 270–277.

O'Neill, M., & Jones, R. S. P. (1997). Sensory-perceptual abnormalities in autism: A case for more research? *Journal of Autism and Developmental Disorders, 27,* 283–293.

Ornitz, E. M. (1989). Autism at the interface between sensory and information processing. In G. Dawson (Ed.), *Autism: Nature, diagnosis, and treatment* (pp.174–199). New York: Guilford.

Ornitz, E. M., Lane, S. J., Sugiyama, T., & de Traversay, J. (1993). Startle modulation studies in autism. *Journal of Autism and Developmental Disorders, 23,* 619–637.

Ozonoff, S. (1995). Reliability and validity of the Wisconsin Card Sorting Test in studies of autism. *Neuropsychology, 9,* 491–500.

Pierce, K., Glad, K. S., & Schreibman, L. (1997). Social perception in children with autism: An attentional deficit. *Journal of Autism and Developmental Disorders, 27,* 265–282.

Piven, J., & Folstein, S. (1994). The genetics of autism. In M. L. Bauman & T. L. Kemper (Eds.), *The neurobiology of autism* (pp. 18–44). Baltimore: Johns Hopkins University Press.

Piven, J., Nehme, E., Simon, J., Barta, P., Pearlson, G., & Folstein, S. E. (1992). Magnetic resonance imaging in autism: Measurement of the cerebellum, pons, and fourth ventricles. *Biological Psychiatry, 31,* 491–504.

Piven, J., & O'Leary, D. (1997). Neuroimaging in autism. *Child and Adolescent Psychiatric Clinics of North America, 6,* 305–323.

Pivik, R. T., Broughton, R. J., Coppola, R., Davidson, R. J., Fox, N., & Nuwer, M. R. (1993). Guidelines for the recording and quantitative analysis of electroencephalographic activity in research contexts. *Psychophysiology, 30,* 547–558.

Post, R. M., Weiss, S. R. B., & Leverich, G. S. (1994). Recurrent affective disorder: Roots in developmental neurobiology and illness progression based on changes in gene expression. *Development and Psychopathology, 6,* 781–813.

Poustka, F. (1998). Neurobiology of autism. In F. R. Volkmar (Ed.), *Autism and pervasive developmental disorders* (pp. 130–168). New York: Cambridge University Press.

Prior, M., & Ozonoff, S. (1998). Psychological factors in autism. In F. R. Volkmar (Ed.), *Autism and pervasive developmental disorders* (pp. 65–108). New York: Cambridge University Press.

Rapin, I. (1997). Autism. *New England Journal of Medicine, 337,* 97–104.

Rapin, I., & Katzman, R. (1998). Neurobiology of autism. *Annals of Neurology, 43,* 7–14.

Ritvo, E. R., Freeman, B. J., Scheibel, A. B., Duong, T., Robinson, H., Guthrie, D., & Ritvo, A. (1984). Lower Purkinje cell counts in the cerebella of four autistic subjects: Initial findings in the UCLA-NSAC autopsy research report. *American Journal of Psychiatry, 143,* 862–866.

Ritvo, E. R., & Garber, J. H. (1988). Cerebellar hypoplasia and autism. *New England Journal of Medicine, 319,* 1152 (abstract).

Royeen, C. B., & Lane, S. J. (1991). Tactile processing and sensory defensiveness. In A. G. Fisher, E. A. Murray, & A. C. Bundy (Eds.), *Sensory integration theory and practice* (pp. 108–136). Philadelphia: F. A. Davis.

Rumsey, J. M., & Hamburger, S. D. (1988). Neuropsychological findings in high-functioning men with infantile autism, residual state. *Journal of Clinical and Experimental Neuropsychology, 10,* 201–221.

Sandman, C. A., Barron, J. L., Chiez-DeMet, A., & DeMet, E. M. (1991). Brief report: Plasma-endorphin and cortisol levels in autistic patients. *Journal of Autism and Developmental Disorders, 21,* 83–87.

Schmahmann, J. D. (1994). The cerebellum in autism: Clinical and anatomical perspectives. In M. L. Bauman & T. L. Kemper (Eds.), *The neurobiology of autism* (pp. 195–226). Baltimore: Johns Hopkins University Press.

Shields, J., Varley, R., Broks, P., & Simpson, A. (1996a). Hemispheric function in developmental language disorders and high-level autism. *Developmental Medicine and Child Neurology, 38,* 473–486.

Shields, J., Varley, R., Broks, P., & Simpson, A. (1996b). Social cognition in developmental language disorders and high-level autism. *Developmental Medicine and Child Neurology, 38,* 487–495.

Smith, I. M., & Bryson, S. E. (1994). Imitation and action in autism: A critical review. *Psychological Bulletin, 116,* 259–273.

Steffenburg, S. (1991). Neuropsychiatric assessment of children with autism: A population-based study. *Developmental Medicine and Child Neurology, 33,* 495–511.

Toga, A. W., & Mazziotta, J. C. (1996). *Brain mapping the methods.* San Diego: Academic Press.

Waterhouse, L., Fein, D., & Modahl, C. (1996). Neurofunctional mechanisms in autism. *Psychological Review, 103,* 457–489.

Westman, J. C. (1990). *Handbook of learning disabilities: A multisystem approach.* Boston: Allyn & Bacon.

Wong, V., & Wong, S. N. (1991). Brain stem auditory evoked potential study in children with autistic disorder. *Journal of Autism and Developmental Disorder, 21,* 329–340.

PART 2

Foundations of the Sensorimotor Approach to Management in Autism

Assessment of Individuals with an Autism Spectrum Disorder Utilizing a Sensorimotor Approach

Scott D. Tomchek

CHAPTER OBJECTIVES

At the completion of this chapter, the reader will be able to:

- Provide the rationale for sensorimotor assessment as part of a diagnostic or intervention planning evaluation.
- Identify evaluation considerations unique to this patient population.
- Identify the main components of a comprehensive assessment of sensorimotor functions.
- Discuss both formal and structured observation assessment of the sensorimotor assessment components.
- Identify the subcomponents of motor performance, visual perception, and adaptive self-help skills.
- Describe the expressions of sensory modulation disorders.
- Identify specialized assessments in autism with sensorimotor components.
- Discuss the impact of sensorimotor functions on the behavioral, social, play, and functional performance of individuals with an autism spectrum disorder.
- Discuss the pertinent scientific literature relating to all of the above objectives.

INTRODUCTION

Sensory and motor function impairments are widely reported in the literature describing children and adolescents with autism spectrum disorders (DeMyer, 1976; Ermer & Dunn, 1998; Haas et al., 1996; Jones & Prior, 1985; Kientz & Dunn, 1997; Kohen-Raz, Volkmar, & Cohen, 1992; Rapin, 1991; Vilensky, Damasio, & Maurer, 1981). Additionally, the timing and sequence of sensory and motor developmental markers are described as both delayed and qualitatively different in individuals with autism spectrum disorders compared to typically developing children (Losche, 1990). These impairments and qualitative differences most often reflect immaturity or differences in central nervous system (CNS) functioning. There is almost universal agreement that autism spectrum disorders have neurobiological underpinnings (Bauman & Kemper, 1994; Coleman

& Gillberg, 1985; Gillberg & Coleman, 1996; Huebner, 1992; Lord, 1991; Minshew, Sweeney, & Bauman, 1997). This has led to a recent effort to extensively investigate and identify CNS abnormalities of both structure and function, the goals of which are to identify a source of these sensorimotor impairments and to establish a possible etiology of autism spectrum disorders. To date, however, the research on these neurobiological underpinnings has been inconclusive (Bauman & Kemper, 1994; Gillberg & Coleman, 1996; Rapin, 1997). These investigative studies are outlined in Chapter 3 and discussed as a foundation for the behavioral, emotional, social, cognitive, sensorimotor, and functional performance aspects seen in autism spectrum disorders.

Given the prevalence of sensory and motor impairments and their impact on behavior and functional performance, assessment of sensorimotor functions is essential as part of the diagnostic evaluation and treatment planning process. This sensorimotor assessment should focus on the detection of soft neurological signs and include an occupational therapist's evaluation of their impact on the individual's functional skills or daily activities (Filipek et al., 1999). The purpose of this chapter is to provide the rationale for, and a thorough description of the process of, sensorimotor assessment of children with an autism spectrum disorder as part of a diagnostic assessment or an intervention planning process. To achieve this purpose, initial discussion focuses on the rationale for sensorimotor assessment. Evaluation considerations, such as reason for referral, standardized versus nonstandardized instruments, and assessment settings are then explored. Following this, the components of a comprehensive assessment of sensorimotor functions, including neurodevelopmental, motor performance, and sensory processing,

are presented along with assessment of the functional implications of impairments on play and occupational performance. Finally, the use of the information obtained from this assessment is described. Included in all of these discussions is a review of the pertinent scientific literature that supports these assessment procedures.

RATIONALE FOR SENSORIMOTOR ASSESSMENT

As noted in Chapter 1, the term *sensorimotor* describes a broad class of intervention theories that emphasize the role of active, experienced-based learning (Murray & Anzalone, 1991). For the purposes of this book, the term refers to the full range of interventions and refinements arising from sensory integration theory and neurodevelopmental theories. In the process of sensory integration, the brain registers sensory input (e.g., touch, sound, movement), processes that input, and organizes a response to that input. This response may result in a change in the perceiver's behavior, or the perceiver may habituate to the incoming sensory input and therefore make no overt behavioral response. Whichever the response, sensory integration supports this ongoing process of learning. Adaptive responding, meaning situation appropriate, to varied sensory stimulations in multiple situations is the ultimate evidence of adequate sensory integration. Adaptive motor responses and skilled motor output are also included here and predicated on intact sensory integration. Children with sensory integrative impairments may have difficulty orienting to and registering sensory input, filtering stimuli, or habituating to familiar stimuli. They may struggle to organize a response to the sensory environment that is logical and appropriate from an observer's viewpoint. With inaccurate sensory processing in the CNS, praxis and motor output impairments may manifest in delayed gross and fine motor development and diminished sensory discrimination abilities (such as visual perception, tactile discrimination, and auditory discrimination).

Historically, with the exception of specifically analyzing stereotypies as part of a "restricted behavioral repertoire" (American Psychological Association, 1994), sensorimotor assessment has not been a major component of the diagnostic evaluation process in autism spectrum disorders (Filipek et al., 1999). Filipek and colleagues (1999) felt that this limited emphasis on sensorimotor assessment was related to the meager systematic empirical research in this domain. Further, they questioned the contribution of previously available literature to differential diagnosis.

Recently, however, with a greater understanding of the neuropsychological relationship in autism, more emphasis has been placed on sensorimotor assessment in both diagnostic and intervention planning evaluations. Coupled with this is ongoing empirical research in these domains, with investigators focusing on many aspects of both sensory processing and motor performance. While some studies identified broad sensory processing impairments (Adrien, Ornitz, Barthelemy, Sauvage, & Lelord, 1987; Baranek, 1999; Dahlgren & Gillberg, 1989; Elliot, 1990; Ermer & Dunn, 1998; Kientz & Dunn, 1997), others defined more specialized skill impairments for motor planning/praxis (Leary & Hill, 1996; Minshew et al., 1997), motor imitation abilities (Rogers, Bennetto, McEvoy, & Pennington, 1996; Stone, Lemanek, Fishel, Fernandez, & Altemeier, 1990; Stone & Lemanek, 1990) and repetitive motor stereotypies (Adrien et al., 1987; Elliot, 1990; Ornitz, 1985). Attention and arousal impairments

were also reported and can be explained as relating to sensory processing impairments (Dawson & Lew, 1989; Rapin, 1991). A growing body of recent literature has begun to document effective intervention strategies; sensory and motor issues are often addressed in integrated and comprehensive interventions programs for autism, in addition to language, cognitive, and behavioral issues (e.g., Greenspan & Wieder, 1999; Ozonoff & Cathcart, 1998; Rogers, 1998).

Based on this growing knowledge base and understanding of sensorimotor performance, greater value has been placed on the findings of a thorough sensorimotor assessment as part of both diagnostic and intervention planning evaluations. Of particular importance in an assessment is the documentation of the qualitative aspects of sensory processing and motor performance, rather than simple assessment of developmental milestones (Filipek et al., 1999). Evaluation of sensorimotor functions should focus on identifying patterns of sensory and motor performance that could provide insight into the possible expression of underlying neurologic deficits. That is, an assessment of developmental milestones answers questions about skill development, sequence, and chronological level; in contrast, sensorimotor assessment answers questions about why skills may be delayed or qualitatively different. An integration of these findings guides the therapeutic process.

Of particular importance is the role of the occupational therapist in the comprehensive assessment process. Occupational therapists take a holistic approach when working with a child and family, addressing both physical dysfunction and mental health/behavioral aspects of development. This approach is grounded in a thorough understanding of task analysis and the process of human and environmental adaptation; both skills are fundamental to the occupational therapist's clinical reasoning. Task analysis and facilitation of adaptation allow for the promotion of maximal independence in the performance of human occupations. Given these strengths, occupational therapists have specific expertise in evaluating the impact of sensorimotor findings on the individual's functional skills and daily activities (Filipek et al., 1999).

Assessment of sensorimotor functions focuses on four major domains. Fundamental neurodevelopmental skills are assessed; these skills are the foundation of motor output and reflect sensory processing. Second, the impact of the neurodevelopmental findings on motor skill is assessed. Motor assessment (gross, fine, visual-motor) is vital when there is a potential developmental delay, qualitative difference in performance, dysfunction, or skill regression. The assessment of sensory processing abilities should address the presence of sensory defensive behaviors, sensory registration and modulation impairments, and sensory integrative functioning. Of significant importance, as one component of the sensory processing assessment, is a thorough assessment of praxis (motor planning), as deficits have been frequently documented in individuals with autism through adolescence (Rogers et al., 1996; Stone et al., 1990; Stone & Lemanek, 1990). Finally, the impact of the sensory and motor strengths and weaknesses on occupational/functional performance is assessed.

Many of the findings from a sensorimotor assessment are beneficial in differential diagnosis and can provide an understanding of the behavioral manifestations seen in the individual being evaluated. This information can also provide insight into the specific learning style of the child or the factors essential to learning. The utmost goal of sensorimotor assessment, whether for diagnosis or intervention planning purposes, is to document the strengths and weaknesses for prognostic and program planning, development of appropriate interventions, and provision of modifications (Filipek et al., 1999; Kientz & Miller, 1999).

EVALUATION CONSIDERATIONS

Reason for Referral

Occupational therapists are requested to complete sensorimotor assessments on individuals with an autism spectrum disorder for a number of reasons. The reason for referral, in many cases, is dependent on the setting in which the practitioner functions (Nelson, 1982). In some settings, occupational therapists are perceived as specialists in sensorimotor performance and sensory processing, but in others their role is more generally focused on the overall development of sensorimotor and occupational/functional performance. According to Nelson, whether the therapist functions more as specialist or generalist likely depends on a number of variables, including: (a) the placement of the individual with autism (e.g., at home with the family, at school, in a group home, in a long-term institutional placement); (b) the characteristics/presentation of the individual with autism (e.g., age, IQ, language ability, behavioral profile); (c) the roles of other professionals in that setting (e.g., psychologists, speech-language pathologists, developmental pediatricians, special educators); and (d) the theoretical frame of reference held by the settings and therapist. While in almost all cases the evaluation is ultimately requested to document the strengths and weaknesses of an individual for appropriate program planning, correctly identifying the reason for referral helps practitioners define their role and ensure that more specialized referral questions are answered.

Because diagnosis is best made by a number of evaluators assessing many domains (Stone & Ousley, 1996), a practitioner likely functions on a multidisciplinary or interdisciplinary team as one component of a diagnostic evaluation. As part of this team, it may be requested, for instance, that emphasis be placed on addressing sensory processing (including praxis) and occupational/functional performance rather than assessing motor milestones. Additionally, fostering the understanding of team members of any sensory processing dysfunction and its impact on the behavioral observations made during the evaluation process may be critical for differential diagnosis. For example, during an interdisciplinary assessment of a very driven and active toddler, the child is found to have cognitive, motor, and communication delays. When discussing potential diagnoses for the child, much of the discussion by the team members revolves around the impact of the child's impulsivity and activity level on motor planning and task performance. These behaviors, if viewed as difficulties in arousal regulation, may be described as sensory modulation impairments or a regulatory disorder rather than an attention deficit hyperactivity disorder (ADHD); consequently, the conceptualization process and intervention planning for this child will be significantly different.

In many cases, the purpose of the multidisciplinary evaluation process is to both establish, or to rule out, a diagnosis and to provide a comprehensive assessment of specific strengths and weaknesses in skill domains for individualized treatment planning. In these situations, team members likely have well-defined roles and expectations in assessment because individually assessed skill areas are interrelated with the skill areas assessed by other team members; findings from any discipline can be interpreted differently. A conceptual integration of findings from several disciplines may provide a clearer understanding of the presentation of the individual with an autism spectrum disorder and dictate appropriate intervention. For instance, a psychologist functioning independently and working from a strict behavioral frame of reference may interpret a "self-stimulatory behavior" or stereotypy as a behavior to be extinguished. However, that stereotypy, when analyzed by an occupational therapist, may be interpreted as a self-regulatory mechanism to maintain optimal arousal in a classroom setting. As a team, the decision to provide the child with additional supports in the classroom to assist with self-regulation may stem from an integrated interpretation.

Whether a referral is made for diagnostic or treatment planning purposes, the practitioner is usually asked to document the strengths and weaknesses of the individual. Defining roles ensures that more specialized domains are assessed and all referral questions are answered. Sharing this information and teaming with the other professionals and the family of the individual with an autism spectrum disorder allows for appropriate diagnosis, program planning, and intervention development.

Standardized versus Nonstandardized Instruments

During a sensorimotor assessment, the testing situation is a social communication process. Inherent to the diagnosis of autism are qualitative social interaction and communication skill impairments. Additionally, individuals with autism have been described as distractible, demonstrating variability in skill performance, having a low tolerance of incoming sensory stimuli, and impervious to the usual verbal and even tangible motivators used to ensure optimal performance (Cook, 1991; Rapin, 1991). A standardized testing process thus draws on the weaknesses rather than the strengths of the individual with autism; consequently, the testing process is often not well tolerated.

Because of these problems, many children are too readily labeled "untestable" when initial efforts at testing fail (Schopler, Reichler, & Lansing, 1980). Attempts at having a child perform a certain task may elicit a refusal, scream, performance of another action with the presented item(s), or tuning out of the tester. Often, it is difficult for children with autism to focus on the appropriate stimulus (Cook, 1991) or to respond to typical social responses (e.g., eye contact) from the examiner (Cook, 1991; Miller, 1996). Given these circumstances, some practitioners and researchers feel that evaluations should be conducted within the child's natural setting, using nonstandardized procedures (e.g., parent interviews) rather than standardized instruments to obtain information on the child's functional performance (Cook, 1990; Kientz & Dunn, 1997; Kientz & Miller, 1999; Prizant & Wetherby, 1993). Other practitioners embrace the notion of testing in the natural setting with nonstandardized procedures but also acknowledge the need to adapt standardized instruments to clearly outline a child's individual abilities (Filipek et al., 1999; Schopler et al., 1980).

Again, we need to remember that the goal of a diagnostic or intervention planning evaluation is to identify the unique strengths and weaknesses of an individual in a number of skill areas. Whether using standardized or nonstandardized instruments, the focus of the assessment process should be on

obtaining this information. A variety of strategies should be used, including direct assessment, naturalistic observation, and structured caregiver interview (Filipek et al., 1999; Rutter & Schopler, 1988).

When utilizing direct assessment, adaptations to the typical testing situation, environment, and materials will likely be necessary to obtain the most accurate measure and to ensure optimal performance of the individual (Filipek et al., 1999; Schopler et al., 1980). Additional visits may be necessary for the child to adapt to the environment or the evaluator, and to transition into the process of testing (Filipek et al., 1999). Directions, especially verbal ones, may be too difficult for the child to comprehend, and therefore the evaluator may need to adapt the directions using more simple or nonverbal directives (Schopler et al., 1980). For example, you want to assess directional reach and quality of grasp and release during container play. When you place a box on the table and hand the child several blocks, you say, "Put all the blocks in the box." If the child does not understand the directive, he or she may throw the blocks, mouth them, stack them, or do nothing with them and leave the table. When you make the directive easier by saying "Put" and pairing it with a point toward the box, the child then puts the blocks in the box. By simplifying the command, you obtained the desired information on directional reach and release and also gathered information on the child's receptive language abilities and learning style that can be used to guide the rest of your evaluation. A child may not be able to sit in a chair to respond to items presented at a table for a number of reasons. If the child appears to need more sensory input as a means of achieving optimal arousal, providing him or her with movement by presenting items while he or she is seated on a platform swing or large equilibrium board may work. Presenting items alongside the child while he or she is in free play may elicit spontaneous interaction with the item, at which time a directive may be given or task can be modeled.

In making the above adaptations, the standardization of an instrument is likely to be abandoned, which should be noted in the written report. However, the testing process is adapted to increase the chances that the results accurately represent the child's unique abilities while providing information on relative weaknesses. Because successful learning is based on utilizing a child's strong skills to foster growth in areas of weakness, accurately defining these variables is the first step in ensuring appropriate differential diagnosis, program planning, and intervention development.

Evaluation/Assessment Settings

Possible settings for an evaluation/assessment of an individual with autism are embedded in the previous discussion and expanded on in this section. Sensorimotor assessment often relies heavily on behavioral observation and task analysis. Global judgments regarding the status of behavior, balance, coordination, praxis, and sensory processing of an individual can be made through skilled observation. Many think this observation is most useful to the diagnostic and intervention planning process and most accurate when accomplished within the child's natural setting(s) (Kientz & Dunn, 1997; Kientz & Miller, 1999; Rutter & Schopler, 1988; Watson & Marcus, 1988). Analysis of performance in the natural setting allows for observation of the child's typical behavior and performance in functional everyday activities that are a familiar part of his or her daily routine. Because chil-

dren with an autism spectrum disorder often have difficulty transitioning to new surroundings and working with new people, an analysis of behavior in the natural environment is also desirable to reduce the effects of the change in setting (e.g., clinic) on a child's usual behavior and performance. Observation in multiple settings can provide significant information about how a child functions as well as how the differences in settings change behavior and performance. Videotaping the child across settings (e.g., home, school, clinic) is often utilized to allow for these observations.

COMPONENTS OF A COMPREHENSIVE ASSESSMENT OF SENSORIMOTOR FUNCTIONS

The sequence of assessment needs to be flexible for children with autism. A comprehensive sensorimotor assessment requires integration of information about the sensory and motor abilities of the child and the impact of these strengths and weakness on performance or occupational functioning. Rather than a sequential pattern of assessment, the process of sensorimotor assessment is evolving, meaning it unfolds at multiple levels. Observations of play or social functioning provide data about sensory and motor abilities; similarly, direct observation of sensory and motor abilities provides insight into strengths and impediments to play and social functioning. The practitioner is involved in this ongoing integration, using multiple theories and frames of reference, throughout the assessment (Watling, Dietz, Kanny, & McLaughlin, 1999). Organizing the components of a comprehensive assessment of sensorimotor functions is challenging because the process must be flexibly sequenced. Nonetheless, for the purposes of this chapter, these components of assessment are somewhat arbitrarily organized in the following broad categories: components common to sensory and motor abilities; motor performance, sensory processing, including visual perception; and assessment of functional performance.

Components Common to Sensory and Motor Functions

Behavioral Expressions

During all aspects of a comprehensive sensorimotor assessment, observations of the behavior displayed by the child are made. These observations are used in differential diagnosis and to give insight into other components of the assessment (e.g., play, sensory processing, praxis). Additionally, they provide information about how a child responds to his or her environment and, thus, his or her unique learning style.

Throughout the assessment session, qualitative differences in the child's interaction with other people and the environment should be noted. Specifically, observations of social attention and responsiveness should be made. Use of eye contact should be monitored. Children with autism have been found to have diminished eye contact in general and to use eye contact communicatively less frequently than children without an autism spectrum disorder (Adrien et al., 1987; Gillberg, 1990; Miller, 1996; Osterling & Dawson, 1994). Further, visual orientation and attention impairments have also been described; children with autism tend to look at and respond less to others in the environment, even at 12 months of age (Baranek, 1999; Osterling & Dawson). Deficits in joint attention have also been noted in young children with autism at one year of age (Osterling & Dawson).

Specific observations about how the child interacts with his or her environment should also be recorded. In their study, Adrien and colleagues (1987) found that the behavioral features of ritualistic use with objects, rubbing of surfaces, body rocking, repetitive jumping, ignoring of objects, and absence of response to stimuli differentiated children with autism from both normal children and children with mental retardation. Children with autism may show an intense attachment to or prolonged play with an object (Reber, 1992). Conversely, they may have a short attention span and shift their attention frequently from toy to toy (Rapin, 1991; Reber).

Stereotypies should also be documented. The presence of repetitive motor stereotypies, unusual body posturing, object stereotypies, and self-injurious behaviors can be reported by caregivers or noted through observation (Adrien et al., 1987; Rapin, 1991, 1996; Reber, 1992). Hand flapping, finger mannerisms, toe walking, head banging, and body rocking have been specifically reported in the literature. In one study (Rapin, 1996), motor stereotypies were present in more than 40% of the 176 children with autism and in more than 60% of those with lower IQ. These stereotypies often manifest during the preschool years (Lord, 1995) and have been associated with children with autism of lower cognitive ability (Howlin & Rutter, 1987).

The behavior of the child may also provide clues about sensory processing. Using an applied sensory analysis, the therapist should examine the sensory antecedents, both long term and short term, for adaptive and maladaptive behaviors. Observation of adaptive or maladaptive behavior may guide interpretation of sensory processing abilities. The consequences of adaptive and maladaptive behavior should also be observed. For example, the child's self-stimulatory behavior may occur following a barely audible (to the examiner) sound (antecedent); the behavioral response (considered maladaptive) may consist of head banging and be followed by the caregiver removing the child from the environment to a time-out area (consequence). Such an observation, when interpreted from a sensorimotor viewpoint, might suggest the hypothesis that the child is hypersensitive to sound and uses deep proprioceptive input to diminish the hypersensitivity. Further, it is felt that the head banging is reinforced by taking the child away from the stimulus. Another child might experience an increasing amount of difficulty with attention and learning as the day progresses, with more tantrums and negative behavior later in the afternoon. One diagnostic hypothesis may be that the child is experiencing difficulty with self-modulating arousal and sensory input, which build up over the day; a logical treatment hypothesis is that the child might benefit from periodic rests in a calming environment to provide environmental supports to modulate arousal. These hypotheses can be tested throughout the assessment and in conjunction with the observations of caregivers and other professionals. Additional suggestions for structured observation of sensory and motor abilities are included throughout this chapter.

Neuromuscular and Neurodevelopmental Status

A comprehensive neuromuscular assessment often initiates the physical evaluation of an individual with an autism spectrum disorder. Active and passive range-of-motion limitations are rare. If present, these limitations are usually noted at the heel cords bilaterally and are related to toe walking. The toe walking, in most instances, relates to the child seeking proprioceptive input in his or her legs rather than the presence of spasticity in the legs. Muscle tone in the trunk and extremities (both proximally and distally) is also evaluated. Because proximal muscle strength and stability are sometimes diminished, strength is commonly assessed through observation of antigravity postures of the trunk and stability in movement patterns. Specific muscle testing is rarely necessary.

To supplement neuromuscular findings, a neurodevelopmental assessment may be conducted. This assessment should include two groups of automated responses as markers for motor dysfunction. The first group of automated responses to be evaluated is the primitive reflexes, which are whole patterns of movement that occur in response to a sensory stimulus (see Exhibit 4–1). These reflexes appear during the late gestational period, are present at birth, and, normally, are integrated into more mature and complex patterns in infancy. Delayed integration of these reflexes has an impact on dissociation between head and extremity movements and thus affects motor performance and coordination. Associated movements (synkinesis) are overflow reactions that are common in children and even in adults during difficult tasks, but an extreme overflow suggests difficulties with neurological maturation and affects coordination. Note that the presence of poorly integrated reflexes can be pronounced, as seen in cerebral palsy, or subtle, as seen in children with autism and other neurological disorders.

The second group of automated responses to be evaluated is the postural reactions. These reactions normally appear by six months of age, following integration of the primitive reflexes, and continue to develop through adult life. Righting, equilibrium, and protective reactions must be evaluated. The coordination of these reactions into functional balance is often observed during free play and the ability to use independent movements for skills.

Exhibit 4–1 A Sampling of Primitive Reflexes

- *Asymmetrical Tonic Neck Reflex (ATNR).* As the child turns his or her head to the side, the arm and leg on the side the child is looking toward tends to extend; the contralateral arm and leg tends to flex. Failure to integrate this reflex leads to difficulties in rolling, crawling, and fine motor skills such as feeding, bilateral hand skill, and writing.
- *Positive Supporting Reaction (PSR).* As the child is bounced or the balls of his or her feet come in contact with a firm surface, the legs extend. Failure to integrate this reflex leads to increased extension of the legs, which may interfere with walking—from preventing it altogether to slowing or diminishing coordination in gait.
- *Tonic Labyrinthine Response (TLR).* As the child changes body position, the muscle tone throughout the body fluctuates. In supine (lying on back), extension tone predominates. In prone (lying on stomach), flexion tone tends to predominate. Failure to integrate this reflex leads to delayed development of equilibrium reactions and diminished postural stability and, thus, delayed skill development.
- *Associated Reactions.* When doing a single movement, overflow of the movement is seen in other parts of the body. Often, for example, the tongue shows associated movements when doing fine motor skills, or it is difficult for the child to do a task with one hand without mirroring the motion in the other hand. The presence of associated movements interferes with skill development (oral-motor, visual tracking, fine and gross motor skills) and bilateral coordination.

Together, the tone, strength, reflex integration, and balance development of a child serve as the foundation for the development of stability and stable movement patterns. If a child is posturally unstable, he or she is likely to use compensatory movement patterns. For example, the child may use a wide base gait pattern or toe walk to increase the proprioceptive awareness in the lower extremities. She or he may also use a midguard posture (arms up) to stabilize the upper thoracic and cervical areas during movement. With postural instability may come insecurity with movement. This child may demonstrate gravitational insecurity and prefer to maintain ground during movement experiences, especially during movement that is imposed on him or her or movement he or she is not in control of (e.g., being pushed on a swing, lifted in the air, bounced on a mattress).

These neuromuscular and neurodevelopmental skills serve as the foundation from which skilled mobility and motor skill are built. Stability of proximal muscle groups is necessary for the development of mobility skills, especially fine hand coordination, gross motor skill development, articulation of sounds and other oral-motor skills, and smooth visual tracking. Deficits identified in basic neurodevelopmental domains likely affect the performance of many motor skills.

Other fundamental neurodevelopmental patterns include bilateral hand use and ability to cross the midline, dynamic and static sitting and standing balance, visual tracking and bilateral visual coordination, oral-motor abilities such as lip closure and tongue motions, ability to perform rapid alternating movements, tremors, and hand dominance. These are often assessed through structured clinical observations (Watling et al., 1999) and are explored in more depth in subsequent sections of this chapter.

Motor Performance

For the purpose of this section, assessment of motor function is divided into the three broad domains of gross, fine, and visual-motor development. These motor performance domains overlap considerably in that the common performance components just described (muscle tone, strength, reflex integration, coordination, etc.) serve as the foundation for skilled motor output. Reliance between these motor skill areas is also significant. For example, stability aspects of gross motor development are vital in fine motor performance because stability provides a solid foundation from which skilled upper-extremity usage is achieved. Both formal and structured observation assessment are described here. Some formalized instruments used to assess gross, fine, and visual-motor development are identified in Table 4–1.

When assessing any component of motor performance, not only are developmental milestones noted but also special attention is directed to the qualitative dimensions of the motor skill. Developmental milestones provide evidence of what the child can and cannot do. A major goal of the assessment should be to determine the source of an observed and documented delay—that is, why

Table 4–1 Standardized Assessment Instruments: Gross, Fine, Visual-Motor, and Handwriting Skill

Instrument	Author, Year	Ages	Domains Assessed

Peabody Developmental Motor Scales (PDMS)	Folio & Fewell, 1983	birth–83 months	Gross Motor:
			  Reflexes
			  Balance
			  Nonlocomotor skill
			  Locomotor skill
			  Receipt and propulsion of objects
			Fine Motor:
			  Grasping
			  Hand use
			  Eye-hand coordination
			  Manual dexterity

Toddler Infant Motor Evaluation (TIME)	Miller & Roid, 1994	birth–47 months	Mobility Motor organization Stability Functional performance Social/Emotional abilities

Bruininks-Oseretsky Test of Motor Proficiency	Bruininks, 1978	4.5–14.5 years	Gross Motor:
			  Running speed and agility
			  Balance
			  Bilateral coordination
			  Strength
			Upper Limb Coordination
			Fine Motor:
			  Response speed
			  Visual-Motor control
			  Upper-limb speed and dexterity

continues

Table 4–1 continued

Instrument	Author, Year	Ages	Domains Assessed
Test of Visual-Motor Skills—Revised	Gardner, 1995	3–13.11 years	Visual motor control for design copying items
Test of Visual-Motor Skills—Revised—Upper Limits	Gardner, 1992	12–40 years	Visual motor control for design copying items
Developmental Test of Visual-Motor Integration (VMI)	Beery & Butkenica, 1997	2–15 years	Visual motor control for design copying items
Minnesota Handwriting Assessment	Reisman, 1999	First and second graders	Rates five qualitative aspects—legibility, form, alignment, size, and spacing—of manuscript or D'Nealian handwriting

the skill is problematic (Watson & Marcus, 1988). Observations made regarding the qualitative aspects of motor control often pinpoint the area(s) of dysfunction and serve as the foundation for intervention planning. In addition to the value of direct observation of motor skill, observation of contextual aspects of motor skill enhances understanding of the source of developmental delays. Several questions can guide this observation process:

- Does the child perform motor tasks only in conjunction with sensory experiences?
- Does motor skill vary greatly depending on attention and motivation?
- Are motor skills performed only after demonstration by the evaluator?
- Is the child's developmental pattern uneven?
- What components of developmental skills are either absent or present to account for the uneven pattern?
- Does the child demonstrate splinter skill development within gross motor (e.g., climbing) or fine motor (e.g., constructional praxis, puzzle completion) tasks?

It is important to gather information and observations about these areas within the context of everyday natural environments. Change in environment alone or minor changes in the equipment used often affects performance of motor skill in individuals with an autism spectrum disorder.

Gross Motor Skill

Gross motor development refers to movements that require the use of large muscle groups. Ambulating, running, jumping, climbing, and ball play are all considered gross motor skills. In neurodevelopmental theory, as described in Chapter 1 and elsewhere, the mobility necessary for these locomotor skills is superimposed on stability. Consequently, the acquisition of these skills, and the quality with which they are performed, depends on the condition of the child's neuromuscular and neurodevelopmental status. Often, the neuromuscular status assessment is considered one component of the child's gross motor status. Accordingly, gross motor assessment includes both tests of developmental milestones and observations of the quality of the child's movement patterns. Balance and stability are measured and observed as the child performs a number of motor tasks. These observations of balance also apply to understanding the vestibular processing of a child, illustrating the link between sensory and motor responses.

Some investigations found that children with an autism spectrum disorder experience gross motor deficits. Postural and movement abnormalities and general clumsiness (DeMyer, 1976; Jones & Prior, 1985) and gait disturbances, including toe walking and arching of the trunk, were noted (Haas et al., 1996; Kohen-Raz et al., 1992; Vilensky et al., 1981). Motor difficulties, especially with ball play, were also reported in children with autism spectrum disorders (Miyahara et al., 1995; Watson & Marcus, 1988).

These gross motor areas are assessed within the context of play-based assessment or strictly through observation. Having a child go through a simple obstacle course, for instance, can provide a wealth of information regarding balance, strength, and postural control. Further, within many clinic settings or natural environments, children have the opportunity to explore through their environment. In doing so, they usually ambulate, run, jump, and climb steps. Situations can also be developed to observe catch and throw abilities. Report of functioning during higher-level bilateral motor tasks, such as riding a bike and swimming, are usually obtained from the caregiver. Throughout the evaluation, developmental milestones are assessed and the quality with which they are accomplished is observed and analyzed.

Fine Motor Skill

Fine motor development refers to movements that require precise or fine motor ac-

tions and require small muscles and more sensory feedback. Grasp of objects, writing, block play, cutting tasks, and dexterity while accomplishing clothing fasteners are all considered fine motor tasks. Some practitioners also include fine oral-motor and visual tracking as fine motor skills. When assessing fine motor skill, it is again important to note the impact of stability and postural awareness. Stable positioning during fine and visual-motor tasks enhances optimal performance, whereas instability diminishes fine coordination.

In the fine motor area, it is common for children with autism spectrum disorders to demonstrate peak skill in certain perceptual-motor activities at or above age level (Watson & Marcus, 1988). These peak skills usually include putting together puzzles, constructional praxis (block design), and disassembling and reassembling toys. Of greater difficulty, however, are perceptual-motor/visual-motor tasks involving tool use (e.g., writing, drawing, cutting).

As in most assessment, the foundations of a developmental skill area are assessed. Many of these foundation skills relating to fine motor task performance are assessed though structured observation, often in a play situation. Table 4–2 outlines the pertinent foundation areas and specific questions that guide these structured observations in fine motor assessment.

In conjunction with these observations, the evaluator can assess the functional application of these foundation skills. Here, the child is asked to engage in purposeful tasks as a means of identifying strengths, weaknesses, and developmental levels. If the child is unable to perform a motor task, it is important to try to ascertain why, as an inability to perform a motor task may stem from one or several limitations including lack of

Table 4–2 Structured Observations of Fine Motor Foundation Skills

Foundation Area	Specific Observations
Hand dominance	• Does the child demonstrate use of a dominant hand, mixed dominance, or no dominance at all? • If the child has mixed or no dominance, does he or she avoid crossing midline?
Grasp and prehension patterns	• Can the child isolate finger motions for prehension of smaller objects? • Does the quality of the child's grasp and prehension abilities differ when he is just manipulating an object, in comparison to manipulating a tool for use (e.g., hammer, pencil, ball)? • Does the child have adequate hand strength to hold onto objects?
Manipulation skill	• What is the quality of the child's in-hand manipulation skill? • Can the child transition objects in his or her hand utilizing transverse palmar (palm-to-finger and finger-to-palm) motions, or does he or she stabilize the object and regrasp?
Purposes of a child's interactions	• Does the child manipulate objects primarily for sensory gratification or for purposeful toy play?
Precision of interactions with objects	• Are tremors present? • Do the child's movements appear ataxic? • Does the child use too much pressure when holding objects? • Does the child have a hard time dampening his or her reach?
Task position and position of the child	• Does the child frequently shift his or her position while interacting with an object? • Does the child frequently turn or reposition a task? • If so, does he or she do either to avoid midline crossing or to position an object for visual inspection?
Coordination of visual tracking with motor efforts	• Does the child use peripheral vision, central vision, or accomplish tasks by feel? • Can the child follow moving objects with his or her eyes?

strength, deficient muscle control, dyspraxia, cognitive limitations, and motivation. Determining the reason for dysfunction allows for appropriate intervention planning.

Visual-Motor Control

There is much overlap between fine and visual-motor skill; often, they are considered one entity. *Visual-motor control* refers to the ability to coordinate visual information with motor output for visually guided movements. Appropriate visual-motor control is predicated on intact visual localization and tracking abilities. Visual-motor control is used to string beads, cut on a line, catch a ball, print within lines, and stay in the lines when coloring a picture. While perceptual-motor tasks that rely on spatial awareness (e.g., puzzles and formboards) usually represent a strength for children with autism spectrum disorders, many children have significant difficulty with tasks requiring visual-motor control (e.g., handwriting, cutting, catching a ball). Some individuals may demonstrate better abilities for design copying items in tests of visual-motor integration but have difficulty when relating these abilities to handwriting. Therefore, it is important to assess each area separately. Fundamental to assessment is the recurrent theme of pinpointing the source of breakdown in task performance. In the visual-motor domain, skills are dependent on adequate attention, visual perception, motor control, and motivation. Questions to ask when analyzing visual-motor performance deficits include:

- Is the child visually attending to the activity?
- Are visual-perceptual deficits affecting performance?
- Does the problem appear to relate more to visual processing or motor control?
- Is this a novel task?
- Does the child lack interest in the task?

Answers to these questions may provide a focus for additional evaluation and treatment decisions.

As can be seen by this discussion of assessment of motor performance, much overlap and interdependence exists among the domains of motor development. The ultimate goal of motor assessment is to identify the unique strengths and weaknesses of the individual with an autism spectrum disorder. Both formal and structured observation assessment determines this vital information. Once skill levels are identified, determining the etiology or source of the documented skill deficiencies provides the basis for program and intervention planning.

Sensory Processing

Sensory processing is a broad term that refers to the way in which the central and peripheral nervous systems manage incoming sensory information from the senses (Lane, Miller, & Hanft, 2000). It encompasses the reception, modulation, integration, discrimination, organization of sensory stimuli, and the behavioral responses to sensory input. Basically, sensory processing refers to the sequence of events that occur as we take in environmental stimulation and respond to it. Individuals with autism spectrum disorders have sensory processing impairments. In this discussion, we focus on dysfunctions of sensory modulation, praxis (motor planning), and some aspects of sensory discrimination. First, the pertinent literature in these areas is reviewed as it relates to individuals with an autism spectrum disorder; next, assessment in each domain is discussed.

Modulation

Sensory processing and *sensory integration* are terms that therapists often use synonymously. Sensory integration, however, is only one component of sensory processing, and refers to the process of combining sensory information from one's body and the environment in a manner that leads to adaptive responding (Lane, 2000; Lane et al., 2000). In this process, sensory information is detected and analyzed within the CNS leading to an appropriate behavioral response. For example, increased attention of the CNS is directed to novel stimuli, but familiar stimuli are less likely to be noticed. This process of continual regulation and organization of reactions to sensory input in a graded and adaptive manner is known as *sensory modulation* (Miller & McIntosh, 1998). Under normal conditions, within a typical nervous system, following modulation there is an adaptive response to the sensory input, which includes maintaining an optimal level of arousal. From this optimal arousal base, maximal performance and skilled occupations can be built.

When sensory modulation is inadequate, the individual has difficulty regulating and organizing sensory information to allow for adaptive responding. For example, attention may be directed to all sensory events in the environment; the individual does not filter out any of the input, which prevents him or her from focusing on the *relevant* sensory events. Problems in regulating and organizing the response to sensory information are described as Sensory Modulation Dysfunction (SMD) (Lane et al., 2000).

In SMD, an individual can demonstrate hyperresponsivity, hyporesponsivity, or fluctuating responsivity. In *hyperresponsivity*, the individual responds to incoming sensations to a greater extent than individuals with typical modulation. This response is caused by an atypical nervous system reaction (Miller & Lane, 2000). Hyperresponsivity may result in the individual responding defensively (autonomic nervous system fight-or-flight response) to a stimulus considered harmless or nonthreatening to most people. Because of this defensive avoidance, hyperresponsivity is also described as sensory defensiveness. Over time, learned patterns and habits develop around avoiding these disrupting sensory events or seeking other sensations that are calming and organizing. These patterns are natural attempts to self-regulate and maintain optimal levels of arousal (Wilbarger & Wilbarger, 1991) but may also result in improved learning in other domains.

Sensory defensiveness may affect all sensory systems. A person may have tactile defensiveness and have difficulty tolerating grooming and hygiene tasks, be bothered by touch of others, have texture preferences for foods and clothing, or avoid interacting with certain substances. An individual may also demonstrate auditory defensiveness and be bothered by loud or specific noises and, in response, cover his or her ears. Visually, an individual may be light sensitive or have difficulty attending to movement or other visual stimuli with central vision; consequently, he or she may visually attend predominately with peripheral vision. Intolerance or fearfulness of movement (gravitational insecurity), especially imposed movement, reflects impairments with modulating vestibular input.

In *hyporesponsivity*, the individual responds to incoming sensations to a lesser extent than individuals with typical modulation; this may result in diminished or delayed responds to sensory input from the environment. These difficulties are also called *sensory registration impairments* by some therapists. A child who is hyporesponsive may walk into objects, step on toys, and knock over a cup of water, then not respond or seem to notice these incidents. Individuals with a high pain tolerance are also thought to be hyporesponsive. Although some children who present with hyporesponsive modulation difficulties are passive, others appear very active or seek supplemental input in an attempt to self-regulate. Some of the stereotypies seen in autism may be the result of poor sensory modulation and may reflect attempts at self-modulation.

Individuals who demonstrate *fluctuating responsivity* present with rapidly shifting hyper- and hyporesponses to sensory input from the environment. This fluctuation prevents the individual from responding adaptively to input. A child with fluctuating responding may enter school in the morning upset and crying after riding the loud and bumpy bus (hyperresponding) but becomes underreponsive and even falls asleep once class starts. These children may have a narrow range of optimal responding.

Modulation impairments are widely reported in the literature describing the behavioral patterns and characteristics of individuals with autism (Adrien et al., 1987; Baranek, 1999; Dahlgren & Gillberg, 1989; Kientz & Dunn, 1997; Ornitz, 1989; Ornitz, Lane, Sugiyama, & de Traversay, 1993; Osterling & Dawson, 1994; Rapin, 1991) as well as by individuals with autism themselves (Cesaroni & Garber, 1991; Grandin, 1992; Williams, 1995). Some investigations noted differences specific to auditory processing, with hyperresponding (Bettison, 1994), hyporesponding (Baranek, 1999; Osterling & Dawson), and fluctuating responding (Rapin) exhibited by individuals. Sensory modulation as a self-regulatory mechanism also accounts some of the diminished eye contact in individuals with autism spectrum disorders (Dawson & Lew, 1989; Miller, 1996).

Other investigations addressed sensory modulation more broadly. Baranek (1999) utilized retrospective videotape analysis in children 9–12 months of age to determine if sensorimotor observations could be used in addition to social behaviors as early infant predictors of autism. Several behavioral items discriminated between children with autism ($n = 11$), children with developmental disabilities ($n = 10$), and typically developing children ($n = 11$). Poor visual attention, social touch aversion, excessive mouthing of objects, delayed response to name, and affect rating were found subtle yet salient predictors of autism at 9–12 months. Several of these items were also used in discriminate analysis to correctly identify the 11 children with autism.

Adrien and colleagues (1987) utilized a modified Behavior Observation Scale (Free-

man et al., 1979) to compare normal children, children who were mentally retarded, and children with autism and very low developmental age to determine the types of behavior that could differentiate these three diagnostic groups. Observations were made during a structured play session and the frequency of these behaviors were recorded. Although many behaviors overlapped among the groups, nine behaviors (rubbing surface, finger flicking, body rocking, repetitive jumping, decreased eye contact, limited or inappropriate social smiling and laughing, using object ritualistically, ignoring objects, and absent responding to stimuli) discriminated children with autism from both normal children and children with mental retardation. These behavioral patterns included subclusters of behavior that might be interpreted as disturbances of sensory modulation (e.g., hyporesponsivity with sensory seeking).

As can be seen, dysfunctions in sensory modulation are well documented in individuals with an autism spectrum disorder. These impairments limit adaptive responding and impact all aspects of daily living performance. Many of the behaviors noted as diagnostic features of autism may stem from a modulation dysfunction. Additionally, inadequate sensory modulation may interfere with the development of sensory discrimination for skills such as visual perception, tactile discrimination, auditory discrimination of speech sounds, and motor planning. Assessment for modulation disorders is presented following a discussion of praxis.

Praxis

Praxis is one result of intact sensory processing. *Praxis* refers to the planning and performance of a motor movement/task or series of motor movements/tasks. Because cognition and praxis are related concepts, the ability to motor plan must be considered in relationship to cognitive ability. If a person has limited cognitive ability, this diminishes his or her overall ability to plan and sequence motions. The ability to plan, sequence, and execute a movement depends on adequate sensory processing of visual, proprioceptive, vestibular, and tactile senses. Dysfunction in praxis is called *dyspraxia* and may cooccur with poor modulation (Lane et al., 2000). However, the diagnosis of dyspraxia requires that the person have the cognitive and motor abilities to perform the task. Thus, dyspraxia refers to disorders of sequencing and planning movement that are delayed or dysfunctional when compared to cognitive and basic motor ability.

Impairments in praxis are also reported in the literature describing the characteristics of individuals with an autism spectrum disorder (Filipek et al., 1999; Rapin, 1991). To this point, investigative studies of praxis focused on motor imitation of body movements, facial expressions, gestures, or motor tasks (Jones & Prior, 1985; Ohta, 1987; Rogers et al., 1996; Stone et al., 1990; Stone & Lemanek, 1990). When investigating motor imitation of hand and arm movements ($n = 11$, Jones & Prior; $n = 16$, Ohta), individuals with autism performed more poorly than cognitively matched controls and often responded only partially to modeled motor actions. Similar findings were noted in another study ($n = 17$; Rogers et al., 1996) assessing motor imitation across four conditions of hand and facial movements and for a pantomime task. The individuals with autism demonstrated deficits on one or more of the conditions in each of the three experimental tasks. Stone and colleagues (1990) conducted direct analysis of imitation abilities for 12 motor tasks in another study. Performance of 22 children with autism was compared to performance of groups of children with mental retardation ($n = 15$), hearing impairments ($n = 15$), and language impairments ($n = 19$), and children who were not disabled ($n = 20$). Imitation skills of the children with autism were significantly lower than those of the children in all the other groups. In this study, motor imitation ability was the most important characteristic differentiating the children with autism from the others. In yet another study (Stone & Lemanek, 1990), parent perceptions of imitation abilities were assessed. Parents of children with autism ($n = 20$) reported significantly less imitation of peers in play when compared to report of parents of children with mental retardation ($n = 14$). Interestingly, no differences were reported for adult imitation in these groups.

Research on Sensory Processing

Some studies investigated sensory processing as a whole (Ermer & Dunn, 1998; Kientz & Dunn, 1997; Tomchek, 1997). In two of these studies (Ermer & Dunn; Kientz & Dunn), the investigators utilized a sensory history, the Sensory Profile (Dunn, 1994, 1999; Dunn & Westman, 1997) in its development phase. The Sensory Profile was used to obtain information about sensory processing in eight categories: auditory, visual, taste/smell, movement, body position, touch, activity level, and emotional/social.

In an initial study, Kientz and Dunn (1997) used the Sensory Profile to determine whether it could discriminate between children with autism ($n = 32$) and without autism ($n = 64$) and which items best discriminated between the groups. They used item analysis to identify the distribution of responses in the groups and conducted multivariate analysis on each domain of the Sensory Profile to identify possible differences between subjects with mild or moderate autism and with severe autism, and those with or without autism. Although no significant between-group differences were noted when comparing the subgroups of children with varying degrees of autism, multivariate analysis did show that children with autism performed differently than children without autism on all categories of the Sensory Profile. Furthermore, 84 of the 99 items (85%) differentiated the sensory processing skills of subjects with autism from those without autism. These items were distributed throughout the categories of the Sensory Profile. Items with the greatest frequencies in the group of children with autism included:

- Is distracted or has trouble functioning if there is a lot of noise around.
- Enjoys strange noise/seeks to make noise for noise's sake.
- Has trouble staying between lines when coloring.
- Avoids eye contact.
- Shows preferences for certain tastes.
- Continually seeks out movement activities.
- Expresses discomfort during grooming.
- Is a picky eater.
- Has difficulty standing in line or close to other people.
- Is always on the go.
- Has difficulty paying attention.
- Needs more protection from life than other children.
- Has trouble "growing up."
- Has difficulty tolerating changes in plans and expectations.
- Is stubborn and uncooperative.
- Has poor frustration tolerance.
- Has difficulty making friends.

These items reflect not only some of the sensory modulation and praxis deficits in autism but also the social and behavior characteristics often utilized in differential diagnosis.

In a follow-up study, Ermer and Dunn (1998) wanted to determine which of the nine factors on the Sensory Profile best discriminate between children with autism or pervasive developmental disorder (PDD) ($n = 38$), children with attention deficit hyperactivity disorder (ADHD) ($n = 61$), and children without disabilities ($n = 1,075$). The results yielded two discriminant functions: one that differentiated children with disabilities from children without disabilities and another that differentiated the two groups with disabilities from one another. Nearly 90% of the cases were classified correctly using these two functions. Specific to children with autism/PDD, four of the nine factors were the best discriminators: sensory seeking, oral sensitivity, inattention/distractibility, and fine motor/perceptual, with a low incidence of behaviors reported within the sensory seeking factor and a high incidence of behaviors noted within the other factors. Based on the findings of this study, the authors concluded that the Sensory Profile is a useful discriminator of certain groups of children with disabilities. See Chapter 1 for additional discussion of these related studies.

In another investigation, sensory processing abilities were assessed in a cohort of children with autism or PDD-NOS ($n = 100$) who were involved in the Autism Project at the University of Louisville Child Evaluation Center (Tomchek, 1997). A 99-item sensory behavior checklist consisting of items compiled from other checklists were completed by the child's primary caregiver. The goal was to collect information regarding sensory processing within auditory, visual, gustatory, olfactory, tactile, and vestibular systems. A six-point Likert scale was used to determine the frequency of behaviors. Item analysis of all 99 behaviors was conducted, as was factor analysis, to identify clusters of behavior typical in this population. Correlation analyses were also conducted on a subgroup of 26 children with available Autism Diagnostic Interview—Research Version (ADI-R) (Lord, Rutter, & LeCouteur, 1994) results, to investigate whether relationships existed between behavior factors and diagnostic criteria. Item analysis results were largely inconclusive. Sensory processing behaviors in children in this sample with autism were either consistent with behaviors anecdotally reported in the literature or revealed behaviors consistent with typical children in another study (Dunn, 1994). Factor analysis for the group as a whole revealed five distinct factors: visual seeking, oral seeking, spatial awareness impairments, olfactory defensive, and auditory defensive. Correlation analysis between these factors and the ADI-R algorithm suggested that the sensory processing factors involving increased oral and visual seeking behavior and auditory defensiveness were inversely related to social skill development (lack of shared enjoyment and failure to develop peer relations) and unusual preoccupations.

Assessment of Sensory Processing

With a better understanding of the sensory processing abilities demonstrated by children with autism spectrum disorders as described in available research, we turn our attention to the assessment of these abilities and inabilities. Similar to sensorimotor assessment for an individual with an autism spectrum disorder, the process likely encompasses both formal and informal measures. Formally, a caregiver report measure such as the Sensory Profile (Dunn, 1999) or Sensory Integration Inventory—Revised (Reisman & Hanschu, 1992) is often used to gather information regarding sensory processing within daily life situations. These caregiver report measures usually utilize a Likert scale to reflect degrees of responsivity to a number of events with sensory components. The responses provide clinicians with an abundance of information about the child's responsivity within each sensory system (e.g., tactile, auditory, visual, vestibular, gustatory) as well as many behavioral/emotional variables. Visual analysis of these instruments is often utilized to summarize and interpret the caregiver report. The Sensory Profile (Dunn), however, allows for scoring and interpretation based on a standardization sample of more than 1,000 children. This information is categorized into three main categories, each with subskills: six domains of sensory processing (auditory, visual, vestibular, touch, multisensory, and oral), five domains of modulation (relating to endurance/tone, relating to body position and movement, of movement affecting activity level, of sensory input affecting emotional responses, and of visual input affecting emotional responses and activity level), and three domains of behavioral and emotional responding (behavioral/social responses, behavioral outcomes, and items indicating thresholds for response). Based on comparison to the standardization sample, a report of a child's sensory processing is classified as typical, as representing a probable difference from typical, or as representing a definite difference from typical.

Information obtained on the Sensory Profile is used in both differential diagnosis and intervention planning. Studies by Ermer and Dunn (1998) identified factors on the Sensory Profile that discriminated between specific diagnoses (PDD, ADHD, and nondisabled) with nearly 90% accuracy. With respect to intervention planning, both the individual processing domains and findings based on the factor analysis of the Sensory Profile are utilized. The separate sensory processing areas are often utilized initially to identify specific sensory processing deficits (e.g., tactile or vestibular processing) that will be the focus of intervention. Findings based on the factor analysis comparisons may also guide intervention; however, these findings address broader sensory processing difficulties, reflecting problems across a number of sensory systems. For example, a child may score high on the factors of poor registration, sensory seeking, and inattention/distractibility. Items from many of the sensory systems are reflected in these items. In treatment planning, for example, one component of the intervention program for this child may be to develop and implement a sensory diet in the classroom to enhance sensory modulation and minimize impulsivity and distractibility. Components of this sensory diet will likely reflect system-specific findings (e.g., while movement is calming to this child, touch excites him or her). Some scores on the Sensory Profile, especially modulation and behavioral and emotional responding, could provide outcome data for monitoring the effectiveness of the intervention program. Because these items are expressed as observable behavioral responses indicative of functional or dysfunctional sensory processing, they may be the target behaviors of intervention programs.

Structured clinical observations are made within the individual's natural environments and across a number of sensory experiences and events. Because environment alone, or its contents, can change how an individual responds to sensory input, these observations may support caregiver reports or provide contrasted information about the effects of an individual's sensory processing within each environment. It is important to note the environmental context in which the observations are made, and, therefore, it is important to observe and record sensory qualities such as the size of the space, light quality and type, fan/heat/air noise, temperature, visual stimulation, and smells in each environment (Kientz & Miller, 1999). These environmental conditions alone may affect an individual's ability to successfully accomplish a task/occupation. For instance, a child may become agitated when transitioning from classroom to classroom when many children are present because of the noise and bumping but tolerate the transition well when alone.

Because optimal arousal is a key to learning, it is important to describe changes in an individual's level of arousal and aspects of praxis as the tasks, environment, or media change. Table 4–3 provides a framework to guide structured observations of sensory modulation and praxis in individuals with autism spectrum disorders.

In addition to a caregiver report measure, an individual may also participate in another standardized measure of sensory processing/integration or discrimination such as the Test of Sensory Integration (DeGangi & Berk, 1983), the Sensory Integration and Praxis Tests (SIPT; Ayres, 1989), and the Touch Inventory for Elementary-School-Aged Children (Royeen & Fortune, 1990) to gather more specialized information. These instruments are usually reserved for individuals with better receptive language abilities in that they rely heavily on the individual's ability to understand directives. Refer to Table 4–4 for a listing of instruments that may be used to formally assess and gather information regarding sensory processing.

These formal assessments also include measures of sensory discrimination or perception. Each domain of sensory processing has a discrimination function in addition to

Table 4–3 Structured Observations of Sensory Modulation and Praxis

Observation Area	Pertinent Questions
Patterns of self-regulation within each environment	• What does the individual do to calm, arouse, and organize himself or herself? • What tasks or environments have a natural calming or arousing response? • Specifically, does the child seek movement, self-vocalize, mouth objects, rock, or flap his or her hands? • What tactile, auditory, visual, and vestibular events does he or she avoid?
Attention to task performance	• Does the child demonstrate sustained attention to certain tasks or tasks with a specific sensory component (e.g., visually stimulating or tactile tasks)? • How does incorporating sensory input into these tasks alter attention?
Changes in social behavior	• Does the child demonstrate differing degrees of joint attention, eye contact, or social referencing with changes in arousal?
Impact of the environment on praxis	• Does the change in equipment/media impair the individual's ability to or quality with which he or she completes the task? • In which environment does the individual best function? • What support or assistance (e.g., touch cues, visual supports, task demonstration) in that environment assists the individual most? • Can the individual imitate a demonstrated motor movement if there is no verbal component?
Quality of movement differences between familiar and novel tasks	• Are spontaneous/reflexive movements more fluid than movements on verbal command? • Does the child have difficulty with task initiation, completion, or both?

an alerting function. For example, in the tactile system, tactile discrimination includes the ability to localize touch, to discriminate aspects of touch (soft, dull, sharp, moving, two-point), to identify objects and shapes using touch, and to discriminate tactile forms (graphesthesia). Similarly, proprioception discrimination involves knowing static joint position or kinesthetic discrimination of direction, distance, and force of movement. Because of the sensory modulation disorders apparent in autism, little empirical research to date has documented these sensory discrimination abilities in children with autism. However, difficulties in sensory discrimination of touch to specific fingers, for example, are likely to be associated with fine motor manipulation difficulties, and poor kinesthetic awareness is likely to influence speed and control of writing and using computer technology. Structured clinical observations, such as finding an object using touch, can be utilized to assess sensory discrimination. Visual perception or discrimination is one specific domain included in a sensorimotor assessment for which several standardized assessments are available. Consequently, visual perception or discrimination is discussed separately in the following section.

Table 4–4 Formal Assessment Instruments of Sensory Processing

Instrument	Author, Year	Ages	Domains Assessed
DeGangi-Berk Test of Sensory Integration (TSI)	DeGangi and Berk, 1983	3–5 yrs	36 items measuring overall sensory integration as well as three clinically significant subdomains: postural control, bilateral motor integration, and reflex integration. These vestibular-based functions are essential to the development of motor skills, visual-spatial and language abilities, hand dominance, and motor planning.
Sensory Integration and Praxis Tests (SIPT)	Ayres, 1989	4–8.11 yrs	Measures visual, tactile, and kinesthetic perception as well as motor performance on 17 subtests: space visualization, figure-ground perception, standing/walking balance, design copying, postural praxis, bilateral motor coordination, praxis on verbal command, constructional praxis, postrotary nystagmus, motor accuracy, sequencing praxis, oral praxis, manual form perception, kinesthesia, finger identification, graphesthesia, and localization of tactile stimuli.
Sensorimotor Performance Analysis (SPA)	Richter & Montgomery, 1989	5–adult	Criterion-referenced assessment designed to provide a qualitative record of individual performance on gross and fine motor tasks. Found useful for clients with a variety of sensorimotor problems, including dysfunction in postural control and movement patterns.
Sensory Profile	Dunn, 1999	5–10 yrs	Standardized method for professionals to measure a child's sensory processing abilities and to profile the affect of sensory processing on functional performance. The profile consists of caregiver report of 125 items grouped into three main sections: sensory processing, modulation, and emotional responses. System and factor analysis information is available.

continues

Table 4–4 continued

Instrument	Author, Year	Ages	Domains Assessed
Sensory Integration Inventory— Revised	Reisman & Hanschu, 1992	14–adult	Screening instrument to identify individuals with developmental disabilities who might benefit from a sensory integrative treatment approach. The inventory consists of 111 items in four sections: touch, vestibular, proprioceptive, and general responses.
Touch Inventory for Elementary-School-Aged Children	Royeen & Fortune, 1990	6–12 yrs	26-item screening scale measuring tactile processing. Individual responses to questions are scored on a three-point Likert scale.

Assessment of Visual Perception

Visual perception is the ability to use visual information to recognize, recall, discriminate, and make meaning out of what we see. Visual-perceptual domains often evaluated include visual discrimination, visual memory, visual form constancy, visual-spatial relation, visual sequential memory, visual figure ground, and visual closure. Refer to Table 4–5 for a description of these domains. Together, these perceptual skills provide vital information that is utilized and relied on by many other systems for optimal functioning. For instance, when climbing stairs, much of the information used to coordinate stability and the motor skill to accommodate the rise in each step and the overall elevation of the flight of steps is derived from visual-perceptual processing.

The formalized assessment of visual-perceptual abilities as part of a sensorimotor assessment in autism is usually reserved for children of school age and older who have higher receptive language abilities and are able to comprehend the oral instructions inherent in these tests. Without receptive language abilities near the five-year level, testing is likely to be invalid because the in-structions may be too abstract or otherwise not comprehended. To maximize performance and obtain the most accurate assessment of the individual's perceptual domains, adaptation or simplification of oral instructions may be necessary. For instance, when giving directions for the visual-spatial relations areas, instead of instructing the child to "find the form that is going a different way" or to "find the form that is not the same as the others," use the simpler terms "wrong" and "different," which the child is more likely to understand. A request to find which one is wrong may produce improved performance. Because we are assessing perception and not receptive language abilities or vocabulary, making these adaptations allows for assessment of the focus area: visual perception. Refer to Table 4–6 for a listing of standardized instruments that may be used to assess these visual perceptual domains.

The instruments listed in Table 4–6 assess nonmotor visual perception in that they do not require motor coordination for the completion of testing. Instead, the child can select among the options by saying the letter that corresponds to his selection. Most children, however, point to their response.

Table 4–5 Description of Visual-Perceptual Domains

Perceptual Area	Description of Ability To:
Visual Discrimination	Differentiate common features in similar forms.
Visual Memory	Recall a stimulus form.
Visual Form Constancy	Discriminate a form even though its size, position, or color is altered.
Visual-Spatial Relations	Differentiate a form that has been rotated.
Visual Sequential Memory	Recall a sequence of forms in the order presented.
Visual Figure Ground	Differentiate a form from its background.
Visual Closure	Identify incomplete figures when only fragments are presented.

Clinical observations can be used to obtain some informal information about the perceptual abilities of children who cannot participate in formal testing. Situations can be devised to assess specific areas, or a child's work can be evaluated. For instance, having a child find a certain toy in a toybox can assess visual figure ground. Asking a child to find or select an item he or she was shown could be used to assess visual memory. Spatial relations difficulties can often be seen when asking a child to accomplish

Table 4–6 Standardized Assessment Instruments for Visual Perception

Instrument	Author, Year	Ages	Visual Domain Assessed
Motor-Free Visual Perception Test—Revised	Colarusso & Hammill, 1996	4–11 years	Discrimination Memory Spatial relations Figure ground Closure
Test of Visual-Perceptual Skills—Revised	Gardner, 1996	4–12.11 years	Discrimination Memory Form constancy Spatial relations Sequential memory, visual Figure-ground Closure
Test of Visual-Perceptual Skills, Upper Limits	Gardner, 1997	12–18 years	Discrimination Memory Form constancy Spatial relations Sequential memory Figure-ground Closure

writing tasks because drawings, letters, and words may be rotated.

Deficits in these perceptual abilities may impact many areas of development, including fine and visual-motor development, reading, and performance of many skills. The information taken in visually guides our ability to reach to an object and the act of grasping that object. During writing tasks, visual information is utilized for spacing, alignment, and formation of all drawings and letters. When deficits in these areas, or in any area that relies heavily on visual input for coordination, are detected, visual-perceptual differences need to be identified through formal or informal testing and included in an intervention plan.

Together, these formal and structured observation measures of sensory processing provide the basis for program and intervention planning. Sensory processing deficits are the primary focus of treatment reported by occupational therapists working with individuals with autism spectrum disorders (Case-Smith & Miller, 1999; Watling et al., 1999). Therapists utilize sensory integrative, sensorimotor approaches, and environmental modification to promote appropriate sensory modulation. Adequate sensory modulation may allow the individual to demonstrate the optimal arousal from which skilled occupations and learning are developed.

Functional and Adaptive Performance

Once the above domains are addressed, how do the findings relate to the individual's functional performance within daily occupations? Ultimately, if deficit areas are noted, yet they do not impair function, services may not be warranted. Depending on the age of the individual being assessed, any number of occupations may need to be assessed. Typically, in childhood and early adolescence, an individual's occupations include performance in play, at school, and for adaptive living and self-help tasks.

Play and Play-Based Assessment

Play is a child's main occupation. Children with an autism spectrum disorder often have a limited play repertoire and, therefore, play needs special attention as part of a sensorimotor assessment (Filipek et al., 1999; Kientz & Miller, 1999; Stone et al., 1990). A child's play skills may vary considerably depending on the surrounding environment and others present in that environment. Therefore, it is ideal to observe play both indoors and outdoors and in both free and structured play situations (Kientz & Miller). Observations should also be recorded regarding how independent play and play with peers differ. These observations should describe situations in which the child interacts with or imitates others. Does the child take turns? How does the child react to other children entering his or her play? Does she or he rely on adult interaction and supervision to guide her or his play? Observations should also be made regarding how much structure and routine the child requires for interaction. Can the child only initiate interaction during play once a routine is established? How does the child react when that routine is changed?

The child's ability to initiate play, to explore many toys, and to play with one toy for a length of time should also be monitored. With these noted, judgments can be made about what motivates the child to play and what kind of play he or she seeks out. Play with objects may be primitive and lack purpose. For instance, a child may not play with a car by pushing it along. Instead, he or she may turn the car over and repetitively spin the wheels. A common form of play in young children with autism is to line objects in rows or sort them (Rapin, 1991; Reber, 1992). In one study (Stone et al., 1990), children with autism spent less total time interacting with toys and using toys appropriately and engaged in fewer functional play acts than all comparison groups of children with mental retardation, hearing impairment, language impairment, or nonhandicapped children. An absence of creative and imaginary play may also be noted. Although children with autism may feed a baby or comb its hair, their pretend play may be repetitive, without a natural evolution into more elaborate scenarios seen in typical same-age peers.

The above observations not only describe a child's play skills but also provide insight into the social, motor, and sensory processing functioning of a child. This information allows for better understanding of a child's motivation to participate in testing and his or her apparent learning style. This understanding can guide the assessment and therapeutic process. Refer to Chapter 7 for a full discussion of play and play assessment in individuals with an autism spectrum disorder.

School and Academic Performance

In children between the ages of two years nine months and five years eight months, the Miller Assessment for Preschoolers (MAP; Miller, 1989) may be used to assess preacademic skills in subjects. The MAP is a standardized screening designed to identify preschool children likely to experience later school-related problems. Its intended use is with children who exhibit mild to moderate preacademic problems but do not have obvious or severe problems. Its use with children with autism spectrum disorders is likely limited to children with better receptive language abilities in that many of the orally given directives are long and complex. As in any formal assessment, however, items from the MAP may be adapted to provide documentation of strengths and weaknesses while recognizing the violation of test standardization.

The MAP evaluates the skills of motor coordination (gross, fine, and oral-motor), verbal language, memory, problem solving, and visual perception. It is widely used with the preschool population and is considered both reliable and valid (Miller, 1982, 1987, 1988). Initial predictive validity studies found MAP scores predictive of school-related behaviors (Cohn, 1986; Lemerand, 1985; Miller, 1986; Miller, Lemerand, & Cohn, 1987; Miller & Schouten, 1988).

The core test consists of 27 items within five performance indices: foundations (basic motor tasks and sensations), coordination (gross, fine, and oral-motor), verbal (language skills), nonverbal (reasoning skills), and complex tasks (combined abilities). A supplemental behavior-during-testing form is a structured mechanism for recording observational data regarding attention, sensory processing, and general behavior. In addition to subtest scores, a total score is obtained that reflects a composite of the index scores. Scores are reported as percentile ranks based on the standardization sample. The child's obtained score can fall into one of three percentile ranges: 0–5%, indicating high risk and warranting referral; 6–25%, indicating possible risk and warranting tracking of the child; and ≥26%, indicating developmentally average performance and no need for further services.

In early-school-aged children, the School Function Assessment (SFA; Coster, Deeney, Haltiwanger, & Haley, 1998) can be used to measure a student's performance of functional tasks that support his or her participation in the academic and social aspects of an elementary school program (K–6). The SFA is a judgment-based assessment that is completed by one or more school professionals who know the student and his or her participation in the academic program well.

The SFA consists of three parts. Part I (participation) is used to examine the student's level of participation in six major activity settings: regular or special education classroom, playground or recess, transportation to and from school, bathroom and toileting activities, transitions to and from class, and mealtime or snack time. Part II (task supports) is used to examine the supports currently provided to the student when he or she performs school-related tasks. Both direct assistance and adaptations are examined separately. Part III (activity performance) is used to examine the student's performance of specific school-related activities. Likert scale scoring is used for individual items within these parts. Criterion scores are obtained and compared to criterion cutoff scores to determine if a child's performance is below that of typically performing peers. Items are written in measurable, behavioral terms that can easily be transferred to the student's Individualized Educational Program (IEP).

Self-Help and Adaptive Living

The child's self-help and adaptive living status are vital domains of emphasis specifically addressed during the assessment process. Several independence measures are available to assess these skills. The Vineland Adaptive Behavior Scales (VABS; Sparrow, Balla, & Cicchetti, 1984) are frequently used as a measure of communication, daily living, socialization, and motor skill. These domains, as well as a cognitive domain, also can be measured utilizing the Battelle Developmental Inventory (BDI; Newborg, Stock, & Wnek, 1984). Similarly, independence levels within physical, self-help, social, academic, and communication domains can be obtained utilizing the Developmental Profile II (DPII; Alpren, Boll, & Shearer, 1984). The Wee Functional Independence Measure (WeeFIM; Uniform Data Systems, 1993) can also be used to assess independence in self-care, sphincter control, transfer, locomotion, communication, and social cognition skill domains. The Pediatric Evaluation of Disability Inventory (PEDI; Haley, Coster, Ludlow, Haltiwanger, & Andrellos, 1992) is a unique assessment of adaptive self-care functioning (ages 0–4½ years) in the domains of self-care, mobility, and socialization because it contains three separate scales of functional skills, caregiver assistance, and modifications. This scoring reflects both the caregiver burden and the use of modifications that promote function (e.g., weighted cup or specialized spoon) that would otherwise require caregiver assistance. All of these self-care assessments are completed primarily as parent report measures.

The VABS has been used in at least one longitudinal study (Freeman, Del'Home, Guthrie, & Zhang, 1999) involving individuals with autism spectrum disorders ($n = 440$) to examine how scores change as a function of age, utilizing human growth modeling statistical techniques. Specifically, the major goal of statistical analysis was to examine the change in VABS scores within the communication, daily living, and social domains as a function of age, and to assess the effect of initial IQ on the change in VABS scores. Results indicated that the natural course of autism is one of improvement over time. Furthermore, whereas individual growth curves for communication and daily living skills were related to initial IQ, improvement of social skills was independent of initial IQ scores.

SPECIALIZED INSTRUMENTS FOR INDIVIDUALS WITH AUTISM WITH A SENSORIMOTOR COMPONENT

The Childhood Autism Rating Scale

The Childhood Autism Rating Scale (CARS; Schopler, Reichler, & Renner, 1988) is a 15-item behavioral rating scale developed to identify children over the age of 24 months with autism, and to distinguish them from developmentally disabled children without autism. Each of the items uses a seven-point rating scale to indicate the degree to which the child's behavior deviates from an age-appropriate norm. At least 11 of the 15 items reflect some degree of sensorimotor functioning in children, including relating to people; imitation; emotional response; body use; object use; adaptation to change; visual response; listening response; taste, smell, and touch response and use; fear or nervousness; and activity level. Other items cover verbal communication, nonverbal communication, level and consistency of intellectual response, and general impressions. Ratings can be made based on observations during developmental testing, classroom participation, parent report, or history.

A diagnostic categorization system was established based on comparison of CARS scores with the corresponding expert clinical assessments of more than 1,500 children. This scoring system allows children to be categorized into one of three categories: nonautistic, mildly to moderately autistic, or severely autistic.

The CARS is widely recognized and used as a reliable instrument for the diagnosis of autism (Filipek et al., 1999). Its authors emphasize that classification using the CARS is not intended as an endpoint in assessment. Instead, it is intended to be the first step in diagnosis and the beginning of the individualized assessment process needed for understanding the unique aspects of a child's problems (Schopler et al., 1988). Many of the areas requiring further assessment fall into the sensorimotor domain.

The Screening Tool for Autism in Two-Year-Olds

The Screening Tool for Autism in Two-Year-Olds (STAT; Stone & Ousley, 1997) is an interactive measure designed to differentiate autism from other developmental disorders in children 24 to 35 months. A 20-minute semistructured play interaction involving 12 activities provides the mechanism to examine play (both pretend and reciprocal social play), motor imitation, and nonverbal communicative development (joint attention, directing attention to objects or events of interest). The tasks used on the STAT best differentiated between children with autism and those with other developmental disorders in studies of matched groups of two-year-olds (see Stone et al., 1990; Stone & Lemanek, 1990). Scoring is directed toward success or failure within each of the three domains and provides for classification as autistic or nonautistic.

The STAT is currently in development but demonstrated strong sensitivity and specificity in a pilot study involving 40 children. In that study (Stone, 1998), the STAT correctly classified 100% of children with autism ($n = 8$) and 97% of children with other developmental delays ($n = 32$), using a criterion of failure on two of the three domains. Current work on the tool is focused on the empirical determination of best cutoffs and algorithm scoring (Filipek et al., 1999).

Ritvo-Freeman Real-Life Rating Scale

Unlike the CARS and STAT, the Ritvo-Freeman Real-Life Rating Scale (RLRS; Freeman, Ritvo, Yokota, & Ritvo, 1986) is not a diagnostic instrument. Instead, it is designed to evaluate the effects of specific treatments on symptomatic behaviors in patients with autism. The instrument contains 47 specific behaviors grouped into five domains or scales: sensorimotor behaviors (stereotypies), social relationship to people (response to interaction attempts, activities; and events in the environment, disturbance of others, change of activities, genital manipulation, isolation of self, response to hugs), affectual reactions (abrupt change, grimaces, temper outbursts, cries, other), sensory responses (sensory processing behavior), and language (verbal and nonverbal).

To evaluate treatment effects, the child is observed using the scale in the same setting, at the same time of day, and on the same day of the week, for 30 minutes. The specific behaviors are coded using a four-point Likert scale reflecting the frequency of behaviors. Mean scores are determined for each scale following a mathematical sign correction to subtract normal behavior items. Visual analysis of a graph is then used to compare baseline and subsequent time periods.

The RLRS has a heavy sensorimotor component (over half of the 47 items). Its easy scoring and limited time requirements lend itself well to the collection of longitudinal data within a school or preschool setting.

The Psychoeducational Profile—Revised

The Psychoeducational Profile—Revised (PEP-R; Schopler, Reichler, Bashford, Lansing, & Marcus, 1990) is an inventory of behaviors and skills designed to identify uneven and idiosyncratic learning patterns in children with autism or related developmental disorders. The test is most appropriately used with children functioning at or below the preschool range and within the chronological age range of 6 months to 7 years; however, useful information can be obtained on children between 7 and 12 years of age if some of their developmental skills are at or below the first-grade level.

The PEP-R provides information on the developmental functioning of a child within seven domains: imitation, perception, fine motor, gross motor, eye-hand integration, cognitive performance, and cognitive verbal.

Skills in these domains are measured by 131 developmental items. The PEP-R also identifies degrees of behavioral abnormality in four domains: relating and affect, play and interest in materials, sensory responses, and language.

The PEP-R kit consists of a set of toys and learning materials that are presented to the child in structured play activities. The examiner observes, evaluates, and records the child's responses during the assessment. Scores (pass, fail, or emerging) are distributed among the developmental and behavioral domains. The resulting profiles depict a child's relative strengths and weaknesses in domains of development and behavior.

This inventory is designed as an educational tool for planning individualized special educational programs. The developmental profiles of children with autism spectrum disorders are characteristically uneven, with passing and emerging scores widely fluctuating among the developmental domains. By identifying developmental age levels in various domains, the PEP-R indicates sensible directions for an individualized curriculum (Schopler et al., 1990). Change over time can be tracked by retesting annually and comparing changes from emerging to passing scores for each domain as well as changes in developmental ages of the child.

USE OF ASSESSMENT DATA FOR PROGRAM AND INTERVENTION PLANNING

As can be seen by the previous discussion, the sensorimotor assessment of individuals with autism spectrum disorders is multifaceted. Therefore, the identified strengths and weaknesses of the individual are also likely to be diverse. The assessment process is not complete, however, until all of these fragments of identified strengths and weaknesses are integrated to provide a clear and holistic description of the individual with an autism spectrum disorder.

In best practice, this integration should be done at least two times, ideally as part of an ongoing program of treatment. Initially, the therapist integrates the information to obtain a clear understanding of the individual with an autism spectrum disorder. Secondly, integrating the sensorimotor information with that obtained by other team members provides a full picture of the individual. Identified strengths can be used to address the noted deficit areas, and thus provide the link between testing and the development of programs and interventions grounded in the uniqueness of an individual child or adolescent (Nelson, 1982). Much of the rest of this book focuses directly on the development and implementation of specific intervention programs for noted sensorimotor deficits. Vital to this process is the completion of a thorough and accurate sensorimotor assessment.

CONCLUSION

Consensus that the autism spectrum disorders are neurobiological in nature is almost total. These neurobiological underpinnings may be the foundation for the sensorimotor impairments widely reported in the literature describing individuals with autism spectrum disorders. Postural and movement abnormalities, general clumsiness, and gait disturbances are reported, as is difficulty with functional application of fine and visual-motor skill abilities. While some investigations broadly identified impairments in sensory processing, others defined more specialized skill impairments for motor planning/praxis, motor imitation abilities, and repetitive motor stereotypies.

Given these performance impairments, a comprehensive assessment of sensorimotor functions, utilizing formalized and structured observation assessments, is imperative to the diagnostic and treatment planning process. Because stability is the foundation on which skilled mobility and motor skill are built, the individual's neurodevelopmental status is initially assessed, followed by assessment of its impact on motor performance (gross, fine, and visual-motor). Visual-perceptual abilities are also assessed. Assessment of sensory processing focuses on sensory modulation abilities and praxis. If deficits are noted, assessment of their impact on functional performance becomes an integral part of the evaluation process. Throughout this assessment, qualitative aspects of behavior, play, and social interaction are noted.

Clearly, the sensorimotor assessment of individuals with autism spectrum disorders is diverse. Therefore, the identified strengths and weaknesses of the individual are also likely to be diverse. Integration of these findings with the findings of other team members allows for individualized program and intervention planning designed to improve noted deficits by utilizing areas of strength. An occupational therapist's expertise in activity analysis and adaptation is vital to this process.

CHAPTER REVIEW QUESTIONS

1. What is the role of the occupational therapist in a multidisciplinary evaluation of persons with autism? How does the sensorimotor assessment complement the evaluation results from other disciplines?

2. Why is a sensorimotor assessment an important component of a comprehensive assessment of children with autism?

3. Describe the process of observing behaviors and interpreting these to analyze the sensory needs and responses of a child with autism.

4. Why is structured observation often used to assess the strengths and weaknesses of children with autism?

5. When assessing domains of motor performance, what structured observations will contribute to understanding patterns of stability and mobility, skill level, and tool use?

6. Give at least one example of hyperresponsivity, hyporesponsivity, and fluctuating responsivity to tactile, auditory, vestibular, and visual stimuli.

7. What is praxis and how is it recognized?

8. Describe the possible effects on self-care and school performance of the following sensorimotor impairments: tactile hyperresponsivity, visual-motor dysfunction, praxis, vestibular sensory seeking, poor visual tracking, and postural instability.

9. Plan a comprehensive sensorimotor assessment for a child you know, or a case study, based on the information presented in this chapter.

REFERENCES

Adrien, J. L., Ornitz, E., Barthelemy, C., Sauvage, D., & Lelord, G. (1987). The presence or absence of certain behaviors associated with infantile autism in severely retarded autistic and nonautistic retarded children and very young normal children. *Journal of Autism and Developmental Disorders, 17,* 407–416.

Alpren, G. D., Boll, T. J., & Shearer, M. S. (1984). *Developmental Profile II.* Los Angeles: Western Psychological Services.

American Psychological Association (1994). *Diagnostic and statistical manual of mental disorders* (4th ed.). Washington, DC: Author.

Ayres, A. J. (1989). *Sensory Integration and Praxis Tests.* Los Angeles: Western Psychological Services.

Baranek, G. T. (1999). Autism during infancy: A retrospective video analysis of sensory-motor and social behaviors at 9–12 months of age. *Journal of Autism and Developmental Disorders, 29,* 213–224.

Bauman, M. L., & Kemper, T. L. (1994). Neuroanatomic observations of the brain in autism. In M. L. Bauman & T. L. Kemper (Eds.), *The neurobiology of autism* (pp. 119–145). Baltimore: Johns Hopkins University Press.

Beery, K. E., & Butkenica, N. A. (1997). *Developmental Test of Visual Motor Integration: Administration and scoring manual.* Parsippany, NJ: Modern Curriculum Press.

Bettison, S. (1994). Auditory training as a treatment for sound sensitivity in autism: Preliminary results. *Special Education Perspectives, 3*(1).

Bruininks, R. H. (1978). *Bruininks-Oseretsky Test of Motor Proficiency examiner's manual.* Circle Pines, MN: American Guidance Service.

Case-Smith, J., & Miller, H. (1999). Occupational therapy with children with pervasive developmental disorder. *American Journal of Occupational Therapy, 53,* 506–513.

Cesaroni, L., & Garber, M. (1991). Exploring the experience of autism through firsthand accounts. *Journal of Autism and Developmental Disorders, 21,* 303–313.

Cohn, S. A. (1986). *An analysis of the predictive validity of the Miller Assessment for Preschoolers in a suburban public school district.* Unpublished doctoral dissertation, University of Denver, CO.

Colarusso, R. P., & Hammill, D. D. (1996). *Motor-Free Visual Perception Test—Revised manual.* Novato, CA: Academic Therapy Publications.

Coleman, M., & Gillberg, C. (1985). *The biology of the autistic syndromes.* New York: Praeger.

Cook, D. (1990). A sensory approach to the treatment and management of children with autism. *Focus on Autistic Behavior, 5,* 1–19.

Cook, D. (1991). The assessment process. In W. Dunn (Ed.), *Pediatric occupational therapy: Facilitating effective service provision* (pp. 35–72). Thorofare, NJ: Slack.

Coster, W., Deeney, T., Haltiwanger, J., & Haley, S. (1998). *School Function Assessment user's manual.* San Antonio, TX: Psychological Corporation.

Dahlgren, S. O., & Gillberg, C. (1989). Symptoms in the first two years of life: A preliminary population study of infantile autism. *European Archives of Psychology and Neurological Sciences, 238,* 169–174.

Dawson, G., & Lew, A. (1989). Arousal, attention, and socioeconomical impairments of individuals with autism. In G. Dawson (Ed.), *Autism: Nature, diagnosis, and treatment* (pp. 49–74). New York: Guilford Press.

DeGangi, G. A., & Berk, R. A. (1983). *DeGangi-Berk Test of Sensory Integration.* Los Angeles: Western Psychological Services.

DeMyer, M. K. (1976). Motor, perceptual-motor, and intellectual disabilities in autistic children. In L. Wing (Ed.), *Early childhood autism* (2nd ed.). Elmsford, NY: Pergamon.

Dunn, W. (1994). Performance of typical children on the sensory profile: An item analysis. *American Journal of Occupational Therapy, 48,* 967–974.

Dunn, W. (1999). *The Sensory Profile: User's manual.* San Antonio, TX: Psychological Corporation.

Dunn, W., & Westman, K. (1997). The Sensory Profile: Performance from a national sample of children without disabilities. *American Journal of Occupational Therapy, 51,* 25–34.

Elliott, C. D. (1990). *Differential Abilities Scale (DAS).* New York: Psychological Corporation.

Ermer, J., & Dunn, W. (1998). The Sensory Profile: A discriminant analysis of children with and without disabilities. *American Journal of Occupational Therapy, 52,* 283–290.

Filipek, P. A., Accardo, P. J., Baranek, G. T., Cook, E. H., Jr., Dawson, G., & Gordon, B. (1999). The screening and diagnosis of autistic spectrum disorders. *Journal of Autism and Developmental Disorders, 29,* 439–484.

Folio, M. R., & Fewell, R. R. (1983). *Peabody Developmental Motor Scales and activity cards manual.* Chicago: Riverside.

Freeman, B. J., Del'Home, M., Guthrie, D., & Zhang, F. (1999). Vineland Adaptive Behavior Scale scores as a function of age and initial IQ in 210 autistic children. *Journal of Autism and Developmental Disorders, 29,* 379–384.

Freeman, B. J., Guthrie, D., Ritvo, E. R., Schroth, P., Glass, R., & Frankel, F. (1979). Behavior observation scale: Preliminary analysis of the similarities and differences between autistic and mentally retarded children. *Psychological Reports, 44,* 519–524.

Freeman, B. J., Ritvo, E. R., Yokota, A., & Ritvo, A. (1986). A scale for rating symptoms of patients with the syndrome of autism in real-life settings. *Journal of the American Academy of Child Psychiatry, 25,* 130–136.

Gardner, M. F. (1992). *Test of Visual-Motor Skills—Revised Upper Limits manual.* Los Angeles: Western Psychological Services.

Gardner, M. F. (1995). *Test of Visual-Motor Skills—Revised manual.* Los Angeles: Western Psychological Services.

Gardner, M. F. (1996). *Test of Visual-Perceptual Skills—Revised (nonmotor) manual.* Los Angeles: Western Psychological Services.

Gardner, M. F. (1997). *Test of Visual-Perceptual Skills Upper Limits (nonmotor) manual.* Los Angeles: Western Psychological Services.

Gillberg, C. (1990). Autism and pervasive developmental disorders. *Journal of Child Psychology and Psychiatry, 31,* 99–119.

Gillberg, C., & Coleman, M. (1996). Autism and medical disorders: A review of literature. *Developmental Medicine and Child Neurology, 38,* 191–202.

Grandin, T. (1992). An inside view of autism. In E. Schopler & G. B. Mesibov (Eds.), *High-functioning individuals with autism* (pp. 105–126). New York: Plenum.

Greenspan, S. I., & Wieder, S. (1999). A functional developmental approach to autism spectrum disorders. *Journal of the Association for Persons with Severe Handicaps, 24,* 147–161.

Haas, R. H., Townsend, J., Courchesne, E., Lincoln, A. J., Schreibman, L., & Yeung-Courchesne, R. (1996). Neurological abnormalities in infantile autism. *Journal of Child Neurology, 11,* 84–92.

Haley, S., Coster, W., Ludlow, L. H., Haltiwanger, J. T., & Andrellos, P. J. (1992). *Pediatric Evaluation of Disability Inventory.* Boston: Department of Rehabilitation Medicine, New England Medical Center Hospital.

Howlin, P., & Rutter, M. (1987). *Treatment of autistic children.* New York: John Wiley & Sons.

Huebner, R. A. (1992). Autistic disorder: A neuropsychological enigma. *American Journal of Occupational Therapy, 46,* 487–501.

Jones, V., & Prior, M. (1985). Motor imitation abilities and neurological signs in autistic children. *Journal of Autism and Developmental Disorders, 15*, 37–46.

Kientz, M. A., & Dunn, W. (1997). A comparison of the performance of children with and without autism on the Sensory Profile. *American Journal of Occupational Therapy, 51*, 530–537.

Kientz, M. A., & Miller, H. (1999, March). Classroom evaluation of the child with autism. *School System Special Interest Section Quarterly, 6*, 1–4.

Kohen-Raz, R., Volkmar, F. R., & Cohen, D. J. (1992). Postural control in children with autism. *Journal of Autism and Developmental Disorders, 22*, 419–432.

Lane, S. J. (2000). Sensory modulation disorders. Manuscript in preparation.

Lane, S. J., Miller, L. J., & Hanft, B. (2000). Toward a consensus in terminology in sensory integration theory and practice. Part Two—Sensory integration: Patterns of function and dysfunction. Manuscript in press.

Leary, M., & Hill, D. (1996). Moving on: Autism and movement disturbance. *Mental Retardation, 34*, 39–53.

Lemerand, P. A. (1985). *Predictive validity of the Miller Assessment for Preschoolers.* Unpublished doctoral dissertation, University of Michigan, Ann Arbor.

Lord, C. (1991). Methods and measures of behavior in the diagnosis of autism and related disorders. *Psychiatric Clinics of North America, 14*, 69–80.

Lord, C. (1995). Follow-up of two-year-olds referred for possible autism. *Journal of Child Psychology and Psychiatry, 36*, 1365–1382.

Lord, C., Rutter, M., & LeCouteur, A. (1994). Autism Diagnostic Interview—Revised: a revised version of a diagnostic interview for caregivers of individuals with possible pervasive developmental disorders. *Journal of Autism and Developmental Disorders, 24*, 659–685.

Losche, G. (1990). Sensorimotor and action development in autistic children from infancy to early childhood. *Journal of Child Psychology and Psychiatry, 31*, 749–761.

Miller, H. (1996, June). Eye contact and gaze aversion: Implications for persons with autism. *Sensory Integration Special Interest Section Quarterly, 19*, 1–3.

Miller, L. J. (1982). *Miller Assessment for Preschoolers.* Littleton, CO: Foundation for Knowledge in Development.

Miller, L. J. (1986). *The predictive validity of the Miller Assessment for Preschoolers.* Unpublished doctoral dissertation, University of Denver, CO.

Miller, L. J. (1987). Longitudinal validity of the Miller Assessment for Preschooler: Study 1. *Perceptual and Motor Skills, 65*, 211–217.

Miller, L. J. (1988). Longitudinal validity of the Miller Assessment for Preschooler: Study 2. *Perceptual and Motor Skills, 66*, 811–814.

Miller, L. J. (1989). *Miller Assessment for Preschoolers—Revised edition.* San Antonio, TX: Psychological Corporation.

Miller, L. J., & Lane, S. J. (2000). Toward a consensus in terminology in sensory integration theory and practice. Part 1—taxonomy of neurophysiological processes. *Sensory Integration Special Interest Section Quarterly, 23*(1), 1–4.

Miller, L. J., Lemerand, P. A., & Cohn, S. H. (1987). A summary of three predictive studies with the MAP. *Occupational Therapy Journal of Research, 7*, 378–381.

Miller, L. J., & McIntosh, D. (1998). The diagnosis, treatment, and etiology of sensory modulation disorder. *Sensory Integration Special Interest Section Quarterly, 21*, 1–3.

Miller, L. J., & Roid, G. H. (1994). *The T.I.M.E.: Toddler and Infant Motor Evaluation.* Tucson, AZ: Therapy Skill Builders.

Miller, L. J., & Schouten, P. G. W. (1988). Age-related effects on the predictive validity of the Miller Assessment for Preschoolers. *Journal of Psychoeducational Assessment, 6*, 99–106.

Minshew, N. J., Sweeney, J. A., & Bauman, M. L. (1997). Neurologic aspects of autism. In D. J. Cohen & F. R. Volkmar (Eds.), *Handbook of autism and pervasive developmental disorders* (2nd ed.) (pp. 344–369). New York: John Wiley & Sons.

Miyahara, M., Tsujii, M., Hori, M., Nakanishi, K., Kageyama, H., & Sugiyama, T. (1995). Brief report: Motor incoordination in children with Asperger Syndrome and learning disabilities. *Journal of Autism and Developmental Disorders, 27*, 595–603.

Murray, E. A., & Anzalone, M. E. (1991). Integrating sensory integration theory and practice with other approaches. In A. G. Fisher, E. A. Murray, & A. C. Bundy (Eds.), *Sensory integration theory and practice* (pp. 354–383). Philadelphia: F.A. Davis.

Nelson, D. L. (1982). Evaluating autistic clients. *Occupational Therapy in Mental Health, 1*, 1–22.

Newborg, J., Stock, J. R., & Wnek, L. (1984). *Battelle Developmental Inventory examiner's manual.* Allen, TX: DLM Teaching Resources.

Ohta, M. (1987). Cognitive disorders of infantile autism: A study employing the WISC, spatial relationship conceptualization, and gesture imitations. *Journal of Autism and Developmental Disorders, 17,* 45–62.

Ornitz, E. M. (1985). Neuropsychology of infantile autism. *Journal of the American Academy of Child and Adolescent Psychiatry, 24,* 251–262.

Ornitz, E. M. (1989). Autism at the interface between sensory and information processing. In G. Dawson (Ed.), *Autism: Nature, diagnosis, and treatment.* New York: Guilford Press.

Ornitz, E. M., Lane, S. J., Sugiyama, T., & de Traversay, J. (1993). Startle modulation studies in autism. *Journal of Autism and Developmental Disorders, 23,* 619–637.

Osterling, J., & Dawson, G. (1994). Early recognition of children with autism: A study of first birthday home videotapes. *Journal of Autism and Developmental Disorders, 24,* 247–257.

Ozonoff, S., & Cathcart, K. (1998). Effectiveness of a home program intervention for young children with autism. *Journal of Autism and Developmental Disorders, 28,* 25–32.

Prizant, B. M., & Wetherby, A. M. (1993). Communication in preschool autistic children. In E. Schopler, M. E. Van Bourgondien, & M. M. Bristol (Eds.), *Preschool issues in autism* (pp. 95–128). New York: Plenum.

Rapin, I. (1991). Autistic children: Diagnosis and clinical features. *Pediatrics, 87,* 751–760.

Rapin, I. (1996). Neurological examination. In I. Rapin (Ed.), *Preschool children with inadequate communication: Developmental language disorder, autism, low IQ* (pp. 58–97). London: MacKeith.

Rapin, I. (1997). Autism. *New England Journal of Medicine, 337,* 97–104.

Reber, M. (1992). Autism. In M. L. Batshaw & Y. M. Perret (Eds.), *Children with disabilities* (pp. 407–421). Baltimore: Paul Brooks.

Reisman, J. E. (1999). *The Minnesota Handwriting Test user's manual.* San Antonio, TX: Psychological Corporation.

Reisman, J. E., & Hanschu, B. (1992). *Sensory Integration Inventory—Revised for individuals with developmental disabilities: User's guide.* Hugo, MN: PDP Press.

Richter, E. W., & Montgomery, P. C. (1989). *The Sensorimotor Performance Analysis.* Santa Barbara, CA: PDP Products.

Rogers, S. J. (1998). Empirically supported comprehensive treatments for young children with autism. *Journal of Clinical and Child Psychology, 27,* 168–179.

Rogers, S. J., Bennetto, L., McEvoy, R., & Pennington, B. F. (1996). Imitation and pantomime in high-functioning adolescents with autism spectrum disorders. *Child Development, 67,* 2060–2073.

Royeen, C. B., & Fortune, J. C. (1990). Touch inventory for elementary-school-aged children. *American Journal of Occupational Therapy, 44,* 155–159.

Rutter, M., & Schopler, E. (1988). Autism and pervasive developmental disorders: Concepts and diagnostic issues. In E. Schopler & G. Mesibov (Eds.), *Diagnosis and assessment in autism* (pp. 15–35). New York: Plenum.

Schopler, E., Reichler, R. J., Bashford, A., Lansing, M., & Marcus, L. M. (1990). *Psychoeducational Profile Revised (PEP-R).* Austin, TX: PRO-ED.

Schopler, E., Reichler, R. J., & Lansing, M. (1980). Assessment and evaluation. In E. Schopler, R. J. Reichler, & M. Lansing (Eds.), *Individualized assessment and treatment for autistic and developmentally disabled children: Teaching strategies for parents and professionals* (vol. 2, pp. 23–41). Austin, TX: PRO-ED.

Schopler, E., Reichler, R. J., & Renner, B. R. (1988). *The Childhood Autism Rating Scale.* Los Angeles: Western Psychological Services.

Sparrow, S. S., Balla, D. A., & Cicchetti, D. V. (1984). *Vineland Adaptive Behavior Scales.* Circle Pines, MN: American Guidance Service.

Stone, W. L. (1998). *Descriptive information about the Screening Tool for Autism in Two-Year-Olds (STAT).* Paper presented at the NIH State of the Science in Autism: Screening and Diagnosis Working Conference, Bethesda, MD.

Stone, W. L., & Lemanek, K. L. (1990). Parental report of social behaviors in autistic preschoolers. *Journal of Autism and Developmental Disorders, 20,* 513–522.

Stone, W. L., Lemanek, K. L., Fishel, P. T., Fernandez, M. C., & Altemeier, W. A. (1990). Play and imitation skills in the diagnosis of autism in young children. *Pediatrics, 86,* 267–272.

Stone, W. L., & Ousley, O.Y. (1996). Pervasive developmental disorders: Autism. In M. L. Wolraich (Ed.), *Disorders of developmental learning* (pp. 379–405). Boston: Mosby.

Stone, W. L., & Ousley, O. Y. (1997). *STAT manual: Screening Tool for Autism in Two-Year-Olds*. Unpublished manuscript. Vanderbilt University, Nashville, TN.

Tomchek, S. D. (1997). *Sensory processing behaviors in children diagnosed with an autism spectrum disorder: An item analysis*. Paper presented at the national meeting of the Autism Society of America, Orlando, FL.

Uniform Data Systems (1993). *The Wee Functional Independence Measure*. Buffalo, NY: Author.

Vilensky, J. A., Damasio, A. R., & Maurer, R. G. (1981). Gait disturbances in patients with autistic behavior. *Archives of Neurology, 38,* 646–649.

Watling, R., Dietz, J., Kanny, E. M., & McLaughlin, J. F. (1999). Current practice of occupational therapy for children with autism. *American Journal of Occupational Therapy, 53,* 498–505.

Watson, L. R., & Marcus, L. M. (1988). Diagnosis and assessment of preschool children. In E. Schopler & G. Mesibov (Eds.), *Diagnosis and assessment in autism* (pp. 271–302). New York: Plenum.

Wilbarger, P., & Wilbarger, J. L. (1991). *Sensory defensiveness in children ages 2–12: An intervention guide for parents and other caretakers*. Santa Barbara, CA: Avanti Educational Programs.

Williams, D. (1995). *Somebody somewhere*. New York: Doubleday.

CHAPTER 5

The Efficacy of a Sensorimotor Treatment Approach by Occupational Therapists

Colleen M. Schneck

CHAPTER OBJECTIVES

At the completion of this chapter, the reader will be able to:

- Understand why the sensorimotor approach to management falls within the domain of concern for occupational therapy.
- Describe the findings with respect to children and adolescents with autism that support a need for using a sensorimotor frame of reference in treatment.
- Define the models for application of the sensorimotor approach to treatment.
- Describe the research that demonstrates the efficacy of occupational therapy using various applications of the sensorimotor frame of reference.
- Appreciate the complexity of research using the sensorimotor approach applied to autism.
- Describe the intervention strategies that may be most appropriate for some forms of sensory dysfunction.
- Understand the implications of this research for treatment.
- Define the needs for further research and understand the guidelines for designing research to test the effects of a sensorimotor approach with autism.

INTRODUCTION AND DEFINITION OF TERMINOLOGY

This chapter has three purposes. The first purpose is to develop a framework for examining the occupational therapy research literature, including defining the terminology, the target behaviors of treatment, and the tenets of the sensorimotor frame of reference. To accomplish this, occupational therapy's domain of concern is identified, establishing occupational therapy's role and focus in sensorimotor functions and treatment. Additionally, the sensorimotor characteristics of children and adolescents with autism are described, sensorimotor treatment approaches are defined and categorized, and occupational therapy services for children and adolescents with autism are depicted.

The second major purpose is to review the research literature and summarize the findings and trends from the current research. To accomplish this, tables are included that summarize the current literature in several categories. Based on these tables and the research results, a narrative review of the efficacy of treatment using the sensorimotor frame of reference by occupational therapists is presented.

The final purpose is to draw inferences from the research on treatment of children and adolescents with autism and to make recommendations for future research. The summary goal is to provide a foundation on which occupational therapists can build the knowledge base necessary for guiding evidence-based practice for people who have autism.

Domain of Concern

The domain of concern of a profession defines the scope and focus of its practice (Kramer & Hinojosa, 1999). Occupational therapists are concerned with an individual's successful participation in his or her daily occupations across the lifespan. To define its domain of concern, the profession of occupational therapy has identified the performance areas, performance components, and the performance contexts that enable persons to engage in meaningful occupation (American Occupational Therapy Association [AOTA], 1994). Performance areas are broad categories of human activity that are part of daily life, including work, school, play/leisure, and activities of daily living. Performance components are abilities in sensorimotor, cognitive, and psychosocial skills that, to varying degrees and in differing combinations, are required for successful engagement in various performance areas. The sensorimotor performance components consist of sensory, musculoskeletal, and motor subcomponents. The

sensorimotor performance components include those parts of human function that depend, in part, on the processing of sensory input. Performance contexts are external to the individual and can support or impede the person's ability to engage in performance areas. For example, performance contexts include the social and the physical environment (AOTA). When individuals cannot adequately engage in occupation, the occupational therapist may analyze the underlying performance components and subcomponents to determine their effect on performance areas. This analysis may explain the problem, assist in planning remediation, or suggest a need to change the performance context to support successful occupation.

If there are deficits in performance, the occupational therapist uses this analysis and clinical judgment to select an appropriate treatment approach or frame of reference (Kramer & Hinojosa, 1999). A frame of reference is a linking structure between theory and application and is a way of organizing knowledge so it can be used for planning and implementing treatment. The sensorimotor frame of reference addresses deficits in sensorimotor components that affect people's occupations. It consists of a blending of multiple approaches, used by occupational therapists, that share a common theoretical base that addresses sensory processing, sensory integration, and related motor output (Ayres, 1972; Farber, 1982; Fisher, Murray, & Bundy, 1991; Oetter, Richter, & Frick, 1995; Stockmeyer, 1967; Williams & Shellenberger, 1994; Wilbarger & Wilbarger, 1991).

Sensorimotor Function in Children with Autism

Sensory Processing Disorders

Sensorimotor performance component deficits are often identified in individuals

with autism. These include sensory processing deficits (e.g., Ayres, 1979; Eaves, Ho, &
Eaves, 1994; Grandin, 1995; Kranowitz,
1998; O'Neill & Jones, 1997; Ornitz, 1974)
and motor impairments (e.g., Jones & Prior,
1985; Smith & Bryson, 1994). (See Chapters 1 and 4 for a full review of sensorimotor
deficits in individuals with autism.) Children with autism commonly have difficulty
with various sensory processing skills, such
as orienting responses, filtering information,
habituation, and interpreting sensory events
in the environment. They may overreact or
underreact to sensory events, or may fluctuate in their responses over time. Many children with autism have difficulties with motor planning and initiation or regulation of
movement (Smith & Bryson, 1994).

Ayres and Tickle (1980) defined two
types of sensory processing disorders in
children with autism. The first was the registration of, or orientation to, sensory input.
They found that children with this type of
sensory processing problem may react normally to sensory stimuli one minute, and the
next minute they may overreact or underreact to the same stimuli; this inconsistent
responding was attributed to inconsistent
registration due to a high threshold for sensory input. This attribution was supported
by Baranek, Foster, and Berkson (1997),
who found that some children with autism
demonstrate a high threshold for registering
sensory input and, as a result, are frequently
underactive to sensation and appear self-
absorbed and passive. In contrast, children
with autism who have a high threshold for
input, seem to crave sensation.

The second sensory processing disorder
defined by Ayres and Tickle (1980) involves
the control or modulation of a stimulus once
it is registered by the child's nervous system.
They observed and theorized that children
with poor modulation may be able to exert
control of behavior at some times but not at
others; they may be overly reactive to sensa-

tion, thereby exhibiting sensory defensiveness. Years ago, Ornitz (1974) hypothesized
that disturbances in sensory modulation
were the primary symptoms of autism and
resulted in disturbances in social relating,
communication, and language. More recently, Waterhouse, Fein, and Modahl
(1996) described the splintered sensory experiences and inadequate sensory integration associated with autism. These authors
theorized that these sensory processing
deficits result in a decreased ability to shift
attention, use working memory, and generalize images of the environment.

Recent studies support sensory processing disorders. Many children with autism
display difficulties with the modulation of
sensory input. In fact, in an extensive chart
review of 200 children with autism, 95% exhibited sensory modulation difficulties
(Greenspan & Wieder, 1997). Recently,
Kientz and Dunn (1997) found that children
with autism were significantly different
from typical children in all sensory categories. These authors reported that the most
frequently occurring sensory problems for
children with autism reflected hypersensitivity to touch and auditory input, a modulation disorder. In a survey of occupational
therapists, Case-Smith and Miller (1999) reported that respondents frequently observed
difficulty in sensory modulation, tactile and
vestibular function, and body awareness
among children with autism. In addition,
children with autism may display other sensory-based disturbances, such as diminished
body awareness and difficulty coordinating
visual and vestibular responses (Dawson &
Lewy, 1989).

Behaviors Attributed to Sensory Processing

Three types of behaviors observed in individuals with autism may relate to sensory
stimulation needs or sensory processing disorders. Although the distinctions are

blurred, the three types are self-stimulatory, stereotypic, and self-injurious behaviors. The presence of these behaviors is thought by some to be incompatible with the establishment of new skills (Lovaas, Litrownik, & Mann, 1971), decrease the likelihood of learning (Koegel & Covert, 1972; Ritvo, Ornitz, & La Franchi, 1968), and hinder development (Ornitz & Ritvo, 1976). Each of the behaviors is discussed and defined in the following section. It is important to define these behaviors because they are thought to satisfy sensory needs resulting from sensory processing disorders and, consequently, were the target behaviors in several research studies.

Self-stimulatory behaviors are a defining characteristic of autism, but they are not unique to it. As stated earlier, children with autism have difficulty maintaining appropriate arousal levels (Lovaas, Newsom, & Hickman, 1987); self-stimulatory behavior may be used as an attempt by the individual to self-modulate arousal (Hutt & Hutt, 1968). A variety of self-stimulatory behaviors, including body rocking, spinning, hand flicking and flapping, head nodding, object tapping, gazing at lights, and mouthing, may be observed. These behaviors appear to be intrinsically driven and may be due to decreased sensory intake. The suggestion is that these behaviors are used by people with autism in an attempt to calm themselves during times of general overarousal. Self-stimulatory behaviors (SSB) may serve individual needs: For some, they are calming; for others, they may be alerting.

Stereotypies are the second type of behavior that may be seen in individuals with autism. These may take on many forms (Berkson, Guthermoth, & Baranek, 1995). A stereotypic behavior (STB) is defined as a disturbance of motility characterized by repetitive yet purposeless movement; these patterns occur with high frequency (Iwasaki & Holm, 1989). Some of the repetitive motor behaviors described previously as self-stimulatory may also fit this description (e.g., body rocking). Although these behaviors may appear similar, the underlying purpose of STB is thought to be a ritualistic, rigid control of the environment rather than self-modulation. Other behaviors, such as unusual object manipulations (e.g., spinning objects), repetitive vocalizations, abnormal focused affections (e.g., affinity for blue objects), rituals (e.g., turning around before opening a door), and behavioral rigidities (e.g., maintaining a certain order) can also be classified as stereotypical behaviors. In an autistic population, STB is reported to be relatively independent of environmental influence and is widely believed to result from a neuropathophysiologic process in the central nervous system (CNS) (Ornitz, Sorosky, & Ritvo, 1970; Ritvo, Ornitz, & La Franchi, 1968). STB may be related to dysfunction of the sensory processing mechanism in the reticular formation and the related neural circuits (Gold & Gold, 1975; Hutt & Hutt, 1968). Appropriateness of sensory input is essential for the reticular formation to maintain an optimal level of cortical arousal for efficient adaptive behaviors. Therefore, either sensory restriction or sensory overload may trigger marked behavior disturbances (Lindsley et al., 1964). Baranek et al. (1997) suggested that tactile defensiveness and some stereotypic behaviors coexist in children with developmental disabilities. These authors found that tactile defensiveness was related to some stereotypic and rigid behaviors and that subjects with higher levels of tactile defensiveness tended to show more sensory stereotypic behavior. These stereotypies included rigid behaviors, repetitive verbalizations, visual stereotypies, and abnormal focused attention. They found no relationship between tactile defensiveness and the motor and object stereotypies.

Self-injurious behaviors (SIB), such as head banging, hair pulling, and biting, are also seen in children with autism. One assumption is that SIB is a form of self-stimulatory behavior and that this self-mutilation may actually be an attempt to stimulate an underactive nervous system. Numerous authors proposed a self-stimulation hypothesis, based on observations and limited study, suggesting that people engage in this behavior as a means of providing their own sensory stimulation (Baumeister & Forehand, 1973: Bloomer & Rose, 1989; Hirama, 1989; King, 1987; Larrington, 1987). The hypothesis was supported in a few studies (Bright, Bittick, & Fleeman, 1981; Larrington, 1987) that have reduced SIB through the use of externally imposed sensory stimulation.

Motor Deficits

Motor deficits commonly seen in children with autism included soft neurological signs (e.g., low muscle tone), decreased visual-motor skills, including eye-gaze abnormalities and visual tracking, decreased movement, poor imitation ability, dyspraxia (Jones & Prior, 1985), and poor endurance. In a survey of occupational therapists, the respondents reported that they observed motor problems, but less frequently than sensory processing problems, in children with autism (Case-Smith & Miller, 1999). The incidence of motor problems reported is still high, with 87% of the respondents reporting that they frequently observed motor planning problems and 67% that they often or always observed other types of motor problems. A sensorimotor approach is often used by occupational therapists to improve the motor deficits described above.

Effect on Functional Skills

Sensorimotor problems, reviewed briefly here and in greater depth in other chapters, can contribute to a variety of functional skill limitations in communication, social interaction, behavioral regulation, and play (Freeman, 1997; Rapin, 1997). Occupational therapists reported more disturbances in play and self-care when they observed more underlying sensorimotor problems in children (Case-Smith & Miller, 1999). Occupational therapists in this study reported that social play was the most significant functional deficit related to sensorimotor problems, followed by delayed development of community life skills. The performance area of self-care, feeding, and hygiene were reported as sometimes delayed because of sensorimotor problems.

When children's sensorimotor skills affect function in performance areas, these needs fall within the occupational therapy domain of concern. Although a list of common sensorimotor deficits was presented here, further studies are needed to describe the sensorimotor skills and deficits of individuals with autism and to relate these to functional performance. Building on existing work, the full range and extent of sensory abnormalities and their effect on function across the autistic population needs to be established. For example, further description of stimulation seeking behaviors is warranted, which will require systematic, concentrated research (O'Neill & Jones, 1997). Additional descriptive information would permit more rigorous study by occupational therapists about the best treatment approaches for specific sensorimotor deficits.

Definitions of the Sensorimotor Approach to Treatment

The term *sensorimotor* refers to approaches to intervention that apply a sensory input to produce a specific motor output (Clark, Mailloux, Parham, & Bissell 1989). In sensorimotor approaches to treatment, controlled sensory input is assumed to influence motor responses and subsequent functional skill. It is thought that abnormal motor responses can be inhibited or facilitated with corresponding changes in the CNS. Sensorimotor treatment approaches are typically used with individuals who have CNS dysfunction. They are based on principles of neuroplasticity and the application of neurological rehabilitation techniques. These theoretical postulates arose from sensory integration theory, first described by Ayres (1972).

For the purpose of reviewing the efficacy of sensorimotor treatment, we identified three main approaches in the literature. Each study is classified as employing one of these approaches: sensory motor, sensory stimulation, and sensory integration. Because these approaches may be used in isolation or in combination with the others, treatment methods overlap. All of these approaches share common theoretical beliefs or postulates on the use of sensory input and sensory integration, differing only in how these approaches are delivered. Recently, several consultative approaches were developed that arise from similar theoretical beliefs; these are included in the research analysis.

Sensory Motor Treatment

The term *sensory motor treatment* (versus *sensorimotor*) is used to distinguish between the broad terminology of the overall sensorimotor approach and this grouping. This approach was described in the literature in two similar, yet distinct, ways. The first description emphasizes the application of handling by the therapist to guide or direct the child's movement in an expected or typical movement. In this approach, the application of specific sensory stimulation with the purpose of eliciting a desired motor response (e.g., a movement or altered muscle tone) is used (Fisher & Murray, 1991). For example,

the therapist may stroke down the spine of the child to elicit a more erect posture. Neurodevelopmental treatment is a sensorimotor approach used widely by occupational therapists in the treatment of neuromuscular disorders.

In addition, the term *sensory motor* is used in a more generic way to refer to a class of intervention theories that use the active, experience-based learning first described by Piaget (Fisher & Murray, 1991). In this approach, the child's direct involvement in activities, designed to elicit the expected or typical movement, allows him or her to practice the skill to be learned. Treatment employing this approach is often provided in groups but can be done individually using sensory and movement activities that are age or ability appropriate. For example, an activity where the child can maintain and practice postural control, such as sitting on a T-stool while blowing bubbles, may be used in treatment. The challenge is to select activities that best match the multiple needs of children with autism. Often, the terms *sensory motor* and *perceptual motor* are used interchangeably.

Sensory Stimulation

This approach involves the passive application of direct sensory stimulation with the purpose of eliciting a more generalized behavioral response, such as increased attention or improved arousal (Fisher & Murray, 1991). Sensory stimulation uses components of sensory motor and sensory integration approaches, but in itself cannot be considered either. During sensory stimulation, clients are passive recipients of the stimulation and the techniques do not need to be presented within the context of a meaningful activity (Murray & Anzalone, 1991). Sensory stimulation techniques can be used with persons who have sensory modulation disorders, with the belief that increased sensory intake may improve sensory modulation ability (Murray & Anzalone, 1991). Examples include brushing the body with soft-bristled brushes, wearing a weighted vest, and rubbing lotion on the arms.

Sensory Integration

Sensory integration (SI) is the process of organizing sensory information in the brain to make an adaptive response (Ayres, 1972). An adaptive response is one that is purposeful, goal-directed, and enables the individual to successfully meet "the just right challenge" and to learn something new (Ayres). The sensory integration frame of reference is used when sensory system processing deficits make it difficult for a child to produce an adaptive response. Although similar in basic goals, the environment and the process of therapy make sensory integration different from sensory motor treatment and sensory stimulation.

Classical sensory integration treatment refers to the individual occupational therapy treatment that Ayres (1972) developed to remediate SI dysfunction in children. Although originally designed for children with learning disabilities, this type of intervention has been used for children with autism (Parham & Mailloux, 1996). The intent of this therapy is to improve the efficiency with which the nervous system interprets and uses sensory information for functional use. The defining characteristics of classical sensory integration treatment include:

- individual treatment
- balance between structure and freedom (treatment is neither predetermined, nor is it simply free play)
- emphasis on the inner drive of the child
- active participation of the child, allowing him or her to choose activities under the direction of the therapist

- therapy involving a special setting and suspended equipment

These characteristics may contribute to the difficulty in studying the effectiveness of the approach—that is, therapy that is individualized and emphasized as child-directed is difficult to describe in treatment manuals, and thus is difficult to replicate; it is also difficult to anticipate the outcome (Tickle-Degnen, 1988).

While sensory integration is a sensorimotor approach, not all sensorimotor approaches to intervention can be called sensory integration treatment. The most significant differences between sensory integration treatment and other approaches are that other approaches use activities done with a group of children, may apply sensory stimulation passively, or do not emphasize the use of suspended equipment in treatment.

Consultative Models

Sensory integration theory has expanded from its classical model and been joined by more recent specialty applications, such as the theory and use of individualized sensory diets (Wilbarger, 1995). Williamson and Anzalone (1997) provided a bridge between the classic SI approach for children with autism and more consultative models. They defined elements of the SI approach as including:

1. Helping parents understand their child's behavior and foster nurturing relationships.
2. Helping parents and teachers modify the environment so that it matches the child's sensory needs.
3. Helping children organize responses to sensory input.

This suggests that occupational therapy using a sensorimotor approach can be applied both in a direct service approach, as previously described, or through consultation to parents, teachers, and children. Consultative models of treatment evolved for several reasons. The Alert Program for Self-Regulation (Williams & Shellenberger, 1994), for instance, was designed to teach children how to identify their own arousal level and seek appropriate sensory stimuli for self-modulation. Other approaches such as the Wilbarger Protocol (Wilbarger & Wilbarger, 1991) and the M.O.R.E. Program (Oetter et al., 1995) evolved as defined intervention strategies to meet specific sensory needs. Consultative models also evolved because occupational therapy in school settings often is provided in groups within the classroom or in a primary consultative model. Suspended equipment for classical SI therapy may not be available in the school setting. Although classroom consultation may necessitate sensorimotor activities of lower intensity, the opportunity for sensory input in the natural environment for a longer duration with increased frequency may have the same effect as the intensity of direct treatment (Kimball, 1999).

These four consultative models are further described. The sensory diet is the type and amount of sensory input any person receives throughout the day (Wilbarger & Wilbarger, 1991). An effective sensory diet helps a person feel calm, alert, and focused. A variety of sensory input through activities in the sensory diet can affect a child's level of alertness. Teaching self-regulation is necessary when the child does not know how to seek appropriate sensory input to maintain an adequate sensory diet. The Alert Program was developed by Williams and Shellenberger (1994) to teach children self-regulation. In this program, children and adolescents are taught to monitor their arousal levels and to provide the needed sensory input to maintain an appropriate

arousal level. Another specialty application, the Wilbarger Protocol, is a method of treatment to decrease sensory defensiveness. It involves direct passive sensory input using a nonscratching brush with pressure, followed by proprioceptive input to all joints. The treatment is usually provided in approximately one minute and is repeated 8 to 12 times per day for one to two weeks. Lastly, the M.O.R.E. Program was designed to integrate the oral-motor and sensory functions of the mouth for maintaining optimal arousal and postural function. For example, sensory input to the mouth (e.g., sucking) may help the child maintain an appropriate level of arousal and upper-body stability to concentrate on the task at hand. Intervention using the M.O.R.E. Program can involve deep pressure to the roof of the mouth, increased resistance of food, sucking activities, and increasing tartness of foods, all to provide oral-sensory and oral-motor work.

Occupational therapists understand the nature of sensory-driven behaviors and can, therefore, design treatment programs for individuals with autism that satisfy a variety of sensory needs. In the treatment of children and adolescents with autism, these sensorimotor approaches and the consultative models may be applied in simultaneous combinations or in a variety of sequences over time. Often, occupational therapists themselves use the terms interchangeably or call all approaches either sensory integration or sensorimotor. Because treatment efficacy can best be determined when the treatment is clearly described, it is important for researchers and practitioners to be clear and consistent in using terminology. Recent efforts by the Sensory Integration Special Interest Section (SISIS) of the AOTA have begun to clarify the terminology of SI theory to establish a consensus on which a research agenda can be built (Miller & Lane, 2000).

Description of Occupational Therapy Services for Children with Autism

Because sensorimotor skills are in the domain of concern for occupational therapists, and children and adolescents with autism demonstrate sensorimotor deficits that lead to performance area problems, a sensorimotor treatment approach is an appropriate choice for occupational therapists. Recent studies find that occupational therapists use a sensorimotor approach in the treatment of children with autism (Case-Smith & Miller, 1999; Watling, Dietz, Kanny, & McLaughlin, 1999). In a survey of occupational therapists working with children with autism, 99% of the respondents reported that they always or frequently used variations on SI in the treatment of children with autism (Watling et al., 1999). Therefore, occupational therapists' emphasis on sensory integration is a unique contribution in the treatment of children and adolescents with autism.

Case-Smith and Miller (1999) surveyed a random sample of 500 occupational therapists in the Sensory Integration SIS and the School System SIS of the AOTA in order to obtain a broad representation of pediatric occupational therapists working with children and adolescents with autism. A return rate of 62% was obtained and 58% (*n* = 202) of the responses were usable for the analysis. The results indicated that the respondents primarily worked in the schools (66%) and that most respondents provided direct services when treating children with autism. Of the responding therapists, 64% provided services for children 0–10 years of age, and that treatment focused on the ac-

quisition of skills such as attention, behavior, sensory processing, and play. These therapists reported that they applied SI and environmental modification approaches most frequently. The respondents who reported more frequent use of and more competence in SI approaches perceived more improvement in children's sensory processing as a result of treatment. Lastly, the therapists reported frequent collaboration with other professionals.

To address sensory processing deficits, respondents (95%) reported using many sensory-based intervention techniques (Case-Smith & Miller, 1999). For example, 95% of respondents "often" or "always" provided services to improve sensory modulation, 84% for vestibular problems, and 92% for tactile deficits. The emphasis of these occupational therapy approaches was to promote the child's ability to modulate sensory input, to decrease sensory defensiveness, and to enhance the child's ability to interact within the social and physical environment.

Case-Smith and Miller (1999) reported a significant and high correlation between the use of SI and environmental modification approaches, suggesting that these approaches were applied together. Occupational therapists help to adapt the child's daily sensory environment so that he or she is better able to modulate sensory input. The use of a SI approach in making recommendations for adapting the environment is an essential role of occupational therapists in schools (Haack & Haldy, 1998) and in early intervention (Humphrey & Link, 1990).

It is important to understand the current practice of occupational therapy services for children with autism when looking at efficacy studies of treatment. Studies indicate that a broad range of sensorimotor treatment approaches comprises the most frequently used intervention strategy by occupational therapists for children and adolescents with autism. Although understanding what occupational therapy practice consists of is the first step, we need to know if interventions are effective and which interventions are most effective for which problems.

THE RESEARCH ON THE EFFECTS OF SENSORIMOTOR TREATMENT

This section presents an overview of research findings on the efficacy of occupational therapy using a sensorimotor approach. In treatment, occupational therapists take a functional approach—that is, they treat problems such as decreased modulation or hypersensitivity to sensory input, not the diagnosis. Consequently, the results of treatment studies on problems found in CNS disorders similar to autism could be generalized, with caution, to the problems of children with autism. Therefore, in this chapter, studies of populations with diagnoses such as learning disorders and mental retardation are reviewed and the findings related to the treatment of individuals with autism. A common feature in all these disorders is some degree of difficulty in processing or integrating sensory information (Gorman, 1997). When reviewing the literature, we identified themes and used them to organize the material into tables and related narrative explanations. For example, we classified each of the efficacy studies, based on descriptions of the treatment in the article, into one of the approaches to sensorimotor treatment just described. This initial classification formed the basis for identifying additional themes in the research literature, such as the frequency of treatment or the specific type of sensory stimulation. Because the descriptions included in the research literature were sometimes unclear and sensorimotor approaches may be provided in combination, this classification system is imperfect and, arguably, could be performed in another manner. Nonetheless, it constitutes a systematic approach.

Research Methods

In reviewing studies on the efficacy of sensorimotor treatment of children and adolescents with autism, it is important to also consider methodological limitations frequently encountered in these studies. Case-Smith and Bryan (1999) reported two methodological problems that must be considered when investigating the effects of treatment for children with autism. The first is the limited ability to use most standardized assessment measures of outcome, because children with autism are often difficult to test on these measures. The second methodological problem relates to the atypical behaviors and the wide variety of behavioral responses and developmental levels exhibited by children with autism; this makes homogeneity of samples and replication of results difficult to obtain. Research is even more difficult to interpret if inferences about the meaning of behavior are drawn. For instance: Is the child engaged in self-stimulatory behavior because he or she is underaroused, or is he or she is responding to overstimulation that can't be modulated? The interpretation may affect the type of therapy provided and, therefore, the outcome of treatment, thus complicating the measurement of outcomes. In addition, operationally defining sensorimotor treatment strategies is difficult because treatment depends on each individual and his or her needs. All of these factors make comparison of studies difficult, replication nearly impossible, and measurement of outcomes inconsistent.

The design of the study is an important consideration with this population. Studies utilizing group designs lose individual effects and, therefore, may not truly evaluate treatment efficacy for all persons with autism. Group studies also may not reveal the clinical significance of the treatment results due to the averaging of results across the group, especially heterogeneous groups. Single-subject design, especially using a rigorous ABA (baseline, treatment, baseline) design, may reveal the clinical significance of treatment while providing descriptive information about the treatment process. The problem in single-subject design research lies in the diminished external validity and generalizability of the results. Given the variability in functioning within this population and the current status of research in sensorimotor interventions, however, single-subject study design may be the most appropriate research design. Despite significant barriers, efficacy research is necessary and should be conducted using careful research design, description of the intervention, and maximum control of confounding variables.

In the studies reviewed for this chapter, several research designs were evident. Many of the studies were, essentially, case study reports. A study with less rigor and specificity in the measurement of change or outcome due to treatment was classified as a case study. Although most of the case studies included reports of behavioral change or improvement in skills, the measurement and rigor of the design did not meet criteria for a single-case study design. Single-case study designs included studies that had at least a baseline and intervention phase with consistent measurement across conditions and a critical analysis of results. Other quasi-experimental and experimental designs were found in the literature and are described in the following tables. Tables were organized by chronological order of the studies. Much of the literature reports on studies performed in a clinical setting rather than in a laboratory setting; the clinical setting offers little opportunity to control confounding variables but does address the question of effectiveness of intervention in typical situations.

Sensory Motor Treatment

A variety of skills were reported to improve in response to sensory stimulation and sensory motor treatment activities in individuals with autism. For example, body image, behavior, balance, and language skills were improved through sensory motor activities (LeShay, 1980; McEvoy, 1987; Willis, 1983). Treatment strategies were described in many articles. Sanders (1993), for example, compared and contrasted the treatment of two boys with autism. For each boy, treatment was directed toward goals of accepting handling, encouraging eye contact, and increasing participation in sensory motor experiences. Sanders felt that a combination of approaches, individualized for each person with autism, enabled continued progress toward these goals, but did not formally test the outcomes of intervention. Pulice (1987) described a multisensory approach that progressed from emphasizing simple eye contact and rocking with the parent and child to practicing perceptual-motor skills, such as assembling puzzles. Cook (1991) reported qualitative data on two four-year-old boys with autism in which sensory motor activities were combined with sensory integration techniques. Significant improvements were reported by the parents and teacher in the quantity and quality of adaptive behavior and skills.

Few studies were conducted that examine the efficacy of sensory motor treatment, as defined for this chapter, for children with autism, and most of these were conducted during the 1980s or before. However, results of these studies suggest that this approach is successful in improving certain skills. Further work is obviously needed. More recent studies compared the efficacy of a sensory motor approach (described as perceptual-motor) to the efficacy of a SI approach. These studies are reviewed later in this chapter.

Sensory Stimulation

Many studies appear to apply sensory stimulation to individuals with autism to achieve several purposes; we categorized the research by these themes of purpose. One theme was the use of sensory stimulation as a reinforcer in behavior management. For example, academic skills were facilitated by the use of visual, vestibular, and vibratory touch as reinforcers (Murphy, 1982), especially in students with lower mental age (Ottenbacher & Altman, 1984). Additional applications of sensory stimulation as a reinforcer are discussed in Chapter 9 and consequently are not included here. The second theme found in the literature was a sensory stimulation approach used to decrease self-stimulatory, stereotypic, or self-injurious behaviors. The third theme was the application of deep pressure to decrease arousal and anxiety. These efficacy studies are organized by these themes for discussion.

Self-Stimulatory and Stereotypic Behaviors

The effects of sensory stimulation on self-stimulatory and stereotypic behaviors are analyzed together because, until recently, these terms were often used interchangeably. Both sensory stimulation and sensory integration approaches were used in the re-

search literature to decrease self-stimulatory and stereotypic behaviors (STB). Although behavior modification was also used to decrease these behaviors, discussion of this approach is beyond the scope of this chapter. The hypothesis supporting much of this research is that a sensory stimulation approach maintains optimal arousal level and thus decreases the need for self-stimulatory behaviors. The sensory stimuli may be prescribed according to a person's inherent sensory needs (Reisman, 1993), often expressed through his or her behavior. Support for these treatment principles is not clear; sensory stimulation was found to increase STB in some studies (e.g., Mason & Iwata, 1990; Morreau, 2000). A review of the research literature related to the effects of sensorimotor treatment in decreasing these behaviors is displayed in Table 5–1.

Several studies demonstrated the effectiveness of sensory integration and sensory stimulation techniques for the reduction of self-stimulatory and stereotypic behaviors. Multisensory strategies were found to decrease self-stimulatory behavior in persons with mental retardation (MR) (Bonadonna, 1981; Storey, Bates, McGhee, & Dycus, 1984) and thereby increase opportunities for using functional skills. Although most of the studies outlined in Table 5–1 were conducted on individuals with MR or severe multiple disabilities, the results, research design, and treatment guidelines may prove useful in treatment planning and research design using sensory stimulation treatment for individuals with autism.

Brockle-Hurst Woods (1990) concluded that twice-a-week treatment of tactile/vestibular stimulation was not adequate to decrease stereotypic behaviors in two adults with developmental disabilities. Other studies that demonstrated effectiveness provided treatment at least four times per week

Table 5–1 Sensory Stimulation To Reduce Self-Stimulatory and Stereotypic Behaviors

Author	Design	Participants	Sensory Input	Outcome
Resman (1981)	Case study	30-year-old man with profound MR	Vestibular, tactile, and proprioceptive stimulation.	Reduced self-stimulation behaviors, increased eye and contact, achieved fine motor and language goals more quickly after four months of therapy.
Bonadonna (1981)	Multiple baseline single-case design (ABA) across subjects	3 persons with severe MR	Vestibular stimulation for 10 minutes/day, 5 days/week for 3 weeks. Rocking in a linear direction in 4 positions at a rate of 40 movements/minute. Vestibular stimuli was chosen based on stereotypic rocking.	Statistically significant reduction of both frequency and duration of rocking behavior both directly after receiving vestibular stimulation and 1 hour after stimulation. Treatment effect persisted for 6 days after the vestibular stimulation was stopped, then gradually returned to baseline rates.
Storey, Bates, McGhee, & Dycus (1984)	Case study	12-year-old girl with profound MR and osteogenesis imperfecta	Providing tactile, olfactory, and gustatory stimulation for 15 minutes 3 days/week for 4 weeks. Treatment designed to increase sensory awareness.	Decreased the frequency and duration of self-stimulatory behaviors during treatment, but resumed self-stimulation behaviors during classroom periods.

continues

Table 5–1 continued

Author	Design	Participants	Sensory Input	Outcome
Iwasaki & Holm (1989)	Pretest-posttest randomized controlled trial experimental design	36 individuals with severe physical disabilities and profound MR, randomly assigned to one of three groups	3 treatment groups: excitatory stimulation, inhibitory stimulation, and control stimulation of informal talk and touch, applied 40 minutes/day for 30 days.	Sensory stimulation effective in decreasing frequency of STB. Neither excitatory nor inhibitory stimulation proved to be more effective at reducing STB than control stimulation. At followup, only the excitatory stimulation group showed an increase in STB from the posttest, whereas the other two groups continued to exhibit a decrease.
Brockle-Hurst Woods (1990)	Single-case design across subjects	2 adults with MR in an institution	Tactile and vestibular stimulation 2 times a week for 7 months.	Although visual analysis showed statistically significant treatment effects, STB continued at a high and variable rate throughout the study; thus, results were inconclusive.
Zissermann (1992)	Case study	8-year-old with autism and multiple disabilities	Controlled deep pressure and tactile input provided through high tight-fitting gloves and a weighted vest.	46% reduction in stereotypic, self-stimulatory behavior when gloves were worn.

(Bonadonna, 1981; Iwasaki & Holm, 1989). Iwasaki and Holm (1989) suggested that an intervention period of 30 days was sufficient to determine if the treatment is effective. However, the long-term effects of the treatment were inconsistent; most studies found that the behavior returned to baseline rates shortly after the treatment was discontinued. Studies are needed to explore both the immediate effects and the long-term effects of treatment and determine how much intervention is necessary before the treatment effects persist over longer periods of time.

Most studies consisted of case reports and single-case designs and used multiple types of sensory stimulation. The research summarized in Table 5–1 indicates that individuals with MR and severe multiple disabilities who receive sensory stimulation may show a decrease in self-stimulatory behavior (e.g., touch and proprioception reduced self-stimulation), with a reduction in both frequency and duration of these behaviors. In these studies, the applied sensory stimulation was often similar to but more intensive than the self-stimulatory behavior observed. For example, vestibular stimulation was used to reduce rocking behavior. This approach to treatment is based on the principle that the STB is communication about the type of input necessary to maintain an appropriate level of CNS arousal; thus, providing a stronger dose of such sensory input was shown to decrease STB. Studies are needed to determine if applying a similar sensory simulation is more effective than using a multisensory approach. Further studies may need to focus on one type of sensory stimulation and its effects on one type of behavior.

In addition, studies are needed to explore whether inhibitory or excitatory stimulation consistently evokes the same treatment outcomes across individuals with different sensory needs. Sensory stimulation may de-crease stereotypic behaviors in the therapy session, but the effects may not persist outside of therapy situations. The maintenance of effects over the long term would likely be beneficial for occupational performance in multiple contexts. It is also necessary to examine if decreased STB is associated with increased functional skills and learning. Lastly, study is needed on the outcome of sensory diets with this population to determine if they decrease self-stimulatory and stereotypic behavior.

Self-Injurious Behaviors

Self-injury is thought by some to develop from persistent attempts on the part of the individual with a developmental disability to find some type of pleasurable sensation that produces a calm, organized state or decreases stress (Reisman, 1993). On the other hand, SIB could also be used by the individual to get attention from others or to control a situation, such as avoiding an activity. Sensory stimulation is a remedial approach to treatment for SIB; its theoretical basis is that applying passive sensory stimulation may eliminate destructive behaviors. The most effective treatment interventions depend on understanding the individual's motivational source (e.g., attention versus sensory stimulation) for such self-injurious behaviors. Lissy (1997) provided an interesting and informative overview of earlier research. Table 5–2 presents a review of studies applying sensory stimulation to decrease self-injurious behavior.

Multiple conclusions can be drawn from the studies displayed in Table 5–2. Several studies incorporated sensory stimulation techniques and demonstrated effectiveness in reducing the amount of SIB. These studies were mostly single-case designs with adolescents and adults and included individuals with MR, developmental disabilities

Table 5–2 Sensory Stimulation To Reduce Self-Injurious Behaviors

Author	Design	Participants	Sensory Input	Outcome
Lemke (1974)	Case study	19-year-old woman with profound MR who had been restrained for several years to prevent self-injury	Tactile stimulation followed by social and motor tasks in 30-minute sessions, 3–4 times/week.	Gains in adaptive behaviors and a decrease in SIB over a 5-month period.
Bright, Bittick, & Fleeman (1981)	Case study treatment was provided as an emergency intervention	28-year-old non-ambulatory man with profound MR with high rates of self-hitting	30 minutes/ day of a combination of tactile and vestibular activities that were determined in prior assessment to be effective in decreasing SIB for the individual.	SIB declined steadily over the five months of sensory stimulation treatment. SIB decreased during treatment from 13 hits/minute to 1 hit/minute. Time out of the restraint on the living unit decreased from 36% to 61% each day over a 7-month period.
Wells & Smith (1983)	Single-case AB design across subjects	4 adult subjects with profound MR, SIB, and SSB	SI of tactile and vestibular input for 30 minutes/day.	Significant decrease in self-injurious behavior. SIB decreased from 13 facial hits to 1 hit/minute in a 5-month period.
McEvoy (1987)	Case study	School-aged students with autism	Massage using deep tactile and proprioceptive input.	Decrease in self-injurious behavior.

Study	Design	Subjects	Treatment	Results
Larrington (1987)	Case study	15-year-old boy with severe MR/autism, numerous long-standing behaviors that were abusive to self and others	2 times/week, reduced to 1 time/week when school started in the fall. Treatment sessions were 45–60 minutes in duration.	Destructive acts decreased and he became calmer, more alert, and more functional; was able to engage in purposeful activities.
Dura, Mulick, & Hammer (1988)	Single-subject design	15-year-old boy with profound MR	20 minutes of passive vestibular input.	Decrease SIB during treatment, no notable differences for posttreatment SIB. Mean rates of SIB decreased to .06/minute during vestibular stimulation and increased to 2.27/minute in the 15 minutes after treatment.
Hirama (1989)	Single-subject, multiple-baseline AB design	8 people with MR	Firm tactile stimulation applied 30 minutes/day.	Significant reduction in SIB.
Mason & Iwata (1990)	Multiple baseline across subjects	3-, 6- and 18-year-old children with MR	A flashing blue or amber light suspended from the ceiling, a rocking chair with a vibrating pillow attached at neck level, cassette tape recorder that played rock or jazz.	Some subjects increased SIB; possible explanation is that individual sensory needs were not taken into account.

continues

Table 5–2 continued

Author	Design	Participants	Sensory Input	Outcome
Brockle-Hurst Woods (1990)	Case study	2 men ages 32 and 38 with profound MR and Down Syndrome	Multisensory stimulation 2 times/week, 50 minutes per session, for 7 months.	Decrease in SIB. The data did not support the efficacy of a reduced number of longer treatment sessions compared to previous research (see Table 5–1).
McClure & Holtz-Yotz (1991)	Case study	13-year-old with autism and severe MR, demonstrated severe self-injurious behaviors, including pinching, biting, and rubbing	Bilateral deep pressure foam arm splints worn during waking hours except during bathing, feeding, and exercise.	Decrease in self-injurious behavior and an increase in social interaction and apparent strong desire to wear splints when removed. On day 53, when splints were permanently removed, self-stimulatory and self-injurious behaviors increased; appropriate interactions decreased.
Reisman (1993)	Single-subject AB design	41-year-old woman with profound MR, impaired vision, CP, and high rates of SIB	Passively applied vestibular, proprioceptive, and tactile input provided for 5 minutes each hour followed by attempts to engage the subject in social interaction and object manipulation.	Both time in restraint and amount of SIB decreased during the treatment phase. Subject was released from restraints, discharged from an institution, successfully lived in a foster home, and engaged in a day program.

(DD), and autism. A variety of sensory stimulation was used, including sustained deep pressure applied through foam arm splints, multisensory input, and tactile and vestibular input. Nonetheless, contrary to theory and the research hypothesis, an increase in SIB was observed in some subjects. Further study is needed to evaluate the type of sensory input provided and the occurrence of increased SIB. Several authors suggested that treatment should be chosen following evaluation of the nature of the SIB so that individual sensory needs can be taken into account. Further studies may need to accurately determine the motivational source for SIB behaviors in individuals with autism to ensure that sensory needs are the basis for the behaviors. Results of these studies suggest that short sessions of planned sensory input daily may be more effective than longer treatment sessions less often. Several studies noted that a decrease in self-injurious behavior was accompanied by an increase in purposeful activities and socialization (Larrington, 1987; Lemke, 1974; McClure & Holtz-Yotz, 1991; Reisman, 1993). These results support the theory that a decrease in SIB behaviors leads to increases in functional skill. In several studies, five months of treatment yielded the desired treatment effect (Lemke, 1974; Wells & Smith, 1983). Long-term effects of treatment are not yet known; further exploration in this area is necessary.

Anxiety and Arousal

One method occupational therapy practitioners use to lessen anxiety and arousal in persons with autism is the application of deep pressure, which is thought to have an overall calming effect that should normalize arousal and reduce anxiety. Studies using deep pressure included experimental designs, although sample sizes were small.

Table 5–3 depicts studies using deep pressure to decrease anxiety and arousal in typical college students and children with autism.

The results of the studies displayed in Table 5–3 suggest that deep pressure may be an effective treatment approach for children with autism with increased anxiety and arousal. Deep pressure input appears to have a calming effect and behavior appears to improve when deep pressure is used (e.g., decreased hyperactive behavior, increased social relating, and improved attention). Edelson, Edelson, Kerr, and Grandin (1999) suggested that a threshold of anxiety or arousal may be required for deep pressure to be beneficial and that those with the highest levels of anxiety and physiological arousal benefit most. This finding supports the ideas of Ayres and Tickle (1980), who noted that SI was more effective for children with autism who had normal or overaroused responses. In studies on the effects of the Hug Machine made available to children as they needed it throughout the day, Inamura, Wiss, and Parham (1990a; 1990b) found that the children did not consistently use the Hug Machine, with the average duration of use being less than two minutes per session. However, greater use seemed to be related to decreased hyperactive behavior in some children. Similarly, Creedon (1994) found that children with autism used the Hug Machine for longer periods and with more sustained pressure on days that were associated with behavior problems, suggesting that the children were able to sense their need for calming sensory input on particularly difficult days. The studies by Inamura et al. and Creedon, however, did not include a control group, physiological measures, or statistical analysis of the results. Although the results of studies using the Hug Machine are promising, the machine used in these studies

Table 5–3 The Effects of Using Deep Pressure To Decrease Anxiety and Arousal

Author	Design	Participants	Sensory Input	Outcome
Krauss (1987)	Pre- and posttest experimental design	23 typical college students, served as own controls	Hug'm apparatus	Measured objective and subjective anxiety. The State-Trait Anxiety Inventory indicated a greater reduction in anxiety levels in the experimental group; however, this reduction was not statistically significant. No significant decrease in heart rate.
Inamura, Wiss, & Parham (1990a & b)	Clinical study	9 children with autism	Grandin's Hug Machine	Greater use appeared to be related to decreased hyperactive behavior in some children.
Creedon (1994)	Clinical study	Children with autism	Hug Machine used by children as needed	Children who used the machine were able to sit more calmly with less aimless action and made more adaptive movements.
Edelson, Edelson, Kerr, & Grandin (1999)	Random controlled trial, subjects randomly assigned to either an experimental (hug machine) or placebo group	12 children with autism	2 sessions per week for 6 weeks—Grandin's Hug Machine	Results suggest that deep pressure may have a calming effect, especially for those persons with autism with high levels of arousal or anxiety. Significant decrease on the tension scale and a marginally significant decrease on the more general anxiety scale.
Morreau (2000)	Single-case ABA design	37-month-old child with autism	Weighted vest used for 2 15-minute periods daily during preschool class over 14 days	Significant increase in attending behavior while wearing the vest, which persisted throughout the preschool class. Increase in STB while wearing the vest. Significant improvement in teacher ratings on Conner's scale (used as measure of arousal). Attention and arousal gradually returned to baseline levels within 8 days of discontinuing vest.

may not be readily available to all persons with autism because of cost. In contrast, the study by Morreau (2000) suggested that a more available form of deep pressure, applied through a weighted vest, may be helpful in improving attention and modulating arousal. Future studies should examine multiple methods of applying deep pressure, such as weighted blankets and vests or backpacks, and the effect of these on physiological arousal and behavioral expressions of arousal. There is a need for consistent measures of constructs such as arousal.

Sensory Integration Treatment

Children with Autism

Although the sensory integration frame of reference is reported to be prevalent in practice with children and adolescents with autism, relatively few efficacy studies of treatment have been published. Both single-case studies and group designs have been conducted. Single-case design and case report studies using sensory integration in individuals with autism are displayed in Table 5–4. Group studies on SI with individuals with autism are reviewed below and overall conclusions are drawn.

Group Studies of Individuals with Autism

Group studies on the effect of sensory integration treatment have begun to suggest which individuals with autism may benefit from treatment. Ayres and Tickle (1980), in a study of 10 children with autism, found that sensory integration was more effective for children who demonstrated normal or hyperresponsiveness to sensory input than for children who demonstrated underarousal or hyporesponsiveness. Greenspan and Wieder (1997) conducted an efficacy study in which SI was one component of a comprehensive clinical program. Those children

with severe involvement made the least progress, while many of the children with few symptoms made outstanding progress. Although the effects of SI cannot be isolated, this study demonstrates that SI can be an important component of a successful comprehensive treatment program.

Studies have examined the effects of the age of the individual with autism on treatment effects. Deterioration in treatment gains about the time of puberty have been reported in approximately a third of children with autism (Gillberg & Schaumann, 1981). In a case study, Ayres and Mailloux (1983) reported a decrease in self-stimulatory behavior of an 11½-year-old girl during occupational therapy using a SI approach. However, these behaviors increased following surgery for scoliosis and the start of menarche. Being aware of this possible regression at puberty is important in decision making for treatment. On the other hand, some adolescents with autism develop insight into their differences at adolescence and actively strive to manage their disorder (Kanner, 1973; MacDonald, 1998). This might be an optimal time for occupational therapists to teach self-regulation and modulation of sensory needs, perhaps through a program such as the Alert Program.

Conclusions of SI Efficacy Studies

Studies of the effects of SI treatment on individuals with autism (as displayed in Table 5–4) demonstrate improvements in the performance areas of self-care, play, and in the performance components of behavior, attention, motor skills, language, and psychosocial interaction. These results are promising and consistent with the reports of occupational therapists that they observed the most significant improvements in sensory processing when they treated children with autism (Case-Smith & Miller, 1999).

Table 5–4 Single-Case Design Studies using Sensory Integration with Individuals with Autism

Author	Design	Participants	Treatment	Outcome
Karsteadt (1983)	Single-case design	Child with autism	Vestibular stimulation compared to fine motor tasks.	Increase in spontaneous verbalizations during sessions of vestibular stimulation versus fine motor tasks.
Reilly, Nelson, & Bundy (1984)	Quasiexperimental	18 children with autism ranging in age from 6.2 to 11.7 years, randomly assigned to one of two orders	Compared SI to fine motor (FM) tabletop activities; children served as own controls; 4 sessions (2SI, 2FM) for 30 minutes; counterbalanced for order.	Fine motor activities elicited significantly more variety of speech, greater average length of utterances, and less autistic speech.
Ray, King, & Grandin (1989)	Single-case design	9-year-old boy with autism	Self-initiated vestibular stimulation provided once daily for 17 days over a 4-week period in 15-minute sessions. Counts during 5 minutes pre- and posttest and 5 minutes of treatment.	Percentage of vocalizations was significantly greater during the time the child was using the stimulation than it was during pre- and posttest.

Kwass (1992)	Case study	3½-year-old girl. Deficits in the tactile and vestibular systems; aversion to water, smells, and many foods. Slept 5–6 hours per night in a reclining chair. Spent hours screaming and throwing tantrums	SI 2 times weekly for 1 hour for 2 years.	Tantrums disappeared and she improved in self-care, gross and fine motor skills, language, and social responsiveness.
Kientz (1996)	Case study	A 3-year-old boy; a 14-year-old boy	Individually designed sensory diet.	Decrease or elimination noted in target behaviors. This author suggests that the implementation of a sensory diet is an important strategy that helps children with autism modulate their arousal level.
Miller (1997)	Single-case AB design	A 3-year-old girl	SI therapy paired with some fine and self-care tasks 2 times/week for 45 minutes each session over 18 sessions.	Statistically significant improvement in parent ratings of attention on the Conners and self-care ability using the PEDI.
Linderman & Stewart (1999)	Single-case AB design across subjects	Two 3-year-old boys with PDD; 3 target behaviors were identified for each child	SI treatment for 11 weeks for participant 1 and 7 weeks for participant 2.	Both demonstrated increase in social interaction, increased approach to new activities, and improved response to holding, hugging, and movement. Decrease in frequency and duration of disruptive behavior; increase in functional behavior, speech, play, and attention to activities.

continues

Table 5–4 continued

Author	Design	Participants	Treatment	Outcome
Jang (1996)	Single-case AB design	5-year-old with autism	3 weeks of SI 2 times/week before structured behavior therapy.	Decrease in SSB (rocking, waving hands, repetitive vocal patterns).
Case-Smith & Bryan (1999)	Single-subject AB design across multiple subjects	5 preschool boys with autism	SI to support behavioral changes. Nonengagement, mastery play, and interaction were measured using counts from videotape. Therapy provided in 1:1 sessions and consultation to teachers for 10 weeks.	3 of the 5 participants made significant improvement in mastery of play. Those who were less impaired demonstrated greater variety of purposeful play behaviors and fewer rigid and stereotyped play behaviors during SI. 4 of 5 participants demonstrated fewer nonengaged behaviors during the intervention phase. None of the children improved in peer interaction but 1 of the children demonstrated significant improvement in interacting with adults; the behavior of 2 others approached significance.

One theme is the consistent report of increased spontaneous verbalizations during sessions of SI providing vestibular stimulation (Karsteadt, 1983; Ray, King, & Grandin, 1989). These authors suggested that children with autism with more overt motor problems have a greater vocal response during vestibular stimulation. In a similar study, not included in Table 5–4, the relationship between vestibular stimulation and language development was studied in a group of 10 preschoolers with MR (Magrun, Ottenbacher, McCue, & Keefe, 1981). These authors found an increase in spontaneous verbal language in response to vestibular stimulation. In contrast, Reilly et al. (1984) found that fine motor activities elicited significantly more variety of speech, greater length of utterances, and less autistic speech than SI. These authors suggested three possible explanations for this finding: (1) sensory input may not have an immediate effect on verbal functions in this population; (2) the children received preexperiment training to verbally respond during fine motor tasks; and (3) the children may have been overstimulated during sensory activities, leading to excessive arousal and diminished vocalizations. Obviously, additional studies are needed to document the level of vestibular stimulation that may elicit vocalizations and the type of sensory problems that are most likely to respond to SI treatment.

Modified sensory integration treatment programs were also reported to result in functional gains when used with persons with MR. Studies report increases in eye contact, frequency of vocalization, quality of postural adaptation (Clark, Miller, Thomas, Kucherway, & Azin, 1978), and language production (Magrun et al., 1981; Neman, Roos, McCann, Menolascino, & Head, 1974).

Two case studies (Kientz, 1996) included an individually designed sensory diet as the treatment intervention. In this approach, the occupational therapist helps the child and the caregivers identify the sensory needs of the child, then develops a systematic schedule of meeting those sensory needs. Results of this study suggested that the development of individualized sensory diets in children and adolescents may be useful in modulating arousal levels and should be further explored.

Current efficacy studies, as depicted in Table 5–4, are mainly descriptive in nature, with a few more rigorous single-case designs. However, the effects of confounding variables, such as developmental changes or the influence of behavioral or other interventions, are not controlled. Future studies of SI efficacy for children and adolescents with autism should include a randomized assignment to control and experimental conditions and the use of consistent and replicable measures of change. SI has been used more widely with children who have learning disabilities (LD). These studies are reviewed because the results enhance overall understanding of the efficacy of sensory integration.

Efficacy Studies Using SI with Children with Learning Disabilities

Children with learning disabilities who were younger, who had more severe fine and gross motor difficulties, who exhibited delays in written language, and who had higher math scores responded with the most gains in occupational therapy using a SI approach (Law, Polatajko, Schaffer, Miller, & Macnab, 1991). Table 5–5 includes a review of studies using SI with children with LD over the past 10 years. See Polatajko,

Table 5-5 The Effects of SI with Children with Learning Disabilities

Author	Design	Participants	Treatment	Outcome
Polatajko, Law, Miller, Schaffer, & Macnab (1991)	2-group random-ized multicenter clinical trial	67 LD children ages 6.0–8.11 were randomly assigned to 2 groups: SI & perceptual-motor (PM).	SI compared to PM. 1 hour/week for 6 months. Examined the effects on academic achievement, motor perfor-mance, and self-esteem.	Both SI and perceptual motor groups increased on academic and motor measures. No differences in treatment.
Humphries, Wright, McDougall, & Vertez (1991)	Pretest and posttest	30 children with LD ages 6–8.1. The majority exhibited vestibular dysfunction.	SI compared with PM and no treatment. 1 hour of SI and PM treatment per week.	SI showed significant improvement in motor skills over the other groups. The researchers measured effects in 4 skill areas: sensorimotor, cognitive, lan-guage, and academics. The results sug-gested that SI was superior to a compa-rable trial of perceptual motor or no treatment in improving certain aspects of gross motor functioning and motor accuracy.
Humphries, Wright, Snider, & McDougall (1992)	Pretest and posttest	103 children with LD and SI dys-function, ages 4.8–8.9.	SI compared with PM. 3 hours of treatment/week.	SI group showed improvement in motor planning; perceptual motor group showed improvement in gross motor skills.
Wilson, Kaplan, Fellowes, Gruchy, & Faris (1992)	2-group random-ized controlled trial, pretest/posttest design	29 children with LD, SI dysfunc-tion, and motor incoordination, ages 5.2–8.6 years.	75 55-minute sessions of individual SI compared with equal amounts	No difference between groups in acade-mics, fine and gross motor skills, or visual-motor skills after 6 months of treatment. The group receiving SI improved slightly on behavioral mea-

			of tutoring during a 12-month period.	sures. The children were tested again after 12 months; although children in both groups showed improvement, there were no significant differences between them except on the behavioral measure.
Humphries, Wright, Snider, & McDougall (1993)	3-group randomized control trial design	Children ages 58–107 months.	Compared SI, PM, or no treatment groups. 72 1-hour sessions for 3 times/week.	Showed no unique advantage for sensory integration treatment; however, SI and PM were superior to no treatment. One factor that may have influenced the results of this study was the type of sensory integrative dysfunction that the children had. Although the groups were randomly assigned, the types of dysfunction were not evenly distributed among them. Those children who were severely involved made the most gains.
Kaplan, Polatajko, Wilson, & Faris (1993)	Combined data from 2 studies	29 children from study 1, ages 5.2–8.6; 67 children from study 2, ages 6–8.11.	Combined results: (1) SI compared to tutoring; (2) SI compared to PM.	SI did not demonstrate significantly greater outcomes than other more traditional methods.
Wilson & Kaplan (1994)	Longitudinal followup study, pretest/posttest	22 of the original 29 subjects. See Kaplan et al. (1993).	Conducted a follow-up study 2 years after completion of the first study, done in 1992, in which SI was compared to tutoring in order to study the effects of treatment after a period of time elapsed.	Neither group showed superiority in maintaining therapy gains, except that gross motor improvement was significantly greater in the SI group.

continues

Table 5–1 continued

Author	Design	Participants	Treatment	Outcome
Fanchaing (1996)	Case study	Adult man with LD.	Reported on a narrative analysis of the life history of a man with LD who had received SI as a child.	The man reported that, through SI and the adaptations he had made, he was able to lead a successful life and achieve his goals. The man continued to choose SI activities to fulfill his needs for sensory input.
Stonefelt & Stein (1998)	Survey research	30 surveys were sent to participants in the Midwest. 77% response rate.	Studied the effectiveness of an SI approach in the treatment of children with LD as perceived by their parents, teachers, and occupational therapists.	Most of the respondents reported that SI was extremely or somewhat effective in helping children improve function in 12 skill areas, especially in coordination and behavior. Other areas in which SI had a significant impact were fine and gross motor skills and balance. This study also suggested that SI was somewhat effective in improving academics. 7 of the 8 occupational therapists reported using another method in addition to SI and noted that a multimodal approach was more effective than SI alone.
Kinnealey (1998)	Case study	3½-year-old girl with sensory defensiveness, and social, emotional, and behavior problems that interfered with age-appropriate roles and learning preschool skills	SI approach focusing on decreasing sensory defensiveness.	She responded well to OT using an SI approach. The Behavioral Style Questionnaire was used to compare pre- and posttreatment behavior, showing improved scores in 6 of 9 areas tested: activity, rhythmicity, approach, adaptability, intensity, and mood. Scores for persistence, distractability, and threshold did not change.

Case-Smith & Miller (1999)	Descriptive, survey design	500 surveys mailed to therapists in Sensory Integration and School SIS of AOTA in the eastern or midwestern U.S.; 58% return rate.	Survey used Likert scale items to measure frequency of performance problems observed in children with PDD, performance areas addressed in intervention, perceived improvement in performance, and frequency of use of and competence in intervention approaches.	Reported improvements in SI, most often in sensory modulation and tactile processing, may indicate that sensory processing is the domain in which children make the greatest gains or the respondents are most aware of these gains. Frequency of direct services correlated with respondents' perceived improvement in SI but did not correlate with improvement in any other performance area. Use of consultation had a low correlation with perceived improvements in SI. Use of SI approaches had a moderate relationship with improvement in SI and a low but significant relationship with improved social skills.
Reeves (1999)	Case study	6-year-old boy with delays in fine motor skills, low frustration level, poor eating behavior, low self-esteem, unusual fears, increased sensitivity to tactile, visual, and auditory stimuli.	9 months of 1:1 SI intervention.	Improvement noted in all areas of concern.

Kaplan, and Wilson (1992) for a complete review of all earlier studies of SI efficacy.

Studies of SI treatment efficacy with children with learning disabilities ranged from case studies to randomized controlled trial designs. These efficacy studies suggest that SI improves motor skills in children with learning disabilities; outcomes may not differ from perceptual-motor treatment (PM) but are better than no treatment. SI was paired with improved gross motor functioning and motor accuracy in a group of children who exhibited vestibular dysfunction (Humphries et al., 1991) and SI improved motor planning abilities (Humphries et al., 1992). No difference between tutoring and SI was found except on a behavioral measure, with those children receiving SI showing greater improvement (Wilson et al., 1992). Results suggest that combinations of therapy techniques may be the most effective. Improvements in sensory modulation and tactile processing were noted by therapists (Case-Smith & Miller, 1999), and SI was perceived by parents and teachers to be somewhat effective in improving academics, coordination, and behavior (Stonefelt & Stein, 1998). Use of consultation as a model of intervention was rated by therapists as having a low correlation with perceived improvements. Studies suggest that children with more severe difficulties made gains (Humphries et al., 1993). In follow-up studies of long-term effects, gross motor improvements were significantly greater for children receiving a SI approach two years after treatment (Wilson & Kaplan, 1994), and improvements in behavior continued for 12 months after treatment (Wilson et al., 1992).

This research with children with learning disabilities suggests that SI may be beneficial for children with autism in improving motor skills, sensory modulation, and tactile processing. However, many of these studies had substantial threats to internal validity, including developmental gains and confounding variables, and threats to external validity, including low statistical power. It is apparent that further studies are needed to determine which children are most likely to benefit from which treatment, and under what conditions.

Meta-Analysis of the Effects of SI

One way to analyze treatment efficacy is through meta-analysis (Kazdin, 1988). This statistical technique, used to analyze and summarize data from more than one study, has emerged as an alternative method of evaluating a body of research. The effectiveness of treatment is examined by quantifying the treatment effect size, using a common metric among different studies. In Table 5–6, meta-analysis studies of the results of sensory integration efficacy research are displayed, synthesized, and analyzed.

The review of these studies suggests that children with learning disabilities receiving SI treatment made gains after intervention; however, they did not significantly outperform other children receiving an alternative treatment, such as tutoring or perceptual-motor training. In fact, SI was found statistically equal to the effect of other alternative treatments (Vargas & Camilli, 1999). The SI group improved as much in reading and other academic measures as did the tutoring group, and the tutoring was as effective as SI in improving motor function (Wilson et al., 1992). In addition, classical SI treatment methods did not show an advantage over adapted SI methods. There was no indication that a better result was achieved by increasing the treatment hours. Studies of the long-term effects of SI indicated that therapy has a more sustained benefit for gross

Table 5–6 Meta-Analysis Studies on the Efficacy of Sensory Integration

Author	Dates of Studies	Studies/Population	Outcomes
Ottenbacher (1982)	1972–1981	8 experimental studies with MR, LD, and aphasia	SI had a positive impact when applied to the populations investigated: MR, LD, and aphasia.
Polatajko et al. (1992)	1978–1992	Included studies that utilized a randomized control group in an LD group	Failed to find statistical evidence that SI improves academic performance of LD children more than a placebo. Of 9 hypotheses tested having a reading-related outcome, only 1 positive result was obtained that favored the SI group. For math ability, only 1 of 6 hypotheses tested achieved significance favoring the SI group. Inconsistent findings with sensory or motor performance, but SI may be similar to perceptual-motor training.
Hoehn & Baumeister (1994)	1981–1993	7 studies with LD	Found only a few instances of notable effects for SI in four categories.
Vargas & Camilli (1999)	1972–1994	76 published articles and 5 master's theses were found that reported results of SI efficacy; 16 SI/NT comparison studies and 16 SI/ Alternative comparison studies were included	The first conclusion was that in the SI/NT comparison, a significant effect was replicated for SI treatment effects in earlier studies, but more recent studies did not show overall positive effects. Second, a larger effect size of SI was found in psychoeducational and motor categories. Third, SI treatment methods were found to be as effective as various alternative treatment methods. A pure sensory integration treatment method did not show advantages over adapted methods. Lastly, with respect to treatment frequency and duration, there was no indication that a better result was achieved by increasing the treatment hours.

motor skills but otherwise is equal to comparison treatment. It is difficult to generalize these findings on SI efficacy in children with LD to children with autism because the conditions are quite different. Nonetheless, this research suggests that improvements in motor skills and behavioral issues may be observed, but they could be obtained using PM treatment approaches. The findings provide ample hypotheses for future theory development. As Parham and Mailloux (1996) pointed out, it is striking that gains made in SI, designed to improve sensory processing, would be comparable to gains made in interventions (e.g., tutoring or perceptual-motor training) that are specifically designed to improve academic or motor skills. It could be that the one-to-one interaction, attention to the needs of the child, or enhanced risk-taking (Tickle-Degnen & Coster, 1995) are more important variables in producing change in children with LD than specific sensory intervention.

IMPLICATIONS OF THESE FINDINGS FOR TREATMENT AND RESEARCH

Occupational therapists are increasingly urged to use evidence-based practice, ensuring that they deliver treatment based on the most credible scientific evidence (Law & Baum, 1998). Evidence-based practice incorporates elements of research utilization, professional judgment and knowledge of individual client characteristics, and preferences in the formation of clinical decisions (Sackett, Rosenberg, Muir Gray, Haynes, & Richardson, 1996). It is important that occupational therapists regularly and critically analyze the studies of treatment efficacy to determine the current state of practice and to plan for future systematic evaluation of treatment efficacy.

Occupational therapy research on treatment efficacy using sensorimotor approaches consists mostly of case reports and single-case design studies, and studies of therapist, teacher, and parent perceptions of outcomes. Although suboptimal, this is consistent with the level of research on autism in other professions, which also generally consists of single-subject multiple baseline designs and small-sample treatment designs (Rogers, 1998). Rogers reminds us that a lack of empirical demonstration of efficacy does not mean that a treatment is ineffective but rather that efficacy has not been demonstrated in an objective way. Research with low statistical power and weak research design is likely to produce contradictory and inconclusive results (Ottenbacher & Maas, 1999). Type II errors in research, which produce high rates of false negative findings, may be due to low statistical power and are common in both occupational therapy and rehabilitation research (Ottenbacher & Maas). Occupational therapy research should be designed with an analysis of statistical power before the research is conducted to ensure that sample size, sensitivity of the measurements, sample heterogeneity, and statistical and experimental designs are likely to demonstrate an effect of treatment if one is present. Without rigorous attention to statistical power analysis, evidence to guide practice is contradictory and, ultimately, impedes progress and the demonstration of the viability of treatment options for individuals with autism.

This chapter presented a narrative or qualitative review of the state of research on the efficacy of sensorimotor treatment approaches. General conclusions about the sensorimotor treatment approaches for children and adolescents with autism can be made from this review. These are based on the published research available today; future research may lead to different conclusions. Here are the conclusions:

1. ***Who benefits?***
   - Children with severe involvement made the least progress in studies where sensorimotor approaches were just one component of a clinical program.
   - SI may be more effective with children with autism who demonstrate a normal or hypersensitive response to sensory input.

2. ***How frequently should therapy be offered?***
   - Sensorimotor treatment may need to be provided frequently in small doses, but effects may be noted in 30 days.

3. ***Effective treatment approaches***
   - Combinations of sensorimotor approaches based on principles in common may be more effective than a single approach.
   - Sensory diets may help modulate arousal in both children and adolescents with autism.
   - Vestibular stimulation may increase vocalizations and decrease stereotypic rocking.
   - Multisensory stimulation strategies may decrease self-stimulatory behaviors, including self-injurious behaviors.
   - Deep pressure may be effective in decreasing anxiety and arousal; those with higher levels of anxiety and arousal may benefit more.

4. ***Functional outcomes***
   - Play skills increased, with the less impaired children showing greater improvement.
   - Improvements were noted in self-care, play, attention, behavior, and social interaction.

- Efficacy studies using SI with children with LD suggest that motor skills improve, but outcomes may not differ from PM treatment; however, outcomes are better than no treatment.
- Improvements were noted in sensory modulation and tactile processing.
- Results suggest that SI does not significantly contribute to improved academic performance more than other methods.

Directions for Future Research

Occupational therapists need to know which interventions are effective and which are not. Further research should be conducted to determine the efficacy of occupational therapy interventions using a sensorimotor approach in facilitating change in multiple contextual environments for clients with autism. Increased understanding of the efficacy of intervention techniques will enable therapists to provide improved services for children with autism. Rogers (1998) suggested that hypothesized variables affecting outcomes, such as age, type of treatment used, intensity of treatment, IQ, language levels, and severity of autism, be rigorously tested and described at the start of treatment. As occupational therapists, we should consider these variables in designing future research.

Criticisms of the validity and effectiveness of sensorimotor treatment approaches for this population stem largely from the lack of empirical research in this area (e.g., Arendt, MacLean, & Baumeister, 1988). The status of this approach is defined, in part, by the status of the research (Tickle-Degnen, 1988). We can influence the perception of professionals and consumers outside of occupational therapy about the benefits of sensorimotor treatment through engaging in rigorous research. Much work needs to be done and many research questions remain unanswered. This chapter may prove to be a useful foundation for such research.

This review of the efficacy research clearly identifies areas of need for future studies:

1. Document the sensory processing of persons with autism (Baranek, 1998).
   a. What is the nature of sensory processing and sensory modulation problems in individuals with autism?
   b. How are these problems different in various groups of individuals with autism?
   c. How does sensory processing and modulation influence occupational performance?
2. More research is needed to determine the sensory processing conditions for which different treatment approaches to sensory dysfunction are most appropriate.
   a. In treatment, does the single sensory mode or the multisensory mode work better?
   b. What is the relationship of self-stimulatory behavior and the response to sensory stimulation?
   c. Does a decrease in self-stimulatory behavior reflect better modulation of arousal levels?
   d. Does a decrease in tactile defensiveness lead to a decrease in stereotypic behavior?
   e. Does dysfunction in registration or modulation require different treatment approaches? Which approaches are most effective for each type of dysfunction?
   f. Do children with hypersensitivity to touch and auditory input respond to sensorimotor interventions? What effects are seen?
3. Further studies are necessary to examine the most effective length of time per individual session, the number of sessions per week, and the duration of treatment. In addition, longitudinal tracking should be conducted to determine the length of carryover of treatment effects.
4. Outcome studies are needed to document treatment effects on functional skills. Studies should focus on treatment that is occupation based rather than be concerned with remediating an underlying problem. For example, qualitative studies investigating life problems in multiple contexts and the effects of treatment on these problems might be conducted.
5. Studies that delineate differences between school-based approaches and medical-based treatment and that compare and contrast the outcomes of each might clarify the contributions of each approach.

As a profession, occupational therapy is beginning to understand what types of sensorimotor approaches may be effective in the treatment of children and adolescents with autism. However, considerable work is still needed in this area so that the best evidence-based practice can be utilized. Through systematic research, occupational therapists can document their knowledge and treatment effectiveness to demonstrate how to best meet the needs of children and adolescents with autism.

CHAPTER REVIEW QUESTIONS

1. List the tenets of the sensorimotor frame of reference for occupational therapy.

2. Compare and contrast the expression and theoretical purpose of self-stimulatory, stereotypic, and self-injurious behavior.

3. Compare and contrast the models of occupational therapy intervention using the sensorimotor frame of reference: sensory motor treatment, sensory stimulation, sensory integration, and the consultative models.

4. What is the most common research design used in the studies displayed in Tables 5–1 through 5–5?

5. Summarize the effects of sensory stimulation on self-stimulatory, stereotypic, and self-injurious behavior.

6. What forms of deep pressure have been used in treatment for children and adults with autism?

7. What principles guide treatment using sensory stimulation to reduce self-stimulatory or stereotypic behavior?

8. Describe two studies that demonstrated that sensory stimulation was effective in reducing self-injurious behavior. List at least three reasons why this treatment may be effective.

9. Summarize the effects of deep pressure on reducing arousal and anxiety.

10. Based on the results of the research displayed in Table 5–4, list at least three functional skills that have improved with the use of a sensory integration approach to treatment.

11. Considering the recommendations for research proposed throughout this chapter, design one research study to examine the effects of a sensorimotor approach to management.

REFERENCES

AOTA (1994). Uniform terminology for occupational therapy (3rd ed.). *American Journal of Occupational Therapy, 48,* 1047–1054.

Arendt, R. E., MacLean, W. E., & Baumeister, A. A. (1988). Critique of sensory integration therapy and its application in mental retardation. *American Journal of Mental Retardation, 92,* 401–411.

Ayres, A. J. (1972). *Sensory integration and learning disorders.* Los Angeles: Western Psychological Services.

Ayres, A. J. (1979). *Sensory integration and the child.* Los Angeles: Western Psychological Services.

Ayres, A. J., & Mailloux, Z. (1983). Possible pubertal effects on therapeutic gains in an autistic girl. *American Journal of Occupational Therapy, 37,* 535–540.

Ayres, A. J., & Tickle, L. (1980). Hyperresponsivity to touch and vestibular stimuli as a predictor of positive response to sensory integration procedures in autistic children. *American Journal of Occupational Therapy, 34,* 375–386.

Baranek, G. T. (1998, June). Sensory processing in persons with autism and developmental disabilities: Considerations for research and clinical practice. *Sensory Integration Special Interest Section Quarterly, 21,* 1–3.

Baranek, G. T., Foster, L. G., & Berkson, G. (1997). Tactile defensiveness and stereotyped behaviors. *American Journal of Occupational Therapy, 51,* 91–95.

Baumeister, A. A., & Forehand, R. (1973). Stereotyped accounts. In N. R. Ellis (Ed.), *International review of research in mental retardation* (pp. 55–96). New York: Academic Press.

Berkson, G., Guthermoth, L., & Baranek, G. T. (1995). Relative prevalence and relations among sterotyped and similar behaviors. *American Journal on Mental Retardation, 100,* 137–145.

Bloomer, M. L., & Rose, C. C. (1989). Frames of reference: Guiding treatment for children with autism. *Occupational Therapy in Health Care, 6,* 5–26.

Bonadonna, R. (1981). Effects of a vestibular stimulation program on stereotypic rocking behavior. *American Journal of Occupational Therapy, 35,* 775–781.

Bright, T., Bittick, K., & Fleeman, B. (1981). Reduction of self-injurious behavior using sensory integrative techniques. *American Journal of Occupational Therapy, 35,* 167–172.

Brockle-Hurst Woods, J. (1990). The use of tactile and vestibular stimulation to reduce stereotypic behaviors in two adults with mental retardation. *American Journal of Occupational Therapy, 44,* 536–541.

Case-Smith, J., & Bryan, T. (1999). The effects of occupational therapy with sensory integration emphasis on preschool-age children with autism. *American Journal of Occupational Therapy, 53,* 489–497.

Case-Smith, J., & Miller, H. (1999). Occupational therapy with children with pervasive developmental disorders. *American Journal of Occupational Therapy, 53,* 506–513.

Clark, F. A., Mailloux, Z., Parham, D., & Bissell, J. (1989). Sensory integration with learning disabilities. In P. N. Clark & A. S. Allen (Eds.), *Occupational therapy for children* (pp. 457–509). St. Louis: Mosby.

Clark, F. A., Miller, L. R., Thomas, J. A., Kucherway, D. S., & Azin, S. P. (1978). A comparison of operant and sensory integration methods on vocalizations and other developmental parameters in profoundly retarded adults. *American Journal of Occupational Therapy, 32,* 86–93.

Cook, D. G. (1991). A sensory approach to the treatment and management of children with autism. *Focus on Autistic Behavior, 5,* 1–19.

Creedon, M. (1994, July). Project SMART: *Sensory modulation, assessment, research, and treatment.* Paper presented at the annual conference of the Autism Society of America, Las Vegas, Nevada.

Cummins, R. A. (1991). Sensory integration and learning disabilities: Ayres's factor analysis reappraised. *Journal of Learning Disabilities, 24,* 160–168.

Dawson, G., & Lewy, A. (1989). Arousal, attention, and the socioemotional impairments of individuals with autism. In G. Dawson (Ed.), *Autism: Nature, diagnosis, and treatment* (pp. 49–74). New York: Guilford Press.

Dura, J., Mulick, J., & Hammer, D. (1988). Rapid clinical evaluation of sensory integrative therapy for self-injurious behavior. *Mental Retardation, 26,* 83–87.

Eaves, L. C., Ho, H. H., & Eaves, D. M. (1994). Subtypes of autism by cluster analysis. *Journal of Autism and Developmental Disorders, 24,* 3–22.

Edelson, S. M., Edelson, M. G., Kerr, D. C. R., & Grandin, T. (1999). Behavioral and physiological effects of deep pressure on children with autism: A pilot study evaluating the efficacy of Grandin's Hug Machine. *American Journal of Occupational Therapy, 53,* 145–152.

Fanchaing, S. P. C. (1996). The other side of the coin: Growing up with a learning disability. *American Journal of Occupational Therapy, 50,* 277–285.

Farber, S. D. (1982). *Neurorehabilitation: A multisensory approach.* Philadelphia: W. B. Saunders.

Fisher, A. G., & Murray, E. A. (1991). Introduction to sensory integration theory. In A. G. Fisher, E. A. Murray, & A. C. Bundy (Eds.), *Sensory integration: Theory and practice* (pp. 3–26). Philadelphia: F. A. Davis.

Fisher, A. G., Murray, E. A., & Bundy, A. C. (Eds.) (1991). *Sensory integration: Theory and practice.* Philadelphia: F. A. Davis.

Freeman, B. J. (1997). Guidelines for evaluating intervention programs for children with autism. *Journal of Autism and Developmental Disorders, 27,* 641–651.

Gillberg, C., & Schaumann, H. (1981). Infantile autism and puberty. *Journal of Child Psychology and Psychiatry, 9,* 365–371.

Gold, M. S., & Gold, J. R. (1975). Autism and attention: Theoretical considerations and a pilot study using set reaction time. *Child Psychiatry and Human Development, 6,* 68–80.

Gorman, P. A. (1997). Sensory dysfunction in dual diagnosis: Mental retardation/mental illness and autism. *Occupational Therapy in Mental Health, 13,* 3–22.

Grandin, T. (1995). *Thinking in pictures.* New York: Doubleday.

Greenspan, S. I., & Wieder, S. (1997). Developmental patterns and outcomes in infants and children with disorders in relating and communicating: A chart review of 200 cases of children with autistic spectrum diagnoses. *Journal of Developmental and Learning Disorders, 1,* 87–142.

Haack, L., & Haldy, M. (1998). Adaptations and accommodations for sensory processing problems. In J. Case-Smith (Ed.), *Occupational therapy: Making a difference in school system practice* (self-paced clinical course) (Unit 4, pp. 1–39). Bethesda, MD: American Occupational Therapy Association.

Hirama, H. (1989). *Self-injurious behavior: A somatosensory treatment approach.* Baltimore: Chess Publications.

Hoehn, T. P., & Baumeister, A. A. (1994). A critique of the application of sensory integration therapy to children with learning disabilities. *Journal of Learning Disabilities, 27,* 338–350.

Humphrey, R., & Link, S. (1990). Preparation of occupational therapists to work in early intervention programs. *American Journal of Occupational Therapy, 44,* 828–833.

Humphries, T. W., Wright, M., McDougall, B., & Vertez, J. (1991). The efficacy of sensory integration therapy for children with learning disability. *Physical and Occupational Therapy in Pediatrics, 10*(3), 1–17.

Humphries, T. W., Wright, M., Snider, L., & McDougall, B. (1992). A comparison of the effectiveness of sensory integrative therapy and perceptual-motor training in treating children with learning disabilities. *Journal of Developmental and Behavioral Pediatrics, 13,* 31–40.

Humphries, T. W., Wright, M., Snider, L., & McDougall, B. (1993). Clinical evaluation of the effectiveness of sensory integrative and perceptual motor therapy in improving sensory integrative function in children with learning disabilities. *Occupational Therapy Journal of Research, 13,* 163–182.

Hutt , S. J., & Hutt, C. (1968). Stereotypy, arousal, and autism. *Human Development, 11,* 227–286.

Inamura, K. N., Wiss, T., & Parham. D. (1990a, September). The effects of Hug Machine usage on the behavioral organization of children with autism and autisticlike characteristics: Part 1. *Sensory Integration Special Interest Section Quarterly, 18,* 1–5.

Inamura, K. N., Wiss, T., & Parham. D. (1990b, December). The effects of Hug Machine usage on the behavioral organization of children with autism and autisticlike characteristics: Part 2. *Sensory Integration Special Interest Section Quarterly, 18,* 1–5.

Iwasaki, K., & Holm, M. B. (1989). Sensory treatment for the reduction of stereotypic behaviors in persons with severe multiple disabilities. *Occupational Therapy Journal of Research, 9,* 170–183.

Jang, D. (1996). *Effect of sensory integration immediately before behavioral therapy sessions on self-stimulation and correctness of response in a child with autism.* Unpublished master's thesis, University of Puget Sound, Tacoma, Washington.

Jones, V., & Prior, M. (1985). Motor imitation abilities and neurological signs in autistic children. *Journal of Autism and Developmental Disorders, 15,* 37–46.

Kanner, L. (1973). *Childhood psychosis: Initial studies and new insights.* New York: Winston/Wiley.

Kaplan, B. J., Polatajko, H. J., Wilson, B. R, & Faris, P. D. (1993). Reexamination of sensory integration

treatment: A combination of two efficacy studies. *Journal of Learning Disabilities, 26,* 342–347.

Karsteadt, K. (1983). The effects of vestibular stimulation on verbalization and attending behavior of an autistic child. *Sensory Integration Special Interest Section Newsletter, 6*(1), 4.

Kazdin, A. E. (1988). *Child psychotherapy: Developing and identifying effective treatments.* Needham Heights, MA: Allyn & Bacon.

Kientz, M. A. (1996). Sensory-based needs in children with autism: Motivation for behavior and suggestions for intervention. *Developmental Disabilities Special Interest Section Newsletter, 19,* 1–3.

Kientz, M. A., & Dunn, W. (1997). A comparison of the performance of children with and without autism on the sensory profile. *American Journal of Occupational Therapy, 51,* 530–537.

Kimball, J. G. (1999). Sensory integrative frame of reference. In P. Kramer & J. Hinojosa (Eds.), *Frames of reference in pediatric occupational therapy* (pp. 119–204). Baltimore: Williams & Wilkins.

King, L. J. (1987). An SI approach to the education of the autistic child. *Occupational Therapy in Health Care, 4,* 77–85.

Kinnealey, M. (1998). Princess or tyrant: A case report of a child with sensory defensiveness. *Occupational Therapy International, 5*(4), 293–303.

Koegel, R. L., & Covert, A. (1972). The relationship of self-stimulation to learning in autistic children. *Journal of Applied Analysis, 5,* 381–387.

Kramer, P., & Hinojosa, J. (1999). *Frames of reference for pediatric occupational therapy* (2nd ed.). Philadelphia: Lippincott, Williams & Wilkins.

Kranowitz, C. S. (1998). *The out-of-sync child.* NY: Skylight Press.

Krauss, K. E. (1987). The effects of deep pressure on anxiety. *American Journal of Occupational Therapy, 41,* 366–373.

Kwass, T. P. (1992). Melissa: A case study for sensory activities in autism. *Occupational Therapy Forum,* (April), 4–8.

Larrington, G. G. (1987). A sensory integration based program with a severely retarded/autistic teenager: An occupational therapy case report. *Occupational Therapy in Health Care, 4,* 101–117.

Law, M., & Baum, C. (1998). Evidence-based occupational therapy. *Canadian Journal of Occupational Therapy, 65,* 131–135.

Law, M., Polatajko, H. J., Schaffer, R., Miller, J., & Macnab, J. (1991). The impact of heterogeneity in a clinical trial: Motor outcomes after sensory integration therapy. *Occupational Therapy Journal of Research, 11,* 177–189.

Lemke, H. (1974). Self-abusive behavior in the mentally retarded. *American Journal of Occupational Therapy, 28,* 94–98.

LeShay, D. (1980). *The integration of speech therapy techniques with those of movement, music, and sensory integration therapies in order to provide communication systems for severely emotionally disturbed children.* Philadelphia: Council for Exceptional Children (ERIC Document Reproduction Service No. ED 196 239).

Linderman, T. M., & Stewart, K. B. (1999). Sensory integrative–based occupational therapy and functional outcomes in young children with pervasive developmental disorders: A single-subject study. *American Journal of Occupational Therapy, 53,* 207–213.

Lindsley, D. B., Wendt, R. H., Lindsley, D. F., Foxx, S. S., Howell, J., & Adley, W. R. (1964). Diurnal activity, behavior, and EEG responses in visually deprived monkeys. *Annals of the New York Academy of Sciences, 117,* 564–588.

Lissy, S. S. (1997). Sensory stimulation as treatment for self-injurious behavior in severe or profound mental retardation. *Developmental Disabilities Special Interest Section Quarterly, 20,* 1–4.

Lovaas, I. O., Litrownik, A., & Mann, R. (1971). Response latencies to auditory stimuli in autistic children engaged in self stimulatory behavior. *Behavioral Research Therapy, 9,* 39–49.

Lovaas, I. O., Newsom, C., & Hickman, C. (1987). Self stimulatory behavior and perceptual reinforcement. *Journal of Applied Behavior Analysis, 20,* 45–68.

MacDonald, V. B. (1998). How the diagnosis of Asperger's has influenced my life. In E. Schopler & G. B. Meisbov (Eds.), *Asperger syndrome or high-functioning autism?* (pp. 367–376). New York: Plenum.

Magrun, W. M., Ottenbacher, K., McCue, S., & Keefe, R. (1981). Effects of vestibular stimulation on spontaneous use of verbal language in developmentally delayed children. *American Journal of Occupational Therapy, 35,* 101–104.

Mason, S. A., & Iwata, B. W. (1990). Artifactual effects of sensory-integrative therapy on self-injurious behavior. *Journal of Applied Behavior Analysis, 23,* 361–370.

McClure, M. K., & Holtz-Yotz, M. (1991). Case report: The effects of sensory stimulatory treatment on an autistic child. *American Journal of Occupational Therapy, 45,* 1138–1142.

McEvoy, C. (1987). *The use of massage therapy in the treatment of self-injurious behavior.* Detroit: Wayne County Intermediate School District (ERIC Document Reproduction service No. ED 308 687).

Miller, L. J., & Lane, S. J. (2000, March). Toward a consensus in terminology in sensory integration theory and practice: Part 1: Taxonomy of neurophysiological processes. *Sensory Integration Special Interest Section Quarterly, 23,* 1–4.

Miller, S. (1997). *The impact of sensory integration on attention and function in a child with autism.* Unpublished special project. Richmond, KY: Eastern Kentucky University.

Morreau, S. (2000). *The effects of a weighted vest on a preschool child with autism.* Unpublished thesis. Richmond, KY: Eastern Kentucky University.

Murphy, G. (1982). Sensory reinforcement in the mentally handicapped and autistic child: A review. *Journal of Autism and Developmental Disorders, 12,* 265–277.

Murray, E. A., & Anzalone, M. E. (1991). Integrating sensory integration theory and practice with other intervention approaches. In A G. Fisher, E. A. Murray, & A. C. Bundy (Eds.), *Sensory integration: Theory and practice* (pp. 354–383). Philadelphia: F. A. Davis.

Neman, R., Roos, P., McCann, B., Menolascino, F. J., & Head, L. W. (1974). Experimental evaluation of sensorimotor patterning used with mentally retarded children. *American Journal of Mental Deficiency, 79,* 372–384.

Oetter, P., Richter, E., & Frick, S. (1995). *MORE: Integrating the mouth with sensory and postural functions* (rev. ed.) Hugo, MN: PDP Press.

O'Neill, M., & Jones, R. S. (1997). Sensory-perceptual abnormalities in autism: A case for more research. *Journal of Autism and Developmental Disorders, 27,* 283–293.

Ornitz, E. M. (1974). The modulation of sensory input and motor output in autistic children. *Journal of Autism and Childhood Schizophrenia, 4,* 197–215.

Ornitz, E. M., & Ritvo, E. R. (1976). The syndrome of autism: A critical review. *American Journal of Psychiatry, 19,* 609–619.

Ornitz, E. M., Sorosky, A. D., & Ritvo, E. R. (1970). Environmental modification of autistic behavior. *Archives of General Psychiatry, 22,* 341–347.

Ottenbacher, K. J. (1982). Sensory integration therapy: Affect or effect? *American Journal of Occupational Therapy, 36,* 571–578.

Ottenbacher, K. J., & Altman, A. (1984). Effects of vibratory, edible, and social reinforcement on performance of institutionalized mentally retarded individuals. *American Journal of Mental Deficiency, 89,* 201–204.

Ottenbacher, K. J., & Maas, F. (1999). How to detect effects: Statistical power and evidence-based practice in occupational therapy research. *American Journal of Occupational Therapy, 53,* 181–188.

Parham, D. L., & Mailloux, Z. (1996). Sensory integration. In J. Case-Smith, A. S. Allen, & P. N. Pratt (Eds.), *Occupational therapy for children* (3rd ed.) (pp. 307–355). St. Louis: Mosby.

Polatajko, H. J., Kaplan, B. J., & Wilson, B. N. (1992). Sensory integration treatment for children with learning disabilities: Its status 20 years later. *Occupational Therapy Journal of Research, 12,* 323–341.

Polatajko, H. J., Law, M., Miller, J., Schaffer, R., & Macnab, J. (1991). The effect of sensory integration program on academic achievement, motor performance, and self-esteem in children identified as learning disabled: Results of a clinical trial. *Occupational Therapy Journal of Research, 11,* 155–176.

Pulice, P. (1987). *Autism and attachment: An attachment-based intervention guide for children with autism and pervasive developmental disorder.* Minneapolis, MN: Minneapolis Children's Medical Center (ERIC Document Reproduction Service No. ED 292245).

Rapin, I. (1997). Autism. *New England Journal of Medicine, 337,* 97–104.

Ray, T. C., King, L. J., & Grandin, T. (1989). The effectiveness of self-initiated vestibular stimulation in producing speech sounds in an autistic child. *Occupational Therapy Journal of Research, 8,* 86–190.

Reeves, G. (1999). Case report of a child with sensory integration dysfunction. *Occupational Therapy International, 5,* 304–316.

Reilly, C., Nelson, D. L., & Bundy, A. (1984). Sensorimotor versus fine motor activities in eliciting vocalizations in autistic children. *Occupational Therapy Journal of Research, 3,* 199–212.

Reisman, J. (1993). Using a sensory integrative approach to treat self-injurious behavior in an adult with profound mental retardation. *American Journal of Occupational Therapy, 47,* 403–411.

Resman, M. H. (1981). Effect of sensory stimulation on eye contact in a profoundly retarded adult. *American Journal of Occupational Therapy, 35,* 31–35.

Ritvo, E. R., Ornitz, E. M., & La Franchi, S. (1968). Frequency of repetitive behaviors in early infantile autism and its variants. *Archives of General Psychiatry, 19,* 341–347.

Rogers, S. J. (1998). Empirically supported comprehensive treatments for young children with autism. *Journal of Clinical Child Psychology, 27,* 168–179.

Sackett, D. L., Rosenberg, W. M. C., Muir Gray, J. A., Haynes, R. B., & Richardson, W. S. (1996). Evidence-based medicine: What it is and what it isn't. *British Medical Journal, 312,* 71–72.

Sanders, D. (1993). Selected literature and case studies supporting the effectiveness of a sensorimotor and behavior modification approach to autism. *Sensory Integration Special Interest Section Newsletter, 16,* 3–6.

Smith, I. M., & Bryson, S. E. (1994). Imitation and action in autism: A critical review. *Psychological Bulletin, 16,* 259–272.

Stockmeyer, S. A. (1967). An interpretation of the approach of Rood to the treatment of neuromuscular dysfunction. *American Journal of Physical Medicine, 46,* 900–956.

Stonefelt, L. L., & Stein, F. (1998) Sensory integration techniques applied to children with learning disabilities: An outcome study. *Occupational Therapy International, 5*(4), 252–272.

Storey, K., Bates, P., McGhee, M., & Dycus, S. (1984). Reproducing the self-stimulatory behavior of a profoundly retarded female through sensory awareness training. *American Journal of Occupational Therapy, 38,* 510–516.

Tickle-Degnen, L. (1988). Perspectives on the status of sensory integration theory. *American Journal of Occupational Therapy, 42,* 427–433.

Tickle-Degnen, L., & Coster, W. (1995). Therapeutic interaction and the management of challenge during the beginning minutes of sensory integration treatment. *Occupational Therapy Journal of Research, 15,* 122–141.

Vargas, S., & Camilli, G. (1999). A meta-analysis of research on sensory integration treatment. *American Journal of Occupational Therapy, 53,* 189–198.

Waterhouse, L., Fein, D., & Modahl, C. (1996). Neurofunctional mechanisms in autism. *Psychological Review, 103,* 457–489.

Watling, R., Dietz, J., Kanny, E. M., & McLaughlin, J. F. (1999). Current practice of occupational therapy for children with autism. *American Journal of Occupational Therapy, 53,* 498–505.

Welch, M.G. (1988). *Holding time.* New York: Simon & Schuster.

Wells, M. E., & Smith, D. W. (1983). Reduction of self-injurious behavior of mentally retarded persons using sensory-integrative techniques. *American Journal of Mental Deficiency, 87,* 664–666.

Wilbarger, P. (1995). The sensory diet: Activity programs based on sensory processing theory. *Sensory Integration Special Interest Section Newsletter, 18,* 1–4.

Wilbarger, P., & Wilbarger, J. L. (1991). *Sensory defensiveness in children aged 2–12.* Denver, CO: Avanti Educational Programs.

Williams, M. S., & Shellenberger, S. (1994). *"How does your engine run?" The Alert Program for self-regulation.* Albuquerque, NM: Therapy Works.

Williamson, G., & Anzalone, M. (1997). Sensory integration: A key component of the evaluation and treatment of young children with severe difficulties in relating and communicating. *Zero to Three, 17*(5), 29–36.

Willis, D. (1983). Balancing learning with pleasure. *Pointer, 27,* 36–37.

Wilson, B. N., & Kaplan, B. J. (1994). Follow-up assessment of children receiving sensory integration treatment. *Occupational Therapy Journal of Research, 14,* 244–265.

Wilson, B. N., Kaplan, B. J., Fellowes, S., Gruchy, C., & Faris, P. (1992). The efficacy of sensory integration treatment compared to tutoring. *Physical and Occupational Therapy in Pediatrics, 12,* 1–35.

Zissermann, L. (1992). The effects of deep pressure on self-stimulating behaviors in a child with autism and other disabilities. *American Journal of Occupational Therapy, 46,* 547–551.

CHAPTER 6

Sensory Integration in Child-Centered Therapy

Sandra L. Rogers

CHAPTER OBJECTIVES

At the completion of this chapter, the reader will be able to:

- Identify the tenets of classic sensory integration therapy.
- Understand the concept of providing a "just-right challenge" to promote learning.
- Appreciate the value of play and a playful attitude in engaging children in self-directed sensorimotor activities.
- Identify the elements and equipment needed within an environment designed for sensory integration therapy.
- Describe modifications to the environment to accommodate for sensory processing disorders.
- Identify strategies and interventions that target vestibular-proprioceptive, tactile, and visual systems.
- Describe strategies for intervention to improve postural-ocular movement and motor planning.
- Appreciate the multiple, almost unlimited, variations that are possible within a sensory integration approach to therapy.

INTRODUCTION AND BASIC TENETS

The purpose of this chapter is to highlight a set of commonly prescribed modalities used in sensory integration (SI) therapy and applied to the treatment of children with autism. The intent is to provide the reader with an understanding of the direct intervention strategies that therapists using a SI approach typically employ. To achieve this purpose, the chapter is divided into sections that include basic tenets and concepts, setting up the therapeutic environment, specific applications for sensory processing disorders, and a case analysis to illustrate the intervention.

Classical sensory integrative treatment is based on six guiding tenets:

1. The use of controlled sensory input elicits an adaptive response.
2. The registration of meaningful sensory input is needed before an adaptive response occurs.
3. Adaptive responses contribute to the development of SI.

4. Better organization of adaptive responses enhances the child's general behavioral organization.

5. Mature and complex patterns of behavior are composed of consolidations of more primitive behaviors.

6. The more inner-directed a child's activities are, the greater the potential of the activities for improving neural organization (Ayres, 1972, 1979).

The implication of these principles is that occupational therapy using an SI approach is an intensive, one-to-one process. Therapy sessions are guided by the therapist–but not rehearsed, because self-direction, presumably, leads to more active participation and more inner-directed activities. The prominent clinical features, identifying children with autism (i.e., impairment of social interaction, impairment of communication, and restricted and repetitive interests and behaviors), require that therapists additionally consider behavioral regulation, control of environmental demands, and a high level of structure during the intervention session to successfully treat the child with autism (Cohen, 1999; Cole, 1998; Watling, Deitz, Kanny, & McLaughlin, 1999).

Each session is prescribed using the strengths of the child and therapist, the goals for intervention, and the constraints presented by the child. Foremost in the clinician's mind is the need to carefully develop interventions after thoughtful evaluation and interpretation of a child's unique set of presenting problems. The clinician is responsible for ensuring a good match between the child's identified impairments and the recommended intervention. Prescriptions for interventions reflect the underlying sensorimotor deficit and the specific outcome expected. For example, a child who demonstrates gravitational insecurity on evaluation and has a goal (set by child and family) of tolerating a gym class with peers would be

provided with opportunities to use suspended equipment, the experiences being graded from very controlled movement to movement on pieces of equipment with less predictability.

Treatment effectiveness for each child is documented by attainment of specified independent living skills, psychosocial skills, and cognitive skills (Mailloux & Burke, 1997). The stated goals should reflect the social, communication, and behavioral constraints typically seen in autism (e.g., poor attention span, poor communication of needs, restlessness, clumsiness, fine motor control impairments, impaired peer interactions, and limited tolerance to social, tactile, environmental changes). These documented changes in pragmatic childhood occupations are an essential part of therapy for reimbursement and family satisfaction with treatment. More important, accurate and systematic documentation can be used to document the efficacy of sensorimotor interventions and congruence with family goals (Cohn, Miller, & Tickle-Degnen, 2000; Fletcher & Fletcher, 1997).

Embedded in the milieu of classical SI intervention is the development of a set of challenging activities that is just beyond a child's skill level ("just-right level") and the achievement of those activities within a play context (Koomar & Bundy, 1991). Koomar and Bundy eloquently captured the complex skills needed to create this intervention in their description of the "art and science" of direct intervention. The essence of SI therapy is to promote a level of participation by the child in activities that are neither too difficult nor too easy to perform. This level is achieved when the child is challenged but not frustrated during a treatment session. To reach the "just-right" challenge, it is essential that a therapist engage in playful behaviors, establish a positive rapport, and use equipment and space creatively. Research indicates that we need to provide both challenges and slightly underchallenging activities that provide brief periods of rest (Dunkerley, Tickle-Degnen, & Coster, 1997).

An additional layer to these principles and to the practice of SI therapy with all children includes integrating play theories into the therapy sessions. This is a particularly challenging aspect of intervention, given the pronounced deficits in play behaviors that children with autism typically display. Theoretical constructs of play are combined with the presentation of play stimuli at the right level for the constraints autism presents (Mailloux & Burke, 1997). As in any sensorimotor intervention session, the activities presented should not only address the identified underlying impairment, reflect SI, and facilitate the stated goals but also be playful and draw on the individual child's skill, interests, and positive emotions (Bundy, 1991; Knox & Mailloux, 1997; Mailloux & Burke, 1997).

Play theories are intertwined with classical SI principles, as both support treatment sessions that:

1. Are intrinsically motivating.
2. Are not ruled by compliance with social norms, expectations, or promise of external rewards.
3. Attend to the means versus the ends of the session.
4. Are free from others' expectations as the child explores new ways to examine a toy or experience.
5. Can change at the whim of the players.
6. Are child centered rather than object centered.
7. Foster instrumental behaviors and nonliteral/pretense behaviors.
8. Exhibit freedom from externally imposed rules.
9. Facilitate active engagement in an activity.

Specifically, engaging a child with autism in SI therapy includes activities in which the child can concretely but positively interact with the play objects or equipment. Additionally, the inclusion of social themes into each session is preferred, as both the deficits commonly acknowledged and the stated goals from families typically include improved social functioning (Cohn et al., 2000).

Surveys of current occupational therapy practice with children who have autism or pervasive developmental delays (PDD) indicate that sensorimotor treatment is the most commonly used type of intervention by occupational therapists who treat children with autism (99%) (Case-Smith & Miller, 1999; Watling et al., 1999). Additionally, these authors found that the majority of sensorimotor intervention is administered on a one-to-one basis in school or outpatient settings for 30–60 minutes. The intervention techniques highlighted here attempt to reflect those clinical realities—that is, ideas that could be appropriately used in current practice are described. The remainder of the chapter is organized around specific treatment interventions and the description of a general play setting for each therapeutic intervention.

THERAPEUTIC ENVIRONMENT

The environment for sensorimotor intervention is critical to creating the just-right therapeutic session for each client (Koomar, 1990). The adequate SI treatment environment includes space for suspended equipment, use of scooters, climbing, running, and jumping; the environment has a wide variety of play objects available, a quiet area designated for reducing stimuli, and a system for adequate control over auditory and visual stimuli.

Play objects within the therapeutic environment often include small manipulative objects as well as large suspended equipment. See Table 6–1 for a listing for play objects commonly featured in a sensorimotor session. Examples of game themes involve hide and seek, follow the leader, musical chairs, obstacle courses, mazes, Simon Says, Twenty Questions (can only shake head yes/no in response to questions), I Spy, hitting targets, and pursuing others. Imaginary play includes pretending that the equipment is, for example, a boat, a whale, a wave, a bucking bronco, a helicopter, or that two people are dueling. The children can also be encouraged to role-model characters, including a superhero, a queen or king, a cowboy, a sports hero, or their favorite television hero. Children can imagine themselves on a fishing trip, climbing a mountain, on a safari, snowboarding, having target practice, being involved with the demolition of a building, building a city, and playing basketball, hockey, or volleyball. The permutations of each activity are constrained only by the therapist's estimation of the child's capability to incorporate appropriate imaginary play (Fink, 1989).

Again, the emphasis on play for the child with autism should be on engagement on positive roles, the clear combination of appropriate social modeling, play behaviors with sensorimotor actions, and clear and concrete goals for the intervention session. Affect may be modeled with exaggeration by the therapist to provide adequate visual cues for the client. Verbalizations should be clear and consistent. The session often has a routine but should avoid overly ritualistic routines, which may interfere with grading or providing additional challenge.

APPLICATIONS FOR SENSORY PROCESSING DYSFUNCTION

In the following sections, each activity is listed for its inherent characteristics that most challenge the identified sensory system. It can be assumed that most of the tasks are multifaceted, stimulating a variety of sensory receptors and enhancing multiple aspects of sensory processing. Each sensory system is listed separately for clarity. Many of the descriptions of specific interventions that follow originated and were first published by A. Jean Ayres (Ayres, 1972, 1979). Others made several important contributions and modifications, and their work is cited (Anderson, 1998; Edelson, Edelson, Kerr, & Grandin, 1999; Fink, 1989; Koomar, 1990; Koomar & Bundy, 1991; Restall & Magill-Evans, 1994; Wilbarger & Wilbarger, 1991; Williams & Shellenberger, 1996).

Vestibular-Proprioceptive Interventions

Vestibular-proprioceptive interventions have been most widely used in classic sensorimotor and SI interventions. Although the vestibular and proprioceptive systems are anatomically differentiated, both contribute to motor performance and to postural control. In fact, the clinician is advised that vestibular system functioning is so closely intertwined with proprioceptive functioning that it is difficult to discriminate between their relative contributions (Fisher, 1991). Consequently, while the interventions detailed here are listed as influencing either the vestibular system or the proprioceptive system, they dovetail with many interventions described as stimulating to both.

The vestibular receptors consist of the semicircular canals, the utricle and the saccule, within the inner ear (Horak & Shupert, 1994). The proprioceptive receptors are distributed throughout the body and include joint receptors, muscle spindles, Golgi tendon organs, and cutaneous mechanoreceptors within the musculoskeletal system (Burgess, Wei, Clark, & Simon, 1982). Given this anatomical structure, movements of the head against gravity tends to stimulate the receptors of the vestibular system and movement of the body against resistance

Table 6–1 Commonly Used Play Objects and Equipment in Sensorimotor Intervention

Object/ Equipment Description	Physical Properties and Gradations	Sensory Modality Elicited by Physical Properties of Object
Bean bags	Outer texture can be soft/plush, vinyl, tacky, Lycra material. Weight, sand, Styrofoam pellets, or lead shot fill. Size of bags also can be altered.	Visual, tactile, proprioceptive.
Dress-up clothes and weighted clothes	A variety of closures (e.g., buttons, snaps, toggles, strings, elastic, hooks); hats, scarves, shoes, large baggy clothes, shiny outfits, dresses, pants, vests, weighted vests, weighted arm bands, leg weights, pompoms. Materials that are sheer, soft, rough, smooth, nubs, shiny, crinkled, pleated (e.g., chiffon, silk, wool, plastic, tweed/raw silk, patent leather).	Visual, tactile, proprioceptive. Also promotes self-care and motor planning.
Balls of all sizes and weights, balloons	Texture of balls can be altered, smooth, oval/egg shaped, knobby. Fabric covers are added to balloons. Different size from ping-pong balls to large gymnastic balls. Weight—beach ball to basketball to weighted ball.	Vestibular, visual, tactile, proprioceptive.
Soap bubbles	Bubble wands with short or long handles; wands that require blowing; large wands that require arm movements to create bubbles.	Visual, tactile, olfactory, vestibular, oral-motor skills, visual tracking.
Shaving cream	To write on body or windows.	Tactile, visual, olfactory.
Plastic and wooden sticks	Weight, length, and shape can vary.	Tactile, proprioceptive, visual.
Hockey pucks, rings	Plastic/lightweight, rings made of rope, weighted hockey pucks.	Proprioceptive, visual.
Orange cones	Weight, size can be altered.	Visual.
Tunnels	Size and material from smooth to rough, can be used, satin, plastic, knit tubular material. Interior construction can also be exposed.	Visual, tactile, proprioceptive, vestibular. Crawling through the tunnel requires motor planning.

continues

Table 6–1 continued

Object/ Equipment Description	Physical Properties and Gradations	Sensory Modality Elicited by Physical Properties of Object
Barrels	Size and material used to design barrel can vary.	Visual, tactile, proprioceptive, vestibular, motor planning equilibrium.
Dry beans, dry rice	Use of total body in beans or beans and rice in small pans is encouraged.	Tactile, visual.
Grooming objects	Wide variety of objects can be used to promote touching face, mouth, arms, and hair.	Tactile, visual, self-care, motor planning.
Ropes, rubber bands or tubing	Facilitate independent movement for climbing and pulling against in swings or on scooter boards.	Visual, tactile, proprioceptive, vestibular, motor planning.
Scooters	Size, type of wheel, and textured material on boards can be altered.	Visual, tactile, proprioceptive, vestibular, auditory.
Swings	A wide variety of swings (e.g., bolster, net, platform, glider, inner tube, whale, variable axis, linear glider, bi-orbital accelerator, sling seat, flexion disc, rubber-dual, trapeze, twirler, spring swings) can be provided.	Visual, tactile, proprioceptive, vestibular, motor planning.
Music and musical instruments	Volume and type of music (instrumental, vocal, classical, folk, jazz, rock, country) or musical instrument can be altered.	Auditory, sequencing and timing.
Paints, markers, chalk, crayons	Size, shape, texture, smell can be varied, e.g., animal markers, triangular shapes, small or large paintbrushes.	Tactile, visual, proprioceptive, motor planning.
Powder, cornstarch	Can be provided in a variety of containers or used with paintbrushes initially. Use to fill balloons for finger squeeze toy.	Tactile.
Fabrics	Yarn, cotton, blankets, velvet, wool, tweed, satin, silk, tube fabric, stockinet, lycra, canvas, sequins can all be incorporated.	Tactile, visual.
Flashlight	Weight of flashlight, power of light, and size of flashlight can vary.	Visual.

continues

Table 6–1 continued

Object/ Equipment Description	Physical Properties and Gradations	Sensory Modality Elicited by Physical Properties of Object
Cart or wheelbarrow	Size, weight, type of wheel, and material used to design carts can be altered.	Proprioceptive, vestibular.
Buckets, baskets, containers	Size, shape (round, square), and differing materials (cardboard, plastic, nets) of buckets can be provided.	Visual.
Magnets	Size and weight of magnets can be altered.	Proprioceptive.
Brushes	Size and bristle material including natural fibers, plastic, stiff, soft, with knobs on the end of each bristle, or densely packed brushes.	Tactile.
Bats	Plastic, wooden, padded, and foam bats are available.	Tactile, proprioceptive.

tends to stimulate the receptors of the proprioceptive system.

Vestibular-proprioceptive disorders include postural-ocular movement disorders, including inability or decreased ability to use prone extension, poor neck flexion with supine flexion, hypotonicity of extensor muscles, poor joint stability, poor postural/balance/equilibrium control, poor kinesthesia sense, and altered responses to postrotary nystagmus (Fisher, 1991). These disorders of basic movement may result in a variety of movement problems, including poor visual tracking, decreased postural control, and poor quality of fine motor output. In addition, gravitational insecurity, intolerance to movement, and excessive seeking of vestibular input suggest vestibular-proprioceptive processing deficits.

Interventions targeting the vestibular system receive a preponderance of attention in SI therapy and are typically viewed as a powerful mode of intervention. On the other hand, interventions targeting the proprioceptive system are often closely associated with active movement (e.g., spatial orientation of body parts, rate and timing of movements, muscle tension, and velocity of movements), so that intervention is designed to challenge motor performance. Interventions for proprioceptive input focus on stimulating large motor movements, which heavily recruit joint receptors.

Intervention offered to provide graded input to the vestibular system typically involves equipment that works in a variety of planes of movement and at a variety of speeds. This includes quick fluctuations while spinning, which stimulate the semicircular canals; slow and rhythmical linear motions in up/down, forward/back, diagonal, and sideways planes, which stimulate the utricle and saccule; and orbital movements, which stimulate all sensory organs in the vestibular system. The premise of providing vestibular stimulation is that appropriately introduced and graded vestibular stimulation normalizes (meaning improves) the vestibular mechanisms mediating postural reactions, which are thought to provide a background for movement (Ayres, 1972, 1979). However, researchers have been challenged to provide documentation of the effectiveness of this theory. Although vestibular interventions are frequently used therapeutic tools that can be graded to offer a variety of challenges to a child, many cautions about the unrestricted use or inappropriate application of vestibular stimulation apply. It is ideal for the client to direct the amount of stimulation received with encouragement, support, and monitoring from a therapist experienced in sensorimotor interventions. Table 6–2 lists of a few of the vestibular stimulation techniques a therapeutic session may incorporate.

Interventions that incorporate the dynamics of activities directed toward specific joint compressions, muscle contractions, and cutaneous mechanoreceptors are designed to target the proprioceptive system. Again, one cannot say which portions of the movement may be more vestibular or proprioceptive, as these systems work in a dynamic dance. The theory is that provision of specific proprioceptive stimulation normalizes muscle length and tension, and allows the child to learn correct motor sequences and to anticipate needed unconscious and bilateral movements (Koomar & Bundy, 1991). The interventions prescribed in a typical sensorimotor session often include the use of resistance to active movement (e.g., bouncing, jumping, running, dancing, swinging, climbing, crawling). Table 6–3 highlights specific intervention techniques a therapist may use in treatment. Equipment, similar to equipment used in vestibular interventions, may include scooter boards, swings, playground equipment, ladders, tunnels, and gymnastic balls.

The critical challenge for any intervention protocol is documentation of positive outcomes of the prescribed treatment. On a pragmatic level, independent skills, like the ability to ride in a car or school bus, participate fully in gym classes with peers, play with friends at a community playground, play tag, and participate in family activities (e.g., hiking, climbing, snow skiing, snow sledding, tricycle/bicycle riding, and going to amusement parks) are laudable goals for treatment designed to improve vestibular-proprioceptive processing. One underutilized mechanism for recording success in therapy may be systematic measurement of changes in behavior (e.g., improved positive affect, self-confidence, and self-management). Systematic methods for recording physiological and psychosocial benefits in addition to motor skill and adaptive skill benefits are needed to provide evidence of treatment effectiveness. It is essential that the clinician focus on goals that maximize the child's occupational competence and use those skills as markers for success in a treatment regime.

Tactile Interventions

Anatomically, the tactile system includes receptors embedded in the skin that provide information to the central nervous system (CNS) about pressure, direction of movement, pain, and temperature. Adequate tactile sensory awareness (tactile perception) and sensory discrimination are critical for anticipating sensory experiences (e.g., being touched by another person) and for responding appropriately. Two types of disorders are identified: tactile defensiveness (inappropriately aversive or negative behaviors in response to non-noxious stimuli) and diminished tactile discrimination (diminished ability to correctly perceive and organize incoming discriminative touch). Children with autism are frequently described as displaying either one or both of these tactile impairments (see Chapter 1). Inappropriate reactions to a variety of environmental tactile stimuli often interfere with an individual's daily routine (e.g., toleration of grooming and reaction to painful stimuli).

Table 6–2 Specific Vestibular Intervention Techniques in Sensorimotor Treatment

Equipment	Positioning	Movement	Modifications to Motion and Sensory Experience
Swings			
Inner tube swing	Seated or prone	Linear, angular, orbital	Inflation level in the inner tube, distance from the floor, child uses rope, rubber tubing, or the floor to initiate and continue movement.
Helicopter/ T-Swing	Seated	Linear, angular, orbital	Peer or sibling can join in ride; therapist assists with child's movement. The material on base of swing and distance from floor can be altered.
Whale swing	Prone	Linear, angular	Child holds onto swing; therapist can provide stability; fabric on surface and distance from floor can be altered.
Bolster swing	Seated, prone, supine	Linear, angular, orbital	Peer or sibling joins in ride on a large bolster swing; child pulls self on swing, using rope or tubing attached to the wall, ceiling, or another swing. The therapist initiates or provides movement for the child, alters fabric on swing surface, alters shape of bolster (round or square) and distance from the floor.
Net swing	Seated, prone, or supine	Linear or angular	Child pulls self on swing using rope or tubing attached to the wall, ceiling, or another swing; therapist assists with child's movement. Size of net swing and material in swing can be changed.
Platform/glider swing	Seated, prone, standing, kneeling, or supine	Linear, orbital	Peer or sibling joins in ride; child pulls self on swing, using rope or tubing attached to the wall, ceiling, or another swing. The therapist initiates or provides movement for the child, alters fabric on swing surface, distance from the floor.

continues

Table 6–2 continued

Equipment	Positioning	Movement	Modifications to Motion and Sensory Experience
Variable axis swing	Seated	Linear, angular, orbital	Child pulls self to upright positions; therapist assists with child's movement; arm movement is facilitated. The material on base of swing and distance from floor can be altered.
Interaction dual swing/Rubber dual swing	Seated	Linear, angular, orbital	Peer or sibling can join in ride and jointly determine the speed and direction of movement. Therapist may assist with child's movement or provide movement. The distance from floor can be altered.
Bi-orbital accelerator swing (seesaw motion)	Seated	Linear, angular, orbital	Peer or sibling can join in ride and jointly determine the speed and direction of movement. Therapist may assist with child's movement or provide movement. The distance from floor can be altered.
Sling seat swing	Seated	Linear, orbital	Child pulls self on swing, using rope or tubing attached to the wall, ceiling, or another swing. Fabric on swing and distance from floor can be altered.
Flexion disc swings/Moon swings	Seated	Linear, angular, orbital	Therapist can assist with child's movement or provide movement. Both distance from floor and material on swing can be varied.
Flying trapeze/Trapeze swing/bars	Standing	Linear, angular, orbital	Child can play games (knocking down objects in path, avoiding objects in path), material on handle can be altered, and therapist can assist with movement.

continues

Table 6–2 continued

Equipment	Positioning	Movement	Modifications to Motion and Sensory Experience
Twirler swing	Seated	Angular, orbital	Child provides movement using rope or tubing attached to the wall, ceiling, or another swing.
Harness swing	Seated	Linear, angular, orbital	Child can step, stand, or spin in harness; provides deep pressure. Therapist can alter distance from floor and facilitate movement.
Tire swing	Seated, kneeling, standing, prone	Linear, angular, orbital	Child pulls self on swing using rope or tubing attached to the wall, ceiling, or another swing; therapist assists with child's movement. The material on base of swing and distance from floor can also be altered.
Spring swings/Frog swings	Seated	Linear, angular, orbital	Child pulls self on swing using rope or tubing attached to the wall, ceiling, or another swing; therapist assists with child's movement. The material on base of swing and distance from floor can also be altered.
Scooter board	Prone, seated, or supine	Linear	Propel self down a ramp, use a plastic mat instead of scooter board, engage multiple children in games (volleyball, follow the leader, obstacle course, tag, crack the whip) on scooters. Pull along rope while lying on back commando style.
Slides	Prone or seated	Linear	Height of slide to ground, material slide is made of (metal, plastic, rolling tubes), method to get to top of slide (stairs, ramp, rope) can be varied.

continues

Table 6–2 continued

Equipment	Positioning	Movement	Modifications to Motion and Sensory Experience
Climbing, rope towers, rope nets, playground ladders	Standing	Angular, linear	Use of rope ladders, metal ladders, and height from ground can be altered.
Suspended bridge	Standing, walking, crawling	Angular, linear	Vary amount of assistance therapists provides.
Trampolines or bounce pads	Standing, kneeling, sitting	Linear	Amount of stabilization provided can be altered; use moon shoes (shoe bases attached to rubber bands and a platform).
Walking	Standing, walking	Angular, linear	Up and down inclined surfaces, walking on a balance beam, walking on a rope on floor, walking on rough surfaces, be pulled on a piece of cardboard and try to surf (go from prone to standing).
Balls	Prone, seated, or supine	Angular	Egg-shaped balls with handles (for bunny hopping), chair balls, ball stand to initiate use of ball, bouncing up and down, use light balls, have child move the ball with his or her head.
Barrels	Prone, supine	Angular	Rolling, crawling through; size of barrel and material barrel is made of may be altered.
Airmats	Prone, seated, supine	Angular	Inflation levels and amount of stabilization provided can be altered.
Rocking in a rocking chair	Seated	Linear	Size of rocking chair, height to floor, material on surface of chair can be varied.
Ride a bike	Seated	Angular, linear	Size can be altered and adaptations for foot and hand placement can be made.
Dancing	Standing	Angular	Alterations can be made to tempo and style of dancing; child can dance with objects like scarves, wands with ribbons.

continues

Table 6–2 continued

Equipment	Positioning	Movement	Modifications to Motion and Sensory Experience
Running	Standing, walking	Linear	Up and down inclined surfaces or on rough surfaces.
Seesaw	Seated	Angular, linear	Peer or sibling can join in ride and jointly determine the speed and direction of movement.
Sit 'n' Spin	Seated	Angular, orbital	Spin while catching objects.
Merry-go-rounds	Seated, kneeling, or standing with arm support	Angular, orbital	Incorporate peers into play, provide stabilization, and allow child to control rate of speed and direction of movement.
Rocking horse	Seated	Linear	Change material on horse, child initiates movement, therapist provides stability and facilitates speed of movement.
Rolling	Prone, supine	Angular	On mats, up or down inclined surfaces.
T-stool	Seated	Linear	Maintain balance while catching and throwing objects.
Tilt boards	Standing or seated	Angular, linear	Maintain balance while catching and throwing objects, surfing; alter the amount of stabilization provided, alter the size of the tilt board, or provide a floor disc (1/2 ball of hard plastic with a flat surface with handles for sitting on the top).

Tactile input in usually prescribed for both conditions—that is, sensory stimulation is provided to diminish tactile defensiveness or to improve tactile discrimination. Intervention typically takes two forms: education and modification to the child's environment, and prescribed activities that allow the child opportunities to modulate defensive behaviors or build discrimination. For sensory defensiveness, if possible, the child can be taught to actively modify his or her environment or to use active coping strategies to modify sensory input (Williams & Shellenberger, 1996). For example, the child might dim the lights or sit away from a group if the sensory stimulation is overwhelming. Direct intervention can be introduced in the form of light touch, deep pressure, discriminative pressure, and firm pressure. Table 6–4 indicates the extensive

Table 6–3 Specific Proprioceptive Intervention Techniques in Sensorimotor Treatment

Intervention	Positioning	Adaptations
Weights	Seated, standing, kneeling, walking	Clothing vests, blankets, hand patches, lap pads, hat, yoke, shoulder pads, weight belt, shoe weights, and weight lifting can be utilized.
Drawing, writing in the air, with weights on, with a variety of writing utensils (pencils, markers, crayons) and in shaving cream.	Standing, seated	
Push or pull objects	Standing, walking	Place heavy objects on chair, push chair over a variety of surface types (smooth to rough). Push or pull a wheelbarrow or cart on level or inclined surfaces. Pulling other children on scooter boards is another alternative.
Climbing	Standing	Use of rope ladders, metal ladders, and height from ground can all be altered; climb up the front of a slide.
Scrubbing movements with resistance	Standing	Scrub mats, tables, and walls with brushes, sponges, and washcloths.
Dancing	Standing	Yoga, dance programs; incorporate shaking body parts, tapping or stomping toes, heel, or foot.
Heavy yard work	Standing, walking	Have child carry sand, soil, help with moving the wheelbarrow, carrying tools, digging with trowel or small shovel, distributing mulch on gardens.
Ball bouncing	Seated, prone	Egg-shaped balls with handles (for bunny hopping), chair balls; provide a ball stand to initiate use of ball, bouncing up and down, use light balls, and have child move the ball with his or her head. Have child hold onto a ball and bounce ball and self against a wall; lie prone over a ball and turn in a circle using hands to propel.

continues

Table 6–3 continued

Intervention	Positioning	Adaptations
Aerobics	Standing	Incorporate jumping, pushups, lateral and linear movements; use stair stepping and situps. Explore the possibility of incorporating martial arts (e.g., Tae Bo, Tai Chi, Karate, and Aikido) into weekly activities, or sports with a heavy proprioceptive component (e.g., boxing and football).
Driving into or hitting objects	Standing, seated, holding on to swing	Jumping into a pile of pillows, diving into water, using a body rebounder, knocking down objects (e.g., plastic bowling pins or large blocks), traveling down a ramp on a scooter board, knocking down a tower when swinging, hitting a ball while swinging.
Wheelbarrow walk	On all four extremities	Combine with relay races or an obstacle course, provide support and stabilization, and use a ball to support chest and walk over the ball.
Crossing monkey bars	Upright	Provide stabilization and support.
Crawling	On all fours or prone	Through a tunnel.
Deep pressure	Seated, prone, supine	Being a sandwich between mats, blankets.
Hitting objects	Seated, prone, supine	Hang balls, balloons from the ceiling and have child hit them, play using bats and balls (e.g., T-ball, softball, soccer, volleyball).
Jumping	Standing	Over a moving rope-snake, jump rope with peers, perform jumping jacks, participate in aerobics classes.

permutations that intervention sessions, designed to target sensory processing disorders, may take. The tactile information in the environment also may need to be modified to allow the individual with autism to engage within a variety of settings. Theoretically, a more balanced sensory environment and graded sensory experiences promote a more balanced response from the child to sensory events (Royeen & Lane, 1991). The right type of sensory input for children with autism was noted anecdotally for improving attention and decreasing anxiety (Edelson et al., 1999). Occupational roles, which can be enhanced by a tactile intervention plan, include the ability to interact positively within a school environment, including social interactions, the ability to participate in a regular classroom environment for education (i.e., sit in a chair, quietly listen to instructions,

Table 6–4 Specific Tactile Interventions

Intervention	Body Area Applied	Specifications or Modifications
Hammock	Whole body	Low to the ground, freestanding; allow the child to initiate movement and contact with the ground.
Ball baths	Whole body or extremities	Use large plastic balls or boxes filled with bean bags, pillows, beans, or rice and have the child move the objects around, or swim with the balls. Use wading pool instead of a box.
Textured surfaces on equipment used in treatment	Whole body	Use carpet, sheepskin, satin, corduroy on swings, barrels.
Providing pressure Deep pressure	Whole body, torso, extremities	Sandwiched between two objects, using floor mats, comforter, sleeping bag, large pillows, or bean bag chairs; roll a large ball over the child; firm contact with equipment, (Grandin Hug Machine) firm pressure on shoulders and make child into a cocoon, or hot dog in a bun, using a sleeping bag, cloth bag, or heavy blanket. Provide a small space to squeeze into, a box with a blanket or cushion, a barrel padded with soft or firm material, teepees filled with cushions, and encourage quiet tasks like reading.
Light pressure	Whole body, back, extremities	Crawl into sleeping bags, lean against or lie against large pillows, sit in beanbag chairs, hold pillows or beanbags in lap, introduce balls, cushions, pillows into a large cloth bag or sleeping bag.
Games Inching along surfaces	Whole body	In prone or supine position, have child be an inchworm and crawl along the floor or mat surfaces.
Rolling on surfaces or walls	Whole body	Have the child be a steamroller and roll over the wall, floor, smooth, rough surfaces, and mats.
Swimming in mats	Whole body	Provide large area of mats and facilitate swimming movements.
Pulling child	Whole body	Use cardboard or plastic to pull child on and off mats and rough or smooth surfaces.

continues

Table 6–4 continued

Intervention	Body Area Applied	Specifications or Modifications
Brushes and surgical scrub brushing techniques	Whole body, back, extremities	Brushes can be altered by providing wide, narrow, variety of bristle size and bristle material (natural fibers, plastic, stiff, soft, with knobs on the end of each bristle, densely packed brushes). Specific programs have been developed for use of a surgical scrub brush.
Textured or tactile mitts	Whole body, torso, extremities	Using a variety of fabrics (cotton, velvet, wool, tweed, satin, silk, stockinet, Lycra, canvas, sequins, sheepskin, corduroy, upholstery fabric), have the child touch various body parts with the fabrics.
Tactile balls	Whole body	Vary size of balls (very large to small), knobby balls, tacky surface, and koosh balls (made of yarn, plastics, netting with both long and short tails).
Vibrators	Extremities and back	Vibrators with variable speeds or use of a Bumble ball.
Fine motor		
Accordion-type connecting tubes	Hands and arms	
Bean bags	Hands and arms	Outer texture can be altered (soft/plush, vinyl, tacky, Lycra material). Weight can be altered (sand, Styrofoam pellets, lead shot). Size of bags can be altered.
Squeeze toys	Hands and arms	Provide a wide variety of shapes, sizes, textures of toys to manipulate and squeeze.
Finding objects in a box	Hands and arms	Use rice, beans, or a combination.
Fingerpainting	Hands and arms	Use powder, shaving cream, lotion, drawing in sand, making sand pictures.
Make snowballs	Hands	Using cornstarch and water, create a loose material to mold.
Use of chalk, other tactile writing materials	Hands	Shapes of markers, pens, and weight of writing utensils can be altered. Use squiggle pen or talking pen to provide feedback to child.
Erase marks written in chalk with hand		Use a chalkboard or the floor.

continues

Table 6–4 continued

Intervention	Body Area Applied	Specifications or Modifications
Hold and fidget with small items	Hands and arms	Jiggle coins, small pebbles, glass beads in pocket.
Touching own hair, hair of others	Head, face, extremities	Done in conjunction with grooming, pretend play, dress-up play.
Showering or bathing	Whole body	Use hand-held shower; allow adjustments.
Petting tame animals	Hands, arms, lap	Dog, cat, ferret, rabbit, bird, reptiles.
Gel filled cushions	Pelvic/hip area	Placed on seats in classroom or home to increase proprioception.
Clothing adjustments	Whole body	Soft fleece, cotton are best choices; seamless socks.
Drawing on body	Back, palm, face	Moderate pressure; draw letters, numbers, shapes, face painting, tattoos.

complete work independently), and the ability to tolerate community settings such as stores, malls, playgrounds, museums, and means of transportation.

As in any sensorimotor intervention, the clinician prepares a treatment plan, based on a thorough evaluation, that reflects the goals for the individual child and represents underlying sensory integrative theories (Royeen & Lane, 1991). The benefits of tactile input were investigated in several studies (see Chapter 5). Researchers documented a variety of improvements to attention, decreased anxiety, decreased hyperactive behavior, improved social and relating behavior, reduction in stereotypic/self-stimulatory behavior, and gradual increases in adaptive skills (Ayres & Tickle, 1980; Baranek, Foster, & Berkson, 1997; Ermer & Dunn, 1998; Field et al., 1997; Linderman & Stewart, 1999; McClure & Holtz-Yotz, 1991; Zissermann, 1992). Further systematic, rigorous documentation of outcomes is essential to providing a base of evidence for tactile interventions using sensory integrative theories.

Visual Processing and Visual Tracking

In typically developing human beings, vision is the primary sense used to gain information about the world. The visual system develops over a period of years and conveys information about size, shape, color, distance, movement, depth, and spatial characteristics. In conjunction with the vestibular system, the visual system is responsible for orchestrating eye movements and head movement. The visual system is anatomically and physiologically linked to the vestibular system, logically linking deficits in vestibular functioning to difficulties with interpretation of visual stimuli, particularly with movement (Kandel & Wurtz, 2000). The visual system consists of the external structures (globe, iris, and retina), optic nerve, visual pathways, and vestibular control of eye movements. The extent of the neurological complexity of vision is slowly being revealed through ongoing research. Over half of the nonhuman primate cortex is concerned with visual information processing; the implication is that the visual system demands intensive processing to handle both the amount of input and the interpretation of stimuli. As with all the senses, developing our understanding of the visual system will undoubtedly help us treat problems in visual attention and vigilance, visual memory, visual defensiveness, and others that are potentially present in many children, including children with autism.

The occupational therapist using SI theory typically construes visual stimuli to mean vestibuloocular-oculomotor control (e.g., vestibuloocular reflex, optokinetic nystagmus, saccades, and convergence), spatial orientation (visual-motor integration), and modulation or registration of visual stimuli (visual attention). Interventions tend to focus on modification of visual information in the environment (e.g., turning off lights) or on developing postural-ocular control (i.e., accurately matching head/eye movements with body movements). Interventions designed for postural-ocular control are described in more detail below. Three primary principles of visual intervention include organization of the environment, providing repeated and consistent experience with visual stimuli, and reducing overall level of stimulation.

Organization of the environment includes limiting visual stimuli through distracting objects. This can be achieved both at home and at school by providing quiet spaces (a cardboard barrel for reading or a study carrel) and by removing objects from tabletops, shelves, and walls. Children may also benefit from strong contrasts between objects (e.g., black paper and white letters, large simple signs) at school to help increase the salience of important visual stimuli. Repetition of stimuli can be effective in establishing retrieval cues for improving visual memory. Finally, reducing stimuli from other sources may allow the child to focus attention on a visual task—for example, using headphones while completing assignments or sitting in a quiet space to limit interactions with others. Additional ideas for altering the environment to accommodate for visual processing dysfunction are summarized in Table 6–5.

Listening/Auditory

Difficulty in communication is a defining characteristic of autistic disorder. The communication and language impairments of people with autism range from failure to develop any functional communication to the development of functional but idiosyncratic spontaneous speech and language. Adequate auditory processing and hearing are essential for typical development of communicative language as well as for nonlanguage auditory processes such as sound perception. In classic sensorimotor intervention, the focus is on intervention to improve auditory perception and to stimulate development of speech, but not on the formation of language for communication, for which Ayres (1972) suggests that a more cognitive approach is appropriate.

Auditory perception can include the analysis of differing sound characteristics, including amplitude and frequency of patterns in sound. The auditory system anatomically consists of the outer ear (pinna), middle ear (malleus, incus, and stapes), inner ear (cochlea), and auditory nerve. It is often assumed that the mechanisms connecting the auditory and vestibular systems, due to their anatomical proximity, have a close relationship. Ayres (1972) suggested that clinical impressions implied that vestibular stimuli have a profound effect on auditory and language capabilities. Although direct connections between the two systems are absent, there is substantial evidence that in CNS processing, the auditory and vestibular systems developed similar embryological

Table 6–5 Visual Interventions To Alter the Environment

Intervention Strategy	Modification or Resource
Watching a fire	
Watching sunset/sunrise	
Watch oil and water toys	Available at novelty or gift shops.
Dim lighting	Install dimmer switches on overhead lights, turn off lights, create small space options with reduced lighting (cardboard barrel with a cutout to sit in for quiet time).
Increased lighting	Use a variety of lighting options, including desk/table lamps, floor lamps, and three-way bulbs.
Clear surfaces	Place papers in drawers or cabinets; clear tables prior to activities.
Read a book	Provide books with large print; use an inclined surface; provide a comfortable reading area.
Watch a movie	Movies can be chosen for their positive visual images or for their contrasting visual images.
Flashlight	Provide a lightweight flashlight with easy on/off switch. Have child identify objects as flashlight is scanned over room. Play flashlight tag with another child.
Dark paper	Use with fluorescent colors or a highlighter, to provide contrast to work surface.
Inclined writing surfaces	Available through educational supply companies and office supply stores. Allow paper tasks to be placed prominently in the field of view.
View an aquarium	Aquariums can be viewed at local zoos or can be purchased and maintained at home.
Use of international signs	Large red circle with slash across it for "no," bathroom sign, large arrows for indicating directions.
Hide and seek	Play with one other child; use a flashlight to seek objects.
Computer games	Turn off screen saver options, use a plain background with dark color, and adjust the screen contrast for the lighting. Games include virtual pool, Kid Pics, coloring pictures.
Computer educational programs	A range of commercially available software is available that can foster visual attention and memory. For example, Reader Rabbit Toddler-Primary School,[®1] Jump-Start School House Series.[®2]
Paper pool	Place finger on the first numbered hole and move to the next hole in sequence, until each hole has been touched. Play with a peer.

[1]Reader Rabbit's Learning System (1997). The Learning Company. One Athenaeum Street, Cambridge, MA 02142. http://www.learningco.com

[2]Jump Start (1998). Knowledge Adventure, 4100 W. 190th Street, Torrance, CA 90504. http://www.KnowledgeAdventure.com

tissue and may share collateral information at the level of the brain stem and cerebellum (Shore, 1999). In typically developing children, auditory stimuli can elicit immediate arousal and orientation to localize the noise source; strong vestibular stimulation is likely to elicit verbalizations. Therefore, disorders in modulation of auditory input or in awareness of auditory input are the primary sensory processing deficits seen in children with autism. Disorders in modulating auditory input may be associated with delayed or atypical discrimination of auditory sounds.

Therapists are concerned with teaching children with autism how to sort out important characteristics of auditory stimuli for communication and with over- or underresponsiveness to auditory input. Children with autism seem to have extraordinary difficulty making sense of auditory speech or sound patterns and often have a number of behaviors driven to avoid or to provide themselves with particular sounds (e.g., avoiding all siren noises or, paradoxically, making high-pitched squeaking noises). The primary strategy of SI intervention for auditory processing deficits involves modifying of the environment to attenuate offensive sounds. Several intervention strategies to alter the environment are displayed in Exhibit 6–1.

Another form of intervention is auditory training, which stems from a similar theoretical base. In this approach, specialized auditory intervention focuses on the use of sounds from which specific frequencies have been filtered out. The child listens through earphones to specially designed sounds; the theory is that auditory hypersensitivity thus will be reduced and improvements in behavior and language will emerge (Bettison, 1996; Hnath-Chisolm, 1997; Musiek, 1999; Tremblay, Kraus, Carrell, & McGee, 1997; Tremblay, Kraus, & McGee, 1998).

Postural-Ocular Movement, Low Muscle Tone, and Primitive Reflexes

In order to move effectively in our environment, we must have adequate postural control. In turn, adequate postural control relies on accurate communication between and integration of the visual and vestibular systems (Koomar & Bundy, 1991). As indicated earlier, disorders of the postural-ocular system are often demonstrated by hypotonia of extensor muscles, poor postural stability, poor righting and equilibrium responses, and difficulty in maintaining positions such as supine flexion or prone extension (Ayres,

---

Exhibit 6–1 Auditory Interventions To Alter the Environment

Interventions	Provide nature sounds.
Listen to classical music.	Provide headphones.
Listen to rock music.	Minimize noise.
Use a personal music player.	Provide white noise.
Avoid/seek noisy places.	Provide auditory training.
Provide fast rhythmic beat.	Teach sing-song speech.
Provide slow rhythmic beat.	Teach rhyming.

1972). Because of the interconnected nature of postural control and the visual system, intervention techniques tend to require complex combinations of strategies prescribed for visual and vestibular-proprioceptive disorders. These interventions typically build on interventions designed to facilitate vestibular-proprioceptive functioning by requiring the child to complete motor skills while positioned in specific ways. For example, use of a scooter board requires that the child lie in prone extension to push a large ball along a specified path. This activity stimulates movement, proprioception, and visual skills. In addition, the use of prone extension patterns of movement assists in integrating primitive reflex patterns and promoting postural stability. When used in combination, such activities also may improve overall motor planning ability for children with a poverty of movement patterns. Ideas of integrated activities for stimulating these sensory systems are displayed in Table 6–6.

CASE STUDY

Background

This illustration is based on a typical case, observed by the author, and provided here to illustrate the process of SI therapy. The case study describes the assessment, treatment planning, and the first few months of therapy. Elliot is a six-year-old boy who was diagnosed with autism shortly after his third birthday. The defining characteristics of his diagnosis involved behavioral, social, and communication deficits. Elliot has one eight-year-old sibling and both parents at home. The unique features of his behavioral repertoire included extreme sensitivity to loud noises, restricted communication skills, need for an extremely structured daily routine, and

intolerance to movement or touching. For example, Elliot panicked, screamed, and became physically combative when he heard blow-dryers or sirens, or encountered large crowds at sporting events. The same behaviors erupted with inadvertent touching; fortunately, this was not as severe as his behavioral reactions to loud noises. His only communication with his family was through crying and screaming. He was attached to his structured daily routine; any deviation from this routine resulted in a cycle of panic, screaming, and physical combativeness. On weekdays, this was not difficult for the family, who had established a structured routine that promoted getting everyone to work or school in a timely manner. However, the structure presented problems with the transition to the weekend, when the family attempted to participate in different activities.

Elliot also resisted or refused to participate in activities that involve unpredictable movement (e.g., he disliked bike riding and using playground equipment but enjoyed car riding). Elliot was receiving educational intervention and his family was involved in implementation of simple behavioral techniques to improve daily functioning for him and the family. Many of these techniques, such as developing structured routines and using simple pictures for communication, provided better management for the family. However, Elliot's intolerance to movement and touching and his extreme need for daily structure, even on weekends, was problematic. In school, Elliot had difficulty with the alphabet and could only imitate simple written words, but he was able to participate in age-appropriate math activities.

Sensory Integration Diagnosis

The family referred themselves to a therapy clinic specializing in SI approaches to

Table 6–6 Interventions for Low Muscle Tone and Primitive Reflexes

Intervention	Movement Facilitated	Positioning	Modifications
Balls			
Kick ball	Flexion	Supine	Hit suspended ball with feet, kick a ball placed on feet to wall or target, catch ball with feet, platform swing.
Catch ball	Flexion or extension	Prone or supine	Hit suspended ball, use bat to hit ball, change ball dimensions, perform catching in swings, use plastic gallon containers with the bottoms cut out to scoop and toss a light ball.
Hold ball with hands or feet	Extension	Prone	Play atlas, hold balls with feet or hands and place them careful toward target/container, perform on a platform or net swing, change dimensions or arms only, place objects in containers, weight balls from heavy to light, done in a net hammock or sling swing (prone), use stick to hit musical instruments, go fishing with magnet rod and fish.
Situps on a gymnastic ball	Flexion and extension	Prone or supine	Hold objects (bean bags, paper) under a chin; peer doubles on another ball and reaches toward client.
Ball pass	Extension, bilateral movements	Prone or supine	Have child use both hands to hold a ball and use the ball to push other balls or objects to other children or to a target.
Suspended ball	Extension, bilateral movements	Standing or seated	Have child use a bat or cardboard tube to hit a light ball suspended from the ceiling.
Balance on large ball	Flexion or extension	Prone, seated	Play statue and try to remain balanced, facilitate a transition from prone to sitting.
Scooters			
Horizontal climbing	Flexion	Seated, supine	Pull self from one end to another of rope secured at both ends.
Helicopter scooter	Extension	Prone, seated	Rope scooters together; child holds onto rope in front of scooter and chain in front is pulled, crack the whip.
Follow a path	Extension	Prone	Propel self down a road using hands or feet only. Place rolled towel under knees in prone, create a maze, alter directionality in the path.
Down inclined surface	Extension	Prone	Use the scooter to go down and onto mat and roll off; use plastic instead of scooter to slide down a ramp, log-roll down inclined surface.
Play games	Extension, flexion	Prone or seated	Play volleyball, follow the leader, obstacle course, tag, crack the whip.

continues

Table 6–6 continued

Intervention	Movement Facilitated	Positioning	Modifications
Knock over objects	Extension		Use self as bowling ball to plastic jugs, plastic bowling pins.
Toss objects into buckets/ baskets/ targets	Extension, bilateral movements	Prone or seated	Use balls or bean bags to make baskets or hit a target.
Alternating arm use	Extension, bilateral movements	Prone	Child uses both arms simultaneously or alternating in windmill fashion to propel self along a course or in a relay race with other children.
Go under objects			Use ropes, tubing, blankets to design obstacle course.
Animal charades			
Crab	Flexion, extension, bilateral movements	All fours	Walking on all fours, reverse directions.
Octopus	Flexion, extension bilateral movements	All fours	Two children work together to reach and toss objects, children can link legs, arms or torsos.
Frog	Extension, bilateral movements	Prone	Child is placed with bolster under chest, rolls forward over bolster to reach for objects.
Dog	Flexion, extension, bilateral movements	Prone, supine, squat, standing	Play tricks, sit (squat), roll over, jump up, play dead.
Kangaroo	Extension, bilateral movements	Standing	Place an object between the child's knees and have him or her hop or use a inner tube band in a figure-8 configuration around thighs.
Elephant or Bear	Flexion, extension, bilateral movements	Flexion	Set child on all fours and have him or her reach for peanuts.

continues

Table 6–6 continued

Intervention	Movement Facilitated	Positioning	Modifications
Rocking horse/ chair/ boat, ball	Flexion, extension	Supine, prone	In supine, make a ball; in prone, make a rocking horse or boat; on all fours, make a table.
Swings	Flexion, extension	Supine, prone, seated	Swinging on trapeze swing, twirler swing, large-diameter rope attached to ceiling; pulling self on swing using rope or tubing attached to wall or other swing; provide resistance with reaching and placing objects (bean bags to target, bucket/basket); rolling balls toward object or person in prone on swing; pulling/swing on rope.
Drawing on body	Flexion	Supine	Child brings knees to chest and draws on knees with soft chalk in supine.
Climbing	Flexion, extension	Upright	Encourage child to use rope ladders or metal ladders. The height from ground can be altered.
T-stool	Extension	Seated	Maintain balance while catching and throwing objects.
Walk around object while holding onto rope attached to ceiling			Stabilize ball in place under a rope attached to the ceiling; have child walk around ball while holding on the rope.
Maze, tunnel crawling	Extension, flexion	Prone, all fours	Child crawls through a tunnel (can vary textures), commando crawls through a maze or forest of bolsters and objects.
Surfboard	Extension	Prone to standing	Child is placed on cardboard and attempts to move from prone to standing while moving on smooth surface.
Hopping	Extension, bilateral movements	Standing	Child hops in and out of a hula hoop or over a rope; hopscotch, alternate feet hopping, alternating hopping with both feet to hopping on one foot, hopping inside a box with both ends cut out; playing follow the leader; place an object between the knees for a challenge while hopping.

facilitate developmentally appropriate skills in conjunction with the community-based educational intervention program already in place. At the therapy clinic, the Sensory Integration and Praxis Tests (SIPT; Ayres, 1989) were administered and revealed a generalized sensory integrative dysfunction. Elliot scored well below average on all 17 SIPT items. This type of score is characterized by consistently low performance, but the administering therapist also identified him as having a pattern of performance consistent with severe deficits in visuopraxis and somatopraxis. On the Touch Inventory for Elementary-School-Aged Children (TIE; Royeen & Fortune, 1990), Elliot had a raw score of 65 (out of 78 possible); his score, when compared to a normative sample, suggested that he responded with much more tactual defensiveness than 100% of the normative sample. Additionally, clinical observations and family and teacher reports supported central deficits in vestibular-proprioceptive processing deficits. The family was encouraged to specify goals for treatment, instead of the more broad goals they had already stated (e.g., improving tolerance to movement and touching and the need for structure). Working with the therapists, the family articulated four specific goals: They wanted Elliot (1) to tolerate going down a slide at the playground; (2) to tolerate standing in line at school and in the grocery store; (3) to play with a peer; and (4) to tolerate a different routine on one weekend day.

Intervention

A general intervention plan was developed that addressed enhanced opportunities to take in tactile, vestibular-proprioceptive, and visual (polymodal) sensory information. Initially, the therapist intended to provide a structured routine to facilitate rapport and trust. The therapist also identified another

child to participate in joint treatment sessions as Elliot's skills developed.

The therapist initiated treatment by showing Elliot a sequence of pictures indicating what each treatment session would be like; she introduced each activity and asked him to do each one, as long as there were no negative behaviors. She identified negative behaviors as a fearful look, crying, or screaming; she immediately terminated the activity if those behaviors ensued. By the second month of weekly one-to-one therapy, Elliot had made progress, but the therapist did not feel that Elliot was ready for a peer. Elliot understood the routine sequence of therapy. Initially, he just sat on the piece of equipment offered and refused to move; now he was beginning to initiate some slow self-propelling movements on suspended equipment and was tolerating a greater range of tactile tasks. In this particular treatment session, the therapist greeted Elliot at the door with eye contact and a handshake, which Elliot was able to return when given verbal cues. He was then shown the pictorial sequence of the anticipated therapy session, which was structured to provide opportunities first for vestibular-proprioceptive activities, second for tactile activities, and third for more complex combined activities.

Elliot chose to use a platform glider swing placed 12 inches from the ground. Sitting on the platform, he was given a rope attached to the wall and used the rope to pull himself in a linear manner while simultaneously tossing bean bags into a basket. He was given verbal cues to look at the basket while tossing the beanbag and was encouraged to cheer for himself each time he made a basket. The therapist encouraged Elliot during this activity while allowing him to move at his own pace. After Elliot showed fatigue and less enthusiasm for throwing the bean bags to the target, the therapist guided Elliot to a quiet area, where he was given an opportunity to explore a variety of objects (e.g., cars and trucks) hiding in a ball bath. Initially, he tolerated only sitting outside a small infant pool with a few balls inside, but he graduated to tolerating getting into the ball bath himself. Elliot is still not vigorous in exploring this environment but, with encouragement, he digs his hands under the balls to find cars and trucks, which he collects in a container. He then moves to a slide and allows the cars and trucks to go down the slide. He must climb the ladder attached to the slide to allow the cars to slide down. While Elliot is not yet ready to go down the slide himself, he is learning to tolerate a portion of the whole activity.

His parents and teacher also keep a sensory diary, at the suggestion of the therapist, in which they report sensory experiences that were positive for Elliot. Initially, few items were listed in this diary. His parents now report that Elliot consistently tolerates a greeting hug from his family members. His teacher reports fewer incidents of upsets during group activities at school. While the goals of therapy are not yet fully met, his family and teachers are more optimistic about integrating Elliot into other school activities that involve groups of children.

The occupational therapist encouraged the family to establish a new routine for each weekend day that was structured but still different from the weekday routine. The family used pictures to communicate the sequence of the day's events, which included running errands, going to a gym, choosing a movie video, and playing outside. Elliot was given frequent cues initially and still has difficulty adjusting to a new routine, but he is becoming tolerant of the new weekend schedule. The therapist is making plans for the introduction of a peer and is moving toward a greater repertoire of tactile and vestibular-proprioceptive tolerance.

CHAPTER REVIEW QUESTIONS

1. Define the concept of a "just-right challenge" and describe how this concept might be used to guide therapy.
2. Why are play and a playful attitude necessary when using a SI approach?
3. Make a list of at least seven items that could be included or added to your environment (e.g., home, school, work site) to make it more conducive to SI intervention.
4. Classify the following activities as primarily stimulating the vestibular or the proprioceptive system: digging in sand, riding the Ferris wheel, pulling carrots from the garden, riding a bike, wearing a heavy backpack, pumping a swing to make it go.
5. Describe one activity that might decrease tactile defensiveness and one that might stimulate tactile discrimination.
6. List at least three techniques to accommodate the environment to promote optimal visual processing or visual-motor skills.
7. Describe several integrated activities that promote postural-ocular movement and motor planning. Put these into a game format for children functioning in the 3-year level, 5-year level, and 7-year level.
8. Plan a 30-minute therapy session for a child you know, or one you have seen on videotape, that utilizes interventions targeted toward at least three sensory systems described in this chapter.

REFERENCES

Anderson, J. (1998). *Sensory motor issues in autism.* San Antonio, TX: Psychological Corporation.

Ayres, A. J. (1972). *Sensory integration and learning disorders.* Los Angeles: Western Psychological Services.

Ayres, A. J. (1979). *Sensory integration and the child.* Los Angeles: Western Psychological Services.

Ayres, A. J. (1989). *Sensory integration and praxis tests.* Lost Angeles: Western Psychological Services.

Ayres, A., & Tickle, L. (1980). Hyper-responsivity to touch and vestibular stimuli as a predictor of positive response to sensory integration procedures by autistic children. *American Journal of Occupational Therapy, 34,* 375–381.

Baranek, G., Foster, L., & Berkson, G. (1997). Tactile defensiveness and stereotyped behaviors. *American Journal of Occupational Therapy, 51,* 91–95.

Bettison, S. (1996). The long-term effects of auditory training on children with autism. *Journal of Autism and Developmental Disorders, 26,* 361–374.

Bundy, A. C. (1991). Play theory and sensory integration. In A. G. Fisher, E. A. Murray, & A. C. Bundy (Eds.), *Sensory integration: Theory and practice* (pp. 46–68). Philadelphia: F. A. Davis.

Burgess, P. R., Wei, J. Y., Clark, F. J., & Simon, J. (1982). Signaling of kinesthetic information by peripheral sensory receptors. *Annual Reviews of Neuroscience, 5,* 171–187.

Case-Smith, J., & Miller, H. (1999). Occupational therapy with children with pervasive developmental disorders. *American Journal of Occupational Therapy, 53,* 506–513.

Cohen, H. (Ed.). (1999). *Neuroscience for rehabilitation* (2nd ed.). Philadelphia: Lippincott, Williams & Wilkins.

Cohn, E., Miller, L. J., & Tickle-Degnen, L. (2000). Parental hopes for therapy outcomes: Children with sensory modulation disorders. *American Journal of Occupational Therapy, 54,* 36–43.

Cole, M. B. (1998). *Group dynamics in occupational therapy: The theoretical and practice application of group treatment* (2nd ed.). Thorofare, NJ: Slack.

Dunkerley, E., Tickle-Degnen, L., & Coster, W. J. (1997). Therapist-child interaction in the middle minutes of sensory integration treatment. *American Journal of Occupational Therapy, 51,* 799–805.

Edelson, S. M., Edelson, M. G., Kerr, D. C. R., & Grandin, T. (1999). Behavioral and physiological effects of deep pressure on children with autism: A pilot study evaluating the efficacy of Grandin's Hug Machine. *American Journal of Occupational Therapy, 53,* 145–152.

Ermer, J., & Dunn, W. (1998). The sensory profile: A discriminant analysis of children with and without disabilities. *American Journal of Occupational Therapy, 52,* 283–290.

Field, T., Lasko, D., Mundy, P., Henteleff, T., Kabat, S., Talpins, S., & Dowling, M. (1997). Brief report: Autistic children's attentiveness and responsivity improve after touch therapy. *Journal of Autism and Developmental Disorders, 27,* 333–338.

Fink, B. E. (1989). *Sensory motor integration activities.* San Antonio, TX: Psychological Corporation.

Fisher, A. G. (1991). Vestibular-proprioceptive processing and bilateral integration and sequencing deficits. In A. G. Fisher, E. A. Murray, & A. C. Bundy (Eds.), *Sensory integration: Theory and practice* (pp. 71–107). Philadelphia: F. A. Davis.

Fletcher, R. H., & Fletcher, S. W. (1997). Evidence-based approach to medical literature. *Journal of General Internal Medicine, 12*(Suppl.), S5–S12.

Hnath-Chisolm, T. (1997). Context effects in auditory training with children. *Scandinavian Audiology, Supplementum, 47,* 64–69.

Horak, F., & Shupert, C. (1994). Role of the vestibular system in postural control. In S. Herdman (Ed.), *Vestibular rehabilitation* (pp. 112–156). Philadelphia: F. A. Davis.

Kandel, E. R., & Wurtz (2000). Central visual pathways. In E. R. Kandel, J. H. Schwartz, & T. M. Jessell (Eds.), *Principles of neural science* (4th ed.) (pp. 523–547). New York: Elsevier.

Knox, S., & Mailloux, Z. (1997). Play as treatment and treatment through play. In B. E. Chandler (Ed.), *The essence of play* (pp. 175–204). Bethesda, MD: American Occupational Therapy Association.

Koomar, J. (1990). Sensory integration treatment in the public school. In S. C. Merrill (Ed.), *Environment: Implications of occupational therapy practice* (pp. 111–142). Bethesda, MD: American Occupational Therapy Association.

Koomar, J. A., & Bundy, A. C. (1991). The art and science of creating direction intervention from theory.

In A. G. Fisher, E. A. Murray, & A. C. Bundy (Eds.), *Sensory integration: Theory and practice* (pp. 251–314). Philadelphia: F. A. Davis.

Linderman, T., & Stewart, K. (1999). Sensory integrative-based occupational therapy and functional outcomes in young children with pervasive developmental disorders: A single-subject study. *American Journal of Occupational Therapy, 53*, 207–213.

Mailloux, Z., & Burke, J. P. (1997). Play and the sensory integrative approach. In L. D. Parham & L. S. Fazio (Eds.), *Play in occupational therapy for children* (pp. 112–125). St. Louis, MO: Mosby.

McClure, M., & Holtz-Yotz, M. (1991). The effects of sensory stimulatory treatment on an autistic child. *American Journal of Occupational Therapy, 45*, 1138–1142.

Musiek, F. (1999). Habilitation and management of auditory processing disorders: Overview of selected procedures. *Journal of the American Academy of Audiology, 10*, 329–342.

Restall, G., & Magill-Evans, J. (1994). Play and preschool children with autism. *American Journal of Occupational Therapy, 48*, 113–120.

Royeen, C. B., & Fortune, J. C. (1990). TIE: Touch inventory for school aged children. *American Journal of Occupational Therapy, 44*, 155–160.

Royeen, C. B., & Lane, S. J. (1991). Tactile processing and sensory defensiveness. In A. G. Fisher, E. A. Murray, & A. C. Bundy (Eds.), *Sensory integration: Theory and practice* (pp. 108–133). Philadelphia: F. A. Davis.

Shore, S. E. (1999). The auditory system. In H. Cohn (Ed.), *Neuroscience for rehabilitation* (2nd ed.) (pp. 131–148). Philadelphia: Lippincott, Williams & Wilkins.

Tremblay, K., Kraus, N., Carrell, T., & McGee, T. (1997). Central auditory system plasticity: Generalization to novel stimuli following listening training. *Journal of the Acoustical Society of America, 102*, 3762–3773.

Tremblay, K., Kraus, N., & McGee, T. (1998). The time course of auditory perceptual learning: Neurophysiological changes during speech-sound training. *Neuroreport, 9*, 3557–3560.

Watling, R., Deitz, J., Kanny, E. M., & McLaughlin, J. F. (1999). Current practice of occupational therapy for children with autism. *American Journal of Occupational Therapy, 53*, 498–505.

Wilbarger, P., & Wilbarger, J. (1991). *Sensory defensiveness in children aged 2–12: An intervention guide for parents & caretakers.* Oak Park Heights, MN: PDP Press.

Williams, M. S., & Shellenberger, S. (1996). *How does your engine run? A leader's guide to the Alert Program for self-regulation.* Albuquerque, NM: TherapyWorks.

Wong, D. L. (1997). *Essentials of pediatric nursing* (5th ed.). St. Louis: Mosby.

Zissermann, L. (1992). The effects of deep pressure on self-stimulating behaviors in a child with autism and other disabilities. *American Journal of Occupational Therapy, 46*, 547–551.

CHAPTER 7

Sensorimotor Aspects of Attachment and Social Relatedness in Autism

Ruth A. Huebner and Gary W. Kraemer

CHAPTER OBJECTIVES

At the completion of this chapter, the reader will be able to:

- Understand the tenets of attachment theory.
- Describe the hierarchical and dynamic system development of relatedness and social behaviors.
- Describe at least one neurobiological system associated with social behavior.
- Appreciate the experiences of a child with autism and the effects of these experiences on the capacity to form social relatedness.
- Define the parent-child interaction processes in forming attachment and social relatedness.
- Formulate ideas for intervention to promote social relatedness for children with autism and families.

INTRODUCTION

The desire to belong with other people, to form attachments with others, to socialize with others, to have relatedness and bonding, is considered a basic motivation for all people (Baumeister & Leary, 1995). Because this drive toward relatedness with others is so fundamentally a characteristic of humans, limitations of social engagement are seen as particularly intriguing, perhaps troublesome. This intrigue with limited social interaction may be one reason why the study of autism is so compelling. Although

autism is marked by several limitations in function, the term *autistic* was chosen to describe the whole disorder based on the social withdrawal and apparent isolation from others. As such, autism is opposite to attachment and social relatedness.

The study of social relatedness was central to the understanding of autism from its earliest descriptions because social dysfunction is the most reliable and consistent symptom of autistic spectrum disorders. In fact, disorders of attachment due to cold and distant parenting were erroneously proposed as the cause of autism by early theorists using a psychoanalytic frame of reference (Bettelheim, 1967). Although some theorists argue that the social deficits of autism are due to cognitive limitations (Happe & Frith, 1996), others argue that they are due to primary problems in social development (Waterhouse & Fein, 1998). All theorists agree that social deficits arise from differences in neurological function. The tenets of the psychobiological attachment theory seek to explain the cognitive, social, and neurological aspects of developing social affiliation (Kraemer, 1997). Because of this, attachment theory is used here as a framework for exploring social relatedness in autism.

Over time, the principles of attachment theory evolved to explain more aspects of social relatedness, cognitive development, psychopathology, and adult affiliative behavior. Early descriptions viewed attachment and bonding as necessary for physical survival; the infant needed to nurse to survive, for example, and bonded to others for physical survival. Bowlby's (1969, 1973, 1979) seminal work formed the basis of current attachment theory; it stressed the psychological implications of attachment, including the process of psychological maturation through parent-child bonds and the grief and loss resulting from breaking of these bonds. Harry Harlow demonstrated that psychological bonds were more powerful than mere survival bonds by showing that infant monkeys attached to a cloth-covered wire "mother" without food rather than a wire "mother" with food. Harlow's research also demonstrated that tactile soothing and comfort was an important component of attachment. Although cloth monkeys had more characteristics of mother monkeys, they did not mother the infant—which, as it turns out, is essential for neurological development. The neurobiological and behavioral differences found in Harlow's monkeys spurred research into the psychobiological implications of attachment.

The necessity of social attachment for nervous system development was demonstrated in infants (Als, 1999), institutionalized children (Carlson & Earls, 1997), and nonhuman primates (Kraemer, 1992). This research shows that infants require adequate mothering for the development of the neural capacity to regulate arousal and state, for cognitive and motor development, and for the development of social relatedness. Touch in a reciprocal relationship with a caring adult person appears to be necessary for the development of the hypothalamic-pituitary-adrenal system (HPA), which regulates neurological state and responses to stress (Carlson & Earls). If a competent infant (one without neurological impairment) does not attach to a caregiver who provides adequate state regulation in the relationship, then the effects surface in the person's cognitive and physiological constitution in a way that may appear to be of a temperamental or genetic origin (Kraemer, 1997) and leave the individual more vulnerable to stress thereafter. These recently added concepts complemented and expanded attachment theory to a reformulation known as *psychobiological attachment theory* (Kraemer, 1992).

Attachment theory was also applied to the study of adults in numerous studies (e.g., Baumeister & Leary, 1995; Lyons & Sperling, 1996; Main, Kaplan, & Cassidy, 1985). These and other studies demonstrate that warm, affectionate bonds with others are key variables in predicting competence, resilience, and hardiness to stressors across the lifespan (Coie et al., 1993; Egeland, Carlson, & Sroufe, 1993). The conclusion that the development of human affectionate bonds is fundamental to physical survival, social and emotional development, cognition, neurological development, and aspects of function throughout the life span is now considered almost common sense because of the preponderance of evidence and literature. Especially in early life, attachment processes are primarily sensory and motor interaction patterns, as primary caregivers feed, rock, bathe, handle, dress, teach, and soothe the infant and young child. Given the essential differences in social relatedness found in autism, the far-reaching implications of attachment for development, and the sensorimotor nature of early attachment, it is critical to consider attachment processes and patterns of social relatedness in relationship to sensorimotor interventions. The purpose of this chapter is to review the premises of attachment theory and the literature describing the development of social relatedness in autism, and to suggest sensorimotor intervention strategies to enhance social relatedness.

To achieve this purpose, we discuss three topics. First, an overview of the theoretical basis of attachment theory and social relatedness is presented. Second, the literature on attachment and social relatedness specific to autism is presented and synthesized to develop an appreciation of the experience of having autism or having a child with autism. Finally, principles for sensorimotor interventions and specific application of techniques to promote attachment and social relatedness are detailed.

OVERVIEW OF ATTACHMENT THEORY

The tenets of attachment theory are richly supported by research on typical and atypical human development and psychological adjustment. In the following sections, the social psychological and behavioral tenets of attachment theory applied across the life span are discussed. Understanding the development of social relatedness promotes an appreciation of the social, cognitive, and neurological outcomes of human interac-

tion. Because people continue to grow and adapt through the life span, we then explore life experiences as an ongoing influence on attachment and subsequent adjustment and social relatedness. In the second section of this discussion, we review the neurobiological antecedents and consequences of attachment. We have attempted to include research based on the study of people and animals to integrate this as a basis for understanding attachment and relatedness in autism.

Social, Psychological, and Behavioral Tenets

Development of Social Relatedness

Personality is our pattern of interaction with others—that is, it encompasses how we relate to others, work with others, share ourselves with others, and what we expect and desire of others. Thus, personality exists only in relationship to others and is generated from our attachments and interactions with others. Genetic and intellectual capacities stimulate the earliest social interactions and influence ongoing reciprocal relationships with others. More important, from this genetic influence, personality is shaped and molded in its core by experiences with others throughout the life span.

Optimal personality development is often described as having an outcome on two related dimensions: a capacity for satisfying and reciprocal interpersonal relationships, and a well-differentiated, positive, and realistic sense of self. These two dimensions of personality are referred to by different authors as *attachment* and *autonomy*, *communion* and *agency*, or *relatedness* and *identity* (Feldman & Blatt, 1996). For children with autism, the capacity for reciprocal interpersonal relationships is diminished by all standards. Although receiving less attention and study, the capacity for autonomy and a well-differentiated sense of self is also diminished. One goal of attachment theory is to explain the development of relatedness, autonomy, and lifelong patterns of social relatedness. Beginning with the work of Bowlby, attachment theory heralded a change in the psychodynamic literature to a focus on the effects of real (rather than fantasy) interpersonal experiences in interaction with temperament to form patterns of social relatedness.

Ainsworth, Blehar, Waters, and Wall (1978) and others (e.g., Chorpita & Barlow, 1998; Main et al., 1985; van IJzendoorn & Bakermans-Kranenburg, 1996) systematically studied the attachment styles of children and their parents. Underlying their work was the premise that attachment, meaning the affectionate bonds we have with others, optimally promotes a sense of security and trust in relationships and forms internal working models of others as, for example, reliable or rewarding. Conversely, suboptimal attachment is associated with insecurity in relationships and internal working models of others as, for example, unpredictable or dangerous. From this basic internal sense of security (called a *secure base*) and trust in primary relationships, the child, adolescent, or adult is free to pursue autonomy. To describe the security in attachment relationships for children, a classification system of attachment styles was developed based on observations of the child's responses to separation from and reunion with their parent (18–24 months is the usual age). The standard test for attachment styles is termed the Strange Situation and involves two separations and reunions between the mother (or father) and the child. The mother and child enter a room with a stranger (and sometimes without a stranger) present; the child plays while the adults talk. After a few minutes, the mother excuses herself and leaves the child with the stranger (who is quiet and responsive, but not interactive) for a specified brief period. The child's behavior for the first minute after departure of the mother is observed and coded. When the mother returns, the child's behavior in greeting the mother is also observed and coded. The codes are used to identify the child's attachment as either a secure style or one form or another of an insecure attachment style (see Exhibit 7–1).

For older children and adults, attachment style can be assessed using numerous measures such as interviews, self-report questionnaires, and reports of early memories (Lyons & Sperling, 1996). In Exhibit 7–1, the attachment styles coded from the Strange Situation for children are displayed in parallel to the same adult attachment style, generally reported in a wide range of literature. The rate of secure attachment style is about 60% of the typical population regardless of socioeconomic status; in samples of adults and children with emotional distress, the rate of secure attachment is about 14% (van IJzendoorn & Bakermans-Kranenburg, 1996).

This attachment style classification system and its predictive validity for multiple social and personality factors have been studied and verified in numerous studies using a wide range of measures; descriptions of this research are well beyond the scope of this chapter. A brief overview of this large body of literature is summarized here to assist the reader in understanding the significance of attachment in development and function throughout the life span. Attachment security was found to be both a risk and a protective factor for the onset of psychopathology by numerous authors (e.g., Coie et al., 1993; Egeland et al., 1993; Masten & Coatsworth, 1998). Securely attached children, including those with a disability, are more likely to develop social compe-

Exhibit 7–1 Attachment Styles for Children and Adults

Infant Strange Situation Behavior	Adult Attachment Style
Secure Attachment Style Explores room and plays with toys before separation. Shows signs of missing parent on separation; may cry. Greets parent actively, often with physical contact, but then returns to play.	***Secure/Autonomous Attachment Style*** Able to discuss attachment experiences, values these, but is objective whether expriences are positive or unfavorable. Realistic expectations of intimate others. Discourse regarding relationships is relevant, orderly, complete, yet succinct. Able to balance relationships with autonomy.
Avoidant Attachment Style Fails to cry or be upset when parent leaves; continues to play. Actively avoids or ignores parent on reunion. Little or no proximity contact seeking, distress, or emotion on reunion. Focuses on toys or environment.	***Dismissing or Avoidant Attachment Style*** Dismissing of experiences and relationships with generalized statements about relationships ("great," "wonderful," "normal") with little detail. Focus on autonomy, power, orderliness. Low expectations of intimacy in relationships.
Anxious or Ambivalent Attachment Style May be wary or distressed prior to separation with little exploration. Preoccupied with parent; difficult separation. May be angry or passive during reunion. Fails to settle and return to exploration; may continue to cry and cling.	***Preoccupied/Emeshed Attachment Style*** Preoccupied with attachment relationships; inhibited autonomy. May have conflicting emotions, including anger or passive helplessness. Long, tangential descriptions of relationships that are sometimes vague and poorly organized. Conflicting expections in relationships.
Disorganized/Disoriented Attachment Style Displays contradictory behavior such as clinging to the parent without looking at the parent. May vacillate between crying and freezing at departure of the parent. May rise up excited to see the parent and then fall and huddle on the floor. This category is used in addition to one of the above types.	***Unresolved/Disorganized Attachment Style*** During discussions of loss or abuse, may show a striking lapse in the discourse such as prolonged silences, magical beliefs, or other lapses in thought coherence. Fits and starts in conversation suggest a struggle to find coherence. This category is used in addition to one of the above types.

Note: Reflects the works of authors including Ainsworth et al., 1978; Feldman & Blatt, 1996; George, Kaplan, & Main, 1996.

tence, trust, a strong sense of self, and resilience against stress. Adults and children with an insecure attachment style have more anxiety and are more prone to depression or decomposition in the face of abuse or trauma (see Lyons & Sperling, 1996, for a review). Children rated as securely attached at 12–18 months of age showed greater emotional openness and fluency of discourse about emotional topics at six years of age (Main et al., 1985). Secure attachment at 18 months was associated with more flexibility, persistence, resourcefulness, and hardiness at four to five years of age (Arend, Gove, & Sroufe, 1979). Other studies (see Huebner & Thomas, 1995, and Lyons & Sperling for a review) demonstrated that securely attached children scored higher on measures of leadership, intelligence, empathy, and curiosity, and lower on measures of aggression. The maintenance of securely attached relationships was associated with ongoing resilience and growth into late adulthood (Staudinger, Marsiske, Baltes, 1993). Conversely, insecurely attached children with anxious avoidant or anxious ambivalent styles were rated by teachers as more hostile, impulsive, and withdrawn; they had more learning disabilities and were more likely to be victimized by other children (Radke-Yarrow et al., 1995; Troy & Sroufe, 1987). In the worst-case scenario, children deprived of attachment experiences because of institutionalization or neglect have severe cognitive impairments; social isolation with huddling, rocking, and wetting; speech pathology; and psychopathic behaviors (Carlson & Earls, 1997; Magid & McKelvey, 1987). Thus, even among children without disabilities, the experiences of attachment and social relatedness are important variables in predicting lifelong competence and resilience.

Disability itself is a risk factor for difference in attachment interaction. Premature infants and infants with disabilities are more likely to be irritable and immature, with poorer motor skills and physiological regulation. These infants are more challenging for their mothers and more vulnerable to maternal and family stressors (Cox & Lambrenos, 1992). Other factors influencing the attachment experiences of children with disabilities include their physical and temperamental characteristics (the presence of a facial deformity or sensory abnormalities

being worst), the family's reaction to the disability, and the amount of social support available to the family (see Huebner & Thomas, 1995, for a review). College students with disabilities were found to have the same needs and desires for relatedness and the same interpersonal skills as their typical peers, but they experienced more emotional distress and decreased satisfaction in primary relationships and expressed more insecure attachment themes in their early memories (Huebner, Thomas, & Berven, 1999).

The attachment style of the parent is strongly associated with the attachment style of the child. From a review of 18 studies, which included 854 parent-child dyads, van IJzendoorn (1995) concluded that adults' attachment style agrees with their child's style on average 75% of the time. Moreover, there was agreement in 65% of cases between the attachment style of the parent prior to the child's birth and the attachment style of the infant at 12 months. Several caveats may explain this strong relationship and also illustrate the complexity of attachment processes. For example, common genetic capabilities for attachment may influence interpersonal relatedness in both parents and the child. Parenting itself may elicit the internal working models of being a child, with the parent likely to recapitulate his or her childhood experiences in his or her interaction with the child. The parent's own attachment style may influence his or her sensitivity to the signals of his or her child. For instance, anxious avoidant adults may be more likely to ignore or misread the attachment signals of their child; because of inconsistent parental responsiveness, the child may be more likely to respond with anxiety and avoidance. The parent with an ambivalent attachment style may vacillate between overindulgence and neglect, fostering similar confusion and ambivalence in the child. The intimate relationship with the child in the attachment process may influence the parent's primary attachment style (Fox, 1995). Stress and stressors may diminish the amount of parental energy available for attachment (Westman, 1991). The environmental context, including the amount of social support and resources, influences the parent's ability to respond to his or her own attachment needs and the needs of his or her child.

Life Experiences and Attachment

There is evidence that attachment style is both relatively stable and relatively changeable over time. Early experiences with caregivers are thought to form internal working models of relationships by age three years. These internal working models have both affective and cognitive schema that seem innately true to the individual and form a template, a set of rules, about the social world. Affective and cognitive relationship schema influence how a person acts and behaves in interpersonal relationships, shape expectations of others in relationships, and guide the interpretation of others' social behavior. Thus, internal working models of relationships are the foundation for our emotional reaction to others and our cognitive expectations and thoughts about others.

Internal working models are, initially, adaptive models; they make sense of the world and the experiences of the child. A child might respond with avoidance, for example, if interpersonal relationships are confusing or punitive; avoidance reduces pain and confusion and allows the child to develop protective autonomy. However, once established, internal working models tend to be self-fulfilling and more resistant to change. For example, if one expects oth-

ers to be hostile, one is likely to act in subtle ways that elicit hostility from others; this elicited hostility confirms the cognitive schema that others are hostile. Thus, the internal working model is a powerful influence on behavior in relationships that serves to elicit behavior in others and confirm the expectations inherent in the working model.

On the other hand, attachment style can be altered by subsequent life experiences—reduced or increased stress, subsequent relationships, success and failure, and a host of other factors—so that attachment is either more secure or more insecure (Fox, 1995). Adults who had difficult childhood attachment experiences may achieve a secure attachment style through working through their experiences; then they are more able to share that secure style of interaction with their own children (Main et al., 1985). Changes in the family environment and the economic stability of the family are associated with predictable changes in attachment style of the children (Egeland, Kalkoske, Gottesman, & Erickson, 1990). Healthy intimate relationships as adolescents or adults tend to promote secure attachment patterns, and individuals may actively strive to change their worldview through multiple self-help measures. Altering or modifying maladaptive templates through which the world is viewed is the goal for psychotherapy interventions using interpersonal and cognitive behavioral strategies. Numerous applications of attachment theory focus on building secure and adaptive internal working models through interpersonal therapy (e.g., Teyber, 1992), cognitive therapy (e.g., Safran & Segal, 1990), and narrative techniques (e.g., Lyons & Sperling, 1996).

As can be seen, many variables influence the development of attachment style and social outcomes over a life span. Figure 7–1 is a representation of the complexity of attach-

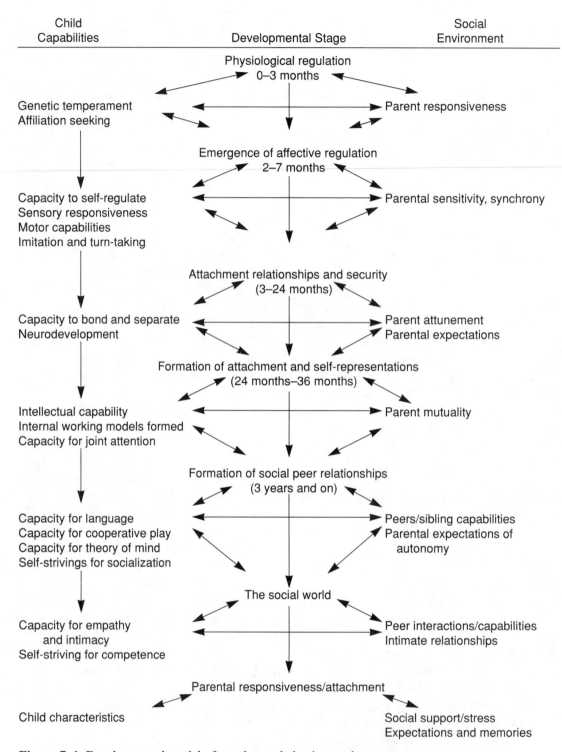

Figure 7–1 Developmental model of attachment behaviors and outcome

ment processes using a dynamic systems model. In this model, a child-centered hierarchy of capabilities is influenced by and influences the social environment, and the social environment influences subsequent child capabilities. In a dynamic system model with both hierarchical and systemwide interaction, a small change in one variable has the potential to influence the developmental trajectory—that is, the child enters the world with a genetic foundation of neurological development and capabilities that influence his or her physiological regulation and temperament, and set an initial developmental trajectory. Some children have more difficulty regulating homeostasis and are more fragile; subsequent responsiveness of the environment in helping the child maintain homeostasis positively or negatively influences the developmental trajectory. Stable homeostasis then promotes brain maturation, security, self-regulatory capacity, and improved social responsiveness. Each developmental stage then affects the subsequent stage in a cyclical and reciprocal fashion.

Similarly, the parent's skills typically develop in response to the influences of hierarchical and systemwide processes. Parent success with regulating the homeostasis of the child affects the parent's sensitivity and sense of competency, and reinforces the synchrony and timing of interactions between parent and child. Parents ordinarily respond with sensitivity to the child's needs for stimulation and rest; they synchronize their care to correspond with their perception of the child's needs and are, presumably, attuned to the arousal state of the child. As the child develops, parents engage in mutual interaction, imitation, and joint attention with the child to teach and model social skills. Parents gradually enable the child's autonomy as the child pursues social relatedness with a

wide range of others. As the child matures, the social environment includes peers, professionals, and intimate others, which influences attachment and further develops a capacity for intimacy, empathy, and the ability to see the world through another's perspective (theory of mind). These well-developed social skills then form the foundation for responsiveness to the infant when the child becomes a parent. Of course, at any point in this process, events and experiences can interfere with the typical developmental trajectory. Disruptions to the attachment process include events specific to the parent (e.g., grief, depression, substance abuse), events between parents (divorce, death of a parent), events in the environment (war, financial strain, stress), and changes in the child's characteristics that interfere with social responsiveness and interaction.

Neurobiological Relationships in Attachment Processes

Genetic Capacities and Subsequent Social Interaction

The child brings to the early parent-child relationship and all social interactions his or her own innate, meaning genetically and biologically predisposed, capabilities that influence the attachment relationship. Capacities for social behavior and attachment that are present in the young child include:

- autonomic and reflexive responses that regulate physiological rhythms, such as breathing, sucking, and swallowing
- state regulation and reactive temperament (Westman, 1990)
- affiliation seeking and responsiveness (Waterhouse & Fein, 1998)
- capacity to process and integrate incoming sensory information

• motor reactivity for skills such as visual tracking, smiling, and timing of interactions in sequence and harmony with others

The experiences emerging from the reciprocal interaction between the infant and primary caregivers provide the foundation for developing increasingly complex social skills and interaction patterns. Additionally, the response of the environment, primary caregivers, and other factors, such as nutrition, may alter these innate capacities in such a way that subsequent altered capacities may appear to be genetic in origin (Kraemer, 1997). Maturing social capabilities and skills include the capacity to form attachment bonds, turn-taking and imitative behavior, the capacity for joint attention, empathy and intimacy, and theory of mind.

In Table 7–1, social capabilities are itemized with implications for autism. Although numerous subcategories exist, those displayed have implications for the management of autism. This table summarizes and was generated from the literature review found throughout this chapter.

Numerous theories might explain the social disorders of autism, but one consistent with attachment theory is based on the cybernetic model or dynamic systems model of autism (Mundy & Crowson, 1997). This model proposes that the child with autism experiences a deviation in neurological development before birth that influences subsequent interactions and results in secondary neurological disturbances that dramatically alter the developmental trajectory. Several neurotransmitter and neural systems models are proposed to explain this primary neurological deficit (see Chapter 3). Although all of these conclusions are speculative because there is no integrated model of the neurobiological basis of social behavior (Waterhouse & Fein, 1998), some details of proposed neurobiological models are presented here to update the reader on the current research and to provide guidelines and rationale for intervention strategies.

Neurotransmitter Models

A role of oxytocin and vasopressin in governing social affiliation was proposed in recent publications. Oxytocin is thought to promote the expression of the affiliative behavior necessary to establish and maintain social relationships; it may support affiliation seeking and responsiveness (Carter, 1998; Insel, 1997). Oxytocin and vasopressin are amino-acid peptides synthesized in the hypothalamus and released by the pituitary gland. Although considered hormones acting on body systems, these two peptides were recently shown to be neurotransmitters or neuromodulators. Receptors for these two peptides are found throughout the limbic system and the autonomic centers in the brainstem (Insel). In a study of prairie voles, which live in monogamous families, compared to montane voles, which are solitary animals, Insel found that oxytocin and vasopressin are active in promoting pair bonding, parental care of the infant, and in regulating the infant's arousal responses (through oxytocin in breast milk). Furthermore, pair bonding and social contact increase the level of brain oxytocin, thus promoting and maintaining ongoing affiliation seeking and capacity for social contact

Because autism is considered primarily a genetic disorder that does not respond consistently to medications targeting other neurotransmitter systems (such as the serotonin system), Insel, O'Brien, and Leckman (1999) proposed that abnormalities in the levels of oxytocin and vasopressin may be prominent in autism. They note that the pattern of influence is consistent with findings

Table 7–1 Social Capabilities with Implications for Autism

Capabilities	Possible Deviation in Autism	Developmental Implications	Management Implications
Physiological timing of sleep/wake cycles, suck, swallow breathing patterns.	Dysregulation of sleep/arousal cycle, respiration, difficulties in feeding (Wieder et al., 1999).	Difficulties are stressors for care providers and infants that may disrupt attachment and early self-regulator ability (Als, 1999).	Carefully observation of the child to see what type of stimuli elicit avoidance or approach. Structure the environment to establish homeostasis.
State regulation to self-modulate arousal and sensory input.	Regulatory disorder with detached and hypersensitive responses are common in autism (Wieder et al., 1999).	Chronic high levels of stress in the infant with resultant secondary problems in neurological development (Mundy & Crowson, 1997).	Parental responsiveness and ability to structure the environment can profoundly influence the outcome. Goal to allow child to experience a calm, positive state with optimal arousal.
Affiliation seeking with responsiveness and capacity for social interaction.	Reduced levels of oxytocin and possibly vasopressin associated with reduced affiliation seeking, responsiveness, and dependence on social reinforcement (Insel et al., 1999).	Social isolation further reduces the levels of these two neuropeptides. Social interactions increase oxytocin, which may enhance affiliation seeking, attachment, and other social behaviors (Carter, 1998).	Provide consistent social intervention and frequent social contact to promote more optimal social interaction and development (Greenspan & Weider, 1999).
Sensory integration of sensations from multiple senses perceived and modulated in a way that promotes understanding of the stimuli and a reasonable response to it.	Sensory processing abnormalities seen in most children with autism including difficulty with hypo- or hyper-sensitivity, diminished sensory memory, difficulty assigning significance to sensory input, and narrow focus on some aspects of stimuli (see Chapters 1 and 3).	The attachment process requires extensive sensory input for care, feeding, nurturing, and learning (Kraemer, 1997). Sensory processing disorders may diminish attachment, learning, and modulation and promote a high arousal level (DeGangi et al., 1997).	Control external environment to reduce novelty and threat. Carefully graded sensory input. Use of proprioceptive input to modulate arousal. Recognize high arousal and anxiety level and reduce this while helping child self-modulate.

continues

Table 7-1 continued

Capabilities	Possible Deviation in Autism	Developmental Implications	Management Implications
Motor functions to permit output of responses in a way that is timed and sequenced.	Difficulties with imitating actions, visual tracking, oral motor control, proximal stability, motor planning, and sequencing or timing of output (e.g., Smith & Bryson, 1994).	Child may not give clear signals to the caregiver about his/her needs and experiences. This reduced or confusing output may effect the synchrony of care by the parent and increase parental stress (Rogers, 1988).	May need to learn to read the child's needs through different or more subtle cues. Parents may need to work harder than is typical to respond with synchrony and mutuality to their child and thus require professional approval, support, and reinforcement for their efforts.
Social behaviors of moving towards others or seeking satisfaction from others.	Strategic social behaviors of asking for help or items and simple proximity seeking is more intact for children with autism. Affiliative social behaviors that are primarily relational are decreased (Grossman et al., 1997).	Affiliative behaviors support emergence of joint attention. Example: "See my toy"—an affiliative behavior—and "Get my toy"—a strategic behavior. Being close to another for security versus being close for affection (Grossman et al., 1997).	Affiliative behaviors may need to be intensified by caregivers. Affiliative responses or approximations could be elicited and reinforced in natural settings. Proximity seeking could be elicited and reinforced.
Joint Attention	Rare for a child with autism to initiate behavior that invites another to share activities only for the social reinforcement of joint attention to a task (Baker et al., 1998).	Joint attention activity is thought to form the foundation for more complex social reciprocity needed for mature social skills.	Actively teach people with autism how to engage with another in social interaction and encourage them to make bids for joint attention from others.
Theory of Mind	Inability to interpret the mental state of another and use this interpretation to guide social interaction (Happe & Frith, 1996).	Skills in empathy and understanding others are the foundation for all mature social interaction skills.	Intensify the communication of positive emotional responses to actively teach people with autism about feelings and how to respond. Teach social skills, use social stories, videotapes, and visual supports.

in autism because these peptides are more abundant in males, more active in the immature brain, and have effects on cell migration and neuronal dendritic formation. As explained in Chapter 3, autism is considered by many to result from problems in cell migration that yield an immature brain. In animal studies, both peptides were found to be important in developing social attachments, some forms of aggression to protect families, and social memory (Insel, 1997). Preliminary evidence suggests that oxytocin plasma levels are abnormally low in children with autism ($n = 20$), and that increased oxytocin plasma levels are associated with higher scores on measures of social behavior for typical children, but not for children with autism (Modahl et al., 1998). Despite these interesting findings, Insel et al. (1999) cautioned that findings from human plasma levels and animal studies cannot be substantiated at this time because definitive research requires techniques too invasive for humans. As Kraemer (1997) and Nelson and Panksepp (1998) explained, the neurobiological systems associated with affiliative behavior are complex and dependent on numerous neurotransmitters that respond independently and differently to developmental experiences; dysfunction may result in labile neurobiology rather than predictably low or high levels of any single neurotransmitter.

Other neurotransmitter models relevant to autism were summarized by Carter (1998), who proposed that two independent neurological systems regulate responses to stress in interaction with social interaction. Behaviorally, humans are social beings who respond to isolation, particularly when under stress, with increasing levels of anxiety and arousal. Hyperarousal is associated with increased levels of cortisol and norepinephrine and a fight-or-flight pattern of behavior, or, paradoxically, a dissociative pattern of behavior (Carter, 1998; Perry, Pollard, Blakley, Baker & Vigilante, 1995). Thus, when under threat, people respond with fight or flight if there is potential for fleeing danger, or they respond with dissociation (numbing, freezing, forgetting) when aggression or flight is futile. Conversely, positive social interaction, especially under stressful conditions, significantly reduces anxiety, cortisol levels, and norepinephrine and increases oxytocin, vasopressin, and other opiates. With long-term secure social attachment (maternal or adult partners), stable, persistent, and higher levels of oxytocin and opiates may enhance positive social affiliation and further reduce anxiety (Carter). This theory explores one potential neurobiological mechanism to explain the protective functions of social support and social attachment identified in a large body of research.

Another proposed neurotransmitter model is based on the balance between inhibitory systems producing opiates in response to proximity with the mother and arousing systems producing noradrenergic transmitters in response to separation from the mother (Smith, 1994). Smith asserted that a primary developmental task of the toddler is to develop its own capacity to modulate arousal and reduce dependence on the mother. In this theoretical model, autonomy is enhanced by rehearsing increasing distances from the mother, which stimulates noradrenergic production and anxiety. Anxiety stimulates return to the mother with an increase in opiate production, which then supports autonomy. Through graded rehearsals of increasing distance and time away from the mother, self-modulation of arousal is developed and neural systems adapted. Smith likened this process to finding an optimal arousal state in which the level of challenge is just beyond a person's skill (a just-right challenge). This balance between neurobiological systems is similar, according to Smith, to concepts described by other authors as flow, optimal frustration, and optimal arousal. This theoretical model may explain one mechanism of lifelong adaptation and learning through active movement into somewhat anxiety-provoking states. Waterhouse and Fein (1998) include ideas similar to Smith's as one component of an integrated model of social behavior in autism. In this integrated model, approach and separation from the primary caregivers are also seen as early message exchanges in which the child communicates fear and the need for comfort in approaching the mother as a source of security, and communicates the need for autonomy in leaving the mother.

Another social neurobiological theory concerns the polyvagal system described by Porges (1997), which controls facial expression and heart rate and inhibits fight-or-flight responses. This system is hypothesized to be related to the level of approach/avoidance in social situations. People with high vagal activity are likely to be more anxious and, consequently, have less energy for social interactions, avoid social interactions, or be inhibited in social situations. In contrast, persons with low levels of vagal activity and anxiety are likely to be uninhibited and even unaware of themselves in social encounters. In this social biological model, a medium level of vagal activity is thought to be associated with optimal social interaction.

These models of social affiliation are based on neurological findings extrapolated from research with animals and with humans. In the following section, a set of related literature is reviewed that illustrates a comprehensive examination of multiple causal theories of social affiliation and dysfunction. This research with nonhuman primates is described here in depth because it was specifically designed to examine premises of the psychobiological attachment theory, relating attachment experiences to effects on neurological development. The studies also illustrate the research methodology that is the foundation of the neurotransmitter models just presented. Although not intentionally designed to study autism, the results of this literature have implications for the disorder.

The Effects of Social Experience on Neurobiology

Kraemer, Ebert, Schmidt, and McKinney (1989) reared infant monkeys from birth in several attachment conditions (i.e., without any objects; with cloth, stationary wire, or moving wire surrogate mothers; with peers; or with their mothers). They measured levels of norepinephrine (NE) in cerebrospinal fluid (CSF) over 21 months. Although monkeys raised with peers had higher levels of CSF NE than those raised without objects or with inanimate surrogate mothers, the monkeys raised by their mothers had nearly twice the levels of CSF NE. Low levels of NE function are thought to be associated with poor overall adaptation, attention disorders, increased vulnerability to stress, and decreased problem-solving ability. In addition, primates raised in social isolation were noted to have eating disorders, lack aggression-impulse control, and demonstrate hypervigilance, body rocking, self-injurious behavior, and a variety of cognitive deficits. Kraemer (1992) integrated the results from many studies on brain biogenic amine systems and concluded that deficits produced by social isolation include disregulation of the NE system, the dopamine system, and the serotonin system, changes in brain cytoarchitecture such as reductions in dendritic branching, and failure to organize an adaptive response to stressors. These findings suggest that numerous neurobiological systems are active in social interaction and are changed in response to social interaction.

Many of these theories and explanations are speculative and generalized freely from studies on animals to humans. Confirmation in human research may never be completed because of the limitations in studying human neurobiology. The proposed relationships between neurotransmitters, neurodevelopment, and neurostructure are theoretical at this point, and the research to describe the processes and relationships of social interaction is itself in its infancy (see Carter, 1998). However, the findings in the literature begin to confirm the original premises of attachment theory by demonstrating that neurochemical changes associated with social affiliation reduce anxiety, promote learning, shape brain development, and may underlie the expression of persistent behavioral styles or personality. Furthermore, this research suggests that if children with autism are born with alterations in the neuromechanisms for attachment, the social contacts of parents may be perceived differently. The result of this primary dysfunction may be the secondary cascade of impairments in many neurological systems, as theorized by Mundy and Crowson (1997) and Kraemer (1992).

As depicted in Figure 7–1, genetic temperament, capacity to be socially attentive and responsive, and self-regulation capabilities influence attachment behaviors and succeeding social outcomes in the young child. Presumably, the neurobiological processes related to attachment influence social development at some level throughout the life span. But the early development of neurological structures is also shaped and formed by attachment experiences. Although attachment experiences and neurological development are reciprocally interactive, development is not deterministic—that is, one can have optimal attachment experiences that optimize neurodevelopment but guarantee neither optimal development nor typical personality expression. At each level of development, different neurological structures and networks are utilized and developed; any neurological structure may have limitations that ultimately affect adult and life span social outcomes. Ensuing neurodevelopment may be constrained so that "normal" outcome is never achieved despite optimal social relatedness experiences. Conversely, children may have suboptimal attachment experiences yet have reserve intellectual capacities, at least one caring adult at a critical period, an intimate other, or other resources associated with resilience and archive positive social outcomes (Egeland et al., 1993; Masten & Coatsworth, 1998). Nonetheless, the early institutionalization of children with autism produced, perhaps, the worst social outcome; the images of severely impaired institutionalized children still permeate our view of autism. A major benefit of early intervention may be that improved experiences of social relatedness promote optimal nervous system development with a more typical developmental trajectory (Mundy & Crowson, 1997).

SPECIFIC FINDINGS IN AUTISM

With this background of the social, psychological, and neurobiological findings related to social attachment and social relatedness, we now review studies specific to autism. Because attachment processes are complex patterns between individuals that are influenced by multiple factors, this review focuses on child characteristics that may influence attachment and on the research on parental responsiveness in autism. Although not reviewed here, additional factors such as societal expectations, environmental supports, and financial and social resources are potent influences on the parents and, later, directly on the child. For example, society's response to autism and the process of navigating the medical and educational systems may be a source of stigmatization or stress, or, conversely, a source of social support, tangible resources, and pride in achievement for parents.

Child Characteristics That Influence Attachment

Within the first year of life, children later diagnosed with autism showed differences in attention, perception, association, imitation, contact, and communication as coded from family videotapes (Lelord et al., 1994). Pertinent to attachment, children in this study showed unstable attention, limited imitation, and contradictory facial expressions and gestures that increased in severity over time. In contrast to these findings, Losche (1990) found no differences in the timing or sequence of development for eight children later diagnosed with autism until the second year of life. Only within the second year of life were videotaped differences noted in their exploration of the environment, range of skills, and social interaction. These findings, although contrasting in themselves, reflect that some parents report knowing that their child was different from early life and others report that their child was entirely normal and easy to care for until the second year. These different findings may also reflect the wide range of symptoms associated with autistic spectrum disorders, subtypes of autism (see Chapter 1), or the unfolding of symptoms with neurological development (see Chapter 3).

Because of the benefits of early intervention for children with autism, the earliest identification of children at risk is desired. To that end, Bagnato and Neisworth (1999)

studied 621 typical and 212 atypical children in 33 states between the ages of 11 months and 71 months. They assessed each child using the Temperament and Atypical Behavior Scale (TABS): Early Childhood Indicators of Developmental Dysfunction (Bagnato, Neisworth, Salvia, & Hunt, 1999), which is designed to detect regulatory disorders. The authors (Bagnato & Neisworth) present normative data from their study to identify children who are at risk, atypical, or may qualify for services; the factor structure generated from this sample corresponded to the categories of the regulatory disorders.

Most important, for this chapter, Bagnato and Neisworth (1999) compared scores of children with autism ($n = 36$), Fragile-X ($n = 12$), and developmental delay ($n = 37$) and found that children with autism showed the highest overall scores, suggesting the most severe regulatory disorders. Children with autism showed the most disturbance in detached regulator behavior, such as tuning out, staring, or being overexcited in crowded places; and hypersensitive regulation, such as having difficulty being soothed and being easily frustrated, angry, impulsive, and irritable. Additionally, children with autism achieved the highest scores of any group on dysregulatory behaviors, such as having difficulty sleeping and crying without an ability to comfort themselves. Although the presence of regulatory disorders before 11 months was not studied by these authors, it seems clear that, by the second year of life, temperamental challenges and regulatory disorders are severe and consistently present in many children with autism. Such temperamental characteristics constitute vulnerabilities in the child's experience and a potential negative influence on the caregiver relationship, but this same caregiver relationship has the potential to modulate and transform early temperamental challenges and enhance the child's self-regulatory capacity (Wieder, Kalmanson, & Fenichel, 1999).

Although research on the effects of motor dysfunction on social interaction is limited, some children with autism may have difficulty in planning, sequencing, and organizing a motor response, suggesting an output disorder (Smith & Bryson, 1994) that may attenuate social interaction. Research has demonstrated significant motor deficits in autism, including the presence of choreiform movements, balance disturbances, incoordination, misarticulation with speech dysprosody, and motor dyspraxia ($n = 10$; Jones & Prior, 1985); poor visual tracking, proximal muscular weakness, and incoordination ($n = 6$; Huebner, Gamradt, & Klund, in preparation) and increased abnormal saccadic eye movements ($n = 10$; Kemner, Verbaten, Cuperus, Camfferman, & van Engeland, 1998); postural abnormalities and immaturity ($n = 91$; Kohen-Raz, Volkmar, & Cohen, 1992); differences in muscle tone and movement during the first two years of life (Lelord et al., 1994); and difficulty detecting eye direction in conversation (Shields, Varley, Broks, & Simpson, 1996). Although these difficulties may be relatively minor in comparison to the sensory disturbances experienced by children with autism, children may be less able to focus their gaze, smile, sequence a vocalization, sustain consistent visual tracking of caregivers, mirror the facial image of others, suck and swallow in rhythm with the feeding cycle, or organize a motor or verbal response. These limitations may produce confusing signals for the caregivers, elicit less reciprocal interaction by the parent, and diminish the experiences of social competence and social control for the child (Rogers, 1988). For some children

with autism, remediation and compensation for motoric limitations may be critical to building social interaction skills.

Other studies described more lifelong patterns of social interaction specific to autism. Mayes and Calhoun (1999) tested 143 children with autism (1.5–14 years, mean age 5 years) using their Checklist for Autism in Young Children. Similar to *DSM-IV* criteria, all children had difficulty with social skills, including social isolation and limited eye contact and reciprocal interaction. Young children tended to perseverate on topics or tasks; older and brighter children were obsessed with thinking and talking about specific topics. Nearly all (83%) had a history of repetitive play or stereotyped behavior and were distressed with change; on average, they exhibited 6.2 (of 10 possible) atypical sensory responses. Unanticipated strengths in simple social interaction were also found. For example, 67% of children with a developmental age of 1.5–3.5 years engaged in pretend play, such as feeding a doll or talking on a phone; 80–95% of the children used some form of gestural communication. These relative strengths afford an opportunity to engage the child in social interaction.

Social Interaction Strengths and Constraints

The social interaction patterns of persons with autism may be described as a pattern of syndrome-specific strengths and constraints. Although children with autism frequently use nonverbal requesting skills (strategic social behavior) and may learn social turn-taking skills, the ability to initiate bids for joint attention (see Mundy & Crowson, 1997, for a review) or engage in social reciprocity (Baker, Koegel, & Koegel, 1998) are particularly limited. *Joint attention* refers to behaviors that engage another person in a shared activity for the primary purpose of social reinforcement and interaction. Behaviors suggestive of joint attention bids are showing toys or objects to others in order to socially share experiences with others, to alternate attention between an activity and a person to engage that person in the joint task, or to invite another to play or engage in a task together. Older and brighter children with autism respond more readily to joint attention bids of others—that is, become engaged in tasks of interest to another, but rarely initiate such interaction with others. Mundy and Crowson proposed that joint attentional activities are a pivotal skill in motivating infants and young children to attend to and engage in their social world. The capacity for joint attention and the initiation of joint attention bids by children forms the foundation of more complex social linguistic and social cognitive skills (Bristol et al., 1996).

Three types of social interaction patterns in autism are described by Waterhouse and Fein (1998): (1) aloof and indifferent to people; (2) passive and controllable without social initiative; and (3) active but odd social interaction—for example, to deliver monologues on topics or to discuss obsessive interests. As Waterhouse and Fein noted, all three of these patterns suggest a fundamental reduction of social reward dependence. With a diminished need for social rewards, bids for joint attention from others may seem pointless to people with autism, but these early social behaviors are the catalysts for developing complex social skills involving language and cognition, such as empathy and theory of mind. This line of logic suggests that the social deficits of autism are due to a truncation of social skill development from a diminished skill to seek or ability to process social experiences. Other au-

thors attribute the social skill deficits of autism to cognitive limitations.

Cognitive Strengths and Constraints

Complex social skills involving sophisticated language and cognition also require high degrees of simultaneous processing of information and of cognitive flexibility in disengaging from one mental focus (a task) and shifting the focus to a new stimulus (a person). These cognitive skills are independent of social experiences, affiliation seeking, and social responsiveness. Ciesielski and Harris (1997) found that, regardless of intellectual capabilities, sequential processing (such as turn-taking and following rules) was much easier for persons with autism than the simultaneous processing of information such as is needed in social interactions. Similarly, Pierce, Glad, and Schreibman (1997) found that children with autism who watched videotaped vignettes of child-child interaction did well on answering questions requiring general attention, but that they had much more difficulty with using two or more cues to interpret stories, suggesting that the social deficits of children with autism stem from a poorer ability to disengage and shift attention and attend to a multitude of dynamic events during social interaction. Shields et al. (1996) found that both children with semantic-pragmatic syndrome and those with autism performed most poorly on tests of social comprehension questions and theory-of-mind procedures, suggesting a fundamental social language disorder. Happe and Frith (1996) described the cognitive difficulty of persons with autism in recognizing emotional expression, matching facial expressions to voice quality, sharing joint attention for social interaction, and imitating emotional responses. One component of social impairment is the theory of mind, which is based on the hypothesis that cognitive deficits make it difficult for people with autism to represent and think about the mental states of themselves and others (termed *metarepresentation* or *mentalizing*). Mentalizing is used to understand self and others and then interact in a way that creates synchrony or reciprocity in relationships. Happe and Frith proposed that this mentalizing deficit is a common cognitive element accounting for the social impairments of autism. In contrast, according to Happe and Frith, the desire to have physical contact with others, such as enjoying tumble play and comforting by others, does not rely on skills in mentalizing about others and is relatively unimpaired in autism.

Summary

Although we can only speculate about the experience of having autism, it is helpful to build empathy by attempting to understand the world from the point of view of a person who does. The literature reviewed in this book and the personal experiences of people with autism give us some clues. Early in life, the world of the child with autism must be distressing; they may experience sleep problems, with fitful or unpredictable sleep, difficulty calming themselves, fatigue, and irritability. Their earliest attempts at gaining control in a social relationship, responding to others, and making their needs known may be frustrated by disorganized or slow output; caregivers may misunderstand the signals, feel confused themselves, or have limited awareness of the child's unique sensory experiences. Sensory input is likely to be overwhelming and confusing. Even small changes may appear as continuously novel stimuli and elicit vigilance and high arousal—but some stimuli are so engaging that they stand out and incur exaggerated interest. Some motions feel good, moving visual objects are interesting, but sounds, some foods, and touching by others may feel noxious, like being stabbed. The worst and most predictably confusing stimuli are people. They speak in loud words that are difficult to interpret; they want to cuddle and kiss and have expectations of how children should respond. People's faces are always changing; the volume of information coming in is overwhelming; trucks, fans, or lighting may be more easily understood. As Waterhouse and Fein (1998) observed, people with autism sometimes respond to social interaction as if it were noxious, a stimulus to be avoided, perhaps an overwhelming stimulus that disturbs homeostasis.

As social expectations become more complex with psychological and neurobiological development, the source of problems in social relatedness also becomes multifaceted. Previous attachment experiences, language abilities, sensory abilities, the development of social skill prerequisites, motor output abilities, and specific cognitive skills interact and synthesize to produce success and competence during any social interaction. Social interaction and social reciprocity require simultaneous and complex information processing, multiple neurological systems, and synchronous responding; it is the most complex human activity. Sorting the contributions of each of these factors to problems in social relatedness is likely to prove a speculative venture for years. Regardless of the fundamental source of these social skill deviations, intervention must strive to develop social attachments, enhance social skill development, and promote social reciprocity using the most current information and best intervention strategies for children with autism. Several strategies have been employed successfully to improve social skills, including teaching specific social skills, facilitating play with typical peers, teaching children with autism to initiate social interactions and sharing, and using special interests or obsessions to engage them with others (Baker et al., 1998).

Parental Responses and Attachment Findings

Typical Parent-Child Interaction Patterns

Few parents are prepared through their own experiences for a child who is born with neurobiological differences that complicate and alter the attachment process. Normally, the timing of the attachment process is predictable. Early in the infant's life, the goal for the child is to maintain state homeostasis; a positive homeostasis is observed in a child who maintains a relaxed flexed posture, has regular breathing patterns, sucks and searches for sucking, has a pink color with limited startle, and has a regular heart rate and blood pressure (Als, 1999). In contrast, signs of distress include extension patterns, irregular respirations, flaccidity, fussing, and frequent fisting. Parental responses are critical to the child as a source of modulation; parents provide the control of the environment to promote homeostasis and establish self-regulation. Calming input from parents include skin-on-skin contact, encouragement of sucking and finger grasping, soothing calm voice quality, gentle slow rocking, swaddling in soft cotton or silk, decreased smells, and reduced lighting (Als). Conversely, some children need more stimulation and arousal for feeding; parents provide stimulation and begin early tactile and verbal interaction with the child.

As the infant matures, he or she begins to engage in longer periods of social interaction with smiling, vocalizing, making eye contact, and following the movements of caregivers. In turn, caregivers elicit and reward the early social contacts of the infant. The parent and child develop a mutually determined rhythm of interaction in which the mother or father and child synchronize levels of vocalization and cuddling. With increasing child maturity, the parent becomes increasingly attuned to the subtle individualized communications of the child and matches his or her behavior to the child's needs and capabilities. Parents and caregivers encourage joint attention, engaging the child in activities of interest to them and joining with the child in the child's play and activities. As the child develops preschool capabilities, parents allow increasing amounts of autonomy and encourage problem solving by the child.

The term *good-enough parenting* refers to the natural cycle of parenting, which is responsive, synchronous, and attuned to the child, but trusting of the child's ability to achieve autonomy and solve problems; the term does not refer to minimal standards of parenting. As parents attend to multiple aspects in their own lives, natural lapses in parenting give rise to opportunities that encourage the development of the child's problem-solving skills and promote autonomy and self-confidence (Smith, 1994). Of course, parents can be overly responsive or underresponsive, making natural opportunities for autonomy either absent or overwhelming. But for parents with a child who has autism, the process of grief and adjustment and the social environment influence all aspects of parent-child attachment (Cook, 1996). Parents need social support and energy to meet their own needs and the needs of all of their children, they need reinforcement from the child or from their social support system, and they need to formulate their own narrative life story of developing success and competence in their parent role.

Attachment Patterns in Autism

The research on parent-child attachment indicates that children with autism do socially bond and affectionately attach with their parents, direct more social behaviors toward their parents, and seek soothing and comfort from parents, and that parents synchronize their efforts to the child's needs. However, the whole story of parent-child attachment and social relatedness in autism is more complex than this.

Sigman and Mundy (1989) found that children with autism displayed attachment behaviors toward their parents but were more vulnerable to separation from parents and less able to self-soothe. In an extensive study of attachment security among 19 children (ages 3–6 years) with autism, Capps, Sigman, and Mundy (1994) found that all of the children showed some signs of attachment to their mothers. However, of the 19, the attachment style of four children could not be classified, one because of the mother's behavior, one because of no real pattern of behavior, and two who were "falling and freezing in stereotyped ways, and directing unusual, indecipherable facial expressions toward the mother" (p. 255). Of the 15 children classified, all were classified initially as showing disorganized/disoriented attachment style. Six of these children were secondarily classified as securely attached and nine were classified as insecurely attached. Of these insecurely attached children, three were truly disorganized and disoriented in their style, two were insecure-ambivalent, two were avoidant, and three could not be subclassified because of their puzzling combinations of behavior. Similarly, Dissanayake and Crossley (1997) found that children with autism displayed much more variability in their responses to separation and reunion across three sessions when compared to typical children, suggesting more unpredictable patterns of social responsiveness. From these descriptions, it seems apparent that the children with autism, even those who were securely attached, interacted with disorganized behavior toward their parents—behavior that could be difficult to read and interpret. This suggests that a key concern for intervention is helping parents of and professionals working with children who have autism to interpret confusing interaction patterns and to persist in attachment efforts despite inconsistent feedback from the child. It is also important for people to recognize that miscommunication by the child or between parent and child is likely to occur in autism even under ideal circumstances.

Joint attention is a more advanced pattern of parent-child interaction that emerges later. Capps et al. (1994), in the study discussed above, found that securely attached children were more responsive to bids for joint attention, made more requests of the parents, and initiated more social interaction with parents than insecurely attached children. However, neither group of children with autism initiated bids for joint attention from the parent. This finding suggests that the formation of an attachment bond is separate from the development of the capacity to make bids for joint attention, which requires more sophisticated internal working models of relationships. Thus, children with autism demonstrated attachment to their parents and interacted with them for social and strategic purposes; however, they rarely sought interaction with them in activities solely for the social interaction and reward inherent in bids for joint attention.

Part of the difficulties in interaction that are seen in autism arise from sensory hypersensitivities (Cohn, Miller, & Tickle-Degnen, 2000). DeGangi, Sickel, Kaplan, and Wiener (1997) compared the mother-child interaction patterns of 94 children (7–30 months of age) with regulatory disorders to 154 typical children in three sensory play conditions (symbolic, tactile, and vestibular play situations). The children with regulatory disorders and their mothers experienced the most distress in the tactile play conditions. The children showed flat affect and more aggression during tactile activities. Both mother and child showed more anticontingent responses during tactile activities. Anticontingent responses are mismatches in synchrony or timing, or failure to read the social signals of the other person. Most of the children with regulatory disorders displayed hypersensitivity to touch. Their mothers reported that they struggled to cope with the defensive reactions to touch that these children exhibited because touch is so fundamental to mother-infant care relationships. Mothers found it difficult and confusing when, for example, the child arched his or her back in response to cuddling; the mothers felt rejected and less in control. In contrast to tactile play, there were no differences between groups in symbolic play; mothers and children in both groups were comfortable in these situations. In the vestibular play situation, the mothers of children with regulatory disorders tended to display a flatter affect and encourage the child's self-stimulation and play using vestibular-based toys. The authors theorized that these mothers were gauging their own responses to their children's behavior. Vestibular activities, although desired by most children, also evoked unpredictable responses to and sometimes led to overarousal of the children. Playing with the children on balls and other moving objects required touch by mothers, which was an aversive stimulus for children; consequently, mothers were wary and encouraged self-play.

Watson (1998) also found that the responses of parents were understandable given the responses of their children. In this study, the language interactions of 14 preschool children with autism and 14 typical children were compared during a 15-minute free play interaction. Not surprisingly, the higher the child's language comprehension age, the more utterances were made during free play. The mothers of children with autism did not differ from the mothers of typical children in the frequency of child-focused utterances, suggesting that they were equally responsive to their children. However, the children with autism displayed much more difficulty in establishing and maintaining joint attention, while "mothers of typically developing children did not have to work as hard to get their children engaged in activities . . . or to shift the child's attention" (p. 57). In addition, the children with autism displayed highly variable behavior during free play, with some extremely active and others focused only on one toy. In both of these situations, the mothers engaged in more "onlooking" behavior toward their child and used more anticontingent responses to redirect, rather than to mutually engage, their child.

Rogers, Ozonoff, and Maslin-Cole (1991) found that the level of security in attachment bonds was positively correlated with the level of cognition, language, and gross motor skill among children with autism. Mothers of securely attached children appeared more sensitive to their children; securely attached children had higher language comprehension and initiated more social interaction with their parents than insecurely attached children, suggesting a link between representational ability and attachment (Capps et al., 1994). These studies suggest that parents are doing many things right and that their responses are synchronous given the behaviors of their children with autism, but that their work is more taxing and influenced by their children's unpredictable and difficult-to-interpret responses. The relationship between attachment and other cognitive skills is complex, and cause-and-effect conditions have not been demonstrated in research with humans. However, we know that secure attachment is associated with improved outcomes for both typical children and children with autism.

Occupational therapists working from a child- and family-centered approach have long advocated that professionals seek to understand the world from both the child's and the parent's viewpoint (Brown, Humphry, & Taylor, 1997; Burke & Schaaf, 1997; Cohn & Cermak, 1998; Cohn et al., 2000; Humphry, 1989; Humphry & Case-Smith, 1996; Miller & Hanft, 1998). It is evident, based on the review presented here, that children (and, perhaps, adolescents and adults) with autism struggle to have their needs met and bring to the relationship vulnerabilities, limitations, and opportunities for interaction. Despite these constraints, children with autism social-bond with their parents. Parents, by the same token, are working hard to connect to and engage their child with autism despite confusing and ambiguous signals and their own struggles with grief and the social stigma attached to autism.

Cohn et al. (2000) found that parents hoped that the collaboration of professional, parent, and child would help their child participate socially, learn self-regulation, and gain competencies. For themselves, parents hoped to learn strategies to support their child and longed for validation of their own competencies as parents. To achieve these parent hopes, professionals need to reduce the burden to primary caregivers and join with the family in a collaborative relationship to determine their specific needs,

dreams, and desires. In the child's best interest, many factors related to the family need to be considered. The stresses and strengths of every family must be understood and respected by professionals. The goals of all family members must be seen as important. Treatment must be flexible. Families need hope and social support. Most professionals need to commit to a long-term relationship with a family for the best collaboration (Mueser, 1996). Movement to a family-centered approach requires changes in many expectations, an increased respect for family expertise, and a sensitivity to parents' need for validation and support without negative judgments by professionals (Lawlor & Mattingly, 1998). This background in understanding children and adolescents, parents, and the relationship between parents, children, and professionals serves as a guide to the following section, which includes specific suggestions for enhancing attachment and facilitating social relatedness for people with autism.

INTERVENTION STRATEGIES FOR IMPROVING ATTACHMENT AND SOCIAL RELATEDNESS

Much of parenting, caregiving, and professional interaction with children involves sensory input through touch, the sound of a voice, the way someone is moved, joint visual attention, eye contact, voice quality, and background noise. Attachment, social relatedness, and personality emerge from the synchronous interaction between two people. Sensory interaction with another is subtle, sensitive, and revealing of the other's inner state. If you are tense, for instance, another adult may not notice your stress, but handling a child conveys the tension, which is likely to be felt and sensed. The act of caring for another involves caring for yourself as well, this facilitates finding a rhythm (the dance of attachment) in which each person feels content in the other's presence. A calm interaction, although more difficult for the child with autism, promotes secure attachment; this calm and relaxed interaction style is the goal of sensorimotor interventions.

Occupational therapists using a sensorimotor approach to management believe that one key to creating a mutually satisfying rhythm of interaction is to value the world from the other's point of view (Cohn et al., 2000). Fundamental to this approach is an acceptance of the child exactly as he or she is, but with a vision of how he or she could become. Sensory defensiveness, stereotypic behaviors, and restricted interests are viewed as opportunities to learn about the child's need and as clues to expanding the child's repertoire of skills and social interaction. This balance between acceptance and vision for change may sound contradictory and is an elusive goal. However, in accepting the child, the child is freed to accept himself or herself too, and the pressure for parents or children to change, to make things normal, is greatly diminished. A vision for change is fundamental to all of parenting; for instance, parents accept nighttime feedings as just right now, but also dream of their son becoming a pilot or hockey player. Special or restricted interests, a poverty of play and functional skills, social communication difficulties, sensory hypersensitivities, and behavioral challenges are facts of life for children with autism and key considerations in developing relationships. Special interests can be expanded on, sensory hypersensitivities need to be respected, behavior needs to be shaped and taught in natural environments, and social communication can be enjoyed. A guiding principle to facilitating social relatedness is to keep the person with autism engaged with people as often as possible and gradually expand the repertoire of skills in small but persistent and incremental steps. The one way to know if any intervention is working is to watch the recipient. If the person with autism is engaged with you, then that task is helping develop socialization and is a just-right challenge. If you, as a parent, professional, or caregiver, feel good about what is happening, then whatever you are doing is building your relationship.

The following is a list of ideas for where to begin and what to do. These are only ideas and most may not be appropriate for any specific person with autism. But try them out and apply the test described above. Are you happy in doing an activity? Do you experience a feeling of acceptance? Is the person engaged with you? If so, you are on the right track.

Social interaction involves a few guidelines. Like medication for children with autism, the rule is "start low and go slow." With any intervention, take small steps, gradually increase the complexity of the activity, and persist in moving toward change. These ideas are embedded in the principle of carefully grading tasks and sensory input to find the just-right challenge for a child, a challenge that promotes adaption and learning and elicits an adaptive functional behavior. Other principles of management and facilitating social interaction are illustrated in the suggestions that follow. These principles of management could be applied in many more ways than suggested here. The principles of using sensorimotor strategies to improve social relatedness in autism, with illustrations, are listed in Table 7–2.

Sensory Defensiveness

Smell, a powerful stimulus with direct input to the limbic system, is sometimes overlooked as a source of sensory sensitivity. Newborns can discriminate their mother, in part, based on smell characteristics. Certain smells may be particularly noxious to peo-

Table 7–2 Principles of Social Interaction Using Sensorimotor Management

Principles of Management	Illustrations Using Sensorimotor Interventions
Reduce sensory overload.	Dim lights, reduce voice volume, whisper, select soft clothing.
Present graded introduction of sensory input to decrease hypersensitivity.	Provide tactile input to the least sensitive areas of the body and gradually increase the time and intensity of the stimulation.
Start low and go slow.	Make small changes in sensory input; for example, add textures to food and slowly increase the amount of texture.
Teach self-modulation.	Teach the child to indicate with a sign, word, or picture when he or she needs to retreat. Reinforce attempts to self-modulate and return to social interaction when calm.
Use proprioception to calm.	Provide regular opportunities for deep pressure and heavy work such as sucking activities, pushing/pulling heavy loads, using a trampoline, and using weighted blankets.
Use visual cues.	Use pictures of emotions expressed by people who are familiar to the child. Label, discuss, imitate, and exaggerate the emotions seen in the pictures.
Expand on restricted activities to engage social contact.	Join with the child in sensory activities such as twirling objects. Imitate the child and then engage the child in twirling objects in new ways or taking turns.
Share control.	Engage the child in turn-taking on any sensory, play, or interactive activity. Give the child as many choices as possible in, for example, what to wear, what to eat, what toy to play with.
Make activities fun.	Use your sense of humor to make things silly in a way that the child will enjoy. Play with humor should be as spontaneous as possible to reduce arousal and hypersensitivity. It's okay to laugh and enjoy your child just as he or she is.
Foster joint attention.	Imitate the child and then ask him to imitate you. Show the child your activities and engage him or her with you. Show interest in the special interests of the child.
Exaggerate social interaction or positive emotional responses.	When playing sharing sensory games with the child, let him or her know clearly when you feel joy, excitement, fatigue, and other emotions.
Teach work skills.	Children with autism need jobs, however small, to build work skills and participate in the family. Have them grate cheese, crush cans, vacuum, etc.

continues

Table 7–2 continued

Principles of Management	Illustrations Using Sensorimotor Interventions
Persist.	Children with autism will respond to your contacts and do learn. Once you start making a change, make it small, but then continue to ask for the response you need in a gentle but persistent way.
Take good care of yourself.	When you are too tired or stressed to do something with your child, do not initiate a request or activity. It's okay to take a break.
Provide and get social support.	Happy parents and caregivers can be more spontaneous and responsive to their child.
Take good care of your marriage and the rest of your family.	The best atmosphere for children to develop interpersonal relatedness is within a happy family.

ple with autism and these should be reduced in the environment. For example, the smell of smoke, strong perfumes, makeup, hair spray, dry cleaning, and certain cooking odors could be noxious to some. It often takes experimentation with different smells to identify pleasurable and noxious smells. Some people with autism smell objects as one way to learn and explore. Sharing a smell can be one way to engage with your child. A principle of intervention, for instance, is to expand on the intrinsically rewarding interests of people with autism. For children who enjoy smelling objects, ask them to smell in different body positions (sitting, standing, lying on stomach), at different angles, with a wide variety of smells, to share smells with another person, pick a favorite smell, or match smells to real objects (e.g., lemon smell to a real lemon).

Auditory input can elicit defensiveness. One of the easiest things to control is your voice quality. Whisper sometimes, especially when the situation is overly charged. Speak in a firm but gentle tone of voice. Sing messages and make up lots of songs to go with daily events—for example, "Now its time to go to bed, go to bed, go to bed.

This is the time to go to bed." Singing the same song for different tasks may help the child learn the tasks, keeps the transitions calm, and provide structure of the environment. Music often is calming. Some children calm to classical music while others seem to prefer a stronger beat. Try music without lyrics at first as a background calming noise. Some children are able to complete their schoolwork with improved attention when wearing headphones with music; musical sounds are predictable, but environmental sounds may be random and distracting.

Fluorescent lighting can be arousing, especially if the lights flicker even slightly. Some people are particularly sensitive to light and may benefit from wearing a brimmed hat when outdoors or even indoors. On the other hand, soft lighting, such as Christmas tree lights, could be calming and engage the child in visual pursuits. Using a flashlight in the dark might be a fun way to highlight faces and social expressions; this type of activity demonstrates a principle of increasing the salience of a social response and simplifying the sensory input. With a flashlight in the dark, you can highlight your face or the face of the child looking in the mirror; by reducing all other stimuli, the child may be able to attend to facial expressions and link these to their own emotions and the emotions of another to build social understanding.

Tactile defensiveness is a particularly difficult problem frequently present for people with autism. Some therapists recommend a specific brushing technique (Wilbarger & Wilbarger, 1991); although research is limited, this technique may reduce tactile defensiveness for some children. Ask your occupational therapist about this. Tactile input is important to people; those who are defensive need as much input or more than people who enjoy touch. Because of this, it is important to provide regular tactile input in a way that is pleasant and acceptable; firm pressure and touch may be pleasant. When the child is relaxed, touching by the parent in a massage or gentle stroking pattern may be helpful. Sometimes it is helpful, for example, to sit the young child across your lap facing you; put your feet up on a table and relax. In this position, you can make maximal eye contact with the child and monitor his or her response. Then, using firm but not hard touch, tactile input can be introduced; start with the least sensitive body areas, such as the arms and legs. As the child tolerates and enjoys the sensory input, progress to touching the more sensitive areas of hands, feet, and face. Use your hands to desensitize the area around the face and then to gradually introduce tactile sensory input into the child's mouth. Some children prefer massage and tactile stimulation using textures such as cotton cloths (Q-Tip, very soft brush, or soft foam for the mouth), silk, furs, and soft brushes, and other children enjoy rougher textures such as corduroy and soft denims. A principle of management involves making activities fun and spontaneous. For example, putting soft cotton socks over your hands to provide tactile stimulation may engage the child in silly play and early self-help training as he or she puts socks on your or his or her own hands. It's important that this time be relaxed and gamelike; talking with the child, labeling body parts, or singing a simple song (e.g., "Now I'm going to touch your nose") may help the child stay relaxed.

After a bath, spend a little extra time towel-drying the child, or let the older child towel-dry himself or herself. If the person is not allergic, apply powders or body lotions with a firm touch may help. Sharing control might include giving the child choices of things to use in this sensory activity (e.g., a blue towel or a white towel; powder or lotion) or a choice of which body part to begin with (e.g., feet, hair, or toes). Use his or her special interests to reduce resistance. For instance, if the child enjoys trucks, a cloth truck (available in stores) could be used to drive over the arms and face; add attachments (a string or cotton balls) to the truck for variation. If the child enjoys spinning or flapping objects, you can imitate him or her (often to his or her delight), then engage the child with you in taking turns with the sensory toy. Although prolonged tickling of any child may seem enjoyable to them, it is always contradicted. Such prolonged tickling is overpowering to any child, especially those with autism, may be sensed as intrusive, and may result in a rebound with excessive arousal. Some intervention strategies use a tickle game that includes brief and frequent touch between caregivers and children in a playful manner. Although this technique may be helpful, it is important to monitor a child's response to any tactile input. Take good care of yourself, too; if you are feeling anxious or rushed, it is best to wait for a more relaxed time than to initiate a social-sensory activity that may be too taxing now.

Some children benefit from having a special place that is calming and quiet. To illustrate the concept of promoting self-modulation and self-soothing, a large box can be set up as a place to go for calming when the sensory input is too much. It's important to teach the person to recognize when he or she is experiencing sensory overloaded and then to teach him or her to self-regulate. If the person with autism engages in self-calming, such as retreating to a quiet corner, using a sucking or chewing activity, or asking for a break, reward him or her for taking care of his or her needs and rejoining in life activities when he or she is ready. Self-soothing and self-calming are adaptive and mature strategies that we all use.

Feeding

Feeding is a natural time for social interaction, but it is difficult when oral-motor difficulties interfere; sensory and motor problems are common sources of feeding difficulties. Sensory hypersensitivity may be paired with spitting, coughing, or difficulty in chewing. Encourage the child to suck or chew on objects or a pacifier between meal. Any sensory stimulation to the mouth reduces sensory hypersensitivity; lack of sensory input increases sensory hypersensitivity. Before meals, spend some time, as suggested above, providing tactile stimulation to the whole body, but then concentrate on the face and around the mouth area. A gentle massage before meals may make feeding go better. Respect the child's tolerance for certain foods while gradually introducing subtle changes. For example, using the principle of starting low and going slow, introduce a tiny amount of applesauce into liquids to provide texture; add a little mashed potato or mashed rice to other foods. Every few days, increase the amount of texture by *just a little*. It's okay if the child spits these out; you cannot force a child to eat anything. Relax and follow the child's lead, but gradually expand his or her repertoire by being persistent and patient. Persistence is a principle; once you introduce a small amount of texture, persist in doing this for as long as it takes—sometimes months.

People sometimes enjoy chewing even when they are hypersensitive, so try a variety of resistant items such as licorice, bagels, beef jerky, and chew toys. You can make a social game of this, with the child reaching toward food held in your mouth or feeding you; this could also be fun. Share control in all social and sensory activities by giving choice about what sensory activity or food to use. Choices can also be presented using pictures of foods, snacks, sensory games, etc.

The child may have motor problems that interfere with feeding. Try these ideas: Sit the child in a more upright position; make sure that you present food when the head is turned toward the center or midline of the body; keep the head flexed forward slightly to promote chewing and swallowing. Thickening liquids using applesauce, pudding, nectars, or baby cereal may help the child swallow. When presenting food, it may help to place the food over the molars rather than in the front of the mouth to encourage chewing and swallowing.

Proprioception

Proprioception input is often calming and can be achieved by passive means or by active motion of the person. Passively, slightly weighted, or tight-fitting garments can help calm a child. Heavy blankets, a cotton rug, bean bags sewn into blankets, or purchased weighted blankets may provide increased proprioception to improve sleep or provide calming. Tucking in blankets around young children and swaddling infants may help.

Some children benefit from using a weighted vest for brief periods; these can be made or purchased. Wearing Lycra tights under clothing or using a backpack may provide deep proprioceptive input. Sometimes people enjoy wearing a winter coat to protect them from being touched; it may also provide deep proprioceptive input. Firm proprioceptive stimulation can be provided with firm hugs and deep massages to the body.

Children and adults derive proprioceptive stimulation through active movement, especially movement against resistance. Children can crawl through cloth tunnels, which can be purchased at fabric stores or made by sewing cloth together; try fur, knits, or other textures for more input. The young child needs opportunities to move outside, to dig in the mud and sand, to push trucks laden with rocks, to push or pull a cart with a small weight or rocks inside, or to ride tricycles and other riding toys. Jumping on a trampoline is calming for many children and adolescents.

As the child ages, work activities can provide much proprioceptive input that may be calming while supporting training in work skills such as attention and task completion. Vacuuming, shoveling snow, sweeping walks and driveways, crushing cans, washing the car, scrubbing floors, carrying in groceries, hand-grating cheese, or using simple tools in the workshop may provide work and proprioceptive activities as well as opportunities for mutual interaction and tangible help in running the home. The job may not be done well at first, but it's more important that the skills are learned and that children contribute to the household. Work activities and play activities are not differentiated in children's minds. Some families embed work and play interaction into their daily routines; such integration may provide assistance to families in completing daily chores while offering children and adoles-

cents opportunities for building work competencies (Primeau, 1998).

Vestibular Stimulation

Children with autism may enjoy vestibular stimulation that comes from rocking, spinning, and swinging so much that it seems to take the child away from interaction with others. Some children may need what seems like excessive sensory input, for reasons we don't fully understand. You can hang a net or hammock swing in the basement, garage, or somewhere in the house where the child can use the swing as much as he or she needs. You can use the time when he or she is swinging or spinning to engage him or her in social interaction with peekaboo games, touching his or her hand when he comes around, asking for more pushing if you are pushing him or her, placing a puzzle piece after every 10 spins, or taking turns with a sibling or peer in swinging. Expand the repertoire of skills and change the activity subtly to increase flexibility. For example, swing with shoes on, socks on, or in bare feet; swing or spin in sitting, kneeling, standing, lying on the stomach, back, or side; swing in a net, on a swing, in a blanket held by two people; swing outside or inside; swing in a pink net, decorate the swing with plastic flowers, hang flags on the swing for July 4th, or decorate the swing with pumpkins for Halloween. The ideas are endless. Consistent and persistent changing of small details related to a special interest is one key to building flexibility and social interaction. Some people benefit from having a rocking chair available to them in many environments. To increase resistance and provide calming proprioceptive input, put weights across the rockers or put the rocker on thick carpeting or in sand.

Teaching Techniques for Social Skills

Visual skills are often strongest for children with autism; these skills offer may possibilities for promoting harmony and calm social relatedness and are used naturally in parenting. Early in life, the social interaction between the infant and parent is highly visual. The parent smiles and demonstrates a highly animated face, in a sense wooing the infant's engagement. Parents show babies things and carry them to see things without expecting them to understand their language or to vocalize in response. Continue to use visual stimulation and an expressive face to engage the child with autism as he or she ages; it is important that you give clear visual signals about your emotional responses and your expectations.

Use visual cues by showing pictures of familiar people, places, and things; make a picture book of familiar people showing emotions such as laughing, crying, being angry, and feeling surprised. Videotape parents and other family members expressing a range of emotions. Let the child watch the videotape repeatedly. Make videotapes of social interactions, such as the many ways of saying hello, how are you, thank you, and goodbye. Videotapes of other social skills, such as playing with a friend, sharing toys, taking turns, and asking questions about another person's interests, can be replayed frequently. Because children with autism may enjoy videotapes, using video recordings of real people in the child's life, with real objects and real places the child goes to may help him or her generalize and apply these skills at the proper time.

Reading and understanding the responses of children with autism may be difficult, and expecting them to read and interpret your responses may be unrealistic. It may be helpful to increase the strength of your emotional responses—that is, to intensify social and emotional responses (without being frightening) so that what you feel is clearer to the child or adolescent likely to misinterpret the subtle cues of social interaction. Most parents want to be assured of the love of their children, but people with autism may have difficulty knowing how to respond consistently to show their affection. It is important to know that the child is attached to you and loves and needs you. Seek support from other parents of children with autism, close friends, or professionals to get the assurance and validation that all parents need. For many reasons, people with autism are sometimes separated from their families for periods, especially as they age. Although separation is stressful, it is important to remember that both families and people with autism may benefit (see MacDonald, 1998, for a personal account). Some lapses in parenting are normal, after all, and may stimulate problem-solving skills, self-striving, and autonomy (Smith, 1994).

Keeping a regular schedule may be the most important way to maintain calm; however, transitions are almost always difficult and changes in a schedule are inevitable. A schedule can be augmented by posting pictures of what will happen throughout the day, singing songs to help transitions to tasks, using timers to help cue when something will occur (if possible, let the child set the timer). Some events, such as getting a haircut, can be troublesome and may need a few days to a week of warning that the event is coming, with regular reminders as the event approaches. Videotapes of such stressful events can be replayed by the child as a way to reduce anxiety and resistance. When it is realistic, give choices on difficult topics—for example, "When do want to get your hair cut, in the morning or after dinner?"

Joint attention can be built around the special interests of the child. If, for instance, the child wants to line up blocks or cars, then join in the task with him or her. It is important not to be an onlooker but an active participant in a gentle, accepting way. Sometimes, simple imitation of the child's activity conveys a sense of acceptance and becomes an opportunity for social engagement. It is difficult for the child to ask you to share in a game, but model this, seeking to expand the shared interest in subtle ways to make it more complex.

Finally, all of us working with children with autism need to remain optimistic and care for ourselves and the parents of the children. It is important for professionals to avoid blaming or judging parents or caregivers negatively in any way (Lawlor & Mattingly, 1998). Blame is unproductive and may prevent professionals from doing their best to assist the family. Parents need help in ways that will make their lives easier; this will free them to have the energy to care for their child. Giving parents therapy assignments may increase their burden and sense of failure and guilt; however, offering guidance in making life simpler may be helpful.

Progress with children who have autism may be so slow that parents and caregivers become discouraged. Keeping a narrative journal of the child's progress or recording monthly videos may be helpful to highlight progress. Regular celebration of the child's progress, along with celebrations of all the family's progress, may help the whole family focus on the positive. Parents need regular time for their own intimate attachment to help them self-regulate and maintain social support and contacts. "Out to Dinner In" may be one method of having a regular romantic evening when financial and social constraints prohibit a real night out. The support and understanding of grandparents should also be cultivated by professionals, as they can be a great help to families.

Sometimes it helps a family to build a narrative of their life story. For example, family members can explore what the child with autism teaches them about their own life or strengths. Focusing on a life journey can elicit adaptive strategies and feelings of success in overcoming challenges.

These are just a few suggestions. Some families may benefit from the periodic help of a mental health professional. Support groups through local chapters of the Autism Society of America may be helpful. For some parents, the child with autism may elicit feelings about their own childhood or a person in their family who was like their child. At these times, it may be helpful to access mental health services to resolve some earlier experiences or to clearly differentiate the child from someone in the past. Social relatedness is best facilitated when all parties feel happy and relaxed in the situation.

CONCLUSION

In this chapter, the concepts of attachment theory were reviewed. Attachment theory can explain the feelings that we all experience in our relationships with others. Our relationships provide a foundation about how we think, feel, and act when we engage with others; these same relationships shape new ways of viewing the social world. Each person with whom we interact teaches us something about ourselves and our social world, and may shape neurological structures to be consistent with our experiences. For children with autism, barriers to social interaction include differences in neurological systems. Although we cannot pinpoint these differences, we know that attachment experiences are a powerful influence on the development of social relatedness and on many aspects of neurological development.

Children with autism attach and bond to their parents; they enjoying comforting from their parents and primary caregivers and seek strategic interaction, but their interaction style is different at least by age two. Turn-taking may emerge, but a capacity for joint attention is often the most fundamental skill lacking. The development of an understanding of the social world from another's perspective (theory of mind) and patterns of social reciprocity are also diminished in autism for a variety of possible reasons.

Because social interaction involves sharing a great deal of sensory stimuli and requires the formation of a motor response to another, the consideration of the sensorimotor characteristics of children with autism is critical in management. Specific suggestions for management include using proprioception to calm and graded introduction of sensory input to decrease hypersensitivity. Careful attention to the sensory needs of people with autism can be embedded in many environments and included as a complement to other treatment approaches. Research is needed to document the impact of these methods; such research is complicated by the individual needs of people with autism, the embedded nature of sensory input with social and language stimulation, and the need to change strategies to correspond with maturation. Nonetheless, embedding sensorimotor interventions in environments is considered a key component of integrated developmental approaches for the effective management of autism (Dawson & Osterling, 1996; Greenspan & Weider, 1997, 1999).

CHAPTER REVIEW QUESTIONS

1. Identify the four attachment styles seen in children and related these to the same attachment style seen in adults.
2. In what ways do early attachment experiences influence brain development and social emotional development?
3. Describe the sensory and motor difficulties that children with autism exhibit and list some ways that these problems complicate the process of attachment.
4. Define theory of mind and relate this to the development of social skills in individuals with and without autism.
5. Describe strategic and affiliative behaviors related to social interactions.
6. Compare the typical attachment of children to the attachment patterns seen in autism.
7. Describe the challenges that parents face in forming attachments and establishing social reciprocity with their children who have autism.
8. Describe the limited social capabilities present in autism and list at least one developmental implication of each limited social capability.
9. Define at least four guidelines for intervention to improve the social interaction of children with autism and give one specific example of how that guideline is used.
10. List at least four problems associated with autism and suggest one sensorimotor intervention strategy for improving social relatedness.

REFERENCES

Ainsworth, M. D. S., Blehar, M. C., Waters, E., & Wall, S. (1978). *Patterns of attachment: A psychological study of the Strange Situation*. Hillsdale, NJ: Erlbaum.

Als, H. (1999). Reading the premature infant. In E. Goldson (Ed.), *Nurturing the premature infant: Developmental interventions in the neonatal intensive care unit* (pp. 18–85). New York: Oxford University Press.

Arend, R., Gove, F., & Sroufe, L. A. (1979). Continuity of individual adaptation from infancy to kindergarten: A predictive study of ego-resiliency and curiosity in preschoolers. *Child Development, 50,* 950–959.

Bagnato, S. J., & Neisworth, J. T. (1999). Normative detection of early regulatory disorders and autism: Empirical confirmation of DC: 0–3. *Infants and Young Children, 12,* 98–106.

Bagnato, S. J., Neisworth, J. T., Salvia, J., & Hunt, F. M. (1999). *Temperament and Atypical Behavior Scale (TABS): Early childhood indicators of developmental dysfunction (TABS Assessment Tool and TABS Screener).* Baltimore: Brookes.

Baker, M. J., Koegel, R. L., & Koegel, L. K. (1998). Increasing the social behavior of young children with autism using their obsessive behaviors. *Journal of the Association for Persons with Severe Handicaps, 23,* 300–308.

Baumeister, R. F., & Leary, M. R. (1995). The need to belong: Desire for interpersonal attachments as a fundamental human motivation. *Psychological Bulletin, 117,* 497–529.

Bettelheim, B. (1967). *The empty fortress.* New York: Free Press.

Bowlby, J. (1969). *Attachment and loss: Attachment* (vol. 1). London: Hogarth Press.

Bowlby, J. (1973). *Attachment and loss: Separation* (vol. 2). New York: Basic Books.

Bowlby, J. (1979). *The making and breaking of affectual bonds.* London: Tavistock.

Bristol, M. M., Cohen, D. J., Costello, E. J., Denckla, M., Eckberg, T. J., Kallen, R., Kraemer, H. C., Lord, C., Maurer, R., McIlvane, W. J., Minshew, N., Sigman, M., & Spence, M. A. (1996). State of the science in autism: Report to the National Institutes of Health. *Journal of Autism and Developmental Disorders, 26,* 121–154.

Brown, S. M., Humphry, R., & Taylor, E. (1997). A model of the nature of the family-therapist relationships: Implications for education. *American Journal of Occupational Therapy, 51,* 597–603.

Burke, J. P., & Schaaf, R. C. (1997). Family narratives and play assessment. In L. D. Parham & L. S. Fazio (Eds.), *Play in occupational therapy for children* (pp. 67–84). St. Louis, MO: Mosby.

Capps, L., Sigman, M., & Mundy, P. (1994). Attachment security in children with autism. *Development and Psychopathology, 6,* 249–261.

Carlson, M., & Earls, F. (1997). Psychological and neuroendocrinological sequella of early social deprivation in institutionalized children in Romania. In C. S. Carter, I. I. Lederhendler, & B. Kirkpatrick

(Eds.), *The integrative neurobiology of affiliation* (pp. 419–428). New York: Academy of Sciences.

Carter, C. S. (1998). Neuroendocrine perspectives on social attachment and love. *Psychoneuroendocrinology, 23,* 779–818.

Chorpita, B. F., & Barlow, D. H. (1998). The development of anxiety: The role of control in the early environment. *Psychological Bulletin, 124,* 3–21.

Ciesielski, K. T., & Harris, R. J. (1997). Factors related to performance failure on executive tasks in autism. *Child Neuropsychology, 3,* 1–12.

Cohn, E. S., & Cermak, S. A. (1998). Including the family perspective in sensory integration outcomes research. *American Journal of Occupational Therapy, 52,* 540–546.

Cohn, E. S., Miller, L. J., & Tickle-Degnen, L. (2000). Parental hopes for therapy outcomes: Children with sensory modulation disorders. *American Journal of Occupational Therapy, 54,* 36–43.

Coie, J. D., Watt, N. F., West, S. G., Hawkins, J. D., Asarnow, J. R., Markman, H. J., Ramey, S. L., Shure, M. B., & Long, B. (1993). The science of prevention: A conceptual framework and some directions for a national research program. *American Psychologist, 48,* 1013–1022.

Cook, D. G. (1996). The impact of having a child with autism. *Developmental Disabilities Special Interest Section Newsletter, 19*(2), 1–4.

Cox, A. D., & Lambrenos, K. (1992). Childhood physical disability and attachment. *Developmental Medicine and Child Neurology, 34,* 1037–1046.

Dawson, G., & Osterling, J. (1996). Early intervention in autism. In M. Guralnick (Ed.), *The effectiveness of early intervention* (pp. 307–325). Baltimore: Brookes.

DeGangi, G. A., Sickel, R. Z., Kaplan, E. P., & Wiener, A. S. (1997). Mother-infant interactions in infants with disorders of self-regulation. *Physical and Occupational Therapy in Pediatrics, 17,* 17–39.

Dissanayake, C., & Crossley, S. A. (1997). Autistic children's responses to separation and reunion with their mothers. *Journal of Autism and Developmental Disorders, 27,* 295–312.

Egeland, B., Carlson, E., & Sroufe, L. A. (1993). Resilience as process. *Developmental Psychopathology, 5,* 517–528.

Egeland, B., Kalkoske, M., Gottesman, N., & Erickson, M. (1990). Preschool behavior problems: Stability and factors accounting for change. *Journal of Child Psychology and Psychiatry, 31,* 891–909.

Feldman, R., & Blatt, S. J. (1996). Precursors of relatedness and self-definition in mother-infant interaction. In J. M. Masling & R. F. Bornstein (Eds.), *Psy-*

choanalytic perspectives on developmental psychology (pp. 1–42). Washington, DC: American Psychological Association.

Fox, N. A. (1995). Of the way we were: Adult memories about attachment experiences and their role in determining infant-parent relationships: A commentary on van IJzendoorn (1995). *Psychological Bulletin, 117*, 404–410.

Greenspan, S. I., & Weider, S. (1997). Developmental patterns and outcomes in infants and children with disorders in relating and communicating: A chart review of 200 cases of children with autistic spectrum disorders. *Journal of Developmental and Learning Disorders, 1*, 87–141.

Greenspan, S. I., & Weider, S. (1999). A functional developmental approach to autism spectrum disorders. *Journal of the Association for Persons with Severe Handicaps, 24*, 147–161.

Grossman, J. B., Carter, A., & Volkmar, F. R. (1997). Social behavior in autism. In C. S. Carter, I. I. Lederhendler, & B. Kirkpatrick (Eds.), *The integrative neurobiology of affiliation* (pp. 440–454). New York: Academy of Sciences.

Happe, F., & Frith, U. (1996). The neuropsychology of autism. *Brain, 119*, 1377–1400.

Huebner, R. A., Gamradt, J., & Klund, M. (in preparation). *Wisconsin Sensorimotor Pointing Assessment: Application to adults with autism.*

Huebner, R. A., & Thomas, K. R. (1995). The relationship between attachment, psychopathology, and childhood disability. *Rehabilitation Psychology, 40*, 111–125.

Huebner, R. A., Thomas, K. R., & Berven, N. L. (1999). Attachment and interpersonal characteristics of college students with and without disabilities. *Rehabilitation Psychology, 44*, 85–103.

Humphry, R. (1989). Early intervention and the influence of the occupational therapist on the parent-child relationship. *American Journal of Occupational Therapy, 43*, 738–742.

Humphry, R., & Case-Smith, J. (1996). Working with families. In J. Case-Smith, A. S. Allen, & P. N. Pratt (Eds.), *Occupational therapy for children* (pp. 67–98). St. Louis, MO: Mosby.

Insel, T. R. (1997). The neurobiological basis of social attachment. *American Journal of Psychiatry, 154*, 726–735.

Insel, T. R., O'Brien, D. J., & Leckman, J. F. (1999). Oxytocin, vasopressin, and autism: Is there connection? *Biological Psychiatry, 45*, 145–157.

Jones, V., & Prior, M. (1985). Motor imitation abilities and neurological signs in autistic children. *Journal of Autism and Developmental Disorders, 15*, 37–46.

Kemner, C., Verbaten, M. N., Cuperus, J. M., Camferman, G., & van Engeland, H. (1998). Abnormal saccadic eye movements in autistic children. *Journal of Autism and Developmental Disorders, 28*, 61–67.

Kohen-Raz, R., Volkmar, F. R., & Cohen, D. J. (1992). Postural control in children with autism. *Journal of Autism and Developmental Disorders, 22*, 419–432.

Kraemer, G. W. (1992). A psychobiological theory of attachment. *Behavioral and Brain Sciences, 15*, 493–541.

Kraemer, G. W. (1997). Psychobiology of early social attachment in rhesus monkeys: Clinical implications. In C. S. Carter, I. I. Lederhendler, & B. Kirkpatrick (Eds.), *The integrative neurobiology of affiliation* (pp. 401–418). New York: Academy of Sciences.

Kraemer, G. W., Ebert, M. H., Schmidt, D. E., & McKinney, W. T. (1989). A longitudinal study of the effects of different rearing environments on cerebrospinal fluid norepinephrine and biogenic amine metabolites in rhesus monkeys. *Neuropsychopharmacology, 2*, 175–189.

Lawlor, M. C., & Mattingly, C. F. (1998). The complexities embedded in family-centered care. *American Journal of Occupational Therapy, 52*, 259–267.

Lelord, G., Herault, J., Perrot, A., Garreau, B., Barthelemy, C., Martineau, J., Bruneau, N., Sauvage, D., & Muh, J. P. (1994). What kind of markers in childhood autism? *Developmental Brain Dysfunction, 7*, 53–62.

Losche, G. (1990). Sensorimotor and action development in autistic children from infancy to early childhood. *Journal of Child Psychology and Psychiatry, 31*, 749–761.

Lyons, L. S., & Sperling, M. B. (1996). Clinical applications of attachment theory: Empirical and theoretical perspectives. In J. M. Masling & R. F. Bornstein (Eds.), *Psychoanalytic perspectives on developmental psychology* (pp. 221–256). Washington, DC: American Psychological Association.

MacDonald, V. B. (1998). How the diagnosis of Asperger's has influenced my life. In E. Schopler, G. B. Mesibov, & L. J. Kunce (Eds.), *Asperger syndrome or high-functioning autism?* (pp. 367–376). New York: Plenum.

Magid, K., & McKelvey, C. A. (1987). *High risk: Children without a conscience.* New York: Bantam.

Main, M., Kaplan, N., & Cassidy, J. (1985). Security in infancy, childhood, and adulthood: A move to the level of representation. *Child Development Monographs, 50*, 66–104.

Masten, A. S., & Coatsworth, J. D. (1998). The development of competence in favorable and unfavorable environments: Lessons from research on successful children. *American Psychologist, 53*, 205–220.

Mayes, S. D., & Calhoun, S. L. (1999). Symptoms of autism in young children and correspondence with the DSM. *Infants and Young Children, 12*, 90–97.

Miller, L. J., & Hanft, B. E. (1998). Building positive alliances: Partnerships with families as the cornerstone of developmental assessment. *Infants and Young Children, 10*, 1–12.

Modahl, C., Green, L., Fein, D., Morris, M., Waterhouse, L., Feinstein, C., & Levin, H. (1998). Plasma oxytocin levels in autistic children. *Biological Psychiatry, 43*, 270–277.

Mueser, K. T. (1996). Helping families manage severe mental illness. *Psychiatric Rehabilitation Skills, 1*, 21–42.

Mundy, P., & Crowson, M. (1997). Joint attention and early social communication: Implications for research on intervention with autism. *Journal of Autism and Developmental Disorders, 27*, 653–676.

Nelson, E. E., & Panksepp, J. (1998). Brain substrates of infant-mother attachment: Contributions of opioids, oxytocin, and norepinephrine. *Neuroscience and Behavioral Reviews, 22*, 437–452.

Perry, B. D., Pollard, R. A., Blakley, T. L., Baker, W. L., & Vigilante, D. (1995). Childhood trauma, the neurobiology of adaptation, and "use-dependent" development of the brain: How "states" become "traits." *Infant Mental Health Journal, 16*, 271–289.

Pierce, K., Glad, K. S., & Schreibman, L. (1997). Social perception in children with autism: An attentional deficit. *Journal of Autism and Developmental Disorders, 27*, 265–282.

Porges, S. W. (1997). Emotion: An evolutionary by-product of the neuronal regulation of the autonomic nervous system. *Annals of the New York Academy of Sciences, 807*, 62–77.

Primeau, L. A. (1998). Orchestration of work and play within families. *American Journal of Occupational Therapy, 52*, 188–195.

Radke-Yarrow, M., McCann, K., DeMulder, E., Belmont, B., Martinez, P., & Richardson, D. T. (1995). Attachment in the context of high-risk conditions. *Development and Psychopathology, 7*, 247–265.

Rogers, S. J. (1988). Characteristics of social interactions between mothers and their disabled infants: A review. *Child: Care, Health, and Development, 14*, 301–317.

Rogers, S. J., Ozonoff, S., & Maslin-Cole, C. (1991). A comparative study of attachment in young children with autism or other psychiatric disorders. *Journal of the American Academy of Child Adolescent Psychiatry, 30*, 483–488.

Safran, J. D., & Segal, Z. V. (1990). *Interpersonal process in cognitive therapy.* New York: Basic Books.

Shields, J., Varley, R., Broks, P., & Simpson, A. (1996). Social cognition in developmental language disorders and high-level autism. *Developmental Medicine and Child Neurology, 38*, 487–495.

Sigman, M., & Mundy, P. (1989). Social attachments in autistic children. *Journal of the American Academy of Child Adolescent Psychiatry, 28*, 74–81.

Smith, I. M., & Bryson, S. E. (1994). Imitation and action in autism: A critical review. *Psychological Bulletin, 116*, 259–273.

Smith, T. S. (1994). Catastrophes in interaction: A note on arousal-dependent discontinuities in attachment behavior. *Social Psychology Quarterly, 57*, 274–282.

Staudinger, U. M., Marsiske, M., & Baltes, P. B. (1993). Resilience and levels of reserve capacity in later adulthood: Perspectives from life-span theory. *Development and Psychopathology, 5*, 541–566.

Teyber, E. (1992). *Interpersonal process in psychotherapy: A guide for clinical training.* Pacific Grove, CA: Books/Cole.

Troy, M., & Sroufe, L. A. (1987). Victimization among preschoolers: Role of attachment relationship history. *Journal of American Academy of Child and Adolescent Psychiatry, 26*, 166–172.

van IJzendoorn, M. H. (1995). Adult attachment representations, parental responsiveness, and infant attachment: A meta-analysis of the predictive validity of the adult attachment interview. *Psychological Bulletin, 117*, 387–403.

van IJzendoorn, M. H., & Bakermans-Kranenburg, M. J. (1996). Attachment representations in mothers, fathers, adolescents, and clinical groups: A meta-analytic search for normative data. *Journal of Consulting and Clinical Psychology, 64*, 8–21.

Waterhouse, L., & Fein, D. (1998). Autism and the evolution of human social skills. In F. R. Volkman (Ed.), *Autism and pervasive developmental disorders* (pp. 242–267). New York: Cambridge University Press.

Watson, L. R. (1998). Following the child's lead: Mothers' interactions with children with autism. *Journal of Autism and Developmental Disorders, 28*, 51–59.

Westman, J. C. (1990). *Handbook of learning disabilities: A multisystem approach*. Boston: Allyn & Bacon.

Westman, J. C. (1991). *Who speaks for the children?* Sarasota, FL: Professional Resource Exchange.

Wieder, S., Kalmanson, B., & Fenichel, E. (1999). Diagnosing regulatory disorders using DC: 0–3: A framework and a case illustration. *Infants and Young Children, 12*, 79–89.

Wilbarger, P., & Wilbarger, J. (1991). *Sensory defensiveness in children ages 2–12: An intervention guide for parents and other caretakers*. Santa Barbara, CA: Avanti Educational Programs.

PART 3

Application of the Sensorimotor Approach

CHAPTER 8

Integration of Sensorimotor and Neurodevelopmental Approaches

Kay Rydeen

CHAPTER OBJECTIVES

At the completion of this chapter, the reader will be able to:

- Understand the basic tenets of both the sensorimotor and neurodevelopmental approaches to treatment.
- Understand the process of integrating sensorimotor interventions with neurodevelopmental treatment.
- Analyze this process when applied in a home setting and to a case study.

INTRODUCTION AND BASIC PREMISES

The theories that support therapeutic interventions are frequently organized around diagnostic categories (Hinojosa & Kramer, 1993). The theory of sensory integration (SI) is most commonly identified with children with learning disabilities; however, it is extended to include individuals with mental retardation, autism, and other neurological and behavioral disorders (Kimball, 1993). The theory behind neurodevelopmental treatment (NDT) developed from work with children with cerebral palsy and adults recovering from cerebral vascular accidents. Today, it is a treatment approach addressing a variety of diagnoses that exhibit motor impairments. As such, SI treatment and NDT stem from theory bases addressing two different diagnostic categories; they may seem divergent in their application.

But practitioners do not treat a diagnostic category per se. Although a diagnosis provides significant information about an individual, the functional skills that a therapist can observe are even more significant. Selecting the treatment approach to use with any one individual, then, is based on how the therapist analyzes and organizes theoretical information to improve function. This organizational structure and analysis is referred to as a *frame of reference*. Research indicates that occupational therapists in pediatric practice use a multitheoretical or pluralistic approach utilizing several frames of reference (Storch & Eskow, 1996). The most common combinations include using SI with NDT.

Combining SI and NDT in the treatment of children with autism can be appropriate, because these children may exhibit dysfunction in both sensory and motor responses. SI focuses on the sensory systems underlying function, and many children with autism exhibit sensory processing difficulties (Ayres, 1979; Fisher, Murray, & Bundy, 1991; Grandin, 1995; Kranowitz, 1998; O'Neill & Jones, 1997). Children with autism also may exhibit problems with movement (Smith & Bryson, 1994), low muscle tone, and compensatory postures secondary to the low tone (e.g., locking an elbow joint in extension to help stabilize the position rather than using muscle cocontraction to stabilize the arm). Neurodevelopmental treatment focuses on such motor behaviors. Although SI is essentially a hands-off approach (the therapist seeks to control the environment) and NDT is a hands-on approach (the therapist guides body movements), they complement one another well. They may be regarded as two sides of the same coin.

Both NDT and SI theory are based on the concept that sensations from the environment are registered and interpreted in the brain, or central nervous system (CNS). These sensations then affect movements or motor responses. In turn, motor responses provide additional sensory input (sensory feedback) to the CNS (Bly, 1996; Reeves, 1992). Within this sensory-motor-sensory loop, as depicted in Figure 8–1, the therapist uses SI treatment to provide the appropriate sensory input to produce a functional motor response, while the use of NDT promotes appropriate motor behavior to enhance the sensory feedback loop. In each case, the goal of intervention is to provide the CNS with the appropriate sensory input to encourage the progressive development of functional skills for daily life tasks.

The common perspectives shared by SI and NDT theory may have emerged from a common history. Both approaches evolved during the same time period and both were influenced by the work of Margaret Rood, an occupational therapist and physical therapist. A. Jean Ayres, the originator of the theory of sensory integration, was an occupational therapy student of Rood's. The Bobaths, who originated the theory of NDT, were influenced by Rood's use of tactile stimulation (Bohman, 1986). Rood emphasized three treatment principles (Trombly, 1989) that are incorporated in both SI and NDT approaches: (1) controlled sensory

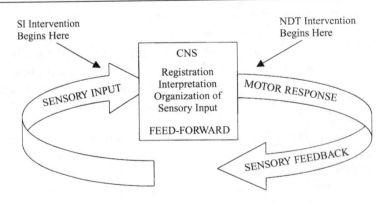

Figure 8–1 The sensory-motor-sensory loop.

stimulation; (2) the use of developmental sequencing; and (3) the need to demand and facilitate a purposeful response through the use of activity. Each approach reflects the use of these principles and these are reviewed in the following sections.

Sensory Integration Theory

A. Jean Ayres, PhD, OTR, began work on her theory of sensory integration in the late 1950s and continued to develop it over three decades. SI theory focuses on the sensory systems that underlie the development of function and skills. These sensory systems go beyond the traditional senses to emphasize three near senses, as depicted in Figure 8–2. The vestibular, tactile, and proprioceptive systems are regarded as the building blocks on which increasingly complex skills develop. Vision and hearing are also regarded as of primary importance, but even these are superseded by the three near senses when we consider the foundational components of skill.

The vestibular system has receptors in the inner ear and neural connections throughout the CNS; input to the vestibular system can influence ocular control, states of alertness, emotional responses, and muscle tone. The receptors respond to gravity and to movement. As Ayres (1979) stated, "Because gravity is always present on this planet, the gravity receptors send a perpet-

The Near Senses

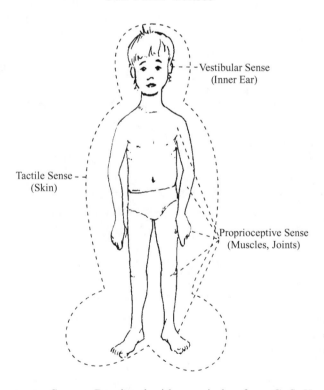

Figure 8–2 The near senses. *Source:* Reprinted with permission from C. S. Kranowitz, *The Out-of-Sync Child,* p. 41, © 1998. A Skylight Press Book.

ual stream of vestibular messages throughout our life" (p. 35). She recognized the vestibular system as a unifying system for the body: "It forms the basic relationship of a person to gravity and the physical world. All other types of sensation are processed in reference to this basic vestibular information" (p. 37). This theoretical assumption has now evolved to incorporate the vestibular-proprioceptive system (Fisher et al., 1991; Kielhofner, 1992).

Proprioception, a word derived from Latin, refers to the perception of sensations that arise from one's own movements. As such, the vestibular system is one form of proprioception, but this term also defines, in a more conventional sense, the sensory information we receive from pressure to our muscles and joints. Proprioception allows us to move our limbs without watching them. Through the influence of the vestibular-proprioceptive system, we are provided consistent information on where our body is in space and where our body parts align. This system provides a "reference point for monitoring and controlling movement" (Kielhofner, 1992).

SI theory includes an understanding of two related tactile systems: discriminative and protective. With discriminative touch, one can reach into a pocket and distinguish a quarter from a dime. With protective touch, one becomes alarmed at the sensation of an insect moving along the skin surface. Both systems alert us to information in our external environment, but it is the development of the discriminative system that contributes to the development of skill.

It is believed that the subcortical process of integrating information from the tactile, vestibular, and proprioceptive systems is basic to growth and learning (Figure 8–3). When these systems, together with vision and hearing, are working well—with the CNS registering, interpreting, and organiz-

ing this information—the mind and body can use that information to develop new skills. The interplay of these senses helps us plan motor movements. Motor planning (praxis) encompasses having an idea about what we want to do (ideation), planning the action (feed-forward) and executing it, and receiving feedback on how well we did.

We are not conscious of SI activity; when our brain successfully integrates and filters the sensory information that is bombarding us at any one moment, we can focus our attention and conscious thought on the task at hand. SI, then, is the organization of sensation for use (Ayres, 1979). It refers to the ability of the brain to organize and interpret sensory stimuli for an adaptive response. It refers to the brain's ability to organize and process sensory input and to use that input to respond appropriately to a particular situation (Trott, Laurel, & Windeck, 1993).

It is believed that in the normal developmental sequence we seek those sensations that we need, and we seek novelty. Children learn about themselves and their world by going through their own discovery process. The theory of SI incorporates Piaget's view that children need opportunities to explore and discover on their own in order to make the appropriate linkages between what they already know and new learning. In normal development, SI and learning occur in an upward spiral, based on a sensory-motor-sensory continuum.

Children with SI dysfunction have difficulties registering or organizing and using the sensory information from the environment. When this process is disordered, problems in learning, development, or behavior may become evident. Children with SI dysfunction frequently show motor impairments, including poor muscle cocontraction around joints, low muscle tone, and decreased balance and equilibrium skills. These functional support

The Four Levels of Sensory Integration

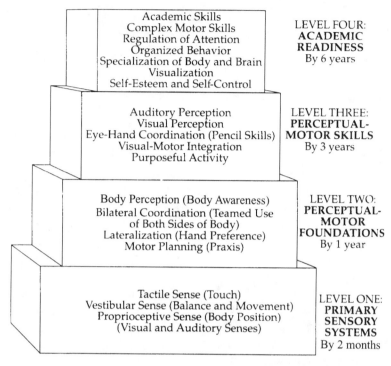

Figure 8–3 The four levels of sensory integration. *Source:* Reprinted with permission from C. S. Kranowitz, *The Out-of-Sync Child,* p. 48, © 1998. A Skylight Press Book.

capabilities (physical capabilities that under-lie and provide support for end-product skills) are addressed in assessment and treatment (Kimball, 1993). Evaluation of SI dysfunction usually consists of both standardized testing and structured observations of responses to sensory stimulation and functional support capabilities.

In SI treatment, the therapist does not seek to physically control the child but, ideally, provides the child with an environment that allows him or her to make choices and explore sensory challenges. These experiences should provide a just-right challenge: neither over- or underarousing the child and providing an experience that is novel yet successful. Within this context, the therapist provides controlled sensory input designed to elicit an appropriate adaptive and functional response. For example, consider a child with poor postural tone who has difficulty sitting in a chair without slumping, holding his or her head in his or her hands, or resting his or her head on a table surface. Within the therapeutic setting, this child may choose to ride a scooter board (a small board, mounted on four wheels, that supports the child's pelvis and abdomen). Riding the board in a prone (stomach down) position encourages the child to hold his or her head, trunk, and legs up against gravity (Figure 8–4). Riding a scooter board down a ramp in this position can be challenging and still fun. Ayres (1979) stated:

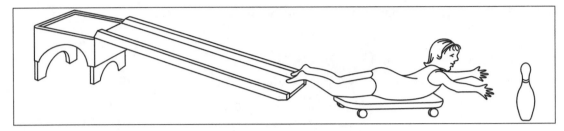

Figure 8–4 The SI approach to facilitating antigravity extension.

As the child speeds down the ramp and levels off onto the floor, the bursts of vestibular input open up pathways to many parts of his nervous system. The strong input activates reflexes that have not been developed in the past. These reflexes hold the head and legs up against the pull of gravity. (p. 144)

The intent of the therapeutic activity in this example is to build antigravity extensor control so that the child will be better able to maintain a functional posture while sitting, enhancing the ability to attend to academic tasks and to maintain the sitting position without struggle. Ayres continued:

When the child has mastered the challenge of going down the ramp and its novelty is starting to wear off, we give him other challenges that require more complex sensory integration and adaptive responses involving motor planning. For instance, the therapist might set up a tunnel for the child to ride through on the scooter board or hang a ball from the ceiling for him to punch as he passes it by. (p. 145)

SI treatment, in its purest sense, includes the use of suspended equipment that swings or undulates in varied directions. The direc-

tion, rhythm, and speed of the movement depends on the goals of the session and the needs of the child. The position of the child on the equipment varies also. Some therapists believe that if treatment incorporating movement is primarily on the floor, the intervention is "sensorimotor" and not sensory integration (Roley & Wilbarger, 1994). Others believe that a child's environment holds multiple opportunities for SI to be facilitated and that suspended equipment is not the defining element in this treatment approach.

Neurodevelopmental Treatment Theory

The theory behind NDT was conceived by the Bobaths in the 1940s. Karel Bobath, an English neurologist, and Berta Bobath, a physiotherapist, developed this theory based on their work with individuals with motor impairments (cerebral palsy and cerebral vascular accidents). Like the theory of SI, it has continued to evolve over the decades. Initially, it supported the use of reflex-inhibiting postures (RIPs) to hold a child with spasticity in a position counter to an aberrant motor pattern. Although successful in reducing hypertonicity, RIPs required total control of the therapist over the child and the positions were static. Children did not learn how to move in more appropriate ways. Today, the NDT approach incorporates more active motion and seeks to facilitate normal movement patterns within functional contexts (Bohman, 1986; Schoen and Anderson, 1993).

NDT is primarily concerned with motor behaviors. It recognizes that with damage to the CNS, normal movement can be affected and decrease one's ability to perform daily life tasks. "Central to NDT is the assumption that abnormal patterns of movement may be changed by altering sensory input to the CNS, thereby altering motor output" (Schoen & Anderson, 1993, p. 57). In seeking to decrease aberrant and inefficient movement patterns, the therapist directly influences a child's movement through handling techniques. *Handling* refers to the use of the therapist's hands on the child, guiding him or her toward more mature motor responses while grading the amount of hands-on control. The therapist tries to help the child feel what it is like to move normally by inhibiting abnormal muscle tone and movement patterns while facilitating normal posture and movement. The therapist uses handling techniques at key points of control. A key point of control can be any part of the body that the therapist uses to influence movement. Often, key points of control are proximal areas on the body (shoulder girdle, pelvis), but they can also be distal areas (hands, feet). The resulting sensory feedback to the CNS from the guided movement is assumed to provide more appropriate sensory input for ensuing motor responses.

As with SI, another assumption central to NDT theory is that change occurs subcortically, utilizing the sensory-motor-sensory loop. The child is encouraged, through graded handling by the therapist or caregiver, to take active control of his or her body during meaningful activities. Control

follows a developmental sequence of cephalo to caudal ("head to tail"), proximal to distal, and gross to fine motor. Evaluation of an individual, as with SI, uses standardized tests and structured observation.

Consider again a child who has low postural tone, as described previously. How would this child be treated using the NDT approach? The child depicted in Figure 8–5 is from an actual NDT case study. This child does not have cerebral palsy, but he cannot maintain a steady antigravity posture. To stimulate more dynamic and active antigravity control in the prone position, the therapist provided support to the child's hips (key point of control) while stimulating maintenance of weight bearing through the arms. This allowed for (sensory) stimulation and feedback of the (functional) protective arm reactions, while stimulating tone around the shoulders. In the future, the child could participate in an activity that utilized this position (e.g., retrieval of a ball to then toss into a bucket), or the therapist could decrease hands-on control.

Combining SI and NDT Approaches in the Treatment of Children with Autism

As this discussion shows, SI and NDT treatment approaches have many common elements. The theories supporting these approaches are based upon principles of normal development and neural functioning. SI focuses on the sensory systems underlying skill development. NDT focuses on the motor behaviors influencing skill development. Both theories are living concepts, changing as knowledge in the neurosciences increases. Both theories recognize the plasticity of the brain and emphasize the use of sensory input to affect changes in motor output. In treatment, SI and NDT require

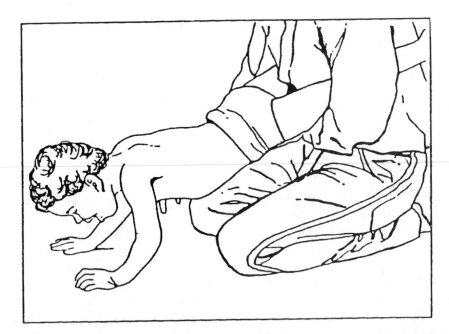

Figure 8–5 NDT facilitation of antigravity postural control in prone position. *Source:* Reprinted with permission from G. J. DeMauro, *The Use of an NDT Approach for a Child with Hyperkinesis, NDTA Network,* September 1992, p. 4, © Neuro-Developmental Treatment Association.

that the child should be as self-directed as possible, as this facilitates the feed-forward component of motor planning, promoting learning and skill.

CASE STUDY

Ryan was referred for occupational therapy services at the age of 5½ years following comprehensive evaluations at two leading diagnostic clinics. He was diagnosed with autism. Parental concerns included language development, toilet training, feeding skills, social skills, and Ryan's responses to frustration (head banging). As an infant, nursing was fatiguing for him and he provided no indications of hunger. When given shots, he never responded to the pain. At the time of referral, he demonstrated low tone in his trunk and in proximal joints. Protective extension responses were delayed. It was difficult for him to assume and maintain anti-

gravity postures in flexion or extension. He preferred to lie down to play. He was noted to crave movement and enjoyed swinging and climbing, but fatigued when activities required maintaining a stable posture. He demonstrated sensory modulation difficulties; he fluctuated between over- and under-responsiveness to environmental stimuli. He could overreact to sounds, visual stimuli, and movement perceived as out of his control (e.g., being tipped). His internal sensory awareness of toileting needs was questionable. He was hyporesponsive to temperature and pain. He was noted to mouth objects, including clothing. He could undress, but not dress. He became frustrated when tasks were unfamiliar and required sequencing.

For all of the difficulties that Ryan was having in growing up, he was a verbal and engaging child. Initial treatment concerns were to provide him with the foundation components that he needed for increased self-care, social, play, and academic skills. These components were identified as (a) postural stability, (b) sensory modulation, and (c) motor planning.

A combined NDT/SI and behavioral approach was found to be appropriate for Ryan. This approach is not appropriate for all children, but for Ryan, it was a good match. He did not object to touch from the therapist, so handling techniques were acceptable to him. Also, he was being served in the home and suspended equipment was not available inside the house. However, a well-designed playground was built in his backyard that afforded a multisensory environment, including suspended equipment.

Developing Foundation Components

Addressing postural stability, Ryan participated in varied games that included the use of a large therapy ball. When he was placed prone on the ball and an NDT approach was used, protective extension and antigravity extension were facilitated. He was provided with tactile cues to prevent hyperextension of his elbows while prone. Prone-on-elbows positions were also used. Inverted positions while supine over the ball were incorporated to increase postural control in antigravity flexion; handling techniques were used to guide Ryan to rotate up to sit. Over time, the handling techniques were graded down from guiding to intermittent tapping to withdrawal of handling cues entirely. Although these inverted positions provided intense vestibular input, at no time did Ryan exhibit fear, although gravitational insecurity was documented in previous reports (perhaps the safety of his home environment eased his comfort in moving backward while inverted).

Ryan was also provided with activities that encouraged him to perform "heavy work" at vertical surfaces. For example, on a summer day, he might paint the brick exterior of his home with a painting roller dipped in water. During the winter, he made Christmas wrapping paper while stamping vegetable prints into paper mounted on a vertical surface. These activities, requiring heavy work of the arms into a vertical surface, promoted increased shoulder stability. These activities also assisted with sensory modulation. As Kimball (1993) stated, "Proprioception is important in sensory modulation and may be either joint compression or traction; thus, any heavy work, along with motor activity, that a child engages in will have a normalizing effect on the child's nervous system" (p. 143).

Obstacle courses were developed to promote postural stability, sequencing, and praxis. Tactile, proprioceptive, and vestibular experiences were always included. During occupational therapy sessions, a game was incorporated into the obstacle course to encourage the repetition of motor movements. When occupational therapy services began, Ryan was always provided with two games from which to choose, building his sense of control. For example, Ryan could choose to assemble a puppet or complete an interlocking puzzle. When Ryan chose to complete a puzzle, he obtained a puzzle piece while inverted over the therapy ball. He then moved through (two to four) obstacle course stations, delivered the puzzle piece to an endpoint, and returned to the therapy ball to obtain another puzzle piece. Once all the puzzle pieces were collected at the endpoint, the therapist and Ryan assembled the puzzle, facilitating not only additional sensorimotor skills (such as visual perception and fine motor coordination) but also cognitive and social/emotional skills (e.g., attention to task, sequencing, categorization, and turn-taking).

Frequently, the therapist was able to promote, within this context, goals developed by the psychologist serving Ryan (goals addressing preacademic skills and social games). For example, if Ryan assembled a puppet, the therapist encouraged the puppet (a.k.a. Ryan) to tell the therapist about the sequence of his day. If Ryan chose to open plastic eggs (filled by the therapist with specific contents prior to the therapy session), he then was encouraged to categorize the contents. Continuing to address postural control, the structure of the endpoint activity might require Ryan to move from squat to stand or to use his arms at an elevated or vertical surface. Monitoring these movements from an NDT perspective, the quality of his movement was recognized as important and tactile cues were provided to facilitate appropriate alignment. For example, squatting with knees braced against one another decreases the demand for cocontraction of leg muscles; squatting with knees aligned over toes is facilitated. Safety was monitored during SI activities that encouraged jumping and rolling within the obstacle courses; Ryan's parents kept foam mattresses in the family room where these sessions occurred to provide a sufficient cushion. Here, the environment was manipulated and Ryan's sensory needs for proprioceptive and vestibular input were the focus.

Ryan enjoyed the games that accompanied structured activities. He was encouraged to talk about what he was doing and often was able to do this. Kimball (1993) noted that encouraging these verbalizations is helpful in building the ideation component of praxis. Over time, Ryan was introduced to a menu of sensorimotor options. He began to develop his own obstacle courses and experiment within them in a playful manner. For example, rather than creep through a fabric tunnel, as he had initially, he began to experiment with locomotion, scooting through on his back, moving sideways, or standing in the stretching tunnel and attempting to walk through it.

Within his home environment, Ryan began to test his postural control. During one treatment session, he attempted to climb the smooth surface of his outdoor slide. Initially, he made no progress in ascending the slide, as he alternately kicked his feet in an attempt to propel himself forward. Allowed the opportunity to continually return to this self-directed challenge, he eventually climbed to the top of the slide. In a single treatment session, Ryan independently pursued a motor goal and met it. Ryan was becoming increasingly confident in his motor skills. As he experimented with postural challenges, he grew more comfortable with play and movement. He pretended to be a monkey while hanging supine from the stairway banister. While rolled (sausagelike) in a sheet for sensory modulation purposes, he pretended to be an inchworm as he walked on hands and feet, raising and lowering his pelvis. A chair draped with a blanket became a car wash as he used commando crawling to pull himself between the legs of the chair. Imaginative play and pretend play were developing for Ryan.

Sensory modulation was always attended to during treatment and guided by the SI approach. Ryan's responsiveness to the environment could indeed swing from underresponsive to alert and attending to hyperresponsive. If Ryan began to chew on clothing (which is one technique for self-calming), resistive foods, such as bagels, were provided. The therapist's voice was recognized as an important therapeutic tool. Tone, rate, volume, and rhythm were monitored to facilitate sensory modulation. Proprioceptive input was constant.

Behavioral Concerns

Behaviors indicative of sensory overload or fatigue were addressed supportively. For example, if Ryan began to scream during a therapy session, it was initially ignored. If it continued, he was provided with increased proprioceptive input, such as joint compression or traction applied by the occupational therapist. This technique was successful, as was the use of a weighted blanket. On the therapist's recommendation, Ryan's parents found that a homemade weighted blanket (sewn into compartments and filled with rice) placed over Ryan helped calm him. When he was inconsolable, they draped the blanket over him and slowly rocked him. Within minutes, his sobbing subsided. If, during an occupational therapy activity, he began to withdraw from participation, a behavior that can indicate sensory overload, he was allowed quiet time. On such occasions, the endpoint activity drew Ryan back to the session. The sensorimotor challenges of the session could be modified, but the activity was always completed. Ryan's apparent need for quiet time was not ignored, yet shutting down was not allowed to divert Ryan from completing an activity he had chosen.

Behaviors that could endanger someone, such as inappropriate throwing, were not tolerated. If Ryan threw a shoe, he was required to retrieve it. Rarely, hand-over-hand guidance was required; hand-over-hand guidance provides increased proprioceptive input as well. The occupational therapist sought to address sensory modulation needs as quickly as possible through more positive interventions and to distinguish sensory needs from testing behaviors. Typically, Ryan responded well to concrete two-part directives, e.g., "No throwing shoes. Get the shoe and park it by the bear." He was allowed time to follow through.

Simple songs, which focus a child's attention, were used to help Ryan transition and to learn rules. These were ditties composed on the spot by the occupational therapist or Ryan's mother. Two examples follow. On the occasion of the therapist's first visit to the home, Ryan attempted to throw a small chair at her when it was time for her to leave. At that moment, a transition song was implemented by Ryan's mother. This song was used consistently until Ryan's behaviors indicated his readiness for it to fade and extinguish. Several minutes prior to the therapist's departure at subsequent sessions, the first verse of the ditty was sung: "Five more minutes, five more minutes, five more minutes, and it's time for Kay to go home." Strict minutes were not adhered to, but Ryan understood the descending sequence of five, four, three, two, one, and "no more." He began to sing along and transitioned easily.

On another occasion, as Ryan grew increasingly more comfortable with movement and experimenting with it, he attempted to stand on the large therapy ball when no adults were near him. This could have resulted in a severe fall. A new ditty was immediately composed: "When you're standing on the ball, when you're standing on the ball, when you're standing on the ball, have a grown-up with you." Rather than discourage Ryan from challenging his motor skills (e.g., "No standing on balls!"), he was allowed to challenge his dynamic postural control under the direct supervision of an adult. Ryan continued to intermittently challenge his body in this way, but then expected an adult to be with him and expected the song to be repeated. The song and the accompanying adult became attached to the activity and ensured his safety.

Home Activities

Ryan's parents became knowledgeable about his sensory needs. They understood the sensory modulating attributes of proprioceptive input and used "heavy work" activities in creative ways when guiding Ryan's play. For example, they encouraged him to place fireplace logs into a small wagon and then pull the wagon by attaching it to his pedal tractor. They encouraged rigorous backyard play, including opportunities to push, pull, climb, swing, jump, and revel in mud. They provided him with structured opportunities to challenge his near senses (e.g., gymnastic classes and horseback riding). Ryan's mother and toddler sister were present during most occupational therapy treatment sessions. Activities during these sessions often included his sibling and many required his mother's assistance, as when fabricating a hammock swing from a sheet, using two adults as the fixation points. Therapy sessions were videotaped, allowing review of Ryan's behaviors, therapy techniques, and intervention results.

Understanding the near senses, Ryan's parents developed a game called "He's Mine." As his home-based occupational therapy services drew to a close, Ryan could tell his parents when he wanted to play this game. With Ryan lying supine on the floor, one parent held Ryan's feet and the other his arms. The parents then began a gentle version of tug-of-war with Ryan, alternately saying "He's mine" and "No, he's mine," to their son's sheer delight.

Results

Therapy services in the home lasted approximately one year. At the end of the year, Ryan was directing the sessions with an increased sense of reciprocal interaction and playfulness. For example, he directed the therapist as follows:

"Dribble the ball on me."

"Swing me, please, please, please."

"Lift me by the feet like a crane."

Reevaluation at one of the diagnostic clinics six months after therapy began noted that Ryan was much more able to follow instructions during testing and he could respond to questions. He did well with tactile discrimination tests, puzzles, and imitation of postures. Postural stability had increased so that he could maintain a prone position with head, upper trunk, and arms lifted for 20 seconds. He continued to lean on the table surface during fine motor activities, but previously he had preferred to lie down for most play. Overall coordination and motor planning were improved. Sensory modulation had progressed, as well as more complex play schemes. Head banging had ceased.

The evaluation noted that Ryan's "parents have developed a good sense of how the sensory and motor systems are impacting his development" and that they were able to design meaningful activities and interventions themselves.

Five months after therapy began, Ryan had a birthday. His usually upbeat mother choked with emotion while saying "He's six years old and not toilet trained." Helping Ryan toilet train became a primary goal. Ryan did seem unaware of toileting needs. Recognition of his need to urinate developed first; bowel movements were irregular. However, his mother noted that shortly after Ryan's SI/NDT treatment sessions, he would have a bowel movement. An experiment was launched, establishing baseline data and documenting elimination patterns following treatment sessions. Medical testing ruled out obstructions or physiological factors affecting his toilet training. Over a three-month period, consistently incorporating SI and NDT activities that required postural control in flexed positions, results indicated that treatment sessions did regulate elimination patterns. At the end of the year of therapy, Ryan was on his way to being bowel and bladder trained.

TREATMENT OF CHILDREN WITH AUTISM IN THE HOME SETTING

Most of Ryan's occupational therapy was conducted in the home. In many circumstances, children with autism learn best in an environment that is highly structured and where extraneous stimuli are limited (Faherty & Fraley, 1999; Ward, 1989). But treating in the home environment does not provide a controlled setting: dishwashers, clothes washers, dryers, vacuum cleaners, radios, televisions, computers, garage doors, doorbells, telephones, air-conditioning units, and furnaces may intermittently contribute a variety of background sounds. Meals are prepared, contributing to wafts of new smells. Family members, neighbors, delivery personnel move into and out of the home; siblings may want to participate in the treatment session. Life does not come to a halt in any home because a family member has a disability. As a therapist working in this setting, one must recognize that one is a guest and that the intimacy of treating in the home provides special challenges and opportunities.

For all the uncontrolled chaos that the home environment may present, one of its assets is that, for most children, this is where they feel most secure. When challenging a child to attempt new tasks, the safety of the home environment can facilitate taking risks. The continuity of the home environment provides a base from which children can explore the new or unfamiliar. "A continuity framework suggests that the opportunities and riches to be derived from new experiences are paradoxically most accessible to very young children when they are linked to familiar experiences, in a setting with adults who provide a secure base from which to explore the unfamiliar" (Sanchez & Thorp, 1998, p. 1).

Another asset of treatment in the home environment is that it provides an immediate avenue to nurture and empower the family. Parents of children with autism typically seek professional guidance relative to the care of their child. This professional help needs to be provided in measured doses; Birkmeier (1994) wrote that, initially, parents need empathy and validation of their abilities as parents. Understanding their grief process, as they recognize the loss of their "perfect" child, is regarded as essential. Let the parents describe what they want their child to do, helping prioritize goals for the child. As treatment approaches and the theories supporting them are explained, parents can become active problem solvers. Recognize that parents "will adopt different strategies for managing daily living tasks with their child depending on their style, their home and work responsibilities, their time, and other family members" (Case-Smith, 1989, p. 2).

A parent, Naomi Angoff Chedd (1994, p. 11), developed a brief list of dos and don'ts for therapists; highlights are as follows:

- Try to tell us something positive at each session.
- Be honest, but be gentle.
- Be patient if other children join the therapy session.
- Tell us if we are doing something fundamentally wrong or something that interferes with treatment goals.
- Be sensitive to us as parents (with dreams for our children), not only as parents of children with special needs.

CONCLUSION

Sensory integration and neurodevelopmental treatment approaches are frequently combined by occupational therapists. This chapter reviewed the development of these two treatment approaches and their complementary aspects. A case study described how these approaches—combined with behavior management techniques—were used with one child with high-functioning autism.

The use of SI and NDT is not appropriate for all children with autism. The selection of a treatment approach is dictated by the developmental level of the child, the life skills the child needs to attain, the foundation component skills the child needs to develop, the priorities of the family, and the experiential and educational background of the therapist. Therapy can look like play and, indeed, it should be play for the child. However, the treatment approach that guides the play requires of the therapist analytical study combined with a sense of educated intuitiveness (Oetter, 1992/1993). Services in the home additionally require the therapist to understand the limits and advantages of serving within that context. The art of therapy stems from the marriage of these multiple elements.

CHAPTER REVIEW QUESTIONS

1. What are two key concepts of sensory integration theory and of neurodevelopmental theory?
2. How are these key concepts applied in the case study on Ryan?
3. How would a professional or other service provider apply the dos and don'ts of home treatment to a case that you might know, or to the case of Ryan?

REFERENCES

Ayres, A. J. (1979). *Sensory integration and the child.* Los Angeles: Western Psychological Services.

Birkmeier, K. E. (1994, July). Nurturing and empowering the family. *NDTA Network, 3,* 3–11.

Bly, L. (1996, September/October). What is the role of sensation in motor learning? What is the role of feedback and feedforward? *NDTA Network, 5,* 1–7.

Bohman, I. (1986, May). The philosophy and evolution of the neuro-developmental treatment (Bobath) approach. *Neuro-Developmental Treatment Association Newsletter,* 1–3.

Case-Smith, J. (1989, March). Working with families in early intervention: New strategies with traditional occupational therapy skills. *Developmental Disabilities, 12,* 2–4.

Chedd, N. A. (1994, September). The way we see it: Families and caregivers speak out. *NDTA Network, 3,* 11.

Faherty, C., & Fraley, G. (1999, February). *Working with autism/PDD.* Lecture presented at the EDIS/DoDDS Tri-Country Conference, Weinheim, Germany.

Fisher, A. G., Murray, E. A., & Bundy, A. C. (Eds.). (1991). *Sensory integration: Theory and practice.* Philadelphia: F. A. Davis.

Grandin, T. (1995). *Thinking in pictures.* New York: Vintage Books.

Hinojosa, J., & Kramer, P. (1993). Developmental perspective: Fundamentals of developmental theory. In P. Kramer & J. Hinojosa (Eds.), *Frames of reference for pediatric occupational therapy* (pp. 3–7). Baltimore: Williams & Wilkins.

Kielhofner, G. (1992). *Conceptual foundations of occupational therapy.* Philadelphia: F. A. Davis.

Kimball, J. G. (1993). Sensory integrative frame of reference. In P. Kramer & J. Hinojosa (Eds.), *Frames of reference for pediatric occupational therapy* (pp. 87–175). Baltimore: Williams & Wilkins.

Kranowitz, C. S. (1998). *The out-of-sync child: Recognizing and coping with sensory integration dysfunction.* New York: Berkley Publishing Group.

Oetter, P. (1992). *Sensory processing issues related to arousal, attention, interaction and learning.* Paper presented at the 1992 Autism Society of America Conference, Albuquerque, NM. (From a summary by Joe McKeon published in *The Advocate,* 1993, Summer, *25,* 18.)

O'Neill, M., & Jones, R. S. P. (1997). Sensory-perceptual abnormalities in autism: A case for more research? *Journal of Autism and Developmental Disorders, 27*, 1997.

Reeves, G. D. (1992, June). *Introduction to sensory integration theory*. Course materials from A Neurobiological Foundation for Sensory Integration, Sensory Integration International, St. Louis, MO.

Roley, S. S., & Wilbarger, J. (1994, June). What is sensory integration? A series of interviews on the scope, limitations, and evolution of sensory integration theory. *Sensory Integration Special Interest Section Newsletter, 17*, 1–4.

Sanchez, S. Y., & Thorp, E. K. (1998). Discovering meanings of continuity: Implications for the infant/family field. *Zero to Three, 18*(6), 1–6.

Schoen, S., & Anderson, J. (1993). Neurodevelopmental treatment frame of reference. In P. Kramer & J. Hinojosa (Eds.), *Frames of reference for pediatric occupational therapy* (pp. 49–86). Baltimore: Williams & Wilkins.

Smith, I. M., & Bryson, S. E. (1994). Imitation and action in autism: A critical review. *Psychological Bulletin, 116*, 259–273.

Storch, B., & Eskow, K. (1996). Theory application by school-based occupational therapists. *American Journal of Occupational Therapy, 50*, 662–668.

Trombly, C. A. (1989). Neurophysiological and developmental treatment approaches. In C. A. Trombly (Ed.), *Occupational therapy for physical dysfunction* (pp. 96–107). Baltimore: Williams & Wilkins.

Trott, M. C., Laurel, M. K., & Windeck, S. L. (1993). *SenseAbilities: Understanding sensory integration*. Tucson, AZ: Therapy Skill Builders.

Ward, J. D. (1989). Infantile autism. In M. K. Logigian & J. D. Ward (Eds.), *Pediatric Rehabilitation: A team approach for therapists* (pp. 83–94). Boston: Little, Brown.

CHAPTER 9

Integration of Sensorimotor and Speech-Language Therapy

Rose M. Geis and Scott D. Tomchek

CHAPTER OBJECTIVES

At the completion of this chapter, the reader will be able to:

- Describe multiple methods for integrating sensorimotor interventions with speech and language therapy.
- Analyze a case study that applies sensorimotor interventions.
- Appreciate the need to integrate a concern for sensory and motor functions within a wide range of environments.

SENSORIMOTOR CHALLENGES AND THEIR IMPACT ON CHILDREN'S COMMUNICATION SKILLS

Children with autism and related disorders are known to have a relative weakness for giving and receiving verbal and nonverbal communicative information. More uniquely, they have a considerable impairment in their ability to direct or share attention with others (Baranek, 1999; Mundy, Sigman, Ungerer & Sherman, 1986; Osterling & Dawson, 1994). Sensory and motor function impairments are also reported in this population of individuals. Specifically, individuals with autism spectrum disorders are described as having broad sensory processing impairments (Adrien, Ornitz,

Barthelemy, Sauvage, & Lelord, 1987; Baranek, 1999; Dahlgren & Gillberg, 1989; Elliott, 1990; Kientz & Dunn, 1997), impairments in motor planning/praxis (Leary & Hill, 1996; Minshew, Sweeny, & Bauman, 1997), limited motor imitation abilities (Stone & Lemanek, 1990; Stone, Lemanek, Fishel, Fernandez, & Altemeier, 1990; Rogers, Bennetto, McEvoy, & Pennington, 1996), and repetitive motor stereotypies (Adrien et al, 1987; Elliot, 1990; Ornitz, 1985).

Given these impairments in both communication and sensorimotor development, intervention by both a speech-language pathologist and occupational therapist is often warranted. These interventions may be most beneficial if collaborative. In joint intervention sessions, the occupational therapist provides structured activities to foster improved bilateral motor integration, facilitate application of fine motor skills to functional tasks, and enhance sensory integrative function. Within this array of activities, the speech-language pathologist facilitates development of functional communication skills and play interaction. As Windeck & Laurel (1989) wrote, the ability to use both speech and language is dependent on central nervous system (CNS) organization of sensory input. Use of visual, tactile, and vestibular input helps the child focus and participate in communication exchanges. Motor planning aspects of sensory integration (SI) are important for fluent speech and nonverbal communication functions as well. SI therapy in conjunction with speech-language therapy promotes full use of gross and fine motor abilities and adds purpose and meaning to movement.

TREATMENT PRINCIPLES OF JOINT OCCUPATIONAL AND SPEECH-LANGUAGE THERAPY

Treatment principles of joint occupational and speech-language therapy are based on individualized evaluation (see later discussion and Chapter 4) and intervention planning, with emphasis on early intervention. These treatment principles address the following:

- Helping the child to understand communication.
- Facilitating understanding of spoken language and situation expectations.
- Giving the child something to talk about.
- Giving the child a means of communication.
- Giving the child a reason to communicate (Kiernan, Reid, & Goldbart, 1987; Jordan & Powell, 1995; Quill, 1995).

These principles also rely on the provision of a calm and structured intervention setting, with the child sharing control during treatment. Developmentally age-appropriate activities are used that involve concrete, meaningful materials incorporating the child's interests. Social skills and affective sharing are taught and modeled during these intervention sessions. The child's level of arousal is carefully modulated to maximize his or her learning potential.

STRATEGIES THAT ARE USED WITHIN THE JOINT THERAPY SESSIONS TO ENCOURAGE COMMUNICATION

Teaching Cause and Effect To Help the Child Understand Communication

In order for the child to understand communication, he or she must understand the cause-and-effect relationship. For example, with picture exchange, the child learns if he or she gives a picture of a cookie to another person (cause), then he or she will get a cookie (effect). If the child says "tickle" to someone (cause), then that person will tickle him or her (effect). If the child points to a desired object (cause), someone will get the object for him or her (effect).

Using Visual Supports To Help the Child Understand Communication

Children with autism and related disorders are, usually, better able to process static or repetitive visual information than the ever-changing acoustic signal. Consequently, using visual supports with these children builds on their area of relative strength. Visual supports can be objects, line drawings, or photographs that give the child information about his or her environment and, in turn, can be used by him or her to give others information. In joint therapy sessions, visual supports may include a choice board of activities, activity schedules, and activity-specific boards that guide the activities. Additionally, directional cards and object markers are often used for indication and management of behavior, time, and space.

Incorporating Motivating Materials, Themes, and Language Concepts into Activities To Give the Child Something To Talk About

It is no surprise that people are more likely to attend to and to communicate about what interests or affects them. It is no different with the children with whom we work. Taking this simple principle and applying it to our intervention can make the difference between a child who learns and one who does not. For example, going down the ramp on a scooter board becomes riding Thomas the Tank Engine or a constructional praxis task (building block designs) becomes constructing the homes of the three little pigs.

Functional vocabulary, linguistic concepts, and word relationships are also taught within the context of joint therapy, with the benefits being reciprocal in nature. SI activities inherently provide opportunities to teach language. For example, positional concepts of *up* and *down* can be targeted as the child goes up and down a ramp on a scooter board. Names of objects and actions can also be presented using simplified verbal mapping and picture representation. Meaningful word relationships can be introduced and reinforced. An obstacle course can be used for motor planning while targeting the semantic relationship of position + object. For example, the child can go in the tunnel, out of the tunnel, under the table,

across the bridge (balance beam), on the mat, off the mat, up the stairs, down the stairs, and between the chairs. In another example, building block designs for constructional praxis can be used to target the semantic relationship of color + object by having the child request a red block or a blue block to complete a design.

Providing Augmentative or Alternative Forms of Communication To Give the Child a Means of Communication

Since many children that we see initially have limited or no functional, communicative speech or gestures, they are significantly compromised in their ability to communicate appropriately and effectively with others. One widely used picture communication system is the Picture Exchange Communication System, developed by Lori Frost and Andrew Bondy (1994). The premise of this system is that children with autism and related disorders have difficulty initiating communication with others, responding to initiations of others, and gaining the attention of another before giving their message. Consequently, the training sequence begins with the child initiating communication to request highly desired items by exchanging a picture of the item for the item itself. This means of communication can be expanded in many ways so that the child can actively participate in the selection of activities, what is done within the activity, and when the activity is repeated or ended.

In addition to picture communication systems, signing and use of the written word may also be effective augmentative or alternative means of communication. A combination of communicative means may be most helpful in some children. Thomas L. Layton and Linda R. Watson provide strategies to assist in the selection of augmentative/alternative communication systems for children with autism in Quill (1995).

The understanding and use of conventional communicative gestures are also taught—for example, shaping the child's reach into a point or a "give me" gesture for an object request. Teaching a "my turn" gesture and encouraging the child to hand a toy to another person are helpful strategies in facilitating the concept of turn-taking.

Strategies To Give the Child a Reason To Communicate

The functions of, or reasons for, communication are many. For the child with autism or a related disorder, protesting objects and actions and requesting objects and actions are the most common communicative functions. These functions regulate the behavior of others, as opposed to regulating social interaction (e.g., greeting and calling) or joint attention (e.g., commenting and requesting or providing information). Using social routines as an intervention context can offer a myriad of opportunities for the child to use and develop a variety of communicative functions.

Providing Choices

The sensory needs of a child with autism or a related disorder may vary greatly from one moment to the next. Consequently, choices of activities are made available to the child via a picture choice board to address a variety of sensory needs. The purpose and use of a choice board is similar to the use of menus in restaurants. We go to a restaurant to satisfy a need—that is, hunger. If the server brought us food without giving us a choice, we would likely feel unhappy and that the choice was not the best one to fill our need. So, thankfully, restaurants have menus to give us choices about what we eat. As the occupational therapist A. Jean Ayres

(1979) wrote, sensory integrative therapy is most effective "when the child wants the stimulus and initiates an activity to get those sensations. . . . The brain is designed to give itself the experiences that are necessary for its own development" (p. 140). The choice board provides the structure for the child to initiate desired activities to meet his or her sensory need. Going back to the restaurant illustration, sometimes too many choices on the menu can be overwhelming; therefore, we may ask the server to suggest something. In the same way, the choices of activities for the child may be narrowed as necessary, or a sequenced picture schedule or written schedule may be used.

Based on our clinical experience, the children typically gravitate toward gross motor activities and away from fine motor activities. The choice board consequently is structured to provide alternating gross and fine motor selections. For less desired, more challenging activities, external tangible reinforcers may be included. Incorporating motivating themes into activities, as noted above, can enhance their desirability. Additionally, SI therapy is most effective when the child directs his or her own actions while the therapist unobtrusively directs the environment (Ayres, 1979). Therefore, besides the picture choice board, activity regulation boards are also provided for the child to show what he or she wants within the activity and when the activity is to end.

Violating Routines and Enticing the Child To Communicate

Refer to Table 9–1 for examples of ways to violate routines or entice a child to communicate. Note that the level of sophistication of communication enticed in this way depends on the means of communication already established or available to the child (pictures, signs, speech).

Table 9–1 Examples of Violating Routines for Communicative Enticement

Targeted Communicative Function	Violation or Communicative Enticement
Request for assistance	Send the child to obtain or assemble the main object of the activity; however, lock the closet where the item is located or put the item in a tightly closed container.
Protest	Give the child an item that he or she does not want or an item other than the one he or she requested.
Request for object	Omit an essential item from an activity.
Request for action	Put the child on a swing, therapy ball, or other piece of equipment that requires your help to make it move, or stop the fun activity to entice a request.
Comment	Include a new toy or object that is generally not present within the activity.
Request for information	Relocate an item without the child's knowledge and then ask him or her to retrieve that item.
Request for cessation	Continue doing an activity that the child is wanting to end.

Providing Opportunities for Social Interaction

Even more challenging to teach are the social interaction and joint attention functions of communication. Greeting, calling, requesting social routine, commenting, requesting information, and providing information are examples of these functions. Additionally, secondary intersubjectivity, a form of joint attention, is a critical skill in the normal development of human communication that involves frequent shifting of the focus of attention from objects to people and back again (Trevarthen, Aitken, Papoudi, & Robarts, 1996). The emergence of this skill is typically seen in children by the end of their first year. This stage of development is characterized by the child seeking to share or exchange experiences with others and leads to the learning of social conventions and language. Dawson and Adams (1984) found that imitation of the child's behavior by another person resulted in an increase in the use of eye gaze and social responsiveness. All of these skills are the early foundations for developing communication skills.

Because intentional communication is inherently social in nature, involving parents, other primary caregivers, siblings, and peers as part of the intervention team provides additional opportunities for social communication within the therapeutic session. This involvement may also build a bridge to generalization across settings and nurture empowerment in significant others. Generalization of skills is always a primary focus throughout the intervention process. Involvement of significant others in therapy sessions provides a way to facilitate skills in a variety of natural settings.

CASE STUDY

This case study illustrates the typical development of a program plan as well as collaborative intervention sessions. Clark, two years, nine months of age, presented for a comprehensive evaluation at the request of his doctor. He was having behavioral, social interaction, and communication difficulties at home and at preschool. His parents noted that his development was quite delayed in comparison to his twin sister's. His parents also described him as very active and as "being in his own little world." At the time of the occupational therapy evaluation, Clark was noted to be active and unfocused. He presented with significant sensory modulation difficulties. In general, Clark was noted to be hyporesponsive to incoming sensory input, though he had paradoxical responses to tactile input. He frequently sought supplemental vestibular input in an attempt to self-regulate, spinning himself repeatedly for up to 10 minutes. He was also observed to frequently circle-run (run in a tight circle). He also sought out tactile input, especially deep proprioceptive input to his head. He was observed to drop objects on his head (dump baskets of toys on his head, mouth/bite objects, rub sand in his hair, rub his head on the carpet, etc). At the same time, he was reported to be hyperresponsive to sticky substances he came in contact with, especially on his hands, and during grooming and hygiene tasks. Clark spent much of his day seeking proprioceptive and tactile sensory input, and therefore he had limited functional toy play.

From a communication standpoint, both receptive and expressive language delays were noted. Clark communicated primarily to request and protest, and did so with primitive forms of nonverbal communication (e.g., tantrum, directing through the use of another's body, and limited eye gaze). He had a limited speech sound repertoire and few intelligible words. Additionally, deficits in social communication, including joint attention and affective sharing, were noted.

From a comprehensive evaluation conducted by a developmental pediatrician, psychologist, speech-language pathologist,

and occupational therapist, the skill levels and diagnoses shown in Table 9–2 were discussed with Clark's family.

As many of Clark's social interaction and behavioral difficulties stemmed from noted impairments in communication and sensory processing, it was thought that he would benefit from joint therapy with an occupational therapist and a speech-language pathologist. Intervention was given weekly, with active home programming for application to other natural settings. The plan of treatment shown in Table 9–3 was developed to guide the treatment sessions.

Example of an Initial Therapy Session

It should be noted that Clark was taught to use picture exchange for requesting desired objects in previous speech-language therapy sessions. The following visual supports were used: activity choice board, activity regulation boards, "all done" box, "goodbye" overlay.

An activity choice board was used to provide Clark with a selection of activities from which to choose. The therapists previously selected Polaroid pictures of activities to address specific sensorimotor skills (e.g., climbing, rolling in a mat, and riding toys). These pictures were mounted on foam board with Velcro. Each picture was labeled at the bottom to pair the written word with the visual picture.

Activity regulation boards and other visual supports were used to guide Clark and allow for choices within the chosen activity. The therapist can use the activity regulation board to direct the child's actions, and the child can use the board to direct the actions of others. For instance, when Clark was participating in a scooter board activity, the activity regulation board was used to direct him up the ramp, down the ramp, to do the activity

Table 9–2 Initial Evaluation of Clark

Clark's Initial Comprehensive Evaluation: Age: 2 years, 9 months (33 months)

Speech-Language Evaluation	*Rossetti Infant Toddler Scale*	*Age Equivalent*
	Receptive Language	8–10 months
	Expressive Language	8–10 months
Occupational Therapy Evaluation	*Peabody Development Motor Scales*	*Age Equivalent*
	Gross Motor	24 months
	Fine Motor	10 months
	Sensory Regulatory Difficulties	
Psychological Evaluation	*Developmental Profile II*	*Age Equivalent*
	Physical	16 months
	Self-Help	12 months
	Social	10 months
	Academic	12 months
	Communication	10 months
Neurodevelopmental	Central Nervous System Dysfunction as manifested by muscular hypotonia and tremors	

Diagnosis: Autistic Disorder

again, and to terminate the activity ("all done"). Within this activity, another activity board was used between rides down the ramp to have Clark select individual pieces of a puzzle (e.g., one animal piece of a multipiece animal puzzle). This puzzle was used as a visual support to show the child how many times he would be performing the activity and to signal termination of the activity (i.e., when the puzzle is complete, the activity is finished). Other visual supports were used to serve more basic functions. For example, individual color cards were used to have Clark match or select a same-color ball for a ball maze activity. In another example, during a swinging activity, visual supports were uti-

Table 9–3 Treatment Plan for Joint Therapy Sessions

Clark's Joint Therapy Plan of Treatment

Communication Goals	1. To comprehend simple directions within familiar routines.
	2. To comprehend functional vocabulary.
	3. To use symbolic means (speech, pictures, gestures) for a variety of communicative functions.
	4. To develop reciprocal communicative and play interactions.
Sensorimotor Goals	1. To facilitate hand dominance and specialized skill in that dominant hand.
	2. To improve functional application of fine motor skill to age level.
	3. To enhance sensory modulation of incoming sensory input to allow for optimal arousal.

lized to have Clark select whether he wanted to swing rhythmically ("swing") or spin ("turn") on the swing. An example of an activity regulation board is shown in Figure 9–1.

An "all done" box was used to bring closure to an activity and signal the transition to the next activity. A box labeled "all done," with a slit in the top and a picture of a stop sign, was placed below the choice board. Clark put the picture of the activity in the box when the activity was finished.

A goodbye overlay was used to show passage of time and to allow Clark to anticipate the end of the session. The Boardmaker computer software (Mayer-Johnson, 1995) was used to generate an 80 3 80 picture of "goodbye." This picture was overlaid with a picture of a woman and a man (representing the two therapists) that was cut into four equal strips and attached with Velcro. The therapists instructed Clark to remove a strip from this visual approximately every 15 minutes, gradually revealing the "goodbye" picture, until all strips were removed, signaling the end of the session. This goodbye overlap is displayed in Figures 9–2 and 9–3.

After 18 months of therapy, Clark's skills were formally reevaluated. The results of this evaluation at four years, three months of age demonstrated that his skill levels had improved both in the rate of development and overall. During that 18-month period, all aspects of development improved at least 18 months. Table 9–4 displays the results of the reevaluation. The amount of progress, expressed in months, from the initial evaluation is included in parentheses.

Following this reevaluation, goals were reestablished to address deficit areas while utilizing strength areas to accomplish the goals. Generally, communication goals con-

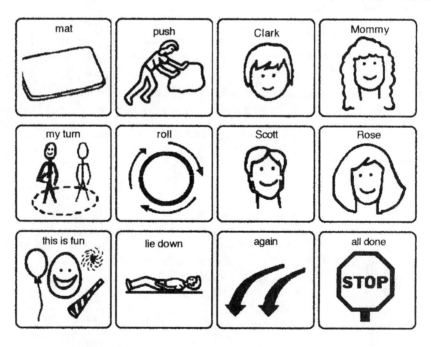

Figure 9–1 Activity regulation board

Figure 9–2 Goodbye overlay. Picture was cut into four strips and attached by Velcro to Figure 9–3.

Figure 9–3 Goodbye overlay. This picture was exposed in four sections. When completely exposed, the therapy session was ended.

Table 9–4 Follow-Up Evaluation after 18 Months of Intervention

Clark's Follow-Up Comprehensive Evaluation 18 Months Later:
Age 4 years, 3 months (51 months)

Speech-Language Evaluation	*Preschool Language Scale—3*	*Age Equivalent (Progress)*
	Receptive Language	33 months (23)
	Expressive Language	29 months (19)
Occupational Therapy Evaluation	*Peabody Developmental Motor Scales*	*Age Equivalent*
	Gross Motor	44 months (20)
	Fine Motor	35 months (25)
	Sensory Regulatory Difficulties	
Psychological Evaluation	*Developmental Profile II*	*Age Equivalent (Change)*
	Physical	42 months (26)
	Self-Help	30 months (18)
	Social	38 months (28)
	Academic	38 months (26)
	Communication	38 months (28)
	Leiter International Performance Scale—Revised	*Scaled Score (x = 10)*
	Figure Ground	6
	Form Completion	15
	Matching	12
	Classification	10
	Developmental Test of Visual-Motor Integration	33 months Standard Score = 67 (x = 100)
Neurodevelopmental	Emerging right-hand dominance, Central Nervous System Dysfunction as manifested by muscular hypotonia	

Diagnosis: Autistic Disorder; Above-Average Nonverbal Intelligence

tinued to focus on increasing the sophistication of communicative means and purposes for communication. Sensorimotor goals focused more on teaching Clark self-regulation to enhance sensory modulation abilities while continuing to improve the functional application of his fine and visual-motor skills during occupational performance.

CHAPTER REVIEW QUESTIONS

1. What is the rationale for combining sensorimotor and speech-language therapies?
2. In what specific ways may joint occupational therapy and speech and language therapy be structured to benefit the child with autism?

3. Based on your particular setting or need (e.g., school setting or parent need) describe at least 3 ways that sensorimotor activities can be used to entice social communication.

REFERENCES

Adrien, J. L., Ornitz, E., Barthelemy, C., Sauvage, D., & Lelord, G. (1987). The presence or absence of certain behaviors associated with infantile autism in severely retarded autistic and nonautistic retarded children and very young normal children. *Journal of Autism and Developmental Disorders, 17,* 407–416.

Ayres, A. J. (1979). *Sensory integration and the child.* Los Angeles: Western Psychological Services.

Baranek, G. T. (1999). Autism during infancy: A retrospective video analysis of sensory-motor and social behaviors at 9–12 months of age. *Journal of Autism and Developmental Disorders, 29,* 213–224.

Dahlgren, S. O., & Gillberg, C. (1989). Symptoms in the first two years of life: A preliminary population study of infantile autism. *European Archives of Psychology and Neurological Sciences, 238,* 169–174.

Dawson, G., & Adams, A. (1984). Imitation and social responsiveness in autistic children. *Journal of Abnormal Child Psychology, 12,* 209–225.

Elliott, C. D. (1990). *Differential Abilities Scale (DAS).* New York: Psychological Corporation.

Frost, L. A., & Bondy, A. S. (1994). *The Picture Exchange Communication System.* Cherry Hill, NJ: Pyramid Educational Consultants.

Jordan, R., & Powell, S. (1995). *Understanding and teaching children with autism.* West Sussex, England: John Wiley & Sons.

Kientz, M. A., & Dunn, W. (1997). A comparison of the performance of children with and without autism on the Sensory Profile. *American Journal of Occupational Therapy, 51,* 530–537.

Kiernan, C. C., Reid, B., & Goldbart, J. (1987). *Focus on language and communication.* Manchester, England: Manchester University Press.

Leary, M., & Hill, D. (1996). Moving on: Autism and movement disturbance. *Mental Retardation, 34,* 39–53.

Mayer-Johnson Publishers. (1995). Boardmaker 1.2 [Computer software]. Solana Beach, CA: Author.

Minshew, N. J., Sweeney, J. A., & Bauman, M. L. (1997). Neurologic aspects of autism. In D. J. Cohen & F. R. Volkmar (Eds.), *Handbook of autism and pervasive developmental disorders* (2nd ed.) (pp. 344–369). New York: John Wiley & Sons.

Mundy, P., Sigman, M., Ungerer, J., & Sherman, T. (1986). Defining the social deficits of autism: The contribution of non-verbal communication measures. *Journal of Child Psychology and Psychiatry and Allied Disciplines, 27,* 657–669.

Ornitz, E. M. (1985). Neuropsychology of infantile autism. *Journal of the American Academy of Child and Adolescent Psychiatry, 24,* 251–262.

Osterling, J., & Dawson, G. (1994). Early recognition of children with autism: A study of first birthday home videotapes. *Journal of Autism and Developmental Disorders, 24,* 247–257.

Quill, K. A. (1995). *Teaching children with autism: Strategies to enhance communication and socialization.* Albany, NY: Delmar Publishers.

Rogers, S. J., Bennetto, L., McEvoy, R., & Pennington, B. F. (1996). Imitation and pantomime in high-functioning adolescents with autism spectrum disorders. *Child Development, 67,* 2060–2073.

Stone, W. L., & Lemanek, K. L. (1990). Parental report of social behaviors in autistic preschoolers. *Journal of Autism and Developmental Disorders, 20,* 513–522.

Stone, W. L., Lemanek, K. L., Fishel, P. T., Fernandez, M. C., & Altemeier, W. A. (1990). Play and imitation skills in the diagnosis of autism in young children. *Pediatrics, 86,* 267–272.

Trevarthen, C., Aitken, K., Papoudi, D., & Robarts, J. (1996). *Children with autism: Diagnosis and interventions to meet their needs.* London: Jessica Kingley Publishers.

Windeck, S. L., & Laurel, M. (1989). A theoretical framework combining speech-language therapy with sensory integration treatment. *Sensory Integration Special Interest Section Newsletter, 12*(1), 1–4.

CHAPTER 10

Facilitating Social Communication through the Sensorimotor Approach

Charlotte A. Hubbard

CHAPTER OBJECTIVES

At the completion of this chapter, the reader will be able to:

- Describe the specific skills of occupational therapists using a sensorimotor approach to intervention that complement the skills of speech and language pathologists.
- Understand the current literature and basic tenets of social communication.
- Understand some techniques to enhance social communication.

INTRODUCTION TO SOCIAL COMMUNICATION

According to the *Diagnostic and Statistical Manual of Mental Disorders* (*DSM-IV*; American Psychiatric Association, 1994), a diagnosis of autism is possible only if the child demonstrates a certain number of behaviors within three domains: social interaction impairment, communication impairment, and repetitive and stereotypical behaviors (Tanguay, Robertson, & Derrick, 1998). All three impact the process of effective social communication. One of the earliest identifying characteristics of autism is the delay or lack of verbal communication. Any person with autism may exhibit communication skills along a continuum from no communicative attempts to either verbal or nonverbal attempts, to functional verbal

communication with mild deviation. A toddler's language may range from no observable evidence of interest in communication with anyone to elaborate verbal communication with only a hint of communication difficulty. When assessing a verbal child with autism, verbal communication is typically composed with accurate grammatical structure and precise speech sound production (Trevarthen, Aitken, Papoudi, & Robarts, 1996). However, the aspects of communication that are typically disordered in a child with autism involve the speech prosodic patterns, the semantics (relationships among word meanings), and pragmatics or social use of communication.

Even though children with autism are very different from each other, they all seem to demonstrate some level of difficulty with social communication (Koegel,

Koegel, Frea, & Smith, 1995). "Social communication is a reciprocal, dynamic relationship based on mutual understanding, enjoyment, and benefit" (Quill, 1995, p. 164). In order for this relationship to occur, more than one person must be involved; all parties should be able to understand and use verbal language, gestures, and paralinguistics, as well as determine the topic within the current social context. In order to effectively continue the conversation, a person with autism must have the cognitive ability to retain in short-term memory what has just been said and associate the words with the social situation and the communicative intent. Cognition also facilitates the child's comprehension of abstract language, such as humor and nonliteral meaning. This chapter focuses on aspects of social communication, assessment, and methods for facilitating social communication.

ASPECTS OF SOCIAL COMMUNICATION

Foundations of Social Communication

In order for effective social communication to develop, the cognitive, emotional, and social skills and neurological processes that are fundamental to communication must be developing and interacting appropriately. One neurological process that is critical in facilitating communication development and academic learning is sensory integration (SI). According to Mauer (1999), "Sensory integration refers to the ability to organize, integrate, and use sensory information from the body and the environment . . . speech and language acquisition depends on multiple sensory processes" (p. 383). SI involves all of the senses (olfactory, gustatory, tactile, vestibular, visual, auditory, and proprioceptive), allowing the brain to compare, associate, and interpret incoming signals to learn about the world. From a communication perspective, as sensory information is interpreted, it is referenced by language symbols and rules and stored in the brain for future use through motor movement or output (e.g., sign language, verbal communication). Often, children with autism have difficulty with SI, which interferes with their communication development and learning.

If sensory information is not effectively transmitted or received in infancy, then the infant with autism, for example, may not feel a wet diaper and, therefore, will not cry to make his or her needs known. This lack of response to sensory input may affect the future use of emotional display. Expression of emotions is the infant's first reflexive vocalization; this is reinforced by the adult and eventually shaped into an attempt to communicate. With additional vocal attempts followed by the adult response, the infant soon learns that responses from the adult can be controlled; thus, communicative intent emerges. Communicative intent—the use of communication for a purpose or for controlling the environment—develops around eight or nine months of age and is the motivation for social interaction and communication. Initially, infants display communicative intent nonverbally, such as raising both arms toward the adult to signal the message "Pick me up." Communicative intent is one reason to communicate; others are discussed in the section on pragmatics.

Some of the cognitive skills that are critical to the acquisition of speech and language are object permanence, imitation, and play. Object permanence, which emerges around one year of age, is the infant's ability to know that an object exists after it is removed from his or her visual field. This skill is important because the young child will need to learn a word as the referent for a particular object or event. This word with its associated sensory information will be stored in his or her brain in order to share it later. Also, object permanence is the conceptual foundation for comprehension and use of the grammatical structure, past tense. The young child will no longer need the object in the present environment in order to discuss it.

Imitation is a learning strategy that enhances the use of memory in young children and provides an opportunity to practice language. Usually, after the first two years of life, excessive use of imitation of speech is eliminated. When it persists, as in autism, it is referred to as *echolalia*. There are various theories as to the function of the echolalia. One is that echolalia is indicative of delayed language development and continues as a learning strategy; however, language does not continue to develop as it does in children without a disability, suggesting more than a developmental delay. Secondly, the social context influences the belief that the child with autism has no other options for responding, like saying "I don't know." A third theory is that the echolalia is a form of self-stimulatory behavior with no communication function (Koegel & Koegel, 1995). When observing children with autism who are physically engaged in activities with another person, it appears that echolalia is an attempt to verbally interact with the other person. However, the communicative intent and interpretation of echolalia is difficult to determine.

Play is a natural context in which young children can learn about their world through sensorimotor stimulation and manipulation of concrete objects. Play is also essential for learning and practicing social rules and skills and for developing friendships. With maturation, verbal and nonverbal social strategies are refined and applied to more complex social situations. Development and use of communication during play is critical for the appropriate development of peer relationships. Around 18 months of age, a particular type of play, known as *symbolic play*, emerges. Symbolic play is an imaginative activity in which one object is used to represent another, such as a shoebox used to represent a doll's bed. This type of play requires abstract thinking and the ability to associate objects, words, or thoughts. A child with autism has difficulty relating to peers during play and engaging in symbolic play. Play requires imagination, flexibility, and spontaneity, which are usually diminished or absent in children with autism. It is often difficult for a child with autism to perceive and understand the subtle social cues necessary for spontaneous play. Therefore, children have difficulty moving beyond highly structured and predictable play, such as stacking blocks to spontaneous play, like pretend tea parties.

Nonverbal Communication

Nonverbal communication is any means used to express oneself that is not spoken language, such as gestures, facial expressions, and body movements. Children with autism typically have difficulty obtaining and maintaining eye contact, which is frequently interpreted as the child not listening to the speaker. However, this is not necessarily the case in children with autism, for whom avoiding eye contact may be a means of avoiding social-communicative interaction (Koegel & Koegel, 1995). Children with autism rarely or never use gestures to communicate unless they have been directly taught. Sign language was taught to a few children with some success, but is not a well-accepted mode of communication among those who do not understand the signs or how to respond in sign.

Facial expressions for the demonstration of emotions are often lacking in children with autism because they have difficulty understanding the abstract meaning in emotions. When emotions appear to be displayed, such as laughter, they are infrequently used for the purpose of communication. These ineffective skills hinder social interactions and communication.

Body language and movements are often inappropriate (e.g., hitting head when given a verbal command) or are inappropriately used in social communication (e.g., arm flapping when a desired food is presented) by a person with autism. However, these body movements serve a communicative function for this person. For example, the arm-flapping behavior could mean that the child is requesting the desired food and hitting the head could be a means of expressing "No, I don't want to do it." Typically, these inappropriate behaviors decrease when the child is given a more acceptable and intelligible means of communication (Koegel & Koegel, 1995).

Communication Comprehension and Expression

A common characteristic of people with autism is a significant delay in the onset of verbal communication. Some children never develop verbal expression, some have limited language, and some have appropriate verbal skills. Because children with autism seldom respond to verbal requests and rarely continue a conversation, their comprehension of spoken language is questioned. However, there are cases in autism in which the individual later developed communication skills and shared the frustration of being unable to respond to or initiate social communication despite their comprehension (Grandin, 1995).

Typically, people with autism who verbally communicate use correct grammar in simple sentence structures. Most often, the articulation or speech sound production is correctly produced. The vocabulary used is typically concrete and basic in sentences used for communication (Trevarthen et al., 1996). Otherwise, many people with autism are capable of reproducing commercials, jingles, and songs exactly the way they are heard. Another prominent characteristic of verbal expression is echolalia, in which the child repeats a portion or all of an utterance. This imitation can occur immediately after the sentence is heard or be delayed for an hour, a day, or a month. The unique aspect of echolalia is that the child repeats the same intonational pattern used in the original utterance. For example, when the adult asks, "Do you want juice, Sam?" the child responds, "Do you want juice, Sam?"

Pragmatic Skills

Probably the most significantly affected area of social communication in autism is pragmatics. Pragmatics is the use of language in social communication, which involves several skills, such as knowing when to speak, when to laugh, when to change a topic, how to take turns in a conversation, and how to repair a communication breakdown. Many of these pragmatic skills, such as joint attention, emerge in infancy. Joint attention requires that the adult and the infant attend to the same object—thus, an early form of topic selection. Once the same object is observed by the adult and the child, then the social interaction and communication can take place concerning the object. Turn-taking is also developed early, especially during vocal play; the infant makes a sound and the adult imitates it, which encourages the infant to produce the sound again. Thus, turns emerge and an early game is formed. Joint attention and turn-taking are the foundation for social communication. In addition, eye gaze, which emerges in the first three months, is basic to joint attention. The infant with autism has difficulty in demonstrating appropriate use of these pragmatic skills.

As the infant matures, other important pragmatic skills facilitate the development of social communication and language. Requesting behavior emerges nonverbally in gestures, such as reaching toward a desired object; this often results in a successful communication attempt and develops the child's sense of control in the environment. Topic initiation and topic maintenance, which require abstract skills of timing and topic extension, are guided by social rules and knowledge of the communication partner. Responding to questions and commenting during conversation are two higher-level pragmatic skills bound by social communication rules. For persons with autism, these skills are often severely impaired and require assessment and intervention.

IDENTIFYING PROBLEMS IN SOCIAL COMMUNICATION

Because people with autism may use either inappropriate or unique behaviors for communication, it is important to understand the communicative intent or the purpose for the attempt at social communication to effectively assess the person's abilities (Quill, 1995). Identifying communicative intent requires careful observation of the behavior, the social situation, and the events preceding and following the behavior. People who spend a significant amount of time with the child (e.g., parents, teach-

ers) often are a great resource for determining communicative intent. In addition, the assessment should note whether the child's pragmatic skills (e.g., requesting) are displayed verbally or nonverbally.

According to Quill (1995), four assessment tools should be used to determine the child's social-communicative interaction ability: a communicative means-function questionnaire, a natural communication sample, a language comprehension inventory, and an interaction analysis. The communicative means-function questionnaire is completed by interviewing the adult about the child's communicative behavior (e.g., reaching for a cookie) when demonstrating a communicative intent (e.g., requesting the desired cookie) in various situations. The natural communication sample requires that 100 spontaneous, child-initiated utterances be recorded along with the context of the communication event and the intent of the social communication. The language comprehension inventory identifies various factors or conditions (e.g., response time given to the child) that facilitate the child's comprehension of language. The interaction analysis assesses the relationship between the communication behaviors of the communication partner and the social-communication skills of the child. For example, an adult who comments on a child's actions usually elicits continuation of conversation from the child, whereas the adult who asks questions about the child's actions usually discourages further conversation. Together with informal observations, these four assessment tools provide a natural and accurate picture of the child's communication ability.

A few published assessment tools are useful in assessing the social communication skills of children with autism. The Communication and Symbolic Behavior Scales (Wetherby & Prizant, 1993) focuses on the pragmatics in social communication; the Sequenced Inventory of Communication Development—Revised (Hedrick, Prather, & Tobin, 1984) and Evaluating Acquired Skill in Communication—Revised (Riley, 1991) assess receptive and expressive language skills in a more natural context, yielding a language age equivalent. The first two tools were designed to assess young children, but are beneficial in determining the communication skills of older children with autism. The last tool was designed for children with disabilities and was developed over six years with 200+ persons with autism between the ages of 2 and 26 years.

FACILITATING SOCIAL COMMUNICATION

General Considerations

Koegel et al. (1995) provided several general suggestions for increasing the success of intervention in children with autism. Communication attempts and verbal language increase when they are reinforced. The reinforcers should be highly preferred by the child in order to increase the frequency of the target responses. If stimulus items are desired and chosen by the child with autism, motivation increases. Motivation also increases when the reinforcer is natural and relevant to the desired response. For example, if a child loves milk, then the child receives it only when he or she says "milk." Natural reinforcers, such as milk, are more likely to generalize to other situations than contrived reinforcers.

Intervention Approaches/Techniques

Because children with autism have difficulty either attending to or comprehending spoken language but have stronger visual skills (Hodgdon, 1995), intervention approaches often focus on using these stronger visual skills. Social communication in children with autism is best facilitated in a setting or situation that is natural for the individual child. One such approach, which incorporates both visual cues and functional communication and attempts to move the communication event toward a more natural setting, is the Picture Exchange Communication System (PECS), developed by Bondy and Frost (1998). PECS focuses on the child's initiation of communication (usually beginning with requests) and rewards this behavior with an effective reinforcer. The communication is initiated by having the child give a picture of the object or activity to the adult, who exchanges the picture for the real object or activity that has meaning in the child's natural environment. For example, Sally loves to swing; therefore, she must give the adult a picture of a swing in order to receive this natural reward. The purpose of this approach is to develop functional communication through pictures, not to develop verbal communication. However, Bondy and Frost reported that some preschoolers who were trained with PECS also developed verbal as well as functional communication.

Another approach to facilitating social communication is through the use of social stories, a technique developed by Carol Gray (1995). Because children with autism have difficulty perceiving the subtle cues and the required social skills in a particular social situation, social stories are individually developed to teach necessary social skills. The social skill selected for the story is usually one that results in a negative interaction within a social context. For example, George grabs a desired toy from another child as he says "Give it to me." Observations are then conducted to determine the basis for the child's inappropriate or limited social behavior. Then a social story is written by the parent or teacher concerning the targeted social skill. Social stories explain to the child the sequence of events, his or her feelings, the feelings of others, or correct social behavior. Drawings or photos depicting the events in the social story are helpful in facilitating comprehension of the targeted social skill. Social stories can be read to or given to the child to memorize or internalize the social rules. George's social story might include his feelings, the feelings of other children, and the steps and words for asking for or waiting for a toy.

In another example, Sarah, who is nine years old, had an appointment with a new dentist in a different location. Her parents were aware that Sarah was calm and enjoyed riding in the car when the route was familiar; however, she screamed and bit her hand when the car turned in a new direction. Her parents were concerned about making this new trip. To develop the social story, they drove the new route to the new dentist, without Sarah, and took photos of each turn and landmark along the way. They wrote a social story about riding to the dentist's office and included the photos in the story. They reviewed the story with Sarah several times and took the social story with them on the day of the appointment. Sarah had a pleasant ride to the dentist's office.

A third approach that promotes social communication is the Natural Language Paradigm, which is a naturalistic language teaching approach incorporating a pivotal response (Koegel, Koegel, & Carter, 1998). Naturalistic language teaching focuses on modifying the environment to increase the number of opportunities children have to use language in a natural situation. For example, the opportunity for natural language to occur is encouraged by placing a child's favorite toy out of reach but within the child's visual field. The child then must ask for or point to the toy in order to obtain it. Pivotal behaviors are those that have an impact on a broad range of functional areas. One major pivotal behavior is motivation. Research demonstrated that children with autism display significant gains in language and fewer inappropriate behaviors when provided with motivation than when not (Koegel, Koegel, & Surratt, 1992). Several key components of the Natural Language Paradigm must be included in order for the approach to be effective. One component requires that the child select the activity or material to be used in teaching the target response. A second component insists that the reinforcer must be the natural outcome of the target response. Once language skills are learned, the third component continues with intermittent reinforcement of the learned skills while introducing new language goals. A fourth component values any attempt to communicate by reinforcing it to maintain the desire to socially interact. This approach can be tailored to meet the individual needs of a child. If a child responds more effectively to visual cues, then pictures or written words can be utilized to facilitate communication. This approach can be effective with verbal and nonverbal children because the communication used by the child does not have to be verbal.

For example, five-year-old Billy typically obtained objects or food by climbing up to get them; he did not request them either verbally or nonverbally. The environment was modified by placing desired objects out of reach but in Billy's visual field. When Billy attempted to climb or reach for the desired object, he had to communicate his request first by pointing to it. This attempt to communicate was rewarded by giving him the desired object. The mode of communication for Billy was pointing, but for other children it might be pictures, sign language, or verbalization.

CONCLUSION

Social communication is a skill that is difficult for people with autism to acquire. Understanding the aspects of social communication as they relate to a particular child is critical in determining the communication skills to be targeted and the intervention approach to be used. These decisions should be determined by a team consisting of, at least, the parents/caregivers, the person with autism, the speech-language pathologist, the occupational therapist, and the educator. Each person with autism is unique and requires individualized attention. Functional social communication is a necessity for a person to live a fulfilling life.

CHAPTER REVIEW QUESTIONS

1. Compare and contrast communicative intent and pragmatic communication skills.
2. Based on ideas found in this chapter, list at least 10 ways that social communication could be elicited.
3. What are the components of a social story? Describe one social skill or activity that might be enhanced by the use of a social story.

REFERENCES

American Psychiatric Association. (1994). *Diagnostic and statistical manual of mental disorders* (4th ed.). Washington, DC: Author.

Bondy, A. S., & Frost, L. A. (1998). The picture exchange communication system. *Seminars in Speech and Language, 19*(4), 373–389.

Grandin, T. (1995). *Thinking in pictures and other reports from my life with autism.* New York: Vintage Books.

Gray, C. (1995). Teaching children with autism to "read" social situations. In K. Quill (Ed.), *Teaching children with autism: Strategies to enhance communication and socialization* (pp. 219–241). Albany, NY: Delmar Publishers.

Hedrick, D., Prather, E., & Tobin, A. (1984). *Sequenced Inventory of Communication Development—Revised.* East Aurora, NY: Slosson.

Hodgdon, L. A. (1995). *Visual strategies for improving communication: Vol. 1. Practical supports for school and home.* Troy, MI: Quirk Roberts Publishing.

Koegel, L. K., Koegel, R. L., & Carter, C. M. (1998). Pivotal responses and the natural language teaching paradigm. *Seminars in Speech and Language, 19*(4), 355–372.

Koegel, R. L., & Koegel, L. K. (Eds.). (1995). *Teaching children with autism: Strategies for initiating positive interactions and improving learning opportunities.* Baltimore: Paul H. Brookes.

Koegel, R. L., Koegel, L. K., & Surratt, A. (1992). Language intervention and disruptive behavior in children with autism. *Journal of Autism and Developmental Disorders, 22*, 141–152.

Koegel, R. L., Koegel, L. K., Frea, W. D., & Smith, A. E. (1995). Emerging interventions for children with autism: Longitudinal and lifestyle implications. In R. L. Koegel & L. K. Koegel (Eds.), *Teaching children with autism: Strategies for initiating positive interactions and improving learning opportunities* (pp. 1–15). Baltimore: Paul H. Brookes.

Mauer, D. M. (1999). Issues and applications of sensory integration theory and treatment with children with language disorders. *Language, Speech, and Hearing Services in Schools, 30*(4), 383–392.

Quill, K. A. (1995). Enhancing children's social-communicative interactions. In K. A. Quill (Ed.), *Teaching children with autism: Strategies to enhance communication and socialization* (pp. 163–189). Albany, NY: Delmar Publishers.

Quill, K. A. (1998). Environmental supports to enhance social-communication. *Seminars in Speech and Language, 19*(4), 407–423.

Riley, A. M. (1991) *Evaluating Acquired Skill In Communication—Revised*. San Antonio, TX: Psychological Corp.

Tanguay, P. E., Robertson, J., & Derrick, A. (1998). A dimensional classification of autism spectrum disorder by social communication domains. *Journal of the American Academy of Child and Adolescent Psychiatry, 37*(3), 271–277.

Trevarthen, C., Aitken, K., Papoudi, D., & Robarts, J. (1996). *Children with autism: Diagnosis and interventions to meet their needs*. London: Jessica Kingsley Publishers.

Wetherby, A. M., & Prizant, B. (1993). *Communication and Symbolic Behavior Scales*. Baltimore: Paul H. Brookes.

CHAPTER 11

Integration of Sensorimotor and Psychoeducational/ Behavioral Interventions

Myra Beth Bundy

CHAPTER OBJECTIVES

At the completion of this chapter, the reader will be able to:

- Describe multiple methods for integrating sensorimotor interventions with psychology.
- Describe the specific skills of occupational therapists using a sensorimotor approach to intervention that complement the skills of psychologists.
- Interpret behaviors and barriers to learning from the sensorimotor perspective and apply a variety of techniques to manage difficult behaviors and promote optimal learning.

THE HISTORICAL INVOLVEMENT OF PSYCHIATRY AND PSYCHOLOGY WITH AUTISM

This chapter briefly travels through the history of psychology's conceptualization of autism and through current trends in psychological intervention in autism on its way to the core intention of the chapter. The core portion includes examples from the literature and from the author's clinical experience combining psychoeducational/behavioral strategies with understanding and use of the unique sensorimotor profiles seen in individuals with autism.

Diagnosis and Description of Autism

Although autism existed before it was officially described, an American psychiatrist named Leo Kanner first described a syndrome he called early infantile autism in 1943 (Mesibov, Adams, & Klinger, 1997). Kanner's original idea was that children with the three behaviors he considered central to autism—social isolation, insistence on sameness, and abnormal language—were born with these differences. That is, he perceived autism as biological in basis (Trevarthen, Aitken, Papoudi, & Robarts, 1998).

Kanner's original three features remained central to psychologists' conceptualization of autism (Mesibov et al., 1997), although a deeper understanding of these features as well as additional difficulties evolved. Laboratory psychologists began documenting symptoms related to sensorimotor functioning when they examined reactions to discrete stimuli by children with autism. Ornitz and Ritvo (1968) noted differences in perception and motor behavior, among other symptoms. Much later, Dahlgren & Gillberg (1989) found that behaviors in the categories of Sensory Functions and Self-Regulation were among those successfully discriminating children with autism and mental retardation from children with mental retardation but no autism. Dawson and Lewy (1989) proposed that difficulties with arousal modulation may impact attentional abilities and ultimately social behaviors and social-emotional development. Waterhouse and Fein (1998), in a recent review of perspectives on social impairment in autism, described a set of theories conceptualizing social impairment in autism as a secondary effect of a primary sensory deficit.

Despite these and other perspectives acknowledging the importance of sensory processing and arousal/regulation differences in autism, the current *Diagnostic and Statistical Manual of Mental Disorders* (*DSM-IV;* American Psychiatric Association, 1994) only considers "odd or extreme responses to sensory stimuli" as characteristics frequently associated with but not necessary for a diagnosis of autism. However, one of the *DSM-IV* diagnostic criteria for autism, "stereotyped and repetitive motor mannerisms," involves sensorimotor functioning.

Psychoanalytic Views

Early psychologists and psychiatrists attempted to explain the behaviors of children with autism in psychodynamic terms—the prevailing theory of the time. These theorists focused on the social differences seen in autism and hypothesized that these differences emerged because of cold, rejecting parenting (Kanner, 1943; Bettelheim, 1967). Consistent with these etiological theories,

the most common treatment approaches involved helping parents, typically mothers, to become less rejecting, or removing children from their parents (Bettelheim, 1967).

Biological and Behavioral Views and Early Interventions

By the 1970s, an increasing number of clinicians and researchers began arguing against the theory that parenting caused autism and proposing biological, neurological, and genetic contributions (Rimland, 1964; Rutter, 1978; Schopler & Reichler, 1970). Some of the most persuasive psychological research included data from a variety of sources and methods showing that parents of children with autism did not show significant differences from other parents on personality measures, marital satisfaction, family cohesion, and other variables (Cantwell, Baker, & Rutter, 1979; Koegel, Schreibman, O'Neill, & Burke, 1983). As views about causation changed, psychological and educational treatment approaches also evolved. Eric Schopler suggested that interventionists work with parents as treatment team members rather than see parents as the focus of treatment (Schopler & Reichler, 1970). Ivaar Lovaas and his colleagues began an experimental program influenced by the proposal that, like other behavior, the behavior of children with autism could be modified by reinforcement, punishment, and other behavior modification techniques (Lovaas, Schreibman, & Koegel, 1974; Lovaas, 1987). Lovaas's work had a major impact on psychological and educational approaches to autism and continues to influence current researchers and practitioners in its use of learning theory and its emphasis on data collection and empiricism.

CURRENT BEST PRACTICE IN PSYCHOLOGICAL/ BEHAVIORAL INTERVENTION IN AUTISM

In recent years, interest and involvement in autism research, assessment, and treatment has increased, so now innumerable intervention approaches, programs, and descriptions exist. Most well-known psychological and behavioral approaches can be loosely categorized as either short-term and focused in nature, or as long-term and global in intervention focus.

Focal Behavioral Treatments

Psychologists are a primary group of professionals involved in the focal behavioral intervention approach, which teaches a specific set of skills or addresses specific behavioral symptoms, such as reducing aggression and task avoidance. These types of treatments often use learning theory to analyze a behavior's function and maintaining factors and to design individualized treatment programs oriented toward change in specific behaviors. The behavioral interventions may involve one or all three of the following strategies, as described by Bregman and Gerdtz (1998): "antecedent interventions" (implemented before a target behavior is likely to occur, in an effort to avert problems); "consequence interventions" (implemented following the occurrence of a target behavior); and "skill development interventions" (behavioral programs designed to teach alternative, adaptive behaviors, to reduce the frequency and severity of maladaptive responses).

These approaches have been used with individuals of all ages and often with those with relatively lower cognitive functioning, because of their higher frequency of severe behavioral difficulties. Literature describing this kind of intervention is plentiful, although most of the research uses either single-case designs or very small samples, so that generalizing results to the whole population of individuals with autism is uncertain (Bregman & Gerdtz, 1998). Some focal work provides detailed descriptions of the use of sensorimotor concepts and is described later in this chapter.

Comprehensive Programs of Behavioral/Educational Treatment

Psychologists are also active participants in and, often, the primary coordinators of comprehensive programs of treatment intended to change the course of autism. These programs attempt to address multiple symptoms of autism, to reduce maladaptive behaviors, and to increase adaptive skills through intervention that is intense both in number of hours and in level of training and number and types of professionals involved. In keeping with the current emphasis on early identification and intervention in autism and other developmental disabilities, the majority of comprehensive programs focus on preschool and early-school-age children. The few programs emphasizing comprehensive lifespan intervention and services, such as the TEACCH program at the University of North Carolina (Mesibov, 1995) and the Eden Family of Services in Princeton, New Jersey (Holmes, 1998), tend to focus on service delivery and applied evaluation of their programs rather than on conducting and publishing studies aimed at proving the efficacy of their overall approach. Positive effects on developmental skills, IQ scores, and functional language and communication have been shown across several comprehensive early intervention models (Dawson & Osterling, 1996; Rogers, 1998).

Dawson and Osterling (1996) reviewed data from several empirically supported comprehensive programs for young children and identified the following common elements:

- Curriculum focusing on areas of attention and compliance, motor imitation, communication, play and appropriate toy use, and social skills
- Highly structured teaching environments with low student-to-staff ratio and systematic strategies for generalizing new skills to many situations
- Predictability and routine in the daily schedule
- Functional approach to understanding and addressing problem behaviors
- Focus on skills needed for successful transition from early intervention program to typical education at the preschool or kindergarten level
- High level of family involvement

Although sensorimotor intervention is not explicitly emphasized, there are references to related strategies in several of the programs reviewed, with various degrees of understanding of sensorimotor concepts implied. These include a statement that children are provided with occupational therapy when appropriate (University of Colorado Health Sciences Center, p. 309), a statement that "self-stimulatory behaviors are handled by ignoring, time-out, shaping" (UCLA Young Autism Program, p. 311), emphasis on improving motor and verbal imitation skills (Princeton Child Development Institute), and, finally, the reviewers' own clinical work and interpretations, using predictability and routine to compensate for "differences in arousal modulation" and using social interactive strategies "designed to

be sensitive to the child's narrow range of optimal stimulation" (Dawson & Osterling, 1996, p. 322).

DISTINCTIONS BETWEEN BEHAVIORAL AND SENSORIMOTOR APPROACHES

Cook (1990) provided an interesting explanation of the difference between traditional behavioral interventions and a sensorimotor approach by discussing task focus. She suggested that a traditional behavioral approach sets up work tasks and setting in a planned fashion and teaches the child with autism to complete the task through practicing it in repeated trials and in multiple settings. For example, as a first step in teaching a child with autism to pull down pants in the bathroom, a behavioral interventionist might give a verbal command (e.g., "Pull down pants") with some degree of visual prompt, physically guide the child to pull down pants, and deliver a reinforcer if the response is correct.

In contrast, the addition of a sensorimotor perspective reduces the direct focus on the task activity (Cook, 1990). Rather than conceiving the task as the primary goal, the interventionist focuses on the sensorimotor experiences that a functional activity can provide. For the toileting example above, a sensorimotor approach might add a program providing controlled movement (vestibular) experiences in home, school, and natural environments such as a playground, with the idea that bending down to get pants requires the ability to tolerate head-down movement (vestibular input) and exhibit dynamic balance. A combined sensorimotor and behavioral approach would hold that while playground activities do not directly practice pulling pants down, the experiences contribute to developing that skill.

APPLICATIONS FOR INTEGRATED SENSORIMOTOR AND BEHAVIORAL METHODS

Many of the psychological or behavioral professionals currently applying sensorimotor activities in autism intervention use sensorimotor activities as consequences for desired behavior (i.e., apply sensorimotor activities as rewards or punishment). However, the professionals rarely note that the sensory experiences they identified can also be used as preventive or facilitative strategies. Others may attempt to modify self-stimulatory behavior, but they typically do not address the underlying causes or purpose of the stereotypies. In contrast, some basic psychological research incorporates a more in-depth understanding of sensorimotor aspects of autism; by its nature, however, this work does not apply this understanding to intervention. For example, Berkson (1998) presented a careful and specific look at the reward systems involved in the self-stimulatory behavior of top-spinning, noting that this particular self-stimulation seems to involve at least two reward systems. The first system involves the visual attraction of the top's complex movement and the second relates to the motor behavior that produces the top's movement. This finding could be applied in numerous situations, including explanding leisure interests of an individual with autism by introducing activities incorporating the sensory properties found to be reinforcing (in this case, finger and hand movement and intense, motion-oriented visual stimuli).

Some of the most sophisticated work integrating an understanding of sensorimotor and psychological functioning in autism was conducted by the applied developmental psychologist Sally Rogers and her colleagues at the University of Colorado Health Sciences Center and the University of Denver. Rogers and Pennington (1991), in a theoretical article, specified motor imitation as a candidate for one of the central deficits in the cascade of effects that produces autism. More recently, Rogers (1998) proposed a variety of social deficits that may result from primary deficits in the ability to plan, sequence, and execute intentional motor movements. Rogers not only theorized about sensorimotor deficits in autism but also incorporated sensorimotor assessment and intervention as part of the Health Sciences Center early intervention program for children with autism (Rogers & Osaki-Bryant, 1995). She described an occupational therapist as an integral member of an interdisciplinary assessment and treatment team and as part of an overall intervention program involving intensive individual teaching, emphasis on social relationships, developmental and interdisciplinary treatment, and emphasis on child initiation, child choice, and child independence. Some of the Health Sciences skill areas that directly involve sensorimotor intervention include acquiring body, facial/oral, and vocal imitations and a variety of gross and fine motor skills. The Health Sciences group also utilizes what they describe as "sensory-social routines"; these are simple interaction routines that are individually developed based on a child's sensory needs to help regulate his or her affect and arousal states (Rogers & Osaki-Bryant, 1995).

Clinically, there appears to be a variety of applications for integrating sensorimotor and behavior change–focused therapy techniques. The application ideas are presented here and organized roughly as they increase in the complexity of conceptualizing behavior and sensorimotor functioning. Many of these examples feature the combination of behavioral functional analysis/assessment and sensorimotor intervention carefully attuned to the needs of the individual with autism.

Sensory Experiences as Consequences

Many straightforward reinforcement surveys focus on materials and activities by form or type—for example, access to a particular object, person, food, etc. However, Dyer (1987) suggested that reinforcers be assessed in terms of stimulus preferences. An individual may enjoy, for instance, a variety of objects, activities, or foods that provide increased stimulation to the oral area. Because of the range of sensory responses in autism and the often strong preference or tolerance for certain types of sensory experiences, this approach provides for an individually designed set of reinforcers and an understanding of the specific reinforcing properties of the materials being used. Although sensory reinforcers may be effective for any individual with autism, individuals with autism at earlier developmental stages, either chronologically or functionally, may be especially likely to respond to and, indeed, to require this type of reinforcer.

Many clinical reports describe using pleasurable sensorimotor experiences as consequences/reinforcers for desired behaviors in children with autism, such as sitting in a chair, working on a task, and attending to adult interaction. This type of application tends to be described most by professionals working under the behavioral intervention framework. For example, Anderson, Taras, and Cannon (1996) described a teaching situation in which a child with autism received tickles, hugs, and candy after correcting imitating the trainer's model. Fisher, Lindauer, Alterson, and Thompson (1998) used toys producing "sensory stimulation similar to stereotypy" along with blocking undesired responses to decrease property destruction in a teenager with autism. Patel, Carr, and Dozier (1998) described using contingent access to the child's actual stereotyped responses to reinforce correct responses in operant teaching trials.

In contrast, if a behavioral functional analysis suggests that a sensory experience is maintaining an undesirable behavior, such as self-injury, removing access to that reinforcing sensory experience may be used to create "sensory extinction" (Kuhn, DeLeon, Fisher, & Wilke, 1999). For example, Van Houten (1993) described an intervention to reduce face-slapping that involved altering the sensory experience of a child with autism. A functional analysis suggested that sensory reinforcement was maintaining the child's face-slapping, so small padded weights were placed on the child's wrists to alter the sensory experience. The intervention was successful in almost completely eliminating the behavior for the next five months of monitoring.

Sensory Experiences as Communication Context

In contrast to the approaches described above, some autism treatment frameworks eschew the idea of adding an "artificial" reinforcer to increase a behavior. These frameworks turn instead to more naturally occurring situations to foster learning, especially to increase social-communication behaviors (Quill, 1995). They might use a pleasurable sensorimotor experience as the context for increasing communicative behaviors—for example, using actions to facilitate concept development and describing, and encouraging a child to use communicative intent and means to request a particular sensorimotor experience (Tomchek & Geis, 1997). Koegel, Koegel, and Parks (1995) described the method of teaching generalization and maintenance of skills that they apply in their work with individuals with autism. Their approach introduces the individual to the positive contingencies that naturally occur in consequence to appropriate behavior in a natural environment. For example, they cite the sensory experience of consuming an ice cream cone as a consequence to learning to request or purchase the item. Another clinical example from the author's experience involves facilitating verbalization through sensory experiences. A 3½-year-old boy with autism receiving discrete teaching trials while seated at a table was struggling with even a basic oral imitation program ("ah," "mm," open mouth, tongue out), until his mother pointed out that he often made sounds while playing on his swing set at home. Moving his oral imitation practice to the occupational therapy room, adding an affectively exaggerated social turn-taking element to the imitation, and conducting it during swinging led to slow but steady progress in verbalizations.

Sensory Conditions as Elicitors

Elicitors are antecedent events that evoke automatic and emotional responses. The behavioral conceptualization of sensory elicitors in autism is an assessment tool first, and thereafter an opportunity for intervention. In his description of behavioral assessment of individuals with autism, Powers (1998) emphasized four main steps: (1) identifying and describing target behavior(s); (2) assessing settings and antecedent and consequent stimuli controlling target behavior; (3) creating and implementing intervention; and (4) evaluating intervention efficacy. His discussion of step 2 highlights the relevance of the sensory functioning of an individual with autism to behavioral analysis. He explained that "elicitors," one category of antecedent stimuli, evoke automatic physiological or emotional responses, such as sweating, increased heart rate, feelings of panic, and desire to escape a situation. Powers (1998) also noted that target behavior maintained by sensory or "automatic" reinforcement, such as arousal reduction or induction, can be quite resistant to intervention. Given the heightened, reduced, or otherwise atypical sensory responses often reported, carefully attending to elicitors may be a crucial step in functional or behavioral assessment for individuals with autism.

A clinical example is a middle-childhood boy with autism who willingly left his classroom with the author to go to a testing room, but then refused to accompany her on the necessary path through the library, instead falling to the floor, holding his ears, screaming as if in pain, etc. An uninformed behavioral interpretation could suggest task avoidance, simple noncompliance, or confusion during a transition as the antecedent for the tantrum. A behavioral assessor more familiar with the sensory differences seen in autism, however, might recognize the echoes, large open space, or other physical aspect of the library's environment as a possible elicitor of unpleasant physical and emotional sensations for this child. In this case, the presence of a strong reinforcer (popcorn) waiting in the testing room, the use of earplugs, and prompting to use familiar coping strategies ("take calm breaths") enabled the boy to cross through the library environment.

Sensory Experiences To Reduce Self-Stimulation

Planned and directed sensorimotor experiences can be used to reduce self-stimulatory behaviors that interfere with a particular activity. For example, the author worked with a young woman with autism and severe mental retardation who displayed hand flapping of such vehemence that she attended to nothing else while flapping. The young woman was referred for behavioral consultation with a goal of reducing hand flapping. Over time, data collection showed that her hands were calm for brief periods after some but not all recess breaks. Further observation suggested that being pushed on the merry-go-round preceded the "quiet hands." This young woman's therapists, educators, and care-givers were able to systematically provide periodic opportunities for an intense vestibu-lar experience (e.g., being pushed on the out-side merry-go-round) and schedule table work or teaching a difficult task immediately after. The young woman's attention and her ability to sit still and use her hands to com-plete tasks was vastly improved for a short time after the intense vestibular experience.

As another example, when asked to con-sult regarding a child with autism who was displaying frequent wiggling and shifting in his desk and other self-stimulation during in-tense work time, the author, in coordination with an occupational therapist, determined that the fidgeting may have been functioning to keep the child alert and attending to chal-lenging paper-and-pencil tasks. Rather than focusing a behavioral program on eliminat-ing fidgeting, the team recommended plac-ing a small inflated cushion in the seat dur-ing table teaching sessions to provide a sensory experience to accomplish the needed alerting with more controlled movement.

Sensorimotor Experiences To Regulate for Cognitive Tasks and Behavior Management

Sensorimotor experiences can be used to obtain and maintain optimal arousal and regulation for a cognitive task that demands increased attention and effort from a child

with autism. For example, learning and cog-nitive profile analysis demonstrates that an-swering questions requiring language com-prehension is frequently a difficult task for children with autism—even those who are quite verbal (Minshew, Goldstein, & Siegel, 1997). Several children assessed by the au-thor became willing or able to put effort into such questions only when provided with a regulating sensory experience, such as sit-ting or being gently pushed into a therapy ball, holding a squeezable ball in their hands, or holding a weighted blanket on their lap.

Simpson and Gagnon (1999) described the behavioral technique of modifying com-mon antecedents to undesired behaviors—that is, identifying the setting or situation that usually occurs before a behavior and changing it. Directed sensorimotor experi-ences or alternatives to sensory bombard-ment can be used in this way to promote arousal regulation as a means of preventing behavioral difficulties (Dalrymple, 1995). For example, if a functional behavior analy-sis shows that tantrums regularly occur dur-ing a recess period for a young child with autism, one hypothesis could be that the child's arousal level became too high for control in this setting of low structure and high physical activity. As part of a preventive strategy, at an early point in the recess pe-riod, directed sensorimotor experiences could be implemented to bring arousal level down to a more manageable level. Similarly, the stabilizing force of a weighted vest might be tried during transitions between activities that seem to increase a child's arousal and anxiety to an unmanageable level.

Sensorimotor Experiences To Teach Cognitive Concepts and Skills for Learning

Sensorimotor experiences can be used to teach desired cognitive-behavioral skills. Durand (1999) pointed out the importance of teaching useful and functional skills to children with autism through the most enjoyable process possible. Sensorimotor activities can facilitate pleasure in learning activities. For example, rather than using physical prompting to teach a child to sit on command, a therapist might put sensory cause-effect toys on the table to elicit the child's approach to the chair. The child's natural approach and eventual compliance with the "sit" command can then be reinforced. Cause-effect toys are those that allow a child's action to create an immediate predictable result. Some popular cause–sensory effect objects are toys that vibrate, play music, or light up when pushed, and motion-activated sound toys.

As a more conceptual example, sequencing and memory for multiple commands, traditionally a skill assessed and addressed by neuropsychologists, psychologists, and others, can be practiced through sequences of sensorimotor activities. If a child with autism resists practicing verbal direction sequences or more functional sequences, like the steps of dressing, he or she may be more willing to try sequences of pleasurable sensorimotor activities represented by concrete locations, such as "Jump on the trampoline, go through the tunnel, and touch the wall." Because of the tasks' contribution to attention and arousal regulation, as described above, young children with autism seem especially likely to willingly take part in these learning activities, in contrast to more table-oriented, less active tasks working on similar skills.

Sensorimotor Experiences for Social Connection

Sensorimotor experiences are an ideal context for establishing socially connected or attachment behaviors between an adult and a child with autism or between two children.

For example, adults can encourage eye contact, proximity seeking/tolerance, or an affective response by providing an adult-controlled but child-responsive sensory activity in an developmentally appropriate format, such as an arm lotion massage, taking turns holding a vibrating toy, or a tactile game.

Although research shows that children with autism clearly show attachment to their primary caregivers, as evidenced by proximity seeking, differential responsiveness, etc. (Dissanayake & Crossley, 1996; Sigman & Mundy, 1989), they are less likely to engage in a class of "sociable" behaviors, including gaze and smile. Sensorimotor games can be used to teach parents to elicit these kinds of positive affective responses from their young children with autism. This is especially true for very young and irritable children with autism. For example, the author observed a highly irritable two-year-old boy diagnosed with autism enrolled in a gymnastics class for toddlers with developmental disabilities. According to his parents, he enjoyed playing with and lining toys by himself, and often laughed during these activities. His mood was negative when others interfered with his activities, however, and he cried inconsolably when he was brought to public places, such as the supermarket, and on his first day at the gymnasium. By the second gym session, however, he showed spontaneous eye contact paired with pleased laughter and response to his name as the gymnastics instructor bounced with him on the trampoline and caught him as he came down a slide. His mother was delighted with the behaviors she observed and reported that she was going to engage in more physically oriented play with him at home so that "he'll respond to me like that."

CONCLUSION

Psychological/behavioral and sensorimotor approaches overlap in theory, practice, and conceptualization of the disorder of autism. An occupational therapist, a physical therapist, a psychologist, or a behavioral interventionist might utilize a sensorily regulated state to increase the preceding behavior of a child with autism. All of these professionals might describe autism as a disorder involving motor-planning deficits and might teach skills embedded in sensorimotor activities. The unique presentations of individuals with autism offer unlimited opportunities for sensorimotor professionals to collaborate with and enhance the efficacy of psychologists using behavioral methods to teach skills and to modify the behavioral symptoms of autism. Some of the straightforward behavioral training and modification strategies in autism can be altered to involve more child choice and more coaxing than commanding with an understanding of sensory fears, motivators, arousal states, and other sensorimotor states. Similarly, psychologists' skills in assessment, functional analysis of behavior, and specialized teaching methods for individuals who do not respond to standard approaches can enhance the ability of sensorimotor professionals to assess and intervene in autism. The future of assessment and intervention in the complex disorder of autism lies in equally complex collaboration between professional disciplines with distinctive yet overlapping theory and methods.

CHAPTER REVIEW QUESTIONS

1. Compare the behavioral and sensorimotor approaches.
2. Give at least one specific application for each the following uses of sensory experiences: consequences, communication context, elicitor, to reduce self-stimulation, to regulate for tasks, to teach concepts and skills, and to facilitate social connections.
3. Compare the behavioral and sensorimotor interpretation of difficult behavior.

REFERENCES

American Psychiatric Association. (1994). *Diagnostic and statistical manual of mental disorders* (4th ed.). Washington, DC: Author.

Anderson, S., Taras, M., & Cannon, B. (1996). Teaching new skills to young children with autism. In C. Maurice, G. Green, & S. Luce (Eds.), *Behavioral intervention for young children with autism: A manual for parents and professionals* (pp. 181–194), Austin, TX: Pro-Ed.

Berkson, G. (1998). Brief report: Control in highly focused top-spinning. *Journal of Autism and Developmental Disorders, 28*(1), 83–86.

Bettelheim, B. (1967). *The empty fortress.* New York: Free Press.

Bregman, J., & Gerdtz, J. (1998). Behavioral interventions. In D. Cohen & F. Volkmar (Eds.), *Handbook of autism and pervasive developmental disorders* (pp. 606–630). New York: John Wiley & Sons.

Cantwell, D. P., Baker, L, & Rutter, M. (1979). Families of autistic and dysphasic children. *Archives of General Psychiatry, 36,* 682–687.

Cook, D. (1990). A sensory approach to the treatment and management of children with autism. *Focus on Autistic Behavior, 5*(6), 1–19.

Dahlgren, S., & Gillberg C. (1989). Symptoms in the first two years of life: A preliminary population study of infantile autism. *European archives of psychiatry & neurological sciences, 238,* 169–174.

Dalrymple, N. (1995). Environmental supports to develop flexibility and independence. In K. Quill (Ed.), *Teaching children with autism* (pp. 243–264). Albany, NY: Delmar.

Dawson, G., & Lewy, A. (1989). Reciprocal subcortical-cortical influences in autism: The role of attentional mechanisms. In G. Dawson (Ed.), *Autism: Nature, diagnosis, and treatment* (pp. 144–173). New York: Guilford.

Dawson, G., & Osterling, J. (1996). Early intervention in autism: Effectiveness and common elements of current approaches: In M. J. Guralnick (Ed.), *The effectiveness of early intervention: Second-generation research* (pp. 307–326). Baltimore: Paul H. Brookes.

Dissanayake, C., & Crossley, S. (1996). Proximity and sociable behaviors in autism: Evidence for attachment. *Journal of Child Psychology and Psychiatry, 37*(2), 149–156.

Durand, V. M. (1999). New directions in educational programming for students with autism. In D. Zager (Ed.), *Autism: Identification, education, and treatment* (2nd ed.) (pp. 323–343), Mahwah, NJ: Lawrence Erlbaum.

Dyer, K. (1987). The competition of autistic stereotyped behavior with usual and specially assessed reinforcers. *Research in Developmental Disabilities, 8,* 607–626.

Fisher, W., Lindauer, S., Alterson, C., & Thompson, R. (1998). Assessment and treatment of destructive behavior maintained by stereotypic object manipulation. *Journal of Applied Behavior Analysis, 31,* 513–527.

Holmes, D. L. (1998). *Autism through the lifespan.* Bethesda, MD: Woodbine House.

Kanner, L. (1943). Autistic disturbances of affective contact. *Nervous Child, 2,* 217–250.

Koegel, R. L., Koegel, L. K., & Parks, D. R. (1995). "Teach the individual" model of generalization: Autonomy through self-management. In R. L. Koegel. & L. K. Koegel (Eds.), *Teaching children with autism: Strategies for initiating positive interactions and improving learning opportunities* (pp. 67–77). Baltimore: Paul H. Brookes.

Koegel, R. L., Schreibman, L., O'Neill, R. E., & Burke, J. C. (1983). The personality and family-interaction characteristics of parents of autistic children. *Journal of Consulting and Clinical Psychology, 51,* 683–692.

Kuhn, D. E., DeLeon, I. G., Fisher, W. W., & Wilke, A. E. (1999). Clarifying an ambiguous functional analysis with matched and mismatched extinction procedures. *Journal of Applied Behavior Analysis, 32*(1), 99–102.

Lovaas, O. I. (1987). Behavioral treatment and normal educational and intellectual functioning in young autistic children. *Journal of Consulting and Clinical Psychology, 55,* 1, 3–9.

Lovaas, O. I., Schreibman, L., & Koegel, R. L. (1974). A behavior modification approach to the treatment of autistic children. *Journal of Autism and Childhood Schizophrenia, 4,* 111–129.

Mesibov, G. B. (1995). A comprehensive program for serving people with autism and their families. The TEACH model. In J. L. Matson (Ed.), *Autism in children and adults: Etiology, assessment, and intervention* (pp. 85–97). Belmont, CA: Brooks/Cole.

Mesibov, G., Adams, L., & Klinger, L. (1997). *Autism: Understanding the disorder.* New York and London: Plenum.

Minshew, N. J., Goldstein, G., & Siegel, D. J. (1997). Neuropsychologic functioning in autism: Profile of a complex information processing disorder. *Journal of the International Neuropsychological Society, 3*(4), 303–316.

Ornitz, E. M., & Ritvo., E. R. (1968). Perceptual inconstancy in early infantile autism: The syndrome of early infant autism and its variants including certain cases of childhood schizophrenia. *Archives of General Psychiatry, 18,* 76–98.

Patel, M. R., Carr, J. E., & Dozier, C. L. (1998). On the role of stimulus preference assessment in the evaluation of contingent access to stimuli associated with stereotypy during behavioral acquisition. *Behavioral Interventions, 13,* 269–274.

Powers, M. (1998). Behavioral assessment of individuals with autism. In D. Cohen & F. Volkmar (Eds.), *Handbook of autism and pervasive developmental disorders* (pp. 448–459). New York: John Wiley & Sons.

Quill, K. (1995). Enhancing children's social-communicative interactions. In K. Quill (Ed.), *Teaching children with autism* (pp. 163–186). Albany, NY: Delmar.

Rimland, B. (1964). Autistic children: Infancy to adulthood. *Seminars in Psychiatry, 2,* 435–450.

Rogers, S. (1998). Empirically supported comprehensive treatments for young children with autism. *Journal of Clinical Child Psychology, 27*(2), 168–179.

Rogers, S., & Osaki-Bryant, D. (1995). The Denver model curriculum. Unpublished manuscript, University of Colorado Health Services Center.

Rogers, S., & Pennington, B. (1991). A theoretical approach to the deficits in infantile autism. *Development and Psychopathology, 3,* 137–162.

Rutter, M. (1978). Etiology and treatment: Cause and cure. In M. Rutter & E. Schopler (Eds.), *Autism: A reappraisal of concepts and treatment* (pp. 327–335). New York: Plenum.

Schopler, E., & Reichler, R. (1970). *Developmental therapy by parents with their own autistic child.* Colloquium on Infantile Autism, Ciba Foundation, London.

Sigman, M., & Mundy, P. (1989). Social attachments in autistic children. *Journal of the American Academy of Child and Adolescent Psychiatry, 28*(1), 74–81.

Simpson, R., & Gagnon, E. (1999). Structuring and management strategies for children and youths with autism. In D. Zager (Ed.), *Autism: Identification, education, and treatment* (2nd ed.) (pp. 175–197). Mahwah, NJ: Lawrence Erlbaum.

Tomchek, S. D., & Geis, R. M. (1997). *Sensory processing, communication, and intervention strategies for the child with an autistic disorder.* Unpublished manuscript, University of Louisville, Kentucky.

Trevarthen, C., Aitken, K., Papoudi, D., & Robarts, J. (1998). *Children with autism: Diagnosis and intervention to meet their needs.* London: Jessica Kingsley Publishers.

Van Houten, R. (1993). The use of wrist weights to reduce self-injury maintained by sensory reinforcement. *Journal of Applied Behavior Analysis, 26,* 197–203.

Waterhouse, L., & Fein, D. (1998). Perspectives on social impairment. In D. Cohen & F. Volkmar (Eds.), *Handbook of autism and pervasive developmental disorders* (pp. 901–919). New York: John Wiley & Sons.

CHAPTER 12

Integration of the Sensorimotor Approach within the Classroom

Leah S. Dunn and Connie Donaldson

CHAPTER OBJECTIVES

At the completion of this chapter, the reader will be able to:

- Describe multiple methods for integrating sensorimotor interventions within educational programs.
- Describe the specific skills of occupational therapists using a sensorimotor approach to intervention that complements the skills of teachers.
- Interpret behaviors and barriers to learning from the sensorimotor perspective and apply a variety of techniques to manage difficult behaviors and promote optimal learning.
- Analyze a case study that applies sensorimotor interventions.

INTRODUCTION

The child with autism diagnosed early in life and attending school from 3 through 21 years of age spends about 20,520 hours in the school environment, assuming a 190-day school year and a 6-hour school day, and excluding summer school, private therapy, and tutoring. Of all the possible interventions for the child with autism, the educational system serves the child for the most time and has the potential for the greatest impact.

The child with autism is guaranteed the right to a free and appropriate education under IDEA, the Individuals with Disabilities Education Act of 1997. Through this federal legislation, the student with autism has access to a multidisciplinary evaluation to determine the need for:

- educational placement in the least restrictive environment
- special education services
- related services, including speech-language pathology, audiology, psychology, recreation, social work, counseling, occupational therapy, physical therapy, orientation, and mobility
- individualized programming

These service needs are designated on an individualized education program (IEP), a summary of the educational interventions for the student, which is updated at least annually.

As a member of the educational team, the occupational therapist evaluates the skills of a student with autism in the performance areas of self-care, work and educational tasks, and play/leisure skills. The occupational therapist also evaluates the sensorimotor, cognitive, and psychosocial components that underlie these skills and the effects of the performance context (environment and temporal aspects) on function, as defined by *Uniform Terminology for Occupational Therapy—Third Edition* (American Occupational Therapy Association [AOTA], 1994). Based on the child's needs and skilled clinical reasoning, the occupational therapist determines the appropriate frame of reference to guide evaluation and to develop an intervention plan. Occupational therapy services are provided along a continuum of care from direct student intervention to assisting the educational team in making modifications to the student's program (AOTA, 1997).

The occupational therapist's education includes the study of the sensory integration (SI) frame of reference. One misconception within the educational field is that an occupational therapist must be "Sensory Integration Certified" to serve the student with autism. This misconception arises from the requirements necessary to become certified to administer and interpret the Sensory Integration and Praxis Tests; the certification process is for this testing procedure only. The entry-level occupational therapist has studied SI theory as part of the educational requirements needed to become an occupational therapist. Although no other certification is necessary for using SI, continuing education provides the occupational therapist with additional knowledge and ongoing development of skills, which is beneficial to students.

In this chapter, a sensorimotor approach using principles from the SI frame of reference is presented. The program was designed for implementation in one school within a Learning Disability–Self-Contained classroom. This class consisted of four students, three with autism and one with attention deficit disorder. The program was also utilized with higher-functioning students with autism, who received services in a resource classroom but were included in regular classrooms at other times during the school day.

Within the context of these two classrooms, the sensorimotor approach to management was based on the belief that students are considerably influenced by the environmental demands of any situation and that fundamental prerequisite skills, including attention, optimal arousal, and self-regulation, are needed for optimal learning. These beliefs about the influences on learning are described in the following sections in relation to the sensorimotor approach to management.

PREREQUISITE TO LEARNING

Effects of Environmental Demands

The environment of the classroom must provide safe opportunities for exploration and support for the prerequisites to optimal learning. Three key elements—the physical environment, the interaction styles of students and teacher, and the learning activities—should be assessed in the classroom and could be modified to support learning. For optimal learning, these elements must be matched to the needs of the child. Richter and Oetter (1990) described progressive matrices that characterize these elements of environmental demands. The four types of environmental matrices, in order of complexity, are the womb, the mother, kid power, and brain power. The exploration of these matrices provides a conceptual framework for analyzing and modifying the environment.

The womb matrix is best described as an area with diminished sensory input, with space or equipment to allow the child to use limited yet rhythmic movement with the body in some flexion, like a modified fetal position. In womb space, the student is able reorganize when experiencing sensory overload. This context is similar to the environment and stimulation that a mother uses to calm her baby. A classroom example is sitting inside a tent for reading.

Interacting with another person or an object positioned 8 to 10 inches away is indicative of the mother matrix, which is one of support and nurturing. Sensory input in this matrix consists, usually, of nonverbal communication such as patting and bouncing—just as a mother plays with her infant. In the classroom, the teacher may sit close to the student to be able to use touch to reinforce correct behaviors or to maintain optimal attention.

As a student develops physically, he or she also develops the need to master the earth and his body. In the kid power matrix, the student is in control and is using his or her body to work against gravity and to develop physical capabilities. Activities seen in the kid power matrix are heavy work, large movements, control and gradation of movement, and movement off the ground. This is easily observed on the playground and during gym class. In the classroom, the primary matrix observed is the brain power matrix. Brain power requires cognition, problem solving, social interaction, complex language, and comprehension.

As noted above, the three elements of the environment—physical environment, interaction styles, and learning activities—must be carefully matched to the needs of the child for optimal learning. Suppose that the educational task is learning to add single digits. The student may interact in a nonverbal manner (mother matrix) and the teacher in a highly verbal manner (brain power). Imagine further that the physical environment includes three other students with instructional aides, all of whom are highly verbal. Finally, consider the educational task of addition, which requires the skills of number recognition and counting using fingers. If the student is experiencing sensory overload—that is, feeling overwhelmed by these incoming stimuli—then his or her ability to filter out irrelevant information, to pay attention to the teacher's verbal instruction, and to learn is diminished.

Using the concepts of the matrix system to promote optimal learning, the teacher may choose to change the physical environment, his or her interaction style, or the learning activity. To change the physical environment to a less demanding matrix, the student might be taught within a small tent, simulating a womb space, or allowed time to engage in heavy work, a kid power activity. The teacher could change his or her interactional style and introduce visual prompts, or use more nonverbal communication consistent with the mother matrix. Alternatively, the teacher could change the activity—for example, show the student the numbers to be added (e.g., 5 + 3), let him or her count the addends separately using tokens (e.g., 5 counting bears tokens and 3 counting bears tokens), and then count all the tokens together, simplifying the demands of a brain power matrix.

Recognizing the environmental demands of the school setting and the student's arousal level enables the educational team to provide an effective strategy to enhance learning. Inappropriate behavior or the student's difficulty with the academic task may be due to the demands on a student to respond in a brain power matrix when the student's nervous system needs kid power–type activities.

Optimal Attention, Arousal, and Self-Regulation

As Mercer and Snell (1997) wrote, "To attend, concentrate, and perform tasks in a manner suitable to the situational demand, one's nervous system must be in an optimal state of arousal for that particular task." Students with autism may display paradoxical attention, with unusually long attention for self-initiated activity but very short attention for specific skill development (Rapin, 1997). Because of this, students with autism were suspected of either perceiving all stimuli as novel and consequently attending to everything, or perceiving all stimuli as non-novel and thus ignoring them (Nelson, 1984). Thus, attention is linked, in part, to arousal and the perception of incoming stimuli.

Maintaining attention for learning in a classroom requires self-regulation. Williams & Shellenberger (1996) defined self-regulation as "the ability to attain, maintain, and change arousal appropriately for a task or situations" (pp. 1–5), and DeGangi (1995) described it as "the internal capacity to tolerate sensory stimulation from the environment and others" (p. 4). Williams and Shellenberger described three levels of self-regulation. First-order regulation develops earliest and is the function of the autonomic nervous system for maintaining temperature, blood pressure, heart rate, muscle tone, sleep/wake cycles, and arousal state. As motor skills emerge, second-order self-regulation develops, including the sensorimotor coordination of suck/swallow/breathe and vocal patterns. Older students and adults still use second-order self-regulation, as evidenced by the number of people who chew pencil erasers while reading. Advanced cognitive skills are required for third-order self-regulation. These include problem solving; expressive language; internal language; organization of space, time, and tasks; and the ability to recognize the need to change arousal state (Oetter, Richter, & Frick, 1993).

The Alert Program

The Alert Program, by Williams and Shellenberger (1996) was developed for use in the educational system and applied in a specific school program. This program is based in theories of arousal and is designed to help the student learn self-regulation. The Alert Program is a curriculum originally designed for 8–12-year-old students with attention and learning issues, but it has been adapted for various populations. Students employing the program learn to recognize the symptoms of an extremely alert state, a just-right state, and a not-alert state, using the analogy of a car engine. Not only does the student recognize his symptoms but also the educational team can use the student's perceptions and self-evaluation to plan educational activities or change environmental demands to optimize the alert state. The Alert Program encourages team members to become detectives to help with planning and recognition of sensory diet strategies that support function (Shellenberger, 1999).

Sensory Diet

The term *sensory diet*, coined by Wilbarger and Wilbarger (1991), is used to describe the sensorimotor requirements for an optimal state of alertness. A sensory diet consists of second-order self-regulation activities. Just as a nutritional diet provides fuel for the body, the sensory diet provides the right combination of sensory input needed for peak performance. Some sensory input is like a snack (low intensity and short duration), such as bubble gum; other sensory input is like a meal (high intensity, such as swinging), providing longer-lasting fulfillment. A sensory diet can be implemented through several means:

- Providing a series of quick sensory tune-ups throughout the day. For example, the entire class could change locations when starting a new activity, providing gross motor movement.
- Attending to interaction with others. For instance, students who are defensive to auditory input and respond to certain tones of voice with fight or flight may need a calming style of interaction. Other students with different sensory needs may benefit from an alerting or a factual interaction. Matching the student's alert state with a teacher's physical ability and interactional style is important in maximizing educational impact.
- Structuring the environment to provide necessary sensory input. Environmental changes like scheduling alternate sedentary and active activities, offering snacks of different texture and tastes, allowing students to lie on a bean bag chair during reading group, and changing the visual distraction in the classroom may provide the necessary input for optimal arousal levels.
- Helping the student develop leisure activities that are appropriate for sensory input (Wilbarger 1995). For example, a student may perform better if he or she

has regular opportunities to swim or ride a horse.

One must be a detective to successfully implement a sensory diet in the classroom. Recognizing outward symptoms of the arousal state is a crucial skill in this detective work. For example, careful documentation of the student's responses to stimuli over time helps identify patterns of behavior, especially because the effects of sensory stimulation can accumulate over time (Wilbarger & Wilbarger, 1991). Consequently, for instance, behaviors exhibited at home may result from the sensory experiences during the school day.

Sensory Input and Management in the Classroom

We can now turn our attention to application of these ideas. In the sensorimotor approach to management, adequate sensory processing is thought to be fundamental for academic learning. Although students with autism have varied intellectual abilities, from above average to well below average, they often have major difficulty with sensory processing, being either hyper- or hyporesponsive to sensory stimuli in all major sensory systems (Dunn & Fisher, 1983; Kientz & Dunn, 1997; see also Chapter 1). These differences in sensitivity may result in a high level of arousal or alertness because of a need to maintain an "ever-ready-to-act" state to avoid noxious stimuli or diminished responsiveness to stimuli. The stimuli may be interpreted as danger, resulting in a fight-or-flight response. Conversely, the nervous system has a built-in safety system that shuts down in response to perceived danger stimuli. In either situation, attention and learning are impaired.

Attention and optimal learning rely on adequate processing of sensory information from the main sensory systems: vestibular, proprioceptive, tactile, visual, auditory, and gustatory. Because any single sensory stimulus may affect more than one system, it is difficult to isolate the effects of each system. The following section nevertheless is organized for simplicity and clarity by sensory system, and presented to illustrate the functions of each system.

Vestibular System

The vestibular system includes the sensory receptors of the inner ear, the sensory processing systems within the brain stem and the cerebellum, and the influence of these systems throughout the brain (Ayres, 1979). The system provides information on the speed and direction of head movement and responses to gravity. It is responsible for letting the student know location, movement, speed, and direction of movement.

A student with a hypersensitive (overly sensitive) vestibular system does not like to move, avoids roughhousing, and often experiences motion sickness. Due to the fear of movement, the student may become distressed during transition times requiring movement, lack basic movement skills, or avoid unfamiliar playground equipment. This student may seek a womb space to avoid movement. In contrast, the student who is in constant motion is suspected of having a hyposensitive (insensitive) vestibular system; this student may crave spinning

and rocking, never becoming dizzy. Aspects of an active or a passive response to sensory input influence this behavioral expression so that, for example, a person with a hyposensitivity to movement may also respond with low sensory registration and disregard of vestibular input (see Chapter 1).

When observing the student with autism during movement, several qualities of the movement should be observed that provide clues to the use of movement to optimize arousal. Is the movement rhythmic and slow, or arrhythmic and fast (starts and stops)? During movement, is the head moving up and down (e.g., jumping), side-to-side or linearly (e.g., swinging), or in rotation (e.g., spinning). Does the movement or movement activity (e.g., going down the stairs) increase or decrease the level of arousal? In Table 12–1, the qualities of vestibular stimulation and their usual effects on arousal are displayed. Because the vestibular system is extremely sensitive, changes of arousal state may occur as much as two hours after the stimulation; this lagged response must be considered when introducing any vestibular stimulation. Within the school setting, several options are available for using vestibular stimulation to change arousal state and attention. A skilled occupational therapist might use swings—several were developed specifically for sensorimotor input—but these require constant supervision by an adult trained in the recognition of autonomic

Table 12–1 The Qualities of Vestibular Stimulation and the Effects on Arousal

Vestibular Input	Calming	Alerting
Flow	Rhythmic	Arrhythmic
Direction	One direction	Multidirectional
Speed	Slow	Fast
Quality	Continuous	Starts and stops
Example	Rocking	Jumping

nervous system symptoms associated with overarousal.

Within the classroom, changing the environmental matrix to a kid power matrix is an excellent way to incorporate movement. The student can practice counting skills while jumping on a mini-trampoline. He or she can sit or lie on a therapy ball or physioroll and reach for manipulatives or complete coloring projects. Rocking or using a glider during reading group can calm a hypersensitive student enough to allow him or her to attend to the reading. Air-filled seat cushion in the student's seat or an inflated inner tube used during circle time can provide enough vestibular stimulation to keep his or her arousal state appropriate. A playground break is always a welcome event. Many classrooms of students with autism benefit from having two to three recesses a day.

Proprioceptive System

The sensory receptors for the proprioceptive system are located in the muscles and joints; they provide feedback on body position and force/extent of movement. The proprioceptive system is stimulated by heavy work or work against resistance or traction to the joints. When pushing and pulling something heavy, the joints are pulled slightly apart or compressed, sending information to the brain about the force and extent of movement. Stimulation of the proprioceptive system is thought to have a calming effect on students if they are overaroused and an alerting effect if underaroused (Ayres, 1979)—that is, proprioception normalizes arousal from either a hyper- or hypoarousal level to a more optimal level.

Firm pressure can be applied by hugging, crawling under heavy bean bag chairs, lying under weighted blankets, and carrying heavy items. Traction can be applied by having the student pull on something heavy,

such as a piece of Theraband attached to his or her desk. Another acceptable way is to have the student deliver the library books to the library using a wagon. Students can stack chairs, wipe tables, and mop floors in the cafeteria. Gardening is an excellent and enjoyable way to provide heavy work and incorporate a science lesson at the same time. Jumping on a mini-trampoline provides proprioceptive input as well as vestibular input. Use of resistive manipulatives (e.g., Legos, bristle blocks, snap blocks, clay) provides proprioceptive input to the hands. Cleaning the chalkboard, doing laundry, and filling the soft drink machine can provide proprioceptive input and prevocational training.

Tactile System

The sensory receptors for the tactile system are located in the skin. The tactile system has both a protective function—to facilitate avoidance of potential danger, like when a spider crawls on your arm—and a discriminative function—to select a nickel from a pile of change in your pocket. A student with tactile sensitivity is relatively easy to identify. This student avoids all touch, does not get hands messy with paint or glue, is particular about his clothing (e.g., long sleeves, long pants, or no shoes), and may hit to avoid touch from his peers. Additionally, this student may have difficulty standing in line or may demand to be the line-leader or door-holder to avoid having someone in front of and behind him or her.

Activities that typically calm a student with tactile sensitivity include those that require firm touch. Light touch can be aversive, but firm touch often produces a positive response in the student with autism (Ayres, 1979; see Table 12–2). Firm touch can be provided in ball tents, rice/bean bins, heavy massage, and pressing between pillows or bean bag chairs, for example.

Table 12–2 The Qualities of the Tactile System and the Effect on Arousal

Tactile System	Calming	Alerting
Pressure	Heavy, firm	Light
Duration	Quick or long	Quick

Visual System

The visual system is responsible for visual acuity, eye movement, and perception. The student who is hypersensitive to visual stimuli may avoid eye contact, squint, and exhibit symptoms of fight or flight (high arousal state) when presented with highly visual stimuli. This student may be constantly distracted by materials on the wall or hanging from the ceiling in the classroom. He or she may insist on wearing a brimmed hat or long bangs. It is recommended that one classroom wall be minimally decorated to allow a safe place for visually defensive students to look in order to better attend to the teacher. Room dividers can be cut from large appliance boxes and placed appropriately to block visual stimuli. Wearing a visor blocks some visual stimuli. Fluorescent lights can be covered with thin, colorful material to filter the brightness, or some lights can be turned off. For some students, it may be necessary to use incandescent rather than fluorescent lighting, which often flickers.

A student with hyposensitivity to visual stimuli requires bright, complex visual stimuli to attend to the educational tasks. Suggestions to increase the complexity of visual stimuli include:

- Placing Christmas tree lights around the educational material (e.g., calendar), turned on only during the instructional time.
- Using laser pens to point out information on the chalkboard.

- Using colored pens and pencils and changeable markers for both the student and teacher.
- Using an overhead projector.
- Using a wipe-off board with colored markers.

Auditory System

The auditory system alerts the student to sounds, prepares the body for attention (Ayres, 1979), and supports communication. Because the school environment has many highly auditory areas, such as hallways, the auditorium, the gym, the cafeteria, the playground, the bus, and the restroom, students who are sensitive to sounds may be in a heightened state of arousal and even a state of fight or flight. It is important to observe the behaviors of the student, which provide clues to understanding his or her response to these sounds (Table 12–3). Students with auditory hypersensitivity can wear headphones, like those designed for skeet shooters, or ear plugs when they must be in these areas. Some children may benefit from listening to music through a headset to screen out the unpredictable sounds around them. Firm pressure (e.g., hugs, squeezes, weighted pillows, weighted blanket, heavy backpack) may provide a calming effect and reduce the sensory overload from the auditory stimuli. Within the classroom, the teacher or occupational therapist can experiment with various sounds played quietly in the background. Classical tapes and relaxation tapes are calming, while swing music and rap tend to be more alerting. Singing

Table 12–3 The Qualities of the Auditory System and the Effect on Arousal

Auditory System	Calming	Alerting
Tempo	Slow	Fast
Rhythm	Regular	Irregular
Loudness	Quiet	Loud

verbal commands can help students attend to the lesson.

Gustatory System

The gustatory system, with sensory receptors located in the mouth and along the digestive tract, is responsible for nutrition and provides feedback on tastes. Oetter et al. (1993) classified the alerting and calming aspects of various therapeutic materials. Oral motor activity and tastes affect arousal states; these effects are displayed in Table 12–4. Activities can be designed to provide the appropriate stimulation (alerting or calming) at appropriate times (snack and meals) during the schoolday. An example of using foods during the day to adjust arousal states is allowing the student to eat pretzels during overly stimulating activities, such as assemblies. Chewing activities provide proprioceptive input, which often normalizes arousal level. Of course, food allergies must be considered when implementing any program involving foods.

Students who are hypersensitive in the oral area are willing to eat a limited number of foods with specific textures or tastes, possibly affecting nutritional status. They may avoid chewing food or closing their mouth around foods. Working with the student in preparing foods can sometimes encourage a greater interest in a variety of foods. Students who do not register the sensory input from the mouth often do not chew food well, have abnormal gag reflexes, stuff food into their mouths, and choke frequently. Both types of students benefit from additional oral tactile activities to enhance oral sensory processing.

CASE STUDY

Within the classroom, it is important to look at the functional abilities of the student from all aspects, not just one theoretical viewpoint (Ayres, 1979; Murray & Anzalone, 1991). This case study illustrates many approaches—sensorimotor, educational, behavioral, and others—used in combination to improve the functional independence of a student with autism.

Background Information

Mark is a seven-year-old student whose autism was identified at the age of five years. Although he attended a preschool program, he did not receive any other early

Table 12–4 The Qualities of the Oral System and the Effect on Arousal

Gustatory (Oral)	Calming	Alerting
Taste	Sweet	Hot, sour, bitter
Oral motor quality	Sucking, chewing	Chewing, crunching

intervention. While in a half-day kindergarten program, he received resource special education services, speech therapy, occupational therapy, and adaptive physical education. Kindergarten was difficult for Mark. Activities such as music class and physical education often resulted in Mark crying, screaming, and trying to leave the room. Due to his outbursts, regular gym class was replaced with one-to-one instruction from the adaptive physical education teacher; speech therapy services were scheduled during music time.

Mark was rigid in his need for specific routines and instruction from the teacher. For example, purple scissors were first used during a cutting activity; subsequently, he wanted to use purple scissors for all cutting activities. Mark's self-stimulatory behaviors of opening windows and turning lights on and off interfered with academic learning. In the resource special education room, he was reluctant to join the other children for group instruction, such as calendar. When his routines were upset, Mark threw himself on the floor ranting. Eating pretzels appeared to calm him during these episodes. Mark was particular about what he ate. He did not eat slippery foods, such as bananas; a typical lunch was chips and a package of cupcakes. Mark chewed on his clothing and the mulch on the playground.

Because of these behaviors, the educational team realized that Mark's current educational placement was not benefiting him; consequently, it was not the most appropriate. The team decided to transition Mark to another school into a self-contained classroom with four other students with autism. To prepare for this change, his new teacher made a book about his new school containing photos of his new classmates, special education teacher, teacher assistants, occupational therapist, speech language patholo-gist, adaptive physical education teacher, principal, and the music/art/library/computer/gym special area teachers. His new special education teacher visited him during the last month of his kindergarten year and during summer school to ease the transition.

Baseline Data in Self-Contained Classroom

To investigate Mark's sensorimotor needs and arousal level throughout the day, baseline data were taken. The occupational therapist instructed the educational team on how to document the behaviors they observed. Educational team members were encouraged to write descriptions of the behaviors they observed on a form adapted from the Alert Program (Williams & Shellenberger, 1996) (see Figure 12–1). Changes in behaviors or environments were indicated on the form. When Mark was difficult to engage in the activity presented, the educational team member noted the time and the behavior on the data collection form. The occupational therapist asked the parents to complete the observation form, too; they were very cooperative. Data were collected 24 hours a day for 10 days to obtain 7 days of full data, including school and a 3-day weekend. Observation data collected at home enlightened the team as to the student's sensory needs. Without the demands of the educational environment, Mark was able to seek out the sensorimotor input that he needed.

While observation data were being collected, the occupational therapist used pictures from the Alert Program (Williams & Shellenberger, 1996) to ask Mark what he liked and disliked. His preferences were confirmed or refuted by his teacher or parent. Additionally, the teacher elaborated on the responses and behaviors that resulted when Mark engaged in one of his favorite

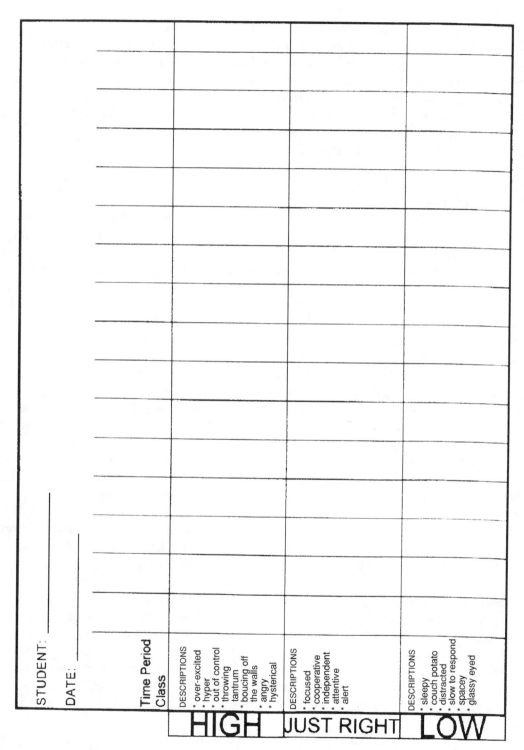

Figure 12–1 Alert level baseline data sheet. *Source:* Adapted with permission from Williams & Shellenberger, How Does Your Engine Run?, © 1994, Therapy Works, Inc.

activities. For example, although Mark really liked to bounce on a therapy ball, his arousal level became too high for classroom work and diminished optimal attention.

The occupational therapist and special education teacher reviewed the observation data to determine what sensory diet activities were needed to help Mark maintain an appropriate arousal state for learning. The initial data collected demonstrated that Mark's attention span was approximately 7 minutes; however, the class was organized in 15-minute instructional sessions. Mark's instructional sessions were modified to include an academic (brain power) task and a sensorimotor (kid power) task to help regulate his level of alertness. The Wilbarger and Wilbarger (1991) Brushing Protocol was implemented every 90 minutes for two weeks and decreased as Mark required it less. Visual prompts and social stories were used to prepare Mark for changes in his routine or his environment.

Mark's teacher wrote the social stories with input from the occupational therapist, speech and language therapist, and parents. The stories were kept at Mark's desk, and an additional copy was sent home. Mark's mother reported that, although he never was interested in books before, he took an immediate liking to his social stories because the stories were about him. At school, the teacher and teacher assistant designated a regular schedule for reading Mark's social stories. Mark quickly memorized the stories. The first stories targeted inappropriate behaviors and explanations of changes in routine. Social stories were also used to teach Mark about the sensorimotor activities that he needed to use to calm himself, encouraging him to learn self-regulation.

The occupational therapist focused her initial therapy sessions with Mark on finding what movement exercises he preferred and additionally were calming. These activities were swinging, jumping on a mini-trampoline, being pressed in the floor mats, crawling in a cloth tunnel, and doing chin-ups on a bar. The teacher and teacher assistants were shown how to do these activities with Mark.

Sensory Diet

In order to teach Mark how to self-regulate his level of alertness in a socially acceptable manner and to take responsibility for his sensory needs, a binder with visual cues was developed. Figure 12–2 is a picture of the binder, which combined both behavioral and sensorimotor approaches. The front of the binder displayed Mark's behavior board, with targeted behaviors identified. Both positive rewards (earning bonuses to get free time) and negative consequences (partial loss of recess time) were used. Although recess was an important and needed event that the team was reluctant to withdraw, it was the only consequence that had meaning for Mark. Additionally, he always retained some recess time to allow him some unstructured, outside down time.

Figure 12–3 demonstrates the use of the Alert Program (Williams & Shellenberger, 1996). On the left side of the binder, the student identified whether his or her engine was running just right, high, or low, and moved the appropriate car to the plastic pocket. If running too high, he or she chose activities from the visual cues under the car; these activities had been determined by experience to calm him or her. If his or her engine was running just right, the student determined that he or she was demonstrating appropriate attention and behavior, earning bonuses on the front of the binder. Because Mark had never been observed to have a low-running engine, no activities chosen to

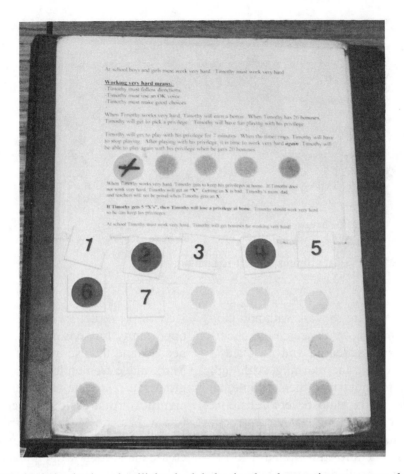

Figure 12–2 Mark's behavior board, utilizing both behavioral and sensorimotor approaches.

alert him were included. The pencil pocket held items that could be used to help Mark keep his engine just right (second-order self-regulation), such as fidget toys and gum. The right side of the binder included a list of strategies to help Mark attend. This system was constantly monitored and adapted to fit Mark's needs. He carried it with him throughout the schoolday.

Due to Mark's intolerance of certain food textures and his pattern of chewing on clothing and mulch, oral motor preferences were evaluated. His need for chewing to calm him was recognized and edible items were made available to replace the nonedible items.

Mark was given a container of pretzels to keep at his desk at all times. He also earned chewy candies and foods throughout the day and was given access to ice for chewing at all times.

Mark's class was highly structured. A visual schedule with a photos of the educational team member he was scheduled to work with during each interval was used. Every 15 minutes, the timer rang and the teacher changed a color card; this cued the students to check their schedules and turn their schedule to match the teacher's color card. When they matched their schedule to the teacher's color card, they saw a photo of

Figure 12–3 Mark's visual prompts for self-regulation.

the person they were to work with and then went to that person. Mark seemed to understand his visual schedule and checked it when he arrived in the morning. Although he appeared to understand the schedule, he had difficulty during almost every transition, especially those requiring leaving the room (music, gym, etc.). At transitions, Mark checked his schedule and flipped it to the next working interval, then threw himself on the floor. When instructed to get up, Mark whined, cried, or screamed. The teacher and assistants quickly learned that trying to reason with Mark only escalated his behaviors.

At the beginning of the school year, the teacher and assistants physically assisted Mark in the transition. It was common for Mark to be in tears, cradled in the teacher's lap, chewing ice until he calmed down and could make the transition. Social stories and sensorimotor strategies were used to help Mark remain calm during transitions. Additionally, he was constantly redirected to his behavior binder to assist him in problem solving during these episodes.

With the structure of the classroom, the opportunity for sensorimotor activity when needed, and the use of the behavior binder, Mark made tremendous gains in this program. Currently, he experiences periods of significant distress only once about every two weeks. As Mark's self-regulation improves, his program will be modified to increase integration with typical peers.

Recognizing and respecting a student's sensorimotor needs has improved the education of students with autism. Investing the time and energy to observe the student and learn the uniqueness of his or her sensorimotor needs pays off in the long run. Each student's needs are as unique as his or her fingerprint. By modifying the educational environment to meet the needs of the student, the educational team makes the first step in building the self-regulating skills needed for the typical educational environment. It takes time and the willingness to change strategies to match the student's needs to ultimately improve integration and success with typical peers.

CHAPTER REVIEW QUESTIONS

1. Describe characteristics of each of the four types of environmental matrices.
2. List at least three ideas for maintaining optimal attention, arousal, and self-regulation to promote optimal learning.
3. List the calming characteristics of sensory input.
4. What concepts or principles of intervention are illustrated in the case study of Mark?

REFERENCES

American Occupational Therapy Association. (1994). Uniform terminology for occupational therapy: Third edition. *American Journal of Occupational Therapy, 48,* 1047–1054.

American Occupational Therapy Association. (1997). Statement: Sensory integration evaluation and intervention in school-based occupational therapy. *American Journal of Occupational Therapy, 51,* 861–863.

Ayres, A. J. (1979). *Sensory integration and the child.* Los Angeles: Western Psychological Services.

DeGangi, G. (1995). *Sensorimotor and attentional deficits: Assessment and treatment for infants and children.* Paper presented at the annual meeting of the Easter Seal Society, Dallas, Texas.

Dunn, W., & Fisher, A. G. (1983). Sensory registration, autism, and tactile defensiveness. *Sensory Integration Special Interest Section Newsletter, 6*(2), 3–4.

Kientz, M. A., & Dunn, W. (1997). A comparison of the performance of children with and without autism on the Sensory Profile. *American Journal of Occupational Therapy, 51,* 530–537.

Mercer, C. D., & Snell, M. E. (1977). *Learning theory in mental retardation: Implications for teaching.* Columbus, OH: Charles E. Merrill.

Murray, E. A., & Anzalone, M. E. (1991). Integrating sensory integration theory and practice with other intervention approaches. In A. G. Fisher, E. A. Murray, & A. C. Bundy (Eds.), *Sensory integration: Theory and practice* (pp. 354–383). Philadelphia: F. A. Davis.

Nelson, D. L. (1984). *Children with autism and other pervasive disorders of development and behavior therapy through activities.* Thorofare, NJ: Slack.

Oetter, P., Richter, E. W., & Frick, S. M. (1993). *MORE: Integrating the mouth with sensory and postural functions.* Hugo, MN: PDP Press.

Rapin, I. (1997). Autism. *New England Journal of Medicine, 337,* 97–104.

Richter, E., & Oetter, P. (1990). Environmental matrices for sensory integrative treatment. In S. C. Merrill (Ed.), *Environment: Implications for occupational therapy practice* (pp. 24–44). Rockville, MD: American Occupational Therapy Association.

Shellenberger, S. (1999, August 26). Personal communication.

Wilbarger, P. (1995). The sensory diet: Activity programs based on sensory processing theory. *Sensory Integration Special Interest Section Newsletter, 18,* 1–4.

Wilbarger, P., & Wilbarger, J. L. (1991). *Sensory defensiveness in children aged 2–12: An intervention guide for parents and other caretakers.* Denver: Avanti Educational Programs.

Williams, M. S., & Shellenberger, S. (1994). *How does your engine run? A leader's guide to the Alert Program for self-regulation.* Albuquerque, NM: Therapy Works.

CHAPTER 13

Play: Engaging Young Children with Autism

Grace T. Baranek, Debra B. Reinhartsen, and Suzanne W. Wannamaker

CHAPTER OBJECTIVES

At the completion of this chapter, the reader will be able to:

- Understand the terminology for play within developmental and process models.
- Describe the strengths and weaknesses related to play competencies and social play interaction among persons with autism.
- Understand the sensory and motor characteristics of autism that influence play behavior.
- Appreciate the complexity of play and describe its relevance to social, cognitive, and sensorimotor development.
- Differentiate between therapeutic interventions using play as a strategy and enhancing play as an outcome.
- Analyze play goals and the characteristics of play spaces, materials, and interpersonal interactions.
- Differentiate between assessment procedures for play competency and for playfulness and identify specific tests used for each procedure.
- Understand and systematically apply current research and multiple play engagement strategies to enhance play competencies and playfulness for persons with autism.

INTRODUCTION

Case Vignette

Jimmy enters a play room filled with new toys he received for his third birthday. He walks past his mother and younger brother without looking at them or indicating a greeting. He immediately runs over to a wooden train set and picks up the train car. He lies down

ACKNOWLEDGMENTS

We thank Dr. Ruth Humphry for her helpful suggestions and constructive comments on this manuscript. Also, we are grateful to Paul, Paul, Jane, and Karl, for their support, patience, and encouragement throughout this process.

on the floor, examines it closely, and then begins to spin the wheels repeatedly with his fingers. This continues for several minutes as he is silent, seemingly transfixed by the spinning wheels. Jimmy's younger brother, Matthew, age 18 months, attempts to get his attention, taking another train car and holding it up for Jimmy to see. "Choo-choo," he says to Jimmy as he shows the train. Jimmy does not respond, but continues his preoccupation with the movement of the wheels. Jimmy's mother playfully interrupts Jimmy and guides his visual attention to the tracks. She places another car on the track and models pushing the train. Gently she moves Jimmy's hand holding his train car toward the track, and he follows suit by placing it appropriately. Jimmy never looks up or changes his expression, but pushes the train along the tracks with regular cues from his mother. Jimmy's mother says, "Train goes choo-choo!" and playfully tickles Jimmy to get laughter and a big smile. The interchange is contagious; Matthew giggles in delight while watching. The three continue to expand the game, playfully moving the trains along the circle of tracks and taking turns repeating "choo-choo!"

Jimmy, like other children with autism, has significant limitations in play skills that produce difficulties engaging in meaningful interactions with his physical and social worlds. The purposes of this chapter are to describe the nature of play in autism based on empirical research and to provide guidelines for play assessment and intervention strategies for practitioners working with young children with autism and related disorders.

DEFINING PLAY

Play is considered one of the primary occupations of a child—one that is not only expected but also encouraged. Play has implications for the child's ability to participate within defined sociocultural roles. Although developmental processes may be similar, play preferences and structures are often culturally specific. For example, types of play exhibited by girls versus boys, or children in the United States versus those in Argentina, may vary tremendously (Bornstein, Haynes, Pascual, Painter, & Galperin, 1999). In the case vignette of Jimmy, for example, it is clear that playing functionally and symbolically with trains is culturally encouraged; however, it is unclear how much Jimmy, given the nature of his disability, is able to perceive the social cues and models that shape the structure of play.

It is easy to recognize that a young child is playing, yet difficult to reach a consensus about a definition of play. Play theorists define play in many ways. One common approach is to elucidate various stages or developmental progressions of play skills, focusing on one or more important dimensions—for example, symbolic play skills or social play (e.g., Knox, 1996; Nicolich, 1977; Parten, 1932; Piaget, 1962; Takata, 1974; Ungerer, Zelazo, Kearsley, & O'Leary, 1981). Such play constructs designate a form or structure and a sequence for play in young children. For example, Jimmy's development indicates cognitive stages of exploratory and manipulative object play, with little ability to engage in the functional or symbolic play expected of a typically developing three-year-old. Like-wise, Jimmy prefers to engage in isolated or solitary play activities, but is capable of slightly more advanced behaviors (e.g., on-looker and parallel play), given adaptations to the social structure.

Other researchers focus on the process of play, stressing characteristics that bring about a playful quality in engagement with persons and objects. The level of intrinsic motivation, internal locus of control, and the ability to suspend reality during play are three key characteristics that enable the playful process and provide individually de-termined meaning to the play activity (Bundy, 1996; Morrison, Metzger, & Pratt, 1996). *Intrinsic motivation* refers to plea-sure as the driving force in play—that is, without regard to outcomes, gains, or exter-nal rewards. For Jimmy's brother, Matthew, it is clear that playing with the trains is an enjoyable game to play with his mother and brother; this is not determined by the out-come, for if that were the case, the activity would end when the train successfully cir-cled the track. *Internal locus of control* pre-scribes that the child is able to determine the choices and direction of the play experience. For example, locus of control becomes more external as Jimmy's mother takes charge of the play interaction. However, it is interest-ing to note that his play competence (devel-opmental stage) may actually increase with this structure, so that characteristics of play-fulness and play competence are not mutu-ally dependent. Finally, the ability to imag-ine and suspend reality allows the child to establish his or her own rules and content of play without constraint from physical mate-rials or props. It is clear that for Jimmy, imaginary play has not developed. Perhaps, with appropriate interventions, Jimmy will be able to use other objects as substitutes for the train to mimic train movements, or use purely imaginative methods to invoke a train scenario.

Play is also defined by what it is not. Some theorists (Bundy, 1996) contrast play with work, which often has a productive out-come, a basis in reality, and is more exter-nally driven for some persons. Thus, play can feel like work to some children if too many demands are imposed, it becomes too predictable, or the child is not allowed to make his or her own choices in the play ac-tivity. Also, play is not synonymous with self-stimulatory or stereotyped actions that afford little adaptive value or are devoid of cultural meaning. Jimmy, for example, has high intrinsic motivation to perform repeti-tive actions (such as spinning the wheels on the train) that may bring about order or sen-sory pleasure and give him a sense of con-trol. Although he may appear to have some characteristics of playfulness, the adaptive value of the activity is limited, and his play competence is quite impaired. Likewise, his ability to participate more fully in the so-cially meaningful play routine takes extra effort from his mother, who playfully in-trudes on his preoccupation, redirects his at-tention, and imposes an extrinsic reward (a tickle) to engage him more successfully.

The ultimate goal for any child with an impairment or disability is to be able to par-ticipate fully with peers and adults within the roles and expectations of society and culture (World Health Organization [WHO], 1999). For all children, play is an expected domain of such participation. Although play seems to evolve naturally for most children, for children with autism, the nature of this neu-rodevelopmental disability poses many chal-lenges that impair particular capabilities (e.g., cognitive skills, sensory processing, language development) and may disrupt the natural acquisition of play skills. Addition-ally, the intrinsic impairments of the child interact with sociocultural and environmental influences (i.e., supports, opportunities, and obstacles) in such a way that the child's capabilities to perform complex sets of activities or play tasks are either facilitated or further compromised, ultimately affecting his or her participation. The neurodevelopmental impairments associated with autism may be severe, but they do not necessarily prevent a child from developing important skills and benefiting from strategies and supports to increase play engagement and ultimate participation in this childhood occupational role. Alternately, remediating impaired functions (e.g., sensory processing, expressive language) does not necessarily translate to better performance and participation in meaningful play. For any practitioner working with children with autism, these points are important to keep in mind as the nature of autism is described and play assessments and interventions are summarized.

THE NATURE OF PLAY IN AUTISM: STRENGTHS AND WEAKNESSES

Much research has been conducted on specific deficits in play competence (e.g., symbolic skills; social interaction) in children with autism over the age of 18 months, whereas fewer studies have looked at the process-oriented aspects of playfulness, or the sociocultural variations of play. Young children with autism, by definition, have significant impairments in play (American Psychiatric Association, 1994). They often display uneven play profiles, with specific areas of strength and weakness, and demonstrate unique differences compared to children with delayed development without autism (Stone & Lemanek, 1990; Wing, 1981). Because play skills are highly associated with level of language development and are critical to successful social participation, play is an important area for practitioners to con-

sider when assessing and intervening with a young child with autism (Restall & Magill-Evans, 1994). Many capabilities or constituent skills are necessary foundations for play; however, in and of themselves, these capabilities are not sufficient to guarantee competent play skills, playful interactions, or successful social participation—that is, play is not a simple summation of these capabilities.

Play strengths and weakness vary tremendously among children with autism and can be best analyzed through an individualized play activity analysis. The information presented in this section summarizes the current research in the field, which frequently focuses on specific constituent skills. This evidence, although limited, in some ways, provides a base of knowledge that aids our understanding of the nature of autism, including areas of strength and weakness that may affect the important childhood occupation of play. The five categories summarized here include: (1) play engagement with persons; (2) play engagement with objects; (3) pretend play; (4) imitation and praxis; and (5) sensory processing, arousal modulation, and attention functions supporting play.

Play Engagement with Persons

The inability to meaningfully engage in interactions with the social as well as the physical world is viewed as one of the primary limitations in children with autism affecting their ability to play. Typical children easily develop capacities to engage and participate in play with other children. Peer participation becomes more interactive and complex as development progresses (e.g., solitary, onlooker, parallel, associative, cooperative [Parten, 1932; Knox, 1996]). Once a child masters associative or cooperative play, earlier participation levels may be utilized less; however, they are not lost, but are retained and applied during appropriate contexts. Likewise, personal preferences and sociocultural variations may determine the amount of time children spend in any particular type of social play participation.

Although many young children with autism are capable of engaging in some play skills, in general, participation in social play is not the child's preferred activity. Play is often characterized by less proximity to peers and isolation in solitary nonsocial play activities (McGee, Feldman, & Morrier, 1997; Stone & Lemanek, 1990). Research shows that children with autism are less likely to seek peer interaction, demonstrate fewer social initiations, and provide fewer responses to social overtures than children with other developmental disabilities (Sigman & Ruskin, 1999). Although there may be several reasons for these difficulties in the peer engagement process, specific impairments in the social-cognitive understanding of complex human interactions is thought to play a role. Specifically, some research in the area of theory of mind (Baron-Cohen, Leslie, & Frith, 1985; Frith, 1996; Frith & Happe, 1994) indicates that children with autism may have trouble taking another's perspective. Because they may have trouble flexibly decoding the meaning of a social-communicative interchange, the resulting social experience becomes fragmented and play is reduced to solitary isolated activities.

Other individuals noted social-communicative and affective limitations that consequently impact the child's ability to engage in meaningful play interactions with others (Loveland & Landry, 1986; Trad, Bernstein, Shapiro, & Hertzig, 1993). Children with autism appear to be more sensitive to changes in their environment than to changes in human faces, affective expressions, or social interactions. Because the human face often holds little interest for the child with autism, he or she does not establish a pattern of mutual gaze with a caregiver. Consequently, parents of children with autism report eye gaze to be abnormal. In a retrospective study (Volkmar, Cohen, & Paul, 1986), 90% of parents reported that their child often, very often, or almost always avoided eye contact. Furthermore, gestures and facial expressions may have little meaning because children with autism have difficulty attributing intention or emotional experiences to others. Adrien (1991, 1992) noted that, when compared to children who are typically developing, children with autism were less likely to seek comfort, share pleasurable events, or experience pleasure when interacting with their parents. For example, in the case vignette, Jimmy seemed to be content to play by himself. His mother had to make a concerted effort to engage him in a tickle game—unlike his brother, who became amused merely by watching his mother tickle Jimmy.

Joint attention, a communicative function that is a basis for shared engagement in social play situations, is usually limited, if not altogether absent. Because of its absence, eye gaze, nonverbal communication, and intersubjectivity (i.e., the building of shared emotional meaning between a child and a caregiver) does not develop as it does in a child who is developing typically (Stern, 1985; Moore, Hobson, & Lee, 1997). The most striking differences between children who have autism and children who are developing typically are the lack of pointing, showing, or using eye gaze alternately between an object and communication partner. Consequently, the use of protodeclarative acts (Mundy, Sigman, Ungerer, & Sherman, 1987) is usually nonexistent. For example, unlike Matthew, who tried to get Jimmy's attention by holding up the train for him to see, Jimmy was content to lie on the floor and spin the wheels of his train. Children with autism seem to understand that other people can be agents of actions—that is, others can help them get something or can swing them (a protoimperative act); however, they appear to have difficulty understanding that the other person has a perspective that could be shared (a protodeclarative act).

Swettenham et al. (1998) confirmed that 20-month-old children with autism looked significantly less at people than children in control groups (typical or delayed) in a free-play task. These toddlers also demonstrated fewer gaze shifts between two persons as well as between an object and a person. Because successful play interactions require joint engagement and smooth coordination of gaze shifts between people and objects, it is likely that specific deficits, such as social orienting and joint attention, profoundly affect play development and the level of playfulness experienced during both social play and object play.

In addition to lack of perspective taking, affective responsiveness, and joint attention, the language deficits of children with autism may affect their flexibility in play and imagination (Wing, 1981). Minsky (1975) speculated that play is derived from shared experiences in the social world, whereas language assumes the role of turning the play into an interaction by creating a shared topic. Because children with autism generally do not learn from shared experiences in the social world, an inability to enter into the language world may result as well. In the case vignette, Jimmy derives sensory pleasure from lying on the floor and spinning the wheels of his train. This activity, which is enjoyable for him, does not require verbal interchange among those present in the room.

Play Engagement with Objects

In typical children, meaningful engagement with objects begins early in life and continues to change in terms of diversity, complexity, and quality throughout development (Piaget, 1962). It is important to note that although typically developing children master new capacities in play, earlier forms of play continue to develop, often expanding in diversity and complexity. Likewise, children's motivation and preferences may also determine the structure of play. For example, a child at three years of age may be perfectly capable of symbolic play but choose to engage in a complex relational play task, such as putting together a non-inset ten-piece puzzle; however, this relational task is much more advanced than the child was capable of as a toddler (e.g., putting a circle in a shape sorter). Thus, understanding play and play interventions for children with autism requires attending to these multiple levels within multiple domains of play.

The play preferences of children with autism often indicate a tendency for more engagement in object play than social play. For example, Tardif et al. (1995) found that young children with autism spent 50.7% of their time in object-focused play, compared to 16.2% time in adult partner play. The children became most involved in the object exchange games in which repetition and turn-taking were inherent characteristics of the interaction. However, these findings should not be misconstrued to imply that object play skills are uniformly proficient in young children with autism. Certainly, an uneven pattern of strengths and weaknesses in object play is described. Play skills dependent on simple manipulation (e.g., object assembly tasks) or visual-spatial qualities (e.g., matching, block design, pattern analysis) are an area of strength compared to object play skills that require representational (pretend) functions or social play interactions (e.g., Hermelin & O'Connor, 1970; Siegel, Minshew, & Goldstein, 1996).

Engagement in object play is often found to be lacking in certain qualitative characteristics such as creativity, flexibility, and diversity of actions demonstrated. For example, Tiegerman & Primavera (1981) found that it was common for children with autism to manipulate objects and toys in a stereotyped fashion. Similarly, Tilton and Ottinger (1964) found that children with autism engaged in significantly more repetitive manual play and oral contacts with toys than did children with mental retardation or typical development. In Jimmy's case, repetitively spinning the wheels of his train seemed to be preferable to playing the tickle game with his mother or interacting with his brother, both of which involved some degree of social interaction. In addition, Stone, Lemanek, Fishel, Fernandez, and Altemeier (1990) studied play behaviors of young children with autism compared to groups of typical and developmentally delayed peers. They derived information about the percentages of time children spent playing with toys, appropriately or inappropriately. Overall, the children with autism used fewer toys, spent less total time playing with toys, and demonstrated fewer functional acts with toys (e.g., pretending to drink from a cup) during play, relative to other control groups. Table 13–1 lists common definitions of object play and descriptions of their first emergence, as well as implications for children with autism.

Many children with autism are noted to have atypical preoccupations with certain materials or sensory features of play objects, and often demonstrate unusual play preferences. Explanations for these types of play engagement deficits with objects are often attributed to either executive dysfunction theories (e.g., Pennington & Ozonoff, 1996; Rogers, Bennetto, McEvoy, & Pennington, 1996), which focus on the lack of planning and flexibility in play behaviors, or sensory

processing and arousal modulation theories, which stress the narrow range of responsiveness afforded by children with autism. Ferrara and Hill (1980) demonstrated that children with autism had better responses to both social and nonsocial toys when they were predictable and low in complexity, indicating support for the notion that these children may have trouble processing complex information and demonstrate lowered thresholds for aversion to novelty. Although novelty is an important motivator for curiosity and play exploration in typical children, for children with autism, it may present unusual challenges for arousal modulation. Arousal modulation and other functions supporting play are revisited below.

Pretend Play

Other difficulties seen in the play of children with autism might be attributed to deficits of symbolic representation, which, by nature, require greater social competence (Dawson & Adams, 1984; Sigman & Ungerer, 1984; Wetherby & Prutting, 1984). One definition cited frequently in the literature specifies that a child is engaged in pretend play if: (a) one object is used as if it were another, e.g., a stick is used as a spoon; (b) properties are attributed to the object that it does not have, e.g., a child pretends a doll is hurt; and (c) absent objects are referred to as if they are present, e.g., while role-playing, a child pretends to have a friend with whom to fight fires (Baron-Cohen, 1987). Although these acts require the capacity of a child to form symbolic representations, they are in fact, three different types of symbolic representation. This is important to consider when interpreting research findings. While numerous studies documented the lack of pretend play in children with autism (e.g., Baron-Cohen; Wing, Gould, Yeates, & Brierley, 1977), others

Table 13–1 Play Definitions and Descriptions

Play Term	Age of Emergence	Definition	Children with Autism
Exploratory/manipulative (also called stereotypic play) (Bergen, 1988; Knox, 1996; Nicolich, 1977; Piaget, 1962; Sinclair, 1970; Ungerer et al., 1981)	<9 months	Explores objects, visually, and tactually; mouthing; waving, banging, and poking and movement of objects from one hand to the other or in space develop later (e.g., throwing, opening, other simple cause and effect.) (Nicolich, 1977; Piaget, 1962; Sinclair, 1970; Ungerer et al., 1981).	Less exploration of objects in unstructured situations (Hermelin & O'Connor, 1970; Kasari, Sigman, & Yirmiya, 1993). In structured situations, exploration is the same (Sigman, Mundy, Sherman, & Ungerer, 1986).
Relational play (Nicolich, 1977; Piaget, 1962; Sinclair, 1970; Ungerer et al., 1981)	8–9 months	Begins to use objects in combination (matches, compares, takes apart), although not considered to be functional (e.g., puts blocks in a container). This play expands to simple construction play later (2 years+), such as using tools. (Nicolich, 1977; Piaget, 1962; Sinclair, 1970; Takata, 1974; Ungerer et al., 1981).	Can produce a range of relational play acts in structured and unstructured situations. Spend more time at relational, functional, and manipulative levels than at symbolic levels (Sigman & Ungerer, 1981). Generating complex actions (praxis) may be difficult in some children (Minshew, Goldstein, & Siegel, 1997).
Functional play (Nicolich, 1977; Piaget, 1962; Sinclair, 1970; Ungerer et al., 1981)	12–13 months	Begins to play with objects appropriately and expected manner (e.g., uses a spoon to feed a doll; pretends to dial phone and bring to ear) (Nicolich, 1977; Piaget, 1962; Sinclair, 1970; Ungerer et al., 1981).	Generally less functional play and fewer diverse acts when children with autism are younger (Sigman & Ungerer, 1984); as they get older developmentally, more functional acts are seen (Lewis & Boucher, 1988).

Symbolic play (Nicolich, 1977; Piaget, 1962; Sinclair, 1970; Ungerer et al., 1981)	13–24+ months	Includes three types of acts: 1. One object used to represent a different object, e.g., a stick for a spoon. 2. Acts implying that a doll is performing an action, e.g., a child pretends that a doll is hurt and crying. 3. Acts that involve an imaginary object, e.g., a child pretends to serve a doll/person imaginary cereal (Nicolich, 1977; Piaget, 1962; Sinclair, 1970; Ungerer et al., 1981).	Generally fewer symbolic acts and less diversity (Mundy et al., 1987; Sigman & Ungerer, 1984) although symbolic acts increase with structure (Sigman & Ungerer, 1984). Seems that if children with autism have language abilities comparable to a five-year-old, they can use symbols in play. They might not use them, however, unless encouraged to do so through structured play (Lewis & Boucher, 1988). Less make-believe play (Stone & Lemanek, 1990). Less dramatic play (DeMyer, Mann, Tilton, & Lowe, 1967).
Rule-governed games (Bergen, 1988)	School age	Social games with rules such as organized sports; skills are developed; projects are constructed.	Often a lack of expressive language, limited play repertoires, limited organization, and poorer imitation skills, and imagination (Kaplan-Sanoff, Brewster, Stillwell, & Bergen, 1988; Nelson, 1984; Powers, 1989).

found that some children with autism are able to enact play routines that resemble advanced forms of pretend play (Jarrold, Boucher, & Smith, 1994; Lewis & Boucher, 1988; Libby, Powell, Messer, & Jordan, 1998).

Specifically, Baron-Cohen (1987) compared play behaviors of children with autism (mean CA = 8.1) to typically developing children (mean CA = 4.1) and children with Down syndrome (mean CA = 7.5). His research findings indicated that the frequency of engagement in pretend play in the group of children with autism was significantly lower compared to the other two groups. Similarly, a study completed by Ungerer & Sigman (1981) looked at four categories of play behaviors in 16 children with autism as compared to children with mental retardation and children who were typically developing. The categories included simple manipulation, relational play, functional play, and symbolic play, assessed in both structured and unstructured free-play situations. Results indicated that all children demonstrated play behaviors in each of the four categories. However, the play of children with autism was characterized primarily by manipulation, relational, and functional play, compared to the other two groups, whose play skills fell largely into the functional and symbolic play categories.

Conversely, Jarrold et al. (1994) found no significant differences between typically developing children and children with autism when evaluating pretend play tasks requiring substitution of one object for another. One possible constraint of this study, however, is that the object substitution occurred in a highly structured play situation, so that the typical demands of spontaneous free play were absent.

In another study, Lewis and Boucher (1988) compared play between children with autism to typically developing children and children with mild learning disabilities. Results indicated no significant differences between any of the children in the amount of time spent in symbolic play. It was noted however, that not much time was spent by any of the groups in symbolic play. Lewis and Boucher speculated that this finding may be due to the nature of the functional toys provided, which were more attractive and larger in number than toys typically eliciting symbolic play.

Similarly, Libby et al. (1998) examined the differences in play behaviors in children with autism, Down syndrome, and typically developing children. Each group of children was matched according to receptive and expressive language skills. No changes in play behaviors occurred over time in the children with autism, while they did for the other two groups. Children with autism also demonstrated significantly more manipulative and exploratory play and less symbolic play as compared to the other two groups. The specific qualities lacking in their symbolic play included making a reference to an absent object and making attributions of false properties to an object.

Although it appears that many children with autism are, in fact, capable of demonstrating pretend play that involves symbolic representation, the amount and nature of pretend play differ from those of children with mental retardation and typical development. It seems that many children with autism are able to substitute one object for another, but have difficulty attributing properties to an object that it does not have and pretending that objects or people who are absent are really present. This inability to suspend reality certainly interferes with a child's ability to effectively engage in meaningful play experiences with others.

Imitation and Praxis

Imitation is one of the most common means by which typically developing children learn to play. Their ability to imitate an action produced by another person helps them internalize some representation of that action. Thus, the ability of a child to share playful imitative experiences with a caregiver is important for symbolic development (Smith & Bryson, 1994; Werner & Kaplan, 1963) and may facilitate self-awareness as well as awareness of others (Barresi & Moore, 1996; Meltzoff & Gopnik, 1993).

Many studies show that children with autism have difficulty imitating simple motor actions (DeMyer et al., 1972; Stone et al., 1990; Stone, Ousley, & Littleford, 1997), although there is evidence that at least some children with autism have intact basic imitation skills (Heimann, Ullstadius, Dahlgren, & Gillberg, 1992), particularly when imitating familiar actions (Dawson & Adams, 1984; Rogers & McEvoy, 1993). Even when present, the quality of imitation appears to be quite poor.

Stone, Ousley, Yoder, Hogan, and Hepburn (1997) found that imitation of body movements was more impaired than object imitation skills in children with autism below 3½ years of age. Furthermore, the researchers found that imitation of body movements was predictive of later expressive language skills, whereas imitation of actions with objects was associated with level of (symbolic) play skills. Children with autism are also noted to have difficulties with laboratory tasks requiring both *immediate* imitation as well as *deferred* imitation (Dawson, Meltzoff, Osterling, &

Rinaldi, 1998). This finding has implications for maintaining learned play actions and generalizing to other contexts. In support of this point, Klin (1992) noted that children with autism had significant limitations in reciprocal social play (e.g., peek-a-boo, pat-a-cake)—games that require the integration of imitation and language to learn—and maintenance of these skills to invoke future play interactions.

Because imitation skills involve the interplay of so many components (social-cognition, motor planning, motivation), the nature of the qualitative differences in imitation between children with autism and other groups is still disputed. Some researchers suggest that praxis difficulties may be influencing this area (Ohta, 1987; Smith & Bryson, 1994). Praxis involves both the integration of sensory information to form appropriate representational capacities (e.g., body perception) and the ability to transfer this representation to initiation of the planned movement. Thus, deficits in sensory processing and/or formation of perceptual representations may affect the ability to engage effectively in play.

Others suggest that unusual play behaviors (e.g., rigid, stereotyped play; preoccupation with certain play themes) seen in children with autism may also be related to deficits in praxis and executive control (Pennington & Ozonoff, 1996; Rogers, 1999)—that is, children with autism may have trouble with formulation, organization/sequencing, and execution of novel motor plans, which are requisites for skilled imitation and object play repertoires. Indeed, compared to controls (matched on IQ), children with autism are less able to imitate a variety of tasks (i.e., static postures and movement sequences; symbolic as well as nonsymbolic object uses) (Ohta, 1987; Rogers et al., 1996). In familiar, more structured, and contextually relevant situations, it appears that performance of children with autism improves (DeMyer, 1976; Rogers et al., 1996). For example, using an object with its functional properties (imitating drinking from a cup) is generally more successful than that of purely symbolic functions (imitating flying the cup like an airplane). Rogers states that problems with inhibition, one aspect of executive control, may specifically account for some of these difficulties such that the child with autism may not be able to switch response sets away from the more automatic or practiced action. Because the majority of studies regarding executive functions were conducted with older children and in decontextualized laboratory settings, the implications for young children within naturalistic play contexts need to be further studied.

Sensory Processing, Arousal Modulation, and Attention Functions Supporting Play

Some of the play difficulties seen in children with autism may be related to difficulties in sensory processing, arousal modulation, and attention to salient stimuli. Distortions in modulation causing over- or underarousal as well as deficiencies in selective attention and attention shifting were noted in studies with older children (e.g., Courchesne et al., 1994; Hutt, Hutt, Lee, & Ounsted, 1964). Retrospective video studies with infants also indicated difficulties with orientation to salient stimuli. Responses to novel social as well as nonsocial stimuli during naturalistic interactions and play experiences with caregivers were found to be problematic (Baranek, 1999; Osterling & Dawson, 1994).

Dawson and Lewy (1989) further suggested that overarousal may add to the symptoms of social withdrawal in children with autism. However, it seems that physiological aversion to stimuli is not a sufficient explanation for poor social play skills, as some studies found that poor social understanding plays a larger role than do physiological contributors for children with autism (Corona, Dissanayake, Arbelle, Wellington, & Sigman, 1998). However, because children with autism seem to respond best to a narrow subset of environmental stimuli, overfocused attention or overselectivity is proposed as an explanation for some of the rigid and stereotyped play evident in this population (e.g., Lovaas, Koegel, & Schreibman, 1979). Likewise, sensory processing disruptions, such as tactile defensiveness, were linked to unusual stereotyped and rigid behaviors (Baranek, Foster, & Berkson, 1997).

Baranek (1998) described a dynamic model of sensory processing (see Figure 13–1) to explain some of the sensory processing difficulties in children with autism that may impact level of engagement in play. This model was developed from Field's (1982) concept of an activation band model and her research with premature infants, which proposes an optimal level of stimulation needed to maintain attention. Separate thresholds for orientation and aversion to sensory experiences may partially determine meaningful engagement in play. The optimal engagement band is thus determined by the width between the two thresholds, which can vary as a function of intrinsic (child-centered) and extrinsic (e.g., temporal context; environment; parental structure) characteristics. Likewise, levels of arousal may fluctuate, interact with these thresholds, and contribute to successful or unsuccessful engagement. In children with autism, the em-

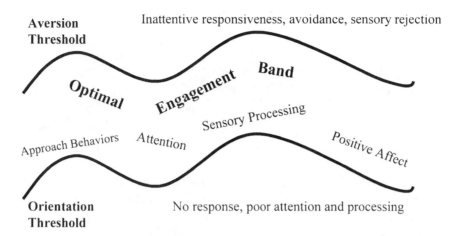

Figure 13–1 Dynamic model of sensory processing. *Source:* Adapted with permission from T. Field and A. Fogel, *Emotion and Early Interaction,* p. 114, © 1982, Lawrence Erlbaum Associates, Inc.

pirical literature (e.g., Dawson & Lewy, 1989; Ferrara & Hill, 1980; Hutt et al., 1964) suggests that this range may be restricted such that the optimal level of engagement for play or other meaningful occupations is compromised (Figure 13–2). For example, increased difficulties in registering and attending to relevant information (e.g., not turning toward a meaningful sound or voice) as well as hyperresponses to or withdrawal from aversive situations (e.g., turning away or covering ears to sound) may be common in autism due to this constricted band. Likewise, the variations in response and extreme fluctuations are possible, as extra intensity in stimulation may be required to get a response (i.e., cross the orientation threshold), but the child then quickly becomes overwhelmed and responds negatively (i.e., crosses the aversion threshold).

PLAY ASSESSMENT

Play assessments for children with autism vary in terms of their format, content, and function. For example, a different assessment process may take place when the pur-
pose is to make a diagnosis rather than to design an effective play intervention plan. Few play assessments were designed specifically for children with autism; thus, it is critical that the practitioner carefully choose tools and methods that not only fit the purpose of the assessment but also are an appropriate match for the strengths, needs, and developmental level of the individual child. If the goal is to promote the child's level of play participation, a top-down assessment strategy is recommended (e.g., Coster, 1998). This strategy involves beginning with an assessment of the child's current level of play participation, followed by a detailed analysis of the complex tasks and activities that are required of the child in play. Finally, if necessary, an assessment of the key constituent capabilities or skills (sensory processing, motor, cognitive, etc.) that support or limit the play process is completed. A careful play activity analysis also includes an observation of the child performing given play tasks within naturalistic contexts and assesses the contributing influences of the temporal, physical, and social environments that limit or support play participation.

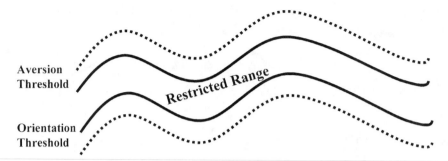

Aversion
Threshold

Restricted Range

Orientation
Threshold

Figure 13–2 Autism: Optimal engagement band is restricted. *Source:* Adapted with permission from T. Field and A. Fogel, *Emotion and Early Interaction,* p. 114, © 1982, Lawrence Erlbaum Associates, Inc.

Because the empirical research demonstrates that play skills vary greatly for children with autism under different conditions, assessing play across multiple contexts (e.g., different days, times, locations, and conditions) and with multiple formats (e.g., parent report, informal clinical observation, standardized structured assessment) may be indicated to get a valid and comprehensive estimate of the child's abilities and to plan adequate individualized interventions. In particular, assessment in naturalistic contexts such as home, school, and playground in the community may be the most ecologically valid, although sometimes more difficult to accomplish. Both social play with adults and peers and object play need to be considered and should be observed under both structured and unstructured conditions. Familiarity and predictability of conditions and toys likely affect the performance of the young child with autism. Including the child's favorite object, toys, or playmates may be one way to ease the stress of an assessment in a clinical setting. In addition to formal and informal observational measures, parent questionnaires, semistructured interviews, and play histories are important to consider. Parents are particularly attuned to their child's strengths and weaknesses, and have the opportunity to observe their child during natural daily routines. Standardized assessments can often provide systematic observations and quantitative comparisons to normative data; however, given the needs of a child with autism, directions or materials may need to be adapted. If the examiner deviates from standardized procedure, test scores must be interpreted with caution.

In many cases, existing assessments and tools, some of which may be autism-specific, others of which are designed for more general use, may be of assistance to the individual practitioner working with young children with autism dependent on the goals of the assessment. Four categories of available tools are described here: (1) play-based developmental assessments; (2) assessments specifically designed to measure one or more domains of play competence (e.g., symbolic play); (3) assessments of play engagement or playfulness; and (4) play-based, autism-specific diagnostic or screening tools.

Play-Based Developmental Assessment

Play-based developmental assessments use play as a vehicle for measuring performance of other constituent skills or developmental capabilities, such as motor, language, and cognitive functions. Play affords a naturalistic context for activities and is a strong motivator of behavior, thus eliciting more mature capabilities and optimal stress-free engagement in the assessment process.

Correlation between play skills and cognitive functions, language, and social skills was documented (e.g., Curcio & Piserchia, 1978; Fewell & Rich, 1987) and, thus, evaluating these skills through play is particularly useful. One example of a broad-based developmental assessment for young children that uses a play-based format is the Transdisciplinary Play-Based Assessment (Linder, 1993). Other assessments utilizing play as a basis for eliciting language abilities include the Rossetti Infant-Toddler Language Scale (Rossetti, 1990) and the Communication and Symbolic Behavior Scales (Wetherby & Prizant, 1993).

Assessments Measuring One or More Domains of Play Competence

Some assessments evaluate play skills directly but vary according to the domain they assess. Because of the strong correlation between symbolic thinking and play in autism (e.g., Jarrold et al., 1994; Riquet, Taylor, Benaroya, & Klein, 1981), domain is particularly important. The Play Assessment Scale (Fewell, 1986) and the Symbolic Play Scale (Westby, 1980) are examples of such tools. The Preschool Play Scale—Revised (Bledsoe & Shepard, 1982; Knox, 1974) additionally includes other play categories such as space management, materials management, and social participation. Both the Play Assessment Scale and the Preschool Play Scale provide developmental ages associated with play types evidenced by the child and determine symbolic play abilities associated with language development.

Assessments Measuring Play Preferences, Play Engagement, or Playfulness

Some assessments focus on the process of play more fully, noting the child's level of engagement in play activities or the level of playfulness experienced by the child during various types of play. The Children's Engagement Rating Scale and Questionnaire (McWilliam, 1994, 1999) was useful in at least one study with children with autism to measure intervention efficacy (Case-Smith & Bryan, 1999). Although several measures of playfulness are available and have been used with young children with other developmental concerns (e.g., Test of Playfulness [Bundy, 1997]; Children's Playfulness Scale [Barnett, 1990; Liberman, 1965]), these are not yet validated for use with children with autism. Finally, some assessments provide a historical account of the child's play preferences (e.g., Play History [Takata, 1974]) or taxonomies of current play preferences and play functions (e.g., Play Preference Inventory [Wolfberg, 1995]).

Play-Based, Autism-Specific Diagnostic or Screening Tools

Play is also used as the diagnostic medium for autism. Specific characteristics inherent to play, such as qualitative impairments in social interaction and communication and restricted or repetitive patterns of behavior, are hallmark areas of identification in children with autism. Consequently, certain play assessments probe for specific behaviors; the lack of these behaviors indicating a potential diagnosis of autism or pervasive developmental disorder (PDD). The Autism Diagnostic Observation Schedule—(ADOS; Lord, Rutter, DiLavore, & Risi, 1999) consists of four modules (no speech/simple phrases, three-word phrases/not yet verbally fluent, verbally fluent for the child/younger adolescent, and verbally fluent for the older adolescent/adult). Other play-based tools that can assist in the diagnostic process are the Screening Tool for Autism in Two-Year-Olds (STAT) (Stone & Ousley, 1997), a second-stage screening tool differentiating children at risk for autism from those with generalized developmental or language delays. The Play Assessment from the Clinical Center for the Study of Development and Learning (CDL) (1998) is a descriptive tool used to augment interdisciplinary developmental assessments. Table 13–2 summarizes types of assessments that are available and may be helpful for use with children with autism. It includes a brief description and intended age ranges. Specific norms and manuals are available from the publishers or authors listed in the references. The practitioner must carefully choose the assessment that best meets each child's needs.

PLAY INTERVENTIONS

As play is largely culturally defined, individual differences in play skills, routines, and social games are to be expected. However, because specific qualitative deficits in play are common to young children with autism, a comprehensive intervention approach is incomplete without directly addressing the qualitative play needs of this population. Many comprehensive educational programs and developmental models (e.g., Greenspan & Wieder, 1999; Rogers & Lewis, 1989; Strain, Hoyson, & Jamieson, 1985) as well as specialized therapies (e.g., occupational therapy, speech therapy, recreation therapy) for children with autism incorporate play interventions; however, the teaching philosophies as well as goals for facilitating play vary tremendously. Some of the elements that are most differentiating are the intended outcomes of intervention; the specific domains of play to be facilitated (e.g., peer play, imaginary play, engagement with objects); the intensity, duration, and format of the intervention; the level of naturalism in the setting; the optimal amount of

structure required to enhance play skills/ interactions; and most effective maintenance and generalization strategies to use. For example, the Treatment and Education of Autistic and Related Communication Handicapped Children (TEACCH) program (Hogan, 1997; Schopler, Brehm, Kinsbourne, & Reichler, 1971) views play as central to the needs of this population, but insists that play needs to be taught in a structured manner. Activities for play are therefore incorporated into daily "work" routines in order to foster specific skills such as symbolic (pretend play) tasks within a structure that is meaningful and organizing to the child. In contrast, the Floortime approach (Greenspan & Wieder, 1999) uses unstructured, child-directed play with techniques such as playful obstruction (e.g., intruding playfully on the child's activity to draw attention to the adult and facilitate a communicative interaction). Other approaches, such as Theraplay (DesLauries, 1978), also utilize child-directed, highly affective play methods to facilitate engagement and communication.

The purpose of this section is to delineate and summarize common elements utilized in play interventions that may be helpful for practitioners working with young children with autism. Although these elements need to be considered simultaneously and in an integrated fashion when designing individualized play interventions for young children with autism, they are described categorically, bearing specific features in mind. As a quick practical guide, Table 13–3 summarizes the elemental components: play goals, play spaces, play materials, play partners, and play engagement strategies.

Play Intervention Goals

Play interventions are used in various ways with young children with autism. Re-

Table 13–2 Play Assessments

Assessment and Author(s)	Intended Age	Description	Applicability for Children with Autism
		Play-Based Developmental Assessments	
The Rosetti Infant-Toddler Language Scale (Rossetti, 1990)	Birth–3 years	Scale designed to assess preverbal and verbal areas of communication and interaction in *interaction-attachment, pragmatics, gesture, play, language comprehension,* and *language expression.* (CR, INTERACT, INT, NST, OBS)	Play behavior (one aspect of the assessment) is used to monitor the child's development of representational thought and language use for children with developmental delays.
Communication and Symbolic Behavior Scales (Wetherby & Prizant, 1993)	Children whose functional communication is 8–24 months. Has been used with children 60–72 months.	Two-part assessment (Caregiver questionnaire and structured interaction component with child) designed to examine *communicative, social-affective,* and *symbolic abilities* of children, monitor changes in child's behavior over time, and provide direction for intervention planning. Also identifies children at risk for developing communication impairments and provides a profile of communication functioning. Caregiver questionnaire is completed prior to assessment. (INT, NR, OBS, QUEST, ST, STRUC)	Assessment results profile relative strengths and weaknesses across communication, social-affective, and symbolic domains for children. This provides useful intervention information for children with autism, as research shows significant deficits in symbolic play are common.
Transdisciplinary Play-Based Assessment (TPBA) (Linder, 1993)	Children of developmental ages 6 months–6 years. Younger infants have also been successfully assessed (at risk and with or without disabilities).	Investigates child's performance across *cognitive, social-emotional, communication and language,* and *sensorimotor* areas during a six-phase play session. Assessment yields identification of service needs, development of intervention plans, and evaluation of	Can be used for any child functioning within the developmental age ranges provided. Linder (1993) indicates success in use with child with autism.

continues

Table 13–2 continued

Assessment and Author(s)	Intended Age	Description	Applicability for Children with Autism
Assessments Measuring One or More Domains of Play Competence			
		progress. Aspects of TPBA can be modified or omitted depending on the need and purpose of the assessment. (INTERACT, INT, OBS, STRUC and UNSTRUC)	
Symbolic Play Scale (Westby, 1980)	17–60 months	Symbolic play/language scale that describes 10 stages in the development of symbolic play activities and the relationships between language and play levels. Information is derived from spontaneous play sample. (OBS, SEMISTRUC)	Assists in assessing developmental levels of language-related cognitive abilities and symbolic representation. These two areas are significantly affected in children with autism.
Preschool Play Scale—Revised (originally titled The Play Scale; Knox, 1974) (Bledsoe & Shepard, 1982)	Birth–6 years	Assessment yields an overall play age (in months) from the combined average of four dimensions of play: *space management, material management, imitation, and participation.* (NST, OBS)	Can be used for children who cannot be tested on standardized tests. This play scale can be used to demonstrate the differences in play behaviors of populations of children.
Play Assessment Scale (Fewell, 1987)	Developmental play ages ranging 2–36 months of age	Assessment includes four sets of toys that are used to elicit spontaneous play actions regardless of the toy. The examiner observes and scores the developmental sequence of play behaviors, then derives a play age score. (NR, OBS, SEMI)	Flexibility in administration procedures allows this scale to be used with children with disabilities who respond poorly to standardized testing and who are under three years of age.

Assessments Measuring Play Preferences, Play Engagement, or Playfulness

The Play History (Takata, 1974)	Has been used on children ages 1.7 years–19.5 years	Play history connects the child's past to the present in order to address future needs while addressing the tie between the individual with internal and external factors that elicit responses. Elements of the play history include five parts: *general information, previous play experiences, actual play examination, play description, and play prescription.* Yields qualitative and quantitative information. (INT, OBS—if desired, SEMI)	Assessment yields a description of the child's play behaviors in order to provide information for intervention and programming. Can be used for children with autism, whose play behaviors and preferences would be used to individualize intervention.
The Children's Playfulness Scale (CPS) (Lieberman, 1965; Barnett, 1990)	School-age children	23-question assessment using judgment of examiner to gain qualitative information regarding five components of playfulness: *physical spontaneity, social spontaneity, cognitive spontaneity, manifest joy, and sense of humor.* Focus is on the playful child rather than the child at play. (QUEST, STRUCT)	Can be generalized to children with autism and used to identify areas in which the child may be lacking in playfulness.
Test of Playfulness (ToP) (Bundy, 1997)	2–10 years	68-item observational assessment to be used and scored by trained examiners observing children engaged in play indoors and outdoors each for 15 minutes in order to systematically examine the playfulness in young children. *Extent, intensity,* and *skill areas* are all assessed within each ToP item. (NST, OBS, UNSTRUC)	Can be used for children across all ages and diagnostic groups. Operationalized categories of playfulness comprise items addressing weaknesses in children with autism (social interaction, communication, and restricted repertoire of behaviors).

continues

Table 13–2 continued

Assessment and Author(s)	Intended Age	Description	Applicability for Children with Autism
Assessments Measuring Play Preferences, Play Engagement, or Playfulness			
Play Preference Inventory (Wolfberg, 1995)	School-age children	Designed to record *play preferences/ materials/themes/activities, interactions with objects,* and *choice of playmates.* Framework for identifying characteristics associated with the symbolic and social aspects of play. (NST, OBS, UNSTRUC)	Views play as a transformational process rather than a linear progression; thus, subtle qualities of play in children with autism are noted (e.g., emerging versus mastery in skills). Developed specifically for children with autism.
Children's Engagement Rating Scale and Questionnaire (McWilliam, 1994, 1999)	School-age children	Rates (1 to 5) the amount of time the child spends in Rating Scale: *advanced, differentiated, unsophisticated, nonengaged,* and *focused attention.* Questionnaire rates (low to high) the domains of *competence, persistent play, undifferentiated engagement,* and *attentional engagement.* (NST, OBS, QUEST)	Measures spontaneous and responsive behaviors in the preschool environment. Has been successfully used to assess engagement in children with autism (Case-Smith & Bryan, 1999).
Play-Based, Autism-Specific Diagnostic or Screening Tools			
Screening Tool for Autism in Two-Year-Olds (STAT) (Stone & Ousley, 1997)	24–36 months	Second-stage screening tool addresses the dimensions of *play, imitation,* and *communication.* Child is scored either pass or fail on all items. Language comprehension is not a prerequisite for assessment. (INT, ST)	Designed as an early screening tool to differentiate children at risk for autism from children with other language or generalized developmental delays.

Play Assessment (The Clinical Center for the Study of Development and Learning, University of North Carolina at Chapel Hill, 1998)	Birth–5 years	Arena-style assessment in which there is a primary examiner while other professionals observe and qualitatively rate behaviors. Predetermined activities are used to measure *socialization, communication, play/stereotypical responses,* and *sensory responses.* (INT, OBS, SEMI)	Tool developed to aid in the developmental assessment and diagnosis of autism in children.
Autism Diagnostic Observation Schedule—Generic (ADOS) (Lord, Rutter, DiLavore, & Risi, 1999)	Nonverbal toddlers to verbally fluent adults of average intelligence	One of four modules is administered based on developmental level and language skills. Flexible administration of *communication, social interaction,* and *play* for possible diagnosis of autism or PDD. Examines presence of atypical behaviors specific to autism and the absence of age-appropriate communication and social skills. (INTERACT, NR, OBS, SEMI, ST)	Diagnostic tool specifically designed for the observation of social and communicative behaviors of children in question of a diagnosis of autism or PDD, based on *DSM-IV* criteria.

Key: *CR:* Criterion Referenced *INTERACT:* Interaction occurs with child *INT:* Interview *NST:* Nonstandardized *NR:* Norm Referenced *OBS:* Observation of child *QUEST:* Questionnaire *SEMI:* Semistructured *ST:* Standardized *STRUC:* Structured *UNSTRUC:* Unstructured

Table 13–3 Practical Considerations for Play Interventions for Young Children with Autism

Play Intervention Essentials	Questions To Ask	Practical Considerations
Play intervention goals	• What are the child's unique strengths and needs? • What is the intended function of the play intervention? • What play outcomes are being targeted?	• Play as a performance motivator (e.g., reinforcement/reward). • Play as a means to facilitate specific constituent skills or capabilities (fine motor, language, cognitive, sensory integration goals, etc.) that may or may not be play related. • Play as participation and a therapeutic outcome (e.g., developing appropriate and specific play skills, such as pretend play or peer play; expanding the play repertoire to be more creative, complex, or diverse; facilitating playful engagement with persons or objects; improving motivation to play, generalizing play skills across social, physical, and temporal contexts).
Play space	• Where and when should the play intervention occur? • How naturalistic should the setting be? • How can the space be modified to enhance the play goals?	• Setting physical boundaries that provide a safe, nurturing environment and support play goals. • Providing appropriate temporal context (e.g., best fit in time of day). • Exaggerating salient physical/contextual features. • Minimizing sensory distractions. • Providing concrete cues for transitions between play activities and play spaces. • Utilizing naturalistic environments. • Adapting physical spaces and contextual features.
Play materials	• What supplies are needed? • How should they be organized and used to meet the goals?	• Capitalizing on the child's unique interests (e.g., toys, themes, reinforcing sensory properties) to increase intrinsic motivation. • Feature-matching materials to goals (e.g., sensory exploration, pretend play, construction play). • Adapting toys, enhancing sensory properties, and creating safe play materials. • Expanding play repertoire (range, diversity, complexity).

Play partners	• Who are the most appropriate play-mates, given the goals?	• Selecting social toys to facilitate engagement with persons. • Organization and presentation of materials. • Familiar versus unfamiliar persons. • Adults versus peers. • Individuals versus groups.
Play engagement Strategies for • social play • object play	• What strategies can enhance social play? • What strategies can enhance object play? • What strategies enhance playfulness during interventions?	• Increasing internal locus of control (providing choices). • Establishing familiar and predictable play routines. • Balancing adult structure with child-directed exploration. • Considering the child's optimal engagement band and specific sensory processing abilities and needs. • Amplifying salient social cues and affective experiences. • Eliciting orientation, joint attention, sharing, and turn-taking. • Reducing complexity of language demands. • Integrating augmented or alternative communication systems into play sessions. • Eliciting spontaneous and self-initiated interactions. • Increasing tolerance of physical proximity and duration of play engagement. • Modeling and imitation. • Play scaffolding and guided participation. • Teaching organizational strategies for initiating, maintaining, and completing play activities. • Expanding play routines and sequences; building creativity and generativity. • Generalizing skills across social, physical, and temporal contexts.

gardless of the type selected, appropriate intervention goals need to be set in order for therapeutic gains to follow. Ultimately, increasing the child's level of participation in play is desired. These goals need to be individualized so that they are appropriate to the child's needs as well as the environment. Three broad but distinct categories of play intervention functions are summarized:

Play as a performance motivator. Play is often used as a reward to keep a child engaged in an activity or to motivate performance in other therapeutic work tasks. This approach is exemplified by numerous behavior-oriented programs (e.g., Applied Behavior Analysis) (Lovaas & Smith, 1989; Maurice, Green, & Luce, 1996), whereby a desired free-play activity may follow a series of teaching drills. The desired play activity is contingent on the child's positive performance in the preceding drills or teaching tasks. Using play as a positive reinforcement can be an effective method of building skills as well as compliance with activities. One limitation surrounding this approach is that children with autism are often impoverished in many aspects of play and thus being afforded free-play time does not guarantee that meaningful engagement with persons or objects occurs. For example, the child may engage in repetitive self-stimulatory activities that have limited therapeutic or adaptive value, as in the case vignette of Jimmy spinning the wheels of the train, which do not meet an adequate definition of play. However, the power of play as a motivator in and of itself cannot be underestimated; play activities and playful interactions are often used by caregivers as a helpful strategy to reward positive performance, divert attention from a less pleasant task, or to regulate the child's behavior in other ways.

Play as a means to enhance developmental skills or performance components. A play intervention approach commonly used by many therapists is using play as a vehicle for teaching other important constituent skills (e.g., fine motor, language, or cognitive functions). For example, a favorite soap bubble activity may be used as the context in which to teach a child communication strategies (e.g., requesting bubbles) in speech therapy; the same activity may be used by an occupational therapist to develop appropriate prehension patterns and functional object manipulation skills (e.g., open bubbles). Although play outcomes are not always the target of this approach, in some cases these components are thought to be foundational to more complex behaviors, including the occupation of play in young children with autism. Although both play as a performance motivator and play as a means for enhancing developmental skills or capabilities can be viewed as using play as a means to an end, this second method uses playful engagement within the therapeutic activity, whereas the first method uses play as a contingency or consequence following performance of a nonplay work task. In either case, it is important to note that teaching specific capabilities, such as motor skills (Mathiowetz & Haugen, 1995) and language skills (Koegel, O'Dell, & Koegel, 1987), may not generalize to broader domains of performance unless they are applied within meaningful naturalistic contexts. Even though a child with autism may learn many constituent skills that are prerequisites to a play task, his or her play may continue to look impoverished, ritualistic, or lacking in spontaneity and pleasure. Thus, engaging in a play task as an integrated whole is certainly more than the sum of its parts.

Play as participation and as a therapeutic outcome of intervention. Because play is important to children's adaptation, well-being, and participation in society, and because children with autism have distinct difficulties engaging in meaningful social and object play experiences, it is a critical target of interventions. Various methods are used to achieve more adaptive and meaningful play in young children with autism. These include interventions that focus on enhancing one or more domains of play competence (e.g., object play, symbolic play) as well as those that view level of engagement in play and playfulness as important outcomes. In the case vignette of Jimmy, both play competence (e.g., functional object play with train) and playfulness (e.g., pleasure from the activity; sense of control over the interaction) were compromised. Expanding on both features is critical in an intervention plan for Jimmy.

For occupational therapists, for example, play is both a therapeutic medium and a desired outcome for young children with autism who have deficits engaging in this important childhood occupation (Reilly, 1974; Parham, 1996). Individually designed and meaningful play activities are thus utilized in contextually relevant play situations to directly enhance playful engagement and participation for young children with autism. Other therapeutic approaches also view play as an important outcome but may select alternate means to developing play skills, such as structured work tasks (e.g., TEACCH program) or teaching functionally related collateral skills (e.g., social-cognitive awareness, communication) before generalizing to broader notions of play or more naturalistic play contexts (Koegel, Camarata, Valdez-Menchaca, & Koegel, 1998). Specific play outcome goals for children with autism may include expanding the variety in the child's object play repertoire; enhancing diversity, complexity, and creativity of play; developing participation in peer play; facilitating playful engagement with persons or objects;

improving motivation to play; and generalizing play skills to negotiate participation across social, physical or temporal contexts.

Play Spaces

Choosing an appropriate play space is critical to intervention goals. The play space defines the physical boundaries, constrains the sensory challenges, and, optimally, provides concrete contextual cues about the function or purpose of the play tasks. This is especially important for children with autism who need salient features to help them with the comprehension and organization of interactions with the physical world. They may demonstrate difficulties with multipurpose, cluttered, or expansive spaces that do not afford specific or meaningful interactions or increase sensory overarousal. Often, children with autism are able to perceive the details in the physical environment but are not able to organize these details into a meaningful whole, which limits effective interactions. The TEACCH model, for example, shows the utility of designing work and play spaces for preschoolers that are defined by the function of the tasks. Clear physical and visual boundaries help define what the play choices are, where the play activity is to occur, and when it is to begin and end. Spaces can be designed by themes such that the dress-up corner is sectioned off from the constructive play area or the art center. A large clinic room filled with sensory integration equipment is better suited to facilitating gross motor play than construction play using small manipulative toys. Moderately small spaces, free of sensory distractions, may facilitate peer play, given appropriate peer training and the availability of socially interactive play objects.

The play space also needs to promote a safe, supportive, and nurturing atmosphere

(Parham, 1996; Wolfberg, 1995). For children with autism, familiarity and predictability are important features, because novel environments may create overstimulation or stressful experiences if imposed without sufficient preparatory strategies. Naturalistic contexts afford meaningful opportunities for play within the desired natural conditions. They are more apt to elicit mature capabilities and to generalize to other situations than are more contrived spaces and conditions. Natural environments in the home, school, or community could be utilized in play interventions in order to meet specific goals. However, naturalistic contexts also increase the complexity and demands on the child with autism that may contribute to disorganized and fewer play initiatives. For example, a child with a low sensory tolerance and poor social-communicative skills may become overwhelmed on the playground during recess activities, when other children are interacting unpredictably with the equipment at the same time. The same child may perform with more advanced play skills or with a more playful affective quality when provided with a smaller peer group, a less active time period, or adaptations to the social routines, sensory demands, or physical boundaries during the play activity. Thus, the affordances in the physical, social, and temporal contexts need to be balanced and matched to the needs of the individual child to promote the best fit and optimal engagement for a therapeutic play intervention to occur.

Play Materials

Play materials also help define the structure, organization, and meaning of play tasks for children with autism and should be chosen carefully to facilitate the intervention goals (Hogan, 1997; Wolfberg, 1995). For example, objects or toys that necessitate a social interaction (e.g., balls; turn-taking board games) are suited to peer play activities, whereas other materials (e.g., puzzles; books) are better suited to developing solitary play or leisure skills. Similarly, the level of play competence and playfulness can be facilitated or inhibited dependent on the materials chosen. Solitary play activities elicit the fewest qualities of playfulness for typical children, however, this may not be the case for children with autism, who tend to prefer solitary play materials. Based on the individual child, an organized system of presenting materials and utilizing a limited amount of play materials may be advantageous as well.

Play objects and materials should be suited to the child's developmental age and unique interests. Appropriate toys that reflect the child's developmental stage or slightly above may be better suited for play interactions and learning than those based on chronological age, which may be too advanced for the child with autism (Lifter, Sulzer-Azaroff, Anderson, & Cowdery, 1993). Deciding whether the child is at the cognitive stage of exploration/manipulation, relational play, functional play, or symbolic (pretend) play may help direct choices of appropriate play materials. If a child is at the stages of exploration and manipulation and primarily focused on the sensory qualities of the play experience, using sociodramatic play activities results in inappropriate interactions with the materials. Objects used also should be responsive to the child's skills or actions in order to maintain play engagement. For example, Play-Doh may be more responsive than modeling clay for a child with poor fine motor skills, thus affording more success with manipulative play activities; simple cause-and-effect toys may respond more quickly to engage a child with a short attention span and limited functional play.

Research indicates that play interactions between children with autism and peers increase when activities reflect the child's preferences (Koegel et al., 1987). Selecting toys, objects, and tasks based on interests (e.g., specific themes, such as trains) or reinforcing sensory properties (e.g., favorite colors, textures, visual features) can be used to increase motivation and interaction while facilitating play goals. Often, exaggerating salient features of materials helps to direct the child's attention and facilitates sensory processing, allowing for optimal engagement. For example, strong visual cues (e.g., bright colors, numbers, or photos) or tactile cues (e.g., textured borders, vibration) can be added to play tasks to promote visibility, clarity, or functional significance.

Play materials for children with autism need to strike a balance between enough novelty and complexity to develop the just-right challenge and enough familiarity and predictability to allow for a stress-free interaction. Likewise, materials that produce aversive or avoidance responses due to their sensory or social qualities need to be adapted. The child's object-play repertoire can be gradually expanded and new dimensions of the materials graded systematically in order to work within the child's optimal band of engagement (see Figure 13–1). Because visual structure is known to be helpful to children with autism who demonstrate strengths in the visual-spatial domain, presenting visual instructions (e.g., object or picture schedules) to augment play tasks and interactions may be helpful. However, level of imposed structure needs to be balanced with choices to allow the child a greater internal locus of control, which is critical to a playful experience.

Materials that are naturally designed to require the assistance of another person (e.g., wind-up toys, tightly closed clear containers with special treats inside, balloons) may be useful to draw attention to another person, a task that is not automatic for many children with autism. The goals of using such materials are to encourage the child to attend to and utilize the adult, spontaneously request help in performing the activity, to participate in the activity, and, finally, to engage in a shared social routine (Klinger & Dawson, 1992). For example, in the case of Jimmy, his mother may activate a small wind-up toy of Thomas the Tank Engine to get Jimmy's attention during playtime. She waits for Jimmy to pick up the train and try to manipulate it unsuccessfully, which requires either handing it to her or vocalizing and looking to her for assistance. If he does not look up naturally, she holds the train near her face and models a request for the activity to continue.

Play Partners

Selection of play partners is a critical issue because most play is culturally defined and occurs within the context of social interactions with caregivers or peers. Often, for children with autism, interactions with familiar adults are easier and more advanced play skills are exhibited than during interactions with peers (e.g., Howlin, 1986). This may be related to the finding that adults tend to be more responsive and persistent than young children and are more effective at adjusting interactions to the needs of the child with autism. However, this same process may cause adults to limit opportunities for the child with autism to initiate play interactions, as adults tend to naturally compensate for the child's difficulties and demonstrate more directives in their play approach (El-

Ghoroury & Romanczyk, 1999). Consequently, pacing and self-monitoring strategies may be needed for the adult play partners to encourage the child to initiate play.

Some interventionists advocate first teaching play skills with high levels of adult structure, then gradually including a peer playmate into the interaction, whereas others advocate an inclusive approach immediately for peers. When using the gradual approach, one peer partner is selected to participate in a cooperative play task once the child with autism is competent with that task; other task complexities, environmental distractions, and increased numbers of peers can be gradually added to a successful situation. Regardless of the restrictiveness of a setting, opportunities to interact with both adults and peers is necessary, as generalization from one to the other may not automatically occur. Furthermore, specific play goals and methods for engaging with playmates need to be elucidated.

Although children with autism clearly benefit from inclusion with typical peers, mere exposure to peers is not sufficient to develop play skills or social competence (El-Ghoroury & Romanczyk, 1999; Myles, Simpson, Ormsbee, & Erickson, 1993). Some research shows that peers need to be trained in appropriate play interaction, modeling, persistent affective engagement, and socialization strategies in order to have demonstrable effect on the skills of the child with autism (Brown, Ragland, & Fox, 1988; McEvoy et al., 1988). Likewise, although there is no definitive guide on whether or not peers should be matched to chronological age or developmental age, it is clear that peer competence is a critical feature for successful play dyads and groups. Thus, much younger peers may not have the social competence to persist in play initiations or play

interactions that benefit the child with autism.

Another important issue is tolerating the proximity of others. If playmates are too intrusive, children with autism just reject or avoid even more. In some cases, active avoidance may be due to such sensory over-arousal, thus maintaining sensory challenges and physical interactions that are within the child's optimal engagement band as well as limiting unpredictability of the sensory experiences. In most cases, however, the social avoidance of children with autism in peer play situations stems from their lack of social-communicative understanding. The language levels may be too complex, or the child may not be able to take the perspective of another (i.e., theory-of-mind deficits). Thus, minimizing the language demands and providing concrete contextual cues may enhance the play engagement process with both adults and peers. Likewise, carefully choosing activities that call for shared participation increases the amount of social initiations from peers. Other play engagement strategies for both social play and object play are described next.

Play Engagement Strategies

Many strategies that facilitate play competence, playfulness, or level of engagement in either social interactions or object interactions during play were elucidated by researchers and practitioners working with young children with autism. It is often difficult to know where to begin. Some strategies may compete with one another. For example, increasing structure can be helpful in teaching a child with autism a new play skill because it decreases the complexity of a task. However, imposing too much adult structure can severely limit the child's internal locus of control; thus, the play task may become a work task (Bundy, 1996). The therapist can provide choices and convey a playful attitude to help set a positive atmosphere for the intervention session.

To ensure a successful intervention, select strategies that are most congruent with the goals of intervention and provide a fit between the child, the task, and the environment. Research shows that children with autism are able to demonstrate more effective interactions when the adult structures or prompts such interaction. This has important implications for play, regardless of whether these difficulties are due to lack of interest, lack of understanding of the social-communicative interchange, or sensory processing overload. However, both solicited interactions and opportunities for the child to initiate social play behaviors without such prompts must be offered. Both therapists and parents may need to be taught self-monitoring strategies that allow for a balance of these functions during play interactions with young children with autism.

Respecting the Child's Sensory Processing Capacities and Working within the Optimal Engagement Band

All play activities inherently provide some level of sensory experience that may have a reinforcing quality and/or a challenging quality. Each child's sensory thresholds for any given play activity should be individually determined, as these vary considerably from child to child and across conditions. Levels of arousal may be affected by a given sensory experience. For example, rough-housing play and tickling are intense and stimulating social activities that raise arousal levels, whereas listening to classical music, looking at a picture book, and

pulling a friend in a wagon may afford more calming effects due to their inherent sensory qualities. Play activities and interactions are needed that provide enough challenge to elicit approach and orienting responses but, at the same time, prevent overstimulation, aversion, and avoidance. Learning and playful engagement occur more successfully when a child is able to approach activities actively, with intrinsic motivation and positive affect. Existing play activities can also be altered to enhance or minimize sensory features or levels of arousal, which, in turn, enhance the fit among the child's needs, the play activity, and the temporal context. For example, roughhousing play may be an alerting activity that could be more therapeutic for a lethargic child in the morning than for an overstimulated child in the evening before bedtime. Intensive play interactions may need to be provided in multiple shorter increments for those children whose attention spans and sensory processing styles afford a narrower band of tolerance for stimulation. As in the case of Jimmy, the tickling helped elicit a positive response during play. However, his mother needs to monitor his reactions closely, pausing from the stimulation to be sure that the tickling does not accelerate to an aversive level that would cause withdrawal from the interaction.

Play Scaffolding

Scaffolding, another play engagement strategy, can be used to increase a child's mutual engagement and participation during play (e.g., Klinger & Dawson, 1992; Wolfberg, 1995). The child's participation is guided or assisted at necessary moments to facilitate a just-right challenge. A just-right challenge provides enough motivation to continue the play activity and to learn but maintains a high level of success throughout the activity. If the challenge is too high, the child may become frustrated; if too low, he or she may get bored. A thorough play activity analysis can assist in identifying where and when to implement such scaffolding strategies. Individualized scaffolding strategies, by their nature, tend to be flexible. They can be used to exaggerate a salient feature of a task or interaction, which, in turn, leads to increased engagement. For example, in the case of Jimmy, his mother is able to prompt him to go to the track by showing him the train car. She then places the car on the track and begins to push it. Although Jimmy does not initiate play with the trains, he watches his mother's actions and is able to follow her lead for a brief time. To encourage his continued participation, his mother may need to repeatedly scaffold parts of the activity or interaction by providing structure to keep the train moving or by encouraging a new challenge, such as moving the train over obstacles in the play scenario. Another scaffolding technique might be to hold one train car in place to help Jimmy successfully connect the next and then take turns with him to complete the task. Jimmy's mother may also pause as she performs an action or verbalizes, thus allowing Jimmy to respond or fill in the blank, e.g., "Train goes...(pause)...choo-choo!" As Jimmy's skills change, the scaffolding strategies will also change.

Imitation and Modeling

Imitation is a fundamental mechanism of social learning and communication. Knowledge of social games, play routines, and functional and symbolic object play behaviors often starts with imitation for all young children. Because children with autism have particular deficits in this area, it is often a direct target for interventions (e.g., Lewy & Dawson, 1992). Some approaches utilize adult-structured drills to teach motor and object imitation skills following a developmental progression, then integrate the skills in more naturalistic contexts. Others focus on exposure to peer models and naturalistic experiences immediately. In either case, it is common to begin with simple imitations and gradually build to ones that are more complex. For children who are unable to imitate any actions or vocalizations, a therapist begins by following the child's lead and imitating his or her actions (mirroring the child with autism). Gradually, the play repertoire is expanded and turn-taking established to promote learning and the social engagement process. Often, developing imitation abilities is easier for children with autism if they can see themselves perform the action and if the action uses an object that is functionally related to the task or provides other contextual cues about its use (e.g., shaking a rattle, putting a piece in a formboard, rolling a car). Later, purely motoric imitations (e.g., touch your head), sequential actions (e.g., jump up and down and turn around), and symbolic actions (e.g., fly the block like an airplane) can be added.

Peer modeling is an effective intervention strategy used to develop play competence and social participation. Modeling, like imitation, involves visually presenting an example of the appropriate behavior or play interaction to be accomplished. For example, a peer could engage in parallel play with the same materials (e.g., Play-Doh) as the child with autism to demonstrate appropriate actions (e.g., roll a snake, cut with scissors, build a snowman). Peer modeling is used to facilitate social initiations, which are particularly difficult for children with autism. Peers can set a physical example or use a verbal script for the child with autism to follow (e.g., greeting a new child). Once the skills are established, the child is given opportunities to expand/adapt the scripts and generalize the skills to other contexts and with other peers.

Facilitating Attention through Highly Salient Sensory Stimuli and Highly Charged Affect

Using highly salient sensory features or exaggerated positive affect may be particularly important to help the child with autism direct attention to the relevant features of a task or respond to and connect affective meaning to the social experience (e.g., experience pleasure from the social interaction). High-affect interventions are successful in gaining a child's initial attention or maintaining gaze during play interaction (Greenspan & Wieder, 1999; Klinger & Dawson, 1992). Using playful vocalizations (e.g., "zoom" while a toy car is moving) that change the rate, intonation, or volume of the voice and exaggerated or surprised expressions (e.g., gasp!) assists in obtaining the child's attention before proceeding with other learning strategies, such as imitation and modeling. Such highly charged social interactions may facilitate the development of positive relationships and increase the chance of getting an appropriate affective response from the child with autism during the social play interaction.

Affective expressions from children with autism may appear diminished in intensity, delayed, or, at times, even labile. Often, positive affect is more apparent during solitary play than during social interactions because the child derives more meaning and reinforcement from object play or repetitive and less complex interactions. Attaching sensory experiences that the child enjoys (e.g., spinning self) to social games (e.g., roughhousing/spinning game with dad) may help to increase motivation and meaning of the social-affective experience. Once the child

successfully maps the affective experience to the social interaction, the sensory features can be faded. Although some research shows that positive affect is seen during social interactions in children with autism, it may be less related to situations involving joint attention (Kasari, Sigman, Mundy, & Yirmiya, 1990). Using concrete cues can help direct the child's attention (e.g., using a flashlight to direct attention across the room; touching the actual toy rather than pointing in the general direction).

Simplifying Language Demands and Augmenting Communication

The ability of children with autism to process visuospatial information is usually superior to their ability to process information auditorally (Wolfberg, 1995). Consequently, when the therapist uses visual aids and simplifies the language demands of a play session, a child can become more fully engaged in a playful manner and focus on success in the social interaction. Several strategies that capitalize on a child's visual strengths can be used.

One strategy is to use scripts (graphic pictures and/or written words) to help structure play and social interactions with typical peers (e.g., Krantz & McClannahan, 1993; Quill, 1997; Wolfberg & Schuler, 1993). For example, place a picture/word sequence of a social interaction that takes place during mealtime on the table in front of a child. Assuming that mealtime is fairly routine, the sequence might depict "Please pass the milk" and "Thank you." Once the child learns that social exchange, encourage him or her to use the same exchange in other environments, then add a new exchange to the mealtime routine. It is important that this type of strategy be individualized so that it matches the (cognitive) strengths or learning style of the child with autism.

Another strategy is to enhance the child's communication abilities using augmented means, such as pictures, objects, or gestures, as symbolic representations of specific concepts. Children with autism often have difficulty understanding or expressing communicative interactions or concepts critical to a play routine. Augmenting the play sessions with a communication system may, therefore, be effective. For example, objects, pictures, gestures, sign language, or a variety of high-tech strategies (e.g., dedicated communication devices and computerized visual displays) may be useful to incorporate with the play interventions so that the transmission of messages between play partners is more easily facilitated (Reinhartsen, Edmondson, & Crais, 1997).

Finally, because processing verbal information or instructions during play sessions may be particularly difficult, reducing the language demands by simply reducing the amount and complexity of language allows the play situation to be more playful and less challenging. It is important to use language appropriate to the developmental level of the child. For instance, if a five-year-old child with autism understands language at a three-year level, it is more appropriate to say "Let's play ball" than "Go get the ball from the toy box so we can play catch."

Expanding Play Routines

Routines, by nature, are comforting and organizing for children with autism. Jimmy's play routine is noted to be restricted to stereotypical interactions with toys within the context of solitary play. One strategy is to begin with the routine that the child prefers or is familiar with and begin to gradually extend or diversify the components of the routine to develop new and more complex play skills (Hogan, 1997). For example, Jimmy may also enjoy lining up small wooden blocks repetitively and is noted to have a relative strength in the area of fine motor skills. The intervention may start to expand his object manipulation (i.e., construction play) routine by introducing stacking two blocks rather than lining them up. Once the child masters the new routine, it is extended again (e.g., stacking several blocks for a tower, building bridges with three to five blocks, imitating larger structures with several dimensions, changing from wooden blocks that are all uniform to Legos or bristle blocks). Likewise, peer interactions can be gradually worked into the routine, adding yet another layer of complexity and diversity. A similar strategy can be employed for a child demonstrating the beginnings of symbolic play. For example, the therapist might begin with simple play schemes that involve only one action, such as the child feeding himself or herself. Gradually, another step is added to the familiar routine, such as stirring with a spoon in the bowl and then feeding himself or herself. Once that is mastered, several steps are added (e.g., stir, feed, make yum sound). Eventually, use of other objects or people as agents (a doll, another human) can be included. After the child becomes adept at familiar routines, the caregiver or other interventionist may progress to novel play sequences.

These can be taught through imitation within the context of a familiar routine and natural context or through imitation of pretend play. Social initiations can also be taught through expansion of simple playful social routines. For example, Jimmy loves tickling. This could be gradually worked into an anticipation game (e.g., "I'm gonna get you"...wait for Jimmy's signal, then provide tickle) or a turn-taking game exchanging tickles. Sharing and turn-taking are especially important skills for children with autism to master in the context of playful interaction. Turn-taking games, once learned, can be utilized to extend the child's actions or help the child generate new ideas for play. For example, in a more advanced child, a Simon Says game could be modified so that each child takes one turn at generating a new action. For less advanced children, using materials may be easier than abstract actions (e.g., make something different with Play-Doh). Initially, the child may need to rely on retrieval of previously modeled or practiced responses (e.g., provide direction about or a picture of making a snake with Play-Doh). Likewise, the adult or peer might try to demonstrate the beginning of an action, but stop or fail the action (e.g., hold cookie cutter, but fail pressing the shape in Play-Doh) to prompt the child with autism to generate a solution and complete the task.

Other Play Organizers

Often, children with autism have difficulty knowing how to initiate, maintain, or discontinue play and benefit from techniques to help them with the temporal or physical organization of routines and play activities (Hogan, 1997; Rogers & Lewis, 1989; Wolfberg, 1995). Setting predictable routines and scheduled playtimes may be helpful for some children, whereas others are able to tolerate change or can engage in play more naturally in the context of embedded family occupations. Some examples of strategies to help organize temporal and motivational aspects of play include:

- Using schedules (picture, word, or object schedules) to organize a sequence of activities and to ensure predictability and ease of transitions.
- Using playful rituals to signal the beginning and end of an activity, or strategies to initiate and close social interactions or games.

- Providing containers, such as start and finish boxes, to indicate where an activity begins and ends, or jigs (i.e., patterns) to provide a concrete learning structure.
- Using auditory signals (e.g., song ends, so stop) or visual signals (e.g., colored light timer is on, so keep going) to indicate the need to maintain or discontinue an activity or transition to a new activity.

Generalization

Children with autism need ample opportunity to practice play skills—beyond what could ever be accomplished in a single intervention session or even a series of interventions. Therefore, embedding play in natural routines and integrating interventions within naturalistic contexts (e.g., home, school, and community) are required for maintenance and generalization (e.g., Goldstein et al., 1988). The most appropriate methods of facilitating generalization are still debated. Some researchers are also investigating the use of self-monitoring strategies in addition to adult structured prompting and praising methods (e.g., Strain, Kohler, Storey, & Danko, 1994) to facilitate social participation within naturalistic contexts and generalization of participation across settings as well as with a variety of play partners.

CONCLUSION

Play is a complex childhood occupation that fosters successful social participation. For many young children with autism, play is an enormous challenge. The nature of the disorder contributes particular challenges in the areas of engagement with persons and objects, pretend play, imitation, and praxis as well as sensory processing, arousal modulation, and attention functions supporting play. Each child's strengths and limitations vary; thus, carefully assessing a child's play and individualizing play goals and interventions is warranted. Facilitating both play competence (skills) and playfulness is important, as these aspects of play are not mutually dependent and, often, both are lacking in young children with autism. A variety of strategies are delineated that provide practitioners guidance in promoting more successful engagement in play for young child with autism. Ultimately, greater participation across social, temporal, and physical contexts is a desired outcome.

CHAPTER REVIEW QUESTIONS

1. How is the development of play and the process of play affected by autism?
2. Give one example of a play task that illustrates each of the play definitions included in Table 13–1.
3. What skills are typically necessary for successful social engagement in pretend play?
4. What capabilities for social engagement in pretend play do children with autism typically display?
5. What are the strengths in play that children with autism display?
6. How can play skills and playfulness be enhanced through the use of structure?
7. Using the dynamic model of sensory processing, describe how a restricted range of arousal influences social and play engagement.
8. What is the difference between play competency and playfulness? Describe one assessment for measuring each of these concepts.
9. What types of play assessments may be most useful for planning play interventions for children with autism? Why?
10. Apply the concepts of designing play spaces and play materials to the design of an environment most relevant to your situation (e.g., home, school, clinic).
11. Design a play experience to increase play interaction between children with and without autism.
12. What strengths and constraints do play activities initiated by adults have for children with autism?
13. Define the purpose of each of the following play engagement strategies: working within the optimal engagement band, play scaffolding, imitation and modeling, facilitating attention, and expanding play routines. Give an example of each play engagement strategy.

REFERENCES

Adrien, J. (1991). Autism and family home movies: Preliminary findings. *Journal of Autism and Developmental Disorders, 21*, 43–49.

Adrien, J. (1992). Early symptoms in autism from family home movies: Evaluation and comparison between first and second year of life using IBSE Scale. *Acta Paedopsychiatrica: International Journal of Child and Adolescent Psychiatry 55*, 71–75.

American Psychiatric Association. (1994). *Diagnostic and statistical manual of mental disorders* (4th ed.). Washington, DC: Author.

Baranek, G. T. (1998, April). *Autism: A window into sensory processing*. Paper presented at the meeting of the American Occupational Therapy Association, Baltimore, MD. (Part of Sensory Integration Special Interest Section [SISIS] institute titled "Sensory modulation, regulation, and processing: What are they?")

Baranek, G. T. (1999). Autism during infancy: A retrospective video analysis of sensory-motor and social behaviors at 9–12 months of age. *Journal of Autism and Developmental Disorders, 29*, 213–224.

Baranek, G. T., Foster, L. G., & Berkson, G. (1997). Tactile defensiveness and stereotyped behaviors. *American Journal of Occupational Therapy, 51*, 91–95.

Barnett, L. A. (1990). Playfulness: Definition, design, and measurement. *Play and Culture, 3*, 319–336.

Baron-Cohen, S. (1987). Autism and symbolic play. *British Journal of Developmental Psychology, 5*, 139–148.

Baron-Cohen, S., Leslie, A. M., & Frith, U. (1985). Does the autistic child have a "theory of mind"? *Cognition, 21*, 37–46.

Barresi, T., & Moore, C. (1996). Intentional relations and social understanding. *Behavioral and Brain Science, 19*, 107–154.

Bergen, D. (1988). *Play as a medium for learning and development*. Portsmouth, NH: Heinemann Educational Books.

Bledsoe, N., & Shepard, J. (1982). A study of reliability and validity of a preschool play scale. *American Journal of Occupational Therapy, 36*, 783–788.

Bornstein, M. H., Haynes, L., Pascual, L., Painter, K. M., & Galperin, C. (1999). Play in two societies: Pervasiveness of process, specificity of structure. *Child Development, 70*, 317–331.

Brown, W. H., Ragland, E. U., & Fox, J. J. (1988). Effects of groups socialization procedures on the social interactions of preschool children. *Research in Developmental Disabilities, 9*(4), 359–376.

Bundy, A. C. (1996). Play and playfulness: What to look for. In L. D. Parham & L. S. Fazio (Eds.), *Play in occupational therapy for children* (pp. 52–66). St. Louis, MO: Mosby–Year Book.

Bundy, A. C. (1997). *Test of Playfulness (ToP) Manual, Version 3.4*. Ft. Collins: Colorado State University.

Case-Smith, J., & Bryan, T. (1999). The effects of occupational therapy with sensory integration emphasis on preschool-age children with autism. *American Journal of Occupational Therapy, 53*, 489–497.

Clinical Center for the Study of Development and Learning (1998). *Play assessment*. Unpublished manuscript.

Corona, R., Dissanayake, C., Arbelle, S., Wellington, P., & Sigman, M. (1998). Is affect aversive to young children with autism? Behavioral and cardiac re-

sponses to experimenter distress. *Child Development, 69*, 1494–1502.

Coster, W. (1998). Occupation-centered assessment of children. *American Journal of Occupational Therapy, 52*, 337–344.

Courchesne, E., Townsend, J., Akshoomoff, N. A., Saitoh, O., Yeung-Courchesne, R., Lincoln, A. J., James, H. E., Haas, R. H., Schreibman, L., & Lau, L. (1994). Impairment in shifting attention in autistic and cerebellar patients. *Behavioral Neuroscience, 108*, 848–865.

Curcio, F., & Piserchia, E. A. (1978). Pantomimic representation on psychotic children. *Journal of Autism and Childhood Schizophrenia, 8*(2), 181–189.

Dawson, G., & Adams, A. (1984). Imitation and social responsiveness in autistic children. *Journal of Abnormal Child Psychology, 12*, 209–225.

Dawson, G., & Lewy, A. (1989). Arousal attention and the socioemotional impairments of individuals with autism. In G. Dawson (Ed.), *Autism: Nature, diagnosis, and treatment*. New York: Guilford Press.

Dawson, G., Meltzoff, A. N., Osterling, J., & Rinaldi, J. (1998). Neuropsychological correlates of early symptoms of autism. *Child Development, 69*, 1276–1285.

DeMyer, M. (1976). The nature of the neuropsychological disability in autistic children. In E. Schopler & R. J. Reichler (Eds.), *Psychopathology in child development: Research and treatment* (pp. 93–114). New York: Plenum.

DeMyer, M. K., Alpern, G. D., Barton, S., DeMyer, W., Churchill D. W., Hingtgen, J. N., Bryson, C. Q., Pontius, W., & Kimberlin, C. (1972). Imitation in autistic, early schizophrenic, and nonpsychotic subnormal children. *Journal of Autism and Childhood Schizophrenia, 2*, 264–87.

DeMyer, M. K., Mann, N. A., Tilton, J. R., & Lowe, L. H. (1967). Toy-play behavior and use of body by autistic and normal children as reported by mothers. *Psychological Reports, 21*, 973–981.

DesLauries, A. (1978). Play, symbols, and the development of language. In M. Rutter & E. Schopler (Eds.), *Autism* (pp. 313–326). New York: Plenum.

DiLavore, P., Lord, C., & Rutter, M. (1995). Prelinguistic autism diagnostic observation schedule (PL-ADOS). *Journal of Autism and Developmental Disorders, 25*, 355–379.

El-Ghoroury, N. H., & Romanczyk, R. G. (1999). Play interactions of family members toward children with autism. *Journal of Autism and Developmental Disorders, 29*, 249–258.

Ferrara, L., & Hill, S. D. (1980). The responsiveness of autistic children to the predictability of social and nonsocial toys. *Journal of Autism and Developmental Disorders, 10*, 51–57.

Fewell, R. R. (1986). *Play assessment scale* (5th revision). Unpublished manuscript.

Fewell, R. R., & Rich, J. S. (1987). Play assessment as a procedure for examining cognitive, communication, and social skills in multihandicapped children. *Journal of Psychoeducational Assessment, 2*, 107–118.

Field, T. (1982). Affective displays of high-risk and normal infants during early interaction. In T. Field & A. Fogel (Eds.), *Emotion and early interaction* (pp. 101–125). Hillsdale, NJ: Erlbaum.

Florey, L. (1976). Development through play. In C. Schaefer (Ed.), *Therapeutic use of play* (pp. 61–70). Northvale, NJ: Jason Aronson.

Frith, U. (1996). Cognitive explanation of autism. *Acta Paediatrica, 416*(Suppl.), 63–68.

Frith, U., & Happe, F. (1994). Autism: Beyond "theory of mind." *Cognition, 50*, 115–132.

Goldstein, H., Wickstrom, S., Hoyson, M., Jamieson, B., & Odom, S. L. (1988). Effect of sociodramatic script training on social and communicative interaction. *Education and Treatment of Children, 11*, 97–117.

Greenspan, S. I., & Wieder, S. (1999). A functional developmental approach to autism spectrum disorders. *Journal of the Association of Persons with Severe Handicaps, 24*(3), 147–161.

Heimann, M., Ullstadius, E., Dahlgren, S. O., & Gillberg, C. (1992). Imitation in autism: A preliminary research note. *Behavioral Neurology, 5*, 219–227.

Hermelin, B., & O'Connor, N. (1970). *Psychological experiments with autistic children*. London: Pergamon.

Hogan, K. (1997). Nonverbal thinking, communication, and play skills from a developmental perspective with some things to remember [On-line]. Available: www.unc.edu/depts/teacch/teacchco.htm

Howlin, P. (1986). An overview of social behavior in autism. In E. Schopler & G. Mesibov (Eds.), *Social behavior in autism* (pp. 63–70). New York: Plenum.

Hutt, S. J., Hutt, C., Lee, D., & Ounsted, C. (1964). Arousal and childhood autism. *Nature, 204*, 908–909.

Jarrold, C., Boucher, J., & Smith, P. K. (1994). Executive function deficits and the pretend play of children with autism: A research note. *Journal of Child Psychology and Psychiatry, 35*, 1473–1482.

Kaplan-Sanoff, M., Brewster, A., Stillwell, J., & Bergen, B. (1988). The relationship of play to physical/motor development and to children with special needs. In D. Bergen (Ed.), *Play as a medium for learning and development* (pp. 137–162). Portsmouth, NH: Heinemann.

Kasari, C., Sigman, M., Mundy, P., & Yirmiya, N. (1990). Affective sharing in the context of joint attention interactions of normal, autistic, and mentally retarded children. *Journal of Autism and Developmental Disorders, 20*, 87–100.

Klin, A. (1992). Listening preferences in regard to speech in four children with developmental disabilities. *Journal of Child Psychology and Psychiatry, 33*, 763–769.

Klinger, L. G., & Dawson, G. (1992). Facilitating early social and communicative development in children with autism. In S. F. Warren & J. Reichle (Eds.), *Causes and effects in communication and language intervention* (pp. 157–186). Baltimore: Paul H. Brookes.

Knox, S. (1997). Development and current use of the Knox Preschool Play Scale. In L. D. Parham & L. S. Fazio (Eds.), *Play in occupational therapy for children* (pp. 35–51). St. Louis, MO: Mosby–Year Book.

Knox, S. H. (1974). A play scale. In M. Reilly (Ed.), *Play as exploratory learning: Studies of curiosity behavior* (pp. 247–266). Beverly Hills, CA: Sage Publications.

Knox, S. H. (1996). Play and playfulness in preschool children. In R. Zemke & F. Clark (Eds.), *Occupational science: The evolving discipline* (pp. 81–88). Philadelphia: F. A. Davis.

Koegel, L. K., Camarata, S. M., Valdez-Menchaca, M., & Koegel, R. L. (1998). Setting generalization of question asking by children with autism. *American Journal on Mental Retardation, 102*, 346–357.

Koegel, R. L., O'Dell, M. C., & Koegel, L. K. (1987). A natural language teaching paradigm for nonverbal autistic children. *Journal of Autism and Developmental Disorders, 17*, 187–200.

Krantz, P., & McClannahan, L. (1993). Teaching children with autism to initiate to peers: Effects of a script-fading procedure. *Journal of Applied Behavior Analysis, 26*, 121–132.

Lewis, V., & Boucher, J. (1988). Spontaneous, instructed, and elicited play in relatively able autistic children. *British Journal of Developmental Psychology, 6*, 325–339.

Lewy, A. L., & Dawson, G. (1992). Social stimulation and joint attention in young autistic children. *Journal of Abnormal Child Psychology, 20*, 555–566.

Libby, S., Powell, S., Messer, D., & Jordan, R. (1998). Spontaneous play in children with autism: A reappraisal. *Journal of Autism and Developmental Disorders, 28*, 487–497.

Lieberman, J. N. (1965). Playfulness and divergent thinking: An investigation of their relationship at the kindergarten level. *Journal of Genetic Psychology, 107*, 219–224.

Lifter, K., Sulzer-Azaroff, B., Anderson, S. R., & Cowdery, G. E. (1993). Teaching play activities to preschool children with disabilities: The importance of developmental considerations. *Journal of Early Intervention, 17*, 139–159.

Linder, T. W. (1993). *Transdisciplinary play-based assessment: A functional approach to working with young children* (rev. ed.). Baltimore: Paul H. Brookes.

Lord, C., Rutter, M., DiLavore, P., & Risi, A. L. (1999). *Autism diagnostic observation schedule.* Los Angeles: Western Psychological Services.

Lord, C., Rutter, M., Goode, S., Heemsbergen, J., Jordan, H., & Mawhood, L. (1989). Autism diagnostic observation schedule: A standardized observation of communicative and social behavior. *Journal of Autism and Developmental Disorders, 19*, 185–212.

Lovaas, O. I., & Smith, T. (1989). A comprehensive behavioral theory of autistic children: Paradigm for research and treatment. *Journal of Behavior Therapy and Experimental Psychiatry, 20*, 17–29.

Lovaas, O. I., Koegel, R., & Schreibman, L. (1979). Stimulus overselectivity in autism: A review of research. *Psychological Bulletin, 86*, 1236–1254.

Loveland, K., & Landry, S. (1986). Joint attention and communication in autism and language delay. *Journal of Autism and Developmental Disorders, 16*, 335–349.

Mathiowetz, V., & Haugen, J. B. (1995). Evaluation of motor behavior: Traditional and contemporary views. In C. A. Trombly (Ed.), *Occupational therapy for physical dysfunction* (4th ed.) (pp. 157–185). Baltimore: Williams & Williams.

Maurice, C., Green G., & Luce, S.C. (Eds.). (1996). *Behavioral intervention for young children with autism: A manual for parents and professionals.* Austin, TX: Pro-Ed.

McEvoy, M. A., Mordquist, V. M., Twardosz, S., Heckaman, K. A., Wehby, J. H., & Denny, R. K. (1988). Promoting autistic children's peers interactions in an integrated early childhood setting using affection activities. *Journal of Applied Behavior Analysis, 21*, 193–200.

McGee, G. G., Feldman, R. S., & Morrier, M. J. (1997). Benchmarks of social treatment for children with autism. *Journal of Autism and Developmental Disorders, 27*, 353–364.

McWilliam, R. A. (1994). *Children's Engagement Questionnaire.* Unpublished manuscript.

McWilliam, R. A. (1999). *Children's Engagement Rating Scale.* Unpublished manuscript.

Meltzoff, A., & Gopnik, A. (1993). The role of imitation in understanding persons and developing a theory of mind. In S. Baron-Cohen, H. Tager-Flushberg, & D. Cohen (Eds.), *Understanding other minds: Perspectives from autism* (pp. 333–366). Oxford, England: Oxford University Press.

Minshew, N., Goldstein, G., & Siegel, D. J. (1997). Neuropsychologic functioning in autism: Profile of a complex information processing disorder. *Journal of the International Neuropsychological Society, 3*, 303–316.

Minsky, M. (1975). A framework for representing knowledge. In D. Winston (Ed.), *The psychology of computer vision* (pp.144–175). New York: McGraw-Hill.

Moore, D. G., Hobson, R. P., & Lee, A. (1997). Components of person perception: An investigation with autistic, nonautistic retarded, and typically developing children and adolescents. *British Journal of Developmental Psychology, 15*, 401–423.

Morrison, C. D., Metzger, P., & Pratt, P. N. (1996). Play. In J. Case-Smith, A. S. Allen, & P. N. Pratt (Eds.), *Occupational therapy for children* (3rd ed.) (pp. 504–523). St. Louis, MO: Mosby.

Mundy, P., Sigman, M., Ungerer, J. A., & Sherman, T. (1987) Nonverbal communication and play correlates of language development in autistic children. *Journal of Autism and Developmental Disorders, 17*, 349–364.

Myles, B. S., Simpson, R. L., Ormsbee, C. K., & Erickson, C. (1993). Integrating preschool children with autism and their normally developing peers: Research findings and the best practice recommendations. *Focus on Autistic Behavior, 8*, 8–18.

Nelson, D. (1984). *Children with autism.* Thorofare, NJ: Slack.

Nicolich, L. (1977). Beyond sensorimotor intelligence. *Merrill-Palmer Quarterly, 23*, 89–99.

Ohta, M. (1987). Cognitive disorders of infantile autism: A study employing the WISC, spatial relationships, conceptualization, and gestural imitation. *Journal of Autism and Developmental Disorders, 17*, 45–62.

Osterling, J., & Dawson, G. (1994). Early recognition of children with autism: A study of first birthday home videotapes. *Journal of Autism and Developmental Disorders, 24*, 247–257.

Parham, L. D. (1996). Perspective on play. In R. Zemke & F. Clark (Eds.), *Occupational science: The evolving discipline* (pp. 71–80). Philadelphia: F. A. Davis.

Parten, M. B. (1932). Social participation among preschool children. *Journal of Abnormal and Social Psychology, 27*, 243–269.

Pennington, B. F., & Ozonoff, S. (1996). Executive functions and developmental psychopathology. *Journal of Child Psychology and Psychiatry and Applied Disciplines, 37*, 51–87.

Piaget, J. (1962). *Play, dreams, and imitation in children*. New York: Norton.

Powers, M. (1989). *Children with autism*. Rockville, MD: Woodbine House.

Quill, K. (1997). Rationale for visually cued instruction. *Journal of Autism and Developmental Disorders, 27*, 697–714.

Reilly, M. (1974). Defining a cobweb. In M. Reilly (Ed.), *Play as exploratory learning: Studies of curiosity behavior* (pp. 117–150). Beverly Hills, CA: Sage Publications.

Reinhartsen, D., Edmondson, R., & Crais, E. R. (1997). Developing assistive technology strategies for infants and toddlers with communication difficulties. *Seminars in Speech and Language, 18*(3), 283–301.

Restall, G., & Magill-Evans, J. (1994). Play and preschool children with autism. *American Journal of Occupational Therapy, 48*, 113–120.

Riquet, C. B., Taylor, N. D., Benaroya, S., & Klein, L. S. (1981). Symbolic play in autistic, Down's, and normal children of equivalent mental age. *Journal of Autism and Developmental Disorders, 11*, 439–448.

Rogers, S. J. (1999). An examination of the imitation deficit in autism. In J. Nadel & G. Butterworth (Eds.), *Imitation in infancy* (pp. 254–283). New York: Cambridge University Press.

Rogers, S. J., Bennetto, L., McEvoy, R., & Pennington, B. F. (1996). Imitation and pantomime in high-functioning adolescents with autism spectrum disorders. *Child Development, 67*, 2060–2073.

Rogers, S. J., & Lewis, H. (1989). An effective day treatment model for young children with pervasive developmental disorders. *Journal of American Academy of Child and Adolescent Psychiatry, 28*, 207–214.

Rogers, S. J., & McEvoy, R. E. (1993, March). *Praxis in high-functioning persons with autism*. Paper presented at the biennial meeting of the Society of Research in Child Development, New Orleans, Louisiana.

Rossetti, L. (1990). *The Rossetti Infant-Toddler Language Scale*. East Moline, IL: LinguiSystems.

Schopler, E., Brehm, S., Kinsbourne, M., & Reichler, R. J. (1971). The effect of treatment structure on development in autistic children. *Archives of General Psychiatry, 24*, 415–421.

Siegel, D. J., Minshew, N. J., & Goldstein, G. (1996). Wechsler IQ profiles in diagnosis of high-functioning autism. *Journal of Autism and Developmental Disorders, 26*, 389–406.

Sigman, M., Mundy, P., Sherman, T., & Ungerer, J. A. (1986). Social interactions of autistic, mentally retarded, and normal children and their caregivers. *Journal of Child Psychology and Psychiatry, 27*, 647–656.

Sigman, M., & Ruskin, E. (1999). Continuity and change in the social competence of children with autism, Down's syndrome, and developmental delays. *Monographs of the Society for Research in Child Development, 64*, 1–130.

Sigman, M., & Ungerer, J. A. (1981). Sensorimotor skills and language comprehension in autistic children. *Journal of Abnormal Child Psychology, 9*, 149–165.

Sigman, M., & Ungerer, J. A. (1984). Cognitive and language skills in autistic, mentally retarded, and normal children. *Developmental Psychology, 20*, 209–302.

Sinclair, H. (1970). The transition from sensorimotor behavior to symbolic activity. *Interchange, 1*, 119–125.

Smith, I. M., & Bryson, S. E. (1994). Imitation and action in autism: A critical review. *Psychological Bulletin, 116*(2), 259–273.

Stern, D. (1985). *The interpersonal world of the human infant*. New York: Basic Books.

Stone, W. L., & Lemanek, K. L. (1990). Parental report of social behaviors in autistic preschoolers. *Journal of Autism and Developmental Disorders, 20*, 513–523.

Stone, W. L., Lemanek, K. L., Fishel, P. T., Fernandez, M. C., & Altemeier, W. A. (1990). Play and imitation skills in the diagnosis of autism in young children. *Pediatrics, 86,* 267–272.

Stone, W. L., & Ousley, O. Y. (1997). *Screening Tool for Autism in Two-Year-Olds (STAT).* Unpublished manuscript.

Stone, W. L., Ousley, O. Y., & Littleford, C. (1997). Motor imitation in young children with autism: What's the object? *Journal of Abnormal Child Psychology, 25,* 475–485.

Stone, W. L., Ousley, O. Y., Yoder, P. J., Hogan, K. L., & Hepburn, S. L. (1997). Nonverbal communication in two- and three-year-old children with autism. *Journal of Autism and Developmental Disorders, 27,* 677–696.

Strain, P. S., Hoyson, M., & Jamieson, B. (1985, Spring). Normally developing preschoolers as intervention agents for autisticlike children: Effects on class department and social interaction. *Journal of the Division for Early Childhood 9,* 105–111.

Strain, P. S., Kohler, F. W., Storey, K., & Danko, C. D. (1994). Teaching preschoolers with autism to self-monitor their social interactions: An analysis of results in home and school settings. *Journal of Emotional and Behavioral Disorders, 2,* 78–88.

Swettenham, J., Baron-Cohen, S., Charman, T., Cox, A., Baird, G., Drew, A., Rees, L., & Wheelwright, S. (1998). The frequency and distribution of spontaneous attention shifts between social and nonsocial stimuli in autistic, typically developing, and nonautistic developmentally delayed infants. *Journal of Child Psychology and Psychiatry, 39,* 747–753.

Takata, N. (1974). Play as a prescription. In M. Reilly (Ed.), *Play as exploratory learning: Studies of curiosity behavior* (pp. 209–246). Beverly Hills, CA: Sage Publications.

Tardif, C., Plumet, M. H., Beaudichon, J., Waller, D., Bouvard, M., & Leboyer, M. (1995). Microanalysis of social interactions between autistic children and normal adults in semistructured play situations. *International Journal of Behavioral Development, 18,* 727–747.

Tiegerman, E., & Primavera, L. H. (1981). Imitating the autistic child: Facilitating communicative gaze behavior. *Journal of Autism and Developmental Disorders, 14,* 27–38.

Tilton, J. R., & Ottinger, D. R. (1964). Comparison of toy play behavior of autistic, retarded, and normal children. *Psychological Reports, 15,* 967–975.

Trad, P. V., Bernstein, G., Shapiro, T., & Hertzig, M. (1993). Assessing the relationship between affective responsivity and social interaction in children with Pervasive Developmental Disorder. *Journal of Autism and Developmental Disorders, 23,* 361–377.

Ungerer, J. A., & Sigman, M. (1981). Symbolic play and language comprehension in autistic children. *Journal of the American Academy of Child Psychiatry, 20,* 318–338.

Ungerer, J. A., Zelazo, P. R., Kearsley, R. B., & O'Leary, K. (1981). Developmental changes in the representation of objects in symbolic play from 18 to 34 months of age. *Child Development, 52,* 186–195.

Volkmar, F. R., Cohen, D. J., & Paul, R. (1986). An evaluation of DSM-III criteria for infantile autism. *Journal of the American Academy of Child Psychiatry, 25,* 190–197.

Werner, H., & Kaplan, B. (1963). *Symbol formation.* New York: John Wiley & Sons.

Westby, C. E. (1980). Assessment of cognitive and language abilities through play. *Language, Speech, and Hearing Services in Schools, 11,* 154–168.

Wetherby, A. M., & Prizant, B. M. (1993). *Communication and symbolic behavior scales.* Chicago: Riverside.

Wetherby, A. M., & Prutting, C. A. (1984). Profiles of communicative and cognitive-social abilities in autistic children. *Journal of Speech and Hearing Research, 27,* 364–377.

Wing, L. (1981). Asperger's Syndrome: A clinical account. *Psychological Medicine, 11,* 115–129.

Wing, L., Gould, J., Yeates, S. R., & Brierley, L. M. (1977). Symbolic play in severely mentally retarded and in autistic children. *Journal of Child Psychology and Psychiatry, 18,* 167–178.

Wolfberg, P. J. (1995). Enhancing children's play. In K. Quill (Ed.), *Teaching children with autism: Strategies to enhance communication and socialization* (pp. 193–218). Albany, NY: Delmar.

Wolfberg, P. J., & Schuler, A. L. (1993). Integrated play groups: A model for promoting the social and cognitive dimensions of play in children with autism. *Journal of Autism and Developmental Disorders, 23,* 467–489.

World Health Organization. (1999). http://who.org. Accessed June 12, 2000.

PART 4

Applications of the Sensorimotor Approach To Improve Function

CHAPTER 14

Sensory Applications for Sleep and Toilet Training

Elaine Fehringer Leone and Sandra L. Rogers

CHAPTER OBJECTIVES

At the completion of this chapter, the reader will be able to:

- Understand the typical development of sleep and toileting readiness.
- Describe multiple methods to simplify sensory and motor demands and enhance toilet training or to modulate arousal and facilitate sleep.

INTRODUCTION

Sleep disturbances are a common clinical feature of children with autism (Hering, Epstein, Elroy, Iancu, & Zelnik, 1999; Patzold, Richdale, & Tonge, 1998; Richdale, 1999; Taira, Takase, & Sasaki, 1998). The most frequently reported deficit is difficulty falling asleep, followed by frequent awakening during sleep, early morning awaking, and nocturnal incontinence. A portion of these sleep problems could be attributed to difficulties in regulating or modulating sensory input and arousal. Similarly, toileting as a self-care skill presents special problems in children with autism. The process of toileting may engender sensory challenges, such as anticipating the need to eliminate, fear of the bathroom, sensitivity in dealing with tactile stimulation (soiled clothing and removing clothing), sitting quietly for two to three minutes, following a relatively complex sequence for hygiene, flushing the toilet, and generalizing toileting skills to novel environments. Thus, both sleeping and toileting rely, in part, on sensory processing, sensory and arousal modulation, sensory discrimination, and, in the case of toileting, muscular stability. These are common daily tasks that, as areas of dysfunction, are particularly difficult for parents and caregivers. The purpose of this chapter is to provide an overview of the sensorimotor strategies that may be helpful in facilitating sleep and toilet training among children with autism. Because these common daily tasks receive scant attention in the published literature, their inclusion here is also intended to highlight their importance for function and to stimulate further study and clinical intervention.

SLEEP

Given that sleep disturbances are often associated with brain stem damage, it is likely that the sleep disturbances of at least some children with autism have neurobiological origins (Rodier, 2000). Many authors documented the persistent sleep problems among children with autism. On the other hand, one researcher indicated that sleep problems may not be as prevalent among children with autism as previously thought, and that sensitivity to normal sleep patterns (nocturnal waking) may be heightened by caregiver concerns about the child's various deficits (Hering et al., 1999). Whether this is true or not, sleep difficulties are problematic for parents and caregivers of children with and without disabilities; a consideration of both typical and atypical sleep patterns is warranted.

Most typically developing children have periodic difficulty with establishing a comfortable sleep routine. Children often experience nocturnal waking, occasional nightmares, and early rising (Pearse, 1999). Consequently, many recommendations for treating sleep dysfunction in children with autism follow guidelines common to typically developing children. Most guidelines encourage familiar and structured sleep routines that are followed clearly by all family members. These habits can be facilitated by choosing a sleep time that is reasonable for the whole family, usually 7:30–8:30 P.M. for the children. Children ages of two to five usually require 12 to 15 hours of sleep per day, with approximately 10 to 12 hours at night. Most children take an afternoon nap of 1 to 2 hours in length, or have a quiet time required until four years of age (Wong, 1997). A typical bedtime routine for any child may include preparatory activities, like having a snack, bathing, changing into pajamas, going to the toilet, brushing teeth, reading a book, listening to quiet music. Caregivers are encouraged to ensure that there is no way in which the child can harm himself or herself if he or she has difficulty falling asleep; avoid frequent checking to determine if the child is asleep (as with any sleep pattern, sleep alternates between deep and light sleep); if a child wakens, provide brief comfort (one minute or less) and assure the child is safe; and set a wake time of 6:00–6:30 A.M. and do not pay attention to the child until that time (e.g., ignore crying; if the child gets out of bed, place him or her back in without a fuss; set a baby gate in the doorway).

As a basic foundation, children with autism should have a structured routine for going to bed and staying in bed, and a set rising time. Additional routines may also be helpful. In order to determine a pattern of sleep, caregivers can complete a sleep diary that documents sleep patterns. Preparation for going to bed should be given adequate time and may need to be almost hypnotic (Pearse, 1999). The child may be allowed to fall asleep to music, have a specific set of motor activities that help him or her wind down, leave a light on, have soothing/familiar objects in bed, have a digital clock and visual cue for time to rise. Another technique that children find useful is a specific routine to decrease arousal level (Williams & Shellenberger, 1996). For example, some children may find that slow rocking with deep pressure from pillows is an effective preparation for sleep (Oetter, Richter, & Frick, 1995). Additional recommendations include use of a water bed, an indoor sleeping bag, a bed tent, several small pillows, and slow and rhythmic deep pressure when the child is ill or has been awake for hours (Pearse). The use of a weighted or heavy blanket may be calming. Some parents reported the use of the following techniques, which provide deep pressure touch: tucking the blankets or sheets in; wrapping the child in a blanket; soothing massage; and clothing the child in tight pajamas, knit tubing (available at local fabric stores), or stretch fabric garments. Simply recognizing that sleep may be enhanced by changing the environment and varying sensory input from clothing, blankets, lighting, movement, and arousing stimuli may help parents and caregivers experiment to find the sensory mix that is best for the child.

TOILETING

This section describes the skills needed for learning both bowel and bladder control and offers suggestions for developing this control. Independence in toileting is a major developmental milestone for any child and his or her family. Mastering toileting is a pivotal skill in acquiring social competence (Lowenthal, 1996). In most families, the advantages of a child with autism learning to use the toilet typically outweigh the difficulties involved in teaching him or her. The primary advantages are improved independence and social acceptance, reduced cost for family, and less required physical care, which increases time available for social and emotional interaction.

Toileting is such a complex process that it is amazing any child learns it before entering the public school system at age five. A task analysis of the steps required for independence reveals that a child must be proficient in dressing, be able to manipulate fine paper, have awareness of bowel and bladder function and sensation, have a well-developed body scheme, and be comfortable with multiple sensory input (e.g., noise, texture, temperature). These are just a few of the critical elements of toileting, but they illustrate the complexity of the task.

Readiness for Toileting

The child with autism often has disturbances of sensory processing and perception, including registration and modulation of sensory input (Ayres & Tickle, 1980). The act of emptying the bladder or having a bowel movement is a sensory experience. Registration of the sensation of bladder fullness is the first step in achieving continence. To develop urine continence, the child must additionally register the following sensations: the start of urination, emptiness of the bladder, and the difference between wet and dry clothing. Children with autism may have difficulty perceiving a full bladder, and the bladder empties reflexively when filled to capacity (Shepherd, Procter, & Coley, 1996). Similarly for bowel movements, the child may not perceive fullness of the lower intestine and may be truly unaware of his or her body emptying the bowel.

As is typical for all children, toilet training follows a developmental pattern that includes progressing from daytime continence to nighttime continence, to reliability in toileting in familiar environments, then to generalizing those skills to other environments. Developmental readiness for toilet training must be assessed carefully before undertaking a training program. For example, results of a longitudinal study of 629 children by Largo, Molinari, and vonSiebenthal (1996) suggested that development of bladder and bowel control is a maturational process that cannot be hastened by undertaking the process before the foundational readiness skills are achieved. Readiness to begin toilet training is determined, in part, by chronological age (at least 18 months) or mental age (at least two years), the child's awareness of elimination needs (changes in behavior after wetting or soiling diapers), the length of time the child remains dry (one to two hours or during napping), the ability to walk, sit, and squat, fine motor abilities adequate for clothing removal, and the regularity of bowel movements. The presence of at least three of these readiness factors may indicate that the child is capable of being toilet trained. If the child does not remain dry for one to two hours, this may reflect water and food intake, which may need to be modified for successful toilet training. At a minimum, the child's calculated mental age should be at least two years, if the chronological age and mental age differ. However, a child who is not aware of elimination needs can still be toilet regulated if he or she has regular elimination habits. These patterns can be detected by keeping a diary (Wong, 1997).

Because children with autism often develop strong aversions to unsuccessful activities, it is especially important to carefully appraise the child's abilities in reference to maturation of bowel and bladder control and other readiness indicators. There are many opinions about the "right age" to start toilet training (Lansky, 1984); however, when approaching toilet training from a sensorimotor perspective, the indicators are sensory, not age-based. The child signals readiness to begin the toileting process through his or her awareness of urination/bowel movements.

Table 14–1 provides a simple guideline for an initial assessment of the child's abilities (Shepherd et al., 1996; Wheeler, 1998). Consulting an occupational therapist yields more definitive information about a child's readiness for toileting.

MANAGEMENT STRATEGIES

Habit Training

Many more opportunities to empty the bladder arise in a day than to move the bowels. Targeting urination at the beginning of training thus may lead to more rapid success and so be paired with more positive feelings than concentrating on the bowel movement. When undertaking bowel training, it is important for the caregiver to determine the child's natural elimination schedule. Many children have bowel movements at about the same time every day. Keeping a record of when the child has a bowel movement for two to four weeks prior to undertaking the actual training process gives the caregiver clear guidelines for incorporating that time into the daily visual schedule and leads to a higher likelihood of successful training or regulation.

Table 14–1 Indicators of Sensory Awareness and Readiness for Toileting

+ and −	Indicator
	Acts differently when clothing is wet or soiled.
	Has bowel movements at predictable times of the day.
	Stays dry for two to four hours during daytime.
	Indicates awareness that urination or bowel movement is occurring.
	Leaves play area and goes to a solitary location while having bowel movement or urinating in diaper or pants.
	Appears interested or demonstrates a change in behavior when near the toilet or sink.
	Appears interested when others are using the bathroom.
	Sits on toilet when placed; initially does so with clothes on.

There are two basic processes for learning to use the toilet routinely after readiness is determined: developing a routine for toileting or habit training, and generalizing skills to novel environments (Wheeler, 1998).

In developing a toileting routine for a child with autism, parents, families, and therapists can often build on the intense desire for predictability that children with autism exhibit. Because of the interest in routines, a sequence of events including preparation, elimination, and completion can be taught as a whole. First, if a schedule is not already in place, establish routine times for eating and for drinking fluids. Diets high in fiber, with foods such as popcorn, fruit, and whole wheat breads, may enhance the need for and ease of routine elimination. Next, the family and educators may need to identify appropriate times for toileting (before naps, bedtime, and after meals). A day schedule can be visually depicted in a series of activities. For example, in the morning, a set of pictographs in the bathroom shows getting up, using the toilet, washing hands and face, brushing teeth, and getting dressed. A more specific routine is to check the daily schedule, enter the bathroom, undress, sit on the toilet, wipe self, flush, dress, wash and dry hands, and return to check the next activity on the schedule (Wheeler, 1998). Establishing a routine time for using the toilet increases the chance for success in toilet training. Utilization of the individual's strongest form of communication is also essential to success. The routine for toileting needs to include the entire sequence of events to enable the child to learn the chain of behaviors required. Habit training is completed using the same steps; however, it is used with the child who is not aware of elimination (no changes in behavior when he or she is soiled). A routine for toileting is followed consistently (matched with typical elimina-tion times) without asking whether the child needs to eliminate.

A recommended strategy for embedding toileting and the use of the bathroom in a complete daily routine is to develop a visual schedule for all activities in a day. Include scheduled times for eating high-fiber foods and drinking liquids to encourage regular elimination. As the child gains independence in using the visual schedule, he or she incorporates the toileting as a regularly occurring part of everyday activity. The attitude that toileting occurs as only part of a broader daily routine tends to diffuse the intense nature of the process and decrease the potential for a power struggle between the child and family or teacher. When undertaking toilet training, the daily schedule is disrupted for both the child and caregiver. Incorporating toileting into a visual schedule tends to help everyone relax and put toileting in perspective—as one small part of a day filled with both favorite activities and less desirable activities (Wheeler, 1998). Whenever possible, surround toileting time with favorite activities. In addition, using positive strategies that pair toileting with pleasant, calming experiences, and positive reinforcement of achievement is essential to success and desensitizing any negative reactions to toileting.

Sensory Strategies

Each child starts the toilet-training process with different tolerance and need for sensory experiences; however, common to many children with autism is the need for routine (Wheeler, 1998). Two of the more intense sensory experiences are sitting on the commode and eliminating, so it is imperative that these tasks be embedded in daily routine and deemphasized. Focusing primarily on these tasks may actually prolong the training process. If the toileting process is approached as a whole, its more intense sensory aspects are likely to be absorbed into a routine.

Flushing can be either an exciting or a scary part of the toileting adventure; the noise and sound can also be an intense sensory experience. Careful observation informs the caregiver when to turn this part of the toileting process over to the child. If the child is fascinated by the sight and sound of the water, flushing can be a powerful incentive for elimination. If, however, flushing elicits sensory defensiveness, the caregiver assumes initial responsibility for flushing and then reincorporates it in the visual schedule when the child is comfortable with the other tasks of toileting.

Because the toileting process is a complex sensory experience, each step may need to be approached by placing a visual cue in the relevant area. For example, handwashing involves stepping onto a stool, turning on the water, getting a squirt of soap, rubbing hands together, placing hands under the stream of water, letting water run over the hands, rubbing the hands together, turning off the water, getting paper or cloth toweling, and throwing away or replacing the toweling. Each part of this process may need to be delineated on a picture strip placed near the sink. In this way, each part of the toileting process is made explicit and incorporated into the rhythm of the child's day.

For some children with autism, sitting on the toilet with bare skin can be a negative and even frightening sensory experience. Luiselli (1996) found that one way to desensitize this issue and lead to successful elimination was to allow the child to sit on the toilet with clothes, including the diaper, still on. The child learned to urinate or have a bowel movement in the diaper while sitting on the toilet. When success was achieved in this fashion, the next steps were to sit on the commode with bare legs and, finally, to remove the diaper. Wheeler (1998) described a child whose mother helped him adjust to defecating in the toilet by cutting a long slit in the diaper, which allowed the waste to fall into the toilet but maintained the snugness of the diaper.

The feel of a diaper may be comforting for some children. It is bulky, fits snugly, and provides pressure around the waist and thighs. To provide a similar sensation when first weaning the child from the diaper, have the child wear underpants, then put a diaper over them. The next step can be to have the child wear thick (or double) training pants, then Lycra panties (these are purchased at a dance store) over them to provide the feeling of bulk and pressure.

If the child's feet do not reach the floor when sitting on the toilet, he or she may become frightened. Enhance proprioception by supplying a foot rest so that the child's feet rest flat on a firm, solid surface. Another means of providing proprioception and improved sense of stability, which may also provide modulation of the sensory experience, is to place a small table or tray over the child's lap while he or she is sitting on the toilet. This allows for the child to engage in a favorite activity while on the toilet and gives firm pressure to the thighs. Some children find it comforting to have a weighted cloth strip placed over their thighs while sitting on the toilet.

Training and regulation for bowel movements requires attention to both the sensory and motor aspects. As noted, some children do not appear to perceive a sense of fullness in the lower intestine. Others appear to register the sensation but avoid defecating because of the strong sensory nature of bowel movements. Initiating and completing a bowel movement requires adequately toned abdominal muscles and the ability to change intra-abdominal pressure through contracting the diaphragm and pushing downward. Bowel training often requires a multipronged approach. In addition to the sensory modulation techniques described earlier, the child may benefit from motor activities that target improving the strength of flexor (thus abdominal) muscles and stability for pelvic control. An anecdotal record of a child engaged in sensory integrative (SI) therapy for several weeks recorded emerging bowel control. The treatment sessions focused on heavy work of the flexor groups, including the abdominal muscles. The goal of treatment at that time was not bowel control, but as the child developed antigravity flexor control, he or she started to have more regular bowel movements and gained an awareness of the urge to have a bowel movement (Rydeen, 1997.)

Other motor aspects to consider in both bowel and bladder training include providing adequate postural stability to allow the child to contract and push with the abdominal muscles and to set the diaphragm to change the intra-abdominal pressure (National Cancer Institute). A potty chair or commode that provides foot support encourages and supports fixation and pushing of the diaphragm. When seated with foot support, an activity such as blowing up balloons encourages diaphragmatic setting and contraction. A warm drink just prior to or at the beginning of sitting on the commode aids relaxation of the muscle fibers in the wall of the intestines and stimulates contraction of intestinal muscles to move the contents of the bowel (Shepherd et al., 1996).

For any child learning to be toilet trained, appropriate dress is clothing that is easy to remove and adjust and is comfortable (Williams & Shellenberger, 1996). This usually means pants with elastic waists, clothing that is slightly large on the child, and clothing made with soft cotton materials. Items needed during toileting need to be within easy reach, including toilet paper, soap, and water faucets. Adaptive equipment that can be used includes plastic protectors for the outside of underpants, potty seats that support the child, and stepstools to allow safe access to the sink area. Environmental adaptations include the alteration of the hot water source to a lower temperature tolerated by the child and lightswitches and door handles within easy reach. The potty chair should be comfortable and secure. Other equipment variations to consider are unscented hand soaps and soft toilet paper.

In some cases, additional techniques may need to be instituted, depending on the child's sensory awareness of elimination. For typically developing children, feelings are associated with toileting, including those of fullness, voluntary control starting urination, and emptying the bladder. If the child has limited awareness of these sensations coupled with poor attention, it may be necessary to institute techniques such as counting to remain on the toilet for a longer period, music for relaxation, or a cue to begin urinating. Some children cannot voluntarily begin the process of emptying the bladder without an additional sensory cue. For these children, applying pressure with the hands on the abdomen over the bladder area or tapping over the bladder region may facilitate the starting and completion of emptying the bladder (Wheeler, 1998). Other needs may include flushing the toilet as the last step in the sequence (allowing a child who is overwhelmed by the sound to leave the room quickly), eating, drinking, and exercising on a routine schedule. Finally, additional cues for unrolling an appropriate amount of paper, flushing the toilet one time, and undressing only as necessary may need to be developed.

Generalizing to Environments

In order to begin generalizing toileting skills from the original learning environment, another routine may be necessary. Because concrete and literal thinking is a characteristic of autism, it is common for children to have difficulty generalizing skills learned at home or school to alternate settings. Specific recommendations for successful toileting in the community include using toileting as a routine part of an outing (going to the bathroom before you leave the house), ensuring that the facility that you are visiting has accessible toilets, using a toileting routine at home that can be generalized to many settings, and supporting communication efforts by having alternative communication devices or cue cards available (Wheeler, 1998). Public restrooms often present a variety of sensory stimuli that can be overwhelming (e.g., loud electric hand dryers, urinals, automatic flushing or sink devices, and unsanitary conditions). Because of this, there is a need to provide stability in the routine that mimics home. For example, the same toilet paper, wet towelettes, a small toy, ear plugs, a Walkman with headphones, drinking cup, or specific snacks may be required. The child may need to carry these items in a backpack or fanny pack.

Because the process of toilet training has many steps, it is important for the caregiver and the child that success be defined in the accomplishment of each small and separate step. Celebrate the mastery of each part of the process; remember that proficiency in each individual step eventually leads to mastery of the whole process. Considering the sensory and motor aspects of sleep and toilet training augments other strategies and provides additional resources to parents and caregivers who wish to enhance sleep and achieve toilet regulation, training, or generalization to other environments.

CHAPTER REVIEW QUESTIONS

1. Compare patterns of sleep between typically developing children and children with autism.
2. What cognitive, motor, developmental, and sensory abilities are necessary for toilet training?
3. List at least four strategies that might be useful in promoting sleep or regulating toileting.

REFERENCES

Ayres, A. J., & Tickle, L. S. (1980). Hyper-responsivity to touch and vestibular stimuli as a predictor of positive response to sensory integration procedures by autistic children. *American Journal of Occupational Therapy, 34,* 375–381.

Hering, E., Epstein, R., Elroy, S., Iancu, D., & Zelnik, N. (1999). Sleep patterns in autistic children. *Journal of Autism and Developmental Disorders, 29,* 143–147.

Lansky, V. (1984). *Toilet training.* New York: Bantam Books.

Largo, R. H., Molinari, L., & vonSiebenthal, K. (1996). Does a profound change in toilet training affect development of bowel and bladder control?

Developmental Medicine and Child Neurology, 38, 1106–1116.

Lowenthal, B. (1996). Teaching basic adaptive skills to young children with disabilities. *Early Child Development and Care, 115,* 77–84.

Luiselli, J. K. (1996). A transfer of stimulus control procedure applicable to toilet training programs for children with development disabilities. *Child and Family Behavior Therapy, 18*(2), 29–34.

National Cancer Institute. (No date). *Constipation, Impaction, and Bowel Obstruction* [On-line]. Available: http://webmd.lycos.com/content/dmk/dmk_article_57746 [2000, February 22].

Oetter, P., Richter, E. W., & Frick, S. M. (1995). MORE.: *Integrating the mouth with sensory and postural functions* (2nd ed.). Hugo, MN: PDP Press.

Patzold, L., Richdale, A., & Tonge, B. (1998). An investigation into sleep characteristics of children with autism and Asperger's disorder. *Journal of Paediatrics and Child Health, 34,* 528–533.

Pearse, J. (1999). *Baby and toddler sleep program.* Tucson, AZ: Fisher Books.

Richdale, A. (1999). Sleep problems in autism: Prevalence, cause, and intervention. *Developmental Medicine and Child Neurology, 41,* 60–66.

Rodier, P. M. (2000). The early origins of autism. *Scientific American, 282,* 56–63.

Rydeen, K. (1997). Personal communication.

Shepherd, J., Procter, S. A., & Coley, I. L. (1996). Self-care and adaptations for independent living. In J. Case-Smith, A. S. Allen, & P. N. Pratt (Eds.), *Occupational therapy for children* (pp. 461–503). St. Louis, MO: Mosby–Year Book.

Taira, M., Takase, M., & Sasaki, H. (1998). Sleep disorder in children with autism. *Psychiatry and Clinical Neurosciences, 52,* 182–183.

Wheeler, M. (1998). *Toilet training for individuals with autism and related disorders: A comprehensive guide for parents and teacher*s. Arlington, TX: Future Horizons.

Williams, M. S., & Shellenberger, S. (1996). *How does your engine run? A leader's guide to the Alert program for self-regulation.* Albuquerque, NM: Therapy Works.

Wong, D. L. (1997). *The essentials of pediatric nursing* (5th ed.). St. Louis, MO: Mosby.

CHAPTER 15

Assistive Technology for Persons with Autism

Jean Kalscheur

CHAPTER OBJECTIVES

At the completion of this chapter, the reader will be able to:

- Appreciate the need for a thorough evaluation and the use of a decision-making model to develop a match between the child, the environment, and assistive technology.
- Describe assistive technology strategies to compensate for the sensory and motor difficulties associated with autism.
- Envision potential solutions to functional problems through the use of assistive technology.

INTRODUCTION

Assistive technology refers to devices, services, strategies, and practices that alleviate barriers faced by persons with disabilities as they go about their daily lives (Cook & Hussey, 1995). The Assistive Technology Act of 1998 (ATA) defines an assistive technology device as "any item, piece of equipment, or product system, whether acquired commercially, modified, or customized, that is used to increase, maintain, or improve functional capabilities of individuals with disabilities" (ATA, 1998). The definition is broad and includes a wide range of products, from a "low"-technology keyguard, which is easily constructed with no electronic or mechanical parts, all the way to a

"high"-technology augmentative communication device, which is complex in design, has electronic parts, and costs several thousand dollars. An assistive technology system can be defined as an assistive technology device, the person using it, and the environment in which the device is used (Cook & Hussey). Technology, by itself, is not a remedy for the problems associated with a disability. It is simply a modality that is available and can be considered when creating solutions for persons having difficulties in their daily living, educational, vocational, or leisure activities.

The current research literature related to assistive technology for persons with autism is limited to case studies or studies using very small sample sizes. Therefore, little definitive information is known about the effectiveness of specific applications of assistive technology for persons with autism. Many assistive technology options exist, but no one device or software program is the consistent answer to any problem. This chapter introduces technology options as a starting point for developing an assistive technology system for people with autism. The chapter is divided into three sections. The first section presents a decision-making model that suggests that the child, the technology, and the environment are all considered when designing an assistive technology system to enhance performance in daily activities. Some characteristics of persons with autism may pose barriers to technology's potential, including sensory sensitivity, difficulty shifting visual attention, and dyspraxia. The second section identifies technology features that can enhance a person's access to the device as related to these characteristics, thus creating a positive interface between the child and the technology. The third section presents assistive technology devices to increase performance in daily activities, including maintaining a schedule, following steps, communicating, controlling the environment, and socializing. Appendix 15–A concludes the chapter, providing contact information for all manufacturers whose products are introduced.

Technology has the potential to yield positive change in functional behavior; however, this is unlikely to occur simply by making the technology available. As important as the technology itself is creating its seamless application through training of the user and the appropriate support persons. An individual's training program needs to match his or her learning style. Because some persons with autism respond positively to a sensorimotor approach, training may incorporate sensorimotor strategies presented elsewhere in this book. Other approaches to learning may also be applied. The scope of this chapter is limited to the technology devices. A parent, teacher, or therapist skilled in intervention approaches to which the learner responds is necessary to elicit the technology's potential.

DECISION-MAKING MODEL FOR ASSISTIVE TECHNOLOGY

Determining an appropriate assistive technology system requires careful consideration of a number of factors by a decision-making team. Team composition varies; its membership is related to the needs of the person with autism and the setting in which he or she functions. For example, a young child attending elementary school may have a team comprising parents, a regular education teacher, a special education teacher, an occupational therapist, a speech therapist, and a school psychologist. A young adult about to leave high school may have a transition team that includes the young adult, a vocational rehabilitation counselor, a representative from the local community college, and the previously mentioned team members. Any team member can bring information about or expertise in assistive technology, because technology use crosses discipline boundaries.

Decisions directed at changing an individual's functional performance are complex. Models can assist the decision-making process by reminding team members what the outcome is, what factors to consider, and how the factors interface. Several models, such as the SETT Framework (Zabala, 1993) and the HAAT Model (Cook & Hussey, 1995), identify the critical features when planning an assistive technology system. These existing models share three essential components: the person who will use the technology, the environment in which the technology will be applied, and the technology device. The model proposed and illustrated in Figure 15–1 includes these components with a core focus of functional life tasks and activities, which can be enhanced through technology devices.

The *child* is the unique individual for whom change in functional activity is desired. Although labeled as a child here for ease of expression, the unique individual could also be an adolescent or an adult. The *environment* is the physical location and social structures in which the activity occurs. The *assistive technology device* refers to any low- or high-technology device, including hardware, software, and the setup necessary to make the technology efficient and effective. The components in isolation are incomplete; improved functional performance occurs only when the three fit together. With this fit, a positive interface is established between the child and technology device, the device and the environment, and the environment and the child. Functional performance is supported by the positive interfaces established among the three components. Each of these interfaces is discussed in the following segments.

Child-Technology Interface

Once team members identify the desired functional outcome, they evaluate the child with autism to identify the unique characteristics that will affect his or her fit with the technology. The team wants to create an appropriate and successful child-technology interface. It is recognized that all persons with autism are unique individuals; however, typical characteristics of persons with autism that the decision-making team can

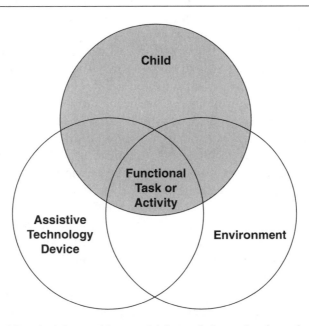

Figure 15–1 Illustrated is a decision-making model for assistive technology showing the three important interfaces that exist between the child and the environment, the child and the assistive technology device, and the device and the environment. At its core is a functional life task or activity that is enhanced through the application of assistive technology.

consider are easily overloaded by sensory input or hypersensitivity to sensory stimuli (O'Neill & Jones, 1997); preference for certain stimuli; difficulty shifting visual attention and diminished visual tracking (Wainwright & Bryson, 1996); and dyspraxia (Hughes, 1996).

Sensory input, or hypersensitivity to it, may easily overload children with autism, suggesting a need to evaluate the child's response to visual and auditory input to make an appropriate match between the child and technology. If sensory input easily overloads a child, we want to create a child-technology interface where the technology gives focused amounts of output to that sensory system most capable of managing it. When a technology device creates sound and movement that are too much for the child, the decision-making team may want to select another that is less stimulating or that lets the user modify the type, amount, and duration of sensory output. Difficulty shifting visual attention and diminished visual tracking suggest a need to slow the presentation of information to a rate that the child manages better. Children with autism who have difficulties with motor planning, or dyspraxia, may need to have the input displays or keys of the assistive technology devices set to be less sensitive to physical contacts that could cause errors. Each of these characteristic problems is discussed in more detail below.

Another consideration that may be relevant is the durability of the technology. Some children, for instance, are extremely active or impulsive and may throw the device aside when frustrated. In such a case, the team wants to be sure the product selected can withstand the treatment it will receive from that child.

The use of technology, especially computer technology, by persons with autism is disapproved by some who fear that computer use may contribute to and reinforce the child's withdrawn behaviors (Bernard-Opitz, Ross, & Tuttas, 1990). This fear is not demonstrated in the research. Computers and multimedia software were found to increase enjoyment in learning, increase motivation, and decrease behavior problems during learning in children with autism (Bernard-Opitz et al., 1990; Chen & Bernard-Opitz, 1993; Heimann, Nelson, Tjus, & Gillberg, 1995; Panyan, 1984).

Technology-Environment Interface

Because technology is always applied in context, the decision-making team must carefully consider the technology-environment interface. The technology must be portable if it is going to be used in different environments. Technology must be compatible with the physical and social environment and with the events in these environments. For example, software that gives voice to word processing programs, called *speech output*, would likely be distracting to others in a classroom environment. This doesn't mean speech output software is eliminated as an option, but it raises the question of the feasibility of incorporating a headset into a planned assistive technology system. Another example is a communication device that supplements or replaces a person's voice. The ease of accessing the volume controls must be considered so a user can speak softly when attending a movie and loudly when participating in a classroom oral report.

Persons in the environment have to be comfortable with technology as a means for a child to accomplish a functional activity. A decision-making team has to discuss their willingness to accept technology as an alternate method and how to introduce technology if people in the environment are wary of its presence. Persons who work with the child must become competent in managing the technology to guide the learning and maintain the equipment. Resources within the environment must support these people. Rewards for using technology, coaching in its applications, and training in its upkeep must also be adequate.

Environment-Child Interface

Creating a positive environment-child interface requires the team to choose the best strategies to teach or train each child how to use the technology and how to incorporate it in his or her daily routine. The strategies for teaching or training are not determined by the technology but by the person's learning abilities and response to the learning situation. Therefore, the same approach used to teach the child in other situations could be applied when instructing in the use of an assistive technology device. For example, one child may be responsive to a behavioral approach when learning new activities, while another child may respond best when his or her restricted interests are incorporated into the training program. Sensory integration strategies can also be incorporated if a child is responsive to them. If a child learns better when desensitized to touch input prior to manipulating objects, this technique should be included when introducing an assistive technology device. Commonly used teaching methods for children with autism include organizing materials, decreasing distractions, giving clear and consistent instructions, presenting material visually, and using community-based teaching (Grandin, 1998; Mesibov, 1996; Ruble, 1993). The reader should find ideas for intervention elsewhere in the book that can be applied when teaching technology use.

In summary, a decision-making team applies the model shown in Figure 15–1 to determine the specific and desired outcome; this decision influences all subsequent decisions. The child's characteristics and skills are examined, along with the environmental constraints and supports, the available technology device options, and available financial resources to implement the technology solution. The effective application of technology requires creative problem solving and agreement on its purpose by those persons involved with the child. Suggestions for technology applications are introduced in the next section.

CREATING A POSITIVE CHILD-TECHNOLOGY INTERFACE

Assistive technology devices, by definition, are used to improve functional capabilities. The role of the technology is not to rehabilitate or change the user's inherent characteristics. Instead, the assistive technology system accommodates the user through adaptations to the device or the environment, or the manner in which the activity is done. Through skillfully applied adaptations, a higher level of function can be achieved. An example of adapting the device is to put a raised dot, using nail polish or puff paint, on the first button to be pressed in a sequence. Using a macro to launch a computer program is an example of simplifying the steps a person has to manage. Background music played through a headset and a study carrel for working are examples of environmental alterations not directly related to the technology that may make the person more functional when using the technology device. In this section, four typical characteristics of persons with autism are discussed in terms of adaptations that can be made (Table 15–1).

Table 15–1 Characteristics of Persons with Autism and Related Adaptation Concepts

Characteristic	Adaptations
Easily overloaded; hypersensitive to sensory stimuli	• Simplify sensory input. • Decrease or eliminate sound. • Decrease visual clutter. • Decrease visual contrast. • Decrease the selection set. • Provide sensory cues to focus attention.
Preference for certain sensory stimuli	• Find a device that gives information using sensory preferences. • Eliminate undesirable sensory information. • Add preferred sensory information to device. • Establish routine placement and arrangement of device.
Difficulty shifting visual attention; decreased visual tracking	• Decrease rate of presentation. • Move all essential visual information into visual field.
Dyspraxic, difficulty motor planning	• Decrease sensitivity of device. • Decrease number of choices on device. • Increase space between choices. • Increase size of targets. • Decrease number of keystrokes. • Place guards over device surface.

Easily Overloaded or Hypersensitive to Sensory Stimuli

The primary adaptation concept for a child with hypersensitivity is to decrease the stimuli to which the child is sensitive. If a child is sensitive to sound, it is helpful to select technology that gives the user control over sound output. For example, a child who likes to watch television but is sensitive to sound and can read may benefit from watching television with closed captioning. On computers, altering the volume, muting the sound, or changing the voice quality of the speech output is managed by accessing the control panels or preference menus. Control panels on a PC with Windows 95/98 are found under Settings on the Start menu; control panels on a Macintosh are located under the Apple on the menu bar.

Children who are easily overloaded when presented with visual stimuli may prefer technology devised with a small selection set—that is, the number of choices available from which the user selects. For example, a standard keyboard has more than 100 keys and, therefore, 100 choices. Having this many choices can be frustrating to a person first learning to type. Keyboards that can be custom designed give the most versatility in altering the number in the selection set. For instance, a child is learning to spell his or her name using a keyboard, and it is decided to decrease the selection set to help focus the learner's attention toward only those keys that are needed for the name. An IntelliKeys keyboard with Overlay Maker software by IntelliTools can be used to create a custom overlay, such as the one in Figure 15–2. If the child's name is Arthur, the

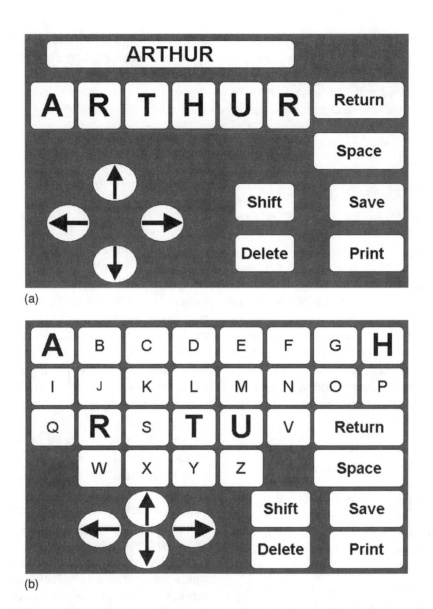

Figure 15–2 The overlays are custom designed to teach beginning writing. In the example, a student named Arthur is guided by the overlays to learn to write his name.

first overlay would have six keys: *A, R, T, H, U,* and *R.* The keys would be presented in the correct sequence and above them would be the word *Arthur* to cue the learner to the letter order. After the correct letter sequencing is achieved, the learner receives a new overlay, which has the five different letters of his or her name presented on an ABC keyboard with the necessary keys highlighted. Custom overlays are relatively easy to produce for various learning needs; they give freedom to decrease the selection set, thus increasing the chances for a new learner to make a correct selection and not be overwhelmed by the number of choices. Custom overlays can also be made with the Discover:Kenx products. Often, these visual overlays are paired with speech output word processing software to add auditory cues to the visual display, depending on the learner's ability to attend to both visual and auditory stimuli.

When selecting software for a child who is easily overloaded by visual stimuli, carefully evaluate the software's screen design. Look for screens that appear uncluttered and for consistency of screen design across all facets of the software. Examples of software designed especially for children with autism are Labeling Tutor, which teaches language concepts, and Train Time, which provides exercises for visual, auditory, and language processing. Basic pictures of items are presented to the learner, who matches the picture and a written word or sound. Both software programs present an uncluttered screen design.

Preference for Certain Stimuli

To create a positive child-technology interface, the preferred stimuli are used to engage the child with the technology. If a child prefers visual input, software applications should include visual displays that are appealing, offer high visual contrast, and display items large enough to attract the user's attention. Some color adaptations can be made to the visual display of a standard monitor through the Accessibility Options menu in the Control Panel of a PC with Windows 95/98. Both the background color of the display and the color of pages in a word processing program can be changed. A learner may prefer a soft pastel background color such as rose or teal with black lettering. Some persons may prefer a high contrast, such as switching from the standard

black type on a white background to white type on a black background (Figure 15–3). Changes made to the monitor display through the control panels affect all software applications on the computer.

Custom overlays using IntelliTools or Discover:Kenx products are another way to increase visual appeal when learning. For example, the software program Dollars and Cents by the Attainment Company teaches money concepts. The software can by accessed using the standard mouse and keyboard; however, a custom IntelliKeys overlay can be purchased that pictures the money on the overlay exactly as real money looks. The software and overlay combination gives high visual appeal, uncluttered choices, and helpful visual learning cues.

For a child with autism who prefers auditory input, select technology with good sound and voice output. Some synthesized speech can sound unnatural and be difficult to comprehend. If possible, listen to the quality of sound produced by the software on the computer system that will be running it, as sound quality is influenced by the computer's sound system. Software that offers a variety of voices and voice speed gives the user the opportunity to select a preferred voice type and speech rate. If a child's technology system is using sound or voice output, a headset can help focus the user's attention to the auditory output and decrease the auditory disruption to others in the environment.

Difficulty Shifting Visual Attention and Diminished Visual Tracking

For a child with autism who has trouble shifting visual attention, the technology and its positioning can decrease the demands on these component skills. The selection set needs to be placed within the visual field of

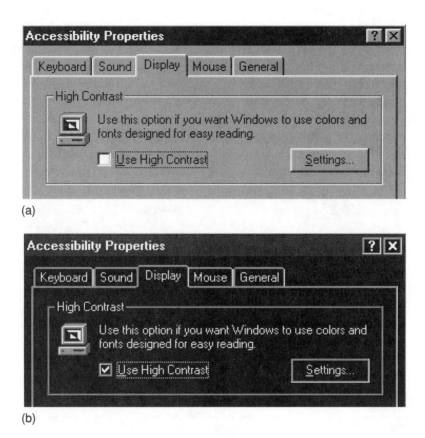

Figure 15–3 A comparison of contrast between black type on a white background and white type on a black background is shown.

---

the user to maximize visual abilities. Typically, the keyboard is positioned below the level of the monitor. A child who does not have touch-typing abilities must continually shift visual attention from the keyboard to the monitor to an assignment sheet or book. It may be helpful to position all three objects in the child's functional visual field. This field may not be the same visual field that the typical adult uses because some children rely on peripheral vision rather than central vision. An arrangement that brings the keyboard, monitor, and assignment sheet close together is to attach the keyboard to a slant board and place papers in a document holder. The keyboard is attached to the slant board with hook and loop closures to pre-

vent it from sliding and positioned directly below the monitor (Figure 15–4). A variety of document holders are available in computer stores. Holders position the work vertically; they can be attached to the monitor or positioned next to it.

Using a keyboard that has the letters presented alphabetically may decrease the amount of visual scanning a child has to do to find the desired keys, especially if the child knows the ABCs but is less familiar with a standard keyboard layout. Both IntelliKeys and Discover keyboards have standard ABC overlays. Keyboards such as Big Keys Plus present the keys in alphabetical order and eliminate most other keys to decrease the selection set.

Figure 15–4 To bring the keyboard and monitor closer together in the visual field, attach the keyboard to a slant board. Photograph taken by Jon McGee.

An on-screen or virtual keyboard can replace the standard keyboard if a child's keyboarding is slow or if errors are high due to difficulty shifting visual attention from the keyboard to the monitor. On-screen keyboard software, like Madentec's ScreenDoors 2000, place a keyboard on the computer monitor (Figure 15–5). The keyboard size can be adjusted, as can the layout of the keys. On-screen keyboards are activated in several ways, such as using the mouse to point and click. If pointing and clicking are difficult, an on-screen keyboard with a dwell feature may be helpful. The user moves the cursor over the desired key and leaves it there for a predetermined amount of time. The dwell time can be adjusted to match individual needs. A third method of activating an on-screen keyboard is to use a touch window. The user points and taps on the touch window to activate the keys.

For children with visual problems, the cursor can be difficult to track because of its small size and undistinguished appearance. Software such as R. J. Cooper's Biggy can alter the size, shape, and display features of the cursor. For instance, a blinking red arrow twice the size of the typical cursor can be easy to visually locate on the screen.

Several technology options are available to assist students to read, including those with diminished visual tracking. Audiotaped textbooks, from elementary to college level, may be obtained from participating libraries of the National Library Service for the Blind and Physically Handicapped. Electronic texts in CD-ROM format are available in many titles, with elementary-grade reading levels most represented—although this is changing as digitized books gain in popularity with many readers. Electronic books

Figure 15–5 An on-screen keyboard such as ScreenDoors 2000 places the keyboard on the monitor, putting it within the user's visual field. Courtesy of Madentec.

such as Don Johnston's Start-to-Finish Series are designed to be interactive for learning enhancement. This book series, for example, highlights words on the screen as a narrator reads them, repeats any word clicked on with the mouse, quizzes the reader, and collects data on reader comprehension. Reviews of electronic books and their interactive features can be found at Web sites like Project LITT. Screen reader software, such as CAST's eReader, reads text from many sources, including scanned text, typed text, and the Internet. Features of screen-reading software include highlighting words, choosing voice preferences, selecting voice speed, and navigating through the document.

Dyspraxia

A child with autism who also has dyspraxia can find a standard keyboard and mouse frustrating to use. An alternative to the mouse is a trackball (Figure 15–6). A trackball remains stationary; the user rolls the palm of his or her hand over the ball to guide the cursor's movement. Clicking and double clicking are accomplished by activat-

ing buttons near the ball. Trackballs eliminate the need for proficiency in pointing, clicking, and dragging. The Penny and Giles trackball comes with a guard, making it especially easy to use.

Keyboard keyguards are a low-technology solution for persons who tend to activate more than one key at a time (Figure 15–7). Keyguards are acrylic covers that sit above the keys. Holes in the keyguard make each key accessible by poking a finger through the hole. Because the keyguard sits above the keys, a user can rest his or her entire hand or drag his or her fingers over it and not activate any keys. A caution is that keyguards restrict keyboarding and persons who have visual perception difficulties can find them confusing when locating a key.

If a keyguard is not a reasonable accommodation for a person with dyspraxia, the sensitivity of the standard keyboard can be altered through the accessibility options in the control panels. When the filter keys or slow keys are turned on, the computer ignores repeated keystrokes or brief keystrokes that occur when a person doesn't accurately target the correct key or repeatedly attempts to depress the same key.

Figure 15–6 A trackball, such as the Penny & Giles Rollerball Light (Don Johnston Inc., Volo, IL), may be easier to use by a person who has difficulty with motor planning. Courtesy of Don Johnston Inc., Volo, Illinois. Photograph taken by Jon McGee.

The size of all on-screen objects, including menu bars and icons, can be increased using the accessibility options in the control panels. Large menu bars and icons are easier to see, locate, and target for a person with diminished motor accuracy or inefficient pointing and clicking with the mouse. If magnification is found useful, screen magnification software offers more choices than the magnification found in the accessibility options. A few tips when selecting magnification software are:

- Be sure the software magnifies in all software applications used by the child.

- Be sure the software has an edge-smoothing feature so that enlarged objects don't become distorted.
- Be sure the software can be easily turned on and off if multiple persons use the same computer and some do not need screen magnification.

Custom-designed overlays for IntelliKey and Discover keyboards can reduce errors caused by decreased motor planning when designed with large target keys placed far enough apart to diminish accidental activation (Figure 15–8). A disadvantage of using custom overlays with large target keys is

(a)

(b)

Figure 15–7 The Mini-Keyboard with Keyguard (ORCCA Technology, Inc, Lexington, KY) may benefit the keyboard user who has difficulty with motor planning or rests or drags the fingers over the keys and accidentally activates them. Courtesy of ORCCA Technology, Inc., Lexington, KY. Photograph taken by Jon McGee.

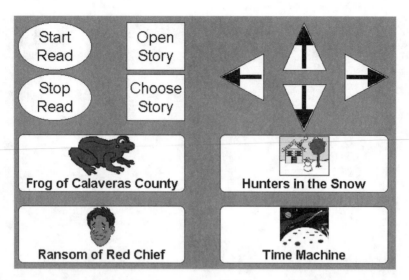

Figure 15–8 This is an example of a custom-designed overlay that used large keys, making them easier to access for a person with motor planning difficulties.

that fewer keys can be placed on the overlay due to space limitations.

ASSISTIVE TECHNOLOGY TO ENHANCE PERFORMANCE IN DAILY TASKS AND ACTIVITIES

This section is divided into six functional activities: maintaining a schedule, following steps or remembering a list, written communication, communication, controlling the environment, and socializing. For each activity, technology-based solutions are offered that are intended to prompt your thinking. The ideas do not imply that they are the only or the best solution, as each assistive technology solution must be individually designed. Many technology devices, hardware, and software are readily obtainable. Technological advances are constantly being made that manufacturers incorporate into better, more effective products. Technology users become accustomed to the ongoing upgrades and changes that occur in technology products. The examples in this section are based on today's products. For the latest in-

formation and detailed descriptions and pictures of any item, contact the manufacturer.

A note of caution is in order. It is easy to be influenced by the allure of technology and to focus on the promise and potential of the device. Try not to let the technology drive decision making; the relevant and important functional outcome activities should direct the decision process. The effective application of technology requires creative problem solving and agreement on purpose by those persons involved with the child. For example, a student has illegible handwriting, making legible handwriting a desirable outcome. Team members immediately suggest voice recognition software, as television commercials and print advertisements make it appear incredibly easy to use. Without looking at all components of the decision-making model presented earlier, this may seem an ideal solution. However, voice recognition software may be an inadequate, expensive technology solution if the team doesn't conduct a closer examination of the child, the environment, and the technology. Voice recognition requires the student to speak out loud, which is not always acceptable in a classroom or study area. The software has to be "trained" to the user's voice patterns. A voice recognition user must have patience and consistency in performance to train the system, and must be able to read to recognize errors needing correction.

Assistive Technology for Maintaining a Schedule

For persons with autism who have difficulty maintaining a daily schedule, technology can provide the necessary assistance to manage routine changes throughout the day. A low-technology solution may be to use an easy-to-carry pocket-sized notebook with two to three sturdy pages. Several horizontal strips of loop-side tape are placed on the front of the notebook and on each inside page. Pictures or symbols representing routine activities are laminated, with a piece of hook-side tape attached to the back. Early in the child's day, the pictures for each routine activity are placed on the front of the notebook in the order in which they occur. The notebook user looks at the first picture on the front strip to know which activity he or she is to be doing. When the activity is finished, the user removes the symbol from the front of the notebook, places it on an inside page, and again refers to the front of the notebook to know the next activity in the routine. The user's ability to recognize the beginning and end of an activity determines the number of activities placed on the front of the notebook at a time. A student who moves from one classroom to the next throughout the day may have symbols that sequence the classes, such as homeroom, math, reading, lunch. For a younger student, routine activities within a classroom may be represented in pictures, such as circle time, learning group, outdoor play. To increase

time management independence with the notebook, the time of day an activity is to occur is printed below the picture or symbol for the activity. The student can also wear a digital watch with an alerting signal set to alert him or her to times in the schedule. When the watch alarm goes off, the user looks at the symbols, matches the digital time on the watch to that on the symbol board, and switches to the next activity in the routine.

An audiocassette player can be programmed to assist a person in maintaining a schedule. A hand-sized player easily fits into a shirt pocket or clips on a belt. An assistant records the schedule of events, cuing the user after each event to "turn off the recording." The user is taught to activate the "play" button at the end of each event to hear the next scheduled activity and then to activate the "stop" button before participating in the activity. To reduce confusion about which button to push, paint the start button green and the stop button red using nail polish or acrylic paints. This technology can be used to teach vocational tasks or to remind a student of a class schedule. If events vary from day to day, a different tape can be made for each day that matches the daily routine events. If the user carries a blank tape, recordings can easily be made to accommodate changes in the typical routine.

A high-technology solution to remembering schedules is an electronic personal planner, which can be programmed and set to alert the user multiple times. These devices are portable and offer many options. They can cue the user with visual and auditory instructions. Successful use of electronic planners requires good cognitive and fine motor skills as well as the ability to reliably follow several steps in sequence to manage the device. Success also depends on having someone available who can program the device to keep it current, if the user requires assistance with programming it. The cost of personal planners may be prohibitive and must be carefully considered, especially if a potential user is inconsistent with assuming responsibility for personal belongings. An example of a personal planner designed for persons with memory and attention disorders is the Planning and Execution Assistant and Training System (PEAT). PEAT cues the user and can adjust a schedule when delays or interruptions disrupt the planned activities.

Assistive Technology for Following Steps or Remembering a List

Two products can assist a child with autism to follow a sequenced activity. The first is an audiocassette recorder on which step-by-step instructions are recorded. The user activates the tape to play the first step of the instructions, stops the tape, completes the step, and reactivates the tape for the next step. The Step-by-Step Communicator, an AbleNet product, is another device that can assist a person in following steps. It is a switch-activated recorder onto which the steps to an activity are recorded. The first activation plays the first step, the second activation plays the second step, etc. The Step-by-Step Communicator is easy to program, easy to activate, and portable.

A list can be recorded on loop tape, which continuously goes back to the beginning after it finishes the recording. A person plays the list while items are gathered. A child who has to gather items for school each morning can use the list to remember his or her lunchbox, bookbag, gym clothes, and house key. A teenager sent to the grocery can use the list to recall the grocery items to pick up.

An advantage of electronic devices is that the steps or lists can be repeated within a single activity or repeated each time the activity is done. These devices deliver a consistent message and never sound frustrated or exasperated by having to repeat the information over and over again. Positive reinforcing messages such as "good job" can be programmed into all devices identified, especially useful when placed after steps known to be difficult for the user.

Assistive Technology for Written Communication

The motor control needed for legible handwriting may not be possible for some persons with autism, and keyboarding can be an alternative method for written communication. There are many kinds of keyboards and several choices for the layout of the keys on the keyboard. Once a keyboard and its layout are selected, applying it in the classroom may require software to facilitate the writing process, such as word completion and word prediction software. Word completion software attempts to predict the word a user is typing by presenting a list of words that begin with the first letter the user types (Figure 15–9). If no words on the list match the user's word choice, the second letter of the word is typed and the prediction list changes. If the word choice appears on the list, the user clicks on the correct choice or enters the number next to the word, and the remainder of the word is entered in the word processing document. Word completion software decreases keystrokes for slow keyboard users and facilitates the correct spelling and use of words for students with learning disabilities. Word prediction software works just like word completion, except it attempts to predict the next likely word based on use patterns. The user of word completion and prediction software must be able to recognize the desired choice

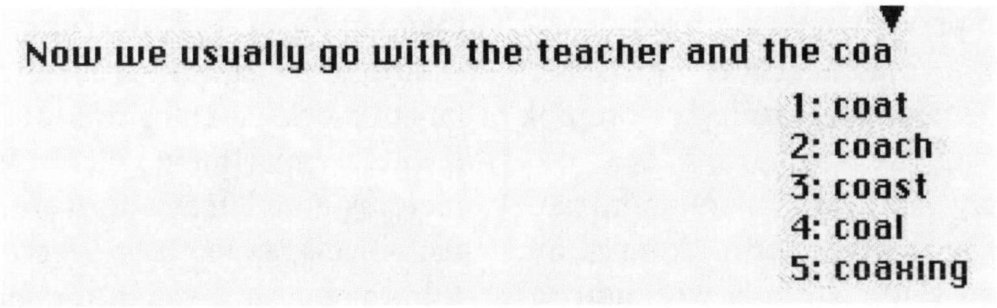

Now we usually go with the teacher and the coa ▼

1: coat
2: coach
3: coast
4: coal
5: coaxing

Figure 15–9 Word-completion software attempts to predict the word a user wants. An example of the word list that appears when typing the word coach comes from Co:Writer software. Courtesy of Don Johnston Inc., Volo, Illinois.

from the options presented. A feature of this software is that it learns the habits of the user; the prediction list becomes a closer match to frequently used words. Two of the many word prediction software options are Co:Writer and Aurora Prediction.

Using multimedia software, children with autism can improve spelling when provided with speech output and visual feedback of the letters and words (Schlosser, Blischak, Belfiore, Bartley, & Barnett, 1998). Speech output is typically a component of word prediction software. Write:OutLoud is often paired with Co:Writer and Aurora Echo gives a voice to Aurora. Speech output means the computer speaks the typed text or the word lists when using word prediction (Figure 15–10). The amount of auditory feedback can be custom selected for the user. The speaking voice can be altered; the program can be set to speak each keystroke word,

sentence, or paragraph, and the number of times a sentence is repeated can be set to user preferences. If students in a classroom use speech output software, a headset is necessary to decrease the distraction to other students.

Assistive Technology for Communication

A continuum of technology, ranging from yes/no symbol cards to technologically sophisticated augmentative communication devices, exists for persons, such as those with autism, whose communication impairment interferes with functional language. To be useful, augmentative communication devices must be readily available to the child and understood by the communication partner. The devices must be portable, easily activated, durable, and easily programmed to meet the child's ongoing language needs. Augmentative communication devices are

When I was in grade school, we often visited my grandparents who lived in Michigan.

Figure 15–10 Talking word processor software, such as Write:OutLoud, highlights and reads the text to the user as it is typed. Courtesy of Don Johnston Inc., Volo, Illinois.

not intended to prevent the child from developing and using oral language skills but rather to supplement the learning or prompt verbal skills.

Children may first learn to communicate by using language cards with pictures on them. However, some children with autism may flip or drum the cards. To decrease self-stimulation, the pictures can be placed inside acrylic picture frames. For example, a child receives a food reward of his or her choice for showing on-task behaviors. When shown the food choices using pictures, the child drums the cards, and if the pictures are laminated, the drumming intensifies. However, when each picture is placed inside an acrylic frame, the child is unable to flip or drum the card. The acrylic frames are light enough to carry and small enough to fit in the pencil pocket of a child's notebook, making them easily available to his or her teachers and aide.

Connecting a word with an object is a beginning communication skill. The compartment communicator by Enabling Devices can facilitate a child's learning to match a concrete object with its name. Compartment communicators have two, three, four, or five compartments. Objects or pictures are placed in each compartment. A message, such as the name of the object in the compartment, is programmed into the switch located in the front of each compartment. The child is asked a question, and when he or she depresses the switch, the prerecorded message is delivered. The compartment communicator can teach language concepts via naming, classifying, and sequencing. The child can express preferences with the compartment communicator. For example, a teacher may set a compartment communicator with four drink choices: white milk, chocolate milk, juice, and pop. Each morning, when making out the class lunch menu, the teacher can ask the children who are nonverbal to indicate their choice by activating the switch. Once a user makes a selection, it is important that a positive consequence follow. Actual objects in the compartments can be replaced with pictures and, later, with words representing the objects, as the user becomes more skillful at using the system for functional communication.

Another device for children first learning to use language is a switch that contains one prerecorded message, such as the BIGmack Communication Aid by AbleNet. Several of these switches can be strategically placed in a classroom. The child learns to activate the switch at the appropriate time for the prerecorded message. One switch might have "good morning" recorded on it, and the user activates it as classmates enter the room. Another switch might have the day's date prerecorded, which the user activates during an activity where children take turns telling the day, date, and weather. A switch may be placed by the door with the message that the child needs to go to the restroom. If a story featuring a repetitive phrase is read to the class, the phrase can be prerecorded so the user can activate the switch as the group chants the phrase.

Some low-technology communication devices, such as the SpeakEasy by AbleNet (Figure 15–11) and the Cheap Talk and 6-Level Communicator by Enabling Devices, help transition a child from using concrete objects to using pictures or symbols. These portable devices can hold from 8 to 48 prerecorded messages. Language symbols are placed over the buttons, which are activated to access the messages.

Assistive Technology To Control the Environment

Controlling the environment for a child with autism can mean turning a radio on and off, selecting a preferred television channel,

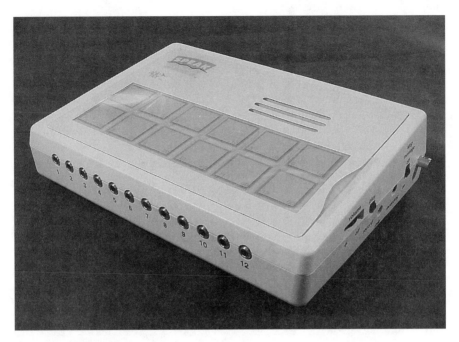

Figure 15–11 A beginning augmentative communication device, the SpeakEasy Communication Aid. Courtesy of AbleNet, Minneapolis, MN. Photograph taken by Jon McGee.

and calling a parent when waking in the morning. Many of these tasks can be accomplished using electronic aids to daily living and strategically located activation switches. Any switch compatible to the child's motor and sensory abilities can be used. The many switches on the market require varying amounts of reliable and controlled movement and sensory capabilities (Figure 15–12). Switches can be secured to a tabletop to prevent them from being cast aside. When teaching a child to use a switch, connect it to something that is extremely motivating to the child to entice him or her to learn the cause-and-effect relationship between activating the switch and activating the desired device. Switches can be made to activate battery-operated toys and appliances by using AbleNet's Battery Device Adapters; they can be made to activate small electrical appliances by plugging the appliance and the switch into AbleNet's Power-Link2 Control Unit. Switches can also be used to operate computer software by using a Switch Interface by Don Johnston. Switches that may be attractive to children with sensory needs include the Vibrating Plate Switch, Texture Switches, and the Koosh Switch by Enabling Devices. When using switches with tactile and proprioceptive input, be sure the additional input is attractive to the child and does not cause a withdrawal or flight reaction.

Switches were reported to be effective with some children as a means to control the environment (Sullivan, Laverick, & Lewis, 1995) and to teach communication of a simple message (Dyches, 1998). Controlling the environment can start with a single switch plugged into an attractive battery-operated toy and an engaging computer software program designed for switch activation. If visual stimulation engages a child, objects with flashing lights are appealing, especially if used in a darkened room. If sound engages a child, tape recordings of fa-

Figure 15–12 A variety of switches are available. Examples include, left to right, a pillow switch, Frog Switch (Toys for Special Children, Inc., Hastings on Hudson, NY), Ellipse Switch (Don Johnston, Inc., Volo, IL), and Jelly Bean Switch (AbleNet, Inc., Minneapolis, MN). A switch can access single switch software through a Switch Interface (Don Johnston, Inc., Volo, IL), shown in the top center of the picture.

vorite music or a radio set to a favorite station can be used. For an older child, switch-activated software may be useful in teaching reliable switch activation or in using a remote switch to activate the television.

Assistive Technology for Socializing

Entertainment software can bring children together in play. Use of a battery-operated toy, a Series Adapter by AbleNet, and two switches can encourage teamwork. The switches must be simultaneously activated to operate the toy. Turn-taking can be practiced through switch-activated software programs such as SwitchIt! Scenes, Creature Antics, and Creature Chorus. These programs can be activated using a keyboard, a switch, or a touch window. In SwitchIt! Scenes, a picture of a switch appears in the lower left or right corner of the screen to cue the player whose turn it is. With each turn, additional animation and sound is added. For older children who use a keyboard, mouse, joystick, or IntelliKeys keyboard, Level Games's arcade-type software, such as Alien Invasion, may be enjoyable. These computer games can be adjusted to the individual user. For example, in Alien Invasion, the alien's speed can be slowed, the firepower to zap the aliens adjusted to a wider spread, the size of the characters enlarged, and high-contrast colors substituted. Each player has his or her own settings based on physical abilities and reaction times, allowing players with different abilities to play together.

Learning about social relationships may have to be specifically taught to children with autism. Grandin (1999) described her experiences using her cognitive capabilities and visualization skills to learn how to act in different situations. Technology can be used to present social skills in a visual format. One example is the use of a custom-designed overlay using IntelliTools Overlay Maker and IntelliPics to teach a child to recognize and communicate his or her feelings. The overlay has six photographs of a child's face showing different emotions. When the face pictures are pressed, a child's voice is heard telling about a feeling.

Videotapes of social interactions can be used to teach social rules. Students can produce the videotapes that demonstrate acceptable and expected interactions in various situations. Virtual reality is a high-technology method that was tried with a very small number of children with autism (Strickland, Marcus, Mesibov, & Hogan, 1996). Virtual reality was considered because it can isolate specific stimuli, it can simplify complex sequences of information, it emphasizes visual skills, and it may make generalization to the real world easier. In one study, two children wore the virtual reality technology, which includes a heavy helmet, when learning about crossing the street. These children were able to immerse themselves in the three-dimensional virtual scenes, identify familiar objects presented via the technology, and locate and move toward objects in the virtual environment. It was not determined if behaviors demonstrated in virtual reality generalized to

the real world. Virtual reality, which allows children to participate in simulated real-world interactions to learn what is expected of them, may have potential as a future learning strategy.

CONCLUSION

A lot of technology is available for all kinds of needs, and most of it is untested in its effectiveness to specifically facilitate the learning of life tasks and activities by children and adults with autism. In this chapter, a decision-making model was presented and ideas were proposed that may address specific functional needs of persons with autism. It is wise and helpful to explore all resources when searching for technology options. *Exceptional Parent* magazine and *Closing the Gap* newsletter provide technology reviews. The Regional Alliance for Technology Access Centers, located in each state, often has software and devices that people can try before making a purchase. It is also wise to talk to people who have implemented assistive technology systems and learn from their experiences. An occupational therapist, speech and language therapist, or special educator may provide additional guidance. Assistive technology is a challenging modality, but it can facilitate independence in persons who learn to use it effectively.

CHAPTER REVIEW QUESTIONS

1. Apply the questions and decision-making model illustrated in Figure 15–1 to a person with autism that you know or have heard about.
2. Describe common adaptations or assistive technology devices that may compensate for a tendency to be easily overloaded by sensory stimuli or for difficulty in motor planning.
3. How does a difficulty in shifting attention interfere with typical computer use? How might this problem be bypassed?

4. Describe at least four assistive technology strategies that might promote written communication, control of the environment, or socializing.

REFERENCES

Assistive Technology Act of 1998, Public Law No. 105–394, Section 3. (1998).

Bernard-Opitz, V., Ross, K., & Tuttas, M. L. (1990). Computer-assisted instruction for autistic children. *Annals of the Academy of Medicine, Singapore, 19*(5), 611–616.

Chen, S. H., & Bernard-Opitz, V. (1993). Comparison of personal and computer-assisted instruction for children with autism. *Mental Retardation, 31*, 368–376.

Cook, A. M., & Hussey, S. M. (1995). *Assistive technologies: Principles and practice.* St. Louis, MO: Mosby.

Dyches, T. T. (1998). Effects of switch training on the communication of children with autism and severe disabilities. *Focus on Autism and Other Developmental Disabilities, 13*(3), 151–162.

Grandin, T. (1998). Teaching tips for children and adults with autism [On-line]. Available: <www.autism.org/temple/tips.html>

Grandin, T. (1999). Social problems: Understanding emotions and developing talents [On-line]. Available: <www.autism.org/temple/social.html>

Heimann, M., Nelson, K. E., Tjus, T., & Gillberg, C. (1995). Increasing reading and communication skills in children with autism through an interactive multimedia computer program. *Journal of Autism and Developmental Disorders, 25*, 459–480.

Hughes, C. (1996). Brief report: Planning problems in autism at the level of motor control. *Journal of Autism and Developmental Disorders, 26*, 99–107.

Mesibov, G. B. (1995). Learning styles of students with autism [On-line]. Available: <www.autism-society.org/packages/educating_children.html> Accessed August 2, 2000.

O'Neill, M., & Jones, R. S. P. (1997). Sensory-perceptual abnormalities in autism: A case for more research? *Journal of Autism and Developmental Disorders, 27*, 283–293.

Panyan, M. V. (1984). Computer technology for autistic students. *Journal of Autism and Developmental Disorders, 14*, 375–382.

Ruble, L. (1993). Methods to enhance learning: Conference notes [On-line]. Available: <www.autism-society.org/packages/edkids_conference.html>

Schlosser, R. W., Blischak, D. M., Belfiore, P. J., Bartley, C., & Barnett, N. (1998). Effects of synthetic speech output and orthographic feedback on spelling in a student with autism: A preliminary study. *Journal of Autism and Developmental Disorders, 28*, 309–319.

Strickland, D., Marcus, L. M., Mesibov, G. B., & Hogan, K. (1996). Brief report: Two case studies using virtual reality as a learning tool for autistic children. *Journal of Autism and Developmental Disorders, 26*, 651–659.

Sullivan, M. W., Laverick, D. H., & Lewis, M. (1995). Brief report: Fostering environmental control in a young child with Rett syndrome: A case study. *Journal of Autism and Developmental Disorders, 25*, 215–221.

Wainwright, J. A., & Bryson, S. E. (1996). Visual-spatial orienting in autism. *Journal of Autism and Developmental Disorders, 26*, 423–438.

Zabala, J. S. (1993). SETTing the stage for success: Building success through effective selection and use of assistive technology systems [On-line]. Available: <http://sac.uky.edu/~jszaba-/JoySETT.html>

Appendix 15–A
Product Manufacturer Information

Manufacturer	Product
AbleNet, Inc. 1081 Tenth Avenue SE Minneapolis, MN 55414-1312 <www.ablenetinc.com>	Step-by-Step Communicator BIGmack Communication Aid SpeakEasy Communication Aid Battery Device Adapter PowerLink2 Control Unit Series Adapter Jelly Bean Switch
Alliance for Technology Access 2175 East Francisco Boulevard Suite L San Rafael, CA 94901 <www.ataccess.org>	Alliance for Technology Access Centers Directory
Attainment Company, Inc. PO Box 930160 Verona, WI 53593-0160 <www.attainmentcompany.com>	Dollars and Cents Spending Money Overlays Making Change Overlays
Attention Control Systems, Inc. 650 Castro Street Suite 120-197 Mountain View, CA 94041 <www.brainaid.com>	PEAT
Aurora Systems, Inc. Box 43005 4739 Willingdon Avenue	Aurora Prediction Aurora Echo

Burnaby, B.C., V5G-3H0,
    Canada
<www.djtech.com/Aurora/
    index.html-ssi>

CAST   eReader/ULTimate Reader
Universal Learning Technology
39 Cross Street
Peabody, MA 01960
<www.cast.org/tools/
    teachingtoolsreader.html>

Closing the Gap   *Closing the Gap* Newspaper and
PO Box 68   Resource Directory
526 Main Street
Henderson, MN 56044
<www.closingthegap.com>

Don Johnston Incorporated   Discover:Kenx
26799 West Commerce Drive   Co:Writer
Volo, IL 60073   Write:OutLoud
<www.donjohnston.com>   Switch Interface

Enabling Devices   Compartment Communicators
Toys for Special Children   Cheap Talk
385 Warburton Avenue   6-Level Communicator
Hastings-on-Hudson, NY 10706   Vibrating Plate Switch, Texture
<www.enablingdevices.com>   Switch, Koosh Switch

Exceptional Parent   *Exceptional Parent* magazine
555 Kinderkamack Road
Oradell, NJ 07649-1517
<www.eparent.com>

Four Leaf Press   Train Time
PO Box 23502
Eugene, OR 97402
<www.autism.com/fourleafpress/index.html>

Greystone Digital, Inc.   Big Keys Plus

Inclusive Technology Ltd.   SwitchIt! Scenes
Saddleworth Business Centre
Huddersfield Road
Delph, Oldham OL3 5DF UK
<www.inclusive.co.uk/index.htm>

IntelliTools, Inc.   IntelliKeys
1720 Corporate Circle   Overlay Maker
Petaluma, CA 94954   IntelliPics
<www.intellitools.com>   IntelliTalk

Laureate   Creature Antics
110 East Spring Street   Creature Chorus
Winooski, VT 05404-1898
<www.laureatelearning.com>

Madentec Limited   ScreenDoors 2000
3022 Calgary Trail South
Edmonton, Alberta
T6J 6V4, Canada
<www.madentec.com>

Millennium Software   Labeling Tutor
3155 Fujita Street
Torrance, CA 90505
<http://members.aol.com/peuapeu/index.html>

National Library Service for the   Audiotaped books
    Blind and the Physically
    Handicapped
Library of Congress
Washington, DC 20542
<http://lcweb.loc.gov/nls/nls.html>

NorthStar Solutions   Level Games's Alien Invasion
1228 Westloop Place
Suite 204
Manhattan, KS 66502
<www.levelgames.com>

ORCCA Technology, Inc.   Mini-Keyboard with Keyguard
462 East High Street
Lexington, KY 40507

Project LITT San Diego State University 6505 Alvarado Road Suite 204 San Diego, CA 92120-1878 <http://edweb.sdsu.edu/SPED/ ProjectLitt/LITT>	Electronic text reviews
RJ Cooper and Associates 24843 Del Prado #283 Dana Point, CA 92629 <www.rjcooper.com>	Biggy
Synapse Adaptive Technology <www.synapseadaptive.com/donjohnston/ pengild.htm>	Penny & Giles Trackball

CHAPTER 16

Employment Options and Techniques in Autism

Kim Sturmfels-Hall

CHAPTER OBJECTIVES

At the completion of this chapter, the reader will be able to:

- Understand the importance of work for all people, including people with autism.
- Describe the process of developing and implementing a life plan for a person with autism.
- Apply adaptations and strategies for improving work capabilities and performance.

INTRODUCTION

If we treat people as they are, we make them worse. If we treat people as they are capable of becoming, we help them become.
—Goethe

Work is a determining factor in a person's place in our society and influences one's psychological identity and sense of well-being (Szymanski & Parker, 1996). The reasons why people work are multifaceted and may include financial necessity, familial responsibility, recognition, being around others, an atmosphere of fun and socialization, and feelings of achievement, autonomy, control, and self-esteem (Maccoby, 1988). According to Maccoby, two of the strongest motivators for work are self-expression and hope. Self-expression provides the opportunity for others to see who we are and what

talents we possess. Hope can be a driving force for work, as we expect that it will bring us pleasure, appreciation, independence, fulfillment, and a sense of optimism. Each person has a unique set of reasons for choosing the type of work that meets his or her needs, values, and desires, and conveys to others his or her identity as a worker.

Despite the universality of the worker role, about two thirds of people with disabilities are not afforded that rite of passage, most often due to society's view of individuals with disabilities (DiLeo, 1993). Among adults with autism, the figures are even worse. Today, only about 18% of adults with autism are working in some capacity (Howlin & Goode, 1998). Fortunately, times and views are changing. Families and professionals are lobbying to help all individuals gain access to the world of work, no matter how severe the disability. People with disabilities are speaking out to convey their desire for full inclusion in society; they want to be self-directed, not other-directed. A young woman with a disability conveys this deep sense of longing for a whole and challenging life; she reflects on her own experiences:

> Our attitude sets our sail, the set of our sail determines our destination. Without the advantage of participation, we have not determined our attitude and we never set sail. We are not talking about getting to the wrong port here, we are talking, never leaving dry dock. You know, when they pull the ship out of the water and hang it up to rehab it? *Major overhaul.* Sometimes you can leave the ship in the water if it is a minor repair. This is like sheltered workshops, still in the water but not really going anywhere. Some people with disabilities live in group homes or with their folks and go to a sheltered workshop setting. I think of this like being tied to the pier, it looks like you are going somewhere, but you aren't leaving the harbor. Big ships, bound for open waters, are taken out of the harbor by tugs. Small, powerful vessels with keen maneuverability and creative captains. This is what supported employment should be. And it is, if the person guiding the process, knows their jobs is to begin the process and not set the sail. If they know their science and how to apply it. If they know what the natural supports are and how to use them. If they have flexible, creative minds and if they know too that the people they are guiding do not

need them for the entire journey, but to facilitate the smooth transition of its beginning. There is a time and a place for dry dock, for wet dock, for being tied to the pier and to set sail. There is nothing wrong with any of these in and of themselves. There is something wrong with a person placed in an environment they did not chose, they do not want, that does not allow for growth and keeps them more dependent than they need to be. (Bogdan, 1995)

This section explores employment for people with disabilities, especially for those with autism. Topics include employment supports and options, the person-centered approach to life planning, financial incentives and disincentives, and case studies illustrating specific techniques to improve employment outcomes.

EMPLOYMENT SUPPORTS AND OPTIONS

Many alternatives exist that enable individuals with disabilities to enter the workforce. Some individuals can navigate the employment process with little assistance and gain competitive jobs. Others need assistance from programs that serve individuals with disabilities. Some Federal legislation, such as the Americans with Disabilities Act (ADA), the Developmental Disabilities Assistance and Bill of Rights Act, the Individuals with Disabilities Education Act (IDEA) Amendments of 1997, the Rehabilitation Act Amendments of 1998, and the Technology-Related Assistance Act, provides financial and legal supports for the full inclusion of individuals with disabilities within our society. Some additional support organizations are listed in Appendix 16–A.

Supported employment may be particularly relevant for people with autism. *Supported employment* is defined as competitive work in integrated work settings for individuals with the most severe disabilities who need ongoing support services in order to perform their job (President's Committee on Employment of People with Disabilities, 1993). Supported employment is also defined in the Rehabilitation Act Amendments of 1998 as competitive work in integrated work settings, or employment in integrated work settings in which individuals are working toward competitive work. According to the Rehabilitation Act Amendments, the work in supported employment should be "consistent with the strengths, resources, priorities, concerns, abilities, capabilities, interests, and informed choice of the individuals, for individuals with the most significant disabilities for whom competitive employment has not traditionally occurred." Other individuals, such as those "for whom competitive employment has been interrupted or intermittent as a result of a significant disability," also qualify for supported employment programs. Such programs, under this law, typically last up to 18 months but can be extended if the individual needs more time (as determined by the individual and the rehabilitation coordinator) due to the nature and severity of the disability. Once the 18-month period is over, continuing support may be provided by a state agency, a nonprofit private organization, or any other appropriate resource.

Supported employment follows one of two models: individual placement and group placement. The individual placement model involves a one-to-one approach where a job coach (also called an employment specialist or employment consultant) provides supports for an individual in an integrated, competitive employment setting for as long as the worker is employed (Wysocki & Neulicht, 1998). Supports provided by the job coach typically include teaching the components of the job, developing job-specific socialization skills, and providing follow-along services to ensure that both the client and the employer are satisfied with the job placement. This individual model of supported employment is the most flexible in meeting the needs of the individual and is considered the least restrictive supportive employment variation (Hanley-Maxell, Bordieri, & Merz, 1996). Group models in supported employment may include enclaves and mobile work crews. Enclaves comprise a group of individuals (usually fewer than eight) who have a full-time supervisor and work in an industry or corporation in an integrated setting (Wysocki & Neulicht). Mobile work crews (typically three to eight individuals with one or two supervisors) travel from site to site in the community and provide services such as groundskeeping and janitorial work (Wolfe, 1992).

Another program option designed for individuals with disabilities is employment in sheltered workshops (also called *community rehabilitation facilities*). Sheltered workshops are intended to be long-term yet transitional placements for individuals with disabilities (Wysocki & Neulicht, 1998). Workers in sheltered workshops perform tasks such as sorting, collating, and basic product assembly. The nonprofit agency that runs the sheltered workshop subcontracts with businesses and pays its employees wages based on their production rate; thus, the pay at a sheltered workshop is usually subminimal wage. Although a source of employment, the best sheltered workshops actively train individuals for increasingly complex work and eventually place them in competitive or supported employment. The drawbacks to sheltered workshops include extremely low wages, limited or inadequate training to prepare individuals to function in an integrated setting (Mcloughlin, Garner, & Callahan, 1994), and isolation from typical employment settings and models.

Although many employment options exist for individuals with disabilities, the question arises: How does one go about deciding which model best meets the need of a particular individual? This is a hard question to answer; the response requires a lot of thought on the part of the person with a disability and their family or caregivers. Table 16–1 includes a list of questions and considerations helpful in making employment decisions. Visiting the various employment programs also provides information valuable to the decision-making process, as does talking with families currently receiving services. Some questions are more appropriate for supported employment options and other questions are more appropriate if visiting a sheltered environment (see Table 16–1). The key to any decision is information adequate to making an informed choice; it is the right of people with disabilities and their families to ask questions. If we believe that people have the right to choose the course that they would like their life to take, then we need to actively involve individuals with disabilities in the decision-making process. Remember, employment programs exist to meet the needs of individuals with disabilities and should respond to those needs.

A typically overlooked option that exists for individuals to be actively involved in their community is to volunteer. Volunteerism has the potential to provide many benefits to the individual with autism as well as to the community. New doors are opened to explore various aspects of the worker role in order to gain a better understanding of the types of employment situations that will help support the individual. The community is having its needs met by tapping an underutilized manpower resource that can provide a valuable service in helping support community organizations.

WHEN TO BEGIN

For persons with autism, it is wise to begin considering employment early in life by building foundational work skills from early on. Gray (1992) outlined some best practices that can be initiated during the school years, including an emphasis on self-evaluation and self-determination. For instance, instead of having a goal that the student will do a task, the student develops the goal and then decides if he or she can do the task independently or with help. If help is needed, the student may indicate what type of help he or she needs (e.g., verbal prompts, visual cues, physical assistance) and, possibly, how frequently help or cues need to be provided. Another example is having the child estimate his or her success prior to a task (e.g., "I will be able to do three [of five]) math problems correctly."). Instead of the teacher or parent checking the task, the child checks the task and calculates his or her success rate, then compares that rate to the prediction. Building simple to more complex self-evaluations into a curriculum or home life from early on develops skills in self-monitoring, which has the added benefit of relieving parents and other care providers from being the only "expert" in task performance. This type of self-evaluation also empowers children to take responsibility and control of their life.

For individuals who are still in school, transition services are a way for them to explore available employment options that exist well before they graduate, beginning at age 14. The IDEA Amendments of 1997 define transition services as a coordinated set of activities for a student with a disability. These services promote "movement from school to post-school activities, including

Table 16–1 Considerations and Questions for Employment Decisions

Question	Considerations
What choices are available within the community?	Talk to rehabilitation/school personnel; see listings in the Yellow Pages; network with other families.
What are the career goals of the individual?	Asking the individual is the best way to find out, or observing skills and talents in many jobs.
What situation is the family/caregiver comfortable with?	Some families are comfortable with more inclusion in the community; others are wary.
Is the mission and vision of the supported employment program compatible with the goals of the individual and his or her family/caregiver?	Observing the individual or group-supported employment program may help.
If the individual does not like the choices of supported employment, what changes can be made?	Read brochures; meet the administration; ask about changes or special needs.
In a sheltered environment, do the individuals in the program appear to be actively engaged in activities?	People should be working most of the day and seeming to enjoy the work and social aspects of the program.
In a sheltered environment, is the atmosphere welcoming, and does it provide adequate supports to help achieve individual career goals?	Are visitors welcomed? Are jobs structured so that work abilities are developed?
In a sheltered environment, is there opportunity for community integration, trials of jobs in the community, and inclusion with people without disabilities?	Some sheltered workshops include people with and without disabilities, include job trials in the community, or train for community-based jobs.
Is the work meaningful? Will it lead to success and skill development?	Work should be real work that is graded for success, skill development, and increased pay.

post-secondary education, vocational training, integrated employment (including supported employment), continuing and adult education, adult services, independent living, or community participation." In planning for transition services, the individual student's needs, interests, and preferences must be considered. Transition services can be broad and include "instruction, related services, community experiences, the development of employment and other post-school adult living objectives, and, when appropriate, acquisition of daily living skills and functional vocational evaluation." The key factors in transition services are to plan early for employment and to use the school years to develop the skills needed to achieve employment goals.

Temple Grandin (1996), an adult with autism, stressed the importance of providing a gradual transition from an educational setting to the individual's chosen employment. Transition services are an excellent way to explore the types of jobs that are of interest to the individual and to gradually familiarize the person with the expectations of the job and within the work culture that her or she has chosen.

PERSON-CENTERED APPROACH TO LIFE PLANNING

The process of choosing an employment option is embedded in a larger process of developing a life plan—that is, a direction to one's life, with an understanding of the skills necessary to achieve it and the supports to develop the skill (Wehmeyer, Martin, & Shands, 1998). Often, a life plan is developed using a team approach to ensure that the needs and dreams of the individual and his or her family are considered and that employment goals match skills and desires. The members of the life planning team may include a special education teacher or a regular education teacher (if the person is still attending school), an occupational therapist, a physical therapist, a professional who may be helping with the employment process, or any other individual who may have valuable knowledge about the individual. Regardless of the professional members on the team, the individual with the disability and his or her family and friends are essential members of the team. These people possess a vast wealth of information concerning the individual. Without their input and insights, it is almost impossible to support him or her in achieving a life plan in the most efficient and effective manner possible.

To formulate a clear picture of all the elements needed to support the individual with autism in the employment process, a metaphor is used here that compares the planning process to an organizational structure. It is paramount that the individual with autism be the president of his or her life planning and employment committee. The family assumes the role of vice president, and the other members play a support role in helping implement the agenda that has been presented. This agenda has many components and is mapped over a series of meetings to help create a clear picture about the direction of the employment opportunities. A secretary for the committee must be appointed to ensure accurate documentation of the business that transpires during committee meetings. Minutes can be taken in a variety of ways, but one essential component is that the thoughts of the committee be posted on the wall during the meeting so that all members have a visual representation of the business at hand (Mount, 1991). This visual representation can take the form of the written word, pictures, or line drawings paired with words; this visual representation is then used to document the flow of the meeting.

The process of developing a life plan is not complicated, but it does require the participation and commitment of all team members in order to address the person's needs for leisure, social opportunities, and work. Many questions may have a different level of priority for each individual with autism and his family. Questions that are typically addressed are:

- What strengths and weaknesses does the individual possess?
- What environments support the unique needs of the individual and what environments do not?
- What are the hopes and dreams of the individual with a disability?
- What are his or her fears?

- What are the hopes and dreams of family members as they relate to the individual?
- What are the family's fears?

Other questions may also be pertinent, depending on individual need. The responses to these questions are documented by the secretary and posted for discussion and refinement. Through this process, a direction for exploring opportunities should emerge.

As the life plan unfolds, the responsibilities for implementing it are shared among the team members to capitalize on the strengths of each. For example, each team member has unique connections within the community at large; these connections may provide answers to questions about social, leisure, or employment opportunities within the community that would support the individual with autism. When it comes to exploring employment options, the contacts of the team members may prove invaluable in opening doors. According to a survey conducted by Louis Harris and Associates, Inc., 52% of adults with disabilities found their jobs through personal contacts, whereas only 5% found their jobs through programs for people with disabilities (Stoddard, Jans, Ripple, & Kraus, 1998). Team members may each have an area of expertise on items such as adaptation of the environment, financial management, or volunteer opportunities that complement the knowledge and connections of other team members.

FINANCIAL INCENTIVES AND DISINCENTIVES

Many families would like their family member with autism to work, but they may be concerned about how work will affect Social Security benefits. This issue should

not be taken lightly, as many individuals rely on the medical coverage they receive under these benefits. The individual may receive benefits under Supplemental Security Income (SSI), Social Security Disability Insurance (SSDI), or both. These two programs differ in how work can affect an individual's benefits, but they both provide work incentives designed to help people with disabilities enter or reenter the work force by protecting their cash payments and Medicaid or Medicare benefits. One resource that is essential for anyone receiving benefits under either of these two programs is the *Redbook on Work Incentives*, which is available from the Social Security Administration. The *Redbook* provides a good overview of the various work incentives. It may be helpful to find someone who knows how to navigate the system well or to gather information and have a good understanding of the system before utilizing these incentives. The *Redbook on Work Incentives* as well as other information related to this issue can be obtained by visiting http://www.ssa.gov/work/workincentives.htm or by contacting your local Social Security Office.

SPECIFIC TECHNIQUES TO IMPROVE EMPLOYMENT OUTCOMES

Worksite accommodations play an essential role in ensuring a successful employment outcome for individuals with disabilities. This section provides concrete examples of possible worksite accommodations for individuals with autism.

Case Example 1: Justin

Justin is a young man with autism and a visual impairment who was hired by a local restaurant to roll silverware, which involves putting a knife, fork, and spoon into a napkin and rolling them together. A job coach worked with him on learning his new job responsibilities. He had a hard time learning where to place the silverware in the napkin and then how to neatly roll the silverware. The job coach analyzed the situation and designed a jig to help Justin learn the process. After a few adjustments to the origin design, the jig was used to teach Justin the proper placement of the utensils needed for each roll. Justin quickly learned how to complete his job tasks and, after a while, no longer needed the jig in order to neatly roll the silverware. The jig was an aid that was used in the initial job training and then was no longer needed once Justin mastered the process. Jigs can be made for many packaging jobs, with placements for different parts, to help the individual learn sequencing skills (Figure 16–1).

Case Example 2: Christine

Christine was recently hired as a clerical assistant at a large company. Her breaks and lunch are scheduled at the same time every day. The employer reported that he was very happy with the work that Christine was doing, but there was a problem with Christine taking her lunch and scheduled breaks at the appropriate time. On talking with Christine, it was determined that she gets busy, loses track of time, and either forgets to go on break or does not remember what time she started her break. The job coach worked with Christine to identify possible solutions to this problem. Christine acquired a watch with multiple alarms, which were set to go off at the beginning and end of break and lunch. This simple adaptation made it possible for Christine to keep track of scheduled breaks and met with the approval of the supervisor.

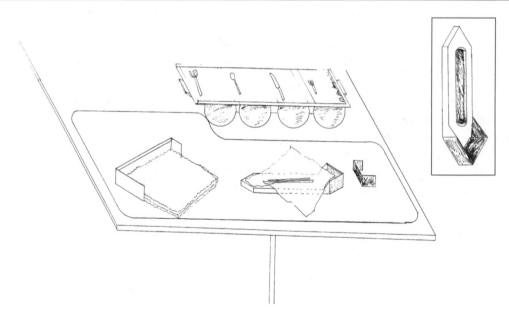

Figure 16–1 System for training in silverware rolling: Utensils, napkins, jig, and closure tab container. *Inset:* Jig for silverware placement.

Case Example 3: Spencer

Spencer was hired by a large drugstore chain to restock inventory. Initially, Spencer needed frequent verbal prompts to remind him of the sequence of the tasks that he was to complete. With the assistance of his job coach, an employment story system was designed that allowed Spencer to prompt himself about the sequence of tasks and what to do when certain situations arose. The employment story in Exhibit 16–1 is an example of the system used to prompt Spencer. Regular readings of this story enabled him to self-direct his day and anticipate the progression of each day.

Another way of presenting this information is to use picture symbols. For some individuals, a visual schedule provides the prompts that they need in order to complete the sequence of their job duties. Once the schedule is shown to the individuals, they may to able to walk themselves through the steps of the process by referring to the pic-

---

Exhibit 16–1 Employment Story for Spencer

When I arrive at work, the first thing that I need to do is put my things away and then clock in. Next, I need to look for my supervisor and get the list of items that I need to stock for the day. Getting a cart and taking it back to the stock area is the next step.

Now, I need to look at the list of items to stock and put the boxes that I need in the cart and push the cart to the aisle that I will start to restock. When I get to the aisle that I will be working in, I need to open the box and take out one of the items. Looking at the item and then finding where it is located in that aisle is the next step. Once I find the item that I will be restocking, I need to rotate the stock that is already on the shelf. After this is done, I want to take the items out of the box and put them on the shelf behind the items that were already on the shelf. If the shelf is full and I still have items left in the box, I should put the box back in the cart. At this time, I need to open the next box and locate the item in the aisle and repeat the same process I used for the other box of items. Once I have restocked all the items that I had in the cart, I need to go back to the stockroom and place any leftover items back where they belong.

It is important to check the time. If it is close to noon, then I need to take my lunch break. If it is not that time yet, then I need to check my list to see what other items I need to restock.

Once I finish stocking all the areas on my list, I need to check with my supervisor to see what else needs to be done. If it is close to 2:00, he may tell me to clock out, but if I have some time left I need to work on the tasks that he assigns me. If it is 2:00 and I have not finished with the tasks that the supervisor has assigned me, I need to let him know what I was able to finish.

Each day before I clock out, I need to check with my supervisor.

When I am stocking shelves or doing other tasks around the store, customers may come up to me and ask questions. I need to make sure that I make eye contact with them when they are speaking to me. If I know where the item is that they are asking for, then I can say, "Please follow me and I will show you where that item is." If I do not know where the item is or am not sure what they are asking me, I can say, "I am not sure, but let me show you where the customer service desk is and they should be able to help you." Once I take them up to the customer service desk, I need to return to the area that I was working in and continue with what I was doing.

continues

Figure 16–2 Visual schedule using Mayer-Johnson symbols. *Source:* Courtesy of Don Johnston Inc., Volo, Illinois.

ture symbols. Figure 16–2 displays the jobs for Spencer in a visual format; this visual schedule was generated using Boardmaker from Mayer-Johnson.

Another challenge for Spencer was remembering the instructions that his supervisor gave him at the beginning of his day pertaining to which areas need to be re-

Figure 16–2 continued

stocked. Two options were devised that could be filled out by the store manager and gone over with Spencer when he arrived. Both options were tried and Spencer chose the first option, a listing of the aisles and the items in each. All the supervisor needed to do was to circle the items that he wanted restocked for that day in each aisle. A copy of that document is displayed in Exhibit 16–2.

The other option was a visual outline of the store. The store manager just needed to highlight the products in each aisle that he wanted

Exhibit 16–2 Stocking List

Aisle 1	**Aisle 6**
Perms	Pet Products
Hair Products	School Supplies
Hair Color	Office Supplies
Hair Sundries	Film
Shampoo	
Hosiery	**Aisle 7**
	Feminine Products
Aisle 2	Lotion
Shaving Products	Eye Care Products
Baby Items	Acne Products
Deodorants	Incontinence Products
Dental Products	
	Aisle 8
Aisle 3	Vitamins
Cards	Tissues
Party Supplies	Analgesics
	Cold and Diet Products
Aisle 4	Antacids
Water	Laxatives
Juice	
Candy	**Aisle 9**
Snacks	Foot Products
	First Aid Products
Aisle 5	Vaporizers
Paper Products	
Trashbags	**Other**
Household Items	Seasonal
Light Bulbs	Cosmetics and Fragrances
Bug Products	Vitamins
Cleaners	

restocked. The visual layout of the store made it easier for Spencer to organize the items that he needed to restock for the day. The visual outline is shown in Figure 16–3.

All of these examples can be adapted in a variety of ways depending on the needs of the individual and the demands of the work environment. It is important to include the individual with autism in the process of deciding which adaptations suit his or her individual learning style best and what he or she feels comfortable using.

When it comes to employment options for individuals with autism, the job spectrum is endless. Each individual possesses unique gifts and talents that can be an asset to a work setting. Sometimes the challenge lies within those persons supporting individuals with autism. Are we truly looking at what the person can do instead of what they can't do? Are we thinking outside of the box about the employment options that exist within the community? Are we looking to create a unique job situation that supports and nurtures the employee with autism? The goal is to make employment a reality for those individuals who want to enter the world of work.

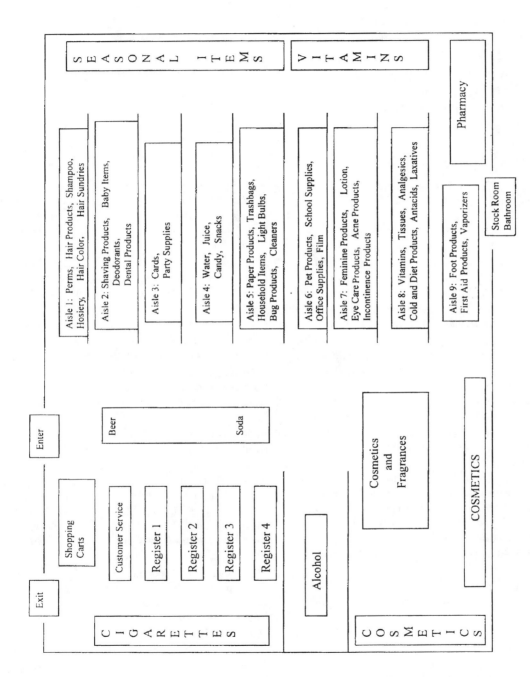

Figure 16–3 Visual outline of the store, created using Microsoft Word.

CHAPTER REVIEW QUESTIONS

1. What does the metaphoric phrase "still in the water but not really going anywhere," found in the young woman's experiences, mean regarding employment and life planning?
2. How would you implement a life planning process with a person who you know or are working with?
3. Write an employment story for your current job.

REFERENCES

Bogdan, A. (1995). Conference handout. Supported employment training network (SET NET). University of Kentucky (distance learning), Lexington.

DiLeo, D. (1993). *The employer's pocket guide to supporting workers with disabilities: Valuing what each of us brings to our work.* St. Augustine, FL: Training Resource Network.

Grandin, T. (1996). *Making the transition from the world of school into the world of work.* [On-line]. Available: http:/www.autism.org/temple/transition.html

Gray, C. (1992). *What's next? Preparing the student with autism or other developmental disabilities for success in the community.* Jenison, MI: Jenison Public Schools.

Hanley-Maxell, C., Bordieri, J., & Merz, M. A., (1996). Supporting placement. In E. M. Szymanski & R. M. Parker (Eds.), *Work and disability: Issues and strategies in career development and job placement* (pp. 341–364). Austin, TX: Pro-Ed.

Howlin, P., & Goode, S. (1998). Outcome in adult life for people with autism and Asperger's syndrome. In F. R. Volkmar (Ed.), *Autism and pervasive developmental disorders* (pp. 209–241). New York: Cambridge University Press.

Individuals with Disabilities Education Act Amendments of 1997. Pub. L. 105–17. [On-line]. Available: http://www.edlaw.net/public/20us1401.html

Maccoby, M. (1988). *Why work? Leading the new generation.* New York: Simon & Schuster.

Mcloughlin, C. S., Garner, J. B., & Callahan, M. (1994). *Getting employed, staying employed: Job development and training for persons with severe handicaps.* Baltimore: Paul H. Brookes.

Mount, B. (1991). *Dare to dream: An analysis of the conditions leading to personal change for people with disabilities.* Manchester, CT: Communitas.

President's Committee on the Employment of People with Disabilities. (1993). *Fact sheet on supported employment.* [On-line]. Available: http://www50.pcepd.gov/pcepd/pubs/fact/supportd.htm

Rehabilitation Act Amendments of 1998. *Findings, purpose, and policy.* [On-line]. Available: http://www.ed.gov/offices/OSERS/RSA/RehabAct.html

Stoddard, S., Jans, L., Ripple, J., & Kraus, L. (1998). *Chartbook on work and disability in the United States.* [On-line]. Available: http://www.infouse.com/disabilitydata/workdisability.html

Szymanski, E. M., & Parker, R. M. (Eds.). (1996). *Work and disability: Issues and strategies in career development and job placement.* Austin, TX: Pro-Ed.

Technology-Related Assistance for Individuals with Disabilities Act of 1988. Pub. L. No. 100–407, 2201, 102 Stat. 1044–1065 (1990).

Wehmeyer, M. L., Martin, J. E., & Sands, D. J. (1998). Self-determination for children and youth with developmental disabilities. In A. Hilton & R. Ringlaben (Eds.), *Best and promising practices in developmental disabilities* (pp. 191–203). Austin, TX: Pro-Ed.

Wolfe, P. S. (1992). Supported employment: A review of group models. In P. Wehman, P. Sale, & W. Parent (Eds.), *Supported employment: Strategies for integration of workers with disabilities* (pp. 63–82). Stoneham, MA: Butterworth-Heinemann.

Wysocki, D. J., & Neulicht, A. T. (1998). Adults with developmental disabilities and work. In M. Ross & S. Bachner (Eds.), *Adults with developmental disabilities: Current approaches in occupational therapy* (pp. 45–87). Bethesda, MD: American Occupational Therapy Association.

Appendix 16–A
Additional Resources

Association for Persons in Supported Employment
1627 Monument Avenue
Richmond, VA 23220
Phone: (804) 278-9187
Internet/Website: http://www.apse.org

Job Accommodation Network (JAN)
West Virginia University
PO Box 6080
Morgantown, WV 26506
Phone: (800) 526-7234
Internet/Website: http://janweb.icdi.wvu.edu

President's Committee on Employment of People with Disabilities
1331 F Street NW, Suite 300
Washington, DC 20004
Phone: (202) 376-6200
Internet/Website: http://www.pcepd.gov

Virginia Commonwealth University Rehabilitation Research and Training Center on Supported Employment
1314 West Main Street
PO Box 842011
Richmond, VA 23284
Phone: (804) 828-1851
Internet/Website:
    http://www.vcu.edu/rrtcweb

PART 5

The Experience of Autism from a Personal Perspective

CHAPTER 17

Parenting, Advocacy, and Living a Full Life

Rita D. Brockmeyer

CHAPTER OBJECTIVES

At the completion of this chapter, the reader will be able to:

- Appreciate and value the impact of autism on a child and the family.
- Describe the common attitudes that pose barriers for people with autism and their families.
- Understand the time people with autism spend in therapy and learning basics and everyday life skills.
- Appreciate the family perspective on choosing interventions.

LABELS AND MORE LABELS, WHY LABEL?

My name is Rita and I am the mother of two children and the stepmother of three. All of these children have taught me much about life and myself. These next few pages are about my son Joseph, who is an eager learner of eight years old and is diagnosed with autism, a Pervasive Developmental Disorder (PDD), including autism, central nervous system (CNS) dysfunction, global developmental delay, dyspraxia, low muscle tone, postural instability, oral motor issues, jaw-lip-tongue dissociation, hypersensitivity and mixed sensitivity within the oral cavity, sensory integration (SI) issues, splintered skills, inability to cross midline, receptive and ex-pressive language differences, left-side deficit, delays in processing, sensory regulatory disorder, sensory modulation concerns, deficits in visual closure, visual tracking, visual-spatial relationships—and the list goes on. This lengthy list sounds like many diagnoses for one child; truly, Tim (my husband) and I have not tried to gather it. It does seem that every time we try to look at something that is going on with Joseph to make informed decisions concerning therapies and interventions, we (parent, professionals, and society) find another label that fits.

Most children and adults with autism have a list of labels that help to express the complexity of autism and the complexity of interventions. Because the list is never the same for any two individuals, the interventions must be tailored for each person and family to maximize individual strengths. Joseph's labels to date of SI dysfunction, autism, and dyspraxia are the most encompassing; these are the basic labels for setting up therapy and interventions. He participates in interventions that are directed toward increasing independent daily living skills and academic performance. My son participates in therapies rather than passively receiving them, just as children participate in, rather than receive, Little League.

The label CNS *dysfunction* is useful because it helps dispel the old Bettelheim (1967) theory of "just bad parents—particularly the mother." Unfortunately, in some people's minds, this myth persists; fortunately, the Bettelheim theory is less believed among professionals and educated society. Research proves that the Bettelheim theory is completely baseless; *autism cannot be caused by parenting, good or bad.* The diagnosis of CNS dysfunction is also useful when working with individuals in my son's school system who are less knowledgeable about autism. The diagnosis of "CNS dysfunction" sounds "medical" and implies a physical and medical involvement, not just the "mental" involvement most people think of when they hear the term "autism." I have found that, in our society, "medical" things are more acceptable than the mysterious and threatening "mental" things. Most people I have met do not realize that a neurologist can also diagnose autism.

For example, the CNS dysfunction label was useful in obtaining physical therapy, which my son needs and benefits greatly from. The attitude of "he does not fall out of his chair and he can walk" as the criteria for *not* doing a physical therapy evaluation is old-fashioned and shortsighted. Physical therapy for Joseph addresses quality of gross motor movement, the ability to balance both when moving and when standing still, postural stability, strength, muscle balance, foot structure, and foot function. Walk up a set of steps with a person who has autism and see if he slams his foot on each step and if his movements going up and down the steps are as smooth as yours. If the movement is not as smooth as yours and the feet are slammed on each step, I would find a good physical therapist for an evaluation. There could be many reasons for this difference, including sensory, motor, foot structure, or muscle compensation patterns. People in all therapeutic fields have varying experience and expertise with autism. As parents, it is important to surround your child with select people who have expertise and who treat your child with respect, the way you want him or her to be treated. I believe that many people on the autism spectrum can greatly benefit from physical therapy, while for others it would not be worth their time and effort. For Joseph, it is worth the investment of time, resources, and effort.

Many complex needs should be addressed by a comprehensive look at what is going on with people who have neurological systems that function a little differently. Once you have an evaluation, the results allow you to make informed choices for your child. It is a great advantage if the individual with autism can participate in the choices of interventions. My son, at age eight, is now making some choices for himself.

I hope that one could get needed services for a child with or without a label. The reality in this country is that diagnostic labels sometimes may help with getting needed services; however, an equal reality is that the same diagnostic label may exclude your child from needed services. Labels are examples of those proverbial two-edged swords. I do not go around announcing that this is my son and then give the list of his labels; this would exclude him from far too many aspects of life.

Of all the labels, dyspraxia is the only one listed by my insurance as covered at all. Nevertheless, although Joseph was diagnosed with dyspraxia three and a half years ago, we have not received one cent of coverage for diagnostic procedures or for occupational, physical, psychological, educational, language, or recreational therapies. Insurance is another battle I will tackle once my child sleeps longer and is more independent. At this time in our lives, I do not have the time to fight every denial of coverage. I believe that most insurance companies know that parents who have children with disabilities do not have the time, energy, or resources to fight to get the rights of coverage for needed services. We have so many needs to address that we continually reassess them to choose where to place our time and effort. Often, we choose daily living skills, communication, education, and the fight to have our child included in society; we choose family time and the needs of all family members. We do not make the insurance denial a priority for our time. Mainly, we are too exhausted to fight. Since the first day of his life, my son basically sleeps only 4 to 6 hours in a 24-hour period, with no naps. When choosing what to address for and with Joseph each day, I tackle the alligator that is up to my waist; the ones around my feet I ignore. I continue to hope that changes in insurance carriers, laws, and policies will result in improved coverage for the therapies Joseph needs.

VISIBILITY, DIAGNOSIS, AND TREATMENT

In spite of all the many labels, *to look at my child, you would not be able to see that he is not typical.* My son and many children with autism look typical and, most of the time, act typically. Joseph and many others on the autism spectrum do not have what we parents call the "third eye in the middle of the forehead." This lack of visibility is both a blessing and a curse. Something as obvious as an eye in the middle of the forehead would make autism easy to diagnose early in life. It would also be easy to see a "cure" when the eye disappeared from the forehead following a particular intervention. If this were the case, I would not mind making people with "cures" rich off the families with a member who has autism—well, at least I wouldn't mind so much. One of the blessings of no third eye is that the person on the autism spectrum does not get quite as many stares in public from others. Another blessing of no third eye is that not all children are pigeonholed into one type of program; potentially, there is a greater opportunity to seek an individualized and effective program.

Families do not get the latent prejudice associated with a disability that is seen by all. For example, a friend of mine whose bright, intelligent three-year-old has Down syndrome, is often asked "How retarded is she?" My friend hates this question, of all the questions, the most. Because of the visibility, she often feels the need to explain behavior or a difference. She noticed that, even when her daughter was very young, people talked down to her, as if she were an infant. They continue to treat her as if she were much younger than her chronological age, which changes her experience and conveys lowered expectations. Many people are uncertain of what she understands. Even though her daughter had delays in walking, it did not mean that she had delays in intellectual prowess. The latent prejudice is the assumption of delay and mental disability

AUTISM

when you see a visual difference. Mental retardation is not an accurate term. For instance, a young woman who works with me and my children, who society has classified as having mental retardation, is one of the wisest persons I have ever met. She has her own pace, but there is nothing slow or unintelligent with her methodological approach to life.

On the other hand, the curse of an invisible life-altering condition is that the disability of a person with autism and the judgment of we parents are always questioned. Many physicians and others in the medical field dismiss early signs and symptoms as "all children develop differently." Similarly, other parents, professionals, friends, and family can also dismiss early signs and symptoms, most commonly by saying "don't compare children," "they all develop differently," or "Uncle So-and-So did that when he was young and there's nothing wrong with him." As parents, we need to advocate and ensure that tools are available to pediatricians for accurately identifying children with autism spectrum disorders earlier. If all children on the autism spectrum had the same difference in physical attribute, no one would be able to deny that the child's early symptoms fall on the autism spectrum.

In addition to being invisible, some symptoms of autism are extremely subtle and hard to categorize. The signs and symptoms associated with autism can wax and wane from hour to hour, day to day, and place to place. Each of the signs and symptoms can range from moderate to severe. I have heard, more than once, that "This child cannot have autism. He looks at me. He has eye contact." Looking back at old videos of the child when younger, usually the eye contact is not as frequent or as long in duration as that of a typically developing infant or child. The eye contact is not usually initiated or sought by the infant or child. Symptoms are *not* just yes-or-no questions; they are also questions about quality and quantity. The sad aspect of this difficulty in diagnosing autism is that many early-intervention opportunities designed for children under three years of age are lost for the child and the family.

Often, the opportunity for early intervention is missed even through preschool and kindergarten. I know of at least three families now seeking diagnosis for high school teenagers and young adults. The average age of identification of autism varies from state to state. In my state, as of 1999, the average age for identification of autism was five years, five months; in some states, the average age is even higher, and in others, lower. Joseph was identified at five years, five months, three years before the 1999 statistic was recorded, earlier than most in my state at that time. Across the United States, we are starting to diagnose autism earlier; however, we still have a long way to go in improving the current system and equalizing it from state to state. In this and many other countries, diagnosis is now more frequent, occurs at an earlier age, and is taking in a wider range of IQ than even 10 years ago.

Joseph was participating in therapies long before any of his diagnoses. At 18 months, Joseph had a multidisciplinary evaluation that concluded that he had splintered skills, his hearing should be checked, and, if his hearing was normal, then speech therapy might be pursued. The reason we took him to this evaluation at 18 months was because he had splintered skills. As a family, this evaluation was of little help. At four years, nine months, we put Joseph's name on the waiting list for another multidisciplinary evaluation and were told that the wait time for the clinic was nine months to a year. With repeated pleading phone calls, one day I lucked out and talked with a sympathetic receptionist, who let us have an appointment at the six-month mark, but not in the traditional order. We were able to see an occupational therapist and a psychologist before we saw a developmental pediatrician or speech-language therapist. This appointment saved us at least three months of wait.

After years of searching, September 11 became the day we will always remember, the day we were given the diagnosis of autism. The diagnosis was presented to us as if it were a death sentence. That day, we also were handed the diagnoses of CNS dysfunction and sensory regulatory disorder; these two diagnoses were presented with a matter-of-fact attitude and an explanation. The professionals at the meeting were solid in their fields and good people—in fact, very good people—but they were afraid to use the *A*-word with us; they talked for an hour concerning all the tests and other subjects. We, the parents, finally had to ask, "Does he have autism?" This took them aback for a moment, and they then gave us the page with the three main diagnoses from the multidisciplinary evaluation, one of which was autism. They said the reason that they did not use the *A*-word was "because most parents shut down and never hear anything else said in the meeting." At the time of the testing, we had asked them to rule out autism or rule it in, once and for all, for our family. Autism should be not treated as "Oh, we do not want to label a child!" or "'Let's save it to the last word when talking to a family!" Neither of these attitudes helps families. Folks, autism is just another diagnosis, and there are many possibilities for treatment and many outcomes. Joseph was the same child after the evaluation that he was before. The label did not change who he is. The label does not change how we feel or think about our son.

The label *did* give us a starting point for researching and evaluating possible inter-ventions. We use an eclectic approach with Joseph; we look at all interventions and keep what works for him and us. We keep a file on the rest for future reference. I always read the actual research on an intervention, along with all the hype. Research data are more important to me than the short papers or the presentations. I have found that, for the disabled community, someone often is selling an idea and making money. The one word I am always skeptical of is *all*. If it works on "all" children with autism, a big red flag goes up. I generally stay away. In the "hype papers," the words *all* and *cure* are used as headlines. In research papers, which the author's peers review, these words are rarely or never used. On the other hand, just because someone uses the hype words does not mean the approach has no merit. I believe many causes equal many interventions equal many outcomes. A cookie-cutter approach will not work. Read and listen to everything with a grain of salt. I still expect Joseph to go to college when he is old enough. I expect him to enjoy life. I expect him to enjoy other people's company, and I expect him to be a taxpayer (he will have a job). A diagnosis or a label does not change who the child or the adult is; it may be a door-opener to find out more about yourself and about them. What are your preconceived notions or prejudices? I know that I had and have preconceived notions.

Sometime the label of autism is nicer than the labels society gives, labels such as "He is lazy"; "He does not finish his assignments"; "He is rude"; "He is disruptive and laughs at his and others' bad behavior"; "He knows exactly what he is doing and thinks he is funny"; "He is just a bad kid"; "He has a bad attitude and will never amount to anything"; "Some days he does just fine; his behavior is fine and so is his academic work. Other days he just is disruptive and refuses to do any academics and we know he is capable"; "I know he can control himself and just refuses to"; "I have no idea why he chooses to be the way he is"; "He must have a bad home situation"; "He is just a rotten apple." Give my son a label of autism any day over the small-minded ignorant prejudices some people come up with. The diagnostic labels were a relief for our family and a starting point from which to better give our son more tools for his life.

FIVE COMMON BUT INACCURATE STARTING ATTITUDES

Be More Strict

The five most common unfounded attitudes our family has encountered because of the curse of physical non-visibility of the autism spectrum are described here. The first is that Joseph just behaves badly at times; a little less leeway and a more strict negative discipline approach will stop that behavior. Some specific thoughts on discipline include: I can control my child; physically control yours. He is spoiled. Negative behavior modification will fix that; it works for my child. He makes a big deal out of nothing. He should be able to handle his emotions better. Just make him do it; you are bigger than he is. You're the mom, he is the child—handle him. Some of these thoughts are said verbally and at other times they are conveyed with that "disapproving look."

Sometimes Joseph's behavior is great and sometimes it is a challenge. A negative discipline approach to Joseph has always been a major disaster. He perseverates on negatives and structure; if negative discipline is done in a structured and predictable way, he will seek the discipline. For example, he belches loudly. If, in response, you always

said that he must go to the timeout chair, then every time he did not know what to do or where he was in space, then he would belch loudly so he would be told what to do. Because getting structure is so important and reinforcing to him, it outweighs any negative experience or punishment that we may perceive. When tried with Joseph, negative discipline has always become a major negative reinforcer, making the behavior more frequent and escalated. On the other hand, totally ignoring an undesirable behavior has the greatest chance of rapidly extinguishing the chance it would be repeated.

Why do you do what you do? Is it because of positive reinforcement (money, promotion, enjoyment, gratification, making a difference, etc.)? Or is it because of punishment (getting yelled NO! at, having things taken away that you like or find comforting, aversive stimuli, pepper on your tongue, electric cattle prods attached to you, being physically moved to a different space you do not understand, etc.)? Does punishment help you to learn or increase the quality of your life? If your job or your learning were associated with negatives, would you want to learn on your own, or would you choose to avoid learning? Joseph is like me; positive reinforcement gets the best results. Negative reinforcement may get the job done, but you will never get any extra or my best work.

He Can Do It Sometimes, So He Should Do It All the Time

The second attitude is "If he can do well sometimes, than he can do well all of the time." This thought is conveyed most often about Joseph's behavior and his academics. Anyone with this attitude needs to study up on SI to understand differences with sensation, motor planning, and modulation. Joseph's performance varies because his processing of environmental stimuli varies—that is, because of inconsistent processing of sensory input, his performance will naturally vary and be inconsistent. I expect Joseph to do well all the time. When he has access to the appropriate tools and interventions, he has the greatest chance to live up to my expectations. What is most important for Joseph's self-esteem is for him to be able to control himself as he desires, not as the disability dictates. Joseph is learning the tools for self-regulation and self-control.

Wrong or Right?

The third attitude is that there is nothing wrong with Joseph. "Look, he can do this—there is nothing wrong with him." I agree with the second part of the statement, that there is "nothing wrong" with my son. Autism is not a right or wrong. Yes, he is different, but you are also different. You may be more typical than he; however, you are still unique, with your own issues. Someone, somewhere accepts you—warts and all; Joseph deserves the same acceptance. Joseph was different even during the first hour of life; Tim and I knew he was different from the get-go. By his 10-day checkup, I was asking the doctor about his differences. My concerns were promptly dismissed as "You are just a new mom." My concerns were that he did not take naps ever, even when he slept only four to six hours a night. He never cried to be fed, changed, or for any other needs. He was far too easy to care for; he was too perfect a child.

It breaks my heart to hear a parent say, "I always knew that there was something wrong with my child." That "what is wrong" is autism. If I could change one attitude in this world, I would change the attitude that autism is a matter of right or wrong. My child may think and function and process

differently, but that does not make it wrong. My son is not "broken"; therefore, he does not need to be "fixed." Autism may be different, but different is not wrong. *Diversity is cause for celebration, not for division.* We may all learn more from someone who is different from us than from someone who is just like us. It is fascinating to meet someone who thinks differently than I do. My son does think differently. *Different is not wrong.*

Crazy and Dangerous

A fourth attitude is that "these people are crazy and dangerous." Joseph is not crazy and poses no danger to anyone else. Crazy and dangerous has no truth to it. Joseph may have been dangerous to himself when he was younger. He sought constant pressure on his head and would get this in any means he could; head-banging and head-pressing were common sources. He would sleep with his head pressed against the end of his crib. He would bang the top of his head on anything and everything. He would press his head hard against the bottom of my chin as hard as he could. Through providing other proprioceptive input, the behavior was no longer needed, so it stopped. I made many giant bean bags and a couple of turtle shells (weight blankets). He often put the giant bean bag on his head and learned how to give self-pressure to his head with his hands; this was safer than the head-banging.

Another safety concern common among parents is stranger danger. Joseph does not know a stranger and never has; this is dangerous to him. Children who have any type of disability are at greater risk from undesirable strangers (particularly those who prey on children); these strangers sense their vulnerability and target children and teenager with disabilities. The danger of crossing streets and the danger in parking lots are still somewhat irrelevant to Joseph. He is not a danger to others. If you go into someone's space when they are out of control and try to hold or move them, you *may* get hit or punched. I respect his personal space and advise you to avoid invading his space without his permission, particularly when he is out of control. We all have a right to personal space.

You Cannot Learn with Autism

The fifth attitude is conveyed by family members, school and church personnel, and friends. All have said, at one time or another, that the diagnosis is wrong because "he does too well" or that "Joseph will grow out of it." The "he does too well" reflects the inaccurate perception and persistent myth that you cannot learn or function with autism. When Joseph was diagnosed, I went home and looked up the definition of autism in two dictionaries. One dictionary, which was quite old, said autism is a mental disorder more severe than schizophrenia. The second dictionary, the 1992 Webster's *Dictionary of the English Language* (Joseph was diagnosed with autism in 1996), defined autism as "a tendency to morbid daydreaming and introspection; uninfluenced by objective norms and realities." I had hoped for a better definition than these, at least something more accurate. Just for the entertainment value, look up *autism,* or similar terms, in the dictionaries in your home and at your work. If you are reading this book, I am sure you would be able to come up with a more accurate definition. This is another area for advocacy: more accurate definitions in dictionaries and other printed materials.

Will children grow out of autism? The answer lies in understanding the wording of pervasive developmental *delay* or a pervasive developmental *disorder*. Autism is pervasive, meaning that it is a lifelong involvement. Some things may be delayed, but that does not mean he will grow out of it or develop to a typical child or adult. Some aspects of autism are not delays at all; they are major differences. The processing of thought in his brain is different; this difference does not change greatly with age. Autism is not a simple delay, but a state of being differently organized. Our society calls such a state a disorder. I believe that interventions can cause brain function enhancement; however, making brain processes completely typical for a lifetime? I doubt it. Autism is from cradle to grave. I do know that, since autism was first described, there have always been groups claiming a cure. This is usually touted for all people on the spectrum, and the only cure comes from this single group. As of 1999, I know of five absolute "cures" being touted by parents, professionals, and the popular media, and one "almost-cure" for most people with autism.

I feel that the definition of a cure comes from improvements in function compared to the misconceptions about autism—that no one on the spectrum will live independently; that all or most are mentally retarded; that all have no sociability and will never have relationships with others; that they will never function in a regular classroom; that they will never be employed, keep a job, and certainly never excel in their fields. Some still-prevailing perceptions of people with autism imply that they will live in caged yards with no eye contact, no language, and no means of communicating, banging their heads on fences. If you have these perceptions and then your child is not like this after an intervention, if your child is loving and caring, if your child can use a means to communicate, if he or she has a social life or academic success, then it is easy to believe that he or she has been cured. The need for a cure only comes about if you believe that having autism and a successful, fulfilled life cannot be used in the same sentence. I believe that many great minds belonged to people who were cast aside by society; those who we labeled as "different," "disabled," "learning disabled," or "poor students." Just do a little research on inventors, scientists, artists, authors, poets, engineers, and other successful people and you will find that many are not normal or typical. *The world would lose much richness if we made all people typical.* The language of "cure" and of "maximizing human potential" may be just semantics, but this language has always been divisive in the community surrounding people with autism and other differently abled persons. Each family has the right to make decisions about interventions that are right for their loved one and their family. Many old myths of autism still live on. Some people choose to be advocates and others have advocacy thrust upon them.

Attitude Adjustment Ideas

My own attitude adjustment has been furthered by reading many books and talking to many people with the diagnosis of autism. My son was slightly verbal and noncommunicative at the time I began reading; I did not know even one of his thoughts. I read Temple Grandin's diagnosed autistic book (Grandin & Scariano, 1986), which in my opinion is a great book for parents of children newly diagnosed with autism. Temple, who has a doctoral degree and autism, has written a vivid description of her personal experiences that have inspired many. Some parts of Temple's book made me laugh because they are so genuine, hit so close to home, and are actually funny. Temple

Grandin has helped my attitude adjustment so much and contributed to, and continues to contribute to, my understanding of autism. I personally owe her a great debt.

Another person with autism to whom I am in debt is a young man named Brad, who shared his thoughts in a cookbook, of all places. *Food for Thought* (1996) inspired me, and I wish to share of few of these thoughts with you. Brad was a nonverbal 18-year-old when he wrote: "Some people who are different wave their hands around or rock back and forth or do other strange things. They may do one simple thing over and over to calm down their nervous system. It would be helpful if you didn't stare or think they were crazy; just allow them to do these things" (p. 261). Another mother of children with autism, for whom I have great and growing admiration, picked the following quote as her favorite. Although we have chosen very different paths for our sons and our families, we both found the same quote valuable. Brad wrote: "Some people who are different are not as smart as you are, some are just as smart and some are smarter. Some tests can tell you how well a person can communicate his smartness, but not how smart a person really is inside" (p. 264). My favorites of Brad's thoughts are these:

> Some people who are different don't mind being different. Even if I could change being different, I doubt I would want to. I wouldn't want to make me a changed person from who I already am, because I think I'm a good person and I like myself....I learned that people wanted to know about me. When they learned how I thought and why I did things, they did things that weren't as confusing to me and

I could understand them better. I learned that I could stay like me and still fit in your world, a little. So I decided it's better to stay like me and fit in a little, than become not like me and fit in a lot. (p. 269)

How do we judge the outcome? An 18-year-old nonverbal man—is this a positive or negative outcome? I am impressed by Brad; I know my attitude. What is your attitude?

WHAT CAN WE ALL DO?

As parents, family, friends, what can we do to help? Teach play by playing when trying to achieve objectives. Teach friendship by being good friends. Teach communication by listening—no matter if it is by words or behavior. Communicate with people who have autism in a straightforward, mutually conversational manner. Regularly include written and drawn communication or whatever facilitates and enhances idea exchange. Communicate person to person; you both deserve it. You cannot have a one-way conversation and consider it communication. If we do not afford people with autism a means of communicating to us, then our effort does not qualify as communication; we must listen even if they do not speak with words. Do not judge, do not demand, but respect them as a person of equal value to yourself. *Yes, of equal value—regardless of age, regardless of behavior, regardless of difference or sameness. There is only one equal, and that is equal.*

INTERVENTION NEEDS AND APPROACHES

Functional Behavior Analysis: Who and Why?

Add to the needs of people with autism the probability that they will be continually asked to do a functional behavior analysis (FBA) on themselves: "Why did you do that?" Although this is probably the only "truly stupid" question in the universe, we all ask it anyway on a regular basis. It took me a few months once Joseph was verbal to stop asking this question. The test for true stupidity is expecting *an accurate split-second self-comprehensive FBA.* If you asked me to do a split-second FBA on why, for example, I am wearing a particular T-shirt, I would say "I wanted to," "Because," or "None of your business."

Joseph Pushes Megan

Here is an illustration of FBA. If you asked Joseph, "Why did you push Megan?" I would expect an answer of "Because" or "Because I wanted to." The actual FBA is more complex and goes more like this:

I was on the tumbling mat in the gym; Megan came onto the tumbling mat. Megan did not belong on the tumbling mat; it wasn't her turn. I did not have the verbal or social skills to ask Megan to leave the tumbling mat, so I used what communication skills I have to restore order. I pushed Megan because this is the only way I have to get back to the structured order—to get her out of my space and into her space. I knew that if I pushed Megan, some adult would come and fix the structure order; Megan would no longer be in my space. An adult will tell Megan and me what to do; it will become predictable again. The predictable environment is of utmost importance for me so I have the opportunity to do what I am suppose to do. I am to do a backward roll; she was in my way. Besides, no one has the Twizzlers out yet and my oral motor needs are driving me nuts. And, who in the heck is the new kid in the class? I have never seen her before and she is making loud, unusual noises, not in perfect pitch. Why did my instructor smell different?

If I rely on Joseph to do an instant FBA and ask, "Why did you push Megan?" I deserve to get the answer "Because!"

Of course, we take this opportunity to teach. First, place something in his mouth for oral motor needs. Next, encourage a more socially acceptable means of communication by giving the needed communication tools. Then, set up a mini-play and practice the skills "Use your words" and "Talk to Megan." Give a perspective of someone else's feelings: "Being nice to Megan makes Mommy happy!" "Let us practice having Megan stand on Joseph's mat; Joseph, say nicely, "'It is my turn; please get back in line, Megan.'" By putting the whole teaching exercise in writing and drawings, this conversation will be more concrete for both Joseph and Megan.

These ideas were borrowed from the social stories concept, organized by Carol Gray (1995) and others, and old-fashioned horse sense. Make the communication visual, direct with the same meaning each time, and keep it simple. With written conversation, we are able to better communicate to Joseph and Megan what they should do and say in this social environmental situation. During a break in gymnastics, I would write a social story, with many opportunities for Joseph's input. We would then find out about the new student and her sounds, and about the instructor's new deodorant. I would explain that it is OK for people to change brands and how Joseph can initiate getting the Twizzler without waiting for an adult. All issues that come up would be included in the written social story conversation. This is a tall order, but it is doable for Joseph—unlike producing an accurate, split-second comprehensive FBA.

Our Communication Skills and Language Use

When we communicate the task at hand to a person with autism, we may choose to use *courtesy* language or *judgmental* language. The choice is ours. An example of a therapist's judgmental language to a three-year-old is: "You must work a little longer. You do not get to play now! Now is a time for work. Pay attention! You must do more words. You are not done yet! No, you cannot do that now." Positive language for the same efforts in communication could be: "Wow! We get to do three more words and next we will play your favorite game of Candy Land! I like playing with you!" I would also use visuals to tell the child what is expected. The shorter positive version accomplishes the communication without telling a three-year-old that he or she is wrong for being interested in exploring something else and for wanting to play. Tell the child exactly what you expect. "Three more words" conveys the message that the task has an end. You express excitement about the three words while you teach the functional sequence of now and next. The nicest point is you are not wasting your time, or the child's time, and you are rewarding the child with the game. Both of you get to have fun. Therapy sessions fly by when you and the child are both having fun; it is play, not work, for both of you, and an opportunity for more learning of the given task. As my grandma would say, "Honey always works better than vinegar when trying to catch a bee."

Communication, Communication, Communication

Expressing one's own emotions and seeing others' emotional state are total mysteries to my son. Explaining emotions to Joseph is like explaining sensory integration to the third of the population whose systems work perfectly; they don't get that sensory input can be jumbled and overpowering and uncontrollable. When people with autism and sensory issues collapse onto the floor and scream, they are doing the best they can do within that particular situation and that particular context. When someone is trying to drag them to do something they do not understand, something that may be severely painful (sound or smell, for example), or something that causes complete fear or absolute terror, an anxiety attack is a given. I know one statement that is absolutely true that I learned from Joseph: *You can never treat sensory issues with behavior methods and expect positive results.* I learned that neither I, Joseph, or anyone else would ever get a positive outcome when applying a behavioral approach for a sensory need. It would be easier to swim up Niagara Falls during the heaviest rain of the spring season than to *NOT* treat sensory differences with sensory methods. It took me a while to figure this one out. Of course, when I was trying to treat sensory problems with traditional parenting behavioral methods, no early intervention was available to us and our only diagnosis was splintered skills.

I wish we all had a wisdom pill that would allow us to pick out the most effective intervention for all situations. We could then distinguish sensory needs, communication, the need for an ordered environment, and other issues with 100% accuracy. As the wisdom pill is not on the market, we just have to muddle through using our brain and our heart. SI therapy does not treat all of the issues of autism, but it does enable Joseph to better control his verbal outbursts, anxiety attacks, and physical collapses. Visual structure, social stories, and other interventions of communication are also a must for Joseph. Sensory interventions are a good tool for Joseph, and he is becoming more independent in his use of them. With Joseph, his behavior is a means of communication and sometimes his *only* means of communication.

Independence

As parents and caregivers, it is up to us to investigate what the behavior is communicating *without judgment, without taking the behavior personally, or placing conditions on it.* The highest hurdle to this approach is not taking the behavior personally. You cannot infer the belief that the person with autism is trying to make you feel bad by his or her behavior. The behavior may seem directed at you. You may even be kicked or have your hair pulled if you get within the personal space and try to hold him or her. I am afraid that I am not explaining this important concept well. To believe that the child is doing the behavior to make you feel bad requires that he or she has a great deal of social understanding. This belief also infers that the child knows another person's perspective of a social situation. If social interactions are a mystery to my child and require years of study for basic understanding, then how could he understand this one complex social interaction perfectly at such an early age? We must not infer the understanding of this complex social interaction—that a person's behavior can affect another's feelings. For example: He is just doing that to make me feel bad; he is doing this to embarrass me; he understands perfectly because he is laughing. These statements imply that the person with autism understands the concepts of "feeling bad," "embarrassment," and "socially appropriate laughter." My son is still working on understanding the emotions of "happy," "sad," and "mad." The concept of making someone feel bad or embarrassed is completely foreign to him. Taking behavior personally is the greatest barrier to seeing what the communication intent of the behavior is and diminishes the meaning of the communication to us. Communications must be a two-way reciprocal event.

My logic for reaction to communication intent that seems atypical is this. I want my child to communicate feelings, needs, and wants. I do not want to discourage communication. If the behavior is for a need, first I fill the need and *then* I attempt to teach him another communication method that is more socially acceptable. My preferred approach is to teach him more independence, so he may be able to recognize and meet his own needs prior to generating a socially unacceptable behavior. This same independence is what we all strive for as we grow. When we are thirsty, we get a drink; when we feel the need for a workout, we go for a walk, a run, or to the gym; when we need to be alone, we seek solitude. Some of Joseph's behavior language I have figured out through careful study and lots of trial and error:

- I throw things or I bump into people or things = I need proprioceptive input.

- I get proprioception = I am back in control = I can now play = I can now learn = I no longer need to bump into people = so I do not bump = I no longer need to throw things = so I do not throw = mom is happy = when mom is happy, everyone is happy.

I am not sure if Joseph will ever consider and understand the last phrases of this equation, but by right of mom privilege I insert it: "If mom ain't happy, ain't nobody happy!"

What I hope Joseph learns in his pursuit of more independence is to run, play basketball, or find some other socially acceptable outlet when he feels like throwing something. For instance, cross country is a great activity that can last a lifetime. The continual training for road racing or marathons is just as beneficial as the races themselves. I hope Joseph's future scenario goes like this:

- I am a more organized, wiser adult.
- I need proprioceptive input to function = I have a scheduled tennis game three days each week = I beat the heck out of the ball three days each week = I get my proprioceptive needs met = I can function = I feel better.
- The side benefit is that tennis is socially acceptable. People think I am an aggressive, dedicated ballplayer. No one says, "Oh look at him! He needs proprioceptive input to function."

CHAPTER REVIEW QUESTIONS

1. What are some common attitudes toward people with autism; what contributes to these attitudes?
2. What are your own attitudes and biases toward people with autism or other differences?
3. Describe at least three sensory differences that Joseph exhibits and how his family has helped him overcome these sensory challenges.
4. Describe at least three ways of interacting with the family or person with autism that may improve success in the interaction.

REFERENCES

Bettelheim, B. (1967). *The empty fortress.* New York: Free Press.

Grandin, T., & Scariano, M. M. (1986). *Emergence labeled autism.* New York: Warner Books.

Gray, C. (1995). Teaching children with autism to "read" social situations. In K. Quill (Ed.), *Teaching children with autism: Strategies to enhance communication and socialization* (pp. 219–244). New York: Delmar.

Northeast Louisiana Chapter Autism Society of America. (1996). *Food for thought.* Monroe, LA: Morris Press. P.O. Box 4762, Monroe, LA 71211. Phone: (318) 343–7698.

CHAPTER 18

My Greatest Wish:
"I Must Play! I Must Play!
I Must Play!"

Rita D. Brockmeyer

CHAPTER OBJECTIVES

At the completion of this chapter, the reader will be able to:

- Understand the genuine and fundamental importance of play.
- Know that because of time commitments, fun, joy, and play must be an integral part of all therapies.
- Describe multiple variations to play activities that create spontaneity and fun for all.

WHY PLAY?

Now, a little about me and where my roots are, and why I think the way I think. My roots, I hope, will let my child have wings.

"I must play! I must play! I must PLAY!"

This is the cry of the young at heart in the Boll home each and every year, during the Christmas season and whenever we are together. My maiden name is Boll. The youngest of my siblings is Anna, 27 years old, and the oldest, Ed, is fast approaching 50, with nine of us in between. We have young children, cousins, nieces, and nephews, all in the home place for the holidays. You might expect that the cry "We must play!" would come from the young, but the call usually starts with Carol, the instigator of fun, who is now 40 years old. At

this age, you might expect that she would no longer run through the house repeating "We must play," and meaning it. You would expect a woman with a master's degree in forestry and a responsible job to have forgotten how to play, and the importance of play. She has not. When she is 90, I expect her to still be the instigator of play. Just watching Carol is a reminder of the free spirit of play and how contagious it is. Many of my other siblings, particularly Fred (youngest brother, now 30 years old), are not far behind in seeking and obtaining fun.

Fun is the lifeblood for the human spirit of our family. Whenever we go on vacation, it is always nice to know that Carol or Fred will be in the same general area. If either is present, there will be play, not just table game play. These two will come up with 8-foot-diameter balls to play volleyball with.

Many of the games are active, different, and always fun. Both Carol and Fred have bachelor's degrees in outdoor education and recreation; this makes them professional players. Carol works for the national forest service on a lake and recreational project in Mississippi. Fred is program director for a camp for children with learning disabilities (differences) and behavior disorders. Carol and Fred have maintained play throughout their whole life. I come from a family that works hard and plays hard. Or is it that they work hard so they can play more? My siblings and my father taught me the value of play, the importance of play throughout a lifetime, and what a great teacher play is. All learning can be fun and joyful; friends and family seek out Carol and Fred for fun.

Another component of play is making time for play, something I learned from my father and his outlook. My dad is the hardest-working person I have ever met. He is 78 years old and has retired at least three times; however, he still works from dawn to dusk in the business that he owns and puts in six 14-hour days in a week. But, I believe that he has not missed a local high school football game in the last 34 years, home or away. My father makes time for play; it is the purest form of play that I have ever witnessed; play is very valuable to him. Sunday afternoon has always been set aside for his play and guarded against any work intrusions. My father, Carol, and Fred understand the importance and joy of play. Each has an ability to make the time to play and to not let the duties of life get in the way of play. People and family like to be around them when they play; because they play often, people like to be with them often.

A GOAL OF PLAY

What do I want most for all my children? What I want for each child is to possess an ability to play. For my son with the list of diagnoses, this wish is more intense. If Joseph can learn to play, then he will never be lonely for long periods of time. Being lonely for short periods of time is typical and is an OK character-building experience for most, but his being alone for long periods of time would concern me. People will be more likely to seek him out if he can play. Joseph will never have the great social ability to seek others out, but if he has a skilled ability to play, friends and family will seek him out. This skilled ability to play will prevent my son from having a lonely life once my husband and I are gone and his sister has a life of her own. The quality of his life will be greatly improved with an ability to play as a child, teenager, young adult, adult, and elderly person. He may be able to make a living because of an extraordinary or ordinary skill in the right work situation with very little office politics. It's OK by me that Joseph will never be good at the complicated social relationships of office politics. However, I want him to have more than a job and an income; I want him to play and for people to want to be around him because of his "play ability." Do you know anyone who is fun to be around, someone that people like to be around? How well do they play?

Play is a great teacher. Play is the teacher of the youngest and the young-at-heart, no matter how many years they live. An ability to play can last a lifetime. An ability to play can enrich a life and all those who touch that life. An ability to play lightens the load and strengthens relationships. An ability to play allows for laughter and learning. *My son has no natural ability to play.* Joseph, before age seven, did not demonstrate any initiation of play, ability to join in and play, or spontaneous imitation of play. The concepts and skills of play, like many things in his life, had to be learned through a multistep sequenced process.

He did not seek out others. He did not have pretend play. He did not seek toys. Although he liked getting things like toys, candy, or books, he had no spontaneous follow-through. He did not eat the candy nor play with a toy, unless the toy was about his special interest (cars and trucks). He loves Halloween; however, he does not eat any candy without a verbal or visual prompt to select, unwrap, and then place it in his mouth. He loves the event of Halloween and understands the process of trick or treat, but if part of the point of getting candy is eating the candy, this has no relevance for him. He does obsess about all the people who do not have their lights on and miss out on the fun of trick or treat.

Joseph was seven before opening Christmas presents was of interest and he showed some curiosity or excitement about what was inside the package. At age eight, Joseph was able to show excitement about presents that he had asked for from St. Nick, but when it came to presents he had not asked for, he often just dropped the present behind him on the floor without appearing to look at the gift. Each year, we have the annual Boll Christmas party on December 26. This year, after the practice of opening presents and showing emotions about presents on the 25th, Joseph showed exceptional, almost exaggerated excitement about both the outside and the inside of gifts on the 26th.

Joseph is a perfectionist, and emotional expression is a mystery to him. He attacks emotions like a detective with great study; once he gets what is supposed to happen, he will do it with more exuberance than most. He learns to celebrate and play through study. In contrast, my three-year-old daughter understands the whole point of Halloween and Christmas without teaching, therapy, visual prompts, verbal prompts, physical prompts, or any other intervention. The ability to play has the potential to open more doors for Joseph then anything else we can do for him. Play is wings of flight and fancy for the young at heart. I want Joseph to always be young at heart and to always have the wings that only play can afford him.

ALL WORK AND NO PLAY!

I believe that the best opportunities for learning and education come through play. Play, learning, laughter, and all other processing and processes take the long way around in my son's brain and neurological system. Nothing comes simply; everything is complex. For most of us, the easy stuff, like "suck, swallow, and breathe," are learned in the first weeks of life. For people like my son, this takes years to learn, and effort to do, and may not be mastered in a lifetime. Many other skills we take for granted require much more intense effort from him. Skills such as walking with an even, steady gait and upper-body coordinated arm swing, sitting in a nonsacral position, chewing and swallowing without choking or packing food in the cheeks, biting off a piece of food with the front teeth or even allowing food to enter the front of the mouth, having food on the back teeth or the roof of the mouth without gagging, being able to use the tongue to facilitate swallowing by pushing food back in the mouth, coordinating swallowing enough water when you are thirsty so you are no longer thirsty are daily hurdles. Add to the difficulty in swallowing and breathing a common social situation in a school setting, with 25 to 30 students and a teacher urging the students to "move along so everyone can drink." Make the water fountain tall, so that you are trying to balance on toes attached to unsteady limbs. Add to this quest to get water impaired communication and impaired social communication. The impaired communication is the inability to say

"I am thirsty." The impaired social communication is the inability to know whom to say "I am thirsty" to, and how to time that request so that the person will be receptive to it. As a child with autism, you go thirsty a lot. I know that Joseph is thirsty often; he will drink 24 ounces of water or more in one sitting when given an opportunity. It is so easy to let this child become thirsty; he requested a drink only once in the first six years of his life.

Joseph must actively try to learn when he is thirsty, hungry, or needs to go to the restroom; he has no ability to communicate this in words or actions to an adult. Does he know when he is thirsty, but have no means of communication to let us know? Or does the long pathway around in his brain not let him know he is thirsty? We may never know which is the barrier. Nonetheless, the intervention is the same: Place a cup of water in front of him anytime you get a drink and do not expect him to get enough water from a fountain. I encourage him to drink at water fountains so he can practice the skills of using them like typical children. However, I still give him the opportunity to drink eight ounces or more of water from a cup.

What about vestibular needs, proprioceptive needs, oral motor needs, motor planning needs, postural needs, temperature needs, textural needs, visual needs, sound needs, and olfactory needs? Without good communication and social communication ability, the chance of him getting these basic needs appropriately met is greatly diminished. Many children and adults with autism have greater needs to be met than a typically developing person. In contrast to Joseph, my three-year-old daughter never goes without food and water, is too cold or too hot, stays in an area that smells bad, wears clothes that scratch, or has any other need unmet. She can immediately identify her needs and dislikes and instantaneously demand that the environment be changed to meet her needs. For example, she makes direct requests: "I am thirsty. Get me some juice." "Mommy, it smells in here. Let's leave." "I do not want to wear this coat. It is hot." "This shirt scratches. Take it off, please." She also initiates environmental changes herself. She changes clothes, gets a cup of something to drink, and takes your hand while pulling you and stating "Come!" Joseph, before the age of seven, never spontaneously initiated any of these requests, either verbally or with gestures.

Coughing must be taught. Blowing one's nose may take years to teach. I almost celebrate when Joseph has a cold; when he has a runny nose, I have an opportunity to teach nose blowing. This is a skill I do not want to try to teach to a teenager or an adult. A 40-year-old with a runny nose and no ability to blow it will not stay employed. High school would not be a fun place with secretions on your face and no personal hygiene skills to wipe your nose or even feel the secretions. This is one battle I would like to have completed by the time he is 10 years old; we are continuing to make progress. Things we have tried in addition to using a nose fluke include blowing out candles with your nose, blowing soap bubbles with your nose, and tooting a flute and other instruments, and whistling with your nose. We have also tried making elephant noises, screaming, and talking with our mouths closed—anything to get air directed out the nose at Joseph's control. If anyone has any other ideas, please share them. I will use any opportunity to teach this skill.

Even wiping your face is a skill. Joseph is getting good at wiping his face during meals. Because we think he may not be able to detect food around his mouth (he has never shown any sign that he can detect food or moisture on his face), we are teaching him to wipe his face every few bites or every few drinks when eating and drinking. This is the same approach we have taken toward time-training for toileting. Both of these methods teach a way to bypass the recognition of need. If he eventually gains the recognition of need, then the skill is already in place; if not, both methods are functional daily skills. Tasks such as dressing, toileting, sleeping, eating, eating neatly, bathing, and drying after a bath all have multiple steps and are complex sequences; each step needs to be taught. None of the simple daily skills we take for granted come simply to Joseph.

Joseph was nonverbal at 41 months when we started language therapy after being on a waiting list for 9 months. Joseph at five years was using sounds and a few words, but was unable to answer yes/no questions or request objects or needs in any way. At five and a half years, he started to combine words in the very early stage of sentence formation. Joseph, by age six, used a moderate number of words with greater sentence structure; he could identify some objects and pictures but, most excitingly, he was able to answer simple questions with a yes and no response that was accurate some of the time. At about six years, three months, Joseph stated calling me Rita. I would have been thrilled if he called me Mug Ugly and knew it was me.

When Joseph was little, Tim and I always discussed how we believed that everything went in (sights, sounds, emotions, words, etc.) and nothing came out of his brain. Prior to Joseph calling me by my first name, he had referred to me just once as Mom and had never used any other word to refer to me. Now that Joseph is older, he refers to me as Mom, Mother, and Rita, and Tim as Dad, Pop, Father, and Tim. Joseph's calling us by our first names has gotten, and contin-ues to get, more social reaction and comments by friends, school personnel, and strangers than any other behavior. Most people want me to be alarmed by this and to stop it. Some people think it is "just not right." They are allowed to think what they want; for me, it is a great gift that my son can call me by any name, can talk, and can make a request. I could not be more thrilled. Saying words was laborious for Joseph at ages six through seven. Now that he is eight years old, the words do not stop; he has many millions of unused words that he has saved over the years to now use. Joseph recently started having conversations. We are still targeting quality conversations, emotional expression, and storytelling. Understanding language and engaging in conversation is intensive work and play for Joseph. He still cannot tell me what happens at school, but maybe someday he will have this storytelling communication skill. Maybe someday Joseph will have the social concept that I am interested in what happens during his day when we are apart. There is always hope.

WHEN DO YOU PLAY?

With all these concerns, plus many more, a person may be in "therapy" many hours each day and in standard therapies many hours each week. Like most other children diagnosed with autism, Joseph has therapies. Skills like associating words with an object, verbal language, and gestural language to communicate needs must be taught and learned. Social language, gestures, facial expressions, social skills, and understanding emotions take many hundreds of hours, or years, to develop. We have a team of people around this child who are all helping Joseph learn these many basic skills; we can call them therapists, doctors, or various other titles. The person with autism is working on all these skills plus reading, math, and other academic tasks at the same time. Plus, he lives in a world that changes every day; all change is difficult and very confusing. All of the basics take time. We only have 24 hours in a day; some of them are for sleep.

If you spend several hours every day working on the basics, when do you play? When do you "work" on play skills? Play skills involve learning language, turn-taking, social skills, and the ability to work with others, be around others, have conversations, develop work skills, get food at a restaurant, get a tire fixed, or date another person. Most important, playing involves learning to not be the odd one, the one who cannot play. All learning starts with play and the best learning stays with play. For Joseph, his work is play; his play is work. If his therapies are not fun and he is not playing with the therapist, then he does not get to play. He does not get to play for that hour of therapy, and he does not get to play during the time of preparing for or getting to and from the therapy; he may have four therapies a day. My son works his whole life on just the basic stuff that is easy for us.

When is he going to learn to play? Why would we, as adults, look at a child and decide he or she needs to work for an hour because the adult is there? Please, teach through play. Even children and adults that are atypical have the right and deserve to play! Can we, as adults, do therapy that looks like play, acts like play, and is fun like play? Can we play and teach skills incorporated in play? Can we incorporate the particular skill that needs to be acquired into play? Can we have fun for that hour of therapy we are with him? I believe that all children can tell when you are working and when you are playing, even children on the autism spectrum. Children need to learn about the emo-

tions of joy through studying you and having fun. They need the sheer joy of the opportunity to play with you for an hour. They need to know that, if you could choose the one place you wanted to be for the next hour, you would choose to be with them exploring the world together. It could be the world of movement, language, math, science, letters, or taking a bath; can the child have fun and learn? I hope we all can play. I know I have more fun playing than working.

PLAY AND SENSORY NEEDS IN THE COMMUNITY

I hope that Joseph will become more independent in meeting his needs. Jogging, throwing shot-put or discus, lifting weights, working out at the gym, and riding a horse are all socially acceptable ways to get one's proprioceptive needs met without requiring sophisticated social skills. Joseph needs to be introduced to these or other sports and skills. Because he does not initiate or seek out anything that is different, we take things that are different and make them familiar for him. If he is going to play, he needs to know the games, rules, social rules, and the environments in which they are played. Joseph is rule-bound, so learning rules is an area of strength for him. The social aspects of "game rules" are that they can be interpreted and that not everyone plays by the exact rules. These "social game rules" are something that he does not understand.

One of the techniques we have used to level the playing field for Joseph physically is playing games that incorporate movement patterns involving diagonal and orbital rotation of muscles and joints. Joseph tends to move in one plane without equal muscle usage in each muscle group, compensating with much overflow of muscle action to achieve movement. The more difficult the task, the more muscular overflow he has. Teaching him to use the muscle groups more evenly through play enables him to have greater physical skills for movement activities involved in more typical play.

To make the unfamiliar familiar, we go into the natural environment. One environment Joseph has explored is horseback riding, which he does weekly. Joseph is able to walk into any stable and be at ease. He is familiar with the rules of a stable: no running, no quick movements when close to a horse, no walking close to the back legs of a horse, and no feeding a horse without asking the owner. He knows how to hold the food if feeding a horse by hand, where and how to pet a horse on the shoulder, and all of the other rules. Joseph was on lead horse at age four and has been participating in lessons since he was five and a half; he now has the social ability and familiarity with stables so that if we stopped lessons tomorrow, he would likely retain his skills. As a teenager, I hope (maybe with assistance, a suggestion, or as part of a group), he could ask a girl if she wanted to go riding with him. It would be a nice, acceptable social interaction that would be a nonthreatening social event for both of them. This would be more communicative and socially acceptable than expressing his interest in a girl by shadowing her with no social approach or by physically bumping into her because he liked her.

The major aspect, which I looked for, in horseback riding was the proprioceptive input of the horses. The horse's gait is the same as the human hip movement, with a greater force. I hoped that the force of the horse walk would stimulate language organization and self-regulation. I believe that it may have helped because he tended to talk more and use more complex sentence structure on the afternoon following horseback riding. Another reason I looked to horse-

back riding was to develop coordination and isolated muscle control in his hand, which is underdeveloped, possibly because he never crawled as an infant. To properly guide a horse, you must hold your arms close to your body, so your arms cannot compensate for lack of strength and control in your hands. You have to use the whole hand and all the separate components of the hand to communicate intricate and subtle instruction to your horse. This may help Joseph develop hand coordination and isolated muscle control.

There are different ways to communicate to a horse. Joseph, over the years, has learned to use his hands and body language to communicate to the horse. Another method of handling a horse is through brute force. We have not allowed Joseph to be taught to bully a horse. Other beneficial aspects of horseback riding include the distance from the ground, for vestibular stimulation, being comfortable with something else moving your body, and developing postural stability. I like the practice for him of being calm for a length of time; calmness is important for him and the horse. He also recognizes the different communication styles of horses—for example, which ones twitch their tail when aggravated and which ones lay their ears back. He has learned how to watch for the movement of the horse's ears to know its emotional state and willingness to listen to his commands. We use these examples from horses to define emotions in people. Horseback riding is great for self-confidence; it gives him something else to be an expert at besides his special interest. Horseback riding also earns the respect of peers and teachers alike, regardless of whether you are or are not differently-abled. Being able to control a horse is impressive. We do this and many other activities or interventions within the community. Sensorimotor interventions do not have to be done with a therapist in a specially designed gym; many life and community-based activities are great for individual sensory integration (SI) regulation. Gymnastics, riding bicycles, tennis, dance, bowling, swimming, and many more activities can be found in most community environments.

The more community-based instruction and interventions I can find, the better. Two primary reasons:

1. Joseph has to live in the community, and activities allow him to be familiar with the community environment.
2. The community has to live with him. If people in the community do not know Joseph or others like him, they will have weird reactions to someone who has differences similar to his.

When you were a child, if you had the opportunity to be in a gymnastics class with a child with autism, not just one class but many classes, you would not have as many questions about autism as you do now as an adult. You would have firsthand knowledge from your everyday community life of the diversity of humans. Knowledge is more powerful than ignorance, even though ignorance is more prevalent.

HOW CAN WE PLAY?

How can we help play? We can help by providing toys that make sense to children with autism, using their intense special interest and favorite color. When Joseph was age one and beyond, he would spin trash can lids. He had to! He was unable to walk by a trash can lid no matter what the setting. In doctors' offices, the red trash cans with the hazard labels on them were not my choice of toy for my one-year-old. As a paramedic for 18 years, I knew what was in those contain-

ers. I bought him a small trash can with a lid that spun to play with at the house. This made Mom a much happier camper. Even though he had his trash can at home, he was not able to resist spinning lids in public restrooms, people's homes, and anywhere that there was a lid that spun, flipped, or swung. We worked on limiting the number of times he could do the spinning, flipping, or swinging to three times—because Joseph always liked the number three. Joseph and I could live with him spinning lids three times and then washing his hands. The other option was to let him spin for hours, which resulted in him throwing a sound and physical limpness fit every time I stopped the activity. I provided a lot of toys that spun. We have many exotic tops in the house for spinning. He has always liked Jo-Jos, especially those with an automatic return. Many infant toys have spinning components. Joseph studied objects as they spun and I feel that he learned something or got something out of watching the spinning movement; my guess is that it was something visual or calming. Just because I did not understand the activity did not mean I had the right to stop it.

Currently, Joseph is eight years old and plays with Hot Wheel racetracks, which is very appropriate for a boy his age. At Christmastime, he watches the train go around the tree with wonder. When he was an infant, he could have watched the Christmas train all day; now, he watches it for about 15 minutes at a time. He still sometimes spins trash lids, but never more than three times. Most of the time, he walks by a trash can and does not need to spin, flip, or swing the top. Joseph used to open and shut doors and flip lights on and off continually; all of these impulses and compulsions are now more at his control. They have evolved from a compulsion to an impulse, to a controllable impulse, to maybe not even a need or want. The greatest thing we can do is to provide toys that help with deficits and emphasize strengths; we can teach by our example. If we are to teach play, then "we must play!"

Special Interest

If you want to get to a mutual ground with a child on the autism spectrum, use his or her special interest. Some people refer to specific special interests as obsessive compulsions. To me and to my son, it is an intense special interest about which he is an expert. Every person with autism that I have ever met has at least one special intense interest. If you know the child's special interests, good. Now you can play! In other words, now you can get something accomplished. If you do not know the interest, listen to the person with autism or ask a family member. Many have a favorite color also. Joseph's interest is in cars and trucks and other things that have wheels. His favorite color is RED and has always been RED—an intense favorite.

Joseph has always had a fondness for the number three. For anyone that hates that their child has a special interest, I have a true story. A friend of mine has a child with multiple diagnoses, none of which is autism. Our boys are alike in many ways, but the big difference is that Joseph has an intense special interest and her son does not have any special interests. My son can be motivated to do almost anything if the special interest is incorporated in the task. Her son does not attempt any task. He has no motivational interest for us to use to give the task meaning for him. I am saying this in a respectful prayer: "Thank God for my son's special interests, the love of red, and the number three." Without them, he and we would not have made such great strides toward independence; they are a true blessing.

Joseph's obsessive-compulsive interest has never been used as a punishment by taking an object away. But boy, have we used that special interest to elicit sounds, words, movement, rest, and a million other milestones! His special interests have been used to motivate him to talk, play, take turns, toilet, dress, eat, bathe, swing—almost everything. Psychologists, occupational therapists, physical therapists, speech-language pathologists, psychiatrists, educators, graduate students, gymnastic instructors, horseback riding instructors, art and music instructors, grandparents, friends, babysitters, his sister, and even his peers have used Joseph's interests to motivate him to comply or to sequence a task for completion. His three-year-old sister uses the interest when she wants Joseph to go outside and play. For example, she gets one of his cars and says, "Let's go play with Freddie the Four-Wheeler outside." He meets the two-step command (go outside and play). Yes, most of Joseph's cars and object have elaborate and specific names. Yes, he knows all of the names and never gets them mixed up; he even knows the day, the year, where, how, and why he got each car and truck. Joseph's recent statement about a toy was: "This is my hot truck I got on the Thursday after my birthday, April 18, two years ago. Jon gave it to me because he is my friend." On the other hand, I am lucky to remember a few of the names and almost always get them mixed up.

Our Home

Our home is never boring because of the people who live there. Joseph is a delightful, extremely fascinating, and eager-to-learn boy. Our daughter is 3 going on 40, and has been a dominant force from her first months. She has a very outspoken take on life; she will never want for anything and will hold her own in this world. My husband, Tim, is involved, loving, supportive, and steady. I would not be able to spend the time needed for Joseph if it were not for Tim. Joseph would not be where he is today without the consistency that Tim brings to his world. Tim and Joseph do many things together; they read, play board games, do math, go fishing, build models, do woodwork, complete home repairs, and do all that father-son stuff.

We have been doing a game night at our home. We play at least one board game during the week, and on the weekends we usually play many more games. The board games are nice because they involve reading and math, the rolling of the dice is good for developing the muscles in the palm of the hand, picking up the dice makes you use both sides of the hand, and you have to take turns playing and communicating. Many board games have great communication skills built into how they are played. Most of all, it is family time and fun. We try to keep certain days and certain parts of the weekends free from therapies and other commitments. We are making time to play as a family and guard this time as special.

THE RITA GUIDE TO HOW TO SELECT TOYS

For every skill, task, or detail to be learned, there are many toys and games to be had. We all have only one life to live; with so many toys and games to play with, we must get started! To begin, use the first four Is: identify the strength, identify the special interest, identify what causes a sensory overload or dislikes, and identify a specific need to be learned. The next five Is are: identify the environment in which the strength can be utilized; identify the environment in which to incorporate the special

interest; identify the environment that avoids a dislike; identify the environment that meets the need; and identify toys, games, activities, and sports that meet the need. The following steps are the six Ls. Look for toys in your house, closet, basement, attic, office, or any other place that stuff is stuffed. Look in grandparents', family members', and friends' stuff places when you have permission. Look in ordinary catalogs. Look in every store you go into, no matter what you are there for. Look in hardware, lumber, gardening, cooking supply, and feed stores; many of these stores have unusual objects that are good for toys. Look in therapy catalogs.

Now that you know some places to look, keep your eyes and mind open and on the lookout; you may find toys in the most unlikely locations. Find toys that you and the one you are trying to teach would enjoy playing with. Many toys and games can do many jobs at the same time. They do not have to be marketed as a toy, but the object becomes a toy when used in play. Often, the least expensive toys are the most effective. Here is an example. We found a pickle picker-upper at a craft store. We use it to develop the thumb as an independent function of the hand. We do not pick up pickles with it, but we use it with the Little Bear Game of Berries, Cherries, Apples, and Pears by Learning Curve to move and pick the fruit. So many toys, so little time! We must play, and play often.

PLAY TOYS AND ACTIVITIES

Visual Skills and Toys

I wish to start with visual skills because they are so important for children and adults with autism. The importance of visual tracking in reading is the ability to follow the sentence line. In the environment, visual scanning is important for finding things, such as a fork or a drink at mealtime. For people who find that the social aspects of humanity are a mystery and that language use is extremely difficult, vision may be most important. When children and adults with autism have more functional vision, the possibility of reading greatly increases. With vision we can enable them to access a library and all the wealth of books for one's consumption. They then have many more possibilities for learning and enjoying that last a lifetime; these possibilities do not rely on social skills. Reading stimulates the mind more than television or computer games. Reading enables people to study simple and complex social situations and repeat them or reread them until they are better understood. Books are good companions; they are completely accepting of the reader, regardless of his or her social skills or abilities. I wish for Joseph that he have access to books and the wealth of knowledge gained by reading. The practical daily skills of being able to find the salt, to find the fork, or to find the cup on the table each required the teaching of a specific sequence and development of new concepts of spatial relationships. I always look for toys that require functional vision; many of these toys also involve movement.

Table 18–1 is the summary of the Test of Visual Perceptual Skills (TVPS) for Joseph at age seven years, nine months. (TVPS is not the only tool for accessing visual skills and may not be right tool for your loved one.) This same test had been given a year earlier and another visual assessment prior to that. We had already been involved with intervention and made great strides toward some of his vision goals. Note that Joseph has exceptional strength in visual memory; this strength can be used to teach him academic and nonacademic tasks. We had been working to develop visual and other sequencing skills (because this had been his weakest skill) with occupational therapy, speech and language therapy, and psychology for three years prior to this test, and are still working on sequencing, probably due to his dyspraxia. Because of home reinforcement and these therapies, his visual sequential memory is now age appropriate. The three current visual deficits of greatest concern are: visual discrimination, visual-spatial relationships, and visual closure. So, we use the strength in visual memory and sequencing to address the deficits using a multidisciplinary approach. I always look for toys to facilitate functional vision because this is a priority I have set for him. Be creative and choose toys that are specific for the person you play with.

Table 18–1 Test of Visual Perceptual Skills (TVPS)—Joseph at Age 7 Years, 9 Months

Subtest	Raw Score	Perceptual Age	Scales Scores	Percentile Rank
Visual discrimination	04	4–10	05	5
Visual memory	12	12–11	15	95
Visual-spatial relationships	08	5–10	07	16
Visual form constancy	07	7–0	09	37
Visual sequential memory	10	7–08	10	50
Visual figure-ground	08	6–11	09	37
Visual closure	04	5–07	07	16

Joseph's Ramp

I look for anything that involves balls or things with wheels that go back and forth; these develop visual tracking and scanning. Joseph's favorite is a piece of eave gutter. You can find plastic gutters in many colors, and lots of other therapeutic toys, at the local hardware store or farm and feed stores. Most items are less expensive in these stores than buying a "therapeutic gutter ramp for visual enhancement" from a therapy catalog. I recommend plastic gutters because they have smooth edges, unlike aluminum gutters, which have sharp edges. If your gutter does have a sharp edge, use many layers of duct tape to cover these. We have both a standard 8-foot piece and a 4-foot piece of gutter.

Set the gutter up in an incline position and start the fun. Roll light balls, heavy balls, cars, trucks, dinosaurs, sandbags, and anything else that fits inside and goes down the gutter. Select the child's favorite objects and items in his favorite color to slide. For one child whose interest was math, we slid the math book down, let him do two math problems, and slid the book down again. This kept his attention on the play much longer than if we used anyone else's special interest. How fast the object slides depends on how high you make the upper end of the gutter; the greater the height, the steeper the incline, the faster the descent. This is an opportunity to introduce practical physics to a young mind—or, if you do not do physics yourself, plain gravitational science. You can make this game as simple or as involved as you like. You can make it mounted or portable. If you have anything outside that you can anchor the top of the eave gutter to, then you can adjust the slope easily by placing objects of different heights under the bottom. You do not have to anchor it at all;

you can lean it against a deck, tree, box, fence, rock, toy, person, or whatever you have in the environment. If you do want to mount it, one possible way is by using the diagram in Figure 18–1. Adjust the speed of the objects according to need by adjusting the slope. This is a slide for Joseph's cars and trucks, red balls, bean bags, Beanie Babies, and all other objects. Rocks, sticks, and wood chips are always favorites.

When using your makeshift ramp, do not let the objects slide toward the face of the person; this is usually frightening and not acceptable. This activity should be a fun way to practice visual tracking and scanning. For Joseph, this activity also involved all of us in lots of social interaction. We used this activity to reinforce and teach turn-taking, which is necessary for social conversation. My son and his younger sister participate in the turn-taking, and we progressed to a three-way turn-taking that included me and them. My son, of course, used cars and trucks (often red ones), and my daughter's dolls joined in, making the trip down on the trucks. As often as possible, I positioned Joseph so that he was watching the object go from his left to right to build tracking for reading. The gutter can be used for both indoor and outdoor fun.

A regular slide can do the same thing, in some ways, as the gutter, but you cannot control the speed of the objects, which tend to go fast down the slide. The child also needs to stand on a box or be held to get visual tracking due to the height of the slide. For some children with autism or SI issues, standing on a box is out because of the height of the box and their anxiety about standing on something off the ground. Some children perceive being held as a threat or find the holding aversive; I would never try to hold them. One little girl I know cannot handle being held by anyone; she panics and

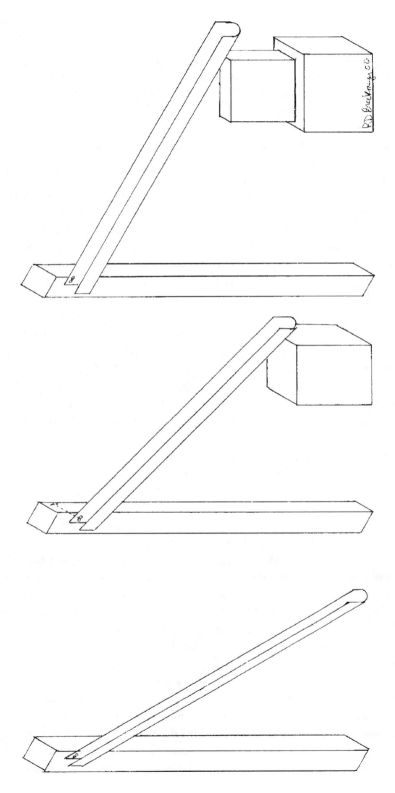

Figure 18–1 Joseph's ramp. Changing the angle will change the speed at which the object descends.

fights when anyone tries to hold her or hug her. Joseph, on the other hand, lets me hold him up so he can see the object. A child-specific approach is vital for these children on the autistic spectrum; for some people with autism, touch is excruciatingly painful no matter how good your intentions. When asked, one adult described touch as feeling like being "burned with a blowtorch," light touch being the most painful. She said she could tolerate touch only when she initiated it. Remember that this activity is fun. If it is not fun, do not do it. You can introduce it in small quantities, using the child's special interest. For Joseph, it took many hours and days to build the skill of visual tracking, and we are still working toward it.

I never expect Joseph to get really involved with an activity the first time he is exposed to it. Joseph is a perfectionist. He wants his participation in any task to be perfect the first time. Initially, he needs to stay toward the outside and study actions and reactions. Everything in his life that is new is a change; all change is bad. It is also hard to be perfect the first time you try anything. I introduce new activities in tiny amounts, a little at a time.

Anything Goes

Anything can be a toy! Water, paint and water, sand, wood chips and sticks, or anything the child will watch may go down the slide. Direct the child or children to the side of the slide so that their eyes are moving left to right to track the object. You may then put large objects down the slide—trucks, large peanut balls, even large rocks or buckets of dumped sand. Big objects are fun and often grab the child's interest and get him or her laughing. Imagination—yours and the child's—is the only limit to what goes down the ramp; use whatever it takes to keep the interest of your audience and gradually ex-

pand the skill and novelty. When doing water, sand, or wood chips, vary the amount going down at a time for different effects. You can add a toy going down with the water, sand, rocks, or wood chips; this will give a specific object to track visually. It is best if everyone enjoys the activity and is entertained, even you.

Rock Migration

In our backyard I have a rock garden, collected from all over the United States and Canada; every one of these rocks, no matter how small or large, has made it down the slide and many of our backyard ramps. They all make different sounds going down each different surface. Joseph and the other children who frequent my backyard (children with labels of autism, Asperger's, Pervasive Development Disorder Not Otherwise Specified [PDD-NOS], Down syndrome, SI issues, and others) all have liked the rocks. The no-cost rocks have been the great backyard hit. In addition, carrying rocks of various sizes and shapes over long distances from all over the yard provides invaluable proprioceptive input. For one child with Asperger's, cerebral palsy, and SI issues, carrying the rocks and the sound of them going down the slide and ramp brings great delight to him.

At first, when my son started carrying the rocks, I was not sure I wanted my rock collection relocated to the bottom of the slide. Some of these old rocks had been picked up on hikes, and I had packed them over many miles. However, even I can be taught to play; let the rock migration begin! The delighted laughter and excitement of these children are worth more than the perfect placement of my rocks in my garden. At the end of the rock play session, the children have almost as much fun carrying the rocks back to the garden as they did rolling them down the ramp. They drop or throw the rocks into my once orderly garden, producing a more random and modern pattern reflective of the group's artistic efforts. The children enjoy the dropping, and the flowers tend to survive despite the pummeling. Flowers are replaceable, but children's laughter is not.

Add Water and Paint for Tactile Input

Remember, this is for fun. You can always put paint, color tablets, or food coloring in water for visual tracking. Use the end of a water hose at the top of the slide or ramp. To use paint, start by putting thick watercolor paints into a dish soap dispenser. Leaving a little soap in the dispenser will help with cleanup later. All cleanup is done with the garden hose once you are finished with the paint. Put in the child's favorite color, or get the child to choose from two colors in two containers to help initiate choice. Show both containers and see if you can encourage the child to pick a color using a color card, gesture, sign language, or any other way he or she has to communicate. You may want to put paint on your hands or on the child's hands for choice. You can put your hand on your child's hand, full of paint, into the water running down the slide. With the paint in the running water, you may visually track the color down the slide. We often stand on the side of the slide to do this. We often put sticks, sand, wood chips, toys, balls, bathtub toys, and foam objects down with the water—whatever is of interest to the child and to you.

The Mud and Muck

You can always work with more than one issue at a time. You may want to make a mud pool at the bottom of the slide to play in. The mud pool may be great for children who cannot stand to have anything on their hands and repeatedly wash them. This is a tactile sensory activity. You can get an inexpensive kiddie pool with rigid sides or just put down a tarp. The mud is simply water and dirt. This does not come out of clothing, so wear mud clothes that you don't care about.

If you are not a mud person, or cannot imagine explaining to parents that you are getting their child covered in mud, or if you are the parent and mud is not your forte, then other options can come close. Sand and water is like being on a beach. Cornstarch and water is a funky mixture and quite different and inexpensive. I buy cornstarch in bulk because you need at least three boxes in a very small pool. Cornstarch is nice even in the larger kiddie pools; it can stay in for days and can be remixed. We usually do this at least a couple of times each summer in swimsuits; cornstarch does not stain and rinses right off of children, clothing, and the pool, slide, and tarp. Cornmeal and water yields a different texture that makes yellow mud; it is grittier than cornstarch or flour. Flour and water is messier than cornstarch, with a totally different texture; it makes white mud. Use at least 10 to 15 pounds of flour. If you use bread flours, the mud is even gummier. You can also add about 2 cups of wheat gluten for an extremely messy, gummy mix. Add just the right amount of water and dry ingredients to get the consistency you want.

For all of these, just dump the substance in the water and have the children mix it in with feet, hands, and bodies. You can add measuring tasks to these muds and mucks. For example, you can teach measuring a cup, a gallon, a tablespoon, 5 pounds, and other weights. You can measure all of the water by counting bucketfuls or gallons. My children love to measure things; they practice and pretend to be scientists and chefs. Although I prefer to do this activity outside where a garden hose is available, I have done it with the child in a bathtub and the muck in a smaller tub beside the child. The real success has been in the backyard, where the whole body can go in the stuff. The backyard is a great place for siblings and neighbor children who hop in and cover themselves with mud and muck also. What fun!

Who would be a candidate for this mud and muck fun? First idea is anybody who wants to have fun. Second idea is any person with autism or SI issues who, after picking up a doughnut, immediately dusts the powder off his hands between each bite or continually dusts his hands when using chalk or other powdery substances. Those children who are fascinated by water may enjoy muck and mud. I started out using small amounts of mud materials; warm water was a must. The first time we did the complete mud pool was a spontaneous effort by the children. They started by relocating the rocks to the pool and then they spied the dirt clods in the recently tilled soil of my tiny vegetable garden. They made a contest out of who could carry the biggest dirt clods across the yard and into the pool. I started by having them walk through the mud once they threw the clod in the water. The parents who were there gradually removed the rocks from the pool and, within an hour, we had the boys and girls covered from head to toe in mud. One of the six-year-old boys had previously not been able to handle any substance on his hands; he continually needed them washed. After the mud and other mucky activities, he was much less anxious about substances on his hands and the frequent washing diminished.

Other Slimes and Slides

Any of the many recipes for play dough and slimes can be made in bulk. I multiply recipes that yield 1 cup of slime until I get 2 to 5 gallons of slime. I sometime keep the slimes slightly warm, making sure not to burn a child. We color the slime using various colors; the children select and add scents or flavors. We then use them as paint. I thin them with extra water for many of our activities. We use our hands and feet to paint grass murals. We often start with painting a group mural of the sun and sky. Then each child paints his or her own mural using his or her special interest. Each child's mural is 20 feet by 20 feet. This activity requires a lot of moving paint with your feet and hands and rubbing onto the textures of the grass. They all get a Polaroid snapshot of them with their mural to take home.

The activity most requested by children with autism and their more typical siblings is slide and slime. This is like Slip and Slide, only we do it with slime. I am brave enough to do this only once or twice a summer. Make gallons of a slimy substance. Let it cool down, divide it into shallow, flat storage containers big enough to stand in, and add color and scents chosen by the children. Importantly, always use each child's favorite color and scent. They can stand in the container and start painting themselves. We usually wear bathing suits. They can paint themselves one or more colors. This is great for teaching body parts, left and right, up and down, and any other concept that is on the child's agenda. For example, you can have them paint the right hand yellow, the right foot red, go up and down on the left leg with green paint, paint their knees blue, and paint back and forth on their tummy. The choices are endless.

To set up the slime slide, go to the hardware store and get the least expensive tarp you can find—they slide best. Land with a slight incline works best, but flat land works just fine too. Anchor the tarp to the ground at the top or where you will be starting to slide. You may use tent stakes; I found that screwdrivers work best. You can buy very long, inexpensive screwdrivers; Tim appreciates it when I do not raid his tool chest. Turn on a sprinkler on low at the top of the tarp; because some children do not like the water to hit them on the face or upper body, set it very low. Once you are slimed, slide! The more the children, adults, and tarp become slimed, the slicker the tarp gets and the less running you need to slide. Between slides, go back and slime yourself. Water, slime, tarp, children, adults = fun.

Please note: I do not take or advocate taking a screaming child, dunking him or her in slime, and sliding him or her down a tarp, saying, "Oh, aren't we are having fun!" Take slow and easy, small steps. Let the child be the guide; if he or she wants to just watch, that is fine. If he or she only wants to get one foot slimy, that is fine too. Many times, I have taken a handful of slime to a child sitting on the deck and let him or her play in a way that is fun for him or her. Gentle, patient, repeated exposure is my approach. If they never have the opportunity to slide and slime, than they never will have the fun of it. Teach everything, but let the child pick up what is of value to him or her.

Slide-and-slime has become a valued summer experience for my son and daughter. To add a visual element, we place objects, often 3-inch balls (red, of course), on the tarp. Joseph has to use his eyes to aim his body toward the ball and use his hands to grab the ball while he is sliding down the slimed tarp. Instead of having a ball coming toward him, he is using his skills, vision, and movement to make a sliding body go toward the ball or other object. We use small cars and trucks and ask him to hold one while he picks up another (to exercise those hand muscles). Whatever works for you, have fun. I look forward to this activity like the children do. I do not believe that you can slide on a tarp in slime and not be a kid again yourself.

PATIENCE, PERFECTIONISM, AND MORE PLAY

Be creative. Be a child yourself. Have fun. Do not expect anything to work the first time you try it, or to work for any length of time. Many people with autism I know are perfectionists. It is hard to be a perfectionist the first time you try anything; Joseph sometimes demonstrates absolute frustration. We often break tasks into small step sequences by breaking them into components, then placing them in an order and reassembling the steps back into a longer chain. This method seems to help with the perfectionist in him. It takes quiet, persistent exposure.

If you let the child guide you, he or she will seek his or her needs and learn a pace that works for him or her; this is a great idea. However, if you have a child with autism, you may have a child who does not initiate anything. My son would lie completely flat on the floor for days rolling a car back and forth. Joseph needs to be continually exposed to a rich environment of options. When he was an infant and toddler, he was happy to stay in his bed all day. I do mean all day, literally! Joseph did not cry to be fed or to be changed; he made no demands on his world. When Joseph was four years old, I remember an occupational therapist asking, "What does he do when you go to a playground?" I thought this a very odd question. My answer was that Joseph did nothing. He did not slide, run, swing, or climb at the playground. At home, on the furniture, he was a climber; he climbed on everything in the house, regardless of height, long before he even walked. At playgrounds, he did not climb. If left alone, he laid down on the ground and stared off into space, not even watching the other children. As far as I could tell, it made no difference to him if he was sitting in his bed or sitting at the park. The answer was the same when Joseph was five.

If you are working with someone like Joseph, I suggest joint play. Because he did not initiate, I did. Shortly after he turned five, when I really learned how to watch for the subtle signs of his needs with greater accuracy, I began initiating play to get the need met. Most of the time, now, he does a great job of initiation for needs or desires; this skill has really developed and continues to develop for him. For example, during our weekly gymnastics class with occupational therapy, Joseph usually makes a beeline for the suspended bolster. When a new series of activities is introduced, there is usually one that he seeks more often than the other options. It is a rare occasion now that I need to initiate for him, or use a verbal or gestural cue, to get him to seek a movement activity.

Catch as Catch Can

How did we play at catching? We started catching objects as they came off the end of the gutter slide to stimulate visual-spatial relationships (also useful in communication) and eye-hand coordination. The spatial relationship aspect of communication involves telling how close to or how far you are from someone when you are talking to them. We also used a social story to explain the social rules of personal space for a stranger, an acquaintance, a close personal friend, and family. However, without spatial awareness, the social explanation of personal space makes little sense. How far away is the object? What is in front of an object? What object is behind another? To help Joseph with the visual concept, we used a regular straight slide, not a spiral slide, because there is more distance to see the object coming with the straight slide. Large stuffed animals were great for learning to catch; they are soft and move more slowly than other objects.

Catching a sibling or a friend going down the slide may also work. However, catching another person may be threatening perhaps because of the physical closeness, and people are likely to move differently each time they slide. Joseph often catches his sister as she comes to the end of the slide; he enjoys this play. Catching has taken quite a bit of modeling. You may have to do it repeatedly or have a typical peer model the catching so the child with autism can watch and study the skill. Do not get discouraged or allow the task to become tedious; it may take days or even years. Balloons are good for catching if the child is not terrified by them. Joseph does not like inflated balloons. One balloon popped on him four years ago, and the thought of the noise is still alarming; he still covers his ears when asked to hold a balloon. Another balloon floated away; he no longer accepts balloons when offered. Other objects for catching are inflatable beach balls, Gertie balls, and Koosh Balls. The Gertie balls come in many colors; our first one was red (of course) and smooth. They also come in different textures; my son's favorite is the bumpy one. Rolling these down the slide and trying to catch them is fun and nonthreatening for Joseph.

Good old throw pillows are great for catching and throwing. Most homes have throw pillows, and catching and throwing these can be a spontaneous activity. Catching is a multiple-step action that involves hands, eyes, fine motor skill, postural stability, and gross motor skill. You have to have a certain amount of postural stability and motor planning to catch a moving object. Joseph has deficits in visual perception, visual-spatial perception, visual closure, motor planning, postural stability, and fine motor and gross motor skills. These have made catching a challenge. We take the skill of catching for granted; his sister was quite good at catching by 18 months. Joseph can now catch most anything, but I would still not throw a baseball at his head and expect him to snag it.

Other visual games that we have played include marble races, both homemade and commercial, and desk toys—the ones for adults that have self-perpetuating movements once you get them started. Zoom balls are great for hands, arms, postural stability, eyes, and practicing having something coming at your face. The Zoom ball looks like a football with two cords running through it to two handles on either side; the ball is passed back and forth using the ropes. Any and all mobiles encourage visual skills. You can make a mobile by suspending objects from a clothes hanger by strings of varying lengths and adding additional hangers and string for balance. Thousands of toys involve movement or spinning. My theory is that by watching movement in play, the eyes practice processing movement; for Joseph, it is somehow an organizing activity. One other benefit of playing using functional vision is that it develops an ability to count using one-to-one correspondence (counting objects accurately).

Much of what I offer here addresses visual perception and skills, but many of these activities support tactile and proprioceptive development as well. Toni Flowers has a book called *Reaching a Child with Autism through Art* (1996). We have adapted many of her great ideas to our driveway and backyard and had fun doing this.

Face Balls

One last example of play is called Faces, Balls, and Shaving Cream. This addresses many concerns in a really enjoyable way. We have used many containers of shaving cream at the top of the slide and ramps in our backyard. We take as many balls as we can find, put faces on the balls with shaving cream (showing different emotions), and the children take turns rolling them down the slide or ramps. We have painted on the balls and on the ramp; the balls roll down onto a paper below and create artwork. In this game, we are getting paint and shaving cream onto hands (tactile tolerance), the shaving cream and paint smell different (olfactory), we are taking turns (communication and game playing), we are talking about emotions (defining emotions and communication), we are practicing facial expressions ("This ball is sad. Can you make a sad face?"), we are visually tracking the ball down the ramp through the paint (visual), and onto the paper and across the grass (visual and cause and effect, as a helper returns the ball to the child). The ball is making different sounds as it hits the ramp and the paper (auditory). We are also throwing (proprioception) and are high off the ground (a little vestibular input, just for good measure). If we end up with a wonderful paint design on the paper, we also have an accomplishment. We can choose what part of the long painting is ours (choice and visual perception) and tear off that section (fine hand coordination). Every single need you can think of could be written up with pages of ideas for toys—olfactory, auditory, visual, touch, taste, proprioception, vestibular—all seven of the senses. I consider humans to have seven senses, which all have potential for toys, games, sports, and especially for play intervention. Play and play often! So many toys, so little time.

CONCLUSION

The title of a book (Bratt, 1991) by a parent of a child with a disability that involved extensive intervention, *No Time for Jello,* influenced my choice of approach for my son and our family. As the lady in the opera *Central Park* sings the great line about "duties and details," we as families cannot let our lives be all duties and details for us or our children. We must play, make time for Jello, and bake at least one batch of iced sugar cookies in a childhood. I have also found great solace in a slogan by MAAP (More Abled Autistic Persons): "Remember you are not alone." I have a MAAP's mug with this saying on it, and on some mornings that is the cup I reach for in the cupboard to hold my important morning coffee. Let us all go forth and play "we are not alone." We can make time for Jello. To all children, childhood is important, and even if you have many duties and details, you only get one chance at a fun-filled childhood while you are young. Children, typical and atypical, have the right to play and have fun learning. Even if you did not volunteer to be an advocate, you can still do advocacy with style. As my sister Carol would say, "We must play! We must play! We must play!" I agree with Carol. I hope you do too.

CHAPTER REVIEW QUESTIONS

1. Why is play important?
2. How does play enhance learning?
3. Why does play enrich learning?
4. How do you use special interests for the enhancement of play?
5. Describe ways to use the strengths of a person for play and learning.
6. Using any play activity, describe at least three ways to vary it and make it more fun, playful, and novel.

REFERENCES

Bratt, B. (1991). *No time for Jello.* Cambridge, MA: Brookline Books.

Flowers, T. (1996). *Reaching the child with autism through art: Practical, fun activities to enhance motor skills and improve tactile and concept awareness.* Arlington, TX: Future Horizons.

The Effects of the Autism Experience on Life View and Philosophy: A Glimpse from One Side of the Looking Glass

Chapter Coordinators
Rita D. Brockmeyer and Myra Beth Bundy

RITA'S INTRODUCTION

What an enriching experience it is to get to know someone with autism! It will enlighten you about yourself and about the wonder of humankind. Each day I learn something new. Come join this fascinating experience in real life. As a parent of a child with autism, I would like to thank you for taking the time to read this book. I hope that it helps you to look at the world from a different vista. Maybe it will inspire you to take a little step into the world of people with autism and not demand that they step completely in your world to have value.

CHAPTER OBJECTIVES

At the completion of this chapter, the reader will be able to:

- Appreciate the perspective of individuals with autism and that of their parents and siblings.
- Describe some of the sensory experiences that people with autism may have.
- Understand the sensory experience of autism from the perspective of a few people on the autism spectrum.
- Appreciate the many ways of thinking about the diagnosis of autism.
- Describe strategies for sensory management of autism.

INTRODUCTION AND CONTEXT

This chapter is a compilation of stories written by parents and siblings of children and adolescents with autism, and of interviews with parents and people with autism. The stories focus on the sensory experiences of people with autism and on broader insights gained from the autistic experience. Prior to sharing these stories, it is important to put them in the context of the history of intervention in autism from a parent perspective, and to add a few ideas about terminology and ways of thinking. These stories and their context are shared with a desire to build understanding, insight, hope, and appreciation for autism among families and professionals. People with autism and their families tell their stories here as a celebration of their lives and their journey.

Trends in Treatment from a Parent Perspective

In the 1960s and 1970s, the standard of treatment for autism was removal from the home and placement in a loving, caring foster home or institution. The approach was to recommend and even insist that parents immediately institutionalize their disabled child once diagnosed. Institutionalization was thought to be best for siblings, for the family as a whole, and for the child. In some parts of this country, families who did not want to participate in this standard institutional approach were advised by some professionals that the outcomes would be negative for their child and for their family. How many parents today would rush out and get a diagnosis of autism if the standard treatment of the 1950s, 1960s, 1970s (or even later) were still in place? Fortunately, not all families or professionals listened to, or followed, this standard recommendation. Many advances have been made in the treatment of autism, yet the field is still in its infancy. We as a society are also in our infancy in researching the pervasive developmental *difference* spectrum. As a society, we have yet to fund the research to get the answers to many questions and, in most cases, we are probably asking the wrong questions. What questions will researchers 20 or 50 years from now be asking? What if we pigeonhole all of our research funds again into answering the wrong question? To prove bad parenting

was a poor use of funds even after it was proven wrong. What are we doing today?

Once autism research began, the goal was to search for and find the silver-bullet "cure" that would work for 90+% of people with autism, or at least over half. Anyone who says, "This will help all" or "This will cure all" is always wrong. One should be very skeptical of those who know how to "treat" our loved one, even before they have spent one minute with the unique person with autism, Pervasive Developmental Disorder Not Otherwise Specified (PDD-NOS), or Asperger's syndrome. In my experience, two groups generally advocate a certain exclusive treatment: those who say, "I do not have a child with autism but have worked with them and this is the only method," and those who tried an intervention for their child and got a desired result. We currently have a few theories on how to identify autism and its possible cause for some people, but we do not have all the answers. My advice is to view everything with hope and skepticism.

In fact, there are probably many causes, many manifestations, and many treatment approaches for autism. The only thing we know as fact is that intervention works better than no intervention. Environmental enrichment opportunities are of benefit. Which intervention is appropriate for any one family is a family decision. For example, some children improve with diet, and others do not. Some families find food supplements (such as DMG) or vitamin therapies helpful, and others do not. Some families choose one of the various forms of applied behavior analysis and discrete trial methods and achieve benefits for the family, while others do not achieve the benefits they anticipated. For some, swimming or horseback riding is of the greatest benefit. Play equipment and sports such as swings, slides, hammocks, therapy balls, small trampolines, bowling, rock climbing, rappelling, canoeing, bicycles, scooters, and tricycles, fit into a family's lifestyle and can be of great benefit to the child and the whole family. Probably more than 100 interventions could be listed that are currently in use. Fortunately, cattle prods and electrical shock are no longer used; they should never have been used. But some people still advocate using slaps on the leg, hot peppers and black pepper in the mouth, and other aversive stimuli. Each family has to ask itself about possible negative side effects of an intervention. Each family decides how to spend its financial, emotional, and the always limited time resources. Each tries to balance what the family needs and what the individual loved one needs, and tries to balance duties and details with fun and laughter.

The families that share their stories here chose many avenues of therapies; no two families approached intervention in the same way. The intensity of interventions also varied. Some of these families have spent 2 hours per week in intense intervention time, while others have spent 40 hours each week. Most of the families have spent an average of 6 to 14 hours per week. As their children changed with age and skills, the time spent in intense therapies also changed. What approaches and amounts of time these families will choose in the future is yet to be determined.

The best way for me to sort out which intervention is of benefit, is to talk with adults diagnosed as on the autism spectrum. They are the real experts. If the adults in the autism spectrum personally select an intervention that they find helpful, then I am inclined to give that intervention more credence. The children, teens, and adults on the spectrum, with whom I have had the privilege to talk or hear, chose a wide variety of individual paths.

This Would Have Been Helpful

When you diagnose a child or an adult, give the family the phone number of another family in their area that has a member with PDD-NOS, autism, or Asperger's syndrome. If a small child receives the diagnosis, send home a vestibular sensory device like a Sit & Spin; or the Dizzy Disk Junior, a small jogging trampoline, and Nancy Gerlach's *Autism Treatment Guide* (1992). This book provides clear, short definitions, resources to read, and contacts for many of the interventions. Give the family a one-page list of resources; the first listing should be the Autism Society of America. This national group can put families in touch with their local autism support chapters or provide information on beginning one themselves. I would also provide resource phone numbers on autism in the state and the region. Because there is probably twice as much bad information about autism as there is good information, these resources will help the parents seek information, get advice, and provide support for them in their choices. The parent or person with autism must decide what is good advice and what is bad advice. I cannot emphasize enough to read and listen to everything with hope and skepticism.

Terminology

After observing my son's years of struggle to communicate his basic needs, I deeply appreciate how difficult communication is. We, as a society, with much terminology at our disposal and centuries of communication skills, have a hard time communicating.

Our terminology can be divisive. The use of the words *autism* versus *Asperger* versus *PDD-NOS* can be divisive among many people. Is there really that much of a difference? Are there major differences among Asperger's syndrome, high-functioning autism, and "more abled autistic person"? The term "high-functioning autism" implies that those who do not qualify for this term are then "low-functioning"—or does it? The same difficulty applies to a "more abled" autistic person; does this imply a "less abled" person with autism? How about the use of the terms "client" or "patient?" How about the terms "therapist" and "therapy?" In a dictionary, *therapy* is often defined as "remedial treatment" or "curative processes." The terms "remedial" and "curative" both imply that something needs to be fixed or is being broken; is this the message we want? I chose not to tell my son at age three that he was going to an hour of remedial treatment, or at age eight that I was taking him for an hour of curative processes. We chose instead to say, "Let's go to language and play and make some sounds." How about a person with autism versus an autistic person? "A person with autism" sounds like autism is an appendage. "An autistic person" sounds like autism is the priority and the person is secondary. Some days my son has autism and some days the autism has him; sometimes he is just a typical eight-year-old boy. Terminology, language, communication....Give us another four centuries and maybe we, as a society of thinking humans, will come closer to the use and mastery of something so elusive, so as not to offend and be divisive. In the previous sentence, should I have written "humans who think" rather than "thinking humans?"

Changing the Way We Think

Following are a few short glimpses of those whose families are altered by the autism spectrum. We, the people with autism, parents, and family members whose stories follow, focus on ability, not disability; strengths, not deficits; possibilities, not boxes. If we identify what steps we or our loved one *can* do, then we can identify what steps to go to next. If we can imagine possibilities, then we can use these steps to achieve these dreams. We have all learned to look and think outside of the box. Let me give you an example of how we have had to change our thinking.

Most of you reading these pages are never going to be brain surgeons. We could, as a group, sit down and make a list of your deficits, the ones that have kept you from being a brain surgeon, such as limited math and science skills, poor desire or motivation, lack of opportunities, etc. We could spend the rest of your life focusing on why you never became a brain surgeon; after all, we have decided that being a brain surgeon is the only positive outcome for your life. As you can see, this will accomplish nothing. Just like our children, siblings, and loved ones, your life has more importance than a singular focus on why you failed to become a brain surgeon. Rather, we focus on the real abilities, the real strengths, and the expanding possibilities for our children and our families.

The following stories were written by family members. It is my privilege to introduce each family and story to you. Artwork or a photo is often included.

STORIES OF PARENTS AND SIBLINGS

Michael

Sherry and Ron are professional educators. Michael's older sister, Karen, is supportive, sweet, smart, responsible, and a joy to be around. In addition to autism, Michael has the diagnoses of obsessive-compulsive

Figure 19–1 Karen and Michael.

disorder and Tourette syndrome. When I first heard about Sherry and her family from another mother, I was told, "You have to meet this woman. She takes the table and chairs out of her dining room each day to put up a tire swing for her child. You will like her. You two will get along." She was right; Sherry does many creative things, and I consider her my very dear friend.

Michael's Story, by Sherry Hoover

The Tire Swing

I took my three-and-a-half-year-old autistic son dutifully to an occupational therapist for an hour every week. Her room was filled with every wonderful sensory toy imaginable. However, Michael refused to take notice of anything except the tire swing. He spent his entire hour making large circles on it. Suddenly it occurred to me that I was paying a dollar a minute to watch him swing. Obviously, he badly needed the sensory input he was getting from swinging. I reasoned: Why couldn't I rig a tire swing myself at home? The occupational therapist reminded me of the extreme importance of padding the ground with foam mats. The last thing he needed, she informed me, was a head injury as well as autism—and she was right. We took pictures of our home setup and she was assured the swing was well constructed and fully padded for his protection.

The outdoor swing was great for the summer and fall months, but we were headed for the winter months (it snows where we live) and he still badly needed this type of sensory stimulation. Spending the winter with an exceptionally hyper child indoors loomed before me. Hey, why not rig a tire swing in my own dining room? It only meant taking down the ceiling fan, replacing it with a hook for the tire, and moving the dining table to the living room for a few hours daily! My husband told me I had finally lost it, but in the end he gave in to my whim.

In the beginning, Michael averaged three hours total on the swing daily. Many people with autism don't get dizzy like other people do, so he was able to maintain long periods of time on it. As I cooked in the kitchen, he swung happily behind me in the dining room.

What happened next? Michael began to swing for shorter and shorter amounts of time. One day, he began to change how he swung on the swing from large circles to linear movements. This was great news, our occupational therapist told me, because it was helping him to develop new brain growth. During occupational therapy sessions, he no longer stayed on the tire swing the entire time; he was busy trying out new toys and equipment. The occupational therapist could also see a significant improvement in his eye contact.

After about five months, he had gone from averaging three hours daily to 30 minutes per day on his swing. And then it happened! One day, as he came off his swing, he began to sway and stagger around the room. Oh my gosh, he was *dizzy*! His brain had finally kicked in and responded as it should have. After the dizziness started, he no longer wanted to swing on the tire swing. It had served its purpose.

Michael's need to circle (spin) returned three years later. This time we bought a product called the Dizzy Disk Junior. It was small and took up very little space. Currently, he averages 20–30 minutes on it daily. He began to experience dizziness again within a matter of weeks of starting to use it.

The "Cubby"

One day, at age three and a half, my autistic son cleaned out the lower half of his closet. He padded it with his favorite blanket, crawled in, and closed the door. He had created his own "cubby" (quiet space). As a parent, I was alarmed because this wasn't normal. However, instead of dragging him out and putting everything back in, I watched to see what would happen. It is amazing what you can learn by quietly watching.

When his environment, our home, got too noisy or just active in general, he would go to his cubby and close the door. When he emerged—anywhere from 10 to 20 minutes later—he was calmer and happier. I began to realize that when he was allowed to have his quiet periods, he was much more social afterward.

When I spoke to his occupational therapist, she told me that when he was in his cubby, his vision got a chance to rest and his ears enjoyed the peace and quiet. So I allowed him to continue using it. What happened next surprised even me. He began to invite (take) his older sister with him. She told me he just wanted to lie down and be peaceful. Later he wanted cookies for them to share in "their cubby." After about two

months, he simply stopped using the cubby. It had served its purpose and he no longer needed it.

Load in the Car for Swimming

We tried activities with my autistic son to encourage fine motor development for two years. By age six, nothing had really helped. Finally, a fellow mom of an autistic child, Rita, reminded me Michael wasn't going to get fine motor development until he had gross motor development. Of course she was right—and boy, did I feel stupid! [Rita's note: There is nothing stupid about Sherry; she has taught me a great deal.]

I chose swimming to encourage gross motor development because Michael loved the water. Water represents security to my child. He is happier in the water than anywhere else and just being in it serves multiple purposes for him. I watch the anxieties of his day slide away in water; he gives in to a totally relaxing, all-body, sensory experience. My entire family loads into the car two to three times weekly for our trek to an indoor pool. Michael loves playing chase with his sister and riding on Daddy's back across the pool. Socially, it is our "family time" and great exercise for all of us.

Initially, Michael played in the shallow water, but later he bravely held onto the ladder and went up and down the deep end of the pool learning to shove off from the bottom. He began to use his arms to swim and we taught him to kick his legs. He could not, however, do both at the same time. It took months of practice before he began to be able to use them simultaneously. An occupational therapist told me this meant that communication between both hemispheres of his brain was occurring throughout his entire body.

How did this help his fine motor development? After about six months of swimming, he began to slowly start gaining control of his individual fingers. He started with his pointer finger and then moved on to the finger beside it. I strongly feel that the swimming laid the groundwork for this progress and plan to continue it for many years. This is a fun activity for Michael and our entire family. We all look forward to loading into the car for the trip to do a swim.

Will

Jim and his wife, Becky, are both lawyers. They have two children, the boy you'll read about here and his older sister. Both parents are active advocates for their children and for other children, with and without disabilities. Jim is a humorous as well as distinguished character. He enjoys reading, as you will be able to discern from his writing. Becky is tireless in her advocacy for all children and is a great comfort and caregiver to her mother. Will is in the third grade and tells wonderful fantasy stories. His sister is energetic and supportive and kind to her brother. Jim writes a weekly column for the Sun, a weekly newspaper in his hometown of Russell, Kentucky. He often writes about Will and autism; here are some of his writings.

Will's Story, by Jim

Sleeping Beauty

There is an English psychiatrist with the sonorous name of Uta Frith. In her book *Autism: Explaining the Enigma*, Dr. Frith (1992) examines the historical record for descriptions of autistic behavior before the 1940s, the time when Drs. Kanner and Asperger separately and coincidentally diagnosed the disorder and coined the term. Frith found many examples of children and adults throughout history described by their contemporaries as possessed by demons or touched by God, as idiots and geniuses, all with what she believes to have been autistic characteristics. One example she uses is the fairy tale Sleeping Beauty. The story, as everyone with a VCR knows, is about the beautiful girl cursed with a sleeping death—not quite alive, not quite dead. Gone from this world, but still with us, waiting behind the wall of thorns for her true love to remove the curse and bring her back to the world of the awake and living. But as the name tells us, she is no ordinary sleeper, but a beautiful one. It is her beauty that adds to the tragedy and compels her prince to try to awaken her.

Children with autism tend to look beautiful. There is a debate as to whether or not this is a true morphology of the disease, but it is very easy for the nonprofessional to observe and is often the first thing people notice when they meet my son, Will. Dr. Bryna Siegel (1998), in her book *The World of the Autistic Child*, writes that people with autism tend to have the appearance to us of a sleeping child—peaceful, serene, calm. Their often placid facial expressions give them an "another-world" look, which has been described as elfin or mystical. Dr. Oliver Sacks (1996), in his book *The Anthropologist on Mars*, speculates that stories of changelings—children left by leprechauns or other magical folk, swapped for a human—may have its roots in the autistic child, who looks and acts as if he or she belongs in another realm.

Will is seven. We have known that he has a form of autism since he was five. He very much loves *Sleeping Beauty*.

There is very little we know for sure about autism. It is a neurobiological disorder, but its cause is unclear. It is not curable. For Will and others, it is an inability to comprehend social language in a flexible way.

People with autism may be of low intelligence, above average (like Will), or near-geniuses, with those astonishing traits called *savant*. (Examples from Hollywood's portrayal of autism: Think of Raymond in the movie *Rain Man*, with his card tricks, or of Forrest Gump, an athletic savant.) Children with autism range from the nonverbal (the preferred term is the more hopeful "preverbal") to the hyperlexic, able to read at levels far above their comprehension. People with autism can lack the ability to understand human emotions. Dr. Temple Grandin, an adult woman with autism, writes that although she watches *Romeo and Juliet*, she just doesn't get the play. (Grandin is a PhD in animal husbandry, the leading designer of humane and efficient meat processing plants in the world.) Grandin coined the expression "anthropologist on Mars" to describe how she watches with puzzlement the social interaction of neurotypical people, just as an alien might observe our strange doings. It is the things we take for granted, the nonverbal clues, the ability to ad lib or make spontaneous decisions, things that we are not taught but just pick up, that some persons with autism must learn as if learning a script.

The title of Grandin's autobiography, *Thinking in Pictures* (Grandin, 1996), describes the visual reasoning common to some people with autism. This visual thinking is one of the reasons she is so successful in her work; she can "see" how a design for her projects should be built. Albert Einstein did not initially work out the theory of relatively in the abstract. He stated that he visualized what it would look like if you rode on a beam of light across the universe.

Einstein lived before adults were diagnosed with autism, but what we know of him personally leads many people familiar with autism to think they recognize him as a template. He thought visually. He cared not for social customs and conventions. He did poorly in math and abstract studies. He favored loose, comfortable clothing, not socially accepted in his time. He performed poorly in many aspects of academic study within structured school settings. He exhibited in all things a childlike joy.

I once told a friend, a retired physics professor, that some believe Einstein to have had autism. He bristled. "Einstein was a very great man!" he thundered. *I assured him I did not think autism and greatness mutually exclusive.*

People often ask what the future holds for Will. I sometimes respond by asking if they know what the future holds for their children. Life has no guarantees. A friend who has a son with autism said that she got the diagnosis when her boy was three. She told an older relative, who said to her, "Better he should break your heart now than when he's seventeen." She thought it horribly insensitive, but I think it rather wise. Being a parent, as Tip O'Neill said about being Irish, means knowing that "sooner or later the world will break your heart." Sometimes, with heartbreaking beauty.

Irony of Word

There is a movie called *Mr. Holland's Opus*, which I have not seen. It is about a high school music teacher whose son—bitter irony—is born deaf. I have not seen the movie, but the irony is not lost on me, as I hope I can explain.

I am told I have a way with words. At least that is what I am told when people are being kind. People who have a way with words can set armies marching, move crowds of people, and create great beauty. But there is a variety of gifts, scripture tells us. Nowhere does it say the gift of gab is chief among the others. In fact, when your car breaks down on a lonely road, the gift of language seems not nearly so important as, say, the gift of large engine repair.

I am glad when people like what I write. I make my living by the written word. And I love a heavy book and a quiet room. But this is not a love my son will ever share, and may not ever understand.

My son Will has autism, and so does not have a way with words. In fact, he struggles to make himself understood, and to understand. Words fail him. Words do not come naturally to most persons with autism. We don't fully understand why that is.

Temple Grandin writes that she thinks not in words but in pictures. Human language is, after all, artificial, abstract, and unnatural. There is no innate correlation between the family dog and the word *D O G*, or the sounds made by those letters. Grandin says that when she hears the word *dog* she thinks not of "dog" in its abstract meaning but of an image of a particular dog, the first dog she ever owned. Another woman I know, who is a visual thinker, told me that when someone uses bad language around her, like when they say the "*S*-word," she actually sees what the word describes. You can understand why bad words upset her.

Rewinding

Occasionally, my wife or I will get a call at our home from people—strangers to us—who have been told that we know something about autism. They are parents of small children whom they suspect of being autistic, and they have typically been told by teachers and doctors and relatives that their fears are unfounded, that the child will "grow out of" the behavior that worries the parents. But with the instinct of parents, they persist, and they are sometimes referred to us.

We assure them that if they do receive the diagnosis, both they and their child will be just fine. We urge them to trust their instincts, and give them the names of psychia-trists and other specialists they can rely upon. We tell them of our own struggles to have our son Will diagnosed. And while I leave the examinations to the professionals, I have my own test. "How does he watch a video?" I ask. The answer usually tells me what the psychiatrist will confirm.

"What's DVD?" my son asks me. It's what we don't have, as we are heavily invested in videos. But while walking through Target and Best Buys, I have noticed that the DVDs are slowly taking over the shelf space of the videos, advancing like kudzu. I remember watching vinyl records being pushed out by cassettes, only to be themselves supplanted by CDs. So while we don't have DVD yet, I know its time will come, and expect it to revolutionize autism as video once did.

This is because DVDs, or so I've been told, allow an almost instantaneous rewind. I suppose even the term "rewind" is archaic, as with a disc there is no winding. And rewinding is what an autistic child likes best.

Most kids sit and watch TV or a video in a state of stupor, but since he was very young, Will has interacted with the set. He puts together props to act out the scenes. When a bit comes on that he likes, he rewinds, acts out, rewinds, acts out, rewinds, rewinds, rewinds, again and again and again. The bits he likes are never very long and are unremarkable, except that he is drawn to them by a power we can't understand.

Other parents of kids with autism tell me it is much the same with them. We don't know why they do this, but most experts agree it has something to do with their quest for order. For people with autism, the world is often a jumble, confusing and unattainable. They are drawn to the things they can safely predict. The older textbooks talk about flapping and spinning and rocking, or a compulsion to line and arrange toys. But while these behaviors sometimes mark our kids, they are outdated. So 1950s. The modern autistic doesn't flap and spin when he or she can rewind, rewind, rewind.

We don't know how often he would do this, and we usually have had all we can stand after the 10th or 15th rewind. We try to explain that it is harmful to the TV, the VCR, and the parents' peace of mind. Sometimes we let him go. Other times we yell and tear out our hair and snap off the TV. Parents, unlike videos, are sometimes hard to predict.

Jake

Patti works at home as a part-time graphic designer and is a mother of two. Jake, age seven years, is diagnosed with high-functioning autism. He is a happy soul who loves to be on the go, especially to gymnastics, swimming lessons, restaurants, and to his many cousins' homes. He likes to watch videos, play with interactive toys, ride his bike, and be around other kids. He is very social (in his own way) and talks a lot, but has difficulty maintaining reciprocal conversations. Jake has a nine-year-old sister, who is bright, with a great natural ability to help and care. Jake's father is a land surveyor. The family enjoys going out to eat, staying at home and spending time together, going to the beach every summer, and spending time with extended family and friends. Patti is an advocate and the newsletter editor for our local chapter of the Autism Society of America.

Jake's Story, by Patti

Swing High

Jake, our seven-year-old, was diagnosed with Autism Spectrum Disorder right before he turned four. He seeks sensory input at school to help keep him focused. One of his favorites in kindergarten was "the swing," a

sort of hammocklike swing suspended from the ceiling on the school stage.

We have a big maple tree in our backyard, and last spring we put up two swings. One is a regular swing with the traditional two strings. The other is a piece of wood, about 18 inches by 8 inches, with a hole drilled in the center. We ran the string through the hole and knotted it and left a little tail hanging down. Jake loves the one-string swing! He often spends 30 minutes to an hour out there by himself, swinging back and forth and around in circles. He also loves us to "pull his tail" and go flying into the lower branches. Now that he has his swing at home, he doesn't seem to need the swing so much at school. He has other favorites there now: the Hop 55—a big bouncing ball with a handle (akin to the Hippity-Hop)—and the scooter board. I always say he is giving himself occupational therapy with his backyard swing!

Erik

Jon McGee is a graphic artist at the University of Kentucky and a musician. He is also a half-brother to 17-year-old Erik, who has a diagnosis of autism. Other members of the family include Erik's mother, a stay-at-home mom who enjoys reading, music, and watching videos, and Erik's stepfather, a professional musician. Erik's half-sister is a recreational therapist who does her job with an enthusiastic and unique flair. Erik is inquisitive and quite talkative. He has talents in reading and remembering specific dates and detailed incidents. However, skills in abstract thinking, abstract academic areas, and mathematics are more challenging for Erik. Jon enjoys corresponding with Erik by e-mail and coming up with ideas to help Erik learn. It is obvious that Jon relishes having Erik as a kid brother and would agree that he has learned more from Erik

Figure 19–2 A crayon drawing done by Jake at age 7. He always uses vivid colors in his drawings, and he always uses both sides of the paper.

---

about what is important in life than he has ever taught Erik. Jon and Erik produce videos together, and Jon supports Erik in his musical pursuits and anything else in which Erik shows interest.

Erik's Story, by Jon McGee

Before the Concept

Long before the concept of early intervention was widely used, Erik was given the diagnosis of autism. Living in a small town, before accurate information about autism was easily accessible, my family and I found ourselves resorting to common sense, creativity, and trial and error in trying to help Erik develop skills and appropriate behavior. At the time, we had never heard the term *sensory integration*, much less what it meant, how it worked, or why Erik acted as he did. The following are some of the ideas we tried and some of the adventures with ideas that worked or didn't.

Throughout his childhood, Erik sought several different intense sensory experiences. He used to love to have me pick him up, turn in circles, run into the bedroom, and bounce him hard on the bed. He wanted this over and over and laughed hysterically when I did it. He also wore out a cheap plastic ball that I bought for him at K-Mart. He rolled and bounced on it for hours. Similarly, he spent hours bouncing on a small exercise trampoline that Mom had originally bought for her own exercise routine. While he was doing these things, he seemed less interested in flapping his arms and fingers (he called it "fun fingers"), shimmying small toys, and what we called "self-stim" behaviors. The ball, trampoline, and similar activities seemed enjoyable for him—like play. We were happy because these things entertained and pacified him, so we tried more things like that—not really thinking specifically of addressing sensory needs.

But of course, not all of the "sensory toys" I bought worked well for Erik. For instance, once I thought I would try giving him a popular toy known as Slime (a gelatinlike acrylic goo). He reacted badly to it; when I opened the container and put it on his hands, he pleaded in panic, "Please get it off!" Needless to say, we have steered clear of Slime-like toys since then.

Physical Touch

Looking back, I see that I have always used sensory ways to relate to Erik. He loved (and still loves) having his neck scratched in a certain way, and this was and is one of the few physical expressions of affection that he requests (by taking my hand and placing it on the back of his neck). When he was younger, I taught him how to give a high five. Typically, I give a pretty good whack, but he always requests that I give him a "soft, not a hard one." In general,

he seems to enjoy play in these physical ways, but I can see what I now recognize as tactile defensiveness in his reactions—he has a love-hate relationship with "thrilling" physical play.

A Cough and a Sneeze

Some of Erik's most challenging behaviors involve sensory sensitivities. We had a very difficult time convincing Erik that it was OK for our mother to cough, clear her throat, or sneeze. He would have a very a lengthy tantrum whenever she made these sounds. This was upsetting to everyone involved, and you can imagine the misery of a cold! We eventually enticed him to stop these reactions by making church attendance reliant on this, if you can believe it! He loves going to Sunday school, but he had to earn it by learning to control his behavior. Autism is a strange disorder indeed.

Dogs and E-Mail

Early on, Erik developed a strong dog phobia, which we are working on to this day. He never had an experience with a dog that any of us considered traumatic, but something about the unpredictability of their movement, their barking, licking, and possibly other aspects terrifies him. We hoped that he would eventually "grow out of it," but his fear only grew stronger. For years, we were unable to attend most outdoor functions or visit people who had dogs as pets. However, this has improved recently through teaching him relaxation and coping skills, using social stories, videotaping familiar dogs, involving dog imagery in his special interests (weddings, photos of family and friends, music), and gradually exposing him to nonthreatening dogs. A lot of this work had to be done via e-mail, as I don't live in the same town as Erik. With careful instruction, he has learned to e-mail and will follow almost any request or instruction given through e-mail. For example, I posted stories and pictures of family and friends with their dogs on the Internet, directed Erik to view these, then had him respond with an e-mail telling me stories about each set of "doggie websites." Then I gave him a scrapbook with the same pictures and information. Occasionally, I prompt him via e-mail to review these materials so we can continue to talk about dogs and have him tell me his personal experiences with dogs. Now Erik can tolerate walking down the street beside a dog on a leash and he can pat a pup. Yeah!

With Age, Change

As Erik grows older, I notice that his sensory problems seem gradually less overwhelming, while motor difficulties seem to increase. For example, while he used to almost constantly do "fun fingers," now finger flicking and object shimmying (repetitively moving a small toy in front of his eyes) has reduced to flipping a straw, which he does only in private situations (at home or at our grandmother's house). On the other hand, I now notice an increasing distinction in his gait (wide based, feet pointed out, awkward). It also seems as though his balance is getting worse, as he has difficulty stepping down from a van, using stairs, and running. He does not have the skill of riding escalators.

Education—Mine

As I gain more information about autism's sensory differences, I'm able to use this to play and work with Erik, but it's also gratifying to look back and see the things our family was doing all along that were fortunately addressing some of his sensory needs just by chance and common sense. By the way, the cheap K-Mart ball has now been replaced by a bona fide big red therapy ball!

Life with Erik

Some of the best things about Erik are his curious and interested approach to life and his trusting and faithful relationships with family and friends. I feel fortunate to have him in my life. I really admire my mother for all the hard work she has put into teaching Erik practical skills and to behave appropriately enough to participate in all kinds of experiences. I admire my stepfather for his unquestioning enjoyment and appreciation of Erik; to him, Erik is the most perfect son imaginable.

Jessie

Allison is a social service worker, just embarking on her career. She has a bachelor's degree in psychology. Her sister, Jessie, is 11 years old and has a diagnosis of autism. Jessie lives with her parents but visits Allison frequently, including staying overnight. Jessie loves to ride bikes, swim, watch Disney videos, play with clay and make small figurines, and listen to music. She loves to sing—including her favorite, the "Meet Me at DQ" commercial song. Jessie's and Allison's most recent accomplishment is learning to play computer video games—a breakthrough after months of work! At school, Jessie is working on addition, subtraction, money skills, and reading. Jessie has words and is able to get her basic needs met by using them, but she doesn't talk socially very much.

Jessie's Story, by Allison

Discipline Discoveries

My mother, Jessie's father, and I have been working together lately on how to control Jessie's behavior. Jessie doesn't really do anything very bad—she just refuses to follow directions sometimes, makes messes, and generally likes to have her own way! As a family, we have struggled with different techniques to control her behavior. Jessie's sensory differences include a really high tolerance to pain. If we tried to spank her, she would laugh! However, we've learned that she does respond to verbal reprimands. She also responds to time out, at least some of the time; that is, if we put her in time out immediately after a bad behavior, she gets upset and really seems to understand that this is a punishment—a response to behavior that we don't like. Her school staff use sensory means to try to encourage Jessie's good behavior. They use brushing, other massage-like techniques, and a sensory diet choice board to help keep her calm. Jesse has become involved in gymnastics through Special Olympics and is doing very well.

Marshall

Terri is a special education teacher with 17 years of experience. Joe is a paralegal and has been a counselor. Marshall loves his parents very much and often tells them so. He has the brightest eyes and a smile that could melt a glacier. Terri and Joe are both activists with our local advocacy group for autism and related disorders. The following is their journey.

Marshall's Story, by Terri Killin

My Son, Marshall

Description: Smart, silly, inventive, caring, tall, picky at times, thin-built, intuitive, investigative, funny, and a loving child. This description is of a normal first grader in many ways. It is my son, Marshall. He is all these things and more. When I say more, I mean he also has Asperger's syndrome. Asperger's Description: inventive, investiga-tive, low social skills, loving. That is also my son.

Marshall is all this and more. He started out the first two years as many children do. He crawled, walked, and talked at the normal times typical of his age. But when he was two and a half years old, he ran a 101-degree fever for two days before the doctors prescribed antibiotics for him. After the fever, he could not walk or talk, and he could barely move. We had to reteach him everything.

After a couple of months in speech therapy and physical therapy, we noticed he wasn't the same child. He was not as responsive or talkative. The speech therapist treated him for apraxia, which is what some stroke victims have after a stroke. When he started talking, he just repeated everything we said to him (this is called echolalia). What had happened to my little boy?

Search for an Answer

We entered Marshall in the early childhood development program in the county in which I teach. They suggested giving him all the services as many times as they could. That is when our job began: to find out what was wrong with him. He had all the services at school, plus what insurance would pay for after school. He had a full day of therapies every day. My husband quit his job to take him to the places he needed to go. Poor little thing, by the time he got home he was bushed. But it was working—we were seeing progress, slowly but surely. We still didn't have any idea why this had happened.

We then asked the doctor to recommend somewhere we could go to find out what was wrong. Had he had a stroke, or was it something worse? During this time, we also noticed that he could hear sounds miles away before we could hear them. Was this some-

Figure 19–3 A pencil drawing by Marshall at age 5. He was instructed to draw his hero, and this was one of the first times he put a face on any of his pictures.

thing to do with his diagnosis? We had to find out. We first went to a neurologist, who said, "Let Marshall stay home from school for a year and he will outgrow it." Then we went to a behaviorist, who said, "Marshall will not get any better and maybe a special school setting is best for him." That didn't satisfy me at all! With my special education background and knowing my child, there was more to him than what the neurologist and the behaviorist were saying.

Our next stop was to seek answers at the State Child Evaluation Center. At this time, my child was potty trained and slowly getting out of echolalia. They took us in at eight in the morning and he was tested all day, with just an hour break for lunch. He was tired and did not know these people, so of course his behavior was more challenging than usual. They came out at about four o'-clock and sat my husband and me down. They explained that because of my special education background I could handle the diagnosis: autism. They stated that he would be in a special school with an assistant and probably would never be potty trained. Balderdash! They also stated that he would never live alone because he would never be able to cross a street safely by himself. Double balderdash! I walked out of there floored and even more determined to find out what was wrong with him, because he was potty trained and making great progress.

Our last stop was in another city's diagnostic center; this was a two-day evaluation and a lot easier. They quit when he got fatigued. The diagnosis: Asperger's syndrome with sensory integration issues. The biggest sensory area of difficulty we could see was the hearing. We explained to them that Marshall had ultrasensitive hearing. This center said that *he would make progress because he could reason.* Thank God! Someone saw my child as I saw him.

Marshall Now

Today, Marshall is in a regular class and has an assistant for math and reading. He goes horseback riding and does gymnastics. His biggest concern still is loud sounds or high-pitched sounds, which really hurts his ears. At school, the assistant and teacher have to be told when the fire alarm or tornado drill alarms are going to go off. He then has a chance to prepare for the sound by covering his ears and being the first out of the building. He loves transportation—cars, trains, and airplanes—but hearing some of the related sounds hurt his ears immensely.

With sounds being his biggest difference, we have found that slowly getting him used to each sound is the best way. We still have not succeeded with the buzzers in basketball games. The basketball buzzer is such a loud sound! He made it to halftime at the last game before tears came down his little face. That was progress for him. He still hears the garbage truck blocks away before we can hear it. He hears trains minutes before we can even strain to hear them.

What you have read about now is the whole of my son: the normal and the Asperger's syndrome. The picky and the ultra-hearing. But when you see him, you can't pick him out from other classmates. Students from the local university have come to his classroom and observed the wrong child until they found out it was him. Terrific! Our, and his, successes come slowly, but they continue to come. We love him dearly and we will help and support his goals always.

Marley

Melissa is a physical therapy assistant and has two boys and one girl. Her husband is a professional hockey coach. Marley's older brother is athletic, loves to read, and is in the educational Quest program. He is the best brother for Marley because he can motivate Marley when no one else can. Marley's three-year-old sister is a character. She bosses everyone around, but Marley is her primary target. Marley has a great talent for ignoring her; he thinks she is funny and does not take her as seriously as she takes herself. Both parents put family and the needs of all members of the family first. Melissa is a level-headed person with a refreshing view of life.

Marley's Story, by Melissa

Different among Different

One of our first indicators that Marley was not typical for Down syndrome was our attendance at two national Down syndrome conferences in a three-year span. The first time, I attended a session for mothers of five-year-olds. During this session, I discovered that my son was not the only child with Down syndrome obsessed with flapping socks. Other moms agreed that there was not a sock in the house that was safe from our sock-flapping children. Two years later, I attended the same conference and went to the mothers' group and was shocked to discover that the other kids weren't flapping socks anymore. They had moved onto social activities and academics. Not only were our family's socks still not safe, but Marley had moved on to tissues. He would take a tissue and meticulously fold it to a preferred flapping size. We would hide the tissues, not buy tissues—anything to try to avoid this behavior. Marley was resourceful. He would go to the neighbors for tissues or bring tissues home from school. Not long after the second conference, Marley was diagnosed with autism by the Children's Health Council of Stanford.

Marley has exhibited many sensory-related behaviors. He went through a serious chewing phase. He would chew on the metal bars of his bunk bed or monkey bars on the playground. I had to stop buying him shirts with buttons because he would chew them all off and I was afraid he would choke. In the absence of buttons and bars, Marley would chew his fingers until they bled and blistered.

Marley always seemed to have oversensitive hearing. He could hear an airplane 30 seconds before anyone else could. My husband thought that because we had named him Marley (after Bob Marley), he just heard rhythm in every piece of sound. Marley used to motor to sound. He would rock out to the dishwasher, the garbage truck, running water, or fans. Rocking out, for Marley, meant sitting on the floor rocking his upper body back and forth. He had the same response to music. The noises in which he could find rhythm were not noxious to him; he just keyed into them. My response to him and his rocking to noise was to help him clap his hands or stand up and dance. Some noises *are* noxious to him. In response to sirens, buzzers, and bells, Marley might cry and shake, become immobilized, or sometimes just lie down and go to sleep.

Raymond

Jo and her husband are both professionals in medical fields. Their son Raymond is one of the smartest young men I have ever had the pleasure to meet. His younger brother, by two years, has a great imagination. Both boys like to bowl, swim, horseback ride, and do gymnastics, and they love T-ball. Raymond is a talented singer with an almost perfect natural pitch. Raymond has the diagnosis of PDD-NOS.

Raymond's Story, by Jo

Visual Thinking

Raymond very proudly brought a picture to me one weekday afternoon. He said, "Mommy, look at my picture. This is a picture of Jesus on the cross. He was sad because he was dying and he had nails in his hands. The large hand is the hand of God that was with him when he died. I drew a golden thumb on it. The little person is me

Figure 19–4 Marley (right) and his two siblings, Castan and Kira.

and I am standing on the clouds in heaven. I am happy. I would go to heaven if I died." He is a very visual thinker; some children with autism or PDD-NOS use art to explain concepts that seem vague to them and to restore order to chaotic thoughts. One speaker I heard described the mind of a person with autism as a collection of many videotapes that play in his mind.

Brushing

Raymond was diagnosed at three years, three months with PDD-NOS. He also has sensory integration difficulties and is a *very active* lad. We began occupational and speech therapies immediately and later added activities to provide him with sensory stimulation and promote motor development, such as horseback riding, tumbling, swimming, and other activities.

During a home visit, Raymond's occupational therapist tried therapeutic brushing to calm him. He *strongly* opposed the tactile stimulation it caused and also seemed to become more hyperactive in response to it. Needless to say, we stopped that!

One year later, at a preschool, brushing was again suggested by the school occupational therapist. It was tried and once again was very disturbing to him. I decided at that time that I would not try it again.

Two years later, Raymond began first grade. Then the dreaded Christmas break that other mothers talk about happened, and Raymond's routine and structure were broken. It became harder for him to focus and much harder for him to transition between activities. This led to several major meltdowns at school as well as daily meltdowns at home. Once again, therapeutic brushing

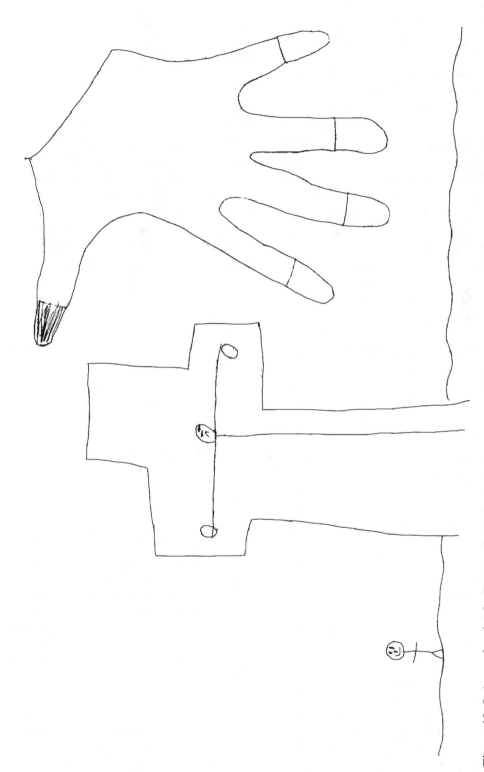

Figure 19–5 A pen drawing by Raymond. While displaying Jesus on the cross and the hand of God, Raymond included himself in the lower left corner, "standing on the clouds of heaven."

was suggested by the original occupational therapist. She said, "Let's try it at school and at home every one and a half to two hours for a few days and if he tolerates it, we'll continue for two weeks." Skeptically, I began the brushing process that Friday afternoon, followed by joint compression. Raymond was very reluctant to try something new, but I somehow was able to convince him. As I brushed his arms, back, and legs while applying deep pressure, I watched a very stressed little boy totally relax. I did not have to encourage him to try subsequent brushing. The following Monday, the instructional assistant began brushing him and using joint compression every couple of hours at school. He became much more successful with transitions and his hyper-aroused state was significantly decreased. At the end of the two weeks, I said to the occupational therapist, "You tell me to stop! It is working and I don't want to change anything!" She explained to me that brushing is designed as a short-term therapy. We decreased, then stopped the joint compression and brushing, and he tolerated that well.

I will definitely use that technique again if he has the need. I am not a very neat person and my house is actually quite messy at times, but my brush is exactly where I can find it if I need it. It can be retrieved at a moment's notice!

This experience has taught me two important things. Occupational therapists are smart people. Also, just because a sensory treatment is unsuccessful one time does not mean it will not be successful the next. We just have to be flexible.

As a parent of a child with PDD-NOS, much of my time is spent anticipating his needs, teaching him social skills to cope with the social demands he experiences, and helping him regulate his sensory system. What a rewarding moment it was for me to see Raymond totally relax under that brush and watch a seven-year-old's cares melt away. What a pleasant memory!

Recess Oh Recess

If you ask Raymond what his favorite part of the schoolday is, he would reply, "RECESS!" Actually, it is probably the most difficult time for him. For someone experiencing sensory or regulatory difficulties, recess is like a record that is stuck or a spinning top that just keeps on spinning. He often becomes saturated with perspiration, usually experiences aggression with other children, and is difficult to manage during this time.

Raymond's school team (principal, teacher, therapists, parents, and other professionals) decided that he somehow needed more structure during this incredibly chaotic time. After much thought, we divided his 30-minute recess into three segments. First came two 10-minute periods where 10 to 12 children participated in a group activity, such as games or relays. The activities are pulled from a large basket of various activities that Raymond carries to the playground. The last 10 minutes consisted of an obstacle course that Raymond helped design using a play structure on the playground. He typically goes through this course three to five times during the 10-minute period. A visual timer is used to show him how much time is left for each activity and when the period is over. Our timer is an 8-inch square that can be seen from a distance. When the red disappears, the time is up. The timer has no sound. This timer provides visual structure as well as reinforcement so the teacher does not have to answer questions constantly.

At first, Raymond was skeptical and didn't want the "changed recess." It quickly became successful, however, and the neurotypical children began to also look forward to the games.

Recess was at the end of the day; when I picked up Raymond, he was not a very sweaty little boy—rather, he was a relaxed and happy one. His social interactions with the other children have also improved. The key to success is collaboration among all the professionals involved with Raymond and the flexibility to make adjustments or changes when needed.

STORIES BY ADULTS WITH AUTISM

The next stories are glimpses into the lives of several people on the autism spectrum. These are insights that I [Rita Brockmeyer] wrote based on interviews and conversations with these individuals. The first story is based on an interview with an adult. The second is based on interviews with a young man with autism and his mother, and the next stories are based on conversations with adults who have autism. As a parent of a child with autism, I am always grateful to adults with autism spectrum differences who take the time to explain to me what my son may not be able to express. I, like many parents and professionals, listen to adults with autism spectrum differences because they can explain in great detail their sensory integration differences. These people are the true experts with the best insight. They have lived with sensory integration differences every day of their life.

Oh the Sound! Hearing Sensitivity— Barbara's Story

I had the privilege of meeting Barbara Moran at the 1999 More Able Autistic Persons (MAAP) conference. Barbara is one of the most fascinating people that I have ever met. We talked for several hours over the two days of the conference. I asked her about her sensory differences; she graciously agreed to share her sensory perceptions and experiences for this book.

Barbara Moran is a delightful woman whose special interests are stoplights and Gothic churches. She is partial to cathedrals and basilicas. Barbara photographs and then draws these churches. In her art, each cathedral or basilica is drawn with its own human characteristics, age, beauty, and complex social interactions. She considers churches to be like artificial life forms. The vivid colors and substance of her drawings are spellbinding. The intensity that Barbara achieves in color, using colored pencils, is greater than the vibrancy that many artists strive for using acrylic paints.

Barbara's hearing is her most affected sense. She describes her experiences like this: Certain pitches, volume, and tones can be painful. The example Barbara used as the most painful sound was a baby crying. To Barbara, a baby crying processes as a bad feeling and the bad feeling perseverates (is persistent and repetitive). The longer the exposure to the sound, the more the sound and feeling continue to repeat itself without stopping. With the perseveration of the bad feeling, she becomes depressed. The depression sometimes lasts for a whole day or a whole week. This perception of a baby crying is the same for Barbara now, as an adult, as it was when she was a child. As a child, she was unable to communicate the pain and depression caused by a baby's cry. If she engaged in behaviors aimed at avoiding sounds as a child, she was perceived as misbehaving by her caregivers, who often told her, "you are being selfish." This did not help her as a child in pain. Her perception of these adults was that "they did not understand it." Barbara's direct quotes are better than my paraphrases. "All sounds from the children are painful." "Noncrying sounds are just as bad as crying sounds, but not as loud." "Children's voices are painful." "The pitch and tone cause pain, and volume makes it much worse." Wow!

How did Barbara adapt her life to live in the noisy world? How does she avoid the debilitating depressions caused by these "bad sounds"? Barbara wears a very high-quality headset like those worn by professional gardeners who use weed-whackers and grass-blowers. As an adult, Barbara can leave a room or an area with "bad sound." As a child or teenager who could not communicate the pain she felt from sounds, she did not have the opportunity to leave an area. As an adult, Barbara can avoid a day or week of depression by changing her location.

Although Barbara also wears tinted glasses, I did not talk to her about her visual differences. I asked her to pick the one sense she wanted to talk about, and she graciously agreed to talk about her hearing as the major affected sense. If you ever meet Barbara at a conference and talk to her, you will learn more from her in a short time than you could in years of study. She is a great resource, a great American treasure, just like her beloved cathedrals and basilicas.

Vision We Take for Granted—Justin's Story

I talked with Justin at the MAAP conference in Indianapolis in the spring of 1999. I then talked to his mother by telephone to put together this collaborative description of Justin's main sensory integration differences. Justin is diagnosed with high-functioning autism.

Visual Overload

Justin is an employed young man with autism. I asked Justin which one of his senses was affected differently. Without a second of hesitation, he answered, "Visual overload." I then asked, "What is visual overload?" He began his description by saying that it was "tunnel vision." This visual overload also includes an intense focus on all things and on all detail of all things. Every detail is of equal focus and importance. For example, when he is walking on a sidewalk and experiences visual overload, he sees the holes in the concrete and the dirt in the holes of the concrete in focus as sharp as the sides of the sidewalk, the street corners, the cars on the street, and any other danger to a pedestrian. There is no filtering out by the eye or the brain of these minute "focus details." As a result, all systems shut down. The motor abilities to walk or to move your tongue to talk are at a complete shutdown. Vision is heightened but is nonfunctional. Complete shutdown of all of the other systems ensues—hearing, motor planning, touch, smell, and all executive functions. At this time, it is impossible to ask someone for help, because his tongue isn't working. It is very difficult to walk during a visual overload.

After Justin's description, I understand better what he means by "visual overload." I know that Justin is adaptive, functional, and employed. What does Justin do to function when he experiences visual overload? Justin offered this example: When he is walking down the sidewalk and becomes visually overloaded, he squints and "stares at a far-away object as far in the distance as possible." This frees up his motor ability to walk for a short distance. This technique works only at the start of the visual overload. Sometimes when he has visual overload, he can squint very hard, and sometimes it helps to watch television. At other times, sleep is the only sure way for the visual overload to subside. According to Justin, sleep is his main adaptive behavior to deal with his visual overload once it has begun. Justin seeks an area that has little or no light—complete darkness is best—and then sleeps to eliminate the overload. "Once you fall asleep, I think the vision reorganizes itself." Justin also said that the use of deep pressure helps.

Justin's adaptive formula for visual overload is little or no light, squinting, a far-off focus on one object, sleep, and deep pressure. The first four on that list are all means of eliminating additional visual input, and the deep pressure provides proprioceptive input for organization of the senses. For Justin, the only major debilitating overload is visual. He explains that there are various degrees of overloads; sometimes the squinting works and sometimes it does not, and only sleep helps. Lying completely still with eyes shut is the only possible course of action, if the overload is severe. The reactions of people around him has a direct effect on the duration of the visual overload. I asked, "What can people do for you that helps or does not help when you are overloaded?" Justin said, "It is so hard to explain while you are overloaded." "People asking questions when I am overloaded do not help." "Trying to get someone to do something for me would not be helpful when I am overloaded." "Even if someone wanted to help, it would be too hard for them to do so while I am overloaded."

How can Justin become more typical when it comes to his vision? One of Justin's statements was, "I do not know what to do to make the overload stop happening." His family continues seeking therapy that will help Justin's vision differences. One avenue they are pursuing is to obtain Earlin lenses for him, which they hope may reduce the frequency of visual overload. However, Earlin lenses are generally not covered by insurance or Medicaid.

Could You Imagine?

Could you imagine being a young child in therapy or school and becoming overloaded visually as Justin describes? How would you ever be able to communicate the overload, given the communication limitations of autism? Could you imagine trying to explain this visual overload to your therapist or teacher? Could you imagine telling your therapist, teacher, or parent you could not comply with their request because of an overload?

Even if you, as a child, could express the experience of visual overload, there is another communication barrier. Justin's mother and I collaborated on the following observation. People tend to dismiss things that are said when coming from the mouth of a person with a disability. People with autism think and speak concretely when describing what has happened and their experiences. Their descriptions include the facts—nothing more and nothing less. In contrast, listeners without autism are abstract thinkers who always add their own perspective to what they hear. Because communication is a two-way street, it is important for people with autism to tell us what it is like, and it is equally important for us to accept the communication as fact, without prejudice or our own abstract interpretations. Working together, we can bridge the communication gap between concrete and abstract thinkers. If we listen openly, without interpretations or judgments, we can learn so much from each other. It never ceases to amaze me how adaptive people with this spectrum disorder become as they get a few more years behind them. Justin is an impressive, very smart, and articulate young man.

Justin's Story and Its Lessons

Justin was diagnosed with high-functioning autism as a junior in high school. It was to his advantage to have a later diagnosis because he was in regular education classrooms until the diagnosis. Justin had the chance for 10 years of school with typical peers. This may account for how well he is doing in the world of employment.

Upon his diagnosis, Justin was placed in a self-contained classroom for children with behavior disorder and mental retardation. Historically, his elementary years took place prior to the 1991 and the 1997 Individuals with Disabilities Education Act (IDEA) rewrites—this is the law that protects the rights of U. S. citizens to an inclusive and an equal education. Prior to this law, most children with autism, and those with many other disorders, were isolated from the general population for educational purposes. One result of this educational isolation was that the first typical social contact for adolescents with autism often occurred after graduation, when competing for employment. For many adults with autism, the complications of employment are the social demands of the job, not the skill demands. Without opportunities to develop typical social skills with typical populations, the ability to keep a job is greatly diminished. For all children and adults, it is important to have children and adults around them who act in socially acceptable ways so that they can model socially acceptable behavior. This is one lesson from Justin's story. The rewrite of IDEA 1997 will hopefully improve the protection of the rights of children and people.

Eye Contact and Mono-Channeling

Recently, as I sat in a group with four other adults, one with the diagnosis of Asperger's syndrome and three with the diagnosis of autism, the conversation turned to the topic of eye contact. Most of the group did not see any social aspect of eye contact; instead, a few of them reported that looking at human eyes is a very intense ex-perience, so intense that if they look at someone's eyes, they could not hear what was being said. They used the term *mono-channeling* to describe this; they defined it as being able to focus on only one sense at a time. If they looked into someone's eyes, they would likely experience sensory overload so that all other sensory systems shut down entirely. That meant that they would not be able to attend to what was being said. All four adapted to the typical society by looking at the eyebrows or ears of people they talked to. They found that, when they did this, they were able to have conversations. Saying "look at my eyes," "look at me," or "look right at me when I am talking" to a person who experiences mono-channeling is really like saying "stop listening," "stop listening," "stop listening." It probably is better to bypass the issue of eye contact by looking at ears or eyebrows. Since that conversation, we have taught Joseph to look at people's eyebrows or ears when talking to them. I prefer to have Joseph listen to me than look directly into my eyes.

A similar story was told by a young woman with a college degree and a diagnosis of autism. When asked what would have been most helpful when she was in school, she replied without hesitation, "When they were giving me directions, it was very difficult if they touched my shoulder." She said that as soon as she was touched, she had to struggle to hear or understand anything that was being said to her. It would have been helpful if her teachers understood that touch caused all other systems to shut down. Even as late as high school, she had no ability to explain this phenomenon to her teachers.

Ann's Story

Ann has a visual aversion to white. Although she is verbal, she is unable to explain why white is "bad" to her. I talked with a verbal adult with autism who I know avoids white, asking him about the color. He said that for him, "white never stayed still." Anything that was white was always moving and this movement made him uncomfortable. Ann has had her aversion to white since childhood, and she is now a young woman in her late teens. She has adapted well to excluding from her life objects that are white. The toilet paper she uses is colored; the napkins and tissues in her home are colored. When as a child she went in for surgery, the nurses found nonwhite linens and scrubs for her. This accommodation made the hospital environment less threatening. This worked for Ann and is the old common-sense approach to a sensory difference. Ann also has an adverse reaction to pastels. We may never know why Ann has these reactions, but I know that if white moved when I saw it, I sure would not use it as toilet paper! Would you?

CHAPTER REVIEW QUESTIONS

1. What challenges did parents of children with autism face in the past?
2. What are some of the current challenges for parents?
3. Make a list of the sensory needs of the children—Michael, Will, Jake, Erik, Jessie, Marshall, Marley, and Raymond—whose stories are included in this chapter.
4. How might the sensory experiences of adults with autism differ from the perceived sensory needs of children?
5. Describe at least three strategies that are used by individuals in this chapter to manage sensory differences.
6. How has your thinking about autism changed after reading this chapter?

REFERENCES

Frith, U. (1992). *Autism: Explaining the enigma.* Williston, VT: Blackwell Publishers.

Gerlach, E. K. (1992). *Autism treatment guide.* Eugene, OR: Four Leaf Press.

Grandin, T. (1996). *Thinking in pictures: And other reports from my life with autism.* Vancouver, WA: Vintage Books.

Sacks, O. W. (1996). *An anthropologist on Mars: Seven paradoxical tales.* Vancouver, WA: Vintage Books.

Siegel, B. (1998). *The world of the autistic child: Understanding and treating autistic disorders.* New York, New York: Oxford University Press.

CHAPTER 20

Living with Sensory Dysfunction in Autism

Penelope McMullen

RITA'S INTRODUCTION: THE TRUE EXPERT

Penelope McMullen is a person I was privileged to hear during a brief presentation at the More Abled Autistic Person (MAAP) conference a few years ago. I was so impressed and had so many questions that I was bold enough to approach her after the presentation. She was overwhelmingly intelligent and gracious, with an obvious desire to help others. After we talked, it occurred to me that I was talking to a true expert. I am humbled at her permission to use a paper she wrote for a graduate course in this book, and impressed with her graciousness and willingness to share her insights. It is a great privilege for me to introduce to you a real expert, someone with a true view from one side of the looking glass.

CHAPTER OBJECTIVES

At the completion of this chapter, the reader will be able to:

- Appreciate the perspective of an individual with autism.
- Describe some of the sensory experiences that a person with autism may have.
- Understand the experience of autism from the perspective of a person with autism.

INTRODUCTION

People with autism suffer from some degree of sensory dysfunction, but this aspect of autism is just beginning to be recognized by clinicians and is not currently included in the diagnostic criteria (Gillberg & Coleman, 1992). Yet some professionals believe that sensory dysfunction is the root cause of autism. As a person with autism, sensory dysfunction is a major factor in my life.

Sensory dysfunction or disorder (SD) is also termed sensory integration dysfunction or disorder, sensory defensiveness, or sensory sensitivity. Wilbarger & Wilbarger (1993) defined it as a combination of symptoms resulting from aversive responses to nonharmful sensory stimuli. I would modify that definition to clarify that the sensory stimuli that are nonharmful to most people may sometimes actually be harmful to the SD person. For example, if a sound or touch is painful, then it is perceived as harmful.

Anderson and Emmons (1996) defined sensory dysfunction as the inability to process or respond appropriately to incoming sensations. I would modify that definition by changing "appropriately" to "normally" because the SD person's responses may be perfectly appropriate for him or her; for example, if a sound hurts, it makes sense for him or her to cover her ears.

Most people can tune out less important stimuli or ignore an annoying sensation. However, the SD person's filters don't function well, so all the senses are on high alert and he or she is constantly bothered by stimuli.

Some part of our nervous system is always on guard to keep us safe, and we may jump when touched by someone we haven't heard approach us. But the SD person is always internally jumpy in regard to one or more types of sensory input. The cause of SD is unknown (Wilbarger & Wilbarger, 1991), but several reasons being explored include genetic predisposition, complications during pregnancy or delivery, environmental toxins, and allergies (Anderson & Emmons, 1996).

Our senses have two types of processing systems: discriminating, which processes information, and alerting, which serves to protect us. From all the incoming information, the brain sorts out what is worthy of attention. Then it asks, "Do I care?" and decides the value of the input. If good, it will have a seek response; if judged bad, it will have an avoid response. Most of this processing is automatic and unconscious. For example, when we see a spider on our hand, we move into a motor reaction without conscious evaluation.

SD is the overactivation of the protective system (Wilbarger & Wilbarger, 1991). If the alerting system is too strong, as in autism, the discriminative system does not get a chance to develop properly, so the perception process gets clouded, which interferes with functional skills (Sears, 1981; Wilbarger & Wilbarger, 1993).

Most people return to normal levels of arousal (a kind of calm alertness) after peaking in response to a stimulus. The SD person takes longer coming back down, so subsequent stimuli have a cumulative effect, until it all builds to a level of intolerance (Wilbarger & Wilbarger, 1993). The SD response can be either hypersensitive, where too much information comes in, or hyposensitive, where the system shuts down after overload and does not let information get to the brain to register.

TACTILE

Tactile defensiveness is an overreaction to touch experiences. It was first described by A. Jean Ayres during a study of hyperactive children with learning disabilities (Sensory Integration International [SSI], 1986; Wilbarger & Wilbarger, 1993). It is also the first to be easily recognized in the infant who does not like being held (Anderson & Emmons, 1996). Many mothers, including mine, thought their babies rejected them because they would not cuddle.

Clothes are a constant problem to the tactile defensive person, especially shoes, socks, wool, elastic, and lace (Wilbarger & Wilbarger, 1993). Most SD people cut off the label tags, which feel like knives (Anderson & Emmons, 1996), but care must be taken that the cut is not frayed and the corners not sharp. I usually have to put my shoes and socks on several times each morning before I get the seams in the socks positioned so they don't hurt my toes. Finding underwear that doesn't scratch is quite a chore. I look for encased elastic, and I often have to replace lace with satin ribbon.

Extreme or reduced sensitivity to pain or temperature is often part of autism (Gillberg & Coleman, 1992). An itch can feel like fire to me, and the slightest summer breeze can send me reaching for a jacket. I'll even wear the jacket with hood indoors when the air conditioning bothers me. Wind is also annoying. Some just don't like the feel or sound of it (Wilbarger & Wilbarger, 1993), but I get paralyzing earaches from wind, so I have joined the ranks of those who wear hoods even in the summer.

Behaviors that develop either to stimulate or to calm tactile input include persistently putting hands in pockets, sitting on hands and feet, and pushing or rubbing against objects, walls, or people (Reisman & Hanschu, 1992). Severe irritation can lead to scratching, pinching, rubbing, slapping or biting oneself, or pulling one's hair. When I bite myself, for example, it is usually to stop a sensation in my hand that is like a cross between a skinned knee and an electrical current; the calming effect of the bite lasts about 20 minutes and then I bite again for another 20-minute reprieve.

Brushing the skin with a soft brush (cornsilk or surgical) before dressing can make clothes more bearable. Brushing, which turns on both kinds of receptors, is followed by joint compression which stops the protective sense and keeps the discriminative sense going. Body massage, acupuncture, and heavy exercise also help calm tactile defensiveness, but tickling makes it worse (Wilbarger & Wilbarger, 1993).

VESTIBULAR

The vestibular system is regulated by the inner ear and helps us move in space. It maintains muscle tone, holds the head upright against gravity, and coordinates the movement of our eyes, head, neck, and body (Anderson & Emmons, 1996; Reisman & Hanschu, 1992; SSI, 1986). Some SD people with underactive or underresponsive vestibular processing have poor posture and awkward movement patterns. The slouched posture with head down and stomach protruding is typical of persons who lack sufficient extensor muscle tone to hold themselves erect (Reisman & Hanschu). I was also constantly frustrated with myself in high school and college for propping my head on my hand while in class or doing homework. I'd try to stop, and then a minute later I'd being doing it again! Throughout my life, I've been admonished to stand up straight. While I could momentarily manage it, I could never sustain it for more than a minute or two. My posture has improved considerably since I've begun chiropractic, acupuncture, Trager, and rolfing treatments, along with working out on weight machines.

A person whose vestibular system is weak experiences gravitational and postural insecurity, seeming to "trip over air" (Anderson & Emmons, 1996; Reisman & Hanschu, 1992; Wilbarger & Wilbarger, 1994). When a child with SD that I know rides his bike, he perceives the tiniest pebble as a huge boulder that will surely topple him. I find myself tending to lean on something (which can also be a need for tactile or proprioceptive input), like pressing my stomach against the sink when washing dishes (which gets me wet, of course!).

Lack of bilateral coordination can be another sign of vestibular problems (Reisman & Hanschu, 1992). I had difficulty with sports like basketball, where I needed to interchange hands easily. And as much as I wanted to, I could not play piano with both hands. Two-footed movements are also problematic, so I was clumsy at ballroom dancing, and soccer was impossible.

"The vestibular system also helps keep the level of arousal of the nervous system balanced. An underdeveloped vestibular system contributes to hyperactivity and distractibility" (Williams & Shellenberger, 1994). People who suffer from this engage in behaviors that stimulate the vestibular system, such as rocking, swinging, twirling, pacing, walking with a bounce, flicking fingers, and running in sudden spurts. They often feel more secure sitting on the floor than in a chair (Reisman & Hanschu, 1992). Other activities that help develop a healthy vestibular system are horseback riding, bicycling, gymnastics, martial arts, aerobics, swimming, weight training, kayaking, wall climbing, and dancing (Wilbarger & Wilbarger, 1993).

PROPRIOCEPTION

This system takes information from our muscles, tendons, and ligaments to give us a sense of where our body is in space and of our body boundaries. This is what helps us bend the knee at the exact angle needed to rise from a chair, step off a curb smoothly, and manipulate pencils, buttons, spoons, and combs (Anderson & Emmons, 1996; Reisman & Hanschu, 1992; SSI, 1986). People who have problems within this system tend not to position themselves squarely on furniture or equipment. I, for instance, find myself askew in a chair about every 15 minutes and consciously "unscrew" and rebalance myself.

The proprioceptive system works with the vestibular system to build muscle tone. While the vestibular system is concerned mainly with extensor tone, the proprioceptive system modulates general background tone throughout the body. SD people have to exert more effort to initiate and sustain movement, so they may become fatigued more easily and appear to be lazy or unmotivated when they try to save energy (Reisman & Hanschu, 1992).

The vestibular sense works closely with the proprioceptive sense in other areas as well. The vestibular system helps to plan a movement and the proprioceptive helps to execute it. We have to know where our body is in space to be able to move smoothly. People with problems in these systems frequently bump into furniture, doorways, and other people. They almost always have bruises somewhere on their body as a result (Anderson & Emmons, 1996).

People with proprioceptive deficits "have difficulty gauging the degree, direction, and subtle adjustments of movements needed for graceful and coordinated actions. They may . . . knock things over [or] under- or over-shoot a target" (Reisman & Hanschu, 1992, p. 19; also Anderson & Emmons, 1996). I was 50 before I learned to catch a football. I was playing with a neighborhood child and I was amazed that I could do it. Baseball was always the worst, I think because the ball goes too fast for my eyes to track it. I was usually the last to be chosen for a team (which is common for SD kids, according to Anderson & Emmons, 1996). Every day I knock my hand into things when I reach for something. Sometimes when I place an object on a table or counter, I knock it off when I move my hand away! Or I'll turn on a light switch and knock it off again while moving my hand away (I know another autistic adult who also does this). At age 50, it is embarrassing when my fork misses my mouth and jabs my lip or cheek. It is frustration with these motor problems that most often causes me to erupt in anger.

Some of the self-stimulating strategies that these SD people develop include hand flapping, jumping, hopping, stomping, climbing, leaning against people or furniture, constant wiggling while seated, and toe walking (which increases the stretch in leg muscles) (Anderson & Emmons, 1996; Reisman & Hanschu, 1992). Socially unacceptable behavior can be lessened if proprioceptive action is planned into the daily routine. Heavy input into joints is calming, such as pushing, jumping, and heavy physical work. In severe cases, self-injurious behaviors can develop, such as head banging, which puts vestibular or proprioceptive information into the head more forcefully. Biting is also common; it stimulates a strong proprioceptive sensation in the jaw (Reisman & Hanschu, 1992).

ORAL

Oral defensiveness is the avoidance of certain textures in the mouth (Wilbarger & Wilbarger, 1993), making the person who suffers with this a picky eater. I don't understand the current craze for crunchy cereals because they scratch my mouth—I like mush! Many of these children (maybe all) have high-pitched mouths, so nothing touches the roof of the mouth (Wilbarger & Wilbarger). The roof of my mouth was so high that I could not breathe through my nose.

Patricia Oetter (1994) is among the therapists who found a connection between oral development and motor skills. When the roof of the mouth is too high, the infant has difficulty getting proper suction when swallowing. Suction is necessary for the development of throat and neck muscles, which in turn influence the back muscles and lungs. So, ultimately, the high palate leads to poor posture and shallow breathing.

The high palate also prevents the jaw muscles from developing properly, so teeth tend to grow out crooked (Oetter, Frick, & Richter, 1994). Because my teeth did not

meet correctly, I could not chew. I mashed the food as best I could using my tongue and upper teeth. But I could not break it down sufficiently, so I often washed it down with water, swallowing chunks that gave me severe gas pains. I hated to eat, and every meal during my toddler years became a battle with my mother.

Around age five, I was hospitalized in a children's psychiatric ward for a couple of days of observation, to find out why I wouldn't eat. They tried all kinds of behavior modification on me, which didn't work. No one thought to look at my teeth, and the diagnosis was that I was just a stubborn child who needed to be disciplined and forced to eat. I was 11 before a doctor finally noticed that I could not chew.

Now doctors check the teeth more often, but few are aware of the sensory problems of eating caused by a high palate. Some therapists discovered that rubbing the roof of the mouth helps develop the receptors there, so the child can more easily adapt to different foods. One child went from refusing to eat to relishing food after just one weekend of sensory therapy (Wilbarger & Wilbarger, 1993). The autistic person always wants something in the mouth, unconsciously seeking oral stimulation; hence, they chew gum, suck candy or straws, smoke, or bite their nails. Oral toys may be recommended for SD children.

AUDITORY

Auditory defensiveness is an oversensitivity to certain sounds (Wilbarger & Wilbarger, 1993). Some clinicians consider the autistic's abnormal response to sound to be the most characteristic of all the sensory problems (Gillberg & Coleman, 1992). School fire alarms, police sirens, vacuum cleaners, and background noises are common problems. I have problems with subways, movie theaters, loud church music, furnaces and air conditioners, and background noises in restaurants, parties, and crowds. I never could handle loud places like dances or outdoor concerts. I lived in one apartment where I had to leave the kitchen every time the refrigerator kicked on. It is not always what I hear that is so bothersome, but the vibration of the sound waves that feels like a rag is being shaken inside my head. Many people, children especially, appear deaf because they simply shut down the auditory sense to avoid overload (Gillberg & Coleman, 1992). My parents were among the many who had their child's hearing tested due to this concern.

Most autistic people have difficulty sleeping, and many babies scream all night. The doctor gave my exhausted mother medication to knock me out, and when it didn't faze me, she took it herself and finally slept. One theory is that the infant hears so acutely that sounds in the dark are scary. Today, parents know to use a night light and play calming music or run a fan to create background white noise.

Often the autistic person has difficulty distinguishing speech sounds. I frequently realize that what I thought someone was saying to me doesn't make sense, and I go back over what was said in my head substituting those sounds I know I confuse. Usually I "translate" quickly, and the other person is not aware of my process. I learned early that I heard better when I watched lips, and I now often tell people I need to be looking at them to hear them.

Auditory Integration Training (AIT), which trains the brain to respond more normally to sound waves, is the preferred treatment in some circles (Rose & Torgerson, 1994). AIT became popular when the account of Georgie Stehli's remarkable recovery from autism was published after she received this treatment from Dr. Guy Berard, who developed AIT (Stehli, 1991). I tried the treatment and it helped for a time but, as with others who tried it, it didn't last and seems to require periodic repetition throughout one's life. At an average of $1,000 per 10-day treatment, repeated treatments are too much a financial burden for many families.

VISUAL

The visually defensive individual is overly sensitive to light, especially bright, flashing, or blinking lights (Wilbarger & Wilbarger, 1993). Fluorescent lights, which are common in schools and workplaces, can be bothersome because they tend to flicker. The SD person notices the flickering long before most others do.

Many visually dysfunctional people do not seem to recognize the things they are looking at (Gillberg & Coleman, 1992). I often look straight at something I'm looking for and not see it. I think this is due to visual overload; there is so much that I cannot take it all in and register for each "this is not it" or "this is it."

The SD person likes to keep furniture and objects in exactly the same place. While Reisman & Hanschu (1992) linked this tendency to perception in the vestibular system, for me it has more to do with visual overload. I have a hard time finding something when I don't already have an idea of where it is, because there are too many other things around from which to distinguish it. I don't like to shop for that reason, and I hate it when I go to buy something I'm familiar with and the packaging is changed so I don't recognize it.

An SD person can also be easily distracted visually and finds it difficult to attend to two kinds of sensory stimuli at the same time (Wilbarger & Wilbarger, 1993). For example, if I am listening to what someone is saying, I do not notice what that person looks like, is wearing, or is doing. If I begin to notice something that I see, I can lose what is being said.

Persons with autism tend to avoid eye-to-eye contact when conversing with someone (Gillberg & Coleman, 1992). I consciously try and often succeed to give eye contact, but if I have to work hard to get my words out, then I have to look away (at space—at nothing, really) in order to concentrate on speaking. If I look at the face, then visual overload interrupts the words.

Scotopic Sensitivity Syndrome can be a part of visual sensitivity. It is a sensitivity to full-spectrum light (Rose & Togerson, 1994), which can affect a person's ability to read because the glare on white paper makes the letters appear to wiggle. Covering the paper with a colored overlay or wearing colored glasses helps many nonreaders to quickly learn and enjoy reading (Irlen Institute, personal correspondence, 1995).

OLFACTORY

I found little written about sensitivity to odors, other than the mere mention of it, though most verbal autistic people talk about it. Some autistic children tend to smell everything, but the reason for this behavior seems to be unknown. Some high-functioning autistic adults have told of their aversion to certain smells, such as perfumes, cigarette smoke, cleaning chemicals, and carpet glue, all of which I experience. In fact, it's more than an aversion; the odors can actually make the autistic person ill. When I begin each semester of teaching at the Santa Fe Community College, I ask my students to not use perfume or cologne and to not smoke right before class.

CONCLUSION

Parents of SD children know there is "something different" about their child, but usually no one understands the parents' concerns. Sensory dysfunction is a relatively new concept in the field of child development, so few doctors, teachers, or therapists understand it (Anderson & Emmons, 1996). Professionals tend to think the parents are overanxious or just can't control their child. But SD is neurological and not the parents' fault. Psychiatrists forgot Freud's advice to rule out possible physical causes first (Wilbarger & Wilbarger, 1994).

In trying to help their child, it is often difficult for parents to know when they are being codependent with the child and when what they are doing is absolutely necessary for survival (Wilbarger & Wilbarger, 1994). Sometimes parents are suspected of child abuse when others hear the wild screaming of an SD child. My family would go outside so the neighbors could see that no one was beating me!

Our world is increasingly invasive with sensory demands. The autistic person perceives the world as irritating, confusing, frightening, torturous, and sometimes dangerous (Wilbarger & Wilbarger, 1994). School is especially challenging, where the child is suddenly thrown into an environment where he or she has to process a wide range of sensory input simultaneously (Anderson & Emmons, 1996; Wilbarger & Wilbarger, 1991). "Even seemingly simple choices and tasks like where to sit, what to draw, or how to feel about something can present a challenge socially, academically, and emotionally" (Anderson & Emmons, 1996, p. 38). Even as an adult, when I enter a room for a meeting, I have to size up the space to decide where I will sit—not facing a window because of the glare, not where a light will be in my face, not close to a loud-speaker, and not in line with a blowing fan or air conditioner or heater. Sometimes, after I have chosen my spot carefully, someone smelling of perfume or smoke will sit next to me and I have to move.

According to Anderson and Emmons (1996), "the struggle can seem never-ending and suffering a way of life" (p. 1). A parent once said she felt hostage to her child. An autistic friend of mine says that "people with autism are held hostage to their bodies and they can't get away from it, ever." For some children, the pressures become too overwhelming and they stop trying. It's important that the people in the child's life understand his or her sensory problems (Wilbarger & Wilbarger, 1993).

SD children appear to have an extremely low frustration level (Anderson & Emmons, 1996), but I question if that is true. So much of life is frustrating that if any "normal" person had that much frustration to deal with, he or she might also fall apart at what seems to be a minor incident but is actually the straw that broke the camel's back.

People with sensory dysfunction are usually lonely. They experience the world so differently from everyone else around them, and no one can mirror their reality. They often know they are different, which adds to their isolation and undermines their self-esteem (Anderson & Emmons, 1996).

Many children learn to compensate for their sensory deficiencies, especially if they live in a predictable and structured environment and if the adults in their lives help them with the alleviation suggestions mentioned earlier. Some become avid readers to tune out the rest of the world. Other techniques that help include frequent snacks, fidget toys, deep breathing exercises, wind instruments, cranial-sacral treatments, and visceral manipulation. It is important to focus on their individual strengths and give plenty of time for any activity (Anderson & Emmons, 1996; Wilbarger & Wilbarger, 1993).

As autistic children grow into adolescence, they tighten up more. More blood rushes to the muscles to flee or fight and thus leaves the central digestive system, causing increased digestive problems. They tend either to be loners or desperately try to appear like everyone else, suffering internal turmoil as a result. Some participate heavily in sports, and some turn to drugs to numb their inner pain (Wilbarger & Wilbarger, 1993).

Those who make it to college often experience a time of depression, as their changed environment is too overwhelming. As adults, SD people usually learn to control their environment to lessen the sensory bombardment. When they can't control the situation, they just endure, which is exhausting (Wilbarger & Wilbarger, 1993).

Sometimes people with SD adapt so well that others around them may not see the real problem but rather just see rigid demands and "strange behavior" (Anderson & Emmons, 1996). "Behaviors" need to be understood in light of realizing that SD people are doing the best they can to just survive and make life bearable (Wilbarger & Wilbarger, 1991).

Elizabeth Anderson and Pauline Emmons (1996) view their SD children as superheroes because of the "strength and courage it takes for them to cope with their disorder" (p. xiii). People with autism are known to have tremendous stamina because they have endured so much. Just like the blind person who develops acute hearing, those with sensory dysfunction, such as in autism, develop skills and strengths in the process of learning to cope with their disability.

CHAPTER REVIEW QUESTIONS

1. How does Ms. McMullen experience sensory dysfunction in the tactile, oral, vestibular, proprioceptive, auditory, visual, and smell senses?
2. Describe strategies to manage sensory differences.
3. How has your thinking about autism changed after reading this chapter?

REFERENCES

Anderson, E., & Emmons, P. (1996). *Unlocking the mysteries of sensory dysfunction.* Arlington, TX: Future Horizons.

Gillberg, C., & Coleman, M. (1992). *The biology of the autistic syndromes* (2nd ed.). New York: Cambridge University Press.

Oetter, P., Frick, S., & Richter, E. (1994). *Oral motor function and its relationship to development and treatment.* Hugo, MN: PDP Press.

Reisman, J., & Hanschu, B. (1992). *Sensory integration inventory, revised for individuals with developmental disabilities: User's guide.* Hugo, MN: PDP Press.

Rose, M., & Togerson, N. (1994). A behavioral approach to vision and autism. *Journal of Optometric Vision Development, 25,* 269–275.

Sears, C. (1981, May). The tactilely defensive child. *Academic Therapy,* 563–569.

Sensory Integration International. (1986). *A parent's guide to understanding sensory integration.* Torrance, CA: Author.

Stehli, A. (1991). *The sound of a miracle.* New York: Avon Books.

Wilbarger, P., & Wilbarger, J. (1991). *Sensory defensiveness in children aged 2–12: An intervention guide for parents and other caretakers.* Santa Barbara, CA: Avanti Educational Programs.

Wilbarger, P., & Wilbarger, J. (1993). *Sensory defensiveness and related social/emotional and neurological problems.* Professional Development Programs workshop in Albuquerque, New Mexico.

Williams, M., & Shellenberger, S. (1994). *How does your engine run?* Albuquerque, NM: Therapy Works.

Index